Story Logic

FRONTIERS OF NARRATIVE

Series Editor: David Herman,
North Carolina State University

Story Logic

PROBLEMS AND POSSIBILITIES OF NARRATIVE

David Herman

University of Nebraska Press : Lincoln and London

Acknowledgments for the use of previously published
material appear on pages xv–xvi, which constitute an
extension of the copyright page.

© 2002 by the University of Nebraska Press. All rights
reserved. Manufactured in the United States of America.

∞

First Nebraska paperback printing: 2004

Library of Congress
Cataloging-in-Publication Data
Herman, David, 1962–
Story logic: problems and possibilities of narrative /
David Herman.
   p. cm. (Frontiers of narrative series).
Includes bibliographical references and index.
ISBN 0-8032-2399-4 (cloth: alk. paper)
ISBN 0-8032-7342-8 (paper: alk. paper)
1. Narration (Rhetoric) I. Title. II. Series.
PN212.H47 2002 808–dc21 2001043074

For Susan, knower of trees, lover of birds, friend to nature

Contents

List of Figures — ix
List of Tables — xi
Acknowledgments — xiii
Introduction — 1

PART ONE: *Narrative Microdesigns*

1. States, Events, and Actions — 27
2. Action Representations — 53
3. Scripts, Sequences, and Stories — 85
4. Participant Roles and Relations — 115
5. Dialogues and Styles — 171

PART TWO: *Narrative Macrodesigns*

6. Temporalities — 211
7. Spatialization — 263
8. Perspectives — 301
9. Contextual Anchoring — 331

Notes — 373
Bibliography — 419
Index — 453

Figures

1. Taxonomy of Events — 41
2. Taxonomy of States, Events, and Actions — 43
3. Typology of Preference Rankings for Action Representations in Narrative — 60
4. Actantial Model Presented in Greimas's *Structural Semantics* — 127
5. One-Many and Many-One Relation between Actants and Actors — 131
6. Semantic Continuum of Thematic Roles — 158
7. Van Valin's Actor-Undergoer Hierarchy — 161
8. Storyworld Chronology for Egoyan's *The Sweet Hereafter* — 240
9. Order in Which Episodes are Presented in *The Sweet Hereafter* — 243
10. Asynchronous Sounds in *The Sweet Hereafter* — 249
11. Modes of Focalization on a Scale of Epistemic Deixis — 327
12. Scalar Model of Narrative *You* — 353

Tables

1. Vendler's Time-Schemata for States, Processes, and Events — 31
2. Vendler's Event Types and a Preference-Based Typology of Narrative Genres — 37
3. Preference Rankings for Nonstative Events — 42
4. Preference Rankings for Coding Strategies — 47
5. Preferred Degrees of Action Specification in Stories — 65
6. Process Types and Participant Roles — 141
7. Outline of Halliday's Process Types — 142
8. Preference Rankings for Process Types — 144
9. Preferred Role Assignments for Protagonists — 147
10. Participant and Nonparticipant Roles — 152
11. Preference Rankings for Role Assignments — 168
12. Preferred Sequences of Narrative Participants/Macroroles — 168
13. Some Modes of Focalization in Narrative — 322
14. Classification of Some Hypothetically Focalized Narratives — 323
15. Some Initial Parameters for Parsing Narrative *You* — 367
16. Additional Parameters for Parsing Narrative *You* — 367

Acknowledgments

There were times when it seemed as though this book would never stop being a process and become, instead, a result. Yet my only measure for the success of the book will be the degree to which it contributes to a larger, ongoing process of inquiry into narrative. I am thus pleased to be able to publish *Story Logic* in the new book series Frontiers of Narrative, which was designed to provide an interdisciplinary context for the study of stories. Ideally, not only literary theorists but also anthropologists and sociolinguists, not only philosophers and historians but also experts in computer science and artificial intelligence, will view the book series as a forum in which to present and debate their findings, a context in which to explore how human beings draw on narrative as one of the primary resources for structuring and comprehending their experiences.

Whatever the role my own book goes on to play in the field of narrative studies, I am grateful to all who encouraged, critiqued, advised, joked with, and in other ways sustained me during the years of thinking, writing, and rewriting that were required to bring *Story Logic* to completion. I thank the many students whose questions and insights helped me sketch out (and in some cases rethink) arguments presented in the book. Particularly helpful were Dan Beckett, Becky Childs, Kirk Hazen, Andy Kunka, Jennifer Liethen Kunka, Mick Philp, and Brett Wetzell. Colleagues of mine on the faculty at North Carolina State University, including Barbara Baines, John Kessel, Leila May, Don Palmer, Kirsten Shepherd-Barr, Walt Wolfram, and R. Michael Young, have also provided crucial support. I single out Walt Wolfram, not only for his friendship and helpful advice on topics pertaining to linguistics but also for the example he sets as a humorist and prankster, as an unfailing mentor to students, and as a dedicated scholar never content to rest on his laurels, considerable though they be.

In the world beyond NC State, I thank the scholars whose research on narrative inspired me to attempt this book and the family members and friends whose support enabled me to carry on with my attempt even when it appeared impossible, hubristic, or worse. In the scholarly realm, I am especially grateful to Marie-Laure Ryan, whose work on narrative has been a major inspiration to me for years; I thank her for her willingness to share ideas and for the exemplary clarity and precision of her own scholarship. While working on this study, I treated Ryan's book *Possible Worlds, Artificial Intelligence, and Narrative Theory* (Ryan 1991) as one of the standards of excellence guiding my efforts. Other standards were afforded by Lubomír Doležel's *Heterocosmica: Fiction and Possible Worlds* (1998) and by William Frawley's *Linguistic Semantics* (Frawley 1992). I firmly believe that using Doležel's, Frawley's, and Ryan's studies as "ideal types" enabled me to write a better book than I would have otherwise.

In addition, I have benefited from discussing many aspects of narrative with Emma Kafalenos, whose careful rethinking of classical narratological theories has been another source of inspiration for my own work. Helpful to me, as well, have been my interchanges with a number of other researchers, colleagues, and kindred spirits over the past several years, including Michael Bamberg, R. A. Buck, Seymour Chatman, Clare Dannenberg, Lubomír Doležel, Chanita Goodblatt, Monroe Hafter, Uri Margolin (who kindly read and provided detailed comments on an earlier version of chapter 6), Manfred Jahn, Brian McHale, Harold F. Mosher Jr., Thomas Pavel, Nikola Petkovic, James Phelan (who commented insightfully on earlier versions of chapters 6 and 8), Gerald Prince, Mick Short, Robyn Warhol, and Jeffrey Williams. I also thank Mr. Taka, Paschkul Clada, Oglethorpe Bigby, Herr Doktor Homunculus, and the notorious Hermanskij.

To my family, however, I owe the largest debt of gratitude. I thank my mother, Virginia Herman, who did not live to see this book through to its completion, but whose life taught me to become the person who wrote it. My father, William Herman, a learned man with sharp wits and a keen sense of the ridiculous, also taught me, and I thank him for being there. My sister, Jennifer Cohen, and her husband, Tim Cohen, have often been in my thoughts during the writing of this book. Kristin Moss and Bob King have been living proof that siblings-in-law can be good friends, too, and I thank Rebecca and Howard Moss (and also Lynne Maples) for so graciously welcoming me into their family. It is Susan Moss, though, who has done the most to make this book possible, and so I dedicate it to her. Susan, Tinker, and the dogwood, ash, red maple, and black walnut trees that surround us are participants in the storyworld I know best, which is also the best storyworld I know.

A research leave awarded to me in the spring of 1999 by North Carolina State University's College of Humanities and Social Sciences greatly assisted me with my research, writing, and revision, as did a research grant from the William C. Friday Endowment at NC State during the summer of 1999. Further, a CHASS Publication Subvention helped defray some of the costs of preparing and producing the manuscript. I gratefully acknowledge these sources of support. The staff at D. H. Hill Library at NC State also provided crucial assistance, and I am especially thankful for the Tripsaver program that enabled me to obtain books and articles from neighboring libraries without having to travel to those libraries myself. I am grateful, too, for the support, professionalism, and expertise of the editorial staff (both past and present) at the University of Nebraska Press, as well as the care and precision with which copyeditor Jane Curran reviewed the manuscript. In addition, the keen insights of the press's readers helped me revise and improve earlier drafts of the book. My special thanks go to M. J. Devaney for her help and encouragement as the Frontiers of Narrative book series evolved from an idea into a proposal and thence into a reality.

Earlier versions of parts of this book appeared in the form of journal articles, and though all this material has been substantially revised since its initial publication, I am grateful for permission to draw on it here:

"Hypothetical Focalization," by David Herman, *Narrative*, vol. 2, no. 3 (October 1994). Copyright 1994 by The Ohio State University. All rights reserved.

"Limits of Order: Toward a Theory of Polychronic Narration," by David Herman, *Narrative*, vol. 6, no. 1 (January 1998). Copyright 1998 by The Ohio State University. All rights reserved.

"The Mutt and Jute Dialogue in Joyce's *Finnegans Wake*: Some Gricean Perspectives," by David Herman, *Style*, vol. 28, no. 2 (1994). Reprinted by permission of Northern Illinois University.

"Textual *You* and Double Deixis in Edna O'Brien's *A Pagan Place*," by David Herman, *Style*, vol. 28, no. 3 (1994). Reprinted by permission of Northern Illinois University.

"Scripts, Sequences, and Stories: Elements of a Postclassical Narratology," by David Herman, PMLA, vol. 112, no. 5 (1997). Reprinted by permission of the copyright owner, Modern Language Association of America.

"Style-Shifting in Edith Wharton's *The House of Mirth*," by David Herman, *Language and Literature*, vol. 10, no. 1 (2001). Reprinted by permission of Sage Publications Ltd.

Story Logic

Introduction

Thanne telle I hem ensamples many oon
Of olde stories long time agoon,
For lewed peple loven tales olde—
Swiche thinges can they wel reporte and holde.
CHAUCER, The Pardoner's Prologue

In this book I develop a broad interpretation of narrative as a discourse genre and a cognitive style, as well as a resource for literary writing. I also work toward an account of narrative understanding as a process of building and updating mental models of the worlds that are told about in stories. In other words, story recipients, whether readers, viewers, or listeners, work to interpret narratives by reconstructing the mental representations that have in turn guided their production. This amounts to claiming, rather unspectacularly, that people try to understand a narrative by figuring out what particular interpretation of characters, circumstances, actions, and events informs the design of the story. But though this last formulation may appear almost tautologically obvious, I believe that, in actual fact, a number of extremely complicated issues are concealed within its surface simplicity—issues that I can only begin to address in the present study.

Understanding long, detailed, and formally sophisticated literary narratives is for many people a natural, seemingly automatic process. Early on, however, artificial intelligence researchers showed that enormously complex linguistic and cognitive operations are required to generate or comprehend even the most minimal stories.[1] In consequence, creating a computer system with genuine narrative intelligence—for example, building an interface that would make users feel as though their interactions with the system were part of an emergent story— would be no mean feat.[2] Even apart from its synergistic relation with such technical work on narrative intelligence, narrative theory remains a vital, self-renewing area of research because of its knack for highlighting in more and more refined ways the interpretive skills required to tell and make sense of stories. I have written this book in the hopes of contributing to the same ongoing effort: the effort to characterize, in ever more precise ways, what narrative is and how people go about understanding it.

In the first part of this introduction, I outline the overall approach of the book by reassessing the relations between narrative theory and two other fields of study, linguistics and cognitive science. Revisiting the way linguistic models have been used by narratologists since the beginnings of structuralist narrative theory, and comparing this cross-fertilization with narrative analysts' more recent borrowing of concepts and methods from cognitive science, I suggest the advantages of an alternative approach. To my mind, both narrative theory and language theory should instead be viewed as resources for—elements of—the broader endeavor of cognitive science. The result: a jointly narratological and linguistic approach to stories construed as strategies for building mental models of the world. The second part of my introduction shifts the focus from metatheory, that is, an exploration of what kind of theory a theory of narrative should be, to an investigation of the idea of "storyworlds," a concept that will be foundational for specific arguments developed over the course of my study. Comparing storyworlds with analogous constructs (e.g., "story," "deictic center," "discourse model," "contextual frame") drawn from a number of research traditions, I attempt to give a sense of the integrative profile of my approach, as well as an indication of its scope and aims.

Narratology and the Architecture of Inquiry

It would be hard to dispute that linguistic models have had a major impact on narrative theory over the past three or four decades—that is, from its very inception. In founding the discipline of narratology (or at least naming it), Tzvetan Todorov's 1969 study of Boccaccio's *Decameron* borrowed categories from traditional grammars to compare narrated entities and agents with nouns, actions and events with verbs, and properties with adjectives (Todorov 1969). Gérard Genette (1980) drew on the same grammatical paradigm in using tense, mood, and voice to characterize the relations between the narrated world, the narrative in terms of which it is presented, and the narrating that enables the presentation. Before Genette and Todorov, Claude Lévi-Strauss (1986) had patterned his concept of *mythemes*, however quixotically, on Troubetzkoy's, Saussure's, and Jakobson's understanding of the phoneme as a bundle of distinctive features. And whereas Claude Bremond (1973, 1980) thought of himself as working to build a logic rather than a grammar of narrative, Roland Barthes's 1966 "Introduction to the Structural Analysis of Narratives" (1977) started from the premise that discourse is the object of a "second linguistics" (Barthes 1977: 83), a linguistics for units of language beyond the sentence, in the context of which "[t]he general language [*langue*] of narrative is one (and clearly only one) of the idioms apt for consideration" (84).

The broad influence of linguistic models on narrative theory, then, is undeniable. But the precise nature, extent, and consequences of this influence—some might say contagion—remain open to question. Indeed, almost as soon as the early narratologists followed other structuralists in conferring on linguistics the status of a "pilot-science" (Dosse 1997, 1:59–66), metatheoretical inquiry into the relations between linguistic and narratological models became a basic research activity, a gesture in part constitutive of the field. There was, it is true, a brief, heady period of what might be called methodological utopianism, a fervent if short-lived belief in the power of linguistic models to revolutionize the study of narrative and more broadly literary and cultural phenomena. Such utopianism can be found in Barthes's 1966 "Introduction," and it is even more palpably evident in his programmatic essay titled "The Structuralist Activity" (1971b), first published two years earlier (cf. Herman 2001b). Almost immediately, however, the goal of narrative theorists modulated from a more or less uncritical celebration of linguistic paradigms into an effort to adapt certain kinds of models for certain descriptive and explanatory tasks.

Remarking that Barthes and Todorov had failed to identify "with precision the basic structural units of a story" (11), Gerald Prince's 1973 *Grammar of Stories* argued that researchers could build a more explicit and more complete model of narrative by replacing traditional grammatical categories with transformational-generative paradigms. Similarly, in 1975, Jonathan Culler's *Structuralist Poetics* comprehensively reexamined the "The Linguistic Foundation" (1975a: 3–31) of work by theorists such as Barthes, Genette, Greimas, and Jakobson. Culler also devoted a chapter to the role of "Linguistic *Metaphors* in Criticism" (97–

109, my emphasis), the title of his chapter suggesting not a knee-jerk assimilation of linguistic models and methods, but rather a reflexive adaptation of certain elements of linguistic theory for certain kinds of narratological and literary-theoretical problems. In 1979 Marie-Laure Ryan was drawing on developments in generative semantics to sketch a second-order critique of Prince's syntactically oriented story grammar, and she was already suggesting ways to refine strategies for refining what was itself a rethinking of structuralist narratology! During the 1980s and 1990s, this process of narratological autocritique (and autoautocritique) accelerated, as exemplified by the diverse contributions of Lubomír Doležel (1998), Monika Fludernik (1996), Manfred Jahn (1997, 1999), Uri Margolin (1984, 1986, 1990b, 1999), Thomas Pavel (1985a, 1986, 1989), Shlomith Rimmon-Kenan (1983, 1989), and Ryan (1991), among others. All of these researchers, despite the diversity of their orientations, arguments, and examples, have addressed core narratological problems by trying to ascertain what sorts of linguistic models can most fruitfully be brought to bear on them.

Doležel (1998), Pavel (1986), and Ryan (1991), for instance, have sought to overturn the structuralist moratorium on referential issues, using tools from model-theoretic or possible-worlds semantics to characterize the world-creating properties of narrative discourse. Meanwhile, Fludernik (1996) has drawn on methods for analyzing oral narrative to argue for a gradualist approach to the study of stories; for her a continuum stretches between the tales exchanged in face-to-face interaction and the most avant-garde literary narratives, with both conversational participants and readers of postmodern fiction using TELLING, VIEWING, ACTING, and EXPERIENCING parameters to organize their understanding of an unfolding narrative—that is, to process the spoken or written discourse as narrative in nature. The same emphasis on cognitively based frames and parameters informs Manfred Jahn's recent efforts to fashion a cognitive narratology. For Jahn (1997), higher-order knowledge representations or frames enable interpreters of stories to disambiguate pronominal references, decide whether a given sentence serves a descriptive or a thought-reporting function, and, more generally, adopt a top-down as well as a bottom-up approach to narrative processing. Readers attach emergent details about a character, situation, or event to a global interpretive frame (e.g., authorial narration, or figural narration) until such time as the details force a more or less conscious reanalysis of the narrative from the perspective of a different or more expansive frame (Jahn 1999).

Approaches such as Jahn's and Fludernik's thus call for updating and enriching narratological theories by incorporating models and tools from discourse analysis, linguistic pragmatics, and cognitive linguistics. As I indicated earlier, this book sketches a different thesis, according to which both language theory and narrative theory can be viewed as resources for—or modular components of—cognitive science. From this perspective, the most pressing task becomes, not characterizing the role of linguistic or cognitive-linguistic models in narrative theory, but rather reorganizing the study of language and narrative in ways that allow for a new interlocking of methodologies, a new synthesis of research methods and aims. Both narratology and linguistics will contribute to rethinking narrative as a strategy for creating mental representations of the world. This sort of redrawing of the architecture of inquiry is, I contend, no trivial pursuit. For one thing, it suggests that narrative theorists should combine several methods of linguistic analysis to study aspects of narrative understanding. For another, it alters and enlarges the horizons of linguistic research itself, recasting language as a crucial interface between narrative and cognition.

In the approach outlined in the present book, the real target of narrative analysis is the process by which interpreters reconstruct the storyworlds encoded in narratives. To invoke terms and concepts that will be spelled out more fully later on in this introduction and in subsequent chapters: storyworlds are mental models of who did what to and with whom, when, where, why, and in what fashion in the world to which recipients relocate—or make a deictic shift (Galbraith 1995; Segal 1995; Zubin and Hewitt 1995)—as they work to comprehend a narrative. As I discuss in more detail below, I here use the term *world* (and *storyworld*) in a manner more or less analogous with linguists' use of the term *discourse model*. A discourse model can be defined as a global mental representation enabling interlocutors to draw inferences about items and occurrences either explicitly or implicitly included in a discourse (Emmott 1997; Green 1989; Grosz and Sidner 1986; McKoon et al. 1993; Webber 1979). By the same token, and like Jahn's cognitive frames, storyworlds—or models for understanding narrative discourse—function in both a top-down and bottom-up way during narrative comprehension. They guide readers to assume that jets, cell phones, and plasma guns do not exist in the world of *Madame Bovary* (Flaubert 1992). But they are also subject to being updated, revised, or even abandoned with the accretion of textual cues, as when the reader of John Lanchester's *The Debt to Pleasure* (1996) gradually realizes that the storyworld is not at all the way its narrator, a homicidal gourmand, says it is.[3]

Fundamentally, then, narrative comprehension is a process of (re)constructing storyworlds on the basis of textual cues and the inferences that they make possible. For heuristic purposes, my study treats this process as decomposable into two broad modeling tasks, each with its associated subtasks, and each requiring a synthesis of narratological and linguistic paradigms for its description and analysis. The first task is that of establishing, at a relatively local level, an inventory of what can be called principles for narrative microdesigns. Such principles bear on interpreters' sense of what is going on—what needs to be mentally modeled—during comparatively short stretches of the unfolding storyworld. These "small" design principles include coding strategies used to apportion particular facets of storyworlds into *states*, *events*, and *actions* (the subject of chapter 1); they also encompass the fashioning of action structures in terms of which individual behaviors can be identified as elements of somewhat larger sequences of occurrences (as discussed in chapter 2). In actuality, techniques for building representations of (sequences of) actions, like some of the other aspects of narrative divided between parts 1 and 2 of the book, straddle the border between local and global principles of storyworld design—between narrative microdesigns and narrative macrodesigns.

My first two chapters, in any event, draw on different theoretical resources to characterize the design principles at issue. Chapter 1 explores narratological ramifications of the way (English) verbs semantically encode states, events, and actions—with actions being interpretable as a subtype of events, consisting of events that are deliberate, executable, and more or less temporally bounded. The chapter suggests that differences between narrative genres—such as epic, news reports, psychological novels, and ghost stories—can be correlated with different preference rankings for states, events, and actions of various sorts. (I return to the concepts of *preference rankings* and *preference rules* below.) Meanwhile, chapter 2 reviews some narratological implications of the models of human behavior developed by theorists of action rather than by researchers in the field of linguistics semantics.

Chapter 3 then turns to cognitive-scientific notions such as *scripts*, *plans*, and *schemata* to extend the approach initiated in my first two chapters. Specifically, chapter 3 examines how interpreters of stories draw on prestored knowledge representations, especially those involving stereotyped sequences of actions and events, to interpret action structures as narratively organized. This chapter also argues that the amount of narrativity a story has—the degree to which it is amenable to being processed as a narrative—can be correlated with how richly it blends what Jerome Bruner (1991) calls "canonicity and breach," or stereotypic and nonstereotypic knowledge. Narrative microdesigns include, as well, *participant roles* by virtue of which individuals and entities more or less centrally and obligatorily involved in what goes on can be distinguished from various sorts of *circumstances* also populating storyworlds. Chapter 4 draws on ideas developed by workers in the fields of functional grammar and linguistic semantics to characterize how readers, listeners, and viewers make inferences about participant roles and relations during narrative comprehension. Interpreters parse storyworlds into participants and circumstances, and then match participants with an inventory of potential roles, as part of the process of building up the subclass of mental representations that I call *action structures*. What is more, participants in storyworlds themselves use *dialogues* and *styles* to accomplish communicative actions that are embedded within the overarching act of narrative communication. Using recent developments in the fields of discourse analysis, linguistic pragmatics, and sociolinguistics, chapter 5 focuses on these metacommunicative dimensions of stories.

The second set of modeling tasks studied in this book encompasses principles for narrative macrodesigns. Relevant here are "large" design principles determining not so much the individual constituents or localized features as the overall contours, the dominant "feel," of the storyworld being mentally modeled. Narrative macrodesigns determine, for example, whether narrated events can be located definitely in time, or whether their temporalization is left strategically inexact, thanks to fuzzy or indeterminate temporal ordering. Drawing on linguistic and philosophical approaches to the problem of time, as well as concepts growing out of research on "fuzzy logic" (Zadeh 1965), chapter 6 discusses these issues under the heading of temporalities, with chapter 7 turning to complementary processes of *spatialization* in narrative comprehension. Although many theorists of narrative have accentuated its temporal properties—such that a story, for Seymour Chatman (1990), can defined as a sequentially organized representation of a sequence of events—chapter 7 argues that understanding a narrative also requires spatializing or "cognitively mapping" the storyworld it conveys. Building on A. J. Greimas's prescient remarks concerning spatial programming in narrative (Greimas 1988; Greimas and Courtés 1983), this chapter incorporates recent linguistic research on spatial reference to argue that making sense of a story entails situating participants and other entities in emergent networks of foreground-background relationships. Story comprehension also entails mapping the trajectories of individuals and objects as they move or are moved along narratively salient paths.

Intimately related to such processes of spatialization are those of perspective taking, discussed in chapter 8. One of the principal means of adopting vantage points on people, places, things, actions, and events, stories index modes of perspective taking by way of personal pronouns, definite and indefinite articles, verbs of perception, cognition, and emotion, tenses and verbal moods, and evaluative lexical items and marked syntax. Focusing on verbal moods in particular as a resource for perspective taking in narrative, chapter 8 shows how some narratives crucially involve "hypothetical focalization," or the use of hypotheses, framed by a narrator or a character, about what might have been seen or perceived in the storyworld.

My last chapter, chapter 9, examines another principle bearing on the macrodesign of storyworlds. I call this principle *contextual anchoring*, or the process by which cues in narrative discourse trigger recipients to establish a more or less direct or oblique relationship between the stories they are interpreting and the contexts in which they are interpreting them. Contextual anchoring, enabled by mechanisms of address, deictic references, and other textual prompts, is thus a way of characterizing the interface between stories and their interpreters. Previous narrative theorists have developed concepts such as "the narratee" (G. Prince 1980b, 1982, 1985, 1987) and "the narrative audience" (Rabinowitz 1996) to help describe this same interface. Using Edna O'Brien's 1970 novel *A Pagan Place* as a case study in second-person narration, chapter 9 argues that earlier narratological concepts can be rethought in productive ways if they are construed as capturing particular dimensions of contextual anchoring. Again, bringing narrative the-

Introduction 9

ory into closer contact with linguistic research on the text-context interface, my discussion of contextual anchoring calls not just for a new synthesis of narrative-theoretical approaches but also for a new interlinking of narratological and linguistic models under the auspices of cognitive science.

As should already be apparent, in order to begin conducting this inventory of local and global principles for storyworld design (an inventory that does not purport to be exhaustive), narrative analysts must address a whole cluster of problems, each quite formidable in its own right. What distinguishes an event from a state? What, exactly, constitutes an action? How do narratives at once depend on and enable interpretation of events as goal-directed actions? On the basis of what cognitive mechanisms do readers or listeners of narratives form inferences about sequential relationships *between* actions, and in what textual features are those inferences anchored? Does narrative itself (operating in a feedback loop of some sort) help shape people's ability to emplot their experiences, to mold their worlds into storyworlds? How do inferences about participant roles bear on the process of narrative comprehension; conversely, how do speech representations in narrative bear on inferences about participant roles? What sorts of textual prompts cue interpreters to draw inferences about the spatiotemporal profile of storyworlds, and how are those inferences additionally constrained by modes of perspective taking also indexed by cues in the discourse? Why does contextual anchoring operate differently in (certain styles of) second-person narration than in first- or third-person narratives featuring a fully characterized intradiegetic narratee? The chapters that follow address these (and related) questions in turn. In the remainder of this introduction, I focus more narrowly on the notion of *storyworld*. My aim is to provide a better sense of my overall approach and how it relates to—adapts, enriches, reconfigures—other frameworks for studying stories.

Storyworlds: A Sketch

I return to my initial definition of storyworlds as mental models of who did what to and with whom, when, where, why, and in what fashion in the world to which recipients relocate—or make a deictic shift—as they work to comprehend a narrative. As a special type of mental or discourse model (the latter term borrowed from research on linguistic pragmatics and natural language processing), storyworlds, again, can be viewed as global mental representations enabling interpreters to draw inferences about items and occurrences either explicitly or implicitly included in a narrative. But this initial formulation leaves much underspecified. What, exactly, is a mental model, a world, a deictic shift, or, for that matter, a narrative? Further, in what ways can the models supporting narrative comprehension, that is, storyworlds, be distinguished from the mental representations on which interpreters draw in trying to understand a word problem on a calculus exam, a six-step recipe for miso soup, a vociferous argument between colleagues at work, or the paragraph of which these very words form a part? And how precisely do textual, visual, auditory, or other cues anchor themselves in—evoke—storyworlds?

To take the last question first, it is worth pointing out that Robert Wilensky (1982) critiqued the entire "story grammar enterprise" (429) as deriving from a basic category mistake, an erroneous identification of narrative with a particular format that can be used to express narrative. For Wilensky, "the notion story refers to actions, events, goals, or other mental objects" and not to words, sentences, or other linguistic objects (425; cf. Emmott 1994, 1997). Since "the notion of storiness can be separated from the notion of a text" (428), Wilensky proposed analyzing narrative structures not in terms of grammatical relations but rather by way of story schemata, "in the sense of mental frame-like structures that define storiness, but which are related to story texts in complex ways. . . . such schemata would not characterize texts, but could only be related to them in very complex ways" (429).[4] Wilensky's critique hinged on a narrow interpretation of grammar as an explanatory (and predictive) apparatus concerned with linguistic patterns only. In a study published around the same time, Jean Matter Mandler (1984) argued for a broader interpretation of grammar as "merely a rule system, describing materials in terms of a set of units and the ways in which the units are sequenced" (19).[5] The units in question need not be linguistic, and story grammars could conceivably be transmedial, or applicable to all semiotic formats supporting narrative. Thus, "[t]he contention of all story grammars is that stories have an underlying, or base, structure that remains relatively invariant in spite of gross differences in content from story to story. This structure consists of a number of ordered constitu-

Introduction 11

ents," which in the case of traditional stories include a setting and an episode, which is in turn decomposable into a BEGINNING that causes a DEVELOPMENT that causes an ENDING (Mandler 1984: 22, 24; cf. Rummelhart 1975).

In his own critique of story grammars, however, P. N. Johnson-Laird (1983: 361–70) restates Wilensky's objection in different terms. Commenting on the problem of categorizing narrative units, Johnson-Laird remarks:

> A real difficulty . . . is to know what counts as an instance of such categories as SETTING, EVENT, REACTION. No story grammarian has ever formulated an effective procedure for determining the membership of such categories. . . . The very fact that one is not certain about [whether a given sentence falls under, say, the category of EVENT or REACTION] illustrates the problem. In a grammar for a language, the categories NOUN, VERB, ADJECTIVE, and so on, can be defined by enumerating the sets of nouns, verbs, adjectives, and so on. . . . If, however, there is no way of specifying the lowest categories in the trees generated by story grammars, then these grammars have little explanatory value. (362–63)

This same problem resurfaces, in another context, in chapter 4; the issue there is how interpreters of stories match individuals and entities with inventories of participant roles (e.g., Agent, Patient, Experiencer). Structuralist theories of narrative actants, such as the one proposed by A. J. Greimas (1983, 1987), acknowledged that relations between roles and entities are both one-many and many-one. One storyworld participant can play any number of roles over the course of a narrative, and conversely many different participants can play a given role. But, in consequence, the theory of actants does not seem to afford a basis for establishing principled, nonrandom relations between textual cues and inferences about participants—or, in Wilensky's terms, between linguistic objects and mental objects. Rather than explaining how interpreters match participants with roles, the theory posits such matches, in an ad hoc way, on the basis of a prior (unstated) gloss of the particular story being analyzed (see chapter 4 and also Hendricks 1967). Likewise, according to Johnson-Laird, workers in the field of story grammar could propose the analyses they did "only because they [assumed an understanding] of the story; such analyses cannot be derived without the exercise of intuition based on such an understanding" (1983: 363).

Yet, as I go on to argue in chapter 4, admitting a one-many and many-one relation between linguistic objects and mental objects is not tantamount to giving up on the effort to map textual cues onto storyworld components. As William Frawley (1992) points out, languages tend probablistically to code things, or more precisely phenomena taking on the role of things in mentally projected worlds, by way of nouns, whereas events tend to surface linguistically as verbs. In other words, the world's languages show (a more or less pronounced) preference for this distributional pattern, although the preferred pattern does not dictate that events or event-like phenomena can never surface in any language in the form of nouns, nor that things or thing-like phenomena can never be coded by way of verbs. Analogously, in stories there are probablistic, preference-based correlations between mental objects and linguistic (or, more broadly, semiotic) objects, not a simple, transparent link between textual cues and narrative micro- and macrodesigns. As discussed in chapter 6, for example, there is more than one way for a narrative to code events as temporally indeterminate or "fuzzy," just as the functions of fuzzy temporality will vary across different kinds of stories. Hence there are multiple, and variable, links between markers of temporal indeterminacy and the states, events, and actions that a narrative may cue recipients to interpret as only partially ordered (or perhaps not ordered at all) in the storyworld. But the complexity of the link between linguistic and mental objects does not negate its existence; nor should complexity be equated with randomness, difficult-to-detect patterning with mere patternlessness. Narrative interpretation does unfold, after all, within certain parameters and does obey certain norms. I would be wrong to construe Claudius as Hamlet's close ally, or read Kafka's *The Trial* as externally focalized, that is, not refracted through the perspective of Josef K. Similarly, some textual cues (e.g., markers associated with dialogues or styles, or prompts enabling interpreters to spatialize storyworlds) will not evoke fuzzy temporality. And different kinds of stories—or stories presented in different media—may show a preference for different subsets of the cues that do mark temporal indeterminacy. Thus the real task for narrative analysts—a task only begun in the present study—is to *chart constraints on the variable patterning of textual cues with the mental representations that make up storyworlds*.[6]

Characterizing the relations between textual cues and storyworlds as multiple, variable, and probabilistic or preference based, however, leaves unanswered a number of the questions with which I began this section. The subsections that follow seek to address those questions by situating the concept of *storyworlds* in the very rich research traditions that have already grown up around narrative.[7]

Storyworld versus Story

The term *storyworld* can be compared, first, with *story*, a term of art used by narratologists to designate *what* happened as opposed to the *way* in which what happened is recounted; the word *discourse* is reserved, in this context, for the *manner* rather than the *matter* of narrative presentation (Chatman 1978). As Gerald Prince (1987) puts it, drawing on many cognate terms that have been proposed over the years by theorists of narrative, story can be defined as

> The content plane of narrative as opposed to its expression plane or discourse [cf. Hjelmslev 1954, 1967]; the "what" of a narrative as opposed to its "how"; the narrated as opposed to the narrating; the fiction as opposed to the narration (in Ricardou's sense of the terms); the existents and events represented in a narrative. . . . [The story consists of the] fabula (or basic materials arranged into a plot) as opposed to the sjuzhet or plot. (91)

As I go on to discuss in chapter 6, in what can be called the classical, structuralist tradition of narratology—a research tradition that had its beginnings in Vladimir Propp's *Morphology of the Folktale* (1968) and Victor Shklovsky's (1990) analyses of plot structure before being systematized by French, Dutch, German, Israeli, and North American theorists in the 1960s to 1980s—the distinction between story and discourse has proven to be an important and much-used resource for analysts of narrative. Chapter 6 discusses aspects of narrative temporality that require a rethinking of classical approaches to the problem of order, that is, the ordering of events in the discourse vis-à-vis the order in which those events can be inferred to have occurred in the story. Here I mean to suggest, in more general terms, the advantages of talking about the storyworld instead of the story.

For one thing, the term *storyworld* better captures what might be called the ecology of narrative interpretation. In trying to make sense of a narrative, interpreters attempt to reconstruct not just what happened—who did what to or with whom, for how long, how often and in what order—but also the surrounding context or environment embedding existents, their attributes, and the actions and events in which they are more or less centrally involved. As I emphasize in chapter 7, this surrounding environment, which is always perspectivally filtered (chapter 8), is not just temporally but spatiotemporally structured, although classical treatments of story tend to emphasize sequence over space. Further, as discussed in chapter 2, to make sense of actions performed by narrative participants, interpreters embed those actions in what Georg Henrik von Wright (1966) called the larger acting situation that forms an essential component of the description of any action. An action becomes perceptible and salient only because of the acting situation, or "opportunity for action," in which it unfolds, and that consists of the state in which the world would have been had it not been for the action at issue (von Wright 1966: 123–24). Hamlet's stabbing of Polonius takes on significance when it is contrasted with the way the world would have been had he not slain the officious adviser. More generally, *storyworld* points to the way interpreters of narrative reconstruct a sequence of states, events, and actions not just additively or incrementally but integratively or "ecologically"; recipients do not just attempt to piece together bits of action into a linear timeline but furthermore try to measure the significance of the timeline that emerges against other possible courses of development in the world in which narrated occurrences take place (cf. Ryan 1991: 109–74). Narrative understanding requires determining how the actions and events recounted relate to what might have happened in the past, what could be happening (alternatively) in the present, and what may yet happen as a result of what already has come about. The importance of such processing strategies in narrative contexts is part of what motivates my shift from story to story*world*.

Storyworlds, Deictic Centers, and Possible Worlds

Also motivating my terminological shift is the very productive use that narrative theorists have made of the idea of *worlds* in recent years. In this respect, I use *storyworld* to suggest something of the world-creating power of narrative, its ability to transport interpreters from the here and now of face-to-face interaction, or the space-time coordinates of an encounter with a printed text or a cinematic narrative, to the here and now that constitute the deictic center of the world being told about. As Erwin M. Segal (1995) puts it, when one reads [or views, or hears] a narrative as it is meant to be read [seen, heard], he or she is often required to take a cognitive stance within the world of the narrative. A location within the world of the narrative serves as the center from which the sentences are interpreted. In particular, deictic terms such as here and now refer to this conceptual location. It is thus the deictic center. DST [Deictic Shift Theory] is a theory that states that the deictic center often shifts from the environmental situation in which the text is encountered to a locus within a mental model representing the world of the discourse.[8] (15; cf. Galbraith 1995; Zubin and Hewitt 1995)

To rephrase this point using a parallel theoretical vocabulary, making sense of narrative requires relocating to the space-time coordinates organizing perception and interpretation of possible worlds more or less distinct from the world that tellers and interpreters of stories treat as actual (Doležel 1998; Pavel 1986; Ryan 1991; see also chapter 8). As Marie-Laure Ryan (1991) has shown, when interpreting fictional narratives, recipients relocate to an alternative possible world, with a number of factors determining the accessibility relations between the fictional and the actual world (31–47).[9] For example, the fictional world may or may not contain the same objects as the world deemed actual, and those objects may or may not have the same sorts of properties. There may or may not be chairs in the fictional world, and those chairs may or may not be larger than forks and governed by the laws of gravity. Hence, in Ryan's terms, "Fiction is characterized by the open gesture of recentering, through which an APW [alternative possible world] is placed at the center of the conceptual universe" (26). Or, as Segal (1995) puts it, "[I]n fictional narrative, readers and authors shift their deictic center from the real-world situation to an image of themselves at a location within the story world. This location is represented as a cognitive structure often containing the elements of a particular time and place within the fictional world, or even within the subjective space of a fictional character" (15).

Meanwhile, interpreting nonfictional (retrospective) narratives entails relocating not to an alternative possible world but to a possible world that is an earlier—and perhaps competing—version of the world deemed actual. More than one story can be told about the discovery of antibiotics or the fall of Rome or what happened in Dublin, Ireland, during the Easter Uprising of 1916. Like interpreters of fiction, interpreters of any of these narratives must relocate from "the environmental situation in which the text is encountered" to a possible world, a storyworld, a deictic center. But fictions encode "stand-alone" storyworlds, which cannot be falsified by virtue of their relation to other storyworlds (cf. Cohn 1999; Ryan 1997, forthcoming). Jean Rhys's *Wide Sargasso Sea* (1993), for example, does not falsify Charlotte Brontë's *Jane Eyre* (1960) but rather supplements it; in this process, which Lubomír Doležel (1998: 199–226) has called "literary transduction," one fictional world extends the scope of another by sketching a "successor world" that may precede the "protoworld" in time, feature a different constellation of participants, and fill in otherwise irrecoverable gaps in the protoworld. By contrast, nonfictional narratives about medical breakthroughs or the rise and fall of an ancient civilization can be compared with and falsified by other, competing accounts of these events. An invidious distinction can be drawn between a narrative about the Easter Uprising that pits the Irish against the Spartans or the Turks and one that portrays English colonialism as the target of the uprising. The storyworlds of historical narratives, in short, stand in a different relation to one another than do the storyworlds of fictional narratives—even when those fictional narratives, through transduction, parallel, complement, or polemicize against other, earlier fictions.[10]

The broader point that I wish to emphasize here is that, as I use the term in this study, *storyworld* applies both to fictional and nonfictional narratives. All narratives have world-creating power, even though, depending on the kind of narrative involved, interpreters bring to bear on those storyworlds different evaluative criteria. Worth stressing, too, is that the power of narrative to create worlds goes a long way toward explaining its immersiveness, its ability to transport interpreters into places and times they must occupy for the purposes of narrative comprehension (Gerrig 1993; Ryan 2000; K. Young 1987). Again, it would be difficult to account for the immersive potential of stories by appeal to structuralist notions of *story*, that is, strictly in terms of events and existents arranged into a plot by the narrative presentation. Interpreters of narrative do not merely reconstruct a sequence of events and a set of existents but imaginatively (emotionally, viscerally) inhabit a world in which, besides happening and existing, things matter, agitate, exalt, repulse, provide grounds for laughter and grief, and so on—both for narrative participants and for interpreters of the story. More than reconstructed timelines and inventories of existents, storyworlds are mentally

Introduction 17

and emotionally projected environments in which interpreters are called upon to live out complex blends of cognitive and imaginative response, encompassing sympathy, the drawing of causal inferences, identification, evaluation, suspense, and so on.

Mental Models, Discourse Models, and Contextual Frames

Most broadly, then, this book construes storyworlds as mental models of a special sort.[11] It will require the whole of this study to outline the nature and scope of the mental models supporting narrative understanding, but a few preliminary comments may help contextualize the account I develop over the course of subsequent chapters.

In his groundbreaking work, Johnson-Laird (1983) describes how mental models emerged as theoretical constructs designed to make sense of inferences, both explicit and implicit (397). Starting from the deceptively simple notion that thinking is the manipulation of internal representations of the world (x; cf. Craik 1943), Johnson-Laird argues that mental models can better account for processes of inference than can the formal rules of a "mental logic" postulated by other researchers (24-34). Indeed,

> It is now plausible to suppose that mental models play a central and unifying role in representing objects, states of affairs, sequences of events, the way the world is, and the social and psychological actions of daily life. They enable individuals to make inferences and predictions, to understand phenomena, to decide what action to take and to control its execution, and above all to experience events by proxy; they allow language to be used to create representations comparable to those deriving from direct acquaintance with the world; and they relate words to the world by way of conception and perception. (1983: 397)

Reviewing constraints on the sorts of mental representations that can be included in the set of possible mental models (e.g., computational tractability, finiteness of size, and parsimony in the mapping of mental models into states of affairs), Johnson-Laird (422-30) proposes a typology that divides mental models into six major types of physical models (relational, spatial, temporal, kinematic, dynamic, and image) and four major types of conceptual models (monadic, relational, metalinguistic, and set-theoretic). Examining the merits of this typology, not to mention its relation to subsequent research in the domain of cognitive psychology, would take me too far afield. Instead, I focus in what follows on some of the implications of a mental-models approach to language comprehension in particular. More specifically still, my concern is how mental models bear on the processing of texts or discourses, including texts or discourses that are narratively organized.

Like possible worlds, which "can be understood as abstract collections of states of affairs, distinct from the statements describing those states" (Pavel 1986: 50), mental models can be characterized in general terms as nonlinguistic representations of the situation(s) described by a sentence or a set of sentences, that is, a discourse (R. Stevenson 1996: 56).[12] In Rosemary J. Stevenson's (1996) account, which is based on Johnson-Laird's work, a mental model

> is structurally similar to part of the world rather than to any linguistic structure, as it represents the state of affairs described by the discourse, not the discourse itself. Information that is not explicitly mentioned in a discourse can be included in a mental model by means of inferences from general knowledge arising in conjunction with the propositional representation [of the discourse]. . . . ThisABSTRACT conceptual representation can be thought of as a mental model of the described situation. (56)

Alan Garnham and Jane Oakhill (1996) insist, similarly, on the difference between the mental representation of a text and its linguistic representations; they also agree with Stevenson in arguing that text understanding is a constructive process, in which "information that is explicit in the text (almost always) has to be combined with relevant knowledge about the world" (316; cf. Speelman and Kirsner 1990; van Dijk and Kintsch 1983: 336–51).[13] What is more, in a mental-models theory of language comprehension, understanding a text can be viewed as an integrative process rather than a concatenation of sentence representations: "The mental model of a text constructed to a particular point forms (part of) the context for the interpretation of the next clause of the text. This process of interpretation changes the context by incrementing the model, and the new model forms (part of) the context for the interpretation of the next clause" (316). As Garnham and Oakhill (1996) see it, the most important aspect of this process of integration is "the establishment of referential links. In the mental models framework, establishing a referential link means identifying something in the world that one of the tokens in the model-so-far stands for as the referent of a linguistic expression in the current clause" (320). Hence the mental-models theory of text understanding claims that the inferences given priority during comprehension are those needed to establish the referents of the referring expressions in the current clause (Garnham and Oakhill 1996: 322). (Below I return to the question of whether additional types of inference need to be prioritized during the processing of a narrative text.)

Ideas associated with the mental-models approach also inform the notion of *discourse models* propounded by linguists adopting a broadly cognitive-scientific approach to language understanding. *Discourse models* can be defined as emergent, dynamic interpretive frames that interlocutors collaboratively construct in order to make sense of an ongoing stretch of talk. At the basis of theories about discourse models is a rejection of what Michael J. Reddy (1979) termed "the conduit metaphor," according to which linguistic expressions and other semiotic formats can be viewed as mere vessels for channeling back and forth thoughts, ideas, meanings (cf. Green 1989: 10–13). Reddy suggested, instead, that sentences are like blueprints, planned artifacts whose design is tailored to the goal of enabling an interlocutor to reconstruct the sets of discourse entities after which the blueprints are patterned. In contrast with the conduit metaphor, which blames miscommunication on a poorly chosen linguistic vessel, the blueprint analogy predicts that wholly successful interpretation of linguistic designs will be rare—given the complexity of the processes involved in planning, executing, and making sense of the blueprints. Just interpreting the blueprints, for example, requires making "inferences about what the utterer believes about what the addressee believes, and about what effect the utterer intends the utterance to have" (Green 1989: 11). But the upshot of substituting blueprints for conduits is a rethinking of what goes on when people use language to communicate. The objective of discourse is not to send ideas back and forth like so many packages, more or less carefully wrapped. Rather, in Bonnie Lynn Webber's (1979) influential account, the "objective of discourse is to communicate a model: the speaker has a model of some situation which, for one reason or another, s/he wishes to communicate to a listener. Thus the ensuing discourse is, at one level, an attempt by the speaker to direct the listener in synthesizing a similar model" (21). More recently, but in the same spirit, Gail McKoon, Gregory Ward, Roger Ratcliff, and Richard Sproat (1993) have characterized

A discourse model [as] the representation of information that is built during comprehension of a text or discourse. As comprehension proceeds through a text, the discourse model is continually updated to reflect the impact of new input on earlier information. . . . [T]he model is made up of the [conceptual] entities evoked by linguistic and contextual information, the relations among the entities, and their accessibilities relative to potential referential cues.[14] (72)

One of the guiding questions of this book is whether *storyworlds*, my term for models built up on the basis of cues contained in narrative discourse, have special properties that distinguish them from other sorts of discourse models.[15] For one thing, storytellers must communicate a model for understanding not only how referents stand in particular relation to one another in the narrated world but also how some of these referents can be construed as participants more or less centrally involved in states of affairs, processes, events. Thus, as Gillian Brown (1995: 142–51) notes, tracking participants in narratives requires more than just incorporating change-of-state predicates into an emergent discourse interpretation; it also requires managing "prototypical expectations" about participant roles encoded in the telling of the story:

> As [people engaged in narrative communication] consider [an] imagined or remembered scene, they scan between the . . . major participants, recalling what they have seen or been told that each of them does. It is these actions which they have seen or been told about which most crucially identify and characterise the individual actors in their continually updated memory of the events. The linguistic identification here is regularly achieved not by distinctive noun phrases . . . but by the sequence of actions which each undertakes, which constitute crucial distinguishing characteristics. (149; cf. G. Brown and Yule 1983: 214–22; Emmott 1997: 37–38; Ryan 1991: 124–47)

Along the same lines, and starting from the premise that any adequate theory of reference in discourse must incorporate the notion of mental representations, Catherine Emmott (1997) has developed powerful new tools for the study of third-person pronouns denoting participants in narratives.[16] Emmott's particular concern is how what she calls *contexts*, or spatiotemporal nodes inhabited by configurations of individuals and entities, constrain pronoun interpretation. Shifts in context—such as shifts from a flashback to the main narrative—alter the pool of potential referents for a pronoun and may enable a pronoun to be interpreted without an antecedent. Information about contexts attaches itself to mental representations that Emmott terms *contextual frames*. An action performed by (or on) a given configuration of participants is necessarily indexed to a particular context and must be viewed within that context, even if the context is never fully reactivated (after its initial mention) linguistically. A participant is said to be *bound* to a contextual frame, and when one particular contextual frame becomes the main focus of attention for the reader, it is said to be *primed*. In the case of *frame modification*, the same contextual frame remains primed, but the frame has to be altered to reflect a change in the participant group. In *frame switch*, one contextual frame replaces another, while in *frame recall* a previously primed frame is reinstated. In turn, frame switch and recall can be either *instantaneous* or *progressive*. Finally, Emmott uses the term *enactors* to name the different versions of participants encountered in narrative flashbacks. Contextual monitoring is necessary to keep track of the current enactor because flashback time is not always signaled by verb aspect, for example. Indeed, there can be frame participant ambiguity (i.e., uncertainty about who is present in a context); another challenge is the monitoring of covert participants in the action (i.e., participants whose presence can be inferred but is not explicitly marked by textual cues).

Emmott's approach suggests, then, that special or distinctive interpretive processes are required to construct discourse models in narrative contexts—to build storyworlds. In essence, the purpose of the present study is to advance the hypothesis that there are, besides the processes that Emmott associates with contextual monitoring, further distinctive processes involved in the creation of storyworlds. My purpose, as well, is to inventory and describe some of these additional requirements for narrative understanding—requirements that impinge, in the form of cognitive preferences, on both narrative microdesigns and narrative macrodesigns. From one perspective, the requirements can be viewed as *problems* of narrative interpretation; from another, as sets of preferences that make it *possible* to make sense of the world in narrative terms.

Drawing on a variety of narratives as my tutor texts, I explore how interpreters of stories use preference-rule systems not only to monitor the roles and relations of participants across shifts in context but also to determine how their attributes and doings (including how and with whom they speak) pertain to larger sequences of states, actions, and events. Further, different kinds of stories display different preferences with respect to the temporal ordering of states, actions, and events. Some narratives seek to minimize temporal indeterminacy (or "fuzzy temporality") of the sort explored in chapter 6; but others, affiliating themselves with avant-garde, experimental narrative genres, openly and productively exploit what I characterize as modes of polychrony. Thus, understanding a narrative requires, in part, using relevant cues to reconstruct the temporal profile of the emergent storyworld—a profile of which definite sequence is only more or less, not absolutely, constitutive.

Other distinctive processes supporting narrative comprehension include those required to spatialize storyworlds; at issue is the use of linguistic or more broadly semiotic cues to map the trajectories (or network of trajectories) emerging over time as entities and individuals trace paths through the narrated world. Again, different kinds of narrative prompt different modes of spatialization. Certain avant-garde narratives, such as Flann O'Brien's *The Third Policeman* (1967), inhibit readers' efforts to locate things in space, relying on, even as they disrupt, default preferences for spatialization. Equally crucial for storyworld reconstruction are interpretive processes associated with perspective taking and contextual anchoring, as described in chapters 8 and 9. To comprehend a story, interpreters must be able to grasp the mode or modes of perspectival filtering that predominate within it. In other words, to understand a narrative, readers, listeners, and viewers must scan for the cues that index the storyworld as seen (or cognized) from a particular vantage-point, or range of vantage-points. Interpreters must also scan for cues that index the storyworld as more or less firmly anchored in the (spatiotemporal) contexts in which it is being interpreted.

A few final remarks about the title of this study. In characterizing the requirements for narrative understanding as both problems of interpretation and possibilities for narrative imagining, I have already tried to explain why I chose the second part of my title.[17] In using the phrase *story logic* in the first part, I mean to suggest that stories both have a logic and are a logic in their own right. The logic that narratives have is the more explicit focus of the chapters that follow; this logic is, as I go on to argue, preference based, with different kinds of narrative preferring different blends of states, actions, and events, different proportions of

Introduction 23

stereotypic and nonstereotypic knowledge, different strategies for distributing participant roles among individuals and entities in the storyworld, and so on. Like other preference-based logics, story logic involves gradient and prototypical situations, properties, and relations, as opposed to absolute, "either-or" situations, properties, and relations. The rules of story logic are preference rules in the sense specified by William Frawley (1992): "a statement in probabilistic form of the relative strength of two or more items for interpretation relative to some property or properties" (57; cf. chapter 1, note 3).

Subtending my claims about the kind of logic that stories have, however, is my claim that stories also constitute a logic of their own. That logic is an unreplaceable resource for structuring and comprehending experience, a distinctive way of coming to terms with time, process, change.[18] Relevant here are ethnomethodological theories about the logic of everyday practices—theories that, in Harold Garfinkel's (1967) original formulation, construe "practical actions as contingent ongoing accomplishments of organized artful practices of everyday life" (11). From an ethnomethodological perspective, the best way to study story logic is to examine how people use stories as contextually situated practices—that is, to investigate how members of story-using groups, which include all human cultures and subcultures, design and interpret narratives in response to the exigencies of their everyday lives. As Garfinkel puts it,

> In exactly the ways that a setting is organized, it *consists* of members' methods for making evident that setting's ways as clear, coherent, planful, consistent, chosen, knowable, uniform, reproducible connections,—i.e., rational connections. In exactly the way that persons are members to organized affairs, they are engaged in serious and practical work of detecting, demonstrating, persuading through displays in the ordinary occasions of their interactions the appearances of consistent, coherent, clear, chosen, planful arrangements. In exactly the ways in which a setting is organized, it *consists* of methods whereby its members are provided with accounts of the setting as countable, storyable, proverbial, comparable, picturable, representable—i.e., accountable events. (1967: 34)

Although this book focuses chiefly on written, literary narratives, I start from the premise that these narratives, too, need to be studied as part of situated practice, in a broad sense. The narratives considered here can be seen as "indexical," in Garfinkel's usage of that term, insofar as they reveal something crucial about the way people use stories as an (organized and artful) everyday activity. True, most of the narratives examined here did not issue from contexts of face-to-face interaction, the usual province of ethnomethodological research. Yet the narratives under study did emerge from humans' shared attempts to make sense of and manage the complexities of experience. It is therefore legitimate, as I see it, to explore ways in which the narratives involve "displays" of members' understandings of the world as "storyable," or subject to narrative imagining. Story logic, in this sense, is the logic by virtue of which people (including writers) know when, how, and why to use stories to enable themselves and others to find their way in the world.[19]

Paired with the foregoing remarks, my epigram from Chaucer suggests that the Pardoner knew what he was doing in making stories—or, more precisely, exempla—the foundation of his hypocritical enterprise. Story logic is a powerful tool for rendering the world cognizable, manageable, and rememberable. But where the Pardoner goes wrong is in his assumption that only "lewed [= ignorant] peple loven tales olde." Narrative is not a cognitive crutch for those who cannot manage to think in more rigorous ways, but rather a basic and general strategy for making sense of experience. Without this strategy, arguably, none of us could "wel reporte and holde" our assumptions, beliefs, values, and hopes. Indeed, Chaucer's *Tales* themselves provide the best proof that the Pardoner errs in thinking himself beyond and above narrative. The Pardoner himself is known and remembered because of the storyworld he inhabits; denigrating narrative, he is a creature of story. And it is with characteristic blindness that the Pardoner uses a narrative in his attempt to stigmatize narrative. It is not going too far, I think, to say that the Pardoner's moral failure consists in his misunderstanding of narrative as (only) an instrument of deception. Stories can certainly be used to mislead and confuse; the Pardoner's *modus operandi* highlights some very real problems of narrative interpretation. At the same time, however, Chaucer's narrative *about* the Pardoner suggests the rich cognitive possibilities that stories afford. What the Pardoner does not grasp, but what his own situation within a narrative underscores, is that stories provide an optimal context in which to dispel confusion about human beings' motivations and aims. Story logic also helps illuminate, and is illuminated by, the wider world in which such motivations and aims take shape.

PART ONE
Narrative Microdesigns

1
States, Events, and Actions

In *Narrative Discourse Revisited*, Gérard Genette wrote that "[f]or me, as soon as there is an action or an event, even a single one, there is a story because there is a transformation, a transition from an earlier state to a later and resultant state" (1988: 19). Genette went on to note, however, that there is "a [narrower] definition of a story requiring very much more: not only a transformation but also a transformation that is expected or desired. . . . [T]o my mind these forms that are specified and therefore already complex are those, let us say, of the interesting story (19; cf. Genette 1980: 25). *Action, event, state, transformation, expectation,* and *interest*—all of these concepts, as Genette's remarks suggest, seem inextricably interlinked with the notion of *story*. But the concepts at issue, and with them the nature and scope of narrative itself, have been further illuminated by recent developments in language theory, the philosophy of action, and cognitive science, among other fields. These developments either occurred after the heyday of structuralist narratology or else were not initially brought within the compass of classical theories of narrative, despite their availability at the time. Accordingly, with my introduction having sketched the nature and overall configuration of storyworlds, this chapter and the four that follow synthesize ideas drawn from several research traditions to create a somewhat more detailed (though by no means exhaustive) inventory of what I have characterized as local principles for storyworld design. In particular, the present chapter focuses in on *states*, *events*, and *actions* as resources for microdesigning narratives. The chapter also initiates a discussion (continued in chapter 2) of the *action structures* in terms of which individual behaviors of story participants can be attached to larger sequences of actions, states, and events.[1]

Verb Semantics and Narrative Theory

Theorists of narrative as diverse as Rachel Giora and Yeshayahu Shen (1994), Thomas Pavel (1985a: 17–24), Vladimir Propp (1968: 25–65), and Marie-Laure Ryan (1991: 124–47) have stressed the importance of actions (and action structures) in stories, arguing that understanding a narrative depends on making inferences about participants' (emergent) motivations and goals.[2] More broadly, Mark Turner (1996: 26–37) has argued that narrative imagining—that is, the use of familiar story patterns to conceptualize novel situations—is one of the most basic cognitive strategies for humans. A fundamental trait of such imagining is its reliance on what might be characterized as a preference rule of the form UNDERSTAND EVENTS AS ACTIONS.[3] For example, in "Last Call," an article published in 1998 in *Sports Illustrated* and centering on the then-imminent dissolution of the Chicago Bulls' championship basketball team, Rick Reilly uses UNDERSTAND EVENTS AS ACTIONS to recount how age had affected the play of Michael Jordan. Reconfiguring an atelic process as a goal-directed action, Reilly writes that "gravity has finally begun to figure him [Jordan] out" (40). For Turner, not just narrative but thinking itself relies on "parabolic projections" of precisely this sort, whereby a source story (say, about actions) is projected onto a target story (about events or processes) to help make the latter more intelligible and tractable.[4] Reformulated in terms of preference rules, Turner's model might be generalized as follows: To tell and comprehend stories is to operate within a system of probabilistic rules in which events are preferentially (but not absolutely or inevitably) viewed as goal-directed actions—these actions in turn forming part of a larger sequence of actions within a storyworld. In recent work on the semantics of verbs, however, language theorists have made fine-grained discriminations between types of events expressible in the English language, among others. Not all of these events are equally amenable to the preference rule UNDERSTAND EVENTS AS ACTIONS.[5] The purpose of the present chapter is thus to explore some of the implications of verb semantics for narrative theory, especially as concerns the core distinction between, states, events, and actions.

Verb Types, Event-Structure, and Narrative

Philosophers such as Donald Davidson (1980, 1985), following precedents set by Edward Sapir (1921), Benjamin Lee Whorf (1956), Ludwig Wittgenstein (1922, 1969), W. V. O. Quine (1960), and others, have emphasized the links between the structure of language and the way humans conceptualize the structure of the world. Thus, for Davidson (1985), people use the grammatical distinction between nouns and verbs as a basis for drawing an ontological distinction between objects and events: "Occupying the same portion of space-time, events and objects differ. One is an object that remains the same object through changes, the other a change in an object or objects. Spatiotemporal areas do not distinguish them, but our predicates, our basic grammar, our ways of seeing do" (Davidson 1985: 176). Similarly, Terence Parsons (1985) argues that "many sentences of English can be assigned logical forms that make reference to, or quantify over, events, states, and processes" (235; cf. Parsons 1990; Davidson 1980: 174–81). My specific concern in what follows is with this last set of mapping relationships—relationships on the strength of which people (in narrative as well as other forms of communication) move apparently effortlessly from manipulating elements of sentence grammar to drawing distinctions between states and events, and between various types of events, in the world. For the moment, I leave to one side the question of what originally got projected into what, words into the world or the world into words.[6] Instead, my focus is on the implications of verb semantics for *storyworld* (re)construction. Here I take my cue from William Frawley's (1992) suggestion that grammatical categories are semantically motivated insofar as they force "some things in the mentally projected world to be coded one way and other things to be coded in another. Nouns select relatively static particulars that persist in unchanged form. . . . Events, on the other hand, are *essentially tied to change*, either changing themselves . . . or bringing about a change in the entities associated with them" (142).

Zeno Vendler's (1967) study of the world-configuring properties of language remains a classic in the field. Extrapolating from syntax and semantics to ontology, Vendler (143) suggested that what grammarians have traditionally categorized as parts of speech constitute linguistic reflexes of what there is in the world.[7] In particular, Vendler adduced the following correlations (where "=" signifies "can be mapped into"):

objects = object nouns [e.g., *Joe, bill collector, bank*]

events, actions, processes = perfective nominal expressions [respectively, *Joe stopped being in debt, Joe got himself out of debt, Joe worked on improving his credit record*] facts = imperfective nominal expressions [*Joe's getting out of debt*; *Joe's being financially solvent*]

Especially consequential for later research was Vendler's investigation of verb semantics vis-à-vis events, actions, and processes. Vendler, in fact, proposed a fourfold distinction between *activity* terms (e.g., used to describe someone running or pushing a cart), *accomplishment* terms (used to describe someone running a mile or drawing a perfect circle), *achievement* terms (used to describe someone reaching the top of a hill), and *state* terms (used to describe someone as female, or North American, or in debt). Further, making the simplifying assumption that events and "their kin" are primarily temporal as opposed to spatial entities (Vendler 1967: 144; cf. Fleischmann 1990: 20–21; Frawley 1992: 62–196), Vendler (106) developed the notion of "time-schemata" to highlight the distinctions at issue:

> for activities: *Joe was running at time t* means that time instant *t* is on *a* time stretch throughout which Joe was running;
>
> for accomplishments: *Joe was drawing a circle at t* means that *t* is on *the* time stretch in which Joe drew the circle;
>
> for achievements: *Joe won a race between t_1 and t_2* means that the time instant at which Joe won the race is between t_1 and t_2;
>
> and for states: *Joe was in debt from t_1 to t_2* means that at *any* instant between t_1 and t_2 Joe was in debt.

Thus, activities, Vendler's rather anthropomorphic label for what might be given the more general name of *processes*, imply *periods* of time that are not unique or definite. By contrast, accomplishments involve definite periods. The process of growing old takes a certain unspecified amount of time, whereas finishing a peanut butter sandwich entails a sequence of actions that falls within a definite temporal span. Analogously, states such as being in debt can be described in terms of situations that hold true of the world for stretches of time, so that at any instant between bankruptcy and solvency Joe can be classified as being in debt. Achievements are more properly event-like in that a team has not won a basketball game until the instant the final buzzer sounds. Table 1 schematizes these points of comparison.

This grid suggests ways to rethink the (socio)linguistic tradition of narrative analysis pioneered by William Labov and Joshua Waletzky (1967; cf. Labov 1972a) some thirty years ago and still exerting signifi-

Table 1. Time-Schemata for States, Processes, and Events (adapted from Vendler 1967)

	Indefinite time periods	Definite time periods	Indefinite time instants	Definite time instants
States			✓	
Activities/Processes	✓			
Accomplishments		✓		
Achievements				✓

cant influence on the study of natural-language narratives (see Bamberg 1997, Herman 1999c; Labov 1997; Linde 1993; Polanyi 1985, 1989). Associating narrative with punctual or at least temporally determinate event types—indeed, in some cases making punctually coded events a criterion for stories—work in this field often assumes that achievements and accomplishments are the hallmarks of storytelling. In an early presentation of his model, Labov (1972a) argued that the skeleton of a narrative is a series of *narrative clauses* that are temporally ordered, that is, separated by temporal junctures. Temporal junctures are hinge points in the temporal structuring of the storyworld; resequencing clauses around such junctures changes a reader's, listener's, or viewer's semantic representation of the narrated events. Thus, *I drove farther south and reached my friend's house* tells a different story than *I reached my friend's house and drove farther south*. Here the (independent) narrative clauses surrounding the conjunction *and* can be distinguished from *free* and *restricted* clauses in that a change in their order produces a change in the story the narrative tells. By contrast, free clauses (something like, say, *The sun shone steadily*) are completely unrestricted as to ordering, whereas restricted clauses (*I got a headache because of the driving*) could occupy several (but not all) possible positions in the discourse without altering the interpretation of the story. In other words, to be processed as narrative versus free or restricted, clauses would preferentially code events as punctual in type, with the implication that "[c]lauses containing *used to*, *would*, and the *general present* [e.g., *That really makes you feel alive*] are not narrative clauses and cannot support a narrative" (362).[8] Likewise, for Livia Polanyi (1985), a story is a fictional or nonfictional narrative account "involving specific past-time events in which the teller may or may not appear as a character" (183). Polanyi goes on to argue that the basic "narrative line" in English language stories is "built up through simple past-time event clauses. These are main clauses that encode instantaneous, noniterative, positive, completive occurrences in the past. Morphologically, these clauses appear in the surface structure of conversational stories in the simple past tense or in a combination of simple past tense clauses and clauses that are morphologically present tense but receive a past-time semantic interpretation" (189–90).

As Marie-Laure Ryan's (1991) work on plot structures suggests, however, it would be erroneous to assume that narrative denies itself the same abundance of semantic resources enabling (or enabled by) other cognitive and communicative modes. Ryan shows that many stories intermix durative and punctual event types to build up rich, highly differentiated representations of temporal progression in the storyworld:

> Some events, like the pulling of a trigger, are nearly instantaneous and largely deterministic, and once initiated, they will almost always reach their completion. These events create clear-cut transitions between narrative states. But other events, like the firing of a time-bomb, are time-consuming processes. The temporal range between their initiation and completion leaves time for the initiation and completion of numerous other processes, some of which may prevent the bomb from going off.... Events with temporal extension introduce a dynamic element in the representation of states and blur the distinction between active and stative propositions.... [Similar sorts of events] will sometimes be coded as an instantaneous change, sometimes as a time-consuming process. (127–28)

In Edith Wharton's *The House of Mirth* (1994), for example, the narrative codes as a long, drawn-out process that stretch of storyworld occurrences that includes Lily Bart's being invited on a Mediterranean cruise by Bertha Dorset, Lily's being used to distract George Dorset while Bertha carries on an extramarital affair with Ned Silverton, and Bertha's publicly humiliating and banishing Lily to deflect attention away from her own conduct (178–211). By contrast, near the end of the novel, the narrative codes as a relatively punctual event Lily's dismissal from the millinery shop where she had made a last-ditch effort to support herself (277–78). With the pace of the narrative increasing in proportion with the desperateness of Lily's circumstances, the firing is coded less as the eventual termination of a lengthy process than as the inevitable and quickly-arrived-at result of Lily's having "been brought up to be ornamental" (278). This example reveals how the *alternation between* different sorts of coding strategies can help build and sustain narrative interest, focus attention on specific characters, highlight particular themes, and so on. Hence, too, the advantages of characterizing narrative genres in terms of hierarchical systems of preference rankings (see table 2 below). In different narrative modes a shift from instantaneous to processural coding or vice versa would generate different sorts of inferences about participants, actions, and events.

True, Labov and Polanyi ground their approach in natural-language data whereas narratological studies such as Ryan's characteristically examine a wide spectrum of narratives: experimental, traditional, fictional, nonfictional, literary, and nonliterary. I concur with Monika Fludernik (1996), however, in construing sophisticated literary narratives as located on a scale that connects the most wildly innovative postmodern novels (or anti-novels) with stories told in canonical instances of face-to-face verbal interaction. And even in the case of oral or conversational narratives, the dominant sociolinguistic tradition seems to place too much emphasis on punctual and temporally determinate event types—in Vendler's terms, on achievements and accomplishments. To put this last point another way, it is important not to confuse preference-rule systems operative in certain narrative modes with those at work in all forms of storytelling.

For instance, in the North Carolina ghost stories I have examined in other work (Herman 1999c, 1999f, 2000a, forthcoming), storytellers regularly use nonindicative verbal moods (not *went*, but *would go*, *used to go*) in their tales, thereby suggesting that certain temporal and ontological properties of storyworlds inhabited by supernatural presences cannot be definitively known. Storytellers use these semantic resources not just to evaluate the action, as Labov (1972a) would have it, but for specialized referential or modeling purposes—that is, to accomplish "fuzzy" or strategically inexact reference to the spatiotemporal positions as well as the behavior of ghosts (see chapter 6). Along the same lines, tellers of ghost stories often show a preference for coding paranormal behavior in terms of activities and states rather than accomplishments and achievements. Thus, one of the Cherokee informants from Graham County NC recounted as follows her experiences of being haunted by extra shadows at night:

(a) And uh, at night time, walking,

(b) if we went outside

(c) and started walking and stuff

(d) and we saw...

(e) You know you have shadows?

(f) [Interviewer replies: "Um hm."]

(g) If you had, a different, *kind* of shadow.

(h) There would be an *extra* shadow a certain way?

(i) There was somebody there

(j) and they were trying to hurt you.

(k) And he [the informant's grandfather] said,

(l) you reach down,

(m) pull up dirt

(n) and just throw it and hit them?

(o) It would kill that person.[9]

In lines (g), (h), and (i), what might be characterized as the onset or inception of the haunting event is in fact coded as a state: in (g) and (h), as the state of having a different kind of (or extra) shadow; in (i), as the state of someone's being in close (and scary) proximity. Further, though line (j) imputes the goal of *hurting* to the supernatural presence, the use of the past progressive tense (together with the meaning of the verb *to try*) codes the potentially hurtful behavior of the ghost as an open-ended activity or process rather than as a definite achievement or even an accomplishment over a determinate time span. These coding strategies reveal that, in cuing recipients to model certain kinds of story-worlds, narrators can resort to preference rules more complicated than the one Turner (1996) identified with narrative imagining as such—namely, UNDERSTAND EVENTS AS ACTIONS. More precisely, stories like the one just mentioned embed Turner's preference rule within a larger system of preference rankings. In interpreting and recounting the appearance of nocturnal shadows as the result of goal-directed actions (or at least activities) of ghosts, the storyteller does display a preference to understand events as actions. Yet in recounting the conduct of the ghosts who cast shadows in the night, she prefers states and processes over achievements and accomplishments, thereby undercutting what might be considered default assumptions about the time schemata that most often correlate with (human or human-like) action.[10] Table 2 sketches a partial typology of narrative genres based on different preference rankings for event types. Before I discuss some of the implications of this typology, a brief methodological digression on the study of genre is in order—especially because I appeal to the notion of "narrative genre" at a number of points in the present study. For one thing, the four generic categories included in table 2 are, of course, meant to be representative rather than exhaustive and to cut across the distinction between oral and written narrative. But beyond that, and to make a more substantive claim, I concur with Todorov's (1990: 12–26) account of literary genres as originating in human discourse. From this perspective the genre of *narrative* can be characterized as deriving, through a series of more or less complicated transformations, from the speech act "telling what happened." The genre of *autobiography* (really, like the genres listed in table 2, a narrative subgenre) derives from analogous transformations of the speech act "telling what happened to oneself." This approach to the problem of genre warrants distinguishing between the *historical existence* of particular genres, on the one hand, and the *semantic and pragmatic properties* underlying people's intuitions that they are in the presence of a given genre in a given situation, on the other hand. (I mention pragmatic properties here because readers of a putative autobiography will engage in wholesale acts of reinterpretation if they learn that the account has been made up by someone intent on deceiving the public, even though nothing about the semantic structure of the text in question has changed. See Ryan forthcoming.) Thus, as Todorov puts it, whereas genres can be preliminarily defined as classes of texts, "any class of objects may be converted into a series of properties by a passage from extension to comprehension. The study of genres, which has as its starting point the historical evidence of the existence of genres, must have as its ultimate objective precisely the establishment of these properties" (1990: 17). In these terms, the account of narrative genres developed here is geared less toward analysis of genres taken historically than toward the analysis of genres taken as sets of properties corresponding with "ideal types"—such as epic construed as an abstract discourse type variably instantiated by particular epics in particular eras and cultures. Indeed, as Todorov stresses, genres taken historically are never pure or wholly illustrative of ideal types, but rather are mixed. Thus, "[a] new genre," for example, "is always the transformation of an earlier one, or of several: by inversion, by displacement, by combination" (15).[11]

In proposing the preference rankings listed in table 2, then, I do not presume to be furnishing a definitive account of all possible instances of the four genres in question. Instead, I offer the rankings chiefly as a means to rethink (and stimulate further debate on) the problem of defining what a genre is—as well as the problem of explaining how readers or listeners intuit stories to be (more or less recognizable) instances of particular narrative (sub)genres.

To return to the proposed typology: epics such as *The Odyssey* and *Beowulf* display a preference for coding events as *accomplishments* gained over the course of long but determinate periods of suffering and heroic endeavor. It takes the entirety of Homer's poem for Odysseus to accomplish his return to Ithaca and victory over Penelope's importunate suitors. But that return and that victory *do* take place. Similarly, Beowulf's victory over Grendel, Grendel's ferocious mother, and (with Wiglaf's help) the dragon guarding the treasure hoard are not announced as punctual events but rather savored as accomplishments whose lengthy but finite durations prove Beowulf's heroic mettle (*Beowulf* 1993). Indeed, if coded as achievements, Odysseus's and Beowulf's actions would not warrant inclusion in the epics that celebrate the valor these two heroes displayed not once but over the course of repeated and individually quite extensive tests. By contrast, news reports preferentially code events as achievements, with backstory (i.e., information about the process by which accomplishments led to the achievement of victory in an election or defeat in a battle) provided as space and time permit. This difference in preference rankings corresponds to the purpose of news stories versus epics—not to celebrate, aggrandize, and memorialize forever, but to announce quickly and, where possible, explain.

Psychological novels, such as Rainer Maria Rilke's *The Notebooks of Malte Laurids Brigge* (1983), draw on yet another preference system in coding experience primarily as states and inchoative processes as opposed to accomplishments or achievements.[12] What takes center stage in Rilke's novel are the morbid, somewhat paranoid psychological qualities or habits of mind displayed by its protagonist as he moves among the poor, the diseased, and the disenfranchised in the streets of turn-of-the-

Table 2. Event Types and a Preference-Based Typology
of Narrative Genres (adapted from Vendler 1967)

Genre	Preference Rankings (by Event Type)
Epic	Accomplishments > achievements > activities > states
News reports	Achievements > accomplishments > activities > states
Psychological novels	States > activities > accomplishments > achievements
Ghost stories	Activities > states > accomplishments > achievements

century Paris. Anything Brigge accomplishes or achieves (writing, stoking the cheap, smoky stove in his shabby room) serves mainly to throw into relief Brigge's current mental state, as well as the processes of remembering, reflecting, analyzing, and so on, that seem to obsess him. Strategies for event coding in the North Carolina ghost stories are similar to those that characterize the preference system supporting psychological novels and are quite different from the strategies associated with epics. Haunting experiences are, it is true, predominantly coded as goal-directed behavior in some sense executed by ghosts. Yet—as suggested by the storytellers' frequent reliance on nonindicative verbal moods (Herman 1999c)—the inception and termination of ghostly behavior often cannot be pinpointed. Tellers of supernatural tales display a nearly equally strong preference for characterizing the world itself as (one in the state of being) subject to haunting at any given moment. To this extent, storytellers report the accomplishments and achievements of ghostly agents not simply or even primarily because they are noteworthy in and of themselves, but also because specific paranormal behaviors can be used to lend support to a general thesis about the nature of things.

The preference rule that Turner associates with narrative as such—UNDERSTAND EVENTS AS ACTIONS—thus proves to be underspecified. For one thing, different narrative modes set distinct preference-rule systems into play. Composing or comprehending an epic poem or tale can be redescribed as a set of preference-based instructions of the form: PREFER TO UNDERSTAND EVENTS AS ACCOMPLISHMENTS, ELSE AS ACHIEVEMENTS, ELSE AS ACTIVITIES, ELSE AS ILLUSTRATIVE OF STATES. The design and comprehension of psychological novels entail a different set of instructions: PREFER TO UNDERSTAND EVENTS AS ILLUSTRATIVE

OF (INTERIOR) STATES, ELSE AS ACTIVITIES, ELSE AS ACCOMPLISHMENTS, ELSE AS ACHIEVEMENTS. Within these distinct preference-rule systems, of course, recounting or interpreting any given incident may require a readjustment of these preference rankings: to interpret Malte Laurids Brigge's stoking of his stove as a state would be to read the protagonist's homodiegetic account as hallucinatory and thus drastically unreliable. Further, a particular hierarchical ranking of preferences is not tantamount to a complete absence of interaction between coding strategies. Interpreting weather-related events as malevolent accomplishments by an irate Poseidon requires making inferences, too, about the god's psychological state. The preference-rule systems corresponding to different narrative genres are thus (like the conventions traditionally associated with the concept *genre* itself) globally but not always locally operative. Capturing such cognitive preferences and their distributions across narrative genres requires—in accordance with the general thesis of this book—not so much a colonization of linguistics by narratology, or vice versa, as a modularized approach to the study of language and narrative. The challenge is to balance respect for the autonomy of each module against the need to understand their interactions, as they jointly vehiculate thought.

As I indicated earlier, a second broad problem with Turner's formulation of the preference rule UNDERSTAND EVENTS AS ACTIONS is that it does not provide a sufficiently fine-grained account of states, events, actions, and how they relate to one another. It is time to specify these aspects of narrative semantics more precisely, drawing on work that postdates Vendler's pathbreaking study and that throws additional light on the interactions between language, narrative, and thought.

Frawley's Taxonomy: Actions as Nonstative Events

Note that in Vendler's scheme, action is not a basic category of event, since for the philosopher it is not goal directedness or executability, but rather temporal extension and definiteness that serve as parameters for classifying event types. From this perspective, "action" is simply too gross a concept to be useful for semantic analysis, actions being subdivisible into achievements, accomplishments, and, in some cases at least, activities, depending on the time schemata involved. More recent work on verb semantics, however, separates actions from states and

States, Events, and Actions 39

other types of events, analyzing them in ways that can be productive for narrative theory (see, e.g., Dowty 1979; Duchan 1986; Frawley 1992; Givón 1993; Parsons 1990; van Voorst 1988). This subsection and the next draw on some of this recent work to outline two accounts of action and of the relationship between actions and other sorts of events. The first approach, articulated by William Frawley (1992), distinguishes between stative and nonstative events and defines actions as a particular kind of nonstative event. The second approach, developed by Talmy Givón (1993), distinguishes between states and events and defines actions as a particular kind of event. Together the two approaches suggest the need to refine previous narratological accounts of narratives as (sequentially ordered) representations of (sequentially ordered) events. True, as discussed in the next chapter, narrative crucially involves coding what happens in mentally projected storyworlds as sequences of deliberate, goal-directed behaviors—behaviors that unfold as part of a larger pattern of states, events, and actions, or alternatively stative and nonstative types of events. But a comparison of Frawley's and Givón's taxonomies shows that this formulation still leaves much to be specified. Depending on the approach adopted, states can be categorized into permanent and temporary conditions; events can be subdivided into causes, motions, and actions that may in turn be (more or less) temporally bounded or unbounded; and actions can be split into temporally bounded and unbounded types of acts. In this connection, rather than trying to adjudicate between Frawley's and Givón's accounts, I show how each opens up new avenues of inquiry for narratologists.

Frawley's (1992: 149–96) taxonomy of events makes a first broad division between entities and events. Just as entities tend overwhelmingly to surface as nouns in human languages, "[n]ot all verbs are actions, but when actions are expressed, they overwhelmingly tend to surface as verbs" (141). In English, verb inflections are the chief grammatical resource for expressing information about tense (or relationship between the time frame of what is spoken of and the time frame of the speaking) and aspect (or the temporal contour of the action being described, e.g., whether it is punctual, iterative, or durative). By the same token, a dominant concern with temporality is what distinguishes events from entities: "Nouns represent *entities*, a cover term for all relatively atemporal regions or individuals, including persons, places, and things. Verbs encode *events*: a cover term for states or conditions of existence (e.g., *be sad*), processes or unfoldings (e.g., *get sad*), and actions or executed processes (e.g., *sadden*)" (141). For Frawley, then, states, as well as causes, actions, and motions, are a type of event that languages encode by way of verbs (145–81). Figure 1 diagrams Frawley's scheme and lists verbal constructions exemplifying the four event types.[13]

In this scheme, stativity and nonstativity are properties having to do with the internal structure of events, rather than properties associated with atemporal versus temporal phenomena as such.[14] In particular, though stativity and nonstativity admit differences of degree, "[s]tative events are internally uniform, in marked contrast to actives, which appear to be heterogeneous and internally structured" (147). At stake is thus a difference of scope: for statives the scope of the event is the event as a totality, whereas for actives the scope of the event includes its components, or constituent subprocesses. Think, for example, of the difference between *Susan likes willow oaks* and *Susan planted the willow oak*. These semantic distinctions provide additional insight into why, as a cognitive and communicative mode, narrative has been traditionally—though, as I argue in the following subsection, somewhat too grossly—associated with events rather than states. Stories do not just identify and record elements of the storyworld as undifferentiated totalities. Instead, they focus on heterogeneous, causally intertwined subprocesses some of which can, in more or less tellable ways, fail, get interrupted, be thwarted by antagonists, and so on.[15] There is a vast difference between, on the one hand, (a set of) stative propositions about Joe (e.g., *Joe is in debt*, *Joe is happy*, *Joe is thirty-two years old*, *Joe lives in New Jersey*, *Joe is plagued by green behemoths in his sleep*) and, on the other hand, a sequence of nonstative propositions (*Joe lost all his money on the stock market*, *Joe moved to New Jersey*, etc.) tracing the logic of Joe's changing states by detailing the subprocesses that produce the termination of one state, the onset of the next, or the coexistence of both.

Under Frawley's rubric of nonstative events fall those expressed by verbs of motion (to be taken up in detail in chapter 7); causatives expressing some relation of determination between two (or more) events, with a prior event resulting in or giving rise to a subsequent event; and actions, or nonstative events that, unlike statives, can be controlled, executed, or carried out via the carrying out of a series of different subprocesses resulting in some effect. Different narrative modes es-

Figure 1. A Taxonomy of Events (adapted from Fawley)

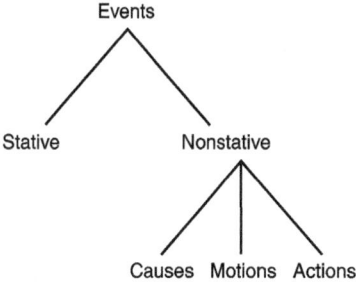

Stative event: Susan likes trees
Cause: Susan had the trees protected
Motion: Susan walked from the trees to the house
Action: Susan planted the trees

tablish different proportions between—or, alternatively, create different preference rankings for—stative events and nonstative causes, motions, and actions (see table 3 below). Arguably, however, narrative cannot accommodate a system of preferences in which statives intermix with causes and motions but not with actions at all. By definition, psychological novels focus more attention on mental and characterological attributes and their causes than on what participants DO or on how they MOVE from one spatiotemporal region of the storyworld to another. What Rilke's Malte Laurids Brigge does once inside his shabby flat, or what paths of motions he takes through the streets of Paris, figure less importantly than the states of mind he is in while he acts and moves. Yet if he did not act at all—that is, if he did not perform *any* deliberately initiated, internally structured, and more or less temporally bounded actions—Rilke's novel could not properly be called a narrative. It would be, instead, a mere tabulation of Brigge's psychological states or a bare list of his successive movements in space. Meanwhile, whereas actions play a prominent role in both epic accounts and news reports, news stories prioritize causes to a degree epics do not. An epic celebrates heroic actions in battle and may recount *how* they were accomplished the better to memorialize them for an audience, but a news report focuses attention on *why* the Chinese embassy in Belgrade, for example, was mistakenly bombed during NATO's recent air campaign against the Serbs. In the case of ghost stories, narrators regularly invoke a specialized version of Turner's (1996) preference rule for narrative imagining: not UNDERSTAND EVENTS AS ACTION, but rather UNDERSTAND MOTIONS AS AC-

Table 3. Preference Rankings for Nonstative Events (by genre)

	Epic	News reports	Psychological novels	Ghost stories
Causes	L	P	P	L
Motions	L	L	L	P
Actions	P	P	L	P

I, D, L, P = Illicit, Dispreferred, Licit, Preferred

TIVITIES. In other words, storytellers cue their listeners to infer that movements of objects along trajectories in the storyworld are a function of temporally unbounded ghostly activities, that is, of hauntings.

Table 3 diagrams the relevant preference rankings for nonstative types of events across these four representative genres. Causes, motions, and actions are labeled (in order of increasingly high preference rankings) ILLICIT, DISPREFERRED, LICIT, and PREFERRED for each narrative mode. This schema assumes, first, that stative events are universally present in stories. Insofar as stories recount interesting or tellable transitions between states (e.g., Achilles is alive → Achilles is dead; George Hurstwood [in Theodore Dreiser's *Sister Carrie* (Dreiser 1997)] is a well-to-do manager of a Chicago restaurant → George Hurstwood is destitute and homeless in New York City), a narrative without stative events is inconceivable. So what distinguishes narrative modes is their preference for different distributions of nonstative event types. Second, the schema assumes that in no narrative genre are actions dispreferred (or, *a fortiori*, illicit). Rather, the scale for action preferences ranges from licit to preferred, with lower scalar values corresponding not to other narrative genres but to nonnarrative modes.

I turn now to Talmy Givón's (1993: 89–145) analysis of the semantics of English verbs to present another perspective on event types. Givón's taxonomy provides the basis for a somewhat finer-grained classification of event types, as well as another way of characterizing the systems of preference rules associated with different kinds of stories.

Givón's Taxonomy: A System of State, Event, and Action Parameters

Like Frawley, Givón highlights the features of executability and goal directedness in classifying actions as a particular type of event. For

Figure 2. A Taxonomy of States, Events, and Actions (adapted from Givón 1993)

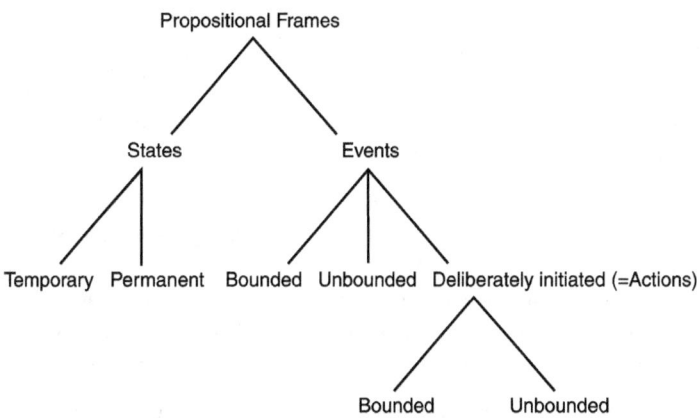

Temporary state = Joe is in debt
Permanent state = Joe is human
Bounded event = High tide crested at 9 p.m.
Unbounded event = Global warming was making ocean levels rise year by year
Bounded action = Joe paid off his debt
Unbounded action = Joe worked at extricating himself from debt

---

Givón, verbs constitute the basic "propositional frame" or semantic core of clauses. Verbal clauses can be divided, broadly, into verbs coding experience in terms of states and verbs expressing events, defined as changes of state over time. States themselves may be either permanent or temporary, and events further subdivided into "fast" or bounded events that involve changes from a definite initial state to a definite terminal state; "slow" or unbounded events coded as ongoing processes without clear temporal boundaries; and actions (themselves either bounded or unbounded) consisting of events deliberately initiated by an active participant or agent. Figure 2 diagrams Givón's taxonomy and lists verbal constructions that exemplify the relevant coding strategies.

It is instructive to compare this account of verb semantics with definitions of narrative that attribute to stories the core property of *representing events or changes of state* (see, e.g., Chatman 1978, 1990;

G. Prince 1973, 1982, 1987; Rimmon-Kenan 1983). Such definitions are widespread in the narratological literature. Gerald Prince (1987), for instance, defines narrative as "[t]he recounting ... of one or more real or fictive events communicated by one, two, or several (more or less overt) narrators to one, two, or several (more or less overt) narratees" (58). Alluding to the distinction between story (or fabula, or the narrated, or what is told) and discourse (or sjužet, or the narrative, or the way something is told), Prince writes:

> The story always involves temporal sequence (it consists of at least one modification of a state of affairs obtaining at time t_0 into another state of affairs obtaining at t_n).... Moreover, in a "true" narrative as opposed to the mere recounting of a series of changes of state, these situations and events also make up a whole, a sequence ... having—to use Aristotle's terminology—a *beginning*, a *middle*, and an *end*. (1987: 58–59)

Givón's idea of propositional frames and his taxonomy of event types, however, suggests that some further specifications are in order. A story can be described as a sequentially presented set of propositions, each using various types of verbal constructions to create different propositional frames. (In the case of visual narratives, one could speak instead of a sequence of images whose narrative content viewers can use propositions to summarize or paraphrase.) From this perspective, there is no such thing as a "narrative proposition"; rather, there are particular ways of sequencing propositions (or propositional frames) that are more or less recognizably narrative in nature. Prince's important insight is that a sequence of state-oriented propositional frames (*Gregor Samsa felt himself to be a negligible presence in his family and in the world. . . . Gregor lacked the kind of interactions needed by human beings. . . . Gregor continued to be exceedingly unhappy*) will be less recognizably narrative than a sequence of frames that code experience in terms of events leading (suspensefully) from certain initial states through "middle" states to other, terminal states (*Gregor Samsa felt himself to be a negligible presence in his family and in the world. . . . Then one day he woke up and found himself transformed into some sort of beetle. . . . Then his family began to revile him as an odious insect*).

Note, however, that defining narrative as the representation of events or changes of state still leaves several questions unanswered. Are the states at issue temporary or permanent? Are the events that lead from source to target states bounded or unbounded?[16] Or are those events, in

States, Events, and Actions   45

fact, deliberately initiated actions, and if so, are they actions of the bounded or the unbounded sort? Assigning different values to these state, event, and action parameters will yield vastly different sorts of narratives. To continue with the example of Franz Kafka's *Die Verwandlung* (*The Metamorphosis*; 1984b), introduced in the previous paragraph: What helps explain the enduring appeal—and unnerving quality—of Kafka's story is the way its central (bounded) event involves a change of state that is dispreferred in the realistic or naturalistic narrative genres to which Kafka's tale in most respects belongs. Much of the story marshals details about Gregor's surroundings and family life— what Roland Barthes (1982) called "reality effects"—to cue readers to reconstruct a storyworld in which the ordinary laws of physics are valid. But the tale's opening lines, together with cues that re-emerge later in the narrative, suggest a mode of transformation more typical of Ovid's *Metamorphoses* than a realistic or quasi-realistic fiction from the modern era. Specifically, the story traces a change involving the loss of what ordinarily counts as a permanent state (Gregor is a human at time t_0) and the acquisition of a new "permanent" state (Gregor is an insect at time t_1) without the disappearance or replacement of the storyworld entity (in this case a participant) undergoing such wholesale alteration. Schematically, the event transpires as $Gregor_x$ is human → $Gregor_x$ is insect, not $Gregor_x$ is human → $Gregor_y$ is insect. To put this same point still another way, in the strange logic of Kafkan events, a predicate that normally operates in binary fashion (human/inhuman, or ± human), being either applicable (+) or inapplicable (-) to storyworld entities at any given time, functions in a gradient way (less human ↔ more human), being more or less applicable to one and the same entity over time. The shock effect of Kafka's tale thus derives from the way it subverts expected coding strategies—coding strategies that much of the story cues readers to use—and allows a bounded event to bring about a radical change of state that in naturalistic genres requires the extinction of the participant/entity involved.[17]

More generally, whereas tables 2 and 3 indicated that differences of narrative genre can be correlated with different (hierarchical systems of) preference rankings for event types, the taxonomy I have adapted from Givón suggests another, more comprehensive basis for classification. What may best discriminate between narrative modes are preferred or, minimally, allowable collocations of propositional frames. At issue are a total of six state, event, and action parameters; values assigned to those parameters in a given story dictate whether the narrative (preferentially) codes experiences in terms of temporary or permanent states, bounded or unbounded events, and bounded or unbounded actions. More precisely, values for these parameters determine which *coding combinations* might be labeled once again (in order of increasingly high preference rankings) ILLICIT, DISPREFERRED, LICIT, and PREFERRED in a particular narrative mode. It would require quantitative analysis—that is, counting how many verbal clauses of each type a given narrative contains—to assign exact values to the relevant parameters and thereby check for genre-specific patterns. In advance of an investigation of this sort, table 4 offers a preliminary schematization. It correlates coding preferences with the four genres discussed previously and also, for the sake of comparison, with Kafka's *Metamorphosis* and Edmund Spenser's allegorical poem *The Faerie Queene* (1981).

All narratives, it seems, involve combinations of states, events, and actions, but different kinds of stories display preferences for different kinds of combinations. Epics focus on accomplishments and achievements, trafficking in species of temporal boundedness that encompass both actions and events in order to celebrate the enduring valor of Achilles or Beowulf or the persistence and wily intelligence of Odysseus. In turn, though bounded events do regularly occur in epics (Beowulf dies from wounds inflicted by the dragon; Achilles dies from the injury to his heel), the imperative to celebrate and memorialize *acts* of heroism results in a dispreference for coding strategies relying on unbounded events. (The epic genre is thus the narrative kind in which Turner's preference rule UNDERSTAND EVENTS AS ACTIONS perhaps finds its widest scope.) The psychological novel, for its part, displays a distinct preference for combining unbounded actions (e.g., Henry James's characters' attempts to negotiate the complexity of interpersonal relations) with permanent and especially temporary states (e.g., + female, + American, more or less status conscious, more or less susceptible to the manipulativeness of false friends). By contrast, bounded actions are dispreferred in this novelistic genre, which foregrounds states of mind and (relatively unbounded) processes of reflection, evaluation of others' behavior and probable motives, and so forth. News reports typically show a preference for yet another combination of coding strategies. They place a premium on bounded actions and events; states, ongoing

States, Events, and Actions 47

Table 4. Preference Rankings for Coding Strategies (by genre)

	Epic	News reports	Psych. novels	Ghost stories	Kafka	Spenser
TS	L	L	P	L	L	P or D*
PS	P	L	L	P	P	L or P*
BE	P	P	L	L	P	P or D*
UE	D	L	L	L	L	L or P*
BA	P	P	D	L	L	P or D*
UA	L	L	P	P	L	D or P*

TS = Temporary state   BA = Bounded action
PS = Permanent state   UA = Unbounded action
BE = Bounded event   I, D, L, P = Illicit, Dispreferred, Licit, and Preferred
UE = Unbounded event

*Coding preferences vary across evolving (foregrounded) and static (backgrounded) participants, the main plot line and its branchings, and levels of the allegory

processes, and continuous activities are licit but more properly the province of backstory.

Meanwhile, in an allegory such as book 1 of Edmund Spenser's *The Faerie Queene* (1981), coding preferences vary across the episodes contained within multiple plot lines—or rather, within multiple branchings from a main plot line involving the education of the protagonist, Red Crosse Knight. Alternation between coding strategies serves to differentiate evolving (foregrounded) and static (backgrounded) participants and also to highlight moral and spiritual differences between participants in each group. In book 1, the Knight's picaresque journey to find the beautiful Fairie Queene (aka Queen Elizabeth) entails a sequence of bounded actions more or less successfully performed; it also entails, in some instances, the acquisition of temporary psychological and moral qualities (states of despair, weakness, pride, and so on) that threaten the protagonist's very soul. Coding of this sort can be contrasted with that used for villains such as Archimago, a figure for Satan and chief architect of all that is potentially deceptive in the realm of the senses, and Duessa, the Knight's duplicitous temptress. Participants such as these two exemplify permanent moral attributes that they can only (temporarily) strive to conceal in attempts to ensnare their Christian foes. Further, the very structure of allegory, in which "the events of a narrative obviously and continuously refer to another simultaneous structure of events or ideas, whether historical events, moral or philosophical ideas, or natural phenomena" (Frye 1974: 12), necessitates a sort of double coding of what happens in the storyworld. On the one hand, what occurs can be conceptualized as a sequence of temporally bounded actions and events (e.g., Red Crosse Knight defeats the dragon-like Error and her vicious mother-eating progeny; Red Crosse Knight and Una part ways because of a deception practiced upon them by Archimago); on the other hand, the "true," noumenal reality consists of an ongoing struggle of good against evil, Christian against infidel, as well as a massive chain of events ongoingly triggered by Satan's pride, rebellion, and fall.

Finally, note once again the similarity of the coding preferences in Kafka and the North Carolina ghost stories mentioned previously. In both cases, ostensibly permanent and binarized states (± human, ± dead) are coded as temporary and gradient. The chief difference is that, whereas Kafka's text portrays Gregor's mind-bending transformation as a temporally bounded *event*, ghost stories code supernatural occurrences as *behavior* with a temporally unbounded profile. Haunting (unlike the change that instantaneously befalls Gregor) is a goal-directed activity, but it is difficult to map onto points of inception and termination that fall at definite points within a span of time. When compared with the epic mode, this example again suggests that Turner's general preference rule for narrative imagining—UNDERSTAND EVENTS AS ACTIONS—describes less a universal property of stories than a preference that will be ranked higher or lower depending on how it functions within a broader system of coding preferences. The event of Gregor's transformation is less amenable to being coded as an action than are events interpreted as instances of (temporally unbounded) paranormal activity.

As table 3 indicates, in none of the narrative genres discussed does a state, event, or action parameter warrant the preference ranking of ILLICIT. This provides a way of accounting for the pervasiveness, adaptability, and persistence of narrative as both a communicative mode and a cognitive style. Stories encompass—and, arguably, foster use of—all of the coding strategies made possible by the semantic resources (e.g., verbs) of a language.[18] In other words, narrative provides an organic, naturally occurring context in which all of the strategies can be used more or less frequently and in various combinations to build storyworlds more or less richly differentiated into states, events, actions. Narrative, in short, furnishes a forgiving, flexible cognitive frame for constructing, communicating, and reconstructing mentally projected worlds—the only worlds, arguably, that any of us can ever know. The problem of what makes a narrative a narrative, a problem that is one of the major concerns of my next chapter, thus cannot be addressed at the level of individual propositions or propositional frames. Instead it must be addressed at a higher level of narrative structure—that is, the level of coding *combinations*.

This "discourse perspective" on stories contrasts with approaches that draw on traditional grammatical frameworks (Todorov 1969), structuralist linguistics (Barthes 1977), or transformational-generative grammar (G. Prince 1973, 1982) to propose analogies between sentence-level and narrative structures. The difficulty with such approaches, arguably, is that moving from sentences to discourses does not just require an adjustment of scale or scope; this shift also necessitates, in some cases, using quite different descriptive and analytic tools.[19] In the case of the syntactic structure of sentences, it may indeed be possible to make judgments about grammaticality (see, e.g., Chomsky 1965) and to establish degrees of acceptability for sentence forms. Take, for example, a speaker who needs to design a sentence that expresses his or her surprise at finding someone who generally hates hummus suddenly ready to eat it. As the following sentences suggest, some candidate constructions do in fact merit the ranking of ILLICIT in this communicative scenario—even though *which* of the grammatically LICIT sentences is PREFERRED for a specific utterance will depend on what contextual circumstances obtain:

To amenable you hummus are eating strangely. (I)

You are amenable to strangely eating hummus. (D)

You, strangely, are amenable to eating hummus. (L or P) [uttered to a group of people, with a gesture toward a specific person in the group]

Strangely you are amenable to eating hummus. (L or P) [uttered to foreground the strangeness of the act of eating hummus]

You are amenable to eating hummus, strangely. (L or P) [uttered to stress that the hummus hater's willingness to eat hummus is indeed, strangely enough, a fact about the world]

By contrast, narratives do not have a "syntax" of the sort structuring these sentences. All available coding strategies are LICIT in stories at a local level. As narratologists have long recognized, however, at a higher level of narrative structure stories (or more precisely users of narrative) disprefer chaining together a disproportionate number of state-oriented propositional frames. Thus, to *be* a narrative, a set of sequentially ordered sentences or images designed to encode a storyworld must satisfy requirements operative at a higher or discourse level. A future task for narratologists is to embark on quantitative analyses of these global constraints. It may then be possible to establish actual preference rankings for relative *proportions* of states, events, and actions both across different kinds of stories and across narrative as opposed to nonnarrative discourse.

Beyond the Semantics of Verbs

Although research on verb semantics can help illuminate the preference-rule systems that support narrative imagining, building or reconstructing a storyworld encompasses much more, of course, than choosing between various coding strategies made available by the grammar of verbs. In particular, whereas verbs offer important clues as to what constitutes a state, what an event, and what an action in the worlds mentally projected during narrative comprehension, there is not necessarily a one-to-one correspondence between a story's textual format and the mental models that its form prompts readers to reconstruct. Rather, a particular textual format may evoke a variety of mental representations, and conversely a given mental representation can be correlated with a variety of textual formats. Depending on the context, *I walked* can evoke a representation of my taking a stroll through the neighborhood, escaping from a low- or medium-security correctional facility, leaving a restaurant without paying, or participating in a college graduation ceremony. In turn, I can code all of these occurrences in ways that emphasize or de-emphasize my agency, convey an impression of their being more a state or condition in which I found myself than an action I may have precipitated, and so on. The next chapter explores this problem in connection with *actions* specifically, already revealed to be of central importance to the logic of stories.

Davidson (1980) pinpoints the difficulties besetting any attempt to define the nature and scope of action on the basis of verb semantics alone:

> I drugged the sentry, I contracted malaria, I danced, I swooned, Jones was kicked by me, Smith was outlived by me: this is a series of examples designed to show that a person named as subject in sentences in the active (whether or not the verb is transitive) or as object in sentences in the passive, may or may not be the agent of the event recorded.... [And] very often a sentence will record an episode in the life of the agent and leave us in the dark as to whether it was an action [e.g., he coughed, squinted, sweated, or tripped over the rug]. (44)

Davidson's point here is that we know whether these events are actions only after we know more than what the verb in each sentence tells us. As Davidson puts it, "By considering the additional information that would settle the matter, we may find an answer to the question of what makes a bit of biography an action" (44). But exactly what sort of "additional information" is required in this connection? What *does* make a bit of biography (interpretable as) an action? And for that matter, what conditions have to be satisfied for a sequence of actions to be construed as a biography? These questions are the chief concerns of chapters 2 and 3.[20]

2

Action Representations

Although Genette did not distinguish between actions and events in the quotation that began the previous chapter, ideas drawn from work on the semantics of verbs have already shown the need for some finer discriminations when it comes to building mental models of what goes on in storyworlds. As Davidson's (1980) comments suggested, however, being able to draw distinctions between states, events, and actions is more than a matter of linguistic competence, requiring something beyond the ability to use and understand the verbs of a language.[1] Verbs provide a clue to, but not a completely reliable index of, the ways in which users of a language carve up the structure of the real; the same goes for verbs vis-à-vis the structure of storyworlds. In language use generally and narratives specifically, a person's mastery of verb forms, tenses, and moods is only part of a broader cognitive capacity enabling him or her to model, express, and comprehend ways in which things exemplify certain properties or states, undergo certain kinds of transformations, or are embedded in more or less complicated patterns of purposive behavior.[2] Accordingly, building on the semantic theories sketched in chapter 1, the present chapter tries to situate in a broader context of cognitive skills and dispositions the use of state-, event-, and, especially, action-oriented propositions in stories. Focusing for the time being on the links between narrative and action, I insist on the distinction between linguistic markers or tags for narrated actions, on the one hand, and the mentally projected *action representations* that various linguistic formats can be used to tag, on the other hand. From this perspective, actions provide localized principles of design with which verbs tend probabilistically to collocate; that is, they are microdesigns that commonly surface in written narratives as verbal or at least verb-like expressions. Analogously, entities or individuals are microdesigns with which nouns tend to collocate, usually surfacing in narrative discourse as nominal or noun-like expressions (cf. Frawley 1992: 62–139).[3]

The first part of this chapter explores narratological consequences of ideas developed, mainly by philosophers, under the auspices of *action theory* (see, e.g., Danto 1985; Davidson 1980; Davis 1979; Goldman 1970; Rescher 1966; von Wright 1966; and, for important narratological extensions of action theory, van Dijk 1976 and Doležel 1998). As I did with theories of verb semantics in chapter 1, I survey and discuss the implications for narrative analysis of several action-theoretical models. Jointly these models imply that the idea of *action* itself needs to be decomposed into several other, more carefully specified concepts. The chapter then turns from representations of actions as such to representations of sequences of actions. Here I draw on Arthur Danto's (1985) suggestive distinction between *atomic* and *molecular narratives*, along with an analogous distinction drawn by Georg Henrik von Wright (1966) between *action descriptions* and *biographies*. The final part of the chapter prepares the way for chapter 3 by introducing the concept of *action structures*, which can be defined as higher-order narrative units based on inferences about participants' (emergent) beliefs, desires, and intentions. These units, or principles of organization, allow listeners and readers to connect non-adjacent events into a coherent, psychologically plausible whole. For, as David Rummelhart (1975) puts it, "[S]ome higher level of organization takes place in stories that does not take place in strings of sentences" as such (213).

Whereas core concepts of action theory shed light on minimal or atomic narratives and also help distinguish them from larger-scale or molecular narratives, coming to terms with what von Wright calls *biographies* and what Danto labels *molecular narratives* requires additional, more properly cognitive-scientific principles of explanation. My next chapter shows how such principles can be used to explain, in particular, the difference between sequences of occurrences that compose a (molecular) narrative and sequences that do not.

Action Theory and Narrative Theory

In his *Essays on Actions and Events* (1980), Davidson poses what are perhaps the central questions of action theory: "What events in the life of a person reveal agency; what are his deeds and his doings in contrast to mere happenings in history; what is the mark that distinguishes his actions?" Significantly, telling a story entails trying to forestall questions of a very similar sort on the part of a reader, listener, or viewer. Action theorists themselves have compared analyzing actions with telling narratives about what agents have done. As von Wright (1983) puts it, "To understand behavior as intentional . . . is to fit it into a 'story' about an agent" (42; cf. Danto 1985; Davis 1979: 96–102). Stories, in other words, rely implicitly on the same conceptual systems that action theorists strive to make explicit through philosophical argumentation. Insofar as they distinguish between act-types and act-tokens, create taxonomies of act-types, and so on, action theorists can be compared with architects (or perhaps architecturally minded archaeologists) mapping the structures and supports of human action. By contrast, storytellers can be likened to guides who invite readers, listeners, and viewers to create, inhabit, familiarize themselves with, and hence better appreciate exemplary as well as exceptional varieties and modes of action. Action theorists study what conditions have to hold for an event to be deemed an action; stories focus on what it means for a particular action or sequence of actions to have happened (or not to have happened) under a particular set of conditions, whether fictional or nonfictional.[4] Hence, in the sections that follow, I draw on several action-theoretical approaches to highlight ways in which competency at forming action representations is an essential requirement for creating and comprehending storyworlds.

Actions, Results, and Acting Situations

In his pathbreaking studies of the logic of action, von Wright (1966) defines acting as intentionally bringing about or preventing a change in the world. In turn, change occurs when some state of affairs either ceases to be or comes to be. Thus, for von Wright, giving a complete description of an action requires describing three items: (a) the initial state, or the state in which the world is at the moment when action is initiated; (b) the end state, or the state in which the world is when the action has been completed; and (c) the state in which the world would have been had it not been for the action in question (123–24). In the case of the act of brushing my teeth, for example, (a) would be my having unbrushed teeth, (b) would be my having brushed teeth, and "factoring out" the act of brushing would produce (c) a world state S in which, counterfactually speaking, my teeth remain unbrushed. As the logic of action predicts, in the case of my *preventing* myself from brushing my own teeth, (b) would be the negation of the end state of the act of brushing my teeth, while factoring out my own agency produces not-S.

Especially consequential for narrative theory is von Wright's emphasis on the importance of item (c) for action representation. Whereas the end state is simply the *result* of the action, von Wright calls the pairing of the initial state and the end state (a pairing that yields item [c]) the *acting situation* or, alternatively, the *opportunity* of action (124). Grasping an acting situation or opportunity for action, then, is tantamount to being able to formulate a counterfactual conditional statement about what would have happened had it not been for what an agent did on a given occasion. So to build a logic for action sentences, one must model not only "sentences describing results of action but also . . . sentences describing states which are, or are not, transformed through the action" (von Wright 1983: 111). Likewise, in the field of narrative analysis, a number of researchers (e.g., Bremond 1980; Labov 1972a; G. Prince 1988 and 1992; Ryan 1991) have stressed that narrative imagining always takes place against a backdrop consisting of representations of things that might have happened in the storyworld but did not. Early on in the history of narratology, and around the same time von Wright was developing his theories of action, Claude Bremond (1973, 1980) characterized the logic of narrative possibilities in terms of elementary triads that can be combined through conjunction, alternation, or embedding to produce larger narrative sequences. Individual triads consist of the opening of a possible course of action (a state of virtuality corresponding to the more or less explicit formulation of some goal); the actualization or non-actualization of this virtuality (through the performance or non-actualization of some act or set of acts); and, in the case of actualization, the attainment or non-attainment of the goal being pursued, through a successful or unsuccessful implementation of acts.

In Kate Chopin's *The Awakening* (1993), for example, a possible course of action opens when the roles of wife and mother begin to chafe at Edna Pontellier, and she starts yearning for a new mode of life. This state of virtuality is actualized when, instead of allowing her hopes and desires to remain mere wishes or fantasies, Edna takes steps to liberate herself from her husband's influence and control. But her efforts end with what many readers have interpreted to be an act of suicide on Edna's part, resulting (at least in one sense) in the non-attainment of her goal. Combining von Wright's and Bremond's models, one might say that Edna's actions take on narrative interest because of the acting situations in which they unfold. Admittedly, a narrative with the complexity of *The Awakening* involves much more elaborate world states than the simplified cases examined by von Wright and other theorists of action (e.g., Goldman 1970). But this does not negate the value of acting situations (i.e., constellations of narrative possibilities) as an explanatory principle. Thus, by pairing the result of Edna's actions, her death, with the initial state of her unhappiness, one can generate any number of counterfactual conditional statements underscoring the salience of the agency that Edna did, in fact, exert in the storyworld: for example, *If Edna had not acted on her initial impulses, she might have lived a long, unhappy life*; or again, *If Edna had not had an affair with Alcée Arobin, she might have drifted back into her passionless, stifling marriage with Léonce*.

More than this, however, analysts of stories have shown that it is part of the nature of narrative to indicate, in a more or less explicit and sustained way, that the actions being recounted are embedded in acting situations. For instance, Gerald Prince (1992) notes that "though narrative is primarily concerned with what happened rather than what might have happened" (34), nonetheless many stories employ a device that Prince calls "the disnarrated" to dwell on "events that *do not* happen though they could have and are nonetheless referred to (in a negative or hypothetical mode) by the narrative text" (30; see also chapter 8 below). The disnarrated thus makes "explicit the logic at work in narrative whereby, as Claude Bremond emphasized, every narrative function opens an alternative, a set of possible directions, and every narrative progresses by following certain directions as opposed to others" (36). Thus, to return to *The Awakening*, in a passage recounting Léonce's concern about how his wife's behavior may affect their public image, Chopin uses the disnarrated (read: foregrounds the Pontelliers' acting situation) to spotlight the consequentiality of Edna's acts, as well as the importance of contrary-to-fact speculation in people's mental lives: "He was simply thinking of his financial integrity. It might get noised about that the Pontelliers had met with reverses, and were forced to conduct their ménage on a humbler scale than heretofore. It might do incalculable mischief to his business prospects" (Chopin 1993: 114). Negative sentences can likewise foreground acting situations over results of actions, indicating how paths chosen by storyworld participants acquire their significance from the place they occupy within a network of paths *not* chosen. As William Labov (1972a) puts it in his account of mechanisms of evaluation in oral narratives, "Negative sentences draw upon a cognitive background considerably richer than the set of events which were observed. They provide a way of evaluating events by placing them against the background of other events which might have happened, but did not" (381).[5] Hence, in recounting occasions on which Robert Lebrun does *not* come to visit Edna, and thereby tracing the acting situation embedding his non-appearances, Chopin hints at the cognitive background that Edna herself draws upon in assessing the meaning of Robert's failure to visit: "Robert did not come that day. She was keenly disappointed. He did not come the following day, nor the next. Each morning she awoke with hope, and each night she was a prey to despondency" (125).[6]

For her part, Marie-Laure Ryan (1991: 148–74) has drawn on possible worlds semantics to argue that the number of virtual or unactualized states, events, and actions in a narrative increases in proportion with its tellability. The more fully a narrative sketches the acting situation(s) of its participants, as opposed to merely reporting the results of their actions, the more likely the story will be deemed worthy of narration (and attended to) by its recipients. Or again, to cite the principle Ryan characterizes as *"seek the diversification of possible worlds in the narrative universe"* (156), a story's tellability is positively correlated with the number of "virtual embedded narratives" it contains, with virtual embedded narratives defined as "story-like constructs contained in the private worlds of characters" (156). These constructs, for Ryan,

> include not only the dreams, fictions, and fantasies conceived or told by characters, but any kind of representation concerning past or future states and events: plans, passive projections, desires, . . . and beliefs concerning the private representations of other characters. Among these embedded narratives, some reflect the events of the factual domain, while others delineate unactualized possibilities. The aesthetic appeal of a plot is a function of the richness and variety of the domain of the virtual, as it is surveyed and made accessible by those private embedded narratives. (156)

On this view, a narrative that dwelled solely on results, in von Wright's sense, would exhibit either very little tellability or even no tellability at all. It would, to invoke the pragmatic model of H. P. Grice (1989), violate

Action Representations 59

the maxim of Relation. The maxim of Relation is Grice's way of capturing the intuition that communicative and other behaviors are commonly assumed to be done for a (situationally appropriate) *reason*. Likewise, one of the default assumptions of storytelling is that there is no reason simply to record the results of actions without indicating—or using the context of the telling to indicate—what was interesting or unusual or remarkable about the accomplishment of those results in the particular circumstances in which they were accomplished. What makes Chopin's tale tellable, then, is not that the protagonist's acts result in her death, but that her acts trace a path through a constellation of story-like constructs corresponding to Edna's and other participants' hopes, anxieties, desires, beliefs, and plans. Edna places so much hope in Robert, only to have it dashed; she worries about her children but will not allow her own identity to be absorbed into theirs; she plans a life for herself as an autonomous being passionately devoted to art, but in the end, unlike Mademoiselle Reisz, she cannot bring that plan to fruition.

Ryan argues that the inherently greater tellability of plots involving elements such as unsuccessful action, broken promises, and deception (as compared with plots featuring successful plans, fulfilled promises, accurate knowledge, etc.) is confirmed by the occurrence of these plot elements in all cultures, periods, and genres (158). Ryan's theory predicts that narratives achieve tellability by inscribing actions in acting situations, thereby defining the lower boundary past which a story devolves into a mere listing of results and ceases to be a story at all. But there is also an upper limit of tellability. Past some point, presumably, a narrative could focus so much attention on opportunities for action (as opposed to acts performed) that once again it might cease to be recognizable as a narrative. To reinvoke the vocabulary of preference rules established in chapter 1, narrative disprefers both unadorned results and the unchecked proliferation of acting situations. By the same token, the universality of certain plot elements across narrative genres does not entail that all genres prefer those elements in the same way or to the same degree.

Figure 3 provides a partial typology of preference rankings for modes of action representation in stories. As the diagram suggests, in each of the three representative genres a dual focus on (or blending of) results and acting situations is preferred, with a concomitant dispreference for representations assuming the form of either simple results or total act-

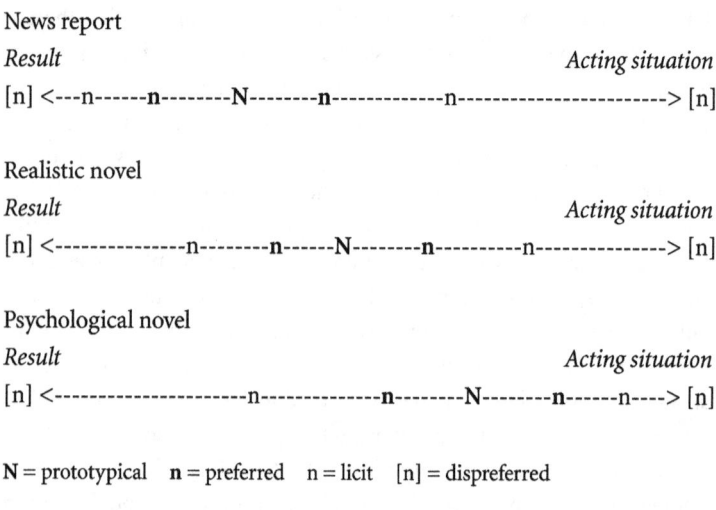

Figure 3. A Typology of Preference Rankings for Action Representations in Narrative (by genre)

N = prototypical   **n** = preferred   n = licit   [n] = dispreferred

---

ing situations. Yet a prototypical narrative (or N) of each sort strikes a different balance between results and opportunities for action, thereby shifting the location of the band in which preferred modes of action representations fall. At a global level (though not necessarily at the level of individual actions, of course), news stories tolerate more result-oriented representations than do psychological novels. Meanwhile, the broad and continued popularity of the realistic novel derives, perhaps, from the way its prototypical and preferred action representations are centrally located on the scale. (*The Awakening*, arguably, can be positioned somewhere between the realistic and the psychological novel. Compare the interpretations of Gilbert 1998, May 1998, and Wolff 1998.) As in chapter 1, I construe narrative as a forgiving, flexible cognitive and communicative frame in which, whatever the genre, a broad range of representational techniques are at least licit if not preferred. All the same, figure 3 suggests that differences among genres correspond to statistically different distributions of result- and opportunity-oriented techniques for representing actions.

Up to this point, I have focused mainly on narratological consequences of the contrast between results and acting situations. The next subsection further decomposes both of these concepts, drawing on other instruments of description and analysis developed by action theorists. In particular, I explore ways of specifying basic parameters for acting. Values assigned to these parameters determine how, in a given case, results are to be mentally projected as the outcome of actions performed in storyworlds, which are characterized in turn by an ordered succession of acting situations.

Parameters of Action

Von Wright (1983: 117) suggests that the logic of actions is a logic of action sentences having a schematic prototype—specifically, "agent *a* on occasion *o* does action *p*." Distinguishing between process actions and achievement actions (recall the discussion of Vendler's contrast between activities and achievements in chapter 1), von Wright (1983: 173–74) names eight elementary types of achievement actions that can be expressed through sentences whose form encodes an agent:

(a) producing a given state of affairs;

(b) leaving the state to continue absent;

(c) sustaining the state;

(d) letting the state cease to obtain;

(e) destroying the state;

(f) leaving the state to continue present;

(g) suppressing the state; or

(h) letting the state come to obtain.

Note that one and the same storyworld behavior can be recounted via different types of action-sentence formats. Continuing on with the example of *The Awakening*, Edna's final act of swimming far out to sea (a) *produces the state of affairs* S_1 in which Edna (according to many readers) is dead by virtue of suicide. But her act also (e) *destroys the state of affairs* S_2 that existed just prior to her death and that consists of Edna's being alive, just as the act (b) *lets continue absent* yet another state S_3: namely, the state of Léonce's being cognizant of his wife's anxieties, desires, and needs. Meanwhile, each action-sentence format can match up with several kinds of storyworld occurrences. For example, any number of Edna's actions can be conceived as state sustaining (c). Her not communicating with Léonce (a mode of *not* acting) sustains the state of their incompatibility, as does, in effect, her moving out of the house they had been sharing in New Orleans, her having an affair with Arobin, and her subsequent attempt to initiate a relationship with Robert Lebrun, all very different modes of acting. There would thus seem to be both a one-many and a many-one relationship between what I am calling action-sentence formats and what recipients mentally model agents as *doing* in storyworlds.

Yet from this it does not follow that action representations are merely randomly (i.e., unpredictably) correlated with textual cues in narrative discourse. Rather, in the case of reading or hearing or viewing a story, general and basic cognitive principles guide the matching of action representations with textual (or, more broadly, semiotic) cues. Such cues can be more or less detailed and trigger action representations in a more or less explicit way. Consider, in this connection, the parameters for action description that Nicholas Rescher (1966) specifies. For Rescher, whereas an action can be represented in more and more elaborate ways, perhaps to an indefinite extent, "this can be viewed as the increasingly detailed presentation of a limited and manageable number of distinctive characteristic aspects of action" (218). In particular, Rescher lists the following as elements of the canonical description of an action:

1. Agent (WHO did it)

2. Act-type (WHAT did he or she do?)

3. Modality of Action (HOW did he or she do it?)

   a. Modality of manner (IN WHAT MANNER did he or she do it?)

   b. Modality of means (BY WHAT MEANS did he or she do it?)

4. Setting of Action (IN WHAT CONTEXT did he or she do it?)

   a. Temporal aspect (WHEN did he or she do it?)

   b. Spatial aspect (WHERE did he or she do it?)

   c. Circumstantial aspect (UNDER WHAT CIRCUMSTANCES did he or she do it?)

5. Rationale of Action (WHY did he or she do it?)

   a. Causality (WHAT CAUSED him or her to do it?)

   b. Finality (WITH WHAT AIM did he or she do it?)

   c. Intentionality (IN WHAT STATE OF MIND did he or she do it?)
   (Adapted from Rescher 1966: 215)

Rescher's list of action characteristics, which mirrors the "pentad of key terms" (*Act, Scene, Agent, Agency, Purpose*) developed by Kenneth Burke in his 1945 book *A Grammar of Motives* (Burke 1969), also confirms von Wright's argument that descriptions of acts have to encompass both results and acting situations. Whereas items 3a and 3b (and possibly 4a and 4b as well) bear principally on results, items 4c and 5a-c bear principally on the acting situation in which a result is achieved. The larger issue here, though, is that building and re-creating storyworlds depends crucially on assigning values to at least some of these basic parameters of (human) action. In fact, another way to account for differences among narrative genres is to examine how they enable and constrain readers', listeners', or viewers' attempts to "fill in" Rescher's slots for action descriptions.

In principle any action told about in a narrative can be analyzed into values satisfying these slots. Inversely, telling a story about actions in a storyworld is tantamount to enabling recipients to fill in at least some relevant values, thereby generating more or less exhaustive action representations. Not all of the values have to be specified, however, for a given act to be identified and understood. Some can be inferred pragmatically from the slots that do get filled in. For example, in the case of *The Awakening*, the final scene of the novel does not explicitly identify Edna's swimming out into the sea as a token of the act-type of suicide. Nor can the reader be sure of the exact rationale of the action, at least with respect to causality (5a). Chopin alludes to Edna's aims (5b) and state of mind (5c)—that is, she walks down to the beach on Grand Isle "rather mechanically" because she "had done all the thinking which was necessary after Robert went away, when she lay awake upon the sofa till morning" (136)—but does not detail precisely what those aims and intentions are. Yet the text does contain information about the modality of the action (3a and b: Edna swims out into the ocean like a sort of sea worshipper and without heed to her own limitations as a swimmer), along with the circumstances of its performance (3c: Robert Lebrun has left Edna a note indicating that he cannot be her lover, and furthermore her own children "appeared before her [imagination] like antagonists who . . . sought to drag her into the soul's slavery for the rest of her days" [136]). In turn, the information provided by the narrative licenses assigning values to parameters left "open" or unspecified by the text, whereby an inference that Edna commits suicide can be drawn. The possibility of framing alternative interpretations of the novel's ending, along the lines suggested, for example, by Sandra Gilbert (1998: 364), confirms that Chopin's account of Edna's final moments is indeed an underspecified or "moderately open" action representation—in the sense described in my next paragraph.[7] More generally, one can say that the number of slots that are filled in during the representation of an action in a narrative is not—or at least is not necessarily—directly proportional with a recipient's ability to comprehend that action.

Debatably, differences among narrative genres can be correlated with differences in the number and kind of slots for action description left open in a story. To put the same point another way, different sorts of stories differently trigger inferences used to complete action representations that are naturally and normally *underspecified*, to varying degrees, in narrative discourse. Table 5 outlines genre-based contrasts of representational technique; as one moves down the list, one moves toward genres that enable the mental modeling of increasingly detailed action representations. As already indicated, table 5 constitutes a scale spanning stories that cue predominantly open (PO), moderately open (MO), moderately specified (MS), and predominantly specified (PS) action representations. The schema assumes that narrative genres can be defined on the basis of the degree of action specification they globally prefer, though once again individual action representations within a particular kind of story could exploit any of these representational techniques. As the diagram suggests, furthermore, neither fully open (FO) nor fully specified action representations (FS) are licit within the system of preferences associated with narrative imagining. Certain experimental or avant-garde literary narratives do skirt the endpoints of the scale, however. In that way they work to skew the entire preference-rule system toward one or the other extreme, or even to distend the system of preferences outward in the direction of both extremes. This countering or undermining of standard preferences can likewise shift the location of the "preference band" in which, for each narrative genre, preferred degrees of action specifications fall. For example, through repeated exposure to novels like Robbe-Grillet's, readers may come to readjust their canons of tellability not just for narratives with predominantly specified actions but also for narratives with moderately specified ones. In particular, readers may come to revise downward their sense of the minimal threshold of tellability for states, events, and actions recounted in stories.

Table 5. Preferred Degrees of Action Specification in Stories (by genre)

FO	Nonnarrative [texts have no identifiable agents/actions; some experimental or avant-garde literary narratives—e.g., Djuna Barnes's *Nightwood*, Virginia Woolf's *The Waves*, James Joyce's *Finnegans Wake*—trace the boundary between fully and predominantly open action specifications, their narrative logic based on a countering or even undermining of prototypical expectations about narrative itself]
PO	Highly allusive and elusive literary narratives such as the ones just named; narratives told by people with learning disabilities or brain disorders (Duchan 1986; Hamilton 1994)
MO	Detective fiction, mysteries, "whodunits," riddles, ghost stories, "replays" in Erving Goffman's sense (Goffman 1974; K. Young 1999)
MS	Allegories, insinuated or elliptical stories, mildly mythopoeic novels such as *The Awakening* (cf. Gilbert 1998), "novels of ideas"
PS	News reports, realist fictions, fictionalized histories, nonfiction novels, science fiction, biographies and autobiographies, popular romance novels
FS	Nonnarrative [texts are descriptively oversaturated, violating preference rules associated with tellability or reportability, i.e., that which makes states, events, or actions worthy of recounting; some experimental or avant-garde literary narratives—e.g., the novels of Robbe-Grillet and other instances of the Nouveau Roman—trace the boundary between fully and predominantly specified action representations, their narrative logic based on a countering or even undermining of prototypical expectations about narrative itself]

FO = fully open
PO = predominantly open
MO = moderately open
MS = moderately specified
PS = predominantly specified
FS = fully specified

This scalar model of action representation in narrative bears importantly on two further issues, to be discussed in my next two subsections. The first issue pertains to linguistic and literary-theoretical accounts of the problem of implicit information in stories, among other discourse types. My proposal that narratives involve neither fully open nor fully specified action representations, but rather strategically underspecified ones, parallels and extends the account of "gapping" developed by Lubomír Doležel (1998: 169–84) in connection with the semantics of fictional worlds. The present model, like Doležel's, distinguishes between textual markers for and mental representations of actions; it also focuses on the asymmetric relationship between formal cues and the action representations that they evoke. The second issue pertains to action theory itself and concerns how ontologically parsimonious a theory of action should be—whether in, say, taking a swim out into the ocean I should be characterized as performing one action or a sequence of many (interlinked) actions. This question, I argue, cannot be addressed without attending to the *contexts* in which, or for the purposes of which, one is building or reconstructing a specific action representation. In particular, given the interconnectedness of narration and action, the degree of parsimoniousness with which one should represent acts varies with the *kinds of stories* that one is trying to tell about an agent's behavior in a storyworld.

Gapping and the Underspecification of Action

As table 5 indicates, narratives trafficking in even the most prolific—and prolifically detailed—action representations will underspecify those actions textually. A cardiologist's write-up cannot capture *every* action performed by or on a patient and still be considered a proper case history; it would devolve, rather, into medically useless banalities. Likewise, a news report or a conversational narrative standardly omits certain elements of action that in most circumstances can be assumed as known by readers, listeners, or viewers. Except under very special conditions, in reporting that Joe used his hand to alert other drivers that he would be making a left turn in his car, I need not recount how his gesture required the transmission of electrical impulses from Joe's brain to his fingers, or detail the exact spatiotemporal coordinates occupied by his hand prior to and during the signaling gesture. Or, as Jonathan Culler

(1975a) has noted, in recounting to a friend what I did yesterday and mentioning that I took a walk in the afternoon, I would probably not say: "Then, at around three o'clock, I raised my left foot two inches off the ground while swinging it forward and, displacing my center of gravity so that the foot hit the ground, heel first, strode off on the ball of my right foot, etc." (143; this modified version of Culler's example is taken from Gerald Prince 1992: 28). To the contrary, actions in stories are characteristically underspecified by the textual formats used to recount them. They thus exemplify the broader phenomenon of *gapping* that reader-response theorists such as Wolfgang Iser (1978) have discussed in connection with literary texts in general. From this perspective, all reading can be characterized as a process of filling in gaps, with much modern literature having, according to Iser, the special purpose of enhancing the extent to which readers are aware of their own role as cognitively creative, gap-filling beings.

I concur with Doležel (1998: 169–84), however, in distinguishing between two dimensions of *gappiness* that can easily be run together in this context. On the one hand, there is the always—the necessarily— more or less incomplete textual presentation of storyworlds. On the other hand, there is the more or less complete reconstruction of aspects of storyworlds—here, actions—that recipients use available textual cues to access. As already suggested, the openness of action *representations* does not necessarily vary in proportion with the degree of gappiness attaching to the *narration* of acts. Rather, as Doležel argues in a more general way in his account of the relative "saturation" of fictional worlds, *gappy* textual formatting can enable as well as constrain the mental modeling of storyworlds. In the manner predicted by Paul Grice's (1989) pragmatic model, the textual format of a narrative always licenses inferences (or "implicatures") about what is implicitly meant but not explicitly articulated during the process of narration.[8]

As Doležel remarks, fictional worlds (i.e., storyworlds that claim for themselves an actuality status of virtual or irreal as opposed to actual or real) are inevitably incomplete: "Finite texts, the only texts that humans are capable of producing, are bound to create incomplete worlds" (169). No one building a fictional world can hope to specify every facet of the world, to characterize every element of it exhaustively and from the ground up. Rather, creators of fictional worlds must rely on readers, listeners, or viewers to draw a vast number of inferences about the world under construction—inferences that enable recipients to supply crucial information not explicitly available in the text. For example, even though Chopin's narrator nowhere states as much in the text of *The Awakening*, I assume that Edna Pontellier is human, has two rather than six or twenty-four eyes, is not equipped with a canine kidney or the spleen of an ancient Egyptian, has a brain structure analogous to that of other humans trying to make their way in the world, and does not have a secret and uncanny ability to speak the Klingon language, some sixty or seventy years before the science fiction series *Star Trek* was even created.

Such considerations prompt Doležel (1998: 173) to articulate two guidelines for a principled semantics of literary (and other) texts. Research in this area should insist, first, that there are "markers of implicit meaning in the explicit texture" or textual formatting of a work, and second, that implicit meaning in a work is recovered from this explicit texture by way of specifiable, rather than random and therefore unpredictable, procedures. I have already touched upon the second guideline in my discussion of inferences that can—indeed, must—be drawn about information left in implicit form in *The Awakening*. What Marie-Laure Ryan (1991: 48–60) calls "the principle of minimal departure" can be construed as a procedure for recovering just this sort of unstated information. Operating in close conformity with Grice's (1989) maxims of Quantity and Relation, Ryan's principle predicts that "we project upon [fictional] worlds everything we know about reality, and ... make only the adjustments dictated by the text" (51). Hence, unless cued to do so by Chopin's text, I will not assume that during those unsatisfactory conversations Edna has with her husband in the first part of the novel, she is secretly issuing a Klingon battle cry *avant le lettre* or speaking out of her left index finger rather than her mouth.

Yet—and this bears more squarely on the issue of *action* representations—fictional worlds are also characterized by differences in the degree to which they can be "saturated," in Doležel's phrase. Again, all texts display instances of "zero texture," whereby "a gap arises in the fictional-world structure" (169). However, "particular fictional texts vary the number, the extent, and the function of [these] gaps by varying the distribution of zero texture. . . . The variable saturation of fictional worlds is a challenge to the reader, a challenge that increases as the saturation decreases" (170). Doležel himself goes on to note some specifically action-theoretical implications of his model: "in action descriptions any of the factors of acting can be deleted. . . . If, for example, the agent is not expressed in the constructing texture of an action (say, by the use of a passive construction), we infer his or her existence" (175). What table 5 further suggests is that preferences for degrees of action specification—Doležel might speak here of degrees of saturation of action descriptions—can be probabilistically correlated with differences among narrative genres. In addition, the present account underscores that the relative richness of the "explicit texture" of a narrative is not a reliable index of the degree to which actions themselves can be mentally projected as specified or open. Even though the final scene of *The Awakening* fails to fill in several key parameters of action, Edna's motives and aims can be readily recovered on the basis of information supplied by the text. Conversely, when the explicit texture of a narrative becomes so rich as to exceed preference rules associated with tellability, it may constrain or even curtail, instead of enabling, a recipient's capacity to form richly specified action representations. Arguably, like Culler's hypermeticulous storyteller, I diminish rather than enhance your ability to model actions in a storyworld if I recount to you not only that Joe moved his hand to signal an upcoming left turn in his car, but also that electrical impulses of such and such a frequency and amplitude traveled a particular distance from his brain to his fingers; that the location of his hand shifted from 14.56 to 14.57 feet above sea level during the peformance of the signal; that, as he signaled, Joe also involuntarily performed six separate respiratory acts; that his torso shifted from such and such a position to another, infinitesimally less upright position during the signaling; and that his gesture differed from other act-tokens of signaling in respect of its duration, intensity, and visibility to sparrows on the wing.

Austere, Moderate, and Prolific Individuation of Actions

Not only do action representations reveal a non-isomorphic—yet principled—relationship between textual cues and mental models. What is more, studying how narratives cue recipients to build models of acts can throw light on what an action really is. In particular, it can help action theorists address the problem of how many actions should be identified as such within a given stretch of purposive behavior. In synopsizing previous work in the field of action theory, Lawrence H. Davis (1979:

30–41) distinguishes between what he calls austere, moderate, and prolific theories of action. More precisely, researchers have proposed more or less parsimonious models for *individuating* actions—for analyzing human behavior into more or less fine-grained complexes consisting of particular acts. For austere theorists such as Davidson (1980), signaling with one's hand that one is making a left turn in a car would constitute a single action. Davidson uses the analogy of an accordion: "The accordion, which remains the same through [the moving of one's hand to accomplish a signal], is the action; the changes are in aspects described, or descriptions of the event. . . . [T]his welter of related descriptions corresponds to a single descriptum" (58–59). Furthermore, for Davidson the only real explanations of actions such as using one's hand to signal are causal in nature, to be phrased in terms of *reasons* agents have for doing what they do. (As Davidson puts it [11], giving a causal explanation of actions is the only way to connect reasons and actions.) I signal with my hand because I intend to take a left turn and want to alert others that I am doing so, perhaps in order to avoid an accident or because I am oddly unaware that my car comes equipped with electrical turn signals. But in any event, in using my hand to signal a turn, I am doing just one thing: signaling the upcoming turn. To hold otherwise, Davidson suggests (58), would be to confuse features of the description of an event (specifically, an action) with features of the event itself. I can describe my act of signaling in many ways, but the act itself remains an act.

By contrast, for prolific theorists such as Alvin I. Goldman (1970), austere individuation of acts lacks descriptive adequacy and explanatory precision. For Goldman, actions must be differentiated into basic acts (or basic act-tokens) and the acts (nonbasic act-tokens) generated by them. There are, in turn, different classes of what Goldman calls "level generation," by which basic act-tokens generate higher-level or nonbasic act-tokens. Goldman (20–48) identifies four such types of level generation: causal, conventional, simple, and augmentative. In the case of moving one's hand to signal a left turn, the basic act-tokens of movements do not causally but rather conventionally generate the act-token of signaling. Meanwhile, if I turn on my electrical turn signal by nudging the turn-signal lever with my fingers, then moving my fingers *does* causally generate the act-token of engaging the turn signal. Simple level generation can be contrasted with both the causal and the conven-

Action Representations 71

tional types. For example, if I engage my electrical turn signal ten times and Joe engages his eight times, then my act-token of engaging my turn signal ten times "simply" generates the act-token of engaging my turn signal more times than Joe does. Finally, in the case of augmentation, one act-token augments another if it entails the one it augments, but not vice versa. For instance, the act of riding a bicycle in the summer entails the act of riding a bicycle, but not the other way around. Thus the act of riding a bike in the summer augments the act of riding a bike. What emerges from Goldman's prolific account, overall, is a much more richly individuated taxonomy of actions than the one that emerged from Davidson's austere approach. In building or interpreting a given action representation, I need to stratify it into basic and nonbasic act-tokens. I also need to indicate or ascertain just how the former generate the latter, whether causally, conventionally, simply, or through some process of augmentation.

The third, moderate theory of action steers a course between the prolific and austere theories. For moderate theorists such as Davis and Irving Thalberg (1977), when an act-token causally generates another act-token, there are two separate actions involved; but when an act-token noncausally generates another act-token (as in the case of manually signaling a turn with one's hand), then only one action is involved (Davis 1979: 33). Moderates, however, must then accept that two events such as Joe's making an obscene gesture at me while driving and my becoming angry in consequence constitute the single action of Joe's making me angry (cf. Davis 1979: 35). Gestures, after all, conventionally rather than causally generate other act-tokens. But why is this one action whereas Joe's stepping on my toe and my becoming angry as a result would count as two actions, the second causally generated by the first? Why should accounts of actions causing other actions have to be richer—that is, less parsimonious—than accounts of actions conventionally or simply generating other actions?

This last question points up the broader issue with which I am chiefly concerned here. Specifically, if one assumes that principles for individuating actions do not necessarily hold across all contexts of action representation—in other words, if one assumes that contexts for describing and explaining actions produce their own norms for describing and explaining—then one need not decide between an austere, prolific, or moderate account of how actions are to be individuated in every possible case. In stories, the scalar model outlined in table 5 suggests that the degree to which actions are individuated and, once individuated, specified will vary with the style of narrative imagining in which the representation of the act occurs. A news report, medical case history, or nonfiction novel is far more likely to individuate and specify actions prolifically than *Finnegans Wake* or, for that matter, a medieval allegory concerned more with the religious connotations of acts than with the nature of the acts themselves. By the same token, an action representation that seems prolific in the context of *Finnegans Wake* might seem austere in the context of a cardiologist's write-up of a patient's case history. Thus, it is not only that different degrees of parsimoniousness are called for by different contexts for action representation, but also that parsimoniousness is itself a scalar predicate rather than an absolute quality. Relative prolificness or austerity cannot be measured apart from the context in which a given action is being represented. As one might also put it, among its other considerable powers, narrative has the ability to blunt Occam's razor.

I wish to make an even stronger claim (or formulate a more controversial research hypothesis) in this connection, however. As suggested by von Wright's intuition that "[t]o understand behavior as intentional . . . is to fit it into a 'story' about an agent" (1983: 42), narrative affords one of the most frequently and naturally occurring contexts for building and reconstructing action representations. I would go still further and assert that developing a viable theory of action hinges on developing a viable theory of narrative—or rather, that action theory is properly a part of a cognitive science also informed by narratological models and methods. Understanding an action is tantamount to fitting it into a story about an agent, yes. But beyond this, actions could arguably not be mentally projected at all in the absence of what can be characterized as narratively based norms for act individuation. At stake are context-specific norms for mapping into a set of discrete, more or less richly profiled acts—acts located in a storyworld—what would otherwise be an undifferentiated mass or agglomeration of behavior. Different kinds of stories, as suggested previously, do call for different kinds of act individuation. More fundamentally, though, there could be no such individuation unless some style or other of narrative imagining guided the process by which regions of (purposive) action are marked off within the general field of behavior. Actions, in this hypothesis, should be characterized not as prefabricated building blocks of storyworlds, but rather as construction materials that have to be fashioned—custom-fit—in a manner dictated by the kind of narrative being told.[9]

From Singular Actions to Action Sequences

The present section marks a shift of focus, moving from the problem of individuating, describing, and explaining (relatively) singular actions to the problem of accounting for *sequences* of actions. In examining the way actions fit into larger sequences, the section skirts the border between local and global design principles for storyworlds, narrative microdesigns and narrative macrodesigns. Along the way, it provides additional evidence for the need to work toward an integration of narrative theory and action theory—and for that matter, for the interconnectedness of the very notions of *narrative* and *action*. I draw on two theoretical vocabularies in investigating action sequences: one sketched by von Wright (1966) to situate individual actions in a larger history of acting situations, and the other outlined by Arthur C. Danto (1985) to account for the role of narrative in historical explanations. Von Wright contrasts action descriptions with biographies; Danto draws an analogous distinction between atomic and molecular narratives. Both of these vocabularies point up the need to articulate criteria for narratively as opposed to nonnarratively organized sequences of actions and events.

Action Descriptions versus Biographies

In von Wright's (1966: 124–32) nomenclature, the smallest descriptive unit is the state description and the largest is the biography, with the other units scaled as follows:

state description
action
acting situation
life situation
life/biography

To review: state descriptions identify an *initial state* that, as a result of an *action*, gets transformed into a *terminal state*. But state descriptions themselves are, by definition, static. Insofar as it provides a synchronic description of what state or states obtain in the world at a given slice of time, a "state-description describes a 'momentary life'. . . . In this life nothing happens. Therefore there is no room for action in it" (126). By moving up to a larger descriptive unit, the action, analysts can account for relationships *between* states. Thus, in taking a swim out into the ocean, Edna Pontellier exerts a form of agency that transforms an initial world state S_1 (= Edna is alive) into a terminal world state S_2 (= Edna is dead). In turn, by surveying the whole complex of initial state/action/terminal state, readers can grasp the acting situation in which Edna's act occurred. If Edna had not taken her swim, then S_1 would not have undergone a transformation into S_2. As a descriptive unit, the acting situation therefore encompasses more than the action taken alone. It allows the analyst to build a counterfactual scenario consisting of any number of world states that might have obtained, but did not. What Edna did stands out in relief against a broader cognitive background consisting of what the world would have been like if she had not done what she did.

Meanwhile, an agent's *life situation* encompasses more than the discrete acting situations in which the agent finds himself or herself compelled to act. As von Wright puts it, "An agent's life-situation at any given stage of his life's journey is . . . determined, one could say, by his total life behind him and by what would be nature's next move independently of him. This notion of a life-situation is a generalization of our previous notion of an acting-situation" (1966: 126–27). From this perspective, the richness and complexity of Edna's life situation in *The Awakening* increase as the narrative progresses—as do the richness and complexity of the cognitive background on which readers draw in making inferences about the significance of Edna's actions at successive stages of the novel (compare, in this connection, the model of narrative progression developed by Phelan 1989, 1996). Edna's act of moving out of Léonce's house into the "pigeon house" (Chopin 1993: 104–16), for example, causes different world states to obtain than it would have if Edna had performed that action earlier in the novel, before her incipient awakening on Grand Isle, for instance. For, during the temporal stretch separating her experiences with Robert Lebrun on Grand Isle and her moving out of Léonce's house, Edna's life situation has expanded through the accretion of many more acting situations.

With an acting situation thus viewed as a limiting case of a life situation (128), a *life* can be defined as a sequence of life situations, that is, "a succession of courses of action taken by a certain agent on a sequence of successive occasions" (125). For the description (as opposed to the living or experiencing) of a life von Wright reserves the term *biography* (125). In von Wright's words,

> The biography [of an agent] describes a succession of stages through which the world passes. But it also describes the agent's actions (and omissions) since it tells us, too, how the world would have been but for him. A biography of one agent is compatible with the existence of other agents in the world. But the contributions of other agents appear, in the biography, merely as changes (and not-changes) "in nature." We cannot tell which actions those other agents performed. For, we are not told what would have happened but for those agents. (125–26)

A biography can thus be contrasted with a *history*; the latter designates "a succession of total states through which the world actually passes," whereas the former can be constructed only if one knows "not [just] how the world actually changes, but also how it would have changed from one occasion to the next, had it not been for the agent" (126). *The Awakening* is, in this sense, a biography of Edna Pontellier and not a mere history of changes in the world Edna occupies. It records the effects of Edna's actions on a world that, as the text prompts us to infer, would have been quite different without her. Conversely, evoking what Doležel (1998: 37–54, 74–95) would call a multiperson as opposed to a one-person narrative world, the novel represents many of the changes in Edna's circumstances not as natural occurrences but as contributions made by other agents. Léonce trivializes Edna and her feelings; Arobin actively courts her; Robert at first flirts with her but finally, when given the chance to have a real instead of an imaginary relationship with Edna, rebuffs her. Chopin's text, in other words, traces several biographies insofar as they impinge on the central biography or description of Edna's life.

Not only does this multibiographical profile distinguish Edna's world from one-person worlds such as (initially, at least) Robinson Crusoe's. Further, it points beyond *action sequences* to *action structures*—a concept to be taken up in the final section of this chapter as well as in chapter 3. Action structures derive from inferences about participants' ongoing, sometimes complementary, sometimes conflicting beliefs, desires, and intentions. These textually cued and mentally modeled constructs are what enable sequences of actions to be conceptualized and identified as, in addition, narratively organized sequences. Given the importance of such action structures for narrative comprehension in particular, theorists of action may need to rethink von Wright's use of the word *biography* for action sequences in general.

Von Wright's usage of the term implies that (without explaining how or why) the chain of acting situations constituting a life is narratively structured. But a succession of acting situations need not have the structure of a story. For example, one could in principle extract from the total biography of an agent a succession of acting situations that would presumably still qualify as a (partial) biography, in von Wright's terms, but that would not be narrative in nature. This "selective" biography might consist only of the following chain of acting situations: the agent, by brushing her teeth twice a day, repeatedly transforms the world state of her having unbrushed teeth at time t_{n-1} into the world state of her having brushed teeth at time t_n. Debatably, this succession of acting situations (Agent X had unbrushed teeth at time t_{n-1}; then she brushed her teeth and had brushed teeth at time t_n; then she again had unbrushed teeth at a subsequent time t_{n+1}; etc.) could not properly be called a narrative. There is no narratively remarkable *conflict* involved—unless an interpreter of the sequence used the preference rule UNDERSTAND EVENTS AS ACTIONS to cast Sloth, Inertia, Not Feeling Like Brushing, and so on, as conniving opponents of Dental Hygiene. By the same token, to qualify as a narrative, the action sequence would have to highlight not just the way the world would have been had X not brushed her teeth but also the *riskiness* of her allowing it to take that alternative course, what with Tooth Decay and Recession of the Gums lurking in the wings. Both of the modifications just mentioned, however, require importing into the action sequence a level of structure not accounted for by the idea of *biography* as such. To rephrase my point, in the context of a life description, recording a succession of acting situations is a necessary but not a sufficient condition for narrative.[10] The action sequence recorded must in addition be figured as *not* coming off without a hitch, as involving obstacles overcome and not overcome, as consisting of actions thwarted as well as actions achieved, and as having in general a pattern or trajectory that heightens the recipient's awareness of all the many things that can go wrong in life, and do—with or without the possibility of their being redressed in the open-ended fullness of time.

Atomic versus Molecular Narratives

A more explicit treatment of the relationship between singular actions, action sequences, and narratives can be found in the model developed by the philosopher Arthur Danto (1985). There are, to be sure, significant parallels between von Wright's theory of actions and Danto's account of the role of narratives in historical inquiry. Just as von Wright conceives of actions as transforming an initial into a terminal world state, Danto conceives of a story or "narrative description" as "filling in the middle between the temporal end-points of a change" (234). Further, just as in von Wright's scheme accounting for an acting situation requires grasping the whole complex formed by the initial state, the action, and the end state, what Danto refers to as "narrative descriptions" explain neither an earlier event nor the later event it leads to, but rather the *connection between* the earlier and later event (235). In part because of his focus on the nature of historical knowledge, however, Danto's primary concern is with *narratives that explain what happened* to produce a change from an earlier state to a later state. This emphasis can be contrasted with the one inflecting von Wright's theory—that is, an emphasis on the conditions that have to hold for a change to be considered the result of an action. Whereas von Wright's chief concern is to formulate the conditions for valid *descriptions* of actions or—at the limit—lives, Danto focuses instead on what he calls *narrative explanations* of actions that have occurred.

True, von Wright does claim that "[t]o understand behavior as intentional ... is to fit it into a 'story' about an agent" (1983: 42). Yet, as I have already begun to suggest, he does not specify exactly what he means by *story* in this connection or render explicit the link between action description and narrative accounts of actions. Not even in his comments on *biography* does von Wright define what gives an account of a sequence of actions the coherence standardly associated with a narrative or life story about an agent. Rather, the succession of acting situations that constitutes a life situation seems to unfold mainly as an additive process, as an accretion of actions performed within a chain of acting situations that all involve the same primary agent. Danto, by contrast, chooses narrative over action as the root concept of what remains, however, a theory of action. He also sketches a theory of "narrative predicates" that captures key logical properties of narrative accounts—though the theory may only go part way in explaining what makes a sequence of actions a story.

Danto's model for narrative explanations of actions (233–56) encompasses three elements (which can again be paralleled with the three items that von Wright holds to be essential ingredients of action descriptions):

(i) x is F at t_1

(ii) H happens to x at t_2

(iii) x is G at t_3

From this perspective, elements (i) and (iii) constitute the explanandum (or thing to be explained), while (ii) is the explanans (or thing that does the explaining). In the case of the explanandum of Austria's being a sovereign nation in 1937, but then a province of Germany in 1938, the explanans is the *Anchluss* forcibly imposed on 11 March 1938 by the Nazi regime and annulled in 1943 by the Moscow Declaration. Again, in seeking to explain Edna Pontellier's transformation from a fairly dutiful wife who does not know her own mind at the beginning of *The Awakening* into a bold shaper of her own fate at novel's end, I can adduce the "awakening" that readers infer to be happening to (or in) Edna during the temporal interval Chopin's novel records. Or again, at the level of relatively singular actions versus that of relatively extended action sequences, my being hungry yesterday at 7:00 A.M. but no longer hungry fifteen minutes later at 7:15 A.M. can be narratively explained by my recounting how I ate breakfast in the meantime. Notice that in all three contexts for acting, whether singular or sequential, I am not explaining what *in general* can transform a sovereign nation into the province of another nation, make a submissive wife into a woman concerned to take charge of her own life, or turn a hungry person into a sated one. Rather, instead of simply marking places where general laws can be inserted to account for the explanandum in each case, my explanations can "be regarded as the *result* of taking an explanation sketch which makes use of general laws already, these marking the place where the description of [a particular] *event* is to be inserted" (Danto 1985: 238). Narrative comes into play, that is, "where we are certain of the law but uncertain as to what precisely happened, the narrative then consisting in an account in which the *general* knowledge of what *kind* of thing must have happened is replaced by the specific knowledge of what specific thing, of the required kind, *in fact* occurred" (238).

Given these considerations, the schema presented in the previous paragraph can be refined (Danto 1985: 251–56), with three components of narrative explanations now reformulated as

(i) Fa,

(ii) y,

(iii) Ga

where "Fa and Ga together, and in that order, represent a change in a. This change may not be covered by a general law, but once reference is made to y—a causal episode—then some general law is being appealed to, some general assumption is made, to the effect that y-like things cause a-like things to change from F to G" (251). As already suggested, one interpretation of Chopin's novel—an interpretation that a number of scholars (Gilbert 1998; Showalter 1993; Stange 1998; Yaeger 1998) have shown to be a plausible—construes Edna (a) as having particular experiences (y) transforming her from dutiful wife (F) to autonomous woman (G). As a narrative explanation of Edna's metamorphosis, this feminist reading of *The Awakening* appeals to a general causal principle accounting for what enables women to shift from submissiveness to self-direction in a given case. The principle in question might be articulated in terms of the following probabilistic "law": "The more women become cognizant of marriage as a contingent social convention rather than a pregiven, natural, and immutable aspect of reality, the more likely they are to assert their autonomy and demand from their spouses equal treatment, the freedom to make their own choices, etc." It is some such causal principle that supports the extrapolation from y in particular to y-like things in general; appeal to this principle, and others undergirding inferences about what happens over the course of Chopin's novel, also helps motivate feminist arguments that the task of interpreting specific texts can in the long run generate whole new paradigms for interpretation (see, e.g., Donovan 1998; Kolodny 1986; Robinson 1986; Showalter 1977). Furthermore, Danto's model of narrative explanation provides independent support for a claim made earlier in this chapter—namely, that action representations should be viewed as custom fit to the purpose of the story being told, not as prefabricated building blocks of storyworlds. Actions, for Danto, cannot be characterized apart from schemata for narrative explanation. Rather, "[o]ne chief task of narration is to set the stage for the action which leads to the end, the description of which is the explanation of the change of which beginning and end are termini" (248). I therefore constitute an action *as* y by slotting it between Fa and Ga. For example, I constitute an action as the act of eating breakfast to sate my hunger by slotting it into a narrative account of how I went from being hungry before breakfast to not being hungry afterward.

Thus, if one views actions as in effect a byproduct of narrative explanations, what I have been calling singular actions can be more accurately termed *atomic narratives*. Such actions have a beginning, middle, and end, and Danto (252) graphically represents them thus:

F G

/ . /

Here the slash marks represent the termini of a change in the world, and the dot represents the action (or, in more schematic terms, the instantiated causal principle) that gets narratively constructed as producing the change in question. As Danto notes, however, there can be *sequences* of changes that no single cause serves to explain. In such cases, where one is dealing with a sequence of causes, each accounting for a successive change, the term *molecular narratives* suggests itself. Take, for instance, the decline and fall of the Roman Empire. Although this historical explanandum can be accounted for by way of a chain of atomic narratives—such as the one fashioned so voluminously and so influentially by Edward Gibbon (1932)—there need be no single causal principle whose scope ranges over every atomic narrative (or singular action) in the chain.[11] Danto (252) represents such molecular narratives diagrammatically as

F G H I

/ . / . / . /

where the three successive changes are F → G, G → H, and H → I. It is worth quoting Danto at some length:

> In a molecular narrative, each unit / . / is covered by a general law of the sort at least that I have characterized above, but there need not be any general law which covers the entire change. There may be a question as to why we require the notion of a molecular narrative, and cannot consider any such molecular narrative as simply an end-to-end series of atomic narratives. The answer to this is plain. It is because we are interested in

the *larger change* (in the above representation) [F → I], of which the intermediating changes are *parts*." (252)

Hence, H → I, the last unit in this chain of atomic narratives (e.g., the last, camel's-back-breaking wave of invading huns), might very well explain I (the fall of Rome). Yet "the fact is that we are not specifically interested in I as such, but in the change [F → I], and for this change the cause cited is not sufficient" (252-53). Likewise, in what I am calling action sequences as opposed to singular actions, the analyst is interested not in any particular action but in a more or less extended span of actions, interpretable as elements of an emergent whole. As Roland Barthes (1977: 101-2) already recognized some thirty-five years ago, and as I discuss in further detail in chapter 3, an action sequence can thus be described as a "logical succession of actions" that readers, viewers, or listeners match with a "title" or "nominal whole" (e.g., *Betrayal, Conflict*) while building mental representations of storyworlds.

But what, exactly, distinguishes a mere succession of individually, narratively explainable actions from a molecular narrative, in which atomic narratives link together to form a whole, a *Gestalt*, that is more than the sum of its parts? In other words, what makes relatively singular actions identifiable—manipulable—as components of the larger action sequences that can be viewed as the backbone of any story? This problem is not directly addressed by Danto's point about historians' and others' shifting focus of interest: to say that one is sometimes interested in larger sequences of actions rather than the individual actions comprised by them does not explain how one is able to shift back and forth between these quite differently scaled units of description and analysis. Instead, the solution to the problem seems to lie, for Danto, in his account (342-63) of "narrative predicates"—that is, "predicates which are true of objects and events at a given time only if certain objects and events occur at a time future to them and failing which they are retrospectively false" (349-50).

For example, a person's having terminal cancer is a future-referring but nonnarrative predicate because this predicate can be true of that person even if he or she does not actually die from cancer, but rather from a car wreck or a stroke. By contrast, the narrative predicate "being Edna Pontellier's future lover" could not be truthfully ascribed to Arobin, at *any* point in the novel, if the two characters had only socialized at the race track without ever becoming romantically involved.

From this perspective, what makes an action sequence a molecular narrative is a tightly knit interconnection—indeed, a logical interdependence—between earlier and later actions that is not found in mere successions of doings. Or, as it might also be put, what sets a (molecular) narrative apart from a chronicle or a list of individually, narratively explainable occurrences is that, in properly narrative contexts, "we include mention of an earlier event because we believe that the later event would not have happened as it did had the earlier event not happened as *it* did" (355). Inversely, if the future were already knowable, if what is to happen later were not contingent upon what we do now, "each event [would become] independent of each event and we [would be] back, in description, to the structure of a chronicle: a list of occurrences" (356).

Danto's model captures important logical properties of narrative predicates; the logical behavior of these predicates stems from their being embedded, irreducibly, in *sequences* of actions and events. But arguably, story logic is itself irreducible to the logical characteristics of predicates that encode temporal relationships between earlier and later segments of a narrative sequence. It is not just that, as I discuss in chapter 6, some narratives exploit varieties of "fuzzy temporality" that place in question the very notion of narrative predicates, as Danto has defined them. What is more, although the logico-grammatical principles governing the use of narrative predicates can help map the temporal disposition of storyworld components, they do not afford a detailed enough account of how action sequences are mentally modeled. Or rather, narrative predicates can be said to bear more directly on the product than on the process of modeling. My next task is to work toward a finer-grained analysis of how inferences about action sequences enable, in their turn, the cognitive *activity* of storyworld construction.

Action Sequences and Action Structures

As both the previous and the present chapter have suggested, actions can be defined as a special type of event. Unlike other event types, actions are *executed* by agents working to accomplish more or less immediate goals. Pace Genette, then, a narrative consisting solely of a transformation of events would not, in fact, be a narrative. Stories, rather, interweave states, events, and actions, with different narrative genres creating different patterns of propositions about states, (intentional) behaviors, and (unintended) occurrences, as well as more or less underspecified representations of actions. In addition, stories depend vitally on sequences of actions. To model these sequences as stories as opposed to mere lists of actions, recipients build *action structures* (Giora and Shen 1994) anchored in broad cognitive principles and dispositions. Again, action structures can be defined as higher-order narrative units or principles of organization based on inferences about participants' (emergent) beliefs, desires, and intentions. Goals or desires (i.e., target states, actions, or events) and the plans designed to reach them are, in turn, closely connected with participants' beliefs about the world. Action structures are what allow listeners, readers, and viewers to connect nonadjacent occurrences and to construe them as elements of an ongoing, coherent narrative.

The importance of action structures for narrative comprehension is the topic of my next chapter, but it can be illustrated, preliminarily, by way of the recent film *Waking Ned Devine* (1998). What makes it possible to comprehend this film is the viewer's re-creation of an action structure that connects (among other incidents) the event of Ned Devine's death and the scene in which Michael O'Sullivan speeds naked through the countryside on a motorcycle. These nonadjacent incidents assume their place in a coherent psychological whole because of a goal G (*Assume the identity of the dead Ned Devine in order to collect on a winning lottery ticket*) that Michael seeks to accomplish through a plan P (*Beat the lottery agent to Ned's house so that Michael will appear to be living there by the time the agent arrives in his car*). Action structures are in this sense the scaffolding on which people can gain more or less temporary footholds while building storyworlds.

Yet if events alone do not make for narrative, neither can a discourse or a text consisting wholly of actions be called a story in the strict sense.[12] If a *narrative* were merely to draw a map that led from a source state to a target state through a sequence of actions, each with its own preconditions and effects, the result would approximate not a story but instead (a description of) a plan, a recipe, a set of navigational instructions, or the like. To continue with the example of *Waking Ned Devine*, what makes Michael's and Jackie O'Shea's actions and experiences worthy of narration is the way in which they arise as a consequence of Ned's unforeseen death, are impinged upon by other unpredicted events brought about by the actions of other participants (e.g., the lottery agent just happens to reappear during the funeral for Ned Devine), intersect with Michael's and Jackie's psychological and personal attributes, as well as those of other inhabitants of the village of Tullymore, and generate unexpected effects that jeopardize their own scheme to impersonate Ned (e.g., Michael and Jackie's initial success at fooling the lottery agent requires them to engage in a more complicated and risky attempt to involve the whole community of Tullymore in their ploy). Combined with events such as Ned's dying from shock over winning the lottery, these multiple and in some cases incompatible plans (with their attendant goals and subgoals) create a rich blend of intentions, actions, and occurrences—a blend whose richness, arguably, increases in proportion with the memorableness and tellability of the story in which it occurs. Granted, the recent work on the concept of *narrativity* that I go on to review in chapter 3 indicates that narrative itself is a fuzzy predicate, with particular stories being only more or less, never absolutely, amenable to processing *as* stories.[13] Yet a minimal condition for narrative can be defined as the thwarting of intended actions by unplanned, sometimes unplannable, events, which may or may not be the effect of other participants' intended actions. This is another way of expressing the intuition that stories prototypically involve *conflict*, or some sort of (noteworthy, tellable) disruption of an initial state of equilibrium by an unplanned and often untoward event or chain of events (Hendricks 1977; Herman 1999a, 2000a; Kafalenos 1995, 1997, 1999; Propp 1968; Todorov 1968).

How narrative sequences at once depend on and transgress patterns of expectation is the central issue to be explored in chapter 3. Structuralist narratology lacked the resources to address this issue squarely. Revisiting it now can yield new ways of thinking about just what a story is.

3
Scripts, Sequences, and Stories

This chapter further characterizes the action structures that enable sequences of actions to be understood as (and, on the production side of things, fashioned into) what Danto called molecular narratives.[1] Building on the approaches outlined by theorists such as Jackson G. Barry (1990), Edward Branigan (1992), Monika Fludernik (1996), Manfred Jahn (1997, 1999) and Marie-Laure Ryan (1991), the chapter reviews classical, structuralist accounts of narrative sequences and attempts to enrich the narratological models with the concepts of *scripts*, *frames*, and *schemata* developed in Artificial Intelligence (AI) research. Workers in cognitive science and AI (e.g., Mandler 1984; Minsky 1975, 1988; Schank and Abelson 1977; Schank 1990; van Dijk and Kintsch 1983) have used these ideas to describe knowledge representations storing past experiences; such representations can assume either a static (frame-like) or a dynamic (script-like) form. As stereotyped sequences of events, scripts, in particular, help explain the difference between a mere sequence of actions or occurrences and a narratively organized sequence, that is, a molecular narrative. Narrative at once anchors itself in and deviates from experiential repertoires stored as scripts, unfolding as an interplay between what Jerome Bruner (1991: 11–13) calls "canonicity and breach."[2] In other words, a sequence of actions, states, and events qualifies as a narrative by virtue of how it situates remarkable or tellable occurrences against a backdrop of stereotypical expectations about the world. Action structures can be thought of as mental models allowing storytellers and recipients to accommodate such blends of tellability and stereotypicality. They enable inferences of a crucial sort to be drawn. At issue is what—given a particular textual format, and given prior knowledge of the way the world is or at least seems to be—participants in a story can be interpreted as doing or as trying to do. At issue, too, is how participants' behavior can be construed as a response to other actions and to unintended events, whether those actions and events are figured as completed, incipient, or ongoing within the storyworld.

Further, capturing the difference between narratives and stereotyped sequences of events or scripts is tantamount to defining *narrativehood*, or what makes a story a story. Capturing the variable quality of this contrast—that is, accounting for the way different kinds of narratives orient themselves differently toward stereotyped sequences of actions and events—is tantamount to defining *narrativity*, or how readily a narrative can be processed *as* a narrative. The final part of the chapter suggests how examination of the script-story interface can enable a rethinking of both the historical development of narrative techniques and the differences among narrative genres at any given time. Storytelling strategies have arguably helped shape, and been shaped by, changes in humans' shared strategies for categorizing and organizing experience.[3]

A digression on method seems warranted here. The reciprocal historical influence of scripts on stories and stories on scripts suggests the need for two complementary approaches within narratology. There is a need, first, for the synchronic study of story logic viewed as part of humans' basic cognitive endowment. And there is also a need for diachronic investigation of this universal yet ever-changing use of stories to organize and comprehend experience (cf. MacNeil 1996)—with the world's narrative literature providing a (partial) record of such evolving patterns of story usage. Although the final part of the current chapter does outline some directions for diachronic research on scripts and stories, it should already be apparent that this book pursues mainly a synchronic approach to story logic.[4] Even so, the approach sketched here does not presume to be exhaustive or definitive. Rather, the book as a whole works toward an *interestingly narrow* account of core principles of storyworld design—principles with both relatively local and relatively global scope.

My account can be construed as *narrow* to the extent that it argues that narrative is this, not that; that narrativity increases or diminishes in correlation with these or those specific factors; that stories show a preference for these, not those, combinations of coding strategies; that narratives characteristically depend on some, as opposed to other, design principles—even though, as the literary narratives examined in part 2 of my study suggest, the principles at issue should be viewed as enabling as much as constraining storyworld construction. In turn, to the extent that my account is narrow it can be considered *interesting*—in a methodological if not necessarily a reader-response or aesthetic sense. The narrower an account of story logic, in the sense just detailed, the more readily it can be falsified, proven wrong, by readers having experience with and intuitions about narratives from diverse traditions, epochs, (sub)cultures, and interactional situations. Thus to put oneself in the position of being wrong, but interestingly wrong, is to work toward sharpening the debate about the nature and scope of narrative imagining, including how it differs from other cognitive and communicative styles, what textual or more broadly semiotic formats it typically prefers and disprefers, whether or not its most fundamental mechanisms have changed over time, and so on.

Sequences versus Stories

Early on narratologists such as Claude Bremond and Roland Barthes, inspired by Vladimir Propp's 1928 groundbreaking *Morphology of the Folktale* (1968), began to elaborate the idea of the narrative sequence and to catalogue some of the sequences they viewed as common, if not universal, ingredients of narrative. This work addresses several questions. What makes certain sequences of events stories and not descriptions, deductions, or, in Bremond's phrase, "lyrical effusions" (1980: 390)? Are some narrative sequences more amenable than others to processing as stories? Can certain kinds of stories meet the minimal criteria for narrative yet lack other features required for the stories to be deemed valuable, interesting, or "effective" (Labov 1972a: 370) as narratives (cf. Bruce 1978; Labov and Waletzky 1967)?

Consider the following set of propositions:

1. A monkey screeched. Sunlight blazed down upon sea. The rancher gazed proudly at his bison.

This string of sentences may strike me as a bad parody of surrealist description, perhaps, but the sentences do not describe occurrences that can be construed as part a narrative sequence, strictly speaking. Nor will anyone confuse a syllogism such as example 2 with a story:

2. Susan is a narratologist. All narratologists are structuralists. Therefore Susan is a structuralist.

Further, note that certain conversational openings are used so often that they prompt an interlocutor to co-construct a particular, canonical sequence of utterances, as in

3. Speaker A: How are you doing?

Speaker B: Pretty good, how about you?

Speaker A: Oh, pretty good.

Such two-party sequences are distinguished precisely by their overt unremarkableness, their patent avoidance of any information that might be deemed interesting and thus worthy of narrative communication or telling. Such non-, even anti-informative sequences typically occur in contexts in which neither party wants or offers stories.

But on the basis of the following sequence (consisting of one action performed by a human agent, a second by a nonhuman agent, and a third by an agent whose nature, thanks to the passive construction, remains unspecified), a Gothic tale or maybe an allegorical fable begins to take shape in my imagination:

4. A black-caped figure prowled among the houses. An owl screeched. Three children were borne away into the night.

Example 4 does not explicitly relate what the black-caped figure did while prowling around, but the sequence furnishes enough of a propositional scaffolding for me to reconstruct the prowler's nefarious intent, cuing me to infer that the owl screeches just when the prowler abducts the three children. By contrast, though a set of cooking instructions might detail acts and occurrences that follow a particular temporal sequence, it cannot be said to tell a story:

5. Remove pizza from box and inner wrapper.... [P]lace on preheated cookie sheet. Bake for 16–18 minutes or until center cheese is melted and edges are golden brown.[5]

Given their illocutionary status as commands, the sentences in example 5 outline a bare pattern for potential events, a skeleton plan for action, issuing step-by-step directives bearing on the realization of an unrealized but desired goal (i.e., the golden brown pizza). The sequence therefore tells us not what happened, in the manner of a story, but rather how to make something (good) happen, in the manner of a prescription or, more precisely, a recipe. The frozen pizza instructions differ from the following sequence, whose constituent sentences declare instead of direct. Example 6 organizes a set of individually highly reportable actions and events into a structured whole that most of us would recognize to be (part of) a story:

6. Mary's fingernails tore at his [Bigger Thomas's] hands and he caught the pillow and covered her entire face with it, firmly. Mary's body surged upward and he pushed downward upon the pillow with all of his weight. . . . His eyes were filled with the white blur moving toward him in the shadows of the room. (Wright 1993: 97-98)

What sets examples 4 and 6 apart from 1, 2, 3, and 5? Why would most people construe 4 and 6 as narrative sequences and the others as a description, a syllogism, an exchange of greetings, and a recipe? Is some critical property—something definitive of story—built into 4 and 5 but manifestly absent in 1, 2, 3, and 5?

In the sections that follow, after reviewing classical approaches to the problem of defining narrative sequences, I argue that analysts of stories can gain new insights into the problem by using AI research on the knowledge structures variously termed *schemata*, *scripts*, and *frames*. For AI specialists such as Dennis Mercadal (1990), a script is a "description of how a sequence of events is expected to unfold. . . . A script is similar to a frame in that it [a script] represents a set of expectations. . . . Frames differ from scripts in that frames are used to represent a point in time. Scripts represent a sequence of events that take place in a time sequence" (255). Further, *schema*, a "term used in psychology literature which refers to memory patterns that humans use to interpret current experiences," can be defined as "a synonym for framelike structures" (254; cf. Bartlett 1932).[6] This research suggests that the mind draws on a large but not infinite number of "experiential repertoires," of both static (schematic or frame-like) and dynamic (or script-like) types. Stored in the memory, previous experiences form structured repertoires of expectations about current and emergent experiences. Static repertoires allow me to distinguish a chair from a table or a cat from a bread box; dynamic repertoires help me to know how events typically unfold during common occasions such as birthday parties and to avoid mistaking birthday parties for barroom brawls or visits to the barber.

Thus cognitive scientists have studied how stereotypical knowledge reduces the complexity and duration of processing tasks bound up with perceiving, inferring, and so on (Bobrow and Norman 1975; Charniak and McDermott 1985: 393-415; Grishman 1986: 140-58; Mercadal 1990: 109, 255; Minsky 1975 and 1988: 244-72). In this research tradition, understanding can be described as "a process by which people match what they see and hear to pre-stored groupings of actions that they have already experienced" (Schank and Abelson 1977: 67). Scripts are the knowledge representations that store these finite groupings of causally and chronologically ordered actions—actions that are required for the accomplishment of particular tasks (e.g., eating a meal at a restaurant, making an omelette). The performance of a long or complicated task usually necessitates more than one script; no one can do heart surgery or build a particle accelerator without recourse to a vast assortment of complexly interrelated scripts. Likewise, comprehension of a text or a discourse—a story—requires access to a plurality of scripts. In the absence of stereotypes stored as scripts, readers could not draw textual inferences of the most basic sort—for example, that a masked character represented as running out of a bank probably just robbed it.

From this perspective, what distinguishes narrative sequences, such as examples 4 and 6, from nonnarrative sequences, such as 1, 2, 3, and 5, is not simply the form assumed by each. Narrative also depends on how the form of a sequence is anchored in—or triggers a recipient to activate—knowledge about the world. It is not that stories are recognizable only if and insofar as they tell me what I already know; rather, stories stand in a certain relation to what I know, focusing attention on the unusual and the remarkable against a backdrop made up of highly structured patterns of belief and expectation.[7] Telling and understanding narratives is a certain way of reconciling emergent with prior knowledge; describing, arguing, greeting, and giving recipes are other ways.

My analysis therefore centers on the interrelations between linguistic form, world knowledge, and narrative structure. Two sets of factors, as already noted, fall under my purview. The first set, associated with what I call *narrativehood*, bears on what makes readers and listeners deem stories to be stories. These factors are criterial for narrative; they determine which sequences of actions, events, and states qualify as narratives. Narrativehood, from this perspective, is a binary predicate: something either is or is not a story. More specifically, the property of narrativehood attaches to sequences of states, events, and actions that involve an identifiable participant or set of participants equipped with certain beliefs about the world seeking to accomplish goal-directed plans. The difficulties participants experience in trying to accomplish these plans—whether because of overambitious goals, erroneous beliefs, unpredicted obstacles, conflicting plans hatched by other participants, mutually inconsistent desires, or other problems—confer on sequences the noteworthiness or tellability distinguishing a story from a stereotype. *Action structures* are mental models of such participant-oriented patterns of effort, conflict, trouble, and, in some cases at least, resolution of conflict and overcoming of trouble.

Meanwhile, the second set of factors to be considered here bears on the narrativity of narrative sequences, definable as a function of "formal and contextual features making a narrative more or less narrative" (G. Prince 1987: 64). Narrativity, then, is a scalar predicate: a story can be more or less prototypically story-like. Maximal narrativity can be correlated with sequences whose presentation features a proportional blending of "canonicity and breach," expectation and transgression of expectation. Conversely, a story's narrativity decreases the more its telling verges on pure stereotypicality, at one end of the spectrum, or on a wholesale particularity that cannot help but stymie and amaze, at the other end.

Narrativehood can thus be conveniently paired with narrativity to suggest the contrast between, on the one hand, the minimal conditions for narrative sequences and, on the other, the factors that allow narrative sequences to be more or less readily processed as narratives. After discussing how narrativehood is a function of the way linguistic, textual, or more broadly semiotic features cue recipients to activate certain kinds of world knowledge in certain contexts, I attempt to characterize the scale of narrativity. Sequences that have a minimal narrativity, which distinguishes them from nonnarrative sequences (of zero narrativity, by definition), are less readily configured into chronologically and causally organized wholes—less readily interpreted as stories—than are sequences with higher degrees of narrativity. Narrativity is a function of the more or less richly patterned distribution of script-activating cues in a sequence. Both too many and too few script-activating cues diminish narrativity. Further, narrative genres are distinguished by different preference-rule systems prescribing different ratios of stereotypic to nonstereotypic actions and events. An avant-garde work by Robbe-Grillet or Joyce's *Finnegans Wake* can be said to prefer a lower ratio of stereotypic to nonstereotypic behaviors and occurrences—and thus to *display less narrativity*—than a news report, a classical epic, or a novel by Dickens. Conversely, reciting the sequence of actions and events that were required for me to take a shower this morning would involve so high a ratio of the stereotypic to the nonstereotypic that it, too, would display little narrativity. All other things being equal, then, the greater the number (and diversity) of the experiential repertoires set into play during the processing of a sequence S, and the more that S nonetheless deviates from or militates against expectations about what was likely to occur or be done, the more narrativity will the processor be likely to ascribe to S.

As the final part of the chapter indicates, the concept of scripts yields insights into more than just the structures and functions of particular literary narratives. In addition, by examining different modalities of the script-story interface, theorists of narrative may be able to rethink the historical development of narrative techniques and to understand better the differences among narrative genres at any given time. In particular, a script-based approach to literary history may suggest ways of reframing the concept of intertextuality as a tool for investigating not so much networks of links or fields of analogies as relations among dominant and recessive world models, in addition to the bearing of these models on the texts that presuppose and encode them. Since, however, the early narratologists anticipated subsequent research on knowledge structures, my goal here is not to dismiss classical narrative poetics as an outmoded framework for analysis, but rather to argue for its continued usefulness within certain limits. Indeed, rethinking the problem of narrative sequences helps underscore the overall purpose of this book: that is, to promote the development of an enriched theory of narrative that draws on concepts and methods to which the classical narratologists did not have access, or that they did not integrate into their research.

Narrative Sequences

This section attempts further to substantiate my claim that cognitive-scientific research can help address the problem of how to define narrative sequences—to isolate what makes a string of actions and events not just a sequence but a story. I begin by reviewing structuralist approaches to the problem and then discuss how this structuralist foundation provides crucial support for a more cognitively oriented approach. The structuralists were not *wrong* about narrative sequences; rather, they were *right within certain limits*. Their models' limits of applicability are what now need to be explored and charted.

Structuralist Approaches

As Bremond (1980: 387) remarks, for Propp the basic unit or "narrative atom" is the function; narrative functions are actions or events that, "when grouped in sequences, generate the narrative." In Propp's words, the function "is understood as an act of character, defined from the point of view of its significance for the course of the action" (1968: 21). Actions are thus the basic constituents of functions, functions the constituents of sequences, and sequences the constituents of stories or, in Propp's case, Russian folktales. To invoke a descriptive lexicon that A. J. Greimas derived from Propp: a story or tale can be analyzed into a set of actants whose specific deeds, realized linearly in the syntagmatic chain of the discourse, encode a more abstract pattern of actantial roles—a pattern formed by paradigmatic relations linking particular acts performed over the course of the narrative (Greimas 1983: 147–48, 176–256; cf. Lévi-Strauss 1986: 812–16). The logico-semantic properties of such actantial roles—Subject, Object, Sender, Receiver, Helper, Opponent—derive from their functional orientation within that emergent totality known as *plot*.[8] In the Proppian tradition, therefore, narrative sequences are representations of the particular acts and events realized linguistically or textually in narrative discourse. For example, in sequence 6 the story is not (or not simply) that Bigger Thomas smothers Mary Dalton out of fear of detection by the awesome white blur of her blind mother; such a paraphrase refers only very elliptically to a network of actantial relations. This network governs the play of functions structuring 6, which is in turn constituted as a narrative sequence precisely by its actantial structure.

However (and to broach issues discussed more fully in chapter 4), this model does not indicate how to match linguistic or textual units with the function(s) they purportedly fulfill in any given sequence.[9] Ideally the procedure for correlating formal units with functions and roles would be explicit and would yield uniformly reproducible results; but the functional profile of Bigger Thomas's deeds in sequence 6, for instance, is so multifarious as to generate competing, even contradictory, interpretations. In the sequence at issue Bigger is simultaneously villain and hero, agent and patient (as a rather heated classroom discussion of Wright's novel recently demonstrated to me). Propp himself recognized this problem and discussed it under the heading of the double morphological meaning of a single function (1968: 66–70; cf.

Doležel 1972, 1990; Kafalenos 1999). Propp's solution was to try to find constraints that, rooted in the very structure of the tale as genre, predetermine the order of the functions occurring in a given tale.[10] Such constraints would allow interpreters to correlate acts with functions in more than just an *ad hoc* way. Thus, though functions might be omitted or inverted in a particular tale (cf. Mandler and Johnson 1977: 129–35; Stein 1982: 494–96), "[m]orphologically, a tale (*skázka*) may be termed any development proceeding from villainy (A) or a lack (a), through intermediary functions to marriage (W*), or to other functions employed as a dénouement. Terminal functions are at times a reward (F), a gain or in general the liquidation of misfortune (K), an escape from pursuit (Rs), etc." (Propp 1968: 92).

Yet Propp's solution came with a price; it severely limited the relevance of the model by anchoring it too firmly in a specific narrative genre (Bremond 1973: 11–47; cf. Doležel 1972: 65–66). The approach also gave an overly deterministic coloration to narrative sequences, a problem that Bremond's work on virtuality or non-actualization in sequences tried to address. Part of the interest and complexity of narrative depends on the merely probabilistic, not deterministic, links between some actions and events (Doležel 1972: 63–64; Culler 1975b: 136; Ryan 1991: 109–74). As suggested by the notion of *acting situations* (von Wright 1966) reviewed in chapter 2, part of what makes a story worth telling is that things might not, in fact, have turned out the way they did. Bigger Thomas might not have smothered Mary Dalton, or Mary's mother might have stayed out of the room in the first place; or, in example 4, the black-caped figure might have abducted the entire village. To put the point more generally and more strongly: if faced with a set of sequences made up of various initial conditions and various outcomes premised on those initial conditions, recipients will be inclined to view as stories precisely those sequences in which the outcome is *not* strictly determined by the initial conditions. Hence Gerald Prince (1982) defines narrative as "the representation of at least two real or fictive events or situations in a time sequence, neither of which presupposes or *entails* the other" (4, my emphasis).

But the chief difficulty with the Proppian model, and possibly the source of its other limitations, is that Propp tried to locate the criteria for narrative *in the form* of the tale itself, in the ordered incrementation of its functions and sequences. Francophone structuralists later came to recognize that although linguistic or textual form may trigger recipients' interpretation of a sequence as a story, the form of sequences is not a sufficient condition for a story. Thus, even as Tzvetan Todorov (1977b) articulates a formal definition of the narrative sequence—"A sequence implies the existence of two distinct situations each of which can be described with the help of a small number of propositions; between at least one proposition of each situation there must exist a relation of transformation" (232)—he refers back to Viktor Shklovsky's postulation of the "existence, in each of us, of a faculty of judgment (we might say, today, of a competence) permitting us to decide if a narrative sequence is complete or not" (231). A sequence can be processed as a narrative not just because it has a certain form but also because its form cues readers, listeners, or viewers, in structured, nonrandom ways, to interpret the sequence as a narrative. A similar dual commitment to form and context appears in Roland Barthes's "Introduction to the Structural Analysis of Narratives" (Barthes 1977). On the one hand, the essay sometimes sounds like glossematics (Hjelmslev 1961), as when Barthes calls the narrative sequence "a logical succession of nuclei [that is, the nondeletable elements of a story] bound together by a relation of solidarity: the sequence opens when one of its terms has no solidary antecedent and closes when another of its terms has no consequent" (101). (One of his examples is the picking up and putting down of a telephone receiver.) On the other hand, Barthes describes such sequences as "essential headings" of "the narrative language within us" (102). People learn that language precisely by assimilating a lot of different narratives and storing them in the memory as narrative schemata, in terms of which we are then able to read and process other stories (cf. 116–17). Sequences thereby become "naming operations" that allow interpreters to "grasp every logical succession of actions as a nominal whole" (102; Barthes 1971a: 8–9); they are the product of people's prior and ongoing negotiations with narrative discourse, not the atomic or molecular constituents of a discourse that was narratively structured before anyone ever got to it.

Hence, in his essay titled "Action Sequences," Barthes (1971a) wrote:

> the label put on the sequence—constituting its essence—is a systematic witness evolving from the vast classifying process of language; if I attach the label *abduction* to a certain sequence, it is because the language itself has classified, summed up the diversity of certain actions in one concept

which it transmits to me, the coherence of which is incontestable. The concept of abduction which I compile from a variety of thinly strewn actions in the text coincides, then, with all the abductions I have read previously.... Thus, finding the label [involves] discovering the *connection* between the total past of language and the specific present of the text. (9)

It is true that at this point Barthes unduly restricts the source and scope of stereotypical knowledge, associating it not with a storing of past experience in general but only with "the total past of language," and more specifically with what the recipient of a narrative has already *read*. From this perspective, "The concept of stereotype—the product of a secular culture—is the true motivating force of the narrative domain, entirely founded on the impressions which experience (*much more bookish than practical in nature*) has left on the mind of the reader, and the memory of which constitutes its essence" (1971: 11, my emphasis). But in *S/Z* (1974) Barthes would broaden the concept of stereotype to include practical as well as bookish experience. He there associates narrative sequences with just one of the codes that can be brought to bear on stories to enhance their readability, that is, the "proairetic" code by means of which we try "to give a . . . name to a series of actions, themselves deriving from a patrimonial hoard of human experiences" (204). Whereas Propp sought to isolate the minimal formal constituents of Russian folktales, Barthes came to argue that experiential repertoires are what allow recipients to recognize a *rescue*, an *abduction*, or any other sequence when they see it in the making. In turn, people's ability to design and interpret stories depends on their recognition of things such as rescues, abductions, and other more or less stereotyped sequences of events, against which a tellable story emerges in the manner of a foreground made perceptible and comprehensible by a background.

Similarly, Bremond (1980) aimed for "a logical reconstitution of the starting points and directions of the narrative network" via "a tableau of model sequences, much less numerous than one might imagine and from among which the storyteller must necessarily choose" (389–90). Bremond explicitly based his model sequences upon "human behavior patterns acted out or undergone" (406). "Although it is a technique of literary analysis," wrote Bremond, "the semiology of narrative draws its very existence and wealth from its roots in anthropology," such that "to the elementary narrative types correspond the most general forms of human behavior" (406). Subsequent research has, however, provided richer, more nuanced ways of talking about Barthes's patrimonial hoard of human experiences and Bremond's human behavior patterns. Among these are the knowledge structures that have been termed scripts, or standardized event sequences.[11] Articulated with the classical accounts, research on scripts can help analysts rethink the problem of narrative sequences and, more generally, envisage new directions for narratology after structuralism.

Cognitive-Scientific Perspectives

Building on Frederick Bartlett's (1932) analysis of memory as the organization of prior experience into patterns of expectations for current experience (201–14), cognitive scientists have explored how stereotypical situations and events are stored in the memory and used to guide interpretations of the world. I know what to do when the waiter comes up to me in a restaurant because I have been in restaurants before and remember the standard roles of waiter and customer in that setting (Schank and Abelson 1977: 42–46). Every trip to a restaurant would be an adventure, and would consume far too many cognitive resources, if I never mastered the appropriate restaurant scripts. As Roger C. Schank and Robert P. Abelson (1977) put it, "Some episodes are reminiscent of others. As an economy measure in the storage of episodes, when enough of them are alike they are remembered in terms of a standardized generalized episode which we will call a script" (19; cf. van Dijk 1981: 179–83). Thus,

> A script is a structure that describes an appropriate sequence of events in a particular context. A script is made up of slots and requirements about what can fill those slots. The structure is an interconnected whole, and what is in one slot affects what can be in another. Scripts handle stylized everyday situations. They are not subject to much change, nor do they provide the apparatus for handling totally novel situations.[12] Thus, a script is a predetermined, stereotyped sequence of actions that defines a well-known situation. (Schank and Abelson 1977: 41; cf. Schank 1990: 7–12)

Significantly, the concept of scripts was designed to explain how people are able to build up complex (semantic) representations of stories on the basis of very few textual or linguistic cues. Thus when I read

7. John went to Bill's birthday party. Bill opened his presents. John ate the cake and left (Schank and Abelson 1977: 39);

or even

8. Mary was invited to Jack's party. She wondered if he would like a kite (Minsky 1986: 261);

I can make an astonishing number of inferences about the situations and participants involved—fill in the blanks of the story, so to speak—precisely because the sequences unfold against the backdrop of the familiar birthday-party script. The "terminals" or "slots" associated with that script allow me to make certain default assumptions (e.g., that guests give presents at birthday parties) and so reconstruct the story from merely skeletal sequences. But the research on scripts suggests that it would be misguided to search for some purely formal property that makes sequences 7 and 8 narrative. Instead, it is the *relation between* the (form of the) sequences and the party script that accounts for my intuition that 7 and 8 are in fact stories or at least parts of stories.

The notion of scripts provides a finer-grained vocabulary for describing what earlier narratologists characterized as readers' tendency to organize event sequences into stories. As Seymour Chatman (1978) put it, "[T]he interesting thing is that our minds inveterately seek structure, and they will provide it if necessary. Unless otherwise instructed, readers will tend to assume that [pace E. M. Forster (1927)] even 'The king died and the queen died' presents a causal link, that the king's death has something to do with the queen's" (45–46). In this case stereotypical knowledge about grief and its (sometimes fatal) effects allows interpreters to read sequentiality and causality—and *eo ipso* narrative—into two past-tense clauses linked by a simple conjunction.[13] More generally, since no recounting can be exhaustive, every act of telling arguably requires that a recipient use scripts to help set the narrative in motion, to co-create the story. Birthday-party scripts, for example, enable readers, listeners, or viewers to "fill in" the background against which an incident at a particular party can stand out and acquire tellability. For instance, John may have eaten so much cake at Bill's party (in sequence 7) as to have made himself sick.

But how might this script-story interface be characterized in greater detail? Not just any sequence can cue a reader to activate a particular script. Consider this sequence:

9. John went to a get-together for Bill. After some food and festivities, John went home.

If I told you example 9 out of the blue, I could not reasonably expect you to infer from the cues provided that it is a story about a birthday party—that John and Bill are children, that parents probably supervised the gathering, that the festivities were over in time for the partygoers' early bedtimes, and so forth. So the formal features of sequences constrain the kinds of scripts that can be indexed to this or that story, and conversely they limit the sorts of stories that can be predicated on any script. However, attempting to specify the nature of the constraint in question raises the problem of narrativehood, of what makes a narrative a narrative. For the form of a sequence is neither a necessary nor a sufficient condition for activating specific components of world knowledge during the processing of that sequence.[14]

Suppose that a group of parents have been discussing their children's birthday parties for a while, and then one of the parents says:

10. John went to Bill's. John ate so much he got sick. Then John had to go home.

Presumably the other parents would conclude that example 10 is a story about a birthday party, even though no explicit textual cues license that inference. Thus a particular set of cues need not be present in a story for recipients of it to activate a given script. A discourse context—the total context of utterances exchanged during an occasion of talk—can imbue sequences it contains with narrative functions that they might not possess in isolation or, for that matter, in other discourse contexts. But neither is the presence of particular textual cues a sufficient condition for a script to be activated. Example 8—

8. Mary was invited to Jack's party. She wondered if he would like a kite (Minsky 1986: 261)—

would set the birthday-party script into play in many contexts. Yet it would not do so if presented in, for instance, an account of the retirement of a chief meteorologist named Jack whose colleague Mary runs a program for observation kites.

As the birthday party examples suggest, the knowledge structures regulating the design and interpretation of narrative sequences have foundational status; strings of sentences representing actions and events can be interpreted as stories only insofar as they are embedded in global semantic frameworks subtending all thought, speech, and behavior. The question then becomes how far, and in what fashion, scripts constrain the textual, linguistic, or more broadly semiotic production of particular stories. At what point would examples 4, 6, or 7, for example, become just too skeletal for reconstruction as narrative sequences? In each case, which cues are definitive of a story, and why? I can begin to address these questions by moving from the problem of the membership criteria for the category of narrative to degrees of narrativity—to the way that different tellings or versions of a story can strike readers, viewers, or listeners as more or less narrative. The factors bearing on narrativity may in turn help illuminate the nature of narrativehood. There may be a threshold past which differences of degree effectively become differences of kind; beyond that point a sequence may begin to display so little narrativity that it can no longer be processed as a story at all.

The Problem of Narrativity: A Thought Experiment

Narratologists differentiate between "tellability" (or "reportability") and what they term "narrativity." Situations and events can be more or less tellable; the ways in which they are told can be more or less readily processed in narrative terms or, to put the same point another way, can display different degrees of narrativity. Thus, whereas both predicates are scalar, tellability attaches to configurations of facts and narrativity to sequences representing configurations of facts.[15] For example, the facts surrounding a bank robbery are likely to be deemed more tellable than the facts connected with the gradual movement of a shadow across the ground over the course of a day—although some postmodernist writers have tried to teach readers otherwise (e.g., Robbe-Grillet 1957; see also the final section of this chapter). But if there are two representations of the facts of the robbery, one (i.e., one version of the story of the robbery) may be deemed to have more narrativity, to lend itself more readily to processing as narrative than the other. Imagine an outside observer's fast-paced account compared to a drawn-out disoriented account by a badly shaken victim.

But what is it, exactly, that makes one version of a story more narrative than another? What formal or contextual variables correlate with differing degrees of narrativity? Since I cannot engage here a full-blown analysis of all the variables associated with (degrees of) narrativity, a brief thought experiment instead may suggest ways to mark off gradations on the scale of narrativity—the continuum stretching from sequences that are nearly impossible to process as narratives to those immediately identifiable as such.[16]

Consider the sequences 11–15, read as much as possible according to the grammar of English (letting, for example, the morpheme -*ed* function as a formal marker for (past) verbal tense, *then* and *and* serve as logico-temporal operators, and *a* and *the* function as indefinite and definite articles, respectively):

> 11. A splubba walked in. A gingy beebed the yuck, and the splubba was orped.

A rudimentary action structure is apparent in this sequence: after the entrance of an actant (the splubba) who had not been previously introduced in the context of the discourse, another new actant (the gingy) does something called beebing to something called a yuck, and this leads to the splubba's being or becoming "orped."[17]

> 12. A splubba fibblo. Sim a gingy beebie the yuck i the splubba orpia.

In sequence 12, only the indefinite and definite articles are decipherable. The result is a drastically impoverished action structure, or rather a set of discourse entities that cannot readily be organized into any configuration of actions and events. Nevertheless, the distribution of indefinite and definite noun phrases—patterned in the way that given and new information is parceled out in a discourse (Emmott 1994: 158–61; Firbas 1964, 1992; E. Prince 1981, 1992; Schiffrin 1994: 197–226)—prompts me to read a kind of narrative structure into 12, along the lines of "first this, then that," or perhaps even "this, then because of this, that," although I do not know the meaning of *this* and *that*. Still, I am warranted in saying that sequence 12 has less narrativity than 11. It is not that 11 is more intelligible than 12; for it is not as if, in 11, I know what *beebed* and *orped* mean. Rather, in 12 the deletion of a particular class of morphosyntactic features (verb inflections) removes some of the formal components that cue me to read 11 as an ordered sequence of causally linked events. Arguably, the narrativity of 12 has decreased in proportion to the deletion of such cues.

Sequence 13, however, displays zero narrativity:

> 13. Oe splubba fibblo. Sim oe gingy beebie ca yuck, i ca splubba orpia.

This string does not meet the criteria for narrativehood; in other words, example 13 does not qualify as a narrative sequence, however minimal or impoverished. It lacks sufficient grammatical structure for recipients to infer actants and entities populating a storyworld, let alone read an action structure into one temporal stretch of that storyworld. By contrast, sequence 14 exhibits more narrativity than either 11 or 12 (and *ipso facto* 13), and 15 displays more than 14 because 15 narrates a fully recoverable, if not fully believable, storyworld:

14. A splubba walked in. A gingy pulled the lever, and the splubba was instantaneously inebriated.

15. A bad man walked in. Then a benificent sorcerer pulled the lever, and the bad man was instantaneously inebriated.

In comparison with example 11, 14 provides additional formal cues for the use of particular kinds of world knowledge—specifically, stereotyped sequences of events such as *pulling a lever* and *becoming inebriated*—during the processing of the sequence. These supplementary cues include a higher percentage of recognizable noun phrases, allowing me to identify more of the entities populating the storyworld. In addition, the entire morphology of the verbs, and not just their inflections, is grammatical, so I can situate story referents in what is at least an incipient action structure—one that involves one participant (the gingy) acting in a way that affects the other (the splubba), though the motivations or goals behind the gingy's action as yet remain unclear. Processing sequence 15, a completely grammatical sequence, requires more (and more diverse) experiential repertoires than does processing 14, in which fewer story elements are expressed grammatically and thereby made available for comparison with pre-stored scripts. In 15, a more fully realized action structure enables mental modeling of occurrences in the storyworld. The action structure in question is constituted by the interplay between three elements: (a) the verbs contained in the string, (b) the event sequences encoded in my memory as scripts, and (c) the way in which the verbs embed behaviors and occurrences in a pattern of conflict (good versus evil, ill will versus beneficent countermeasures, etc.), which stands out as a foreground against the background afforded by (b).

The sequences should thus be ranked 12, 11, 14, and 15 in order of increasing narrativity. In 11 and 12 there are markers, more or less prominent, of narrative (e.g., operators indicating *if-then* relationships, in-

Scripts, Sequences, and Stories 103

dices of given and new information); I know that I am in the presence of a story without knowing what that story means, what it is or might be all about. In 15 these markers furnish the formal scaffolding for a sequence whose content does lend itself to reconstruction along narrative lines. This increased narrativity stems in turn from the nature and scope of the scripts (and frames) activated during the interpretation of the sequence, from *being a bad man* to *walking in* to *performing sorcery*. Accordingly, the present thought experiment provides grounds for making the following claim: Up to a certain threshold that also needs to be specified (and past which the already-known begins to outstrip the remarkable or reportable), there is a direct proportion between a sequence's degree of narrativity and the range and complexity of the world knowledge set into play during the interpretation of (the form of) that sequence. As long as it does not cross the threshold (or violate the preference-rule system) separating tellable stories from well-worn stereotypes, a sequence rooted in a plurality of scripts will be more easily processed as a narrative, will be deemed more story-like, than one only fitfully anchored in the knowledge frames (Minsky 1988: 263) bound up with grammatical competence.

Inversely, just as there is a lower limit of narrativity, past which certain "stories" activate so few world models that they can no longer be processed as stories at all, refusing to be configured into action structures drawing on pre-stored scripts and frames, so there is an upper limit of narrativity, past which the tellable gives way to the stereotypical, and the *point* of a narrative, the reason for its being told, gets lost or at least obscured (G. Prince 1983; Labov 1972a). Everyone has had the experience of being bored by a film whose plot twists are all too easily predicted, or by a conversational narrative in which commonplace incidents take the place of what should be genuinely reportable doings and occurrences. In such cases stereotypicality outstrips remarkableness, with canonicity leaving no room for breach. Then again, some narratives can be said purposely to weaken or diminish their own narrativity, not so much by deleting cues for script activation or trafficking in banalities as by setting so many diverse, even conflicting, scripts into play that processors experience cognitive overload and find themselves unable to structure oversaturated sequences into coherent, narratively organized wholes. Brian McHale (1998) has suggested using the term *weak narrativity*, patterned after Gianni Vattimo's notion of "Il pensiero debole" 'weak thought' (Vattimo and Rovatti 1988), to characterize texts (e.g., Bernard 1994; Greig 1994; Hejinian 1991; Muldoon 1991) in which there is a proliferation of minor narratives (jokes, anecdotes, historemes) oftentimes working at cross purposes with one another. Along the same lines, my next section examines varieties of script usage in literary narratives; it draws a correlation between texts' degrees of narrativity and the extent to which they call into question, formally as well as thematically, the stereotypic knowledge that their very processing requires—that is, the cognitive background against which they stand out as foreground.

For its part, my thought experiment has indicated that a sequence's degree of narrativity is a function not of script use alone but also of a shifting constellation of formal and contextual (in particular, cognitive) factors. At stake are a wide range of variables operating at many levels of narrative structure, including morphosyntactic features of the language in which a story is told or written, the grammatical encoding of information about story referents as given or new, the extent to which the form of a sequence facilitates script-aided recognition of a coherent action structure, and the pertinence of intrasequential details to broader, intersequential patterns built up on the basis of generic expectations. The thought experiment brings into focus, too, a specific research strategy for a narratology after structuralism. Using Hjelmslevian parlance, Gerald Prince (1980a: 50-51) argues that what defines narrative as such is the form of its content side, not the form or substance of its expression side (cf. Hjelmslev 1954).[18] But, as the experiment suggests, the processing of a sequence as a story can be aided or impeded by features pertaining to its mode of expression. A fuller investigation of narrativity, then, should use the resources of language theory and cognitive science to study how the (form of the) expression side of stories interacts with (the form of) their content side. In other words, to understand why some sequences are more narrative than others, we need new ways of modeling the interrelations between what classical narratology divided into story and discourse, *fabula* and *sjužet*.

Finally, the foregoing experiment suggests that narrative competence itself can be redescribed as a nested structure of processing strategies operating at different levels—or during different phases—of story comprehension. Spoken or written sequences take on the profile of stories because of the way their form triggers knowledge about (a) the grammar of the language in which they are related, (b) standardized event sequences, among other sorts of experiential repertoires, and (c) other, prior sequences (and groups of sequences) mediating encounters with any particular string. Ranking these processing strategies, that is, determining their order of importance or the stages at which readers and listeners resort to them in interpreting a narrative, constitutes its own research project.[19] The last section of this chapter examines some interconnections between strategies of types b and c, mentioned above—between script-based strategies and strategies rooted in knowledge about intersequential relations. My last section thus shifts from local to global modes of script use, from principles for microdesigning narrative sequences to genre-related principles bearing on narrative macrodesigns. Although schematic, my discussion demonstrates, I hope, that the script concept can be productive not just for narrative theory but also for the practice of literary interpretation.

Indeed, in setting out the problem of narrative sequences, I have already appealed to knowledge based upon intersequential, or generic, patterning. Arguably, generic factors help account for my inclination to process sequence 4—

4. A black-caped figure prowled among the houses. An owl screeched. Three children were borne away into the night—

as a narrative and not as a description like sequence 1:

1. A monkey screeched. Sunlight blazed down upon the sea. The rancher gazed proudly at his bison.

Gothic tales I know predispose me to read a coherent action structure into the former sequence; by contrast, in example 1 my search for analogous textual or generic models results in my tending not to organize intrasequential events into a narrative. As already indicated, moreover, a cognitively oriented approach to literary narratives suggests that genres—and, for that matter, changes in narrative technique over time—can themselves be redescribed as script-based macrodesigns. Narratives can anchor themselves in stored world knowledge in vastly different ways, whether they activate it for their processing or encode it as themes. Hence focusing on the script-story interface may yield new perspectives on the study of literary history and cast new light on the generic categories to which narratives are typically assigned.

Scripts and Literary Narrative

Barthes and Bremond were not the only researchers who worked toward implementing scripts, *avant la lettre*, in literary-theoretical contexts. For example, in his own explication of structuralist poetics, Jonathan Culler (1975a) developed a broadly script-based account of the operations of reading as strategies of naturalization. For Culler, "to naturalize a text is to bring it into relation with a type of discourse or model which is already, in some sense, natural and legible" (138). People read, then, by naturalizing, and they naturalize by using scripts. In fact, according to the structuralist notion of *vraisemblance*, the real itself can be redefined as "the text of the natural attitude"—as a text, or set of scripts, comprising the "most elementary paradigms of action" (Culler 1975a: 140–41; cf. W. Martin 1986: 67–71). Working in a somewhat different (broadly phenomenological) research tradition, Wolfgang Iser (1978) reached similar conclusions. For Iser, it is not merely that every text potentially presents interpretive schemata, at the formal level, in terms of which acts of reading unfold. What is more, "social norms and contemporary and literary allusions all constitute [further] schemata which give shape to the knowledge and memories" triggered by the text as we process it (143). In other words, "[r]eading is not a direct 'internalization' [of the text], because it is not a one-way process, and our concern will be to find means of describing the reading process as a dynamic *interaction* between text and reader" (107). As Iser's analysis suggests, this interaction is mediated by scripts and other kinds of world models. More recently, R. A. Buck (1996) has drawn on schema theory and the related discourse-analytic notion of "social scripts" to show how readers process literary dialogues through strategies of "contextual delimitation" (70). Branigan (1992), Fludernik (1996), Jahn (1997, 1999), and Ryan (1991) have likewise thrown light on cognitive dimensions of narrative processing. For example, as discussed in my previous chapter, Ryan's "principle of minimal departure" (48–60) captures how readers, listeners, or viewers use world models to make default assumptions about a storyworld, unless explicitly cued to do otherwise by a text, discourse, or film.

Such research has begun to indicate the explanatory potential of the script concept for the study of literary narrative. Yet more attention needs to be given to the reciprocal relation between scripts and literary texts—a relation recently commented on by Cesare Segre (1995). On the one hand, literary texts "formalize and consecrate the schemata drafted by collective experience"; but on the other hand, "the way we schematize reality is partly determined by literary clichés, which easily spread to all levels of culture" (26). Although Segre's formulation is suggestive, it stops short of explaining how scripts shape the design and interpretation of literary texts, and how literary texts in turn affect the production and dissemination of scripts. To this end, I propose the following two hypotheses, one diachronic and the other synchronic in emphasis, which could be used to generate research strategies for the study of story logic:

> (a) The nature and scope of the world knowledge required to process literary texts change over time, as do the ways in which the script-story interface itself gets encoded or thematized in texts. Such changes correspond to shifts in the relations among recessive, dominant, and emergent narrative techniques.

> (b) Contemporaneous texts can relate differently to prevailing scripts. Texts can pertain more or less critically and reflexively to the scripts circulating when the texts were written. For narrative, these variations correspond to generic classifications used to categorize stories.

Literary history produces an ever-expanding corpus of texts, whose varying designs reveal shifting conceptions of how many (and what sorts of) scripts should be activated during textual processing. The formal impetus, the constitutive gesture, of literary fiction has been the rejection or at least the backgrounding of scripts in which prior texts were anchored and the complementary foregrounding of new scripts matched to changing ideas about narrative. Thus Miguel de Cervantes's 1605 work *Don Quixote* (1964) opens with a semicomic indictment of the delusive power of outmoded scripts—in particular, those of chivalric romance (46–47, 56–59, 62–64, 83–84). Interpretation of the subsequent series of action sequences requires scripts grounded in an awareness of human potential and limitations rather than the more restricted world knowledge undergirding idealized quests, knightly courtesy, and so on. Cervantes's novelistic narrative distinguishes itself from romance by demanding richer and more numerous experiential repertoires from readers who would co-construct his fictional world. Madame de Lafayette's 1678 work *La Princesse de Clèves* (*The Princess of Clèves*; 1994) marks a similar rejection of fictional romance, but Lafayette's strategies of script multiplication and enrichment differ from Cervantes'. Lafayette's text displaces action sequences from the public to the private realm, recentering world models around the affective domain. In particular, the novel's anti-romantic profile, its quest for *vraisemblance*, derives not from comic de-idealization but from its focus on the complexities and vicissitudes of male-female relationships, as encapsulated in the Princess's famous, ill-fated "confession" to Monsieur de Clèves (Lafayette 1994: 65–68) and her rejection of Nemours toward the end of the novel (100–105). Literary fabulation, here as in Cervantes, roots itself precisely in what previous texts did not convey about human (inter)actions. Yet vastly different formal principles regulate the proliferation of alternative scripts. In the case of Lafayette, script multiplication yields a narrative whose processing requires (and fosters) the re-modeling of gender-pertinent actions and reactions.

Such changes in scripts and stories are reciprocal: the need for narrative innovation stems from the dominance of certain kinds of world knowledge that, although initially of limited relevance or scope, have been reinforced, consolidated, and generalized by prior narrative techniques. Thus, by the time of Denis Diderot's 1773 work *Jacques le fataliste et son maître* (*Jacques the Fatalist*; 1986), not the romance but rather the novel itself is the repository and source of outworn scripts. A product of the Enlightenment's rethinking of the respective claims of truth and fiction, knowledge and myth, Diderot's text features a narrator who repeatedly insists that he is not writing a novel (51, 214) and who implies that to have verisimilitude, a fiction must *not* conform to novelistically patterned sequences of actions, such as pitched battles between heroes and villains (22, 30, 49). Diderot's anti-novel resists such stereotyped action sequences, and promotes script multiplication and enrichment, by constantly foregrounding the contingency, even indeterminacy, of the narrated events, sometimes hesitating between alternative accounts of happenings in the storyworld (251–54). Narrativizing the philosophical concerns of the Encyclopedists, especially Enlightenment debates concerning determinism versus free will, *Jacques the Fatalist* contains sequences so designed as to activate several competing processing strategies simultaneously and thus to provoke a reconsideration of linear, deterministic models of human behavior.[20]

Later literary developments suggest that there are other ways of reconfiguring the relations between world models and narrative techniques and other reasons for doing so. For example, Gustave Flaubert's 1857 work *Madame Bovary* (1992) displays specifically realist strategies for innovating upon narrative form through script enrichment. Much of the devastating irony of the text derives from the contrast between, on the one hand, Emma Bovary's narrowly circumscribed (and grossly oversimplified) store of world knowledge and, on the other hand, the richer and more comprehensive scripts encoded at other levels of narrative structure, notably through the actions and projected actions of the worldly, cynical Rodolphe during his seduction of Emma. Given that Emma acquires many of her world models and interpretive strategies through Romantic fictions (41–46), Flaubert's text suggests not just the cognitive inadequacy but also the destructive power of Romantic paradigms, which prove to be as restricted in scope as the ones that had Don Quixote tilting at windmills. For its part, Sartre's *La Nausée* (*Nausea*; 1938) transforms the anti-novel into a metanovel. Thematizing the very search for ordered event sequences as a symptom of bad faith—distinguishing between the radical fluidity of existence and the stories through which human beings inauthentically seek to congeal it (Sartre 1964: 37, 39–40)—Sartre's narrative is about the impossibility as well as the undesirability of narrative. Given that the idea of the passage of time is "an invention of man" 'une invention des hommes' for Roquentin and that "[e]very existing thing is born without reason, prolongs itself out of weakness and dies by chance" '[t]out existant naît sans raison, se prolonge par faiblesse et meurt par rencontre' (132, 133; Sartre 1938: 168, 169), telling stories about human lives is an inherently and perniciously (self-)delusional project. The less authentic my attitude toward existence, the more scripts in which I am enmeshed and hence the more stories that I unfortunately begin to understand (Sartre 1964: 56–57, 95–96). Yet the text's thematic profile is at odds with the processing strategies needed to co-create the action structures around which its themes are clustered. Thus the experience of Sartre's narrative form is fundamentally dialectical, forcing recipients to adopt a stance that is at once authentic and inauthentic: they can reconstruct Roquentin's rejection of previous world models, his striving for a condition of absolute scriptlessness, only by anchoring such gestures in a variety of experiential repertoires.

From Diachronic to Synchronic Implications

To be sure, fuller implementation of the script concept in the study of literary history would require an expanded comparison of shifts in narrative form with changing world models, as well as a more comprehensive survey of ways in which the interplay between scripts and stories can itself figure as a theme. The diachronic investigation of script use across time needs to be supplemented, however, with a synchronic investigation of script use across different genres at the same time, in accordance with my second research hypothesis. The recall of previously interpreted sequences, which are recognizable as narratives by virtue of the world knowledge they activate, enables the processing of other sequences as members of larger narrative classes (the diary novel, autobiography, travel narrative, etc.). Thus differences in genre can be correlated with differences in the processing strategies at once necessitated and promoted by particular kinds of sequences. Such strategies, which eventuate in generic codes (cf. Todorov 1990), can be more or less multidimensional; in particular, different types of sequences relate more or less critically and reflexively to the world models on which their interpretation simultaneously depends.

A few representative sequences may provide a blueprint for further research on the orientation of narrative genres toward prevailing scripts. Sequences 16, 17, and 18 are excerpted from works written within fifteen years of one another. The first sequence belongs to the genre of children's fiction, the second to that of autobiography, and the third to that of experimental literary narrative. In progressing through this series, recipients must use increasingly multidimensional or reflexive processing strategies. The processing of narratives is more complex when they inhibit what might be termed the naive application of scripts and promote, instead, reflection on the limits of applicability of the scripts being invoked. The three series recount action sequences—respectively, *getting one's head stuck in a jar*, *confronting armed soldiers*, *going down on all fours and acting like a dog*—that could be transposed into other narrative genres. Correlatively, generic differences stem not from narrative content as such, but rather from the complexity and duration of the interpretive routes that readers take in formulating narrative content (e.g., through story paraphrases like the ones just offered).

Sequence 16 is taken from A. A. Milne's *Winnie-the-Pooh* (Milne 1926). Here Winnie-the-Pooh's craving for honey has tempted him into his and Piglet's Heffalump Trap, where he gets his head stuck in the jar of honey intended as bait for the nonexistent but much-feared Heffalumps:

> 16. And all the time Winnie-the-Pooh had been trying to get the honey-jar off his head. The more he shook it, the more tightly it stuck. *"Bother!"* he said, inside the jar, and *"Oh, help!"* and, mostly *"Ow!"* And he tried bumping it against things, but as he couldn't see what he was bumping it against, it didn't help him; and he tried to climb out of the Trap, but as he could see nothing but jar, and not much of that, he couldn't find his way. So at last he lifted up his head, jar and all, and made a loud, roaring noise of Sadness and Despair. (67)

This sequence suggests one of the crucial features of the genre of children's fiction: the genre is so designed as to establish and inculcate particular world models (for example, those associated with delaying immediate gratification or resisting the gratuitous fabrication of monsters). This genre's primary function is not to problematize a world that readers only think they know, but rather to help them acquire more strategies for getting to know it. Far from presuming the script expertise supporting more elaborate narrative experiments, children's fictions consolidate and reinforce the scripts on which narrative competence itself depends. Such fictions teach reading by teaching scripts.

Sequence 17 comes from Maud Gonne MacBride's 1938 autobiography, *A Servant of the Queen* (1983), and recounts events surrounding the Irish Civil War:

> 17. So in the war, when I was an old woman in Dublin and bullets were flying and crowds swayed like corn ears in the wind, it never occurred to me to take cover; and because I literally felt no fear, nothing ever happened to me, though some who took cover were wounded. Outside General Mulcahy's house in Portobello, the Woman's Prisoners' Defence League had organised a great protest meeting against the murder of prisoners of war for which Mulcahy was held responsible. The Free State soldiers were drawn up inside the railings; some shots had been fired over our heads; a woman's hat had been pierced by a bullet. I heard an order given and the front line of soldiers knelt down with rifles ready,—some of the young soldiers were white and trembling. I got up on the parapet of the railing and smiled contempt at the officer. He had curious rather beautiful pale grey eyes and a thin brown face. We gazed at each other a full minute. The order to fire was not given. (15)

Admittedly, part of what distinguishes sequence 17 from 16 is the way MacBride's text organizes its reality effects (Barthes 1982); the narrative features a more densely populated storyworld with an independently verifiable history and geography, the parameters of which are established by spatiotemporal indices such as *in the [Irish Civil] war*, *Dublin*, *Portobello*, and *Free State soldiers*. As a result, reconstructing the action sequence encoded in 17 necessitates considerably more script expertise, familiarity with a greater variety of world models, than does processing 16 as a story. More than this, however, because it belongs to the genre of autobiography, interpretation of passage 17 requires, to a greater degree than does reading *Winnie-the-Pooh*, reliance on and reevaluation of a particular class of world models: namely, scripts and frames bearing on the formation and maintenance of selfhood (Lejeune 1988; Linde 1993: 127–91).[21] MacBride's text not only activates experiential repertoires but also compels reflection on their explanatory scope—on the kinds of stories about the self that they do or do not help readers comprehend (cf. Herman 1995b). At once invoking and suspending male-authored and male-centered paradigms for heroic action, interpretation of the sequence enriches the repertoire of behaviors that can be used to typify female actants (e.g., facing down a group of armed soldiers). The text thereby exploits existing scripts to generate additional models for understanding who women are and what they can do.

Sequence 18, taken from the ending of Djuna Barnes's highly experimental 1937 novel *Nightwood* (1961), requires processing strategies that are even more multidimensional:

> 18. The dog, quivering in every muscle, sprang back, his tongue a stiff curving terror in his mouth; moved backward, back, as she came on, whimpering too, coming forward, her [Robin's] head turned completely sideways, grinning and whimpering. Backed into the farthest corner, the dog reared as if to avoid something that troubled him to such agony that he seemed to rise from the floor; then he stopped, clawing sideways at the wall, his forepaws lifted and sliding. Then head down, dragging her forelocks in the dust, she struck against his side. He let loose one howl of misery and bit at her, dashing about her, barking, and as he sprang on either side of her he always kept his head toward her, dashing his rump now this side, now that, of the wall. (170)

It could be argued that sequence 18 exploits prevailing scripts more critically and reflexively than 17 and that generic differences between 18 and 17 can be measured by the scope and frequency of the script suspensions cued by the narratives' form. At stake in *Nightwood* is a gamut of world models, including those bearing on questions of per-

Scripts, Sequences, and Stories 113

sonal identity. The passage conveys a strikingly particularized action structure, which dissolves both human and animal behavior into microsequences of atomistic gestures. The sequence thus provokes a reconsideration of, among other aspects of script construction and usage, the canons of tellability (at what level of detail should event sequences be stored or told? what counts as an action or an event?), models for understanding women's and for that matter human identity (to what extent can scripts indexed to nature and culture be transposed? how have such script transpositions contributed to cultural as well as cognitive stereotypes about identity?), and the very concept of purposive action (why would someone mimic and thereby terrorize a dog? on the basis of what world models can readers make sense of such event sequences?).

While constituting only prolegomena for a future narratology, this chapter suggests that a rethinking of classical approaches to the problem of narrative sequences will entail a more careful investigation of the interface between scripts and stories. As I argue throughout this book, although narratology does contain structuralist theory as one of its "moments," it should work to enrich the older approach with research tools taken from other areas of inquiry, while in turn lending its own conceptual toolkit to those other areas. The result will be not simply new ways of getting at old problems in narrative analysis but a rearticulation of the problems themselves, including the root problem of how to define stories. In particular, reinterpreting narrative as an interface between language and thought can throw new light on some of the most basic issues facing analysts of narrative. This reinterpretation suggests that scripts and stories are in some sense mutually constitutive; recipients' ability to process a narrative depends on the way it anchors itself in—but also plays itself off—knowledge representations of various sorts. Narratologists should thus study how interpreters of stories are able to activate kinds of knowledge with or without explicit textual cues to guide them. At the same time, researchers should investigate how literary narratives, through their forms as well as their themes, work to privilege some world models over others. After all, if the right kind of children's story caught on, people might finally stop worrying about Heffalumps. And in time, splubbas might circumvent the dreaded pulling of the yuck.[22]

4
Participant Roles and Relations

This chapter focuses on the roles of and relations between storyworld participants, an important subset of which includes those participants traditionally described as *characters*.[1] I choose the term *participant* advisedly, for my aim is to multiply lines of connection between narratological approaches to character, on the one hand, and linguistic theories about what are sometimes called the "logical participants" of propositions expressed in clauses and sentences, on the other hand.[2] The chapter begins by reexamining A.-J. Greimas's influential account of narrative actants (Greimas 1983, 1987; Greimas and Courtés 1983; cf. Budniakiewicz 1992, 1998a, 1998b, 1998c, 1998d). I argue that despite some significant limitations, Greimas's work, along with the research informing it, laid the foundations for a cognitively oriented approach to participants that synthesizes linguistic and narrative-theoretical models. I then go on to sketch what such an approach might look like. Extending recent linguistic research on grammatical structures at the level of clauses and sentences, I shift from structuralist ideas of narrative actants to the broader notion of storyworld participants, characterized as elements or individuals involved (in various ways) in processes encoded in narrative discourse.[3] Taken in this sense—and to invoke some of the functionalist ideas that I adapt from M. A. K. Halliday (Halliday 1967, 1976, 1994; cf. Fawcett 1980; J. R. Martin 1996a, 1996b) below— participants can be distinguished from the *circumstances* in which the processes are represented as occurring. My approach thus leads back to some of the basic insights of Lucien Tesnière (1976), from whose 1959 study of structural syntax Greimas borrowed in developing his theories. Tesnière, too, distinguished between what he called the *actants* and the *circonstants* of processes encoded in utterances; these terms correspond, respectively, to the participants involved in the processes and to the time, place, manner, and so on, in which the processes unfold (Tesnière 1976: 102–15).

In addition to sketching a functionalist approach to storyworld participants, my chapter draws on other linguistic research concerned with the logico-semantic dimensions of predication in natural language (Cook 1989; Fillmore 1968, 1971, 1977; Frawley 1992: 197–249; Jackendoff 1987; Kiefer 1992; Malmkjaer 1991; Van Valin 1993). Focusing on the interface between syntax and semantics, this research suggests that sentence elements can be viewed as arguments assigned particular thematic or "case" roles by way of predicates encoded in the language. I argue that storyworlds acquire part of their structure by way of analogous roles assigned to their participants. More precisely, mental representations can be assembled into storyworlds only when it is possible to assign roles to participants, and to do so in a manner specified by further preference-rule systems supporting narrative comprehension. Circumstances in storyworlds, meanwhile, can be interpreted as such because they take on *nonparticipant* roles.[4]

To anticipate arguments developed below: with respect to participant roles and relations, story logic involves a two-stage parsing procedure. First, in mentally modeling what is being narrated, readers, viewers, or listeners use textual cues to distinguish participants from circumstances, that is, nonparticipants. Then they use those same cues to match participants (and also nonparticipants) with an inventory of roles deriving from the types of processes involved and from how those processes are instantiated in particular events. The matches that result afford a sense of how participants relate to one another and to circumstances in the storyworld. Morever, these role assignments have to be monitored and updated during narrative comprehension since a given participant's role can change; such role changes may also alter the network of relations between various participants and between participants and circumstances. Thus, as even this preliminary sketch should indicate, in order to grasp the action structures described in chapters 2 and 3—in order to create higher-order narrative units based on interpretations of characters' (emergent) beliefs, desires, and intentions—recipients must frame and reframe inferences about participant roles over time. Interpreters must also work to infer what roles participants impute to themselves and to others through analogous, but storyworld-internal, processes of inference.

There is, of course, an entire tradition of narratives—stretching from Ovid's *Metamorphoses* to Franz Kafka's *Die Verwandlung* (*The Meta-*

morphosis) to Virginia Woolf's *Orlando* to Patrick Modiano's *Le Place de l'étoile* (*The Place of the Star*) to David Lynch's *Lost Highway* and beyond—in which the individuals and entities concerned are more or less radically altered by transformative processes in their respective storyworlds. Even in the face of multifarious, sometimes vertiginous, shifts in the outward manifestation of participants, however, interpreters manage to build cohesive links between episodes. They do so by using mental models based on roles and relations to organize their understanding of the unfolding narrative. Specifically, following a cognitive preference to assume constancy of participant roles in the absence of textual cues indicating otherwise, readers impute to the "before" and "after" versions of participants the statuses of, respectively, source and target, adjusting for a change of circumstance rather than a wholesale shift in participant identity.[5] At issue, though, is just how interpreters are able to use textual cues to track participants across such changes of circumstance. The exact nature of the textual cues enabling this sort of monitoring activity, along with the nature of the activity itself, is the focus of the present chapter, which aims to underscore the centrality of participant roles and relations to narrative understanding.

Contexts for My Approach

My approach raises methodological issues that it might be productive to address here at the outset, as well as in the pages that follow. It does not go without saying that one can (or should) use theories centering on *clause*- and *sentence*-level phenomena to account for the structure and comprehension of narrative *discourse*. In this context it is important to stress that, despite Roland Barthes's (1977) claim to the contrary, a discourse is not a long sentence; nor is a sentence an abbreviated discourse (cf. Herman 2001b). Certain linguistic properties emerge only at the discourse level—for example, the referential (more precisely, anaphoric) functions of a definite description recurring several times in an extended discourse and evoking an item previously mentioned:

> I wrote a book. Then *the book* was reviewed. Then I regretted writing *the book*.

Conversely, as already suggested in chapter 1, whereas sentences can be deemed well- or ill-formed, discourses (e.g., narratives) are not subject to the same sorts of grammaticality judgments. In the present chapter, however, I assume not that participants and nonparticipants in sentences and discourses are isomorphic, but rather that processing strategies triggered by sentence-level cues are *scalable*, with at least some of the same processes extending to discourse-level cues as well.[6] According to this latter assumption, interpreters of narrative, when scanning a text for markers of participant roles and relations, draw on core cognitive resources also used to parse sentence- and clause-level encodings of processes, participants, and circumstances. To assert that discourse processing depends on some of the same resources as sentence processing is not tantamount to asserting that, during the interpretation of a story, readers map sentence structures *directly* into discourse structures when trying to make sense of narrative participants.

Meanwhile, in her careful exposition of Greimas's theory of actants, Therese Budniakiewicz (1992) notes disparities between the way that theory was implemented and Greimas's claim that "the actantial model was hypothesized essentially from the syntactical structure of the sentence" (19). According to Budniakiewicz, her analysis of what Greimas characterized as subject and object actants proves "that the actantial categories are not derived from sentence syntax but are conceptual notions stemming from the practical syllogism of action, its teleological inversion, and its opposition to (or union with) one or more practical syllogisms" (1992: 22; cf. 27–109). As Budniakiewicz (1998b) puts it elsewhere, "[O]ut of the three sources used to generate the actantial model [i.e., Propp's *Morphology*, Etienne Souriau's (1950) analysis of character functions in drama, and Tesnière's syntactic theories], the linguistic constellation of actants carries the least evidentiary weight and does not support the myth surrounding the model that maintains it was derived from sentence structure" (6). Below I draw on Budniakiewicz's critique to motivate a rather different rethinking of the theory of actants. I concede that Greimas's appeal to linguistic models such as Tesnière's was not as well grounded as it might have been, so that his intuitions about the scalability of those models remained underdeveloped.[7] Unlike Budniakiewicz, however, I argue that Greimas was fundamentally on the right track when he alluded to correspondences between narrative actants and individuals involved in the various kinds of processes that clauses and sentences can be used to express.

More generally, since my discussion of participants and circumstances bears on issues traditionally studied under the rubric of character (and, for that matter, "setting"), it may be useful to provide at least a thumbnail sketch of how my account pertains to the extensive body of research on character in literary narrative. Shlomith Rimmon-Kenan (1983: 29–42) has divided this research tradition into approaches that highlight the mimetic (or verisimilar) status of characters and approaches that highlight their semiotic (artificial or constructed) status. Whereas humanists such as A. C. Bradley (1965) used mimetic criteria to interpret and evaluate Shakespeare's fictional participants, celebrating them for their lifelikeness, structuralist narratologists began by underscoring the constructedness of characters, their irreducibly semiotic status, when viewed as nodes in a network of signs. It was not just that the structuralists followed Aristotle and the Russian Formalists in making character "a function of plot, a necessary but derivative consequence of the chrono-logic of story" (Chatman 1978: 113).[8] More than this, viewing characters as autonomous textual entities, theorists such as the Barthes of *Mythologies* used their conception of character to rethink human identities as myths, as sign complexes whose contingent, conventional meanings had become naturalized, that is, transmuted into what simply is (Barthes 1972). In this sense, the structuralists viewed techniques for character analysis as part of a larger semiological revolution whose aim was nothing less than to demythologize identity itself.

For his part, James Phelan (1989) has shown the advantages of reapportioning characterological research into a tripartite study of characters' mimetic, synthetic (= semiotic), and thematic dimensions. Cues associated with a character's mimetic dimensions prompt readers to interpret her as an individual; cues associated with her thematic dimensions, as a representative figure; and cues associated with her synthetic dimensions, as an artificial construct (1–23). For Phelan, these dimensions can take on more or less central or dominant functions and can come to predominate in different ways, during the progression of a narrative. Thus, in Italo Calvino's *If on a Winter's Night a Traveler*, the synthetic dimensions of character have functional dominance, whereas in the portrayal of Winston Smith in George Orwell's *1984* the character's thematic dimensions predominate (Phelan 1989: 27–50, 133–62). Further, as discussed by Bernard Paris (1998) in his 1974 study of what he analogously called the *mimetic*, *thematic*, and *formal* functions of character, differences between classes of narratives—that is, narrative genres—can be correlated with predominant modes of character presentation. Novels of psychological realism, for instance, are marked by a predominance of mimetic over thematic modes of character presentation, with "the main characters exist[ing] primarily as mimetic portraits whose intricacies escape the moral and symbolic meanings assigned to them" (231).

Uri Margolin (1986, 1987, 1990a, 1990b, 1995) has further explored the conceptual underpinnings of this line of inquiry, emphasizing that character itself is a theory-dependent construct rather than an independently existing entity with essential properties or dimensions waiting to be described. As Margolin puts it,

> Proceeding along a scale from signifier to signified or textuality to representation, one can distinguish four theoretical models of LC [literary character] in current poetics, each of which serves as an explication of one aspect of our intuitions in this area. The four are (A) character as a topic entity of a discourse, (B) character as an artificial construct or device, (C) character as a thematic element, and (D) character as a nonactual individual in some fictional (possible) world.... All four ... conceptions of LC are anchored in self-consistent, well-developed theoretical frameworks.... We may profitably regard the four conceptions, and the theories underlying them, not as either/or truths, but as cognitive instruments, tools, or points of vantage, all of which coexist at any given time as options for the theorist. (1990a: 454–55)

Elsewhere, however, Margolin (1990b) focuses in on three theory-dependent definitions of character and argues for the descriptive and explanatory advantages of defining character as a non-actual individual in a fictional world rather than as a Greimassian actant or a "narrative instance" of the sort specified by classical narratology, which grouped narrative agents alongside the instances of narrator and narratee. From this perspective, an ontological approach to individuals in narrative worlds provides the most finely tuned instrument for capturing "constitutive conditions for individuals in narrated states of affairs" (849–57ff.), including their existence, attributes, uniqueness or singularity, and modes of transformation over time. In essence, the account developed in the present chapter combines Margolin's ontological perspective with a modified version of Greimas's theory of actants, reconceptualizing participants as role-bearing individuals bound up with processes instantiated as events in mentally projected storyworlds.

I believe that this way of approaching participant roles and relations affords a rich synthesis of linguistic and narrative-theoretical tools—a synthesis that can, in turn, throw new light on how narrative helps organize humans' understanding of the world. Debatably, the cognitive strategies enabling interpreters to discern and monitor participant roles and relations in stories have the same provenance as—are fundamentally continuous with—those used to make sense of participant structures in social situations generally. As Margolin (1986) suggests, interpreting and playing a part in any social situation require "distinguishing the roles assigned to agent and patient in the pattern of social interaction in which they find themselves, e.g., clerk and applicant, [along with] their institutionalized interrelations and standard role expectations" (211; cf. Fairclough 1989, 1995). Greimas makes an even stronger version of this claim in *Structural Semantics*, arguing that in the absence of the semantic information generated by inferences about participant roles, both cognition and communication would be impossible. As I go on to argue, this strong claim is consistent with recent linguistic and cognitive-scientific research suggesting that "meanings are relativized to scenes" (Fillmore 1977: 59)—though Greimas's approach goes one step further by making stories the primary instrument for building such participant-based scenes.

To invoke Greimas's terms, actants are what enable language users to extract a cognizable *semantic microuniverse* from the ungraspable totality of a *semantic universe*, that is, to build a *manifested* universe of meaning from the materials provided by the *immanent* universe of meaning (Greimas 1983: 135–53). Whereas the immanent semantic universe consists of a limitless combinatorial matrix of sememes (minimal units of meaning based on various contrastive relations), and whereas this immanent universe "constitutes the world of qualities, that type of opaque screen on which innumerable effects of meaning come to be reflected," the manifested universe "is subject to a model which organizes its functioning by combining the sememes into messages" (143). Narrative actants, as I go on to discuss in the next section, represent Greimas's attempt to capture a limited, stable inventory of semantic roles out of which this sort of organizing model might be fashioned. For Greimas, it is not just that the functions of syntactic elements can be compared with the roles played by characters in a drama (198; see also below); more than this, any cognizable "semantic microuniverse can be defined as a universe, that is to say, as a signifying whole, *only to the extent that* it can surge up at any moment before us as a simple drama, as an actantial structure" (199, my emphasis). It is because Greimas came to view actants as a sort of transcendental condition for semantic microuniverses, a sine qua non for meaning making, that narrative and narratology became such central concerns in the so-called Paris School of Semiotics that grew up around Greimas after his appointment as *directeur d'études* at the École Pratique des Hautes Études in 1965 (Budniakiewicz 1992: 1–25; 1998d). My next section argues that, although Greimas had good intuitions in insisting on this story-based approach to sense making, he lacked the conceptual and methodological resources to capture exactly how participant roles and relations bear on narrative understanding, which for the Paris School became an essential precondition for understanding as such (cf. Greimas 1990a: 28–33; 1990b: 43–58).

Actants Reconsidered

This section revisits the structuralist approach to character that can be traced back through Barthes, Greimas, and Todorov to the groundbreaking work of Vladimir Propp. After presenting the fundamentals of this classical approach, whose root concept is the idea of actants that Greimas adapted from Tesnière, I highlight problems that motivate my terminological (and methodological) shift from actants to participants in the sections that follow. Whereas some of these problems are theory-internal, deriving from the way Greimas formulated his actantial model, others emerge when the theory is brought into contact with neighboring fields of study, especially research on functional grammar and on thematic roles in clauses and sentences.

Fundamentals of the Theory of Actants

In a certain sense, structuralist narratology began with the attempt to create a systematic framework for describing how characters participate in the narrated action. In his *Morphology of the Folktale*—a text first published in 1928 and one of the works associated with Russian Formalism that would exercise such a profound influence on Francophone narratology—Vladimir Propp (1968) followed Aristotle in subordinating character to action or plot.[9] Proposing a descriptive vocabulary based on the "functions" performed by characters in stories, Propp conceived of the function as "an act of character, defined from the point of view of its significance for the course of the action" (1968: 21). A function is thus a participatory slot in the syntagmatic unfolding of a narrative, and "character" is a relatively loose (if traditional) way of talking about kinds of slots and the relational networks linking them together. Arguing that many seemingly diverse functions join together to create a few, typifiable "spheres of action," Propp developed a typology of seven general roles (the villain, the donor, the helper, the sought-for-person and her father, the dispatcher, the hero, and the false hero) that correspond to the ways in which characters can participate in the plot structures found in the genre of the folktale (Propp 1968: 79–80). Propp's subordination of characters to the action—his shift from personalities to participatory roles—provided the basis for structuralist accounts of actants.

Rooted in contemporary linguistic theory, these accounts were also resolutely anti-psychological, displacing attention from the interior states to the manifest deeds of participants in a story.[10] Actants represented a new, linguistically informed approach to the very old problem of literary character. Typically defined as "fundamental role[s] at the level of narrative deep structure" (G. Prince 1987: 1), "*actants* are general categories [of behavior or doing] underlying all narratives (and not only narratives) while [*actors*] are invested with specific qualities in different narratives" (Rimmon-Kenan 1983: 34).[11] Further, as Budniakiewicz (1998a) notes, an actant "need not appear as an anthropomorphic being or human actor. Unlike the term *character* that *actant* replaces, it applies not only to human beings but also animals, objects, or concepts" (10). (As I discuss below, theories of thematic roles in linguistic semantics, like theories of participants in functional grammar, also uncouple agency, patiency, and other participant roles from the predicate "humanness.") The actantial model first appeared in its canonical form in 1966 in Greimas's *Sémantique structurale* (*Structural Semantics*) (1983). Refined by Greimas in his 1973 essay "Actants, Actors, and Figures" (Greimas 1987) and in other, later work (Greimas and Courtés 1983; cf. Budniakiewicz 1992, 1998d), the model was widely influential and was adopted (and adapted) in much subsequent narratological research.

The theory of actants originally set forth in Greimas's *Structural Semantics* appeared in the same year that Roland Barthes recommended that "the structural analysis of narrative be given linguistics as founding model" (1977: 82; cf. Barthes 1996). It is thus worth reemphasizing that although Greimas (himself trained as a lexicologist) was the first to invoke the term *actant* in connection with stories, he borrowed the term from the syntactic theories of Lucien Tesnière. In *Éléments de syntaxe structurale* (Tesnière 1976), Tesnière had likened the utterance[12] to *un petit drame* 'a small drama' and had written:

> Comme un drame en effet, il comporte obligatoirement un *procès*, et le plus souvent des *acteurs* et des *circonstances*. Transposés du plan de la réalité dramatique sur celui de la syntaxe structurale, le procès, les acteurs et les circonstances deviennent respectivement le *verbe*, les *actants* et les *circonstants*. Le *verbe* exprime le *procès*.... Les *actants* sont les êtres ou les choses qui, à un titre quelconque et de quelque façon que ce soit, même au titre de simples figurants et de la façon la plus passive, participent au procès. ... Les *actants* sont toujours des *substantifs* ou des équivalents de substantifs. Inversement les substantifs assument en principe toujours dans la phrase la fonction d'actants.[13] (1976: 106; propositions 1–6)

> Like a drama, it comprises necessarily an *action* and most often *actors* and *circumstances* as well. Transposed from the plane of dramatic reality to that of structural syntax, the action, actors and circumstances become, respectively, the *verb*, the *actants* and the *circumstants*. The *verb* expresses the *action*.... The *actants* are beings or things that participate in the action—in whatever capacity and whatever style this might entail, even if it is as mere walk-ons and in the most passive way imaginable. *Actants* are always *nouns* or the equivalents of nouns. Inversely, in a given phrase nouns always assume, at least in principle, the function of actants. (my translation)

The way Greimas appropriated Tesnière's work in *Structural Semantics* helped shape—enabled but also constrained—the course of structuralist research on actants. Synthesizing Propp's and Tesnière's ideas, Greimas revisited one of the theoretical postulates informing *Morphology of the Folktale*: namely, the assumption that if characters are to be described in a systematic as opposed to an *ad hoc* way, they should be viewed not as clusters of qualities or traits, but rather as arguments in a kind of behavioral calculus, or alternatively units in a grammar of action, a syntax of doing.[14] Adopting the Barthesian view that "a narrative is a long sentence, just as every constative sentence is . . . the rough outline of a

Participant Roles and Relations 125

short narrative" (Barthes 1977: 84), and confirming Barthes's claim that structuralist analyses of narrative seek to bring the "actant under the . . . categories of the grammatical (and not psychological) person" (109), Greimas drew on Tesnière's work to interpret actants as elements or arguments that are distributed in narrative "sentences" in patterned, predictable, and functional ways (cf. Culler 1975a: 82). In other words, Tesnière's syntactic model provided Greimas with a formalism for actantial analysis, a system whereby participants could be annotated not as essences with a meaning but as role bearers whose combinations and interactions produced larger narrative structures.

On the face of it, then, Greimas used the idea of actants to reframe and radicalize the "syntactic" approach Thomas Pavel (1985b) has attributed to Propp. Just as "syntax discovers combinatory patterns of abstract categories . . . independently of the lexical units which may form the actual sentence," so "Propp's analyses approach the object from a syntactic perspective; each folk narrative belonging to the corpus is shown to manifest the same abstract structure, independently of the particular motifs in the story" (87). Yet Greimas's chief concern is not the "syntax" of stories. Rather, the theory of actants starts from a double premise: that to make sense of narratively organized discourse, interpreters must make inferences about participant roles and relations, and that to draw these inferences, interpreters extrapolate from principles used to parse the syntax and the semantics—the structure and meaning—of clauses and sentences. Reciprocally, Greimas's approach suggests that narrative, and in particular its participant structure, helps bring into focus aspects of the syntax-semantics interface at the level of clauses and sentences. Although I concentrate for the time being on the specifics of Greimas's account, I return below to broader implications of this nexus where discourse structure, narrative participants, and the syntax and semantics of natural language all intersect.

Initially, Greimas identified a total of six actants to which he thought all particularized narrative actors could be reduced: *Subject*, *Object*, *Sender*, *Receiver*, *Helper*, and *Opponent*.[15] But if reducing narrative-specific actors to "a restricted number of [general] actantial terms" (Greimas 1983: 202) is a prerequisite for any account that seeks to specify the organization of a semantic microuniverse, it is only a necessary and not a sufficient condition. Indeed, insofar as they failed to go beyond drawing up actantial inventories, previous researchers such as Propp and Souriau developed theories that were "at the same time excessively and insufficiently formal": "to define a genre only by the number of actants, while setting aside all the contents, is to place the definition at too high a formal level; to present the actants under the form of a simple inventory, without questioning the possible relationships between them, . . . is to renounce analysis too early, by leaving the second part of the definition, its specific features, at an insufficient level of formalization" (Greimas 1983: 202).[16] Figure 4 represents the scheme Greimas originally proposed as a way to get beyond merely listing actantial roles. Explicating this scheme, Greimas remarks that "[i]ts simplicity lies in the fact that it is entirely centered on the object of desire aimed at by the subject and situated, as object of communication, between the sender and the receiver—the desire of the subject being, in its part, modulated in projections from the helper and opponent" (1983: 207). These underlying actantial categories lend structure to any particularized narrative scenario through a process that Greimas calls "thematic investment" (or alternatively "semic investment"). Or rather, interpreters are able to make sense of scenarios as semantic microuniverses only insofar as they, first, use the actantial model to extract a narrative "message" from the limitless combinatorial matrix of sememes and, second, invest (or perhaps reinvest) the role-related components of the model with particularized properties, such that the Subject involved can be construed as having a specific desire for a specific kind of Object, and the Sender, Receiver, Helper, and Opponent as "a class of variables constituted by supplementary investments" (207).

Greimas's approach does seem to capture, in broad outline, important aspects of narrative understanding. For example, in telling a story about my day at work, I am likely to organize the narrative by casting myself as a Subject seeking out a particular Object that I had or still have hopes of Receiving from a Sender, and in my quest for which I have been aided by Helpers but impeded by Opponents. I may recount how I asked my supervisor for a promotion, for instance, but was blocked in my efforts by (what I perceive to be) his or her longstanding grudge against me. Alternatively, I may be the supervisor in question and recount how, seeking to maintain high standards for the advancement of employees, I have refused to promote someone whose work habits have militated against my goals. Interpreters of either of these accounts will be able to make sense of them, arguably, only by matching particular actors with

Figure 4. The Actantial Model Presented
in Greimas's *Structural Semantics*

Sender — Object → Receiver
              ↑
Helper → Subject ← Opponent

the inventory of roles that I am using to design the storyworld. An interpreter will not understand the first narrative—will not be able to reconstruct the storyworld—if he or she tries to match the supervisor with the actant "Helper," or for that matter "Object." More generally, as a first step toward detaching a cognizable microuniverse from the general flux of experience, both I as teller and my interlocutor as interpreter have to create a delimited, cognitively manageable set of participant roles. Yet the microuniverse cannot take shape until I and my interlocutor go on to assign those roles to the specific entities (boss, worker, longstanding grudge, standards for advancement, promotion, etc.) that we mean to integrate into it.

Similar constraints can be shown to bear on the processing of more complicated literary narratives. Take the actant "Opponent," a category that Greimas initially (if tentatively) included in the actantial model that organizes narrative comprehension. "Opponent" can be used to generate narrative-pertinent descriptions of actors that have been particularized in very different ways—from Claudius in *Hamlet* to the Devil in *The Brothers Karamazov* to Léonce Pontellier in *The Awakening*. Indeed, to construe Claudius as Hamlet's Helper is to misconstrue the narrative—to configure the participants into a possible storyworld, a conceivable microuniverse, but not the storyworld Shakespeare's play cues readers or audiences to reconstruct. Inversely, in the case of Henry James's "The Jolly Corner" (1996), readers who match Alice Staverton with the actant "Opponent" would be likely to generate more or less idiosyncratic paraphrases of James's tale. To persist in interpreting Staverton as antagonist to Spencer Brydon, one would have to disregard a whole gamut of textual cues suggesting that she is facilitating Brydon's strange quest for the Object of his desire: that is, knowledge of the self that he would have become had he not left New York, some thirty years previously, for a life in Europe. The characters' tender encounter in the closing pages of the story would be difficult to make sense of if interpreted as evidence of opposition rather than cooperation.

Problems with the Theory of Actants

However, complex narratives such as "The Jolly Corner" expose crucial problems with Greimas's theory of actants. Some of these problems Greimas recognized and acknowledged from the start; others come to light if the theory is reexamined through the lens of linguistics. For one thing, there is the question of how many—and what particular kinds of—actantial roles need to be specified in an account of the organizing model that interpreters use to build microuniverses, that is, reconstruct storyworlds. It does not go without saying that the six-actant model exhaustively describes the participant roles and relations structuring a narrative such as "The Jolly Corner," let alone those found in all narrative genres and subgenres. As I discuss in my next section, recent linguistic research on thematic roles or semantic "cases" suggests that clauses and sentences encode more than just six participant roles. This research also affords a different (and, arguably, more principled) basis for matching participants with roles.

Note that even in his original formulation of the actantial theory, Greimas hesitated over the categories of "Helper" and "Opponent," remarking that for these categories, in contrast to the other four, "we lack a syntactic model" (1983: 205)—that is, sentence-level analogues. Further,

> What is also striking is the secondary character of these two actants. . . . [W]e could say . . . that they are circumstantial "participants," and not the true actants of the drama. . . . [T]o the extent that functions are considered as constitutive of actants, there seems to be no reason why one could not admit that the aspectual categories [marked by adverbs such as *willingly* versus *unwillingly*, and *well* versus *badly*] could be considered as *circumstants*, which would be the hypotactic formulations of the actant-subject. In the mythical manifestation which concerns us, it is well understood that helper and opponent are only projections of the will to act and the imaginary resistance of the subject itself, judged beneficial or harmful in relationship to its desire. (Greimas 1983: 206)

Considerations of this sort no doubt led Greimas (1987), in his 1973 version of the actantial model, to rename Helpers and Opponents as "positive and negative auxiliants" and to deny them the status of actants proper (Budniakiewicz 1998a: 10). In this modified version of the theory, "[a]n Opponent is a true actant and no longer an auxiliant when he or she is also a quester like the Subject and has aims that are at cross-purposes with those of the Subject," with the crossing of these "two chained and superimposed programs" of Subject and anti-Subject splitting "the narrative into a dual narrative; their opposition to each other makes the narrative not only dual but polemical" (Budniakiewicz 1998a: 10, 11).

These criteria, however, do not necessarily provide a decision procedure (or even a reliable rule of thumb) for determining when a negative auxiliant warrants the label "Opponent." The same goes for the question of when an Opponent should be construed instead as negative auxiliant. In "The Jolly Corner," it is not clear whether Brydon's alter ego is a true anti-Subject, or only the projection of an egomaniacal, hypervigilant Subject who confers that status on an auxiliant, that is, his house. Indeed, it may be that James's story is, in a certain sense, *about* the fuzziness of the line demarcating what Greimas described as opponents and negative auxiliants. Alternatively, the tale might be paraphrased as self-consciously blurring the line between participants and nonparticipants, actants and circumstants, and thereby impeding readers' efforts to reconstruct a storyworld in which participant roles and relations can be exactly specified. James's story may, in other words, cue readers to build a microuniverse whose signature element is its Subject's inability to create a determinate microuniverse. True, Greimas's nomenclature has helped me "get at" what is so striking and innovative about James's tale. Arguably, though, any account of participant roles and relations should be held to stricter descriptive and explanatory standards. The onus is on the theorist to specify how interpreters elevate auxiliants to the status of helpers or opponents or, more generally, how interpreters distinguish between different classes of participants and between participants and nonparticipants.

Questions of this sort—questions about the appropriate number and kind of actants, as well as related questions concerning the procedure for matching actants with actors and circumstants with non-actors—underlie Greimas's own remarks on the possible "syncretism" of actants (1983: 203–4, 211–12; cf. Greimas 1987: 106–7; 111–13; Coste 1989: 134–37; Rimmon-Kenan 1983: 35). The notion of syncretism captures the one-many and many-one relation between actants and actors, narrative-pertinent roles and particularized role bearers. Figure 5 represents the two varieties of syncretism. On the one hand, an actor can embody more than one actantial role; for example, a given storyworld participant can be both Subject and Object over the course of a narrative. In the first part of "The Jolly Corner," Brydon is a Subject pursuing its particularized object of desire, in his case self-knowledge—that is, knowledge of the self that he would have become had he not left New York for Europe many years before. But midway through the story, there is (at least on one interpretation of the tale) a sudden and terrifying role reversal. Seeing a door pulled shut that he feels certain he left open during one of his nocturnal attempts to flush out his alternate, New York City self, Brydon constructs an inverted microuniverse—an embedded storyworld—in which he is now Object of the predatory anti-Subject he had been pursuing. On the other hand, any actantial role can be embodied by more than one participant; for example, several different individuals or entities can be Objects in a narrative. Thus, over the course of James's story, Brydon pursues several different Objects: financial independence (by converting one of his New York properties into an apartment building), knowledge of the self he might have become, escape from the threatening vigilance of the hypothetical self that he later projects as his pursuer, and finally (it seems) a life with Alice Staverton. Indeed, her dreams marked by visitations from Brydon's alter ego, Staverton seems to hold out hope for another, more accommodating microuniverse: one in which Brydon's two "selves" might share pride of place as syncretized Subjects, instead of being intolerably polarized into Subject and anti-Subject, with the repressed anti-self jeopardizing the integrity of the conscious ego.

For his part, Greimas speculated that the way syncretic "fusions" pattern in narrative discourse might provide the basis for a typology of (sub)genres (1983: 204). To extrapolate: in comparison with the psychological novel or tale, epics and romances offer quite limited possibilities for syncretism vis-à-vis the Subject. Odysseus, Aeneas, Beowulf, and Sir Gawain may pursue Objects instantiated by a variety of individuals in their respective storyworlds, encountering variously particularized Helpers and Opponents along the way. However, such protagonists do not typically ramify into imagined selves, proliferate into Subjects and anti-Subjects, in the manner of James's Spencer Brydon, Robert Louise Stevenson's Doctor Jekyll and Mr. Hyde (1905), Oscar Wilde's dual-profiled Dorian Gray (1998), or Charlotte Perkins Gilman's increasingly

Figure 5. The One-Many and Many-One
Relation between Actants and Actors

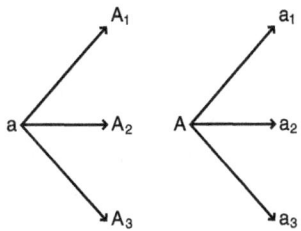

A = an actantial role (Subject, Object, etc)
a = a particularized actor (Brydon, Staverton, etc.)

hallucinatory, self-divided narrator-protagonist in "The Yellow Wallpaper" (1980). Hence differences between narrative genres and subgenres might be correlated with different preference-rule systems governing the fusion of actantial roles. (Below, in my next two sections, I provide additional arguments for viewing narrative genres as systems of preferences for assigning roles to participants in storyworlds.)

Yet the potential syncretism of actants reveals the limits as well as the possibilities of the Greimassian theory. William O. Hendricks (1967) formulated the problem as follows. Whatever their stated intentions, both Propp and Claude Lévi-Strauss (e.g., Lévi-Strauss 1986) base their analyses of folktales and myths not on plots but on plot synopses—textual synopses or interpretive glosses whose bearing on the tale or myth under examination is never explicitly spelled out. Hence, for Hendricks, both theorists step beyond the limits of what could be called principled discourse analysis insofar as they fail to specify "[t]he exact relation, in terms of sentence-constituency, etc., between the synopsis and the text [being synopsized]" (1967: 43). By the same token, what Greimas calls the syncretism of actants could be described—less charitably—as a fatal looseness of fit between narrative structure and the actantial model itself. Or rather, syncretism is a sign that matching actants with actors is the *result* of an ongoing interpretive process, not what enables the process of interpreting stories to be *initiated*, as some of Greimas's methodological statements seem to suggest. Redescribing actors as actants is for Greimas the sine qua non of storyworlds; but insofar as there is a distinction to be drawn between syncretized and nonsyncretized manifestations of actants, interpreters' ability to match roles with role bearers is the outcome of further inferential procedures that in turn need to be explained. In consequence, the target of the theory of actants should be precisely those further inferential procedures, which remain unexplained (indeed, unexamined) in Greimas's initial approach.[17] And in the absence of any account of the procedures in question, applications of the actantial model will be, contrary to Greimas's aims, ad hoc instead of systematic.

This same point can be phrased another way. As everyone can attest, one of the defining features of narrative, whether oral or written, is its ability to support a more or less extensive plurality of glosses; such interpretive richness is what makes narrative such a pervasive vehicle for cognition and communication, accounting for its longstanding preeminence as an instrument for ethical, historical, and other forms of instruction. Narrative, in short, both derives from and helps reinforce the *reinterpretability of human experience*. Thus, insofar as it allows for the possibility of fusing multiple actantial categories with one actor, and of fusing multiple actors with one actantial category, Greimas's theory does capture something crucial about the nature of narrative. But it accomplishes this in a way that militates against the theory's own objectives — in particular, its goal of articulating the organizing model in terms of which all microuniverses are constructed and cognized. The real organizing model, debatably, is not the one Greimas discusses overtly, but rather the unstated, implicit model that undergirds and motivates his account, guiding the paraphrases that he presents as naked descriptions of textual structure and determining which actors he labels as Subjects or Objects (or both) in a given story.

Issues highlighted by the syncretism of actants suggest that the conceptual machinery as well as the overall objectives of Greimas's initial approach need to be rethought. As Budniakiewicz shows (1998c: 438–41), Greimas himself eventually drew on other research to rethink the linguistic (i.e., Tesnièrean) framework in which he originally tried to cast the problem of actants. In particular, Greimas and other members of the Paris School (e.g., Budniakiewicz 1992: 22–25, 52–74, 141–201) turned to theories of the practical syllogism and of legal and polemical contracts, attempting to capture some of the interpretive processes that

Participant Roles and Relations 133

remain unanalyzed (or underanalyzed) in early formulations of the actantial model (cf. White 1996). Here, however, I pursue a different route. Returning to traditions of linguistic research that had just started to emerge (e.g., in Tesnière's work) when Greimas first formulated his theory, I shift from a theory of actants to an account of participant roles and relations in narrative contexts. This shift, I believe, affords a more principled inventory of participant roles than Greimas's, and the inventory is more generalizable across a variety of narrative genres. Further, addressing more squarely the process by which interpreters use textual cues to match particularized actors with roles contained in the inventory of participants, my approach exploits the notion of preference-rule systems to account for possibilities for role overlap.

Reassessing the relation between syntax, semantics, and discourse-level phenomena in narrative, I assume in what follows that any theory of storyworld participants must account for interactions between bottom-up and top-down interpretive processes. Inferences about textual cues encoding roles and relations enable storyworlds to take shape over time, but those same inferences are at once constrained and enabled by the emergent ecology of storyworlds. Although Bruner's (1991) emphasis on the "hermeneutic composability" of stories has helped bring such Janus-faced part-whole relations to the attention of narrative theorists, Greimas's actantial model did not adequately take into account reciprocal relations of this sort. (Neither did the Aristotelian/Proppian tradition of subordinating character to plot, or parts to wholes.) My aim in the remainder of this chapter is to throw additional light on the reciprocity of (inferences about) participants and storyworlds; combining linguistic and narratological concepts under the auspices of cognitive science is, I believe, the best strategy for accomplishing that aim.

From Actants to Participants

Drawing on linguistic research that does not inform Greimas's theory of actants, the rest of this chapter sketches an enriched account of participant roles and relations in stories. I discuss, in the present section, broad issues surrounding the idea of participants in linguistic research—an idea that has been used to capture interactions between syntax and semantics at the level of clauses and sentences. I turn then to

M. A. K. Halliday's functionalist account of the linguistic encoding of processes, participants, and circumstances and outline the relevance of functionalist models for narrative analysis.[18] Arguing for the scalability of the interpretive processes brought to bear on clause- and sentence-level structures, I prepare the way for the following and final section of my chapter, which draws on logico-semantic theories of predication to complement the functionalist paradigm with an account of narrative participants based on thematic roles. Throughout my focus is on how interpreters make sense of narratives by monitoring participant roles and relations both within and across temporal slices of emergent storyworlds.

On the Notion of "Participants"

A few preliminary comments about the notion of "participants" are therefore in order. In a way paralleling Tesnière's original usage of the term *actant*, recent linguistic research has invoked this concept to describe interactions between semantic and syntactic properties of clauses and sentences. The basic idea here is that clauses and sentences do not simply have a particular grammatical structure specified by the linguistic system to which they belong; they also encode information about how entities or individuals carry out or play a role in events—with an event being definable in this context as a particular instantiation of a more general process (Frawley 1992: 197–201; Lamb 1999: 158–61; see also note 3 in the current chapter and chapter 1). Syntax is the domain that specifies the *grammatical roles* of elements in clauses and sentences—such as subject, object, indirect object. Yet a syntactic theory concerned with grammatical roles alone could not specify how clauses and sentences encode semantic information about what are sometimes called the *thematic roles* (also *participant roles*, *semantic roles* or *case roles*) played by individuals vis-à-vis events—such as Agent, Patient, Instrument, Goal.[19] In the present chapter I adapt Frawley's (1992: 201–28) terms *participants* and *nonparticipants* as names for two general categories of thematic roles. Note that Frawley's nonparticipants correspond with what Tesnière (1976: 125–29) originally called *circumstants*. Participants encompass roles played by individuals construed as being centrally and obligatorily involved in events; nonparticipants, roles played by individuals construed as being only peripherally and optionally involved.[20]

In a sentence such as *I kicked the wall*, for example, the grammatical roles of subject and object and the thematic roles of Agent and Patient do in fact match up (*I* = subject, Agent; *the wall* = object, Patient). But semantic structure cannot always be "read off" syntactic structure in such a direct, linear way. In a sentence such as *The prisoner was killed*, the grammatical role of *the prisoner* is subject, but the thematic role of this noun phrase is Patient. Or again, a theory of language structure concerned only with grammatical roles would explain the distinction between transitive and intransitive verbs by accounting for differences in their syntactic behavior with respect to other components of the clause. Transitive verbs take a direct object in contradistinction to their intransitive counterparts, as exemplified by the difference between *I borrowed money* and *I aged*. But though this approach to the transitivity-intransitivity distinction would capture important differences in the way subjects relate grammatically to objects across verb types, it would not account for why the *I* in *I aged* functions as Patient, whereas the *I* in *I borrowed money* functions as Agent. To specify whether a verb is transitive or intransitive is to leave unspecified how the clause or sentence containing the verb encodes other, semantic information about participant (and, in some instances, nonparticipant) roles.

As the previous sketch suggests, the relation between grammatical and thematic roles is, like the relation between actors and actants, both one-many and many-one. The subject of a clause or sentence can be (among other roles to be discussed below) either an Agent (*I borrowed money*) or a Patient (*I aged*), just as the role of Patient can be realized either by a subject (*I aged*) or an object (*I kicked the wall*). But rather than merely acknowledging possibilities for role overlap (or syncretism, in Greimas's terms), linguists working in this area have tried to develop principled accounts of such complex interactions between syntax and semantics. I now review two (interlinked) approaches to the problem at hand, one based on models developed in the context of functional grammar and the other on logico-semantic theories of predication. Although the two approaches draw on somewhat different resources to inventory, characterize, and justify participant roles, they share a broadly cognitive orientation to the way those roles intersect with grammatical structures.[21] Combining the functionalist and semantic approaches to participant roles affords the basis for a rich, integrative account of an important aspect of narrative understanding—namely, the way interpreters make sense of storyworlds by monitoring how entities participate in previous, ongoing, and emergent events.

Functional Grammar, Process Types, and Narrative Participants

This section discusses the functionalist approach to participant roles and relations. Particularly important is the functionalist idea of process types, originally developed to account for interactions between form and meaning at the level of the clause. Though the specifics of Halliday's model have changed over the past several decades, what has remained constant is the suggestion that process types encoded in language not only specify preferences for assigning roles to participants but also constrain possibilities for role overlap. When linked up with the concept of narrative genres, the functionalist emphasis on process types can complement semantic strategies (detailed in my next section) for analyzing how interpreters make principled, nonrandom connections between textual cues and participant roles in stories.

Processes and Participants in the Clause

For Halliday (1994), functional grammar reverses the direction of traditional grammatical explanations: instead of moving from an analysis of the forms of a language to an account of what they mean, functionalist theories proceed from an account of language as a system of meanings to an analysis of the forms by which those meanings can be realized (xiv). Hence functionalist analyses of how grammatical forms express participant roles and relations are grounded in two assumptions. The first is that the language system enables humans to build a mental model of reality as made up of processes of various types; the second, that each such process type specifies a preferred participant structure as well as grammatical forms for expressing it (106–75; cf. Halliday 1967, 1976).

Beginning with some of his earliest work in the field, Halliday (1967) concentrated on participant roles as a key element of the "clause system network," which is one of a number of system networks "representing choices associated with a given constituent type" (e.g., morpheme, word, nominal group or phrase, clause, sentence).[22] Halliday focused special attention on what he called "transitivity systems." These systems "are concerned with the type of process expressed in the clause, with the participants in this process, animate and inanimate, and with various attributes and circumstances of the process and the participants" (1967: 38). Here the term *process* can be interpreted in a broad sense, covering "all phenomena to which a specification of time may be attached—in English, anything that can be expressed by a verb: event, whether physical or not, state, or relation" (1976: 159). Further, Halliday (160) stresses that the term *participant* should not be taken to imply "human being," since a participant is not necessarily human or even animate. Over time Halliday has developed increasingly detailed inventories of process (sub)types made cognizable by the linguistic system; increasingly detailed, too, are his inventories of the participants specified by each sort of process, with those roles finding expression in structures describable at the level of the clause.

Early on Halliday (1967: 38–51) suggested that transitivity systems encompass the three main process types of *directed action*, *nondirected action*, and *ascription*. In turn, these process types assign to the subject of any clause realizing them a participant role or role combination from a role set that included just four possible roles: *Actor*, *Initiator*, *Goal*, and *Attribuant*. For example, a clause such as *she planted the trees* realizes the process type of directed action, and as a result the subject (*she*) can be assigned the dual or syncretized participant role of Initiator/Actor. By contrast, the clause *she appeared content* realizes the quite different process type of ascription, and in consequence what seems to be a structurally identical element of the clause (i.e., the subject, *she*) can be assigned a different participant role—namely, that of the participant to which some state or property is being attributed, that is, Attribuant. Or again, insofar as a clause realizes the process type of nondirected action (e.g., *she walked the dog*), the semantic or participant role of its object can be distinguished not just from its grammatical role but also from the semantic role of the object of a clause realizing, instead, the directed action process type. In *she planted the trees* the object (*the trees*) can be assigned the role of Goal vis-à-vis the action that the subject, as Actor/Initiator, directs. Meanwhile, in *she walked the dog*, the subject of the clause takes on the role of Initiator and the object of the clause can be assigned the role of Actor.

As this last example suggests, whereas Greimas merely noted the possibility of role syncretism in outlining his theory of actants, Halliday's (early) functionalist model uses the notion of transitivity systems to explain such overlap and account for at least some of its distributional patterns. Specifically, Halliday's theory predicts that, in clauses realizing directed action as opposed to those realizing nondirected action, there is a greater likelihood of syncretism of the Initiator and Actor roles vis-à-vis the subject. This is because in directed action (e.g., planting trees) it is difficult to uncouple the Initiator of the action from the participant who performs the action, whereas in nondirected action (e.g., walking a dog) the Initiator and Actor roles are cognized as distinct. More generally, the functionalist approach begins with the intuition that although grammatical and participant roles are heteromorphic (one-many and many-one) rather than isomorphic (one-one), a theory of transitivity systems can reveal principled relations between process types, grammatical structures, and participant roles. The functionalist approach suggests that process types preferentially assign certain kinds of participant roles to the grammatical forms encoding recurring types of process at the level of the clause.

The idea of process types, indeed, is the crucial innovation in Halliday's scheme.[23] Operating under the assumption that "[t]he concepts of process, participant and circumstance are semantic categories which explain in the most general way how phenomena of the real world are represented as linguistic structures" (Halliday 1994: 109), Halliday has worked to refine his taxonomy of process types and the attendant participant roles that they (preferentially but not absolutely) specify. Anticipating the comprehensive model presented in Halliday's 1994 textbook on functional grammar, a paper written in 1969 (Halliday 1976) rethinks the directed action/nondirected action/ascription scheme presented in Halliday's 1967 article and shifts to a new taxonomy of process types: *action*, *mental process*, and *relation*. (Mental process types can be further decomposed into four subtypes: *perception*, *reaction*, *cognition*, and *verbalization*, whereas processes involving relation can be subdivided into those of *identification* and *attribution*.) Realizing these three main types would be clauses such as *she planted the trees*, *she saw the trees*, and *that Tulip Poplar is the tallest tree around*, respectively. As in the 1967 model, recognition of the process type involved is what enables language users to assign participant roles to syntactic elements of the clause and also to predict and manage the possibility of role combinations or overlap.

For example, in the case of mental processes, two new participant roles now have to be added to the role set: *Processor* and *Phenomenon* (Halliday 1976: 164–65; in Halliday 1994, the first of these two roles is renamed "Senser," which parallels the role of Experiencer characterized in my next section.) These roles pattern differently with grammatical forms in mental process clauses than do the roles of Actor, Initiator, and Goal with grammatical forms in action clauses. More than this, though, differences between the two process types can be correlated with different constraints on role overlap in the clauses realizing them. In a clause such as *I liked the book* the subject (*I*) takes on the role of Processor/Senser, and the object (*the book*) is assigned the role of Phenomenon. But if the same clause is paraphrased as *the book pleased me*, the subject (*the book*) now takes on the role of Phenomenon and the object (*me*) that of Processor/Senser. As Halliday points out, examples such as this show that Processor and Phenomenon cannot be consistently mapped into participant roles specified by action clauses: "with *please* the phenomenon seems to resemble the actor and the processor the goal, while with *like* it is the other way round" (165). In other words, the participant structures specified by action clauses do not translate reliably into those specified by mental process clauses, suggesting that distinct strategies for role assignment are involved. And along with those distinct strategies go different constraints on dual or syncretized roles, in particular those of the one role–many forms variety. In action clauses, participants are *things* in the broad sense of persons, objects, abstractions, events, qualities, states, or relations, but in mental process clauses participants can be not only things but also *words*, that is, facts and reports (Halliday 1976: 166). Not only can I see that twilight has arrived or be pleased by a cat; what is more, I can see that Bob is a funny guy or be pleased by what a friend tells me. The role of Phenomenon can thus be assigned to a wider range of entities than can the role of Goal, however those roles might be manifested in the grammatical structure of clauses. Again, then, by anchoring grammatical forms in process types, the functionalist approach reveals patterns in the distribution of (syncretistic fusions of) participant roles—patterns that might otherwise remain undetected.

My next subsection outlines some narrative-theoretical implications of Halliday's functionalist model, which is presented in its most fully developed form in *An Introduction to Functional Grammar* (Halliday 1994). Arguing that *kinds of narrative* can be distinguished on the basis of *preferred process types*, I contend that the process-participant nexus bears importantly on narrative structures and not just the structures of the clause.

Process Types, Narrative Genres, and Storyworld Participants

The present subsection outlines Halliday's most fully developed taxonomy of process types; it also suggests grounds for rethinking narrative genres as preference-rule systems, in which types of process (and associated participant structures) can be assigned preference rankings that contrast more or less markedly with the rankings that define other genres. In other words, comprehending (the roles of participants in) a story requires situating the narrative within a larger system of narrative kinds. In turn, differences between narrative kinds can be plotted against different systems of preferences for process types and the participant roles and relations that they specify.

Halliday's 1994 treatment identifies six process types, some of which encompass additional subtypes. Table 6 lists the relevant process types and subtypes, along with the participant roles specified by each type. The six types of process include three principal types, which "form the cornerstones of the grammar in its guise as a theory of experience," as well as three subsidiary types located at the boundaries between the three principal types. The principal types include *material processes*, or processes of doing; *mental processes*, or processes of sensing; and *relational processes*, or processes of being. Secondarily, there are *behavioral processes*, or "processes of (typically human) physiological and psychological behaviour like breathing, coughing, smiling, dreaming and staring" (139), which skirt the border between material and mental processes; *verbal processes*, or processes of saying situated on the border between mental and relational processsses; and *existential processes*, which represent that something exists or happens and occupy the border between material and relational processes. Further, material processes can be subdivided into *dispositive* (doing to) and *creative* (bringing about) types. Mental processes, meanwhile, include *cognition* (e.g., thinking, knowing, understanding), *affection* (e.g., liking, fearing), and *perception* (e.g., seeing, hearing), and relational processes span three subtypes—*intensive* (x is a), *circumstantial* (x is at a), and *possessive* (x has a)—as well as two modes—*attributive* (a is an attribute of x) and *identifying* (a is the identity of x).

Table 6. Process Types and Participant Roles
(adapted from Halliday 1994)

Process Types (and Subtypes)	Participants
Material (Dispositive, Creative)	Actor, *Goal
Mental (Perceptive, Affective, Cognitive)	*Senser, *Phenomenon
Relational (Three Subtypes = Intensive Circumstantial, Possessive + Two Modes = Attributive and Identifying)	Carrier, Attribute Identified, Identifier
Behavioral	Behaver
Verbal	Sayer, Receiver, *Target
Existential	Existent

* Indicates a participant optionally involved in a process type

Table 7 illustrates each of Halliday's main process types with an example, indicating the roles of the participants involved. Differences in preferred participant roles can be noted across process types. With material processes, participants include an Actor and a Goal. The Actor is obligatory, but the Goal is optional; compare *I kicked the wall* with *I kicked*. Mental processes involve two other participant roles, Senser and Phenomenon. Whereas in material processes no participant need be human or human-like, and the distinction between conscious and unconscious beings is largely irrelevant, mental process clauses code the participant who senses (cognizes, perceives, is affected by) the Phenomenon as human or at least human-like. Further, in mental processes there is greater variability with respect to the types of participants involved. In material process clauses only Goals may be omitted, yielding two variants: + Actor, + Goal (*I kicked the wall*); and + Actor, −Goal (*I kicked*). In clauses encoding mental processes, however, there are three variants: + Senser, + Phenomenon (*I saw the wall*); + Senser, −Phenomenon (*I saw*); −Senser, + Phenomenon (*he did it to shock/annoy/confuse*). In this last example, it would perhaps be more accurate to speak of an "implied" rather than an omitted Senser.) And again, whereas Phenomena can include facts and beliefs as well as things (i.e., different sorts of entity can be fused under the heading of *Phenomenon*),

Table 7. Outline of Process Types, with Examples (adapted from Halliday 1994)

Material processes
    Dispositive: *She [Actor] put the book [Goal] on the table*
    Creative: *She [Actor] wrote the book [Goal]*

Mental processes
    Perceptive: *I* [Senser] *saw the tree* [Phenomenon]
    Affective: *The tree* [Phenomenon] *pleased me* [Senser]
    Cognitive: *His behavior* [Phenomenon] *puzzled me* [Senser]

Relational processes
    Intensive: *The cat* [Carrier] *is finicky* [Attribute]
    Circumstantial: *The cat* [Carrier] *is by the window* [Attribute]
    Possessive: *The cat* [Carrier] *has white fur* [Attribute]
    Attributive mode: (See the previous three examples.)
    Identifying mode: *Oglethorpe* [Identified] *is the villain* [Identifier]; *next month* [Identified] *is July* [Identifier]; *the white fur* [Identified] *is the cat's* [Identifer]

Behavioral processes
    Oglethorpe [Behaver] *grumbled*

Verbal processes
    I [Sayer] *tried to tell everyone* [Target], *but only Oglethorpe* [Receiver] *heard me*

Existential processes:
    There is a cat [Existent] *by the window*

---

material process clauses code participants as things and disprefer fusions between things, beliefs, and facts.

Tables 6 and 7 suggest some other ways of characterizing the link between process types and participant roles. In relational processes, for example, whereas the identifying mode is reversible, the attributive mode is not. Thus, one can say that *Spencer Brydon is the protagonist of "The Jolly Corner"* or *the protagonist of "The Jolly Corner" is Spencer Brydon*, but *Brydon is egocentric* and *egocentric is Brydon* remain asymmetrical. In other words, different modes of expressing this process type differently encode the connection between the participants being brought into relation, whether as Identifier and Identified or as Carrier and Attribute. Further, whereas the Behaver in behavioral processes is a conscious being, like a Senser, behavioral processes themselves are coded more along the lines of doing than sensing. And that doing may shade off into processes of a material, mental, or verbal sort. Behavioral processes thus allow for a certain amount of overlap between the roles of Actor, Senser, and Sayer, as exemplified by forms such as *I watched, I yawned, I frowned,* and *I berated*. By contrast, whereas "behavioural processes are not so much a distinct type of processes, but rather a cluster of small subtypes blending the material and mental into a continuum, verbal processes do display distinctive patterns of their own" (Halliday 1994: 141). For instance, because Sayers can be anything that puts out a signal (e.g., lighthouses, homing devices), verbal processes, unlike mental ones, do not require a conscious participant. In addition, there may or may not be overlap between Receivers and Targets. In face-to-face communication between just two interlocutors, the roles of Receiver and Target often converge: I hear what you intend for me to hear. But when a bystander or eavesdropper intercepts an utterance directed to some other intended Target, who does not pick up on what was said, then the roles of Recipient and Target diverge (cf. Goffman 1981: 124–59). Once again, then, the functionalist approach helps capture distributional patterns for overlapping participant roles, rather than merely noting the bare possibility of syncretism (à la Greimas).

More than this, as table 8 indicates, the functionalist idea of process types can help illuminate interpretive processes brought to bear on discourse- as well as clause-level structures. By extending (or, better, rescaling) the idea such that the focus is shifted from clauses to stories, a functionalist approach to narrative genres suggests that differences between kinds of stories can be correlated with contrastive preference rankings for types of process. Further, process types can themselves be characterized as coding strategies in which different sorts of participant roles and relations are canonical or preferred. How a given story fits into the larger system of narrative kinds thus entails stronger or weaker preference rankings for role assignments vis-à-vis storyworld participants. A narrative's generic affiliations also delimit possibilities for role overlap in a way not accounted for by Greimas's theory of actants.

Table 8 is, of course, a highly schematic outline and does not take into account potential shifts in preference rankings over the course of a narrative. (Contrast table 12 below.) Nonetheless, it does begin to point

Table 8. Preference Rankings for Process Types
in Some Representative Narrative Genres

Narrative Genre	Preference Rankings for Process Types
Epic	Material > Behavioral > Verbal > Mental > ...
Allegory	Relational/Intensive + Identifying > Material > Verbal > Mental > ...
Nineteenth-Century Realistic Novel	Material > Relational / Circumstantial + Attributive > Verbal > Behavioral > ...
Psychological Novel/Tale	Mental > Behavioral > Relational/Intensive + Attributive > Verbal > ...
Detective Novel	Mental > Material > Relational/Intensive + Identifying > Behavioral > ...
Ghost Story	Mental > Existential > Relational/Circumstantial + Identifying > Behavioral > ...

up interconnections between narrative genres, process types, and inferences about participant roles. For example, although ghost stories, psychological novels, and detective novels share an overall preference for mental processes, the larger system of preferences associated with each genre captures important differences between them. James's Spencer Brydon, like the protagonist of a supernatural tale or a detective trying to make sense of what appear to be clues, is crucially an Experiencer of storyworld entities that can accordingly be assigned the role of Phenomena (in James's narrative: the interior spaces and appointments of the house on the jolly corner, the fact that a door that Brydon himself presumably left open appears to the protagonist to have been closed by someone or something else). In ghost stories, however, the existential process type figures more centrally than it does in the psychological tale or in detective novels. It is the business of the storyteller to establish that a ghost did (or does) in fact exist and that it manifested itself in some noteworthy or tellable way. Hence, whereas a story such as "The Jolly Corner" secondarily codes its protagonist and other participants as Behavers whose doings shade off into mental, material, and verbal processes, in ghost stories there is more emphasis on coding supernatural beings as full-fledged Existents in the storyworld. Those Existents are furthermore coded as Identified participants whose being and doing (or Behaving) can be detected at specified locations in the storyworld (see chapter 7 below; cf. Herman 1999f, 2000a). Meanwhile, psychological novels and tales more characteristically overcode Experiencing participants as Carriers whose (psychological) Attributes emerge, in part, during processes of Saying that adjoin somewhat less definite processes of Behaving. Detective fiction foregrounds material processes to a greater degree than do psychological novels or ghost stories, and it typically involves a different subtype of relational processes. Like the criminals they pursue, detectives can be construed as Actors seeking to bring about particular Goals. And whereas participants in psychological tales are Carriers of Attributes, and participants in ghost stories brought into relation with circumstances in which they can be identified as supernatural, more important in detective fiction are intensive, identifying relational processes by which the identity-status of criminal can be imputed to participants categorized as suspects.

Similarly, although mental processes are relatively dispreferred in both epics and allegories, variable preference rankings for other process types help capture differences between these two genres. The same goes for epics vis-à-vis nineteenth-century realistic fiction, which shares the epic preference for material processes but assigns different rankings to subsidiary processes types. Epics code participants primarily in terms of Actor-Goal relations (Odysseus battles the suitors for control over his home on Ithaka; Beowulf seeks one last victory over the dragon guarding the treasure hoard). Allegories, by contrast, show a preference for relational types of process, coding participants mainly as beings that can be Identified as exemplars of abstract qualities or traits. For example, as a participant in book 1 of Edmund Spenser's *The Faerie Queene* (Spenser 1981), Duessa's chief role is to exemplify the evils of duplicity. In contrast, Una exemplifies the unwavering faith to which Red Crosse Knight learns to aspire. Realistic fiction of the nineteenth century shares with epics a favoring of material processes that specify Actor-Goal participant structures. But in contrast with epics, realistic fiction preferentially involves relational processes. At stake, specifically, is that subtype of relational process used to mark participants as Carriers of Attributes deriving from circumstances either explicitly or implicitly represented in the storyworld. In a realistic novel, participants will have traits and dispositions that stem from how, where, and when they have lived. The epic hero is Actor, else Behaver, else Sayer, else Experiencer, but he is not typically a Carrier of properties anchored in circumstances of this sort.

As these last remarks suggest, associating narrative genres with preferred process types helps account for inferences about participant roles across different kinds of stories. By the same token, genres shape the distributional patterns of role overlap. Focusing only on participants having the role of protagonist in their respective narrative kinds, table 9 presents a simplified picture of preferred role assignments in the same six genres displayed in table 8. (Note that, in the case of detective fiction and ghost stories, I have factored out roles not directly pertinent to the coding of the protagonist, or narrator-protagonist.) In setting up table 9, I found that my intuitions about preference rankings for role assignments in each genre became less and less clear as I moved farther down the list (i.e., rightward along the continuum of rankings). It may be the case that certain narrative genres have clear preferences all the way down, whereas others do not. As table 9 indicates, certain modes of role syncretism are far more likely to occur in some genres than in others.[24] In allegory, for example, the protagonist is far more likely to fuse the roles of Actor and Identified than those of Experiencer and Behaver, these last two roles being more typically syncretized in the protagonist of a psychological novel or tale. Similarly, given the contrasting preference rankings of mental and verbal processes in ghost stories as opposed to epics, it is more likely for the protagonist of a tale of the supernatural than an epic hero to fuse the roles of Experiencer and Sayer.

Although I have sketched it only in broad outline here, a functionalist approach to storyworld participants suggests that where a story fits in the larger system of narrative kinds bears importantly on the role assignments that support narrative understanding. Also, a story's generic affiliations both enable and constrain possibilities of role syncretism. To use a phrase that Roland Barthes (1974) coined in another context, participant roles are only "moderately plural," and narrative genres

Table 9. Preferred Role Assignments for Protagonists (by genre)

Narrative Genre	Preferences for Role Assignments (vis-à-vis Protagonist)
Epic	Actor > Behaver > Sayer > Experiencer
Allegory	Identified > Actor > Sayer > Experiencer
Nineteenth-Century Realistic Novel	Actor > Carrier > Sayer > Behaver
Psychological Novel/Tale	Experiencer > Behaver > Carrier > Sayer
Detective Novel	Experiencer > Actor
Ghost Story	Experiencer > Sayer

are what organize their plurality, allowing a semantic microuniverse, a storyworld, to emerge from what Greimas (1983) called the immanent universe of meaning. Narrative becomes possible only when storyworld participants *cannot* be assigned every conceivable role. Hence genre-based preferences for role assignments provide templates for interpreting narrative microdesigns—the role or roles a participant has vis-à-vis other participants at a given moment in the storyworld. As well, generic preferences make possible the narrative macrodesigns to which individual role assignments contribute—the network of roles in which participants can be situated across more or less extended temporal stretches of the storyworld. A story's relation to existing genres predisposes interpreters to expect a predominance of particular sorts of processes and the number and range of participants that they specify. Reciprocally, observing which process types predominate in a narrative triggers inferences about its generic affiliations and guides subsequent efforts to match participants with roles.[25] As I discuss further below, many experimental literary narratives (postmodern novels, metaphysical detective fictions, etc.) produce their effects by evoking generic templates that they also refuse or negate. Other avant-garde narratives produce striking effects by *blending* several generic templates, creating expectations about process types and participant roles that cancel one another out.

I turn now to another tradition of linguistic research that can throw additional light on the crucial role of the concept of "role" in narrative comprehension. Specifically, my next section examines logico-semantic theories of predication at the level of clauses and sentences and argues that they, too, can be scaled up to illuminate how interpreters make sense of participants in a narrative.

Semantic Theory, Thematic Roles, and Narrative Participants

I begin this section with an overview of semantic research on thematic roles. I then focus more particularly on narrative-theoretical applications of the idea of "semantic macroroles" in the context of what has been characterized as the "Actor-Undergoer hierarchy." These key ideas from recent work in linguistic semantics can complement the functionalist approach to storyworld participants, providing additional insights into narrative genres as systems of preferences for role assignments. To highlight similarities and differences between Greimas's theory of actantial roles and the more recent work on thematic roles, I again use James's "The Jolly Corner" as an important tutor text in the pages that follow. (A brief synopsis of James's story can be found above in the section titled "Actants Reconsidered" and also in the following section.)

A First Approach to Thematic Roles

As Budniakiewicz (1992) notes, traditional grammar parses sentences into two main constituents, "the *subject* about which something is said, and the *predicate*, what is being said about it" (27). By contrast, in the predicate calculus originally developed in the field of logic and then imported into linguistic semantics (cf. Allwood, Andersson, and Dahl 1977), every sentence in natural language represents a more abstract proposition that consists of two kinds of terms, *predicates* and *arguments*. From this perspective, "[a]ccording to the number of arguments upon which a predicate operates, it will be classified as a one-place predicate, a two-place predicate, a three-place predicate," and so on (Budniakiewicz 1992: 28). *I kicked the wall* represents a proposition in which *kicked* is a two-place predicate that operates on, or "takes," two arguments (*I, wall*). *I loaned the book to my student* encodes a proposition with a three-place predicate (*loaned*) and three arguments (*I, the book, my student*). Hence, rather than being centered around the subject-object nexus in the grammar of a clause or sentence, predication becomes, in more recent semantic theory, a name for the way arguments, that is, individuals that are independent and can stand alone, instantiate qualities, relations, acts, properties, states, or any other predicate that is inherently dependent on the arguments that "embody, carry out, take, or are linked to" the predicate in some manner (Frawley 1992: 198).

In turn, to accommodate this wide range of predicate-argument relations but at the same time make them describable and explainable, researchers have suggested that arguments connect up with predicates, entities with events, by virtue of a small set of what they variously call thematic, case, or participant roles.[26] For Frawley, such case or thematic roles " 'configure' the projected world of reference, linking arguments to predicates in particular ways," and more generally specifying "how the pieces in any situation go together in our mental models, beyond the variability in the machinery that languages have for putting forms together into *expressions about situations*" (1992: 200). Echoing Fillmore's (1977) suggestion that "meanings are relativized to scenes" (59), Frawley compares the structure and functions of thematic roles with the lenses and settings of a camera—that is, an apparatus that affects "perspective and organization in a photograph by modifying the relationships of the constituents of the picture, zooming in on some, defocalizing others" (200). Thematic roles provide an explanation for why, in a clause such as *I threw rocks at the bridge*, the bridge comes into focus in a way that it does not in a clause such as *I threw rocks on the bridge*. In the first clause, the bridge is a participant, the Goal of an action; but in the second clause, the bridge has the role of nonparticipant or circumstance, the Locative or "fixed locale of the act" (202–3). One of my central claims in what follows is that tellers and interpreters of narratives rely on similar scene-building processes—"zooming" and "defocalizing" strategies—as they configure participants and nonparticipants into storyworlds. In other words, in parallel with Greimas's initial approach to the idea of actants, I contend that processes of role assignment at the level of clauses and sentences are scalable to the level of (narrative) discourse. What Greimas called microuniverses come about when interpreters assign narrative participants (and nonparticipants) roles that are discourse-level analogues of thematic roles. Or rather, participant roles and relations form a template for scene building in stories, while in turn the comprehension of scenes, or temporal slices of storyworlds, requires interpreters to assign participants (emergent) roles and relations.

Arguably, though, in comparison with Greimas's actantial model, logico-semantic theories of thematic roles provide a better foundation for studying how interpreters construe storyworld individuals as participants. In particular, research in semantics establishes a first broad cut between participants and nonparticipants and also affords principles for grouping roles falling within these two main categories. Analogously, interpreters of narrative use textual cues to make inferences about which storyworld entities constitute participants in events, and which constitute circumstances for the unfolding of such participation in events.

Especially relevant, here, is Frawley's distinction between participants inherently selected by processes of predication, on the one hand, and nonparticipants deriving from the larger semantic context of the predication, on the other hand (Frawley 1992: 202, 224). In *she planted a tree in her yard*, for instance, the predication of planting fails if the roles of Actor (*she*) and Patient (*a tree*) are deleted. By contrast, deleting the locale of the planting (*in her yard*) does not compromise the predication, that is, the information about who did what to whom, but rather impinges on the semantic context in which it occurs, the context that furnishes information about the why, where, when, and how of the planting. Of course, Frawley's account centers around clause- and sentence-level structures. Yet narrative comprehension itself can be redescribed, in part, as a process of recognizing and keeping tabs on a more or less extended series of interlinked predications, each specifying (central, obligatory) participant as well as (peripheral, optional) non-participant roles for the storyworld entities involved. The challenge of interpreting a narrative is in large measure the challenge of figuring out what is being predicated of participants, and furthermore how those predications relate participants to other participants and to surrounding circumstances, both at any given moment in the story and also over the course of the narrative as a whole.

In all, Frawley (1992: 201–24) identifies twelve main thematic roles, nine of them participant roles and three nonparticipant roles. Further, the nine participant roles are grouped into three categories, with Agent, Author, and Instrument falling under the category of *logical actors*;

Patient, Experiencer, and Benefactive under the category of *logical recipients*; and Theme, Source, and Goal under the category of *spatial roles*. Nonparticipants encompass three roles: Locative, Reason, and Purpose. (As Frawley notes, other schemes include additional nonparticipant roles, such as Path, Manner, and Time. I use the reduced inventory because my aim is to sketch out directions for future research, not furnish an exhaustive list of all the roles storyworld entities can conceivably be assigned.) Table 10 presents the participant and nonparticipant roles identified by Frawley, briefly characterizing them and drawing on James's "The Jolly Corner" to provide both a sentence-level and (what I take to be) a discourse-level instantiation of each role.[27] In the remainder of this subsection, as well as in the subsections that follow, I argue that some such mapping of sentence-level thematic roles into discourse-level analogues is a crucial aspect of narrative comprehension. As predicted by Greimas's theory of actants, this mapping relation (like the mapping relation that links arguments to sentence-level thematic roles) is both one-many and many-one. Logico-semantic theories of predicate-argument relations, however, provide the basis for a principled explanation of such role overlap and of how interpreters make sense of it.

Assuming that the storyworld encoded in "The Jolly Corner" is a microuniverse that consists of a set of predications made sequentially in the discourse, one might partially characterize that set by way of the following series of paraphrases: P_1 Spencer Brydon returns to New York after an absence of more than thirty years + P_2 Brydon arranges to have one of his properties converted into profit-making apartments + P_3 Brydon speculates obsessively about the self he would have become had he not left New York for a life in Europe + P_4 Brydon reveals to Alice Staverton his fascination with this topic + P_5 Brydon tries to stalk his hypothetical self during nocturnal visits to his childhood home + P_6 It seems to Brydon that his alter ego has turned the tables and begun stalking *him* + . . . P_n. In the complete set individuals other than Brydon (e.g., Staverton, the alter ego, the interior appointments of Brydon's home) may figure as participants. Understanding James's story requires keeping track of what is being predicated of its protagonist (along with the other participants) at different times; it also requires reconciling what is predicated of Brydon at time t_2 with what is predicated of him at times t_1 and t_3—mainly by way of inferences about causal links between

Table 10. Participant and Nonparticipant Roles, with Examples from James's "The Jolly Corner"

PARTICIPANT ROLES

Logical Actors

AGENT: The argument that is the deliberate instigator of the predicate; the primary, involved doer; "the willful, volitional, instigating participant" (Van Valin 1993: 41).

Sentence-level instance: "*he* [Brydon] turned to and fro between this intensity of his idea and a fitful and unseeing inspection, through his single eyeglass, of the dear little old objects on her [Staverton's] chimney-piece" (James 1996: 706).

Discourse-level instance: Brydon, as Agent, searches for his alter ego.

AUTHOR: The argument that is the executor of an act but is not its direct cause or instigator.

Sentence-level instance: "*She* [Staverton] had come with him [Spencer Brydon] one day to see how his 'apartment-house' was rising (700).

Discourse-level instance: Staverton, as Author, executes acts that cater in various ways to Brydon's self-obsession.

INSTRUMENT: The argument that is the means by which a predicate is carried out.

Sentence-level instance: "he [Brydon] turned to and fro between this intensity of his idea and a fitful and unseeing inspection, through *his single eyeglass*, of the dear little old objects on her [Staverton's] chimney-piece" (James 1996: 706).

Discourse-level instance: Brydon views the house on the jolly corner as the means, or Instrument, for self-exploration and self-discovery.

Logical Recipients

PATIENT: The argument that undergoes or is changed or directly affected by a predicate; "the non-willful, non-instigating, maximally affected participant" (Van Valin 1993: 41).

Sentence-level instance: "*He* [Brydon] had been 'sold,' he inwardly moaned, stalking such game as this" [i.e., the figure that he glimpses standing between himself and the outer door] (724).

Discourse-level instance: Once he sees the door pulled shut that he thought he had left open (717-19), Brydon updates his own participant status in the embedded microuniverse in terms of which he mentally models his experiences in the house. Specifically, he ceases to be Agent and becomes, in part, a Patient undergoing what he takes to be actions instigated by his alter ego.

EXPERIENCER: The argument whose internal state or constitution is affected by the predicate.

Sentence-level instance: "Then harder pressed still, sick with the force of his shock, and falling back as under the hot breath and the roused passion of a life larger than his own, a rage of personality before which his own collapsed, *he* [Brydon] felt the whole vision turn to darkness and his very feet give way" (725-26).

Discourse-level instance: Once he sees the door pulled shut that he thought he had left open (717-19), Brydon updates his own participant status in the embedded microuniverse in terms of which he mentally models his experiences in the house. Specifically, he ceases to be Agent and becomes, in part, an Experiencer internally affected by what he takes to be signs of the presence of his alter ego.

BENEFACTIVE: The argument that derives actions or entities from the actions of another.

Sentence-level instance: "It [i.e., the stupor in which Brydon finds himself after passing out when he glimpses his alter ego] had brought *him* to knowledge, to knowledge—yes, this was the beauty of his state; which came to resemble more and more that of a man who has gone to sleep on some news of a great inheritance" (726-27).

Discourse-level instance: Brydon, as Benefactive, derives greater self-knowledge from his encounter with his alter ego.

Spatial Roles

THEME: The argument that is displaced as the result of an initiator's influence and moves from one resting point along a trajectory, often to another resting point.

Sentence-level instance: "Out of that [i.e., Brydon's realization that the doors to the vestibule that he thought were closed are actually open] *the question* sprang at him, making his eyes, as he felt, half-start from his head, as they had done, at the top of the house, before the sign of the other door" (723).

Discourse-level instance: Brydon, the Theme, is transferred from the resting-point on the marble floor where he faints to the window bench where Staverton bends over him lovingly.

SOURCE: The argument that is the point of origin of the displacement that moves the THEME from its initial resting point.

Sentence-level instance: "Out of *that* [i.e., Brydon's realization that the doors to the vestibule that he thought were closed are actually open] the question sprang at him, making his eyes, as he felt, half-start from his head, as they had done, at the top of the house, before the sign of the other door" (723).

Discourse-level instance: The marble floor is the Source from which Brydon, the Theme, is transferred after fainting.

GOAL: The argument that is the destination of the displacement that moves the THEME from its initial resting point.

Sentence-level instance: "Out of that [i.e., Brydon's realization that the doors to the vestibule that he thought were closed are actually open] the question sprang at *him*, making his eyes, as he felt, half-start from his head, as they had done, at the top of the house, before the sign of the other door" (723).

Discourse-level instance: The window bench is the Goal to which Brydon, the Theme, is transferred after fainting.

Nonparticipant Roles

LOCATIVE: The argument that denotes the fixed spatial position of the predicate; its site or static location.

Sentence-level instance: "he [Brydon] sat up, steadying himself beside her [Staverton] there on *the window-bench* and with his right hand grasping her left" (729).

Discourse-level instance: As the story proceeds, ever more particularized entities serve the Locative role: first the city, then the house on the jolly corner, then particular regions within the house.

REASON: The argument that denotes the prior conditions of a predication, i.e., the events or facts that motivate it or bring it about.

Sentence-level instance: "it was strange how with this sense [of returning from a journey after Brydon regains consciousness] what he had come back *to* seemed really the great thing, and as if his prodigious journey had been all for the sake of *it*" (726).

Discourse-level instance: The desire to know what he might have become had he stayed in New York is, as Brydon sees it, the Reason for his nocturnal visits to his house.

PURPOSE: The argument that denotes, not the motivational source of a predication (= REASON), but rather its motivational goal.

Sentence-level instance: "He [Brydon] had made, as I have said, to create on the premises *the baseless sense of a reprieve,* his three absences; and the result of the third [successive absence from the house] was to confirm the after-effect of the second" (714).[1]

Discourse-level instance: Knowledge of what he might have become had he stayed in New York is, as Brydon sees it, the Purpose of his nocturnal visits to the house.

---

1. A perusal of James's story turned up few sentence-level instantiations of the roles of Reason and Purpose. The paucity of entities explicitly coded as Reasons and Purposes in the storyworld underscores the extent to which Brydon's motivations and aims remain obscure, even or especially to himself. Since the story is an instance of what Stanzel (1971, 1984) would call figural narration—i.e., Er-narration refracted through the perceptions and thoughts of a storyworld participant—James's refusal to code entities as Reasons and Purposes accentuates for readers both the necessity and the difficulty of framing inferences about what Brydon's motivations and aims might really be.

---

these discrete temporal slices of the storyworld. What is more, interpreters must distinguish between all these temporally indexed predications and the broader semantic context in which they take shape. In "The Jolly Corner" predications made of storyworld entities select the participant roles (who did what to whom) interpreters must assign to them; nonparticipant roles (how, why, when, and where) derive from the semantic context embedding such predications, that is, the information that James provides about the time and place in which doings occur, about the motivations and aims subtending those doings, and about the specific means by which the doings are brought about.[28]

Overall, then, each predication codes storyworld entities as participants and nonparticipants; each is indexed to a temporal slice of the microuniverse; and each parallels, reinforces, qualifies, or undercuts other predications indexed to earlier and later slices. Even within a single sentence-level predication, however, an argument may be assigned more than one thematic role. Thus, in a predication such as the one encoded in *Oglethorpe bought the computer*, the computer might be assigned the role of either Patient or Theme, whereas Oglethorpe might be assigned the role of either Agent or Source. Conversely, in the case of symmetric predicates such as *kiss, marry, exchange stories with*, and so on, two different arguments take the same role, since in such predicates "the action is mutually distributed among the participants" (Frawley 1992: 232–33).[29] In moving from sentence-level to discourse-level predications, additional complexities emerge. The potential discrepancy between a specific predication and the more or less general *trend* of predications in a narrative reintroduces, at the level of discourse, the by now familiar problem of the one-many and many-one relation between arguments and roles.

For example, over the course of the story, entities assigned nonparticipant roles in the majority of predications may play participant roles in others, and vice versa. In other words, entities that generally surface as nonparticipants in sentences and clauses contained in the discourse may on occasion surface as participants. In James's tale, whereas the role of New York City is predominantly coded as that of a nonparticipant (i.e., Locative), in certain predications the city, with its "newnesses," "queernesses," and "above all . . . bignesses" (James 1996: 697), can sometimes surface as a participant. Thus, one clause codes the city's street addresses as an Agent or, more precisely, as an Agent in an embedded predication that constitutes part of Brydon's mental model of New York: the "dreadful multiplied numberings," among which the de-Americanized Brydon feels lost, "seemed to him to reduce the whole place to some vast ledger-page, overgrown, fantastic, of ruled and crisscrossed lines and figures" (699). More generally, over the course of a narrative one and the same storyworld entity can be assigned several roles. Hence Brydon, whom interpreters of the narrative are likely to construe as its primary Agent, sometimes takes on other participant roles as well—such as that of the Experiencer internally affected by the apparition of his alter ego in the vestibule (725–26), or that of the Theme transferred from the resting point on the marble floor where he faints to the window bench where Staverton bends over him lovingly (726–27). Conversely, as the narrative unfolds, several different individuals in the storyworld play the role of Locative: first the city, then Brydon's house on the jolly corner, then particular regions within the house.[30]

Does, then, a narrative theory informed by semantic research on thematic roles run up against the same impasse that limits Greimas's theory of actants? My next subsection argues otherwise.

Narrative Macroroles and the Actor-Undergoer Hierarchy

To account for one-many and many-one relations between grammatical and thematic roles at the level of clauses and sentences, linguists have developed a "tiered" approach to semantic roles (Foley and Van Valin 1984; Van Valin 1993; cf. Frawley 1992: 235–39). Positing the two semantic "macroroles" of Actor and Undergoer, which can be found at a higher tier of linguistic structure than the tier containing thematic roles of the sort specified in table 10, this approach suggests ways to describe and explain the possibilities for role overlap that remain underexplored in Greimas's theory of actants. In particular, the tiered approach, if scaled to account for interpretive processes brought to bear on discourse-level rather than sentence-level roles, points to an underlying system of preference rules that support inferences about storyworld participants. The tiered approach begins with the premise that it is better to establish a semantic continuum of thematic relations than to work toward a fixed universal inventory of roles. Figure 6 reproduces the continuum sketched by Robert Van Valin (1993: 41). (Note that Van Valin's taxonomy of thematic roles differs from Frawley's, particularly with respect to the participant roles that Frawley grouped under the heading of spatial roles and also the role of Locative, which Frawley classifies as a nonparticipant role. Further, note that Van Valin's Effector corresponds with Frawley's Author.)

As Figure 6 indicates, Agent and Patient provide anchor points for the continuum, and between them fall participant roles ranging from those that are more agent-like to those that are more patient-like. Further, "there is no absolute number of distinctions which every language must make, although there is strong evidence that certain of these distinctions are universal" (Van Valin 1993: 41). All languages, it seems, differentiate between things affected with respect to their state or condition and things affected with respect to their location—that is, between Patients and "things that are clearly at the right end of the scale but are less patient-like, namely themes" (42). Themes get moved around, even if they do not get kicked or diced or raked, like Patients. Meanwhile, on

Figure 6. A Semantic Continuum of Thematic Roles
(adapted from Van Valin 1993)

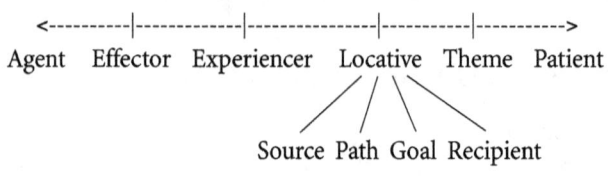

the left end of the continuum are participants (i.e., Frawley's Author and Van Valin's Effector, under which Van Valin subsumes Instruments) that can cause things to happen, without instigating or controlling what happens in the manner of Agents. Farther right on the continuum are Experiencers such as the Brydon that James codes as being shocked by the apparition of his alter ego; such participants are "the locus of an internal event, but [in a way that is] not willful, volitional and instigating" (42). Distinctions on this end of the continuum help capture the difference between English verbs such as *listen to* and *hear* (or *look at* and *see*): the first in each pair codes the subject as both Experiencer and Agent, whereas the second codes the subject as an Experiencer only. More generally, the basic claim here is that figure 6 "represents a continuum of distinctions, and languages may make more or fewer of them than what is listed above.... The same distinctions recur across languages; the same contrasts between experiencer and agent, effector and agent, theme and locative, and so on, are found in language after language" (Van Valin 1993: 42).[31]

The second tier of the model, consisting of the two semantic macroroles of Actor and Undergoer, is designed to account for *relations between* thematic roles that are not captured by the semantic continuum alone. For example, the difference between the active and passive in English can be explained in terms of disjunctive lists of roles that can be assigned to subject and object in each case. In other words, different constraints delimit the possibilities for role assignment and role overlap vis-à-vis subjects and objects in the active as opposed to the passive. The subject of an active verb can be assigned several roles from the role set, including Agent, Effector/Author, Experiencer, or Locative, whereas the direct object of the verb can be assigned the roles of Patient, Theme,

Locative, or Experiencer. Thus, in *Oglethorpe bought the computer*, the subject could be assigned either the role of Agent or of Locative (or, for Frawley, Source), and the object either the role of Patient or of Theme; but the subject of the active verb *bought* cannot be assigned the role of Patient nor the object the role of Agent. Inversely, with passive verbs the roles of Patient, Theme, Locative, or Experiencer can be assigned to the subject, whereas the roles of Agent, Effector, Experiencer, or Locative can be assigned to the object of the preposition *by*. Hence, in *the computer was bought by Oglethorpe*, the subject can be assigned the roles of Theme or Patient but not Agent, and the object of the preposition *by* can be assigned the roles of Agent or Locative/Source but not Patient. In short, there are constraints on possibilities for role overlap built into the structure of language. More precisely, at the level of clauses and sentences, possibilities for role assignment and overlap can be given preference rankings on the basis of the type of verb involved; in turn, those preference rankings can help specify the (jointly syntactic and semantic) behavior of the verbs in question. Active verbs disprefer assigning the role of Theme (even more: the role of Patient) to their subjects, just as passive verbs disprefer assigning the role of Author/Effector (even more: the role of Agent) to their subjects. The result is a preference-rule system accounting for different distributions of role assignment and syncretism in the active versus the passive.

The Actor and Undergoer macroroles help explain why certain kinds of role assignments and fusions are more or less strongly dispreferred—that is, more or less heavily *marked*. Figure 7 represents the Actor-Undergoer Hierarchy in terms of which Van Valin (1993: 44; cf. Frawley 1992: 237) seeks to characterize the preference-rule system in question. As figure 7 indicates, the farther left on the continuum the thematic relation realized by the macrorole of Undergoer, the more marked that realization is. The preference-rule system specifies that the default case is for languages to encode Undergoers by assigning relevant grammatical forms the role of Patient, else Theme, else Locative, else Experiencers, and so on, with the role assignments becoming increasingly marked as one moves away from the default coding of Undergoer as Patient. Inversely, the farther right on the continuum that one places the thematic relation realized by the macrorole of Actor, the more marked that realization is. The preference-rule system specifies that the default case is for languages to encode Actors by assigning relevant grammatical forms the role of Agent, else Effector/Author, else Experiencer, else as Locative, and so on, with the role assignments becoming increasingly marked as one moves away from the default coding of Actor as Agent. Hence "[t]he prototypical actor is an agent, the prototypical undergoer a patient, but effectors, experiencers, locatives and even themes (with intransitive activity verbs of motion) can also function as actor, and locatives, experiencers and themes can also serve as undergoer" (Van Valin 1993: 46). Since they are not themselves thematic roles, but rather prototypes or templates that subsume thematic roles by specifying "potential participants in a predication, potential thematic roles" (Frawley 1992: 235), the macroroles of Actor and Undergoer establish a gradient instead of a categorical relation between syntax and semantics, grammar and meaning. Agents are quintessential Actors, but predications can also code Experiencers, Effectors/Authors, or even Locatives as doing or acting. You can say not only *Oglethorpe is killing me*, but also *New York City is killing me*. Patients are quintessential Undergoers, but Themes and Locatives can also undergo. James's Spencer Brydon undergoes not only when as Patient he is chased (or imagines himself to be chased) by his alter ego, but also when as Theme he is moved from the vestibule to the window bench. Conversely he acts even when, as Experiencer, he senses what he takes to be signs of the presence of his Doppelgänger.[32]

As the examples from "The Jolly Corner" suggest, role fusions in narrative contexts obey an underlying logic that the notion of semantic macroroles, although originally designed for clause- and sentence-level structures, can help explicate. Arguably, something like an Actor-Undergoer hierarchy delimits how many and what kind of participant roles can be fused, at any given moment, in a storyworld entity. In James's narrative, the roles of Patient and Theme coalesce in Brydon only in the second half of the tale, after he sees a door closed that he thought he left open and so infers that he is being pursued by his alter ego. In other words, the fusion in Brydon of the roles of Patient and Theme occurs only after James's figural narration mirrors its protagonist's mental about-face and cues readers to construe him as an Undergoer instead of an Actor. The first part of the story, by contrast, cues readers to interpret Brydon as an Actor, with this narrative macrorole realizing the canonical or default role of Agent (Brydon travels from Europe to New York, takes charge of his properties, induces Alice Staver-

Participant Roles and Relations 161

Figure 7. Actor-Undergoer Hierarchy (adapted from Van Valin 1993)

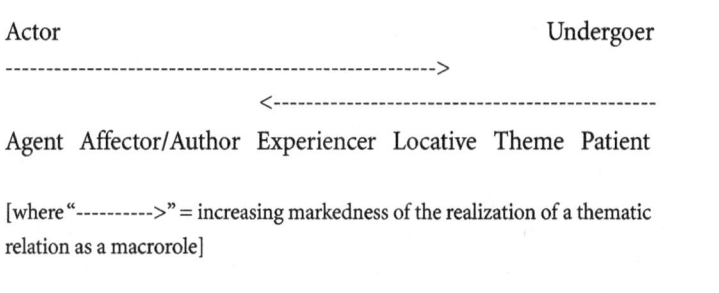

Actor   Undergoer
-->
                    <--
Agent Affector/Author Experiencer Locative Theme Patient

[where "---------->" = increasing markedness of the realization of a thematic relation as a macrorole]

---

ton to accompany him to both of his houses, etc.). Hence, just as it is far more likely for a language to interpret an Agent as an Actor than a Patient as an Actor, the story initially positions Brydon as a participant within a preference-rule system that disprefers the fusion of Agent/Theme or Agent/Patient roles.

The long middle section of the story (James 1996: 709–26) is what prompts readers to reweight their interpretive preferences, or rather enter a differently configured preference-rule system. Although the story's middle section begins by coding Brydon as an Agent, the type of participant that is canonically realized as Actor, as the section proceeds the protagonist begins to assume ever more predominantly the role of Experiencer, which is a more marked participant role when realized as Actor. Note the many clause- and sentence-level predications that assign to Brydon the participant role of Experiencer (all emphases mine): "*He liked* however the open shutters" (713); "*He had felt* it [his ability to perceive things] as above all open to cultivation" (713); "*He knew* after a little while what this was" (716); "*he found himself considering* a circumstance" (717); "*He had* indeed since that moment *undergone* an agitation so extraordinary that it might have muddled for him any earlier view" (717); "*He listened* as if there had been something to hear" (719); "*It seemed to him* he had waited an age for some stir of the great grim hush" (721); "*he recognised* the influence of the lower windows" (723). To anticipate issues that I discuss in more detail in a moment: insofar as (all other things being equal) coding narrative Experiencers as Actors is more heavily marked than coding Agents as Actors, the participant logic of "The Jolly Corner" suggests how patterns of role-assignment are bound up with intuitions about genre. Differences between narrative (sub)genres can be correlated with the way various kinds of stories situate participants along the Actor-Undergoer hierarchy. What would be a marked role-assignment in an epic would be the norm in a psychological tale or novel, where Experiencers are far more often realized as the macrorole of Actor. In "The Jolly Corner" specifically, the predications that prompt readers to assign to Brydon the role of Experiencer have a cumulative effect: they make it harder and harder to sustain the interpretation of Brydon as Actor. As the middle part of the story proceeds, then, the protagonist must be reconstrued as a full-scale Undergoer, taking on first the role of Patient affected by another's actions and then the role of a somewhat-less-affected-but-still-moved-around Theme. This shift in narrative macroroles inverts the markedness relations that hold in the first part of the tale; in a paraphrase of the second part of the narrative, assigning Brydon the macrorole of Actor would be just as marked (read: dispreferred) as assigning him the macrorole of Undergoer in a paraphrase of the first part.

Granted, in the middle section of the story Brydon does perform actions while moving through his house in search of his alter ego, climbing up and down stairs, opening the casement of an upper-story window, peering into dimly lit rooms, and so on. But in portraying Brydon as a hunter whose quarry is a perception, a sought-for glimpse of the person who, counterfactually, he might have become, James codes his protagonist as a radical Experiencer for whom true agency becomes an ever-diminishing role possibility. While trying to "'cultivate' his whole perception" and "bringing it on, bringing it to perfection, by practice" (713) Brydon

> With habit and repetition . . . gained to an extraordinary degree the power to penetrate the dusk of distances and the darkness of corners, to resolve back into their innocence the treacheries of uncertain light, the evil-looking forms taken in the gloom by mere shadows, by accidents of the air, by shifting effects of perspective. (712)

It is perhaps inevitable that as a radical Experiencer of this sort, Brydon would begin to get the impression that "[h]e was kept in sight while remaining himself—as regards the essence of his position—sightless, and his only recourse then was in abrupt turns, rapid recoveries of ground" (714). Seeing the door closed that he thought he had left open, Brydon "took it full in the face that something had happened between" the present moment and the time of his last visitation (717). The door is for Brydon the "sign" (723) that he must reinterpret as Agent the entity to which he had assigned the role of Patient in the microuniverse, the embedded storyworld, with which he had up to that point been working. And the realization of an Agent as Undergoer is, as the Actor-Undergoer hierarchy suggests, heavily dispreferred. Thus Brydon must rethink both his alter ego's and his own narrative macrorole, switching places with the individual he formerly construed as Undergoer.

By the same token, narrative macroroles set up preference-rule systems constraining how many and what kind of storyworld entities can be brought under the heading of a given participant role. Insofar as the middle section of the story begins with Brydon assigning himself the role of Actor and the alter ego that of Undergoer, by extension the narrative macrorole of Undergoer also organizes predications concerning the structure and appointments of the house on the jolly corner. In the resulting preference-rule system, the house initially takes on the role of a Patient that Brydon affects by visiting and penetrating spatially; further, its artifacts (e.g., shutters) are so many Themes that Brydon transfers from one fixed location to another. As Locative, the house encodes the macrorole of Undergoer in a somewhat more marked way: places usually circumscribe actions, rather than being the affected logical recipient of them. However, once the alter ego's macrorole shifts and the preferences for role-assignments are adjusted accordingly, the narrative differently codes the house occupied by and associated with Brydon's alternative self. It now cuts against the grain of the story's participant logic to include the house in the set of individuals interpretable as Patients and Themes. Rather, parallel with Brydon's alter ego, the house begins to surface not just as a backdrop for (Locative) or target of (Patient, Theme) the protagonist's search for self, but also as an active, doing, volitional individual or Agent in its own right, as suggested by James's use of *gloom* as a verb (along with *created*) in the following passage:

> The house, withal, seemed immense, the scale of space again inordinate; the open rooms, to no one of which [Brydon's] eyes deflected, gloomed in their shuttered state like mouths of caverns; only the high skylight that formed the crown of the deep well created for him a medium in which he could advance, but which might have been, for queerness of colour, some watery under-world. (722–23)

164 NARRATIVE MICRODESIGNS

Macroroles, Scene Building, and Narrative Genres

Thus far, I have been using "The Jolly Corner" to suggest that understanding a narrative depends crucially on framing and updating inferences about participant roles and relations. Such inferences are indispensable scene-building strategies, affording those "zoomings" and "defocalizings" that Frawley detected in the semantic "machinery that languages have for putting forms together into *expressions about situations*" (1992: 200). In Fillmore's (1977) account,

> The study of semantics is the study of the cognitive scenes that are created or activated by utterances.... A complete description of the commercial event [for example] would identify the buyer, the seller, the money, and the goods. A prototypic commercial event involves all these things, but any single clause that we construct in talking about such an event requires us to choose one particular perspective on the event.... [T]he choice of any particular expression from the repertory of expressions that activate the commercial event scene brings to mind the whole scene—the whole commercial event situation—but presents in the foreground—in perspective—only a particular aspect or section of that scene. (73, 72, 74)

Likewise, stories activate scenes, or mental models of situations that blend prototypicality and novelty, with the proportion of familiarity and newness determining how much narrativity a story has (see chapter 3 of this book). To build and update such narratively activated scenes, interpreters must assign and re-assign roles to the participants that figure more or less prominently in the scenes in question. As a story progresses, it foregrounds aspects or segments of the scene by cuing interpreters to zoom in on various participants. A different telling of the story—such as one in which Spencer Brydon feels hounded by his alter ego from the first moment of his return to New York—might activate a scene with all the same components but cue readers to zoom in on different components as the most salient ones. Further, narrative macroroles organize the presentation and comprehension of narratively activated scenes by setting up preference-rule systems, which specify more and less canonical role assignments in a given type of scene. Because of these preference-based canons for role assignment, interpreters will be more likely to zoom in on or defocalize some participants than others. In essence, "The Jolly Corner" recounts how its protagonist is compelled to reconceive his life story by zooming in on components of the scene(s) associated with it. Backgrounded (i.e., repressed) components come to the fore, and there is a wholesale readjustment of preferences for role assignment. At another level, by compelling readers repeatedly to confer on an Experiencer the narrative macrorole of Actor, James defocalizes the tokens of Brydon's agency that had previously been foregrounded. Eventually, Brydon's active search for self gives way to a terrifyingly passive mode of Undergoing; concomitantly, the tale cues interpreters to zoom in on Brydon's alter ego as the Agent of a self-knowledge that is violently forced on the protagonist.

Yet canons for role assignment work not only in intranarrative or story-specific contexts, but also in internarrative or generic contexts. Indeed, these canons or preferences help explain what a narrative genre is. A narrative genre can be characterized as a more or less firmly codified set of scene-building strategies; the degree to which those strategies are set into play in a given case is a function of how a story relates to available genres. Take, for example, the genre of detective fiction. Important role-based predictions can be made about stories instantiating this genre, with the genre in turn constituting a preference-rule system for assigning roles to participants in recurrent types of scenes. Thus, in a story activating a prototypical crime-solving scene, assigning the role of Patient or Theme (or even Experiencer) to the detective at the end of the narrative would be less canonical, or more marked, than assigning him or her one of these roles at the beginning. This point can be put another way. Once they have solved the crime, detectives are less apt to be coded as Undergoers—that is, as individuals for whom it is canonical to be affected or moved around—than they are when still impinged on by external forces or faced with a welter of potential clues at the outset of their investigations. The trajectory of the narrative can thus be plotted against a shift of narrative macroroles, with the protagonist moving from Undergoer to Actor and the preferences for role assignments changing accordingly. Meanwhile, experimental or "metaphysical" detective stories (Merivale and Sweeney 1999), such as those authored by Patrick Modiano (1978) and Jorge Luis Borges (1964), exploit this generic preference system in order to innovate on the genre itself. The metaphysical detective, although sometimes living out the macrorole of Actor, is less apt to follow a trajectory that leads from Undergoing to Acting. And even when interpretable as Actor, the metaphysical detective is more likely to realize that macrorole in the form of an Experiencer than in the form of an Agent or even an Effector/Author. Thus, the avant-garde variety of detective fiction can be registered as such and gains its perceptibility and significance because of the way it deviates from patterns of role assignment that are canonical in "garden-variety" instantiations of the genre.

By the same token, however, what distinguishes garden-variety detective fictions (e.g., Hammett's) from other kinds of stories is a broader system of genre-specific preferences for role assignments. A narrative's affiliation with the genre of detective fiction sets into play scene-building strategies anchored in a pattern of preferred role assignments; interpreters expect a shift in narrative macroroles as the protagonist-detective morphs from Undergoer to Actor, with a concomitant shift in participant roles for the criminal, who typically moves from being an Actor (canonically associated with the participant Agent) to an Undergoer (canonically associated with the participant Patient). There are, in other words, a sort of chiasmic reversal of the underlying macroroles of detective and criminal and a corresponding switch in the preferred or canonical role for each participant. It is just as dispreferred or marked for the criminal to be an Agent at story's end as it is for the detective to be a Patient or Theme; and it is just as marked for the narrative to code the Actor-criminal as a Patient at the beginning of the story as it is for the narrative to code the Actor-detective as a Patient (or even Experiencer) at its conclusion. Hence, by affiliating itself with the epic, the realist novel, the psychological tale, the ghost story, or some other narrative genre, a narrative sets different scene-building strategies into play—different preferences for assigning roles to participants (and nonparticipants) at a given moment in storyworld as well as across a longer temporal stretch within that world. In the epic genre, for example, the Actor-protagonist (e.g., Achilles, Beowulf) is preferentially coded as Agent. Or rather, the Actor-protagonist typically participates in the action as Agent, else Author/Effector, else Experiencer—in order of increasingly dispreferred or noncanonical role assignments.

Thus, assigning an epic protagonist the role of Experiencer across long stretches of the storyworld would be much more heavily marked than assigning the same role for long periods to the protagonist of a psychological tale or novel. As confirmed by a protagonist such as Isabel Archer in James's *Portrait of a Lady* (James 1992), the protagonist of the psychological novel is indeed an Actor, but he or she acts mainly by

Experiencing (in the sense of reflecting, anticipating, recalling, realizing, etc.). By contrast, the epic hero is an Actor whose preferred mode of acting is as an Agent defeating Hector, slaying Grendel, and so on. It should be emphasized again that preferred or canonical cases are at stake here, not absolute, one-to-one correlations. Homer's *The Odyssey*, one of the founding instances of the epic genre, codes Odysseus as an Actor whose successful return to Ithaka depends on his ability to adopt the role of Experiencer as well as Agent. By refraining from taking action immediately, and instead adopting the disguise of an old beggar who must endure the insults of Penelope's rude and importunate suitors, Odysseus stages the surprise attack that restores his power and authority (Homer 1999: books 13–24). But the exception proves the rule. In *Beowulf*, the one segment of the text in which Beowulf participates as an Experiencer for any duration is made perceptible (and significant) by virtue of its marked contrast with dominant coding strategies in the text. Just before his fatal battle with the dragon guarding the treasure hoard, Beowulf broods with dark foreboding about his fate.[33] This shift in coding strategies, which assigns the old king the dispreferred role of Experiencer, thus serves to mark off the boundary of Beowulf's very existence, equating the epic hero's loss of Agency with death itself.

Meanwhile, James Joyce's *Ulysses* (1986) creates parodic effects by placing itself in dialogue with the epic genre and with *The Odyssey* in particular. Forging intertextual links between Leopold Bloom and Odysseus (still a recognizably epic hero), Joyce's novel at the same time situates its protagonist in a different preference-rule system for role assignments. Bloom is mainly, not secondarily or intermittently, an Experiencer realized as the macrorole of Actor. Similarly, James's "The Jolly Corner" activates a particularly rich blend of scene-building strategies by positioning itself *between* several narrative genres, including psychological fiction, tales of the supernatural, the detective story, and even epic. At various points in the story, Brydon can be construed as an Experiencer functioning as a protagonist-Actor, a Patient and Theme functioning as protagonist-Undergoer, and an Agent functioning as a protagonist-Actor—one hunting down, in quasi-epic fashion, what he takes to be a weaker version of himself.

More generally, differences between preferred or canonical role assignments help account for the typicality judgments made by readers, viewers, and listeners who are distinguishing between narrative genres

Table 11. Preference Rankings for Role Assignments (by genre)

Narrative Genre	Participants Preferentially Realized as "Actor"
Epic	Agent > Author/Effector > Experiencer
Realist Novel	Agent > Experiencer > Author/Effector
Psychological Novel	Experiencer > Author/Effector > Agent

Table 12. Preferred Sequences of Narrative Participants/Macroroles (by genre)

Narrative Genre	Sequencing of Participants/Macroroles
Detective Fiction	Patient/Undergoer → Experiencer/Actor → Agent/Actor
Metaphysical Detective Fiction	Patient, Theme/Undergoer → Experiencer, Agent/Actor → Patient, Theme/Undergoer → ...
Ghost Stories	Experiencer/Actor → Patient, Theme/Undergoer

and determining how to match a story with a genre. Tables 11 and 12 schematize the preference systems underlying role assignments in some representative genres. To simplify matters, I focus only on participants functioning as protagonists. Table 11 gives a synchronic picture of the participant types preferentially realized as Actor, in any given time slice, across several genres. Table 12 gives a diachronic view of the patterning of canonical role assignments across several other genres; it focuses on how participants and the macroroles under which they can be subsumed typically alter as their respective storyworlds unfold. The arrow (→) means "changes into" or "becomes."

Together with the preceding discussion, tables 11 and 12 provide grounds for rethinking Monika Fludernik's (1996) claim that the factor chiefly responsible for making narrative interpretable as narrative is human experientiality, or "the evocation of consciousness [in terms of] cognitive schema of embodiedness that relates to human existence and human concerns" (12–13). Whereas Fludernik argues that "narrativity is primarily based on a consciousness factor rather than on actantial dynamics or teleological directedness" (30),[34] issues broached in the present chapter suggest a more complicated picture. Stories are interpretable as such because of (in part) their affiliations with one or more narrative kinds, and differences between narrative genres are a function (in part) of systematically patterned preferences for assigning roles to narrative participants. Hence it is important to recognize that the role of Experiencer is just one participant role made possible by the narrative system. That system allows different preference rankings for the role of Experiencer to be matched with different narrative genres. Further, in any given narrative, the role of Experiencer can be assigned a higher or lower preference ranking depending on where a participant is situated in a *sequence* of (macro)roles, different sorts of sequences being canonical for different kinds of narrative. To make experientiality definitive of stories, then, is to place too much weight on a participant role whose degree of salience derives from a larger, preference-based system of roles. Also, if one posits a direct proportion between experientiality and narrativity (or for that matter narrativehood), it becomes harder to account for the genre-specific patterning of narrative macroroles vis-à-vis Experiencing participants. For example, the coding of an Experiencer as an Actor-protagonist functions differently (i.e., in a more marked way) in the context of epic than it does in the context of a ghost story or a psychological novel.

5
Dialogues and Styles

Let us swop hats and excheck a few strong verbs weak oach eather yapyazzard abast the blooty creeks.

Finnegans Wake

Another relatively local principle for storyworld design involves the creation of mental models for speech acts performed by participants. Although research on speech representation in literature predates the heyday of structuralist narratology, the advent of a formalized theory of narrative has led to an explosion of interest in the ways in which stories can embed as well as result from verbal acts.[1] Most broadly, this research is based on the intuition that the ontology of narrative encompasses Sayings as well as Doings, or rather that it includes verbal as well as nonverbal modes of Doing.

Reinvoking Plato's distinction between mimesis and diegesis in book 3 of *The Republic*, Gérard Genette (1980: 162–85; cf. Fludernik 1993a: 30–31) contrasted "narrative of events" with "narrative of words," noting modern-day analogues in the pairs "scene vs. summary" and "showing vs. telling." The first item in each pair corresponds to a reproduction of nonverbal events in the storyworld—though, as Genette points out, given the medium-specific constraints on narratives conveyed in language, so-called showing "can be only a *way of telling*" (166; cf. Booth 1983). The second item in each pair corresponds to a reproduction of verbal events, whereby the narrator "delivers a speech as if he were someone else," in Plato's phrase (quoted in Genette 1980: 162). Although Plato's metaphysical theories prompted the philosopher to campaign against narratives of words, Genette notes that "one of the main paths of emancipation of the modern novel has consisted of pushing this mimesis of speech to its extreme, or rather to its limit, obliterating the last traces of the narrating instance and giving the floor to the character right away" (173). In turn, Brian McHale (1978) refined Genette's scheme by outlining a scale or continuum that stretches from comparatively diegetic to comparatively mimetic types of discourse representation. At the diegetic end of the scale are modes such as diegetic summary ("Joe was unhappy") and indirect discourse ("Joe said he was unhappy"); at the mimetic end are modes such as direct discourse ("Joe said, 'I am unhappy' ") and free direct discourse ("I am unhappy," reported as part of an interior monologue by Joe).

Other researchers have analyzed the functioning of free indirect discourse, in particular, in literary writers as diverse as Fyodor Dostoevsky, Eduoard Dujardin, William Faulkner, James Joyce, and Virginia Woolf (see, for example, Cohn 1978; Doležel 1973; Fludernik 1993a; Herman 1995a; Hernadi 1972; Pascal 1977).[2] As a more or less ambiguous blending of a narrator's and participant's speech styles (as in "Joe was damned unhappy"), free indirect discourse could be described as a hybridized narrative of events *and* words. In this narratorial mode, showing assumes the form of telling and vice versa. Ann Banfield (1982), for her part, argues that free indirect reports of thoughts must be viewed as "unspeakable sentences," given that no linguistic agent, no narrator, could literally "speak" the thoughts of a narrative participant (for a detailed account and critique of Banfield's model, see Fludernik 1993a: 360–97; for additional counterarguments against the "no-narrator" theory, see Ryan 1991: 67–70; 1999: 134–38). By contrast, for V. N. Vološinov (1973) and M. M. Bakhtin (1984), free indirect discourse (or "quasi-direct discourse") exemplifies the inherently dialogical quality of language itself. Rather than violating pragmatic constraints on communication, this type of represented discourse points up the "vari-directional" or "internally undecided" nature of all communicative acts, which reflect in their very structure multiple contexts of utterance, past and future as well as present.

As this brief outline suggests, what is at stake in research on free indirect and other types of represented discourse is an important species of cognitive activity—namely, the activity whereby recipients mentally model varieties of communicative behavior in storyworlds. Further, the research suggests that, by prompting readers, listeners, and viewers to interpret how and why participants are performing communicative acts, narrative discourse can enrich interpreters' understanding of the nature and scope of communication itself. I am, in other words, seconding Bakhtin's (1981a) claim that novelistic discourse is in large part discourse *about* discourse (301–66). In this spirit, using inves-

Dialogues and Styles 173

tigative tools that narrative analysts have yet to exploit as fully as they should, the present chapter explores metacommunicative dimensions of discourse representation that deserve further study. First, I draw on theories from linguistic pragmatics and discourse analysis to examine the *interactional profile* of utterances embedded in narrative discourse; my concern here is the way in which discourse representations in stories typically involve coordinated interchanges between two or more participants. Focusing on the metacommunicative role of fictional dialogue—that is, the way such dialogue has something to say about communication itself—I examine the Mutt and Jute episode in James Joyce's *Finnegans Wake* (1939). This part of the chapter takes issue with the non-, even anti-communicative impetus sometimes ascribed by Joycean scholars to the *Wake*. Second, I draw on sociolinguistic theories of language variation to suggest new ways of exploring the *verbal texture* of represented discourse. In particular, I use the concept of "style shifting" to examine speech representations in Edith Wharton's 1905 novel *The House of Mirth* (1994). Here my concern is with how the format of represented utterances functions to mark aspects of participants' identity, thereby reinforcing patterns of cooperation and conflict encoded at other levels of narrative structure as well. Over the course of the chapter, it will become clear that my initial division between the interactional profile and the verbal texture of represented discourse is merely a heuristic one. For speech styles at once shape and are shaped by contexts of interaction, whereas the coordination of interchanges entails, too, a coordination of styles.

Dialogues

My first concern, then, is with the interactional profile of represented discourse cast in the form of dialogue. By drawing on H. P. Grice's (1989) pragmatic theories about the "logic of conversation," along with models for analyzing discourse, or units of language beyond the sentence, narrative theorists can provide new insights into the way recipients process communicative acts in storyworlds. In particular, theorists can move from fashioning *typologies* of represented discourse to building frameworks for studying the narrative (or more broadly communicative) *functions* of embedded speech productions. Such productions, after all, take shape in the context of interaction between participants. Conversely, studying the mechanisms of fictional dialogue can help illuminate the assumptions, predispositions, and competencies on which all interlocutors rely in communicating with one another. To clarify just what sorts of communicative resources are at issue, I center the first part of my discussion around an experimental, highly ludic fictional dialogue, one that raises questions about the possibilities and limits of dialogue itself.

Dialogue in a Discourse Context

It has been a quarter of a century since Mary Louise Pratt (1977) extended to literary discourse Grice's ideas about language and communication. Even so, Pratt's book did not attempt to account for communicative acts *represented* in literary discourse—such as dialogues—but rather for "the literary speech situation" in a global sense (100–151).[3] By contrast, this section explores the possibilities and limits of pragmatic (i.e., Gricean) and discourse-analytic models vis-à-vis local versus global literary speech situations (cf. Leech and Short 1981: 288–317). Specifically, it examines the extent to which pragmatic and discourse-analytic ideas and methods can be used as a framework for understanding the dialogue between Mutt and Jute in Joyce's *Finnegans Wake*.[4] Although this avant-garde literary narrative sets up obstacles to understanding Mutt and Jute's interchange as a stretch of talk jointly accomplished by the two participants, it also underscores the extent to which the cognitive frame "dialogue" (or "conversation") guides comprehension of narrative discourse. Indeed, by toying with, or problematizing, readers' intuitions about the structures, routines, and purposes of talk itself, texts such as Joyce's not only draw upon but also enrich cognitive prototypes for conversation. Thus, by invoking linguistic models in connection with Mutt and Jute, I work toward a finer-grained conception of pragmatics and discourse analysis as tools for literary interpretation. But I also suggest that literary texts can function as, in effect, models for hypothetical discourse situations. To put this same point another way, literary dialogues like Joyce's stage the principles and mechanisms of dialogue in general, forcing recipients to reflect on their own canons for conversational coherence.

My initial aim is to examine the form and functioning of the Mutt and Jute episode in light of recent linguistic theories about discourse and communication. These theories indicate that when early text-grammatical approaches (e.g., van Dijk 1972) tried to locate within a text or a discourse the principles explaining the coherence of that text or discourse—what makes it more than a mere jumble of sentences, a hodgepodge of statements—they were engaged in a fundamentally misguided attempt.[5] For analysts influenced by Grice's pragmatic theories, coherence is not a property inhering *in* texts, but instead a relation between sentences—or rather utterances—that recipients bring *to* texts in their bid to interpret them (Blakemore 1988: 237; Green 1989).

Perhaps the best way to gain entry into this research domain is to draw a quick sketch of the distinction linguists often make between sentences and utterances—and between semantics versus pragmatics and discourse analysis as the theoretical domains pertaining to sentences and utterances, respectively.[6] (Formal) semantics is commonly defined as the part of grammatical theory that is concerned with the study of the truth-conditional meaning of sentences. By contrast, pragmatics can be defined as "the study of the use of context to make inferences about meaning" (Fasold 1990: 119). Pragmatics is thus that part of grammatical theory concerned with meanings that attach to sentences not through their semantic content, but rather through the contexts in which the sentences are uttered, or more precisely the discourse situations in which sentences are issued as utterances. For example, given sentence (S),

(S) Meredith's cat is aloof but clean,

a particular set of truth conditions holding for (S) can be mapped into the semantic content, the truth-conditional meaning, of the sentence. Meredith's cat must be both clean and aloof—that is, both conjuncts contained in the sentence must be true—in order for (S) to be true. If the cat is aloof and dirty, or friendly and clean, or friendly and dirty, then (S) is false. Schematically, and to invoke the truth-table for "(Meredith's cat is) p & q," the truth conditions of (S) can be represented as follows:

	T	T	T
	T	F	F
	F	T	F
	F	F	F
(The cat is)	aloof (but)	clean	= true sentence
	aloof	dirty	= false sentence
	friendly	clean	= false sentence
	friendly	dirty	= false sentence

But—and this is where pragmatic and discourse-analytic considerations begin to converge—take a stretch of talk in which speaker B happens to utter sentence (S) in response to the prior utterance of sentence (S') by speaker A:

Speaker A: (S') I like dogs because they're friendly

Speaker B: (S) Meredith's cat is aloof but clean

Here the meaning of (S) cannot simply be reduced to its semantic content: what B's utterance of (S) is *doing* in the discourse situation cannot be described solely via the truth-conditional meaning of (S). Rather, (S) takes on an additional *pragmatic* meaning in the context of the larger discourse situation in which it occurs. Sentence (S) carries the implication that B objects to dogs' dirtiness, however friendly they might be, and, *ceteris paribus*, prefers the neat self-sufficiency of cats to the sloppy gregariousness of dogs. By extension, pragmatics is the study of just those aspects of linguistic competence that permit interlocutors to register, and furthermore to calculate or explain, all those features of (S) such that (S) functions as a relevant and meaningful response to A's utterance of (S')—even though nothing about the semantic content of (S) *per se* indicates why the sentence can perform the discourse functions it does in the context at issue.

At issue most fundamentally, then, is the relation between linguistic contexts and linguistic meanings. When speaker B says "Meredith's cat is aloof but clean" after hearing speaker A say "I like dogs because they're friendly," speaker A *assumes* that speaker B has made a nonrandom rejoinder. In other words, Speaker A adheres to what Grice called the "Cooperative Principle," which can be defined (in part) as a default assumption that one's interlocutor is designing and processing utterances in a reasoned or predictable manner. Thus for Grice, "talk exchanges," which can be seen as "a special case or variety of purposive, indeed rational, behavior" (1989: 28),

> do not normally consist of a succession of disconnected remarks, and would not be rational if they did. They are characteristically, to some degree at least, cooperative efforts; and each participant recognizes in them, to some extent, a common purpose or set of purposes, or at least a mutually accepted direction.... We might then formulate a rough general principle which participants will be expected (ceteris paribus) to observe, namely: Make your conversational contribution such as is required, at the stage at which it occurs, by the accepted purpose or direc-

tion of the talk exchange in which you are engaged. One might label this the Cooperative Principle. (26)

This principle helps explain why A attempts to elicit the implied meaning of (or draw a "conversational implicature" from) B's remark, instead of assuming, precipitously, that what B has said is only randomly related to the discourse context at hand and is therefore incapable of being interpreted as a meaningful utterance. The coherence of two or more contiguous statements—such that those statements constitute discourses or conversations—thus derives from interlocutors' assumptions about what roles the statements are performing in particular discourse contexts, together with the linguistic profile of the statements themselves. As Brown and Yule (1983) put it, "[I]n addition to our knowledge of sentential structure, we also have a knowledge of other standard formats in which information is conveyed. We also rely on some principle that, although there may be no formal linguistic links connecting contiguous linguistic strings, the fact of their contiguity leads us to interpret them as connected" (224). Along the same lines, a user-oriented view of coherence underlies what Grice describes as conversational implicatures: namely, meanings that attach, in nonrandom ways, to utterances by virtue of the contexts of those utterances, rather than by virtue of the conventional meaning of the expressions uttered (1989: 22–40; cf. Fasold 1990: 119–46: Levinson 1983: 97–166).[7]

Grice's general approach has had a powerful impact on linguists concerned with units of language beyond the sentence, including dialogues or conversations. Although John J. Gumperz (1982) works mainly in the tradition of interactional sociolinguistics, as opposed to the pragmatic tradition spawned by philosophers such as Grice, J. L. Austin (1962), and John Searle (1969), Gumperz too argues that "[c]ohesion or coherence does not inhere in the text as such. It is the listeners' search for a relationship, along with their failure to find anything to contradict the assumption that a connection must exist, that motivates the interpretation" (33). Gillian Brown and George Yule (1983) put the point even more strongly: "Within chunks of language which are conventionally presented as texts, the hearer/reader will make every effort to impose a coherent interpretation, i.e., to *treat* the language thus presented as constituting 'text.' We do not see an advantage in trying to determine constitutive formal features which a text must possess to qualify as a 'text.' Texts are what hearers and readers treat as texts" (199). The latter formulation represents an extreme version of the position put forth by Grice. Brown and Yule's suggestion that textual coherence, or texthood as such, is purely a function of interpretation, goes against the grain of other trends in discourse analysis. These other trends attempt to describe coherence as a complex interplay between the formal features of utterances and some version of the Cooperative Principle—an interplay that predisposes language users to interpret linguistic forms, and the utterances that embed them, as contributions to some emergent conversational whole.

At issue, more precisely, is a large body of (socio)linguistic research suggesting that what accounts for the cohesiveness of a set of utterances constituting a conversation is the ongoing "interactional achievement" (Schegloff 1981) of the discourse participants themselves.[8] Discourse coherence, on this view, is the product of communicative negotiations of extraordinary, but describable, complexity and variety. For example, Deborah Schiffrin's work on discourse markers, that is, "sequentially dependent elements which bracket units of talk" (1987: 31), throws new light on what Grice characterized as the logic of conversation. For Schiffrin, participants in a conversation must perpetually negotiate an always emergent discourse coherence (23), in which discourse markers (e.g., connectives such as *and*, *but*, and *or*; markers of cause and result like *so* and *because*) "index an utterance to the local contexts in which utterances are produced and in which they are to be interpreted" (326). Such markers help interlocutors situate units of talk in a discourse model—a model that both *explains* what people do when they talk and also emerges as a *result* of their conversational negotiations—spanning speech act, ideational, and other communicative structures. Accordingly, for Schiffrin, "[l]ocal coherence in discourse is ... defined as the outcome of joint efforts from interactants to integrate knowing, meaning, saying and doing" (29). From this perspective, conversational coherence can be redescribed in terms of discourse functions bestowed on utterances by their place in a larger context of talk—a context that those same utterances, however, help to create.

As should be evident from even this preliminary overview, Grice's ideas about cooperation in discourse acquire a more nuanced, more richly differentiated profile in the work of Schiffrin and other post-Gricean analysts of discourse and conversation.[9] Some of the most important of these later developments have been advanced by sociologically minded analysts of discourse. For example, Erving Goffman's early (1955) study of what he called the ritual elements of social interaction set an important precedent not only for Grice's account of conversational cooperation, but also for the influential idea of talk as an economy of turns, a systematic allocation of conversational resources (cf. Sacks, Schegloff, and Jefferson 1974; Schegloff 1981, 1997). Thus Goffman's insight that "[i]n a conversational encounter, interaction tends to proceed in spurts, an interchange at a time, and the flow of information and business is parceled out into these relatively closed ritual units" (1955: 228) directly anticipates work in the conversational-analytic (or ethnomethodological) tradition (see Schiffrin 1994: 232–39). Writing in this tradition, Emanuel Schegloff (1981) notes that

> the operation of continuers [i.e., discourse tokens such as *uh huh*] and of other bits of behavior produced by recipients in the course of, or rather in the enabling of, extended talk or discourse by another, is designed in a detailed way to fit to the ongoing talk by the teller, and "to fit" may involve either "cooperating" with what that talk seems designed to get, or witholding; both of these are fitted to the details of the locally preceding talk, and cannot be properly understood or appreciated when disengaged from it. (86)

Thus, conversation-analytic and more broadly discourse-analytic theorists, by characterizing discourse as a species of cooperative and interactional behavior, have construed conversational coherence as an inalienably social mode of meaning. In their view, what people say and the way they say it are jointly the cause and the result of the particular sociocultural interaction in which they are engaged.[10]

As the following pages go on to argue, Joyce's Mutt and Jute episode likewise suggests that cohesiveness in discourse derives to some extent from (contexts of) interpretation, instead of being wholly given before readers start interpreting. Thus, both discourse analysis and fictional dialogues such as Joyce's highlight that presumption of coherence that interlocutors and readers bring to the utterances comprised by texts, discourses, and conversations. To that extent, both discourse-analytic theories and fictional texts such as the Mutt and Jute episode are metacommunicative in nature: both derive from an attempt to model, in new ways, what it is that people do when they communicate. Specifically, Joyce's text forces recipients to come to grips with their own guiding assumption that, despite the polysemic profile of their remarks, Mutt and Jute's encounter is, in fact, a discourse—and more specifically, a dialogue. On the strength of that assumption, the episode unfolds not as a randomly generated sequence of atomistic utterances, but rather as an ordered set of locutions, structured according to dialogic principles at work in discourse at large—although those principles, here, are importantly inflected by the formal (syntactic, lexical, phonetic) innovations characteristic of *Finnegans Wake* as a whole. Joyce's suggestion, like Grice's, is that people create discourse out of a vast, in principle infinite assemblage of linguistic and encyclopedic elements, and that the threshold at which any given discourse can be labeled as incoherent is in part a function of particular communicative contexts.

Previous Approaches to Mutt and Jute

Commentators on *Finnegans Wake* have typically adopted two sorts of interpretive strategies in discussing the Mutt and Jute episode. On the one hand, scholars such as Bernard Benstock (1963), Kimberly Devlin (1983), and William York Tindall (1969) have assimilated Mutt and Jute to the other paired males who figure at various points in the book—most notably, Muta and Juva in chapter 17—and whose Wakean archetype is the Shem-Shaun polarity.[11] On the other hand, the dialogue between Mutt and Jute has been viewed as an anti-communicative situation in which language regresses into unintelligibility by way of its prehistoric and precolonial past. Thus John Bishop (1986) characterizes Mutt and Jute as figures "who babble and stammer imperceptively like Vico's men" (194)—those "mute primitives" of Vico's divine age that "like so many Mutts and Jutes . . . communicate by grunts, gestures, hieroglyphs, coats of arms, and fables" (Tindall 1969: 9). Tindall goes so far as to suggest that "[c]ommunication between Mutt and Jute, Irishman and invader, proves impossible, for one is 'jeffmute' and the other hardly 'haudibble'" (43).

There are important grounds, however, for insisting on the specificity of the episode; these same grounds do much to support my claim that Mutt and Jute's remarks illuminate the possibilities as well as the problems of communication. In the first place, the episode acquires special significance by being placed near the opening of the *Wake*. The dialogue functions in effect as a paradigm for understanding other communicative acts embedded in the text, as well as the global discourse situation corresponding to *Finnegans Wake* as a whole.[12] Along the same lines, I would urge that Joyce confers prehistoric attributes on Mutt and Jute just because their talk is in a sense an archaeology of human communication—an investigation of the conditions under which discourse has become possible, both in the history of the species at large and in the context of the *Wake* itself.[13] Furthermore, the passages that frame their encounter suggest why researchers should resist designating Mutt and Jute as mere speakers of gobbledygook. Immediately before the dialogue Joyce writes that "The babbelers with their thangas vain have been (confusium hold them!) they were and went" (15.13–14); immediately after, he writes, in quasi-telegrammatic parlance, of "curios of signs (please stoop) in this allaphbed" (18.17–18), such that "When a part so ptee does duty for the holos we soon grow to use of an allforabit" (18.36–19.2). Along Joyce's evolutionary continuum, then, Mutt and Jute's interchange lies somewhere between a properly babelian confusion of tongues, and the telecommunicational technologies made possible by the advent of alphabets.

In this connection, note that Mutt and Jute are represented as participating in "that basic face-to-face conversational context in which all humans acquire language" (Levinson 1983: 63), and that John Lyons has termed the "canonical situation of utterance": "this involves one-one, or one-many, signalling in the phonic medium along the vocal-auditory channel, with all the participants present in the actual situation able to see one another and to perceive the associated non-vocal paralinguistic features of their utterances, and each assuming the role of sender and receiver in turn" (quoted in Levinson 1983: 63). Significantly, though, Mutt and Jute's canonical situation of utterance is *represented* through the medium of written discourse. Again, the text concerns itself, metacommunicatively, with the modes and principles of communication. As Elizabeth Closs Traugott and Mary Louise Pratt suggest (1980: 45), *Finnegans Wake* is a text that persistently exploits the gap between spoken and written discourse, preserving in its verbal texture a sort of iconic heritage of earlier forms of English (as well as forms deriving from other languages), and punning off homonyms, in ways that spoken discourse does not permit. In this connection, Joyce's pun "abcedminded" (18.17) iconically and phonetically connotes a post-alphabetic orientation (and the "absentmindedness" or non-immediacy of which written discourse is perhaps both symptom and cause), but it also incorporates the Old English word for *alphabet* itself (*abecede*). What could be termed the global creolization of Joyce's discourse—elements of some forty different languages pass through a text in which English is an only fitfully "superstrate" or dominant language (Traugott and Pratt 1980: 363)—further attests to Joyce's exploitation of the richer iconicity and greater manipulability of written as opposed to spoken language (Biber 1988: 101–69). Mutt, his own name indicating a highly creolized identity, indicates that the episode itself attempts to come to grips with the evolutionary trend stretching from orality to literacy. As Mutt notes, the spread of written discourse marks not the death but rather the memorialization of oral culture, a "sound seemetery" (17.35) in which written words are inscribed with the ancient legacy of speech.

My larger point, however, is that Joyce's episode should be viewed as an archaeology of intelligible discourse that does not wholly exempt itself from the commitment to intelligibility. Viewed in light of what researchers in pragmatics and discourse analysis have characterized as a crucial interdependence of coherence and context, the conversational mechanisms set into play by Mutt and Jute take on a new aspect. More specifically, the episode can be construed as an extended meditation on how coherence is not a primitive feature of discourse; as the episode suggests, rather, coherence in discourse is the result of contextualizing operations triggered but not wholly determined by the things people say to one another. It is not just that, by multiplying interpretive contexts for Mutt and Jute's remarks, Joyce's text broadens what Gumperz (1982) has called those "culturally possible lines of reasoning" (160) along which human conversations evolve. Joyce's suggestion, furthermore, is that by framing communicative acts centered on the act of communication itself, cultures can increase the scope of what those cultures view as coherent, as reasonable. In short, metacommunicative texts such as Joyce's participate in what I have elsewhere described as an ongoing *rapprochement* between universal grammar and narrative form—a more or less explicit and recoverable conceptual affiliation between language theory and literary experimentation (Herman 1995a).

Dimensions of (Joycean) Discourse

From the start, Mutt and Jute's is a conversation about conversations. Among the topics of their discourse are strategies and procedures for establishing discourse topics. Thus, to adopt for a moment not Gricean but rather Jakobsonian terminology, Mutt and Jute's opening remarks perform both metalingual and phatic functions: the interlocutors check up both on the code to be used for communication and on the physical (in this case, auditory) channel conducting messages from addressor to addressee.[14] Mutt's first concern is to determine what language Jute speaks: "You tollerday donsk? N. You tolkatiff scowegian? Nn. You spigotty anglease? Nnn. You phonio saxo? Nnnn. Clear all so! 'Tis a Jute" (16.5–8).[15] In turn, Jute seeks to confirm whether Mutt is in fact receiving the messages made possible by their mutually stipulated code, and whether he himself will be able to receive Mutt's messages:

Jute.—Are you jeff?

Mutt.—Somehards.

Jute.—But you are not jeffmute?

Mutt.—Noho. Only an utterer.

Jute.—Whoa? Whoat is the mutter with you?

Mutt.—I became a stun a stummer.

Jute.—What a hauhauhauhaudibble thing, to be cause! (16.12–18)

A few lines later Jute conducts another phatic checkup: "You that side of your voise are almost inedible to me" (16.23). In general, the episode unfolds as a read that is also a *Rede*—in German, a speech or a conversation. The text itself represents the activity of reading as a version of more broadly conversational activity: "(Stoop) if you are abcedminded, to this claybook.... Can you rede (since We and Thou had it out already) its world?" (18.17–19). Writing likewise figures as a form of conversational practice: "He who runes may rede it on all fours" (18.6–7).

Besides including conversation as one of its privileged themes, however, the episode as a literary dialogue also enacts techniques for conversing. To put the same point another way, the text is the record of a hypothetical discourse situation, one whose formal peculiarities force recipients to re-evaluate their own conversational models and stereotypes. As Schiffrin (1990a) has it, "Conversations in literary discourse . . . are less representative of actual language use than of models of communicative competence"; conversations represented in literary works such as Joyce's are, according to Schiffrin, "idealized representations of what a conversation should be like" (131). I would emend the latter part of Schiffrin's formulation, however, such that it reads "idealized representations of what a conversation should, might, or could conceivably be like." That is, metacommunicative texts such as Joyce's hold up a range of conversational methods and models for display, encouraging reflection on the whole gamut of interpretive principles undergirding communicative competence.

To highlight some of the metacommunicative dimensions of Joyce's discourse, my next three subsections invoke discourse-analytic categories developed by language theorists in their effort to capture the logic of conversation. At issue are *adjacency pairs*, *turn-taking procedures*, and *topic boundaries*.[16] Using these categories as descriptive guidelines, I work toward an account of the Mutt and Jute episode as evoking a storyworld in which acts of saying bear reflexively on the "real-world" communicative acts that are in turn used to make sense of the episode. In other words, Joyce's is a fictional dialogue that foregrounds the cognitive, interactional, and linguistic resources on which human beings draw in order to engage in dialogue in general.

Adjacency Pairs

Adjacency pairs are typically defined as paired utterances issued by alternating speakers, "of which question-answer, greeting-greeting, offer-acceptance, apology-minimization [of the offense], etc., are prototypical" (Levinson 1983: 303). As Harvey Sacks, Emanuel A. Schegloff, and Gail Jefferson (1974) put it in their pathbreaking essay "A Simplest Systematics for the Organization of Turn-Taking for Conversation,"

> By contrast with [ceremonies, debates, and other such] speech-exchange systems, the turn-taking organization for conversation makes no provision for the content of any [conversational] turn [or "move"], nor does it constrain what is (to be) done in any turn.... But this is not to say that there are no constraints on what may be done in any turn.... [T]he non-fixedness of what parties say should be modified by noting a bias operative in it. The group of allocation techniques which we have called "current speaker selects next" cannot be used in just any utterance or utterance-type whatever. Rather, there is a set of utterance-types, adjacency pair first parts, that can be used to accomplish such a selection; and with the constraint to employ one of those, there are constraints on what a party can say. (710–11)

In this connection, note that Joyce's use of the *Mutt and Jeff* comic strip as an intertext for the episode creates a generic expectation of discourse

Dialogues and Styles 185

in which adjacency pairs will play an important role. Mutt and Jeff were designed to be cartoon versions of vaudeville comic teams trading remarks on stage.[17] Much of the humor of Bud Fisher's comic strip thus derived from Mutt and Jeff's attempts to get the better of one another in argument and in practical jokes. (In one instance, Jeff's wise-guy antics cause Mutt to be burned and suffer excruciating pain, via a barber's steaming hot towel.) Thus Joyce's allusion to the strip creates a context for the "verbal dueling," or "competitive use of language in focused interaction" (McDowell 1985: 203; cf. Labov 1972b; Longacre 1983: 43–76); such banter is one of the hallmarks of an episode in which the discourse participants "excheck a few strong verbs weak oach eather yapyazzard abast the blooty creeks" (16.8–9). Mutt and Jeff's conversation, in other words, is a discourse genre premised on interpersonal conflict (Bavelas, Rogers, and Millar 1985). It stages what Schiffrin (1985) calls "oppositional argument," or "an interaction in which an opposition between speakers creates an extended polarization that is negotiated through a conversation," versus "rhetorical argument," or "a discourse through which a [single] speaker justifies a disputable position" (41).[18] By instantiating a sort of conversational stereotype, operative across both the productions of popular culture and avant-garde literary texts, the comic strip guides readers' interpretation of Mutt and Jute's discourse. Specifically, the stereotype helps recipients comprehend the quasi-ritualistic exchange of what can be recognized as more or less confrontational questions ("Are you jeff?" "somehards" [16.12–13]) and evaluations ("Pride, O pride, thy prize!"; "'Stench!" [17.30–31]). Yet by focusing attention on the process by which such discourse "frames" enable interlocutors to make sense of a current exchange, Joyce's text suggests that what might seem to be conversational primitives—elements of conflict, dispute, banter, and invective—are rather patterns in discourse that prior models teach readers and interlocutors to recognize as well as perpetuate. The episode can be read as a dispute because of its form and because of readers' sense that stretches of discourse cast in that form typically signify dispute.

Adjacency pairs form the minimal units, as it were, of such ritualized or quasi-ritualized abuse, which in turn forms only part of the conversational frame embedding Mutt and Jute's individual utterances. Having prepared readers for the entrance of "this carl [i.e., Jute] on the kopje in pelted thongs" (15.29)—and "What a quhare soort of mahan" he is

(16.1)[19] — Mutt likewise sets up the greeting-greeting adjacency pair that initiates their discourse:

> Jute. — Yutah!
> Mutt. — Mukk's pleasurad. (16.10–11)

Here, the expectation that a greeting follows a greeting, both in vaudeville and in discourse at large, allows readers to negotiate the lexical and phonetic peculiarities of the passage. More precisely, the format of the initial exchange triggers, but does not fully account for, a reading of Mutt and Jute's first, semi-garbled remarks as a salutation. What accounts for that reading are readers' own assumptions about the format of greetings. The same penchant for pattern-recognition enables recipients to identify, and interpret, a number of question-answer adjacency pairs also featured in the episode. After Mutt informs Jute that he "became a stun a stummer" (16.17), Jute responds by asking, "How, Mutt?" (16.18–19).

> Mutt. — Aput the buttle, surd.
> Jute. — Whose poddle? Wherein?
> Mutt. — The Inns of Dungtarf where Used awe to be he. (16.23)

The reason why it would be very difficult to program a computer to read these highly atypical linguistic strings as genuine questions and answers, and why human processors by contrast make sense of them in just those terms, is that readers approach the passage with what might called a presumption of coherence (a.k.a. the Cooperative Principle), which is very hard to translate into machine-readable algorithms.[20] That presumption allows readers to delimit relevant contextual information; in the case at hand, it can be hypothesized that Mutt is blaming his being a "stummer" or stammerer on his fancy for the bottle, but not on butts, puddles, paddles, pods, or poodles. For it would place unusually severe demands on readers' background knowledge and powers of inference to arrive at a viable causal link between, for example, small, well-groomed dogs and a speech disorder.

Yet — and this is the crucial point — at the same time that Joyce's text reinforces the necessity of making a presumption of coherence in interpreting Mutt and Jute's discourse, the episode also compels readers to examine that presumption's force and scope. Given the lexical profile of the lines just quoted, one can only tentatively, not absolutely, exclude butts, poodles, and puddles from the set consisting of likely reasons for

Mutt's stammering. Likewise, when Jute asks "Wid wad for a norse like?" and Mutt replies "Somular with a bull on a clompturf" (17.8–9), recipients are prone to draw on contextual information (once they have it at their disposal) about both the Duke of Wellington and Brian Boru's victory at Clontarf. On the basis of such information, conjoined with Mutt's remark, readers can draw the implicature that Mutt construes Wellington and Brian as historical and conceptual analogues, as "somular." But Joyce's text also encourages recipients to second-guess that very implicature; the text only partly prompts readers to foreground Wellington and Brian over other, only partly virtualized contexts for interpretation, including whatever has to do with wads, clumps, norsemen, and somnolence. In general, the text suggests how adjacency pairs—arguably among the most common conversational patterns of all—are not simply built into discourse. Such patterns, rather, are something that participants construct, and cannot help but construct, *through* discourse.

By compelling readers to interpret as adjacency pairs a series of stichomythic utterances whose semantic relationships are at best highly mediated, the episode illuminates the constraints on conversational turns described by Sacks, Schegloff, and Jefferson (1974). In proportion as the genre of speech exchange known as conversation relaxes constraints on the *content* of individual turns (711), conversation comes to depend on the *formatting* or *organization* of turns for its functioning and coherence, such that "[t]urn-taking organization at least partially controls the understanding of utterances" (728). Likewise Joyce's nonstandard adjacency pairs—his use of discourse tokens that are difficult to subsume under paired utterance types—suggests that meaning and organization in discourse are crucially interdependent, with meaning (and coherence) being a function of organization and vice versa. The organization of a discourse, to put this point another way, is not merely a reflection of its meaning, but rather helps constitute it. A closer examination of turn taking in the Mutt and Jute episode may further clarify the nature of this interdependence between the structures and functions of discourse elements.

Turn Taking

As was indicated in the previous section, adjacency pairs are just part of a larger system for the allotment of conversational moves or "turns."

Collectively, and under the auspices of Sacks, Schegloff, and Jefferson's "Simplest Systematics," these techniques for allocating the resources of talk have been called turn-taking procedures—procedures, that is, for the apportionment of conversations into turns that are divvied up among different participants. Thus, as Levinson (1983) puts it, "One way of looking at the rules [for talk] is as a sharing device, an 'economy' operating over a scarce resource, namely control of the 'floor.' Such an allocational system will require minimal units (or 'shares') over which it will operate, such units being the units from which turns at talk are constructed" (297). Classically conceived, "the turn-taking organization of conversation . . . obliges its participants to display to each other, in a turn's talk, their understanding of other turns' talk. . . . [A] turn's talk will be heard as directed to a prior turn's talk, unless special techniques are used to locate some other talk to which it is directed" (Sacks, Schegloff, and Jefferson 1974: 728). Turn taking, then, is just another way of describing what people who are talking to one another do when they intuit that it is time for one person to stop talking and another to begin.

But consider the following set of turns taken by Mutt and Jute at the very end of their encounter:

> Mutt.—O'c'stle, n'wc'stle, tr'c'stle, crumbling! Sell me sooth the fare for Humblin! Humblady Fair. But speak it allsosiftly, moulder! Be in your whisht!
>
> Jute.—Whysht?
>
> Mutt.—The gyant Forficules with Amni the fay.
>
> Jute.—Howe?
>
> Mutt.—Here is viceking's graab.
>
> Jute.—Hwaad!
>
> Mutt.—Ore you astoneaged, jute you?
>
> Jute.—Oye am thonthorstrok, thing mud. (18.6–16)

Some of these turns form question-answer adjacency pairs of the sort discussed in the previous subsection. What I wish to focus on more particularly here, however, is Joyce's use of typographical cues specific to dialogue.[21] Without the typographical cues—including punctuation, line breaks, and, of course, the name affixed to each utterance—recipients would be hard-pressed to identify Mutt and Jute's contributions as turns at all. Prima facie it is hard to determine in what sense the two interlocutors are taking turns—what joint conversational purpose their individual utterances might be working toward. But the presence of conversational cues in the text prompts readers to model, at least hypothetically, a discourse situation that spans an unusually rich semantic domain over the course of an unusually small number of conversational moves. Mutt and Jute's exchange encompasses Dublin's heraldic designs, earwigs, the ancient Norse parliament in Ireland, the Danish word for *what* (*hvad*), and so on. A turn, in this context, does the work that an entire lecture on escutcheonry or bugs or history would do in another context. In this way, Joyce's text again courts recipients' presumption of coherence—in this case, their assumption that Mutt and Jute's discourse unfolds as a series of nonrandomly generated turns—but at the same time it sketches out an interchange consisting of turns that themselves have the informational content of whole discourses. Reading the episode thus reminds readers that, although interlocutors invariably structure conversations into turns—or interpret them as being so structured—nonetheless the scope or richness of what counts as a turn will vary across different contexts of talk.

Two issues, then, present themselves here: first, Joyce's use of typographical cues to signal that the episode in fact comprises a system of speech exchange; and second, Joyce's emphasis on what might be called the functional overdetermination of individual turns—on the way turns could in principle always do more in a discourse than (strictly speaking) the economy of speech allocation permits. These two features of Joyce's text work against each other. Through the inquits (i.e., the attributions of speech now to Mutt, now to Jute), punctuation, and other typographical cues the text provides a discontinuous chunking, as it were, of discourse that is always reasserting its continuousness, its polyfunctionality, its intractability vis-à-vis the economy of talk set up by a system of speech exchange divided into alternating turns. Interestingly, for internal reasons the classical model of turn-taking procedures lacks the conceptual resources for handling what can be called the semantic density or functional overdetermination of individual turns. Since the focus of Sacks, Schegloff, and Jefferson's "Simplest Systematics" is on the contribution of turn taking to interlocutors' comprehension of an ongoing discourse, their analysis minimizes the importance of content per se relative to conversational coherence.[22] Joyce's text, by contrast, suggests that the organization of discourse into turns—the economy of talk—always operates within or against another economy that can be called "informational." The presumption of coherence that delimits what contextual information participants take into account when designing or interpreting a turn, and that disposes them to view a chunk of discourse *as* a turn in the first place, has a "cost" that can be measured in terms of the relative redundancy or obviousness of their talk. To put the matter another way, and as Grice himself recognized, certain of the conversational maxims required by the Cooperative Principle may at certain times conflict with other maxims *also* required by that same principle (Grice 1989: 26–30), so that in the interest of orderliness of presentation, for example, interlocutors may on occasion have to sacrifice informativeness of content.

My point is that Joyce's text enacts the tension between these two competing economies of talk—call them the economies of cohesiveness and of informativeness—precisely by compelling readers to interpret a sequence of non-obviously related utterances as turns comprised by an ongoing conversation. Of course, other dialogues contained in the book (for example, the washerwomen's conversation in the "Anna Livia Plurabelle" chapter [196–216]) also contain utterances that are difficult to characterize as conversational turns, but that readers must nonetheless interpret as elements of a system of speech exchange. Yet in the Mutt and Jute episode Joyce's use of the typographical cues already mentioned highlight, with special force, the tension between cohesiveness and informativeness in which and by means of which all talk unfolds. (Once more, the placement of the Mutt and Jute episode near the beginning of *Finnegans Wake* is of crucial importance in this connection.) Joyce's ordered alternation of semantically saturated turns—a stichomythic pattern enforced and regulated by the inquits and other cues—again serves a metacommunicative purpose. Specifically, the episode reminds recipients that the system of speech exchange is, as Sacks, Schegloff, and Jefferson (1974) put it, a "local management system" that is also an "interactionally managed system," subjecting the variability of the size and order of turns "to the control of the parties to any conversation" (725–26). What makes for conversational coherence will vary with the informational needs of specific participants during specific stretches of talk; conversely, a (segment of) discourse will be more or less informative according to the success of particular discussants at achieving and maintaining cohesiveness across a particular string of utterances. Analogously, the format of the Mutt and Jute episode suggests that whereas the semantic density of any conversational turn is in principle infinite, that density or richness is pragmatically constrained by the presumption of coherence that here manifests itself typographically in the text.

Topic Shifts

The sometimes encyclopedic profile of Mutt and Jute's remarks points to another important conversational phenomenon—namely, the way interlocutors talk about certain topics, and moreover manage topic shifts, when they are conversing. At issue here is just what Mutt and Jute are talking *about*, at any given point in their discourse, and also how they move on, together, from that to a different topic, or to a different dimension of the current topic. There is in fact a vast body of research on the problem of topic, including any number of attempts to analyze sentences and discourses into topics and comments, or themes and rhemes, or presuppositions and focuses.[23] Van Dijk (1981), for example, defines topic (and the related notions of *episode*, *theme*, and *gist*) as a "global macroproposition" under which a sequence of subpropositions are subsumed in a way that makes them jointly cohesive (180). By contrast, Diane Blakemore (1988), working in the Gricean versus the text-grammatical tradition, suggests that accounts such as van Dijk's fail to recognize "the context dependence of the relations which contribute toward the macro-structure of the text" (234). Instead, Blakemore insists that "context is involved in the recognition of the entailment relations in terms of which the topic of discourse is defined" (234).[24] But what should be stressed is that, generally speaking, discourse participants can "distinguish within a sentence [for example] a part which is somehow 'given,' or 'known,' or 'assumed,' and a part which is commenting on the first part" (van Dijk 1972: 109). Furthermore, "between two contiguous pieces of discourse which are intuitively considered to have two different 'topics,'" "there should be a point at which the shift from one topic to the next is marked" (Brown and Yule 1983: 94–95).

One way to account for the notorious difficulty of *Finnegans Wake* is to say that its design hinders any ready assortment of its discourse components into topics and comments; the text's most abiding topic, in a sense, is that the *way* people talk about things determines *what* they are talking about. Take, for example, this segment of Mutt and Jute's exchange:

> Mutt.—Has? Has at? Hasatency? Urp, Boohooru! Booru Usurp! I trumple from rath in mine mines when I rimimirim!
>
> Jute.—One eyegonblack. Bisons is bisons. Let me fore all your hasitancy cross your qualm with trink gilt. Here have sylvan coyne, a piece of oak. Ghinees hies good for you.
>
> Mutt.—Louee, louee! How wooden I not know it, the intellible greytcloak of Cedric Silkyshag! (16.26–34)

It is possible to glimpse topics, or at least fragments of topics, in the coded references to Brian Boru ("Boohooru! Booru Usurp!"); to the slogan used to advertise Guinness ale ("Ghinees hies good for you," or "Guinness is good for you"); and to the wooden nickels introduced by the British, in the eighteenth century, in an effort to debase the currency of the Irish ("sylvan coyne, a piece of oak"). But Joyce's text frustrates any attempt to divide the discourse into exactly what Mutt and Jute are saying, on the one hand, and exactly what they are saying *about* those discourse topics, on the other hand.

Again, however, Joyce's inclusion of Mutt and Jute's dialogue at the start of the book suggests the need not for abandoning, but rather for reconsidering, the topic-comment distinction and the notion of topic shift. Mutt and Jute's is a dialogue that models readers' own dialogic interaction with the *Wake*. In each case the participants can only partly delimit current discourse topics from other concerns with at least some bearing on the current topics; in each case, too, participants cannot be absolutely sure where previous topics end and new ones begin. But there is considerable evidence for the view that *all* verbal interaction occurs under such constraints—that interlocutors can never be completely certain about what they are discussing with one another, nor when they have stopped talking about that and started talking about something else. Joyce's text helps recipients model an understanding of discourse topics as always only emergent constructs interactively elaborated—not chunks of essential information underlying secondary and derivative remarks, but rather constantly renegotiated agreements concerning which remarks are to function as expansions, modifications, negations, and so forth, of other remarks in the context of a given discourse. By making it hard to figure out just what Mutt and Jute are saying to one another and when (and why), Joyce's text suggests that discourse analysts cannot and should not hope to recover communicative content through a simple algorithm assorting sets of utterances into topics and comments. Instead, they should work toward an understanding of the contextual parameters that determine which elements of communicative content are likely to *function*, in a given discourse situation, as topics or as comments. The episode thus uses a particular (if hypothetical) discourse situation to enable readers to build a model of topics and topic shifts that Levinson describes in the following terms:

> topical coherence cannot be thought of as residing in some independently calculable procedure for ascertaining (for example) shared reference across utterances. Rather, topical coherence is something constructed across turns by the collaboration of participants. What needs then to be studied is how potential topics are introduced and collaboratively ratified, how they are marked as "new," "touched off," "misplaced" and so on, how they are avoided or competed over and how they are collaboratively closed down. (315)

Rather than comprising an all-out assault on conversational coherence, Joyce's text is therefore metacommunicative through and through. Here, part of the process of storyworld reconstruction involves revisiting—that is, updating and enriching—the models on which interlocutors rely when they participate in conversations. What I have argued to be the metacommunicative impetus of Joyce's text, furthermore, gives point to the more or less maddening circumlocutions of which episodes like Mutt and Jute consist. The format of the text stigmatizes the search for pure communicative content—meaning without context, information without processing—as nostalgia for what never was. But readers should resist drawing the further inference that the Mutt and Jute episode is symptomatic of Joyce's ongoing effort to dismantle, from within language, our most entrenched ideas about the communicative functions of language. Instead, by making its interpreters talk about the contexts in which they talk, the episode enriches readers' conception of what discourse can be and do.

Styles

Not just fictional dialogues but also representations of speech styles can perform a metacommunicative role in narratives. Like dialogues, representations of styles cue recipients to draw on their prior models of communicative behavior to make sense of acts of saying in storyworlds, while also inviting a reassessment of those very models. As I go on to argue in connection with my second tutor text, Wharton's *The House of Mirth*, style in fiction is not just a device for characterization or a narratorial format but a way of encoding modes of alignment, opposition, and conflict operating at other levels of narrative structure as well. Style is content. More than this, however, Wharton's styles undermine the commonsensical idea that one selects from among various available styles to communicate who and what one is. Rather, her text shows that it is *by* communicating, *by* stylizing, that interlocutors take on a role as selves. Through verbal interaction participants become the centers of subjectivity that in turn help orient communicative behavior. Content is style.

Toward a Sociological Stylistics

In examining fictional styles in *The House of Mirth*—more precisely, the novel's use of *style shifts* to organize and mark participant roles—I explore a research problem identified quite early on by M. M. Bakhtin. Around 1935, Bakhtin (1981a) wrote that "[a]ny stylistics capable of dealing with the distinctiveness of the novel as a genre must be a *sociological stylistics*" (1981a: 300). Ironically, however, Bakhtin's own dispute with classical stylistic models, his sense that traditional linguistics had little to offer to those concerned with the dialogic profile of utterances, may have at first hindered the cross-fertilization of literary stylistics with later linguistic research on style. For example, one of Bakhtin's chief claims is that the polyphonic texture of the novel cannot be accounted for by way of traditional stylistic models. These models have, according to Bakhtin, turned a deaf ear to the social life of language, to the social provenance of the "voices" represented in the novel and distributed between authors, narrators, and characters. Bakhtin was right in pointing out that Saussurean linguistics, by foregrounding *la langue* over *la parole* and by placing the situated production of utterances outside the domain of linguistic science, had little to say about how a novelistic style might resonate with social meanings. But Bakhtin set an unfortunate precedent (in his early work, at least[25]) by divorcing the study of novelistic style in particular from the broader enterprise of analyzing style in language generally. Discourse in the novel could, with the help of this precedent, be seen as special, unique, characterized by a literariness that somehow set it apart from people's everyday communicative resources. In turn, theorists of the novel influenced by Bakhtin had every reason to underestimate the potential of linguistics to evolve models for understanding style in fiction. Yet researchers can come to terms with the social meanings of style only by developing ways to identify and describe what counts as a style in the first place. A sociological stylistics must still be a stylistics; it will not do to arrest the dialectic of language and society at either pole. Hence, in the study of fictional as well as everyday discourse, positing that all utterances are socially situated does not obviate the need to work toward an understanding of speech styles as formally patterned. Rather, as modern-day research on style suggests, patterning in language is precisely what gives utterances their distinctive social meaning, situating them contrastively against alternative ways of speaking.

Recently, there have been some important advances made in the linguistic analysis of style in fiction, heralding a stylistics of the sort envisioned (if not realized) by Bakhtin. Thanks to the influence of several pathbreaking works in the field (e.g., Fowler 1977, 1986; Leech and Short 1981; Page 1973), theorists of literature have finally begun to consult post-Saussurean scholarship on discourse and style.[26] The result has been a more sustained exploration of discourse-level properties shared by literary and nonliterary texts. A crucial test case, in this respect, is the question of (shifts into and out of) social styles. Not the novel distinctively, of course, but all communicative behavior involves styles, symbolically significant collocations of formal features, whose social meanings need to be investigated. Thus a truly sociological stylistics requires that, in examining style as a transdisciplinary object of study, researchers pool the resources of literary, narrative, and language theory. In particular, theorists can gain a better understanding of the forms and functions of discourse in the novel by attending to recent sociolinguistic and discourse-analytic research on style. This work helps underscore how, in *The House of Mirth*, Wharton represents a range of social styles and uses style shifts to index, among other things, class- and gender-based identities. Strategically managed shifts into and out of speech styles reveal a mutually constitutive relationship between style and identity, patterns of usage and contexts of use. In turn, making sense of the communicative acts represented in Wharton's storyworld necessitates a more general rethinking of the interrelations between styles, contexts, and identities.

Varieties, Registers, and Styles

A brief synopsis of the recent work on style in discourse will faciliate a closer look at Wharton's fictional styles. Indeed, with the advent of sociolinguistic and ethnographic approaches to language study in the 1960s, researchers have sought to distinguish phenomena sometimes grouped together under the single heading of *style*. Specifically, they have tried to demarcate *styles* from *registers* and *varieties* (or *dialects*).[27] All three terms denote patterns of usage that can be contrasted with other such patterns along phonological, grammatical, lexical, and pragmatic dimensions. A variety or dialect, however, is often characterized as a pattern of usage shared by a particular speech community. A dialect thus functions to mark off a speech community, ethnolinguistically, from other, more or less proximate speech communities. Consider, for example, southern varieties of American English. Two of the hallmarks of southern varieties are phonological in nature: the merger of the /I/ and /e/ vowels before nasals (as in the words *pin* and *pen*), and the monopthongization of the /ay/ dipthong in words such as *time* (pronounced [taːm] instead of [taɪm]) (Wolfram and Schilling-Estes 1998: 69). These differences of pronunciation distinguish southern dialects from neighboring varieties. But there are also dialect differences within dialect differences, enabling finer-grained distinctions between microvarieties within an overarching regional, social, or ethnic macrovariety. Thus, members of a Native American speech community in Robeson County, North Carolina, set themselves apart from Anglo-American and African American residents of this tri-ethnic area by attaching an inflectional -s to habitual *be* (e.g., *She bes doing it* versus *She be doing it*). Drawing on semiotic possibilities built into the morphology and syntax of English, these Native American speakers have created a subvariety of English whose distinctiveness vis-à-vis surrounding dialects confirms the community's sense of its own linguistic and cultural uniqueness (Wolfram and Schilling-Estes 1998: 182–83; Wolfram and Dannenberg 1999).

Meanwhile, registers are typically construed as language varieties "viewed with respect to [their] context of use" (Biber and Finegan 1994a: 4). The term *register* thus refers to "situationally defined varieties, as opposed to *dialect*, which refers to varieties associated with different speaker groups" (Biber 1994: 51; Ferguson 1994: 20–21; Hymes 1974: 59; Wolfram and Schilling-Estes 1998: 216). Some researchers have claimed further that registers are topic specific—that is, patterns of usage that manifest themselves "when certain topics are discussed by people with shared background knowledge and assumptions about those topics" (Cheshire 1992: 325; cf. Rickford and McNair-Knox 1994). In general, registers are forms of speech behavior anchored in regularly recurring communicative situations (Ferguson 1994: 20). Shirley Brice Heath and Juliet Langman (1994), for example, have argued that structural features of the register of coaching make it especially suited to fostering shared thinking. These features include not only discourse-level structures such as eventcasts or hypothetical narratives about what might happen in a game situation, but also syntactic structures such as *if-then* conditionals, tag questions (*But the infielders should always be ready. Okay?*), and strategic alternations between inclusive and exclusive uses of the pronoun *we* (Heath and Langman 1994: 90–93, 95–100). Other communicative situations, such as conference talks, sales pitches, and sermons, breed other, less participation-inviting registers.

But what, then, is style? Most generally, the term *style* has been used to differentiate language variation in the speech of individual speakers from language variation across different groups of speakers—that is, intraspeaker from interspeaker variation (Labov 1972c; Wolfram and Schilling-Estes 1998: 214). Style shifting occurs when a speaker shifts, for example, from casual to formal speech or vice versa, shifting from, say, *I wonder, do you happen to have any beer?* to *Give me a beer.* A number of markers allow speakers to recognize where these two utterances fall on the formal-casual stylistic continuum. Whereas the first utterance's lexical content and intonational contour mark it as an indirect speech act designed to minimize a threat to the recipient's face (Brown and Levinson 1987), it being a locutionary act with the surface form of an information-seeking question and the illocutionary force of a directive, the second utterance baldly issues a command, without benefit even of a mitigating *please*. Further, empirical studies suggest that stylistic variation, or what Dennis Preston (1991) calls the "variation space" created by the availability of a range of more or less formal styles, is in some sense parasitic on social class variation. In other words, in a survey of speech styles used by a group of middle- and upper-class speakers only, one can predict less stylistic variation than would be found in a survey of styles used by lower, lower-middle, middle, and upper-class speakers (Preston 1991; Bell 1984).

Is style therefore an epiphenomen of dialect? Actually, it is not clear whether styles can be distinguished from speech varieties or dialects in the first place (Wolfram and Schilling-Estes 1998: 216–17). A bidialectal speaker of a stigmatized nonstandard variety may find that, in order to shift toward a more formal style, he or she has to shift into the standard variety as well. The same holds for styles vis-à-vis registers. In ceasing my informal chat with a member of the audience and beginning my formal lecture at a conference or colloquium, I must arguably adopt a certain mind-numbing academic register in order to effectuate the new style. In short, the terms *dialect*, *register*, and *style* seem to denote overlapping but nonequivalent aspects of discourse usage; they can interact synergistically in a single speech production, indexing the speaker's membership (or claim to membership) in a particular social group, degree of familiarity with a particular type of communicative situation, and status-based need to be more or less formal in speaking with a particular interlocutor.

Style and Identity in *The House of Mirth*

In *The House of Mirth*, gender- and class-based identity is a locus where questions of group membership, competence within and across different sorts of communicative events, and considerations of status and power all intersect. At the novel's opening Lily Bart is, at twenty-nine, still an aspirant to the social and financial security that could be hers if she were to marry into the upper echelons of Old New York Society— however stultifying the marriageable representatives of Old Money (e.g., Percy Gryce) prove themselves to be. Wharton uses her protagonist to explore the injurious asymmetry of a social order in which, as Lily herself puts it, "a girl must [marry], a man may if he chooses" (Wharton 1994: 33). Thus, from the start, Wharton represents the world of early-twentieth-century New York as one experienced in radically different ways by women and men. The "same" setting, event, or configuration of characters is revealed to be not a stable, prelinguistic reality onto which social meanings are foisted verbally and after the fact, but rather a construct built on an ever-shifting basis of subculturally specific norms, presuppositions, beliefs, and inferences.

An ingenious shift in perspective midway through the first chapter (34–35) enables Wharton to portray how the world looks, first through the eyes of the aloof young bachelor Lawrence Selden and then from the vantage point of a woman no longer young by the standards of her peers. Selden, secure in his darkened, book-lined study, is the detached observer of Lily's exotic beauty, aestheticizing her as "a captured dryad subdued to the conventions of the drawing-room" (34). By contrast, though she is "not familiar with the moral code of bachelors' flathouses" (34), Lily knows that she has committed an indiscretion merely by accompanying Selden back to his apartment. Space itself is gendered here, and one and the same setting displays two different profiles simultaneously: a neutral field of observation for the male, a place of perilous exposure for the female. To retain the privilege of circulating herself on the marriage market, Lily must work very hard to keep up appearances and ward off even the most unfounded suggestion of impropriety.

The double standard for men and women—the fact that Selden's affair with Bertha Dorset does not disqualify him from marriage while the mere rumor of an affair between Lily and George Dorset is enough to stigmatize her irreparably—is one of the major sources of conflict in the novel and is encoded in the unfolding of events as well as in manipulations of narrative perspective. Gender, in this text, determines how strictly the sexual code is to be applied. Through its stylistic texture, however, Wharton's discourse also reveals that gender is itself the product of ways of seeing, thinking, and speaking, rather than preceding and explaining human conduct and speech. The novel thus inverts the process by which gender roles are mythologized, in Roland Barthes's (1972) sense of that term—that is, emptied of all history and contingency and reified into a transcendent ground for social interaction, an essence that predetermines men and women to act and talk in specific ways.[28] Instead, Wharton uses style shifts to suggest that to be gendered male or female is to project oneself (and others) as such through stylized communicative acts.

All discourse usage, as already suggested, entails a style or range of styles, and every style commits one to a role—or, in Erving Goffman's terms, a "footing" (Goffman 1981; Herman 1998b, 2001b; Kiesling and Schilling-Estes 1998; Tannen and Wallat 1993)—vis-à-vis the roles implicitly assigned to one's interlocutors by way of stylistic choices. Through shifts of footings and roles, one can align oneself with certain (present or absent) addressees in favor of others. Or, as Goffman (1981) puts it, by changing their footing in discourse, participants change "the alignment that [they] take up to [themselves] and the others present as expressed in the way [they] manage the production or reception of an utterance" (128). It is in this spirit that Deborah Schiffrin (1994: 106–36) examines microinteractional details associated with "speaking for another," a discourse strategy by which one expresses solidarity with the person or principal whose "voice" one animates. Speaking for another is thus a way of "chipping in" without "butting in." More generally, on the basis of roles stylistically imputed to them, addressees can be projected as antagonists, passive lookers-on, partners in collusion, and so forth. Gender roles—modes of alignment and opposition between men and women—are in this sense built interactionally, on a moment-by-moment basis, through style shifts used to establish, limit, or otherwise regulate intersubjective rapport.[29]

Wharton's novel, in fact, features a broad range of social styles, with style shifts indexing conflicts based on class as well as gender. For example, when the charwoman, Mrs. Haffen, tries to blackmail Lily into buying letters actually exchanged between Selden and Bertha Dorset (110–15), Lily adopts a markedly formal style and an impeccably standard speech variety: "'Do you wish to see me?'. . . 'You have found something belonging to me?'. . . 'I don't understand; if this parcel is not mine, why have you asked for me? . . . 'I know nothing of these letters . . . I have no idea why you have brought them here' . . . 'I am sorry you have been in trouble'" (112–113). Here, despite one counterexample in the speech acts just quoted, one of the stylistic features creating an impression of formality in Lily's speech is the absence of contracted verb forms (e.g., Lily says *I am* rather than *I'm* and *you have* instead of *you've*). Further, at the pragmatic level as well as the level of grammar, Lily's style (which could also be described as, in part, a register) is one geared for interchanges between servants and their employers. She resorts to a style that is impolite, in the technical sense, insofar as it is marked by direct, potentially face-threatening questions issued from a position of social superiority. Intruding on what politeness theorists (e.g., Brown and Levinson 1987; cf. Buck 1996; Goffman 1955; Scollon and Scollon 1995) would call Mrs. Haffen's negative face wants, that is, her desire not to be imposed on by others, Lily uses a direct or impolite style to manage a delicate situation, countering any presumption of familiarity or social proximity on Mrs. Haffen's part.[30] Overall she casts herself in the role of a person occupying a socioeconomically superior and hence more powerful position than the would-be blackmailer, who speaks digressively and in a nonstandard dialect: "I brought'em [the letters] to you to sell, because I ain't got no other way of raising money. . . . I seen you talking to Mr. Rosedale on the steps that day you come out of Mr. Selden's rooms" (113).

Note, too, that Lily's speech style is much closer than Mrs. Haffen's to what might be termed the baseline narratorial style established by Wharton's heterodiegetic narrator. Whereas any speech report is in actual fact, as Deborah Tannen (1989) points out, an evaluative *reconstruction* of someone's speech, researchers need to focus more attention on the specifically stylistic aspects of constructed dialogue in literary as well as nonliterary discourse. Here, as in language use generally, what is different is what is salient. Hence I propose the following hypothesis about style shifts in the context of reported speech: *All other things being equal, a reported utterance is evaluated more negatively the more it differs from the degree of formality, type of speech variety, and mode of situational appropriateness of the style in which the report is couched.* In accordance with this hypothesis, the style adopted by the narrator in *The House of Mirth* works to align recipients with Lily and against Mrs. Haffen. The way speech styles subtly but systematically accomplish such alignments helps explain why some commentators have detected a class bias in Wharton's presentation of the social ills of New York (e.g., Robinson 1994).

But the same stylistic alignments explain why other commentators have found the novel to be an important instance of feminist critique. Wharton indexes certain discourse modes (and certain discourse users) as "masculine" by reporting the utterances of male characters—mainly Gus Trenor, Simon Rosedale, and George Dorset—in a style and a register quite distinct from the general narratorial style, from Lily's styles, and for that matter from the styles used by another prominent male character, Lawrence Selden. Indeed, most of the male characters are portrayed as using an altogether different expressive style than the one used by women. The male characters' discourse is often direct, informal, and marked by lexical items and collocations that can be characterized broadly and somewhat imprecisely as "slang," what with their strong group identity associations. Such discourse is shown to be the specialized vocabulary of a highly exclusive in-group, a parlance acquired in clubs built to keep out women (cf. Wharton 1994: 155–56).[31] That said, Selden, an educated professional whose technical legal consultations are, however, reported in indirect rather than direct discourse late in the novel (201–4), comes across as being perhaps Lily's closest stylistic match, male or female. Since his use of the register of legal business is reported rather than demonstrated, Selden's discourse, like Lily's, matches up quite closely with the default narratorial style and register. Likewise, Selden shuns the slang used by Trenor and Rosedale, for example, and maintains a level of formality that parallels Lily's own characteristic speech style. The two characters' shared overall preference for politeness—in the sense of indirectness—in discourse can be seen by comparing their utterances during the encounters that punctuate phases of Lily's descent along the scale of social estimation (26–34, 80–87, 141–42, 209–11, 261–64, 284–89).

The similarity of their styles, then, underscores the poignancy of Selden's and Lily's failure to make a meaningful connection.[32] But it also highlights that though people may be born with a sex, they are molded to assume a gender—in part by using styles to act in concert with or opposition to others who are likewise building a gender in style. Wharton is, after all, a female author orchestrating a wide range of social styles, the very text of the novel suggesting that a speaker's or a writer's sex is not a necessary condition for use of a particular speech style. But neither is it a sufficient condition, as exemplified by the convergence of Lily's and Selden's styles. In other words, Wharton's novel, in contrast with more or less essentialist theories about a distinct "women's language" (cf. Jespersen 1922; Lakoff 1975) but in line with more recent work on language and gender (Cameron and Coates 1988; Cameron, McAlinden, and O'Leary 1988; Coates 1993; Fairclough 1989, 1995; Romaine 1999), suggests that no discourse mode can be categorized as inherently masculine or feminine. Rather, Wharton's representations of speech styles reveal how communicative norms get constructed as gender specific by virtue of the way they create or suppress certain role possibilities, certain types of participant alignment. To put this last point another way, discourse, insofar as it is stylized, works actively to engender the men and women who use and interpret it.

Coates (1993: 106–40) reviews empirical work indicating differences in the learned interactive styles of men and women during mixed-sex conversations, including differences in the frequency of interruptions (men tend to interrupt female interlocutors more than women interrupt their male counterparts), hedged constructions (women tend to use hedges such as *he's wrong, I think* more often than men), and use of backchanneling (female interlocutors are more likely than males to display interest and engagement by saying *uh huh* or *really?* in response to a speaker who currently holds the floor). Thus it "seems that women and men have different sets of norms for conversational interaction, . . . that women and men may constitute distinct speech communities" (140; cf. Cameron, McAlinden, and O'Leary 1988). Wharton's novel suggests a similar disparity between men's and women's interactive styles; it, too, anchors the different role possibilities for males and females in the norms learned over the course of repeated interactions, which are in turn enabled by participants' more or less persistent adherence to the norms at issue. Thus the social situations that Lily finds most discomfiting and disempowering, the ones in which she is least able to take on an active contributing role, are those accompanied by styles that the novel pragmatically and lexically marks as masculine. At issue are speech styles whose users align themselves against—attempt to put themselves in a position of dominance or control over—those who use styles that the novel contrastively marks as feminine. This clash of styles in part *constitutes* the antagonistic structuring of men's and women's participant roles, rather than merely reflecting or signifying it. In other words, Wharton's representations of stylistic clashing place a question mark next to Halliday's (1978) hierarchical arrangement of first-order (or language-independent) versus second-order (or language-dependent) social roles (see note 27). Wharton's style shifts foreground modes of verbal interaction as primary, not secondary, determinants of self-other alignments.

Lily is shocked early on, for example, by one of Rosedale's characteristically bald, face-threatening questions: "How's your luck been going on Wall Street, by the way? I hear Gus pulled off a nice little pile for you last month" (121).[33] Similarly, alone with Lily for a moment at the opera, Trenor makes one of his importunate advances in an offensively direct, slang-laden style:

> Hang going to your aunt's, and wasting the afternoon listening to a lot of other chaps talking to you! You know I'm not the kind to sit in a crowd and jaw—I'd always rather clear out when that sort of circus is going on. But why can't we go off somewhere on a little lark together—a nice quiet little expedition like that drive at Bellomont, the day you met me at the station. (124)

And in the most brutal confrontation described in the novel, Trenor adopts a style radically at odds with the narrator's or Lily's typical styles when he implicates that Lily must give him sexual favors to "pay back" the money he made for her on the stock market:

> I don't doubt you've accepted as much before—and chucked the other chaps as you'd like to chuck me. I don't care how you settled your score with them—if you fooled 'em I'm that much to the good. Don't stare at me like that—I know I'm not talking the way a man is supposed to talk to a girl—but, hang it, if you don't like it you can stop me quick enough—you know I'm mad about you—damn the money, there's plenty more of it—if that bothers you . . . I was a brute, Lily—Lily! (149)

Here Wharton's repertoire of style-marking devices includes slangy words and phrases (e.g., *chucked, mad about you*), oaths (*hang it, damn the money*), and the hesitations and disfluencies signified by dashes—broken-off units of thought no doubt meant to represent the halting delivery of an inebriated, and lecherous, speaker. As Trenor himself indicates, the unprecedented directness and informality of his style, his blatant disregard of his interlocutor's negative face wants, reduces Lily to a staring silence. Judging from her subsequent reaction, it is also a terrified silence, and part of Lily's fear may stem from the sheer alienness of the communicative norms with which her own interactive style has come into conflict. More than this, though, Lily's encounter with Trenor reveals to her with frightening clarity the powerlessness of her own position in social space. The all-too-evident clash of styles exposes a social logic according to which women must respect the negative face wants of men in order to have a place in society, but men, particularly socially well-established men, need not extend the same respect to women. Thus, through Lily's interchanges with characters such as Rosedale and Trenor, Wharton highlights incompatible strategies for doing facework, that is, an asymmetrical observance of politeness requirements. Wharton's novel shows that discordant communicative norms, far from being secondary conflicts that are parasitic on some primary, prelinguistic division between those already equipped with a masculine or a feminine gender, do much to account for the antagonistic role relationships lived out by men and women from day to day.

Significantly, the communicative styles Wharton's novel marks as masculine occur not just in constructed dialogue or reported speech but also in contexts of psychonarration (Cohn 1978) or reported thought, as demonstrated by this passage: "Trenor felt himself wishing that his wife could see how other women treated him—*not battered wire-pullers like Mrs. Fisher, but a girl that most men would have given their boots to get such a look from*" (94, my emphasis). The narrator's report of Trenor's thoughts, again marked by slangy phrases and idioms (*wire-pullers, given their boots*), suggests that the speech style at issue has been internalized by the male characters and become a sort of "mindstyle," to use a term originally proposed by Roger Fowler (Fowler 1977, 1986; cf. Bockting 1994; Leech and Short 1981: 187–208). Trenor's is a way of speaking that reconfirms a way of seeing and vice versa. Yet the very fluidity with which Wharton shifts into and out of this way of seeing and speaking indicates that it is contingently, not necessarily, associated with men as a social group. The novel's proliferation of styles, its polyphony of voices, functions to show that who engages in what style is a matter of culture, not nature.

Styles, Roles, and the Role of Stylistics

In rethinking the scope and aims of classical theories of style—in attending to how such theories neglected sociocultural dimensions of novelistic discourse—researchers should not underestimate the potential of linguistic models to describe and explain the bearing of social styles on discourse in the novel. Minimally, communication consists of the interplay between two things: on the one hand, a linguistic code that is inherently variable; on the other hand, a set of socially defined contexts in which options made available by the code can be used to generate particularized, situated meanings. A style thus represents a socially symbolic patterning, at the discourse level, of features associated with the grammar, phonology, or lexicon of a language. Such patterning is what is involved in the use of a formal, an aggressive, a technical, or a "masculine" style to assume (and prompt others to assume) a certain role on the basis of one's communicative acts. Fictional discourse such as Wharton's *represents* the way styles foster roles and roles, styles.

Accordingly, if the study of style in language can and should inform the study of style in fiction, the converse proposition holds as well. An underexplored area of research for practitioners in the field of critical discourse analysis (e.g., Fairclough 1989, 1995), for example, is the consideration of fictional styles as a resource for analyzing speech styles in general. Most broadly, critical discourse analysis examines language in its relation to power and ideology, with power

> conceptualized both in terms of asymmetries between participants in discourse events, and in terms of unequal capacity to control how texts are produced, distributed and consumed (and hence the shapes of texts) in particular sociocultural contexts. A range of properties of texts is regarded as potentially ideological, including features of vocabulary and metaphors, grammar, presuppositions and implicatures, politeness conventions, speech-exchange (turn-taking) systems, generic structure, and style. (Fairclough 1995: 1–2)

Although my discussion of Wharton's fictional styles has touched on only a few of the questions relevant for critical discourse analysts, it does suggest the pertinence of fictional discourse representations for the study of how language imbricates itself with issues of power and ideology. For Fairclough (1995: 70–83), ideological forces can be located both in language *structures* and language *events*. Such forces can be detected, on the one hand, in the coding strategies that language makes available for people trying to make sense of and express propositions about their experiences. Thus grammatical options such as the choice of intransitive over transitive verb forms, or the passive over the active voice, can work to occlude aspects of human agency in ways that either support or undercut dominant ideologies about the nature and status of the self (Fairclough 1989: 169–96). In the context of a press briefing, *I made mistakes* is a very different sort of statement than *mistakes were made*. On the other hand, language events, including interviews, arguments, lectures, narratives, and other types of "actual discoursal practice," are more or less constrained by dominant social conventions, norms, and histories (Fairclough 1995: 71). When hauled into the police station for questioning, I can either actively challenge or else passively accept the turn-taking protocols that call for me to speak only when spoken to during the interrogation.

By the same token, Wharton's text explores the intersection of communicative styles with both language structures and language events. The discourse situations it represents can be decomposed into factors pertaining to the code as well as the process of communication, including relative standardness of dialect, degree of reliance on slang or occupation-based registers, relative formality of address, and relative proneness to respecting or violating negative face wants over the course of an interaction. Wharton's novel reveals these factors to be partially determinative of class and gender distinctions; the factors locate participants in a social space that is molded by ways of speaking and thinking, rather than being a transcendental, non- or prelinguistic ground for who and what we are. Hence, in fictions such as *The House of Mirth*, style shifts used by narrators reporting participants' utterances, or for that matter by participants reporting other participants' utterances, do not just help make fictional agents vivid and memorable. Beyond this, fictional styles invite reflection on how discourse is an instrument that can either work against or reinforce patterns of conflict—more or less unquestioned hierarchies and antagonisms—operative in society at large. Pointing to the inextricable interconnection between social identities and communicative styles, fictions such as Wharton's reveal that communication is not just the channeling back and forth of ideas, but a way of acting and being acted upon in the world. In this sense, too, discourse in the novel is metacommunicative, or discourse about discourse. Novels formally manipulate social styles to indicate how style as such is a jointly formal and social phenomenon.[34]

PART TWO
Narrative Macrodesigns

6

Temporalities

As I mentioned in the introduction, in the classical, structuralist narratological tradition—a research tradition that had its beginnings in Vladimir Propp's *Morphology of the Folktale* (1968) and Victor Shklovsky's (1990) analyses of plot structure before being systematized by French, Dutch, German, Israeli, and North American theorists in the 1960s–1980s—the distinction between story and discourse has proven to be an important and much-used resource for analysts of narrative. Despite its prevalence throughout the history of narratological research, however, the story/discourse distinction remains an analytic construct whose limits of applicability have yet to be established. The present chapter examines several narratives whose temporal structure suggests the need to enrich classical vocabularies—vocabularies that pose a distinction between, variously, story and discourse, *fabula* and *sjužet*, the what and the way, the narrated and the narrative, the form of content and the form of the expression. What is required is a finer-grained account of how textual cues can prompt interpreters to assign to events in the storyworld a place (relative to one another) in time, for one of the major factors bearing on the global design of storyworlds is the manner in which—or, for that matter, the extent to which—discourse cues prompt recipients to engage in a temporal ordering of events. Other key principles for narrative macrodesigns are discussed in the next three chapters. These include the way stories cue recipients to spatialize storyworlds—that is, to configure them as spatially structured mental models (chapter 7); the way this process of spatialization in turn enables, and is enabled by, strategies for perspective taking that support narrative comprehension (chapter 8); and the way narratives facilitate or impede contextual anchoring (chapter 9). Contextual anchoring is my term for the process by which the format of a narrative triggers recipients to establish a more or less direct or oblique relationship between the stories they are interpreting and the contexts in which they are interpreting them.

One of my claims in the present chapter is that although analysts using structuralist paradigms have developed useful and productive ways of characterizing temporal aspects of narrative, they have not focused enough attention on how readers can sometimes be prompted to assign storyworld events not a definite but only a more or less determinate location on the story's timeline. There are narratives, such as the three discussed in this chapter, that ascribe to certain events an inexact position within the chronological sequence that recipients mentally model as part of the process of interpreting the story itself. More precisely, some narratives exploit what I go on to describe as "fuzzy temporality," one subtype of which involves temporal sequencing that is strategically inexact, making it difficult or even impossible to assign narrated events a fixed or even fixable position along a timeline in the storyworld. After reviewing Gérard Genette's original proposals concerning the relation between story time and discourse time, I characterize narratives that order events in a fuzzy or indeterminate way as stories engaging in a "polychronic" style of narration. Their interpretation highlights the need for new tools for describing and explaining the temporal dimensions of storyworld (re)construction.

I develop the concept of fuzzy temporality in parallel with research on fuzzy logic, a field of inquiry designed to enrich classical systems of logic. Work on fuzzy logic stems from Max Black's early (1937) contribution to the logical analysis of vague expressions, as well as Lofti Zadeh's (1965) description of fuzzy sets, which are sets whose elements belong to them not absolutely but to different degrees, such as the set containing human males who are tall or the set containing people who are happy with their jobs (cf. Kosko 1986, 1992, 1993; Morgan 1998). As Bart Kosko (1992) notes, "Fuzzy theory holds that all things are matters of degree," reducing "black-white logic and mathematics to special limiting cases of gray relationships" (3). Fuzzy logic thus operates on the basis of multivalence as opposed to bivalence. Three-valued logics, for example, derive from a system based on the values True, False, and Indeterminate, in contrast to bivalent classical logics based on the values True and False.[1] As I suggest below, when it involves events being assigned indeterminate temporal positions in a storyworld, fuzzy temporality likewise reconfigures the concepts of "earlier" and "later" as special limiting cases in a multivalent system. What I am calling polychronic narration entails a three-value system spanning Earlier, Later, and Indeterminate, where, again, Indeterminate is shorthand for Indeterminately-situated-vis-à-vis-some-temporal-reference-point-X.

To conclude this overview of the chapter, and to give a better sense of the scope and aims of my analysis, I reproduce some insightful comments that Uri Margolin made on an earlier draft of the chapter. Margolin noted that a given set of events or other temporal elements can be ordered in (at least) four different ways. There can be *full* or unequivocal ordering (e.g., ABC), where "for any two events it is possible to decide whether one is earlier, later, or contemporaneous with the other"; *random* ordering, where "all mathematically possible arrangements are equally probable"; *alternative* or *multiple* "equiprobable (or not) orderings," where "it might be 60% probable that their temporal order is ABC and 40% that it is ACB"; or *partial* ordering, where "[s]ome elements of the set can be uniquely sequenced relative to all others, some only relative to some others, and some relative to none." In this last case, one might know that A is earlier than B but not know the temporal position of C relative to either; or else one might be able to include B in a temporal interval A-C, but not be able to situate B vis-à-vis other events falling within that same interval, e.g. B_1, B_2 . . . B_N. (For information about some of the linguistic and philosophical research subtending Margolin's comments, see Salmon 1992; Sklar 1998; Q. Smith 1998.)

As I go on to discuss, the present chapter explores ways in which the temporal ordering of events in narrative can either be *inexactly coded* (as in two of my tutor texts, Anna Seghers's "Der Ausflug der toten Mädchen" and Atom Egoyan's *The Sweet Hereafter*) or else *coded as inherently inexact* (as in my third tutor text, D. M. Thomas's *The White Hotel*). Within these two types of inexact or "fuzzy" ordering, the second arguably more radically indeterminate than the first, an additional distinction needs to drawn between multiply ordered as opposed to partially ordered events—to invoke Margolin's third and fourth categories. As I use it here, the scope of the term *polychrony* covers this entire semantic range. It includes both the more and less "radical" types of inexactness in coding, as well as both the multiple and the partial ordering of events. Polychrony can thus entail self-conscious, self-subverting modes of narration in which alternative or multiple ways of sequencing events are entertained (Seghers; Thomas). And it can also entail modes of narration that make it possible to reconstruct a global sequence or overall temporal interval, yet militate against interpreters' efforts to establish temporal positions for particular events within that larger span of time (Egoyan).

Story Time, Discourse Time, and Fuzzy Temporality

Despite impressive results yielded by the distinction between *story* and *discourse* in analyses of plot structure, exposition, and narrative temporality (e.g., Chatman 1978, 1990; Genette 1980; G. Prince 1982; Sternberg 1978), there is still a lack of consensus concerning the scope and validity of these narratological terms of art and their cognates.[2] Theorists have disagreed about the best way to label the difference between the chronological series of events recounted in a story and the manner in which those events are organized in the recounting. At stake is what to call—and how best to characterize—the difference between the subject and the method of narrative presentation. More important, charges of Platonism have been leveled against the very proposal to distinguish between a decontextualized set of events and the contextualized presentation of those events in a particular narrative.[3] In making such a distinction, theorists seem to commit themselves to the view that some abstract story subtends all the possible discursive manifestations of a given narrative—that all the recountings of the narrative of Cinderella can be reduced to a single, idealized story instantiated by all those "versions" of the tale. Yet the mode of telling also bears crucially on— indeed, alters—the matter told. Empirical investigations of conversational narrative suggest that retellings involve less a telling again of the same story on different occasions than a telling of (more or less) different stories on each new occasion (Chafe 1998; Metzger 1998). Further, as Gérard Genette (1997) has shown in connection with specifically literary retellings, a narrative "hypertext" can be characterized in terms of more or less pervasive, more or less radical transformations of the "hypotext" on which it draws but to which it can in no sense be reduced. At stake, in the case of stories, are intermodal transformations that produce theatrical or film versions of written narratives, as well as intramodal transformations by which a first-person narrative is retold in the third person or a narrative with four participants is reduced to one with three. Given the richness and diversity of the species of transformation that Genette himself documents, narrative hypertexts should perhaps be construed less as so many discourse-level "instantiations" of one and the same story or hypotext than as acts of narration each of which expands the range of contexts in which the original hypotextual paradigm can be used as a template for interpretation. Put briefly, in the case of literary rewritings, it is sometimes hard to know just where story ends and discourse begins.

Similarly, in recent discussions about focalization, homodiegetic narrators, and other narrative phenomena, theorists have disagreed about where to draw the boundary between "story space" and "discourse space."[4] Some researchers have suggested that the story/discourse distinction should be viewed as a more or less valuable heuristic device rather than a hard-and-fast rule dictating how to read stories—and analyze narrative structures—in all cases. Indeed, readers' or listeners' fluctuating responses to a story may result from changes in the narrator's orientation with respect to story space. Rigidly bracketing the telling from the told—setting up an impermeable ontological barrier between the domain of the narrating and the domain of the narrated—could therefore vitiate the phenomenology of reading. Any such method of analysis might very well be at odds with the felt experience of interpreting narrative worlds.

That said, however, classical methods have produced some striking results. By distinguishing between the what and the way, story and discourse, narratologists have been able to demonstrate how storytellers exploit different ratios between story time and discourse time to create different narrative effects.[5] Setting up what proved to be an influential descriptive framework, and using Marcel Proust's *A la Recherche du temps perdu* (*In Search of Lost Time*) as a kind of theoretical model as well as a particular case study, Genette (1980) originally discussed the ratios between story time and discourse time under the headings of *duration*, *frequency*, and *order*. Thus, the telling can have more or less duration with respect to the told; that is, the discourse can proceed at a rate faster or slower than that of the story. A narrative summary, for instance, abbreviates happenings in the storyworld; by contrast, a narrative pause represents a hiatus in the action while the narrator comments on or evaluates the narrated world, and in a narrative scene events are represented at a pace that iconically matches their "real-time" speed. Functionally speaking, longer or shorter duration can cue readers to focus on some narrative details as more salient than others. When a storyteller passes over events quickly or fails to mention them altogether, story recipients regularly infer those events to be of relatively little importance vis-à-vis the narrative as a whole. Of course, some narratives exploit this inferential habit in self-conscious and subversive ways, attaching the greatest significance to things that do *not* get told (at least not at first). Think of stories recounted by manifestly and perversely unreliable narrators such as the homicidal gourmand in John Lanchester's *The Debt to Pleasure* (1996); gappy or paraliptic detective fictions that omit important clues in order to maintain narrative suspense; narratives of past trauma that, like the stories examined in the present chapter, arrive at causes only after painfully extended explorations of effects; and postmodern narratives centering on the unknowable and the nonnarratable.

Further, events in the storyworld can be narrated with different sorts of frequency. A singulative telling tells once what happened once (the more general formula would be telling n times what happened n times); a repetitive telling tells n times what happened once; and an iterative telling tells once what happened n times (see Rimmon-Kenan 1983: 56–58). As departures from the baseline mode of singulative narration, repetitive telling helps signal the importance of an event or series of events whose significance might otherwise be underappreciated, whereas iterative narration suggests (among other things) the interrelatedness of events that might otherwise be interpreted as unconnected or disanalogous. For example, as a way of weighting certain events in her life story more heavily than others, Chaucer's Wife of Bath narrates repetitively that her husband Janekyn badgered her with recitations of texts by antifeminist authors. And as Genette points out, Proust's *Recherche* is itself a highly illustrative instance of iterative (homodiegetic) narration, there used as a strategy for superimposing temporal frames—a way of subordinating isolated events to the ongoing temporal flux from which they take their shape and derive their meaning.

Again—and more significant for the concerns of this chapter—a given chronological sequence can be told in different orders (can be ordered in different ways). As Genette (1980) puts it, "To study the temporal order of a narrative is to compare the order in which events or temporal sections are arranged in the narrative discourse with the order of succession these same events or temporal segments have in the story, to the extent that story order is explicitly indicated by the narrative itself or is inferrable from one or another indirect clue" (35). Hence the sequence ABC can be told chronologically as ABC, the sequence of the telling exactly matching the order of the events being recounted. Through analepsis (flashback), the same sequence can be narrated BCA. Through prolepsis (flashforward), it can be told as CAB.[6] Genette calls such departures from chronological sequence "anachronies"; these departures from linear narration have not only a "reach" that bears them more or less far from the present into the past or the future, but also a wider or narrower "extent" insofar as they can cover a duration of the story that is more or less long. In functional terms, proleptic storytelling, by eliminating or reducing narrative suspense, requires an interpretive reorientation on the part of readers. In texts such as Muriel Spark's *The Prime of Miss Jean Brodie* (1961), where the narrative periodically leaps into the future to show the delayed effects of Miss Brodie's teaching on her pupils, proleptic narration prompts, not the question "What happened?" but rather the question "How (and why) did these events happen?" For its part, analeptic narration yields "returns," or "retrospective sections that fill in, after the event, an earlier gap in the narrative" (Genette 1980: 51), as well as "recalls," where the narrative explicitly retraces its own path (54). Such narrative maneuvers encourage a reviewing of the past through the lens of the present (and vice versa). Sometimes they even erode the boundary between what has happened and what is happening—as in a novel such as A. S. Byatt's *Possession* (1990), where, in a manner detailed below in chapter 8, current events prove to be inextricably interlinked with events that occurred a century earlier.

In general, Genette's categories of duration, frequency, and order capture important ways in which narratives cue recipients to build *temporally organized* models of the situations, events, and entities told about over the course of the story. By being paced faster or slower, narratives can trigger inferences that some domains within the storyworld are more salient than others. Similar sorts of inferences can be cued by events that are repeated, compressed, or omitted in the narration. And the more or less nonchronological presentation of events can point up causal or other interconnections between occurrences that readers might be otherwise inclined to model as separate, unrelated. A temporal category that does not figure in classical frameworks, however, is the fuzzy temporality that necessitates different techniques for storyworld reconstruction. What I am calling fuzzy temporality can manifest itself in a variety of ways. For example, a story may purposely leave vague how many times a certain kind of event took place, or whether a particular instance of narration involves, in Genette's terms, a *scene* or rather a scene slowed just enough to constitute a *stretch*. Indeed, as I discuss more particularly below, inexactness with respect to the ordering of events in the storyworld constitutes a narrative strategy not easily described in classical terms. Inexactness of ordering prompts readers to model a world in which the temporal position of certain events remains indeterminate.[7] Equally uncertain are the temporal and causal relationships obtaining *between* indeterminately ordered events. Yet narrative prototypically roots itself in such temporal and causal relationships, being a vehicle for cognizing events-in-sequence. Stories marked by fuzzy temporal ordering, as one might also put it, introduce a specialized, reflexive modeling system (cf. Lotman and Uspenskij 1986)— one that spotlights the possibilities and limits of narrative's own capacity to model a world as consisting of events ordered in time.

Of special relevance here are thus the "ambiguous structures"—those complex and sometimes radically indeterminate modes of anachrony— that Genette discovered in Proust's ingenious experimentations with narrative time. Such structures start to manifest themselves when anachronies are embedded within one another to produce, in the *Recherche* as well as other texts, a baroque temporal syntax that puts the notions of before and after into question. Genette points out that

> the very ideas of retrospection or anticipation, which ground the narrative categories of analepsis and prolepsis in "psychology," take for granted a perfectly clear temporal consciousness and unambiguous relationships among present, past, and future. Only because the exposition required it, and at the cost of excessive schematization, have I until now postulated this to always have been so. (1980: 78–79)

The case of Proust is more complicated, however. In Proust's novel it is not just that certain "proleptic analepses and analeptic prolepses are so many complex anachronies," which "somewhat disturb our reassuring ideas about retrospection and anticipation" (Genette 83). Beyond this,

> we also find in the *Recherche* some events not provided with any temporal reference whatsoever, events that we cannot place at all in relation to the events surrounding them.... Here no inference from the content can help the analyst define the status of an anachrony deprived of every temporal connection, which is an event we must ultimately take to be dateless and ageless: to be an achrony. (83)

It is noteworthy that Genette here ascribes *timelessness* to what are in effect *temporally indefinite* or "unplaceable" events. Writing again of Proust, he remarks that "To be unplaceable they [the events that "we cannot place at all in relation to the events surrounding them"] need only be attached not to some other event (which would require the narrative to define them as being earlier or later) but to the (atemporal) commentarial discourse that accompanies them" (83). Arguably, however, temporal indefiniteness should not be conflated with timelessness or achrony: not knowing the exact temporal positions of several events occurring within a larger narrative sequence does not make those events achronic. Further, both the achronic and the temporally indefinite (i.e., the only partially temporally ordered) should be distinguished from the temporally multiple. In some cases of complex anachrony at least, what is at stake is not a complete absence of sequence or the lack of definite sequence but instead a kind of narration that exploits indefiniteness to pluralize and delinearize itself, to multiply the ways in which the events being recounted can be chained together to produce "the" narrative itself. Both in cases of temporal indefiniteness and cases of temporal multiplicity—where the narration anchors events in multiple temporal frameworks and thereby promotes competing ways of sequencing those events—narratologists might be warranted in using the term *polychrony* rather than *achrony*.[8]

As the three narratives discussed in this chapter demonstrate, there is more than one mode of polychronic narration, as well as different ways of putting polychrony to use in different narrative contexts. In the first place, one can draw the distinction just mentioned—between a partial as opposed to a multiple temporal ordering of situations and events in the storyworld. But this distinction is crosscut by another: namely, between modes of narration that inexactly code the temporal position of events through partial or multiple ordering and modes of narration that code the temporal position of events as intrinsically inexact. The first two sections of this chapter explore how both modes of polychrony (i.e., multiple and partial ordering) function in narratives that inexactly code the temporal sequence of happenings in the storyworld; the final section examines a storyworld in which events themselves are coded as irreducibly temporally multiple.

Functionally speaking, refusing to assign situations and events a definite location in time can, in some contexts, highlight the difficulty of narrativizing traumatic occurrences. In broad terms, this is the function of temporal indeterminacy in two of the narratives under examination, Anna Seghers's "Der Ausflug der toten Mädchen" ("The Excursion of the Dead Girls"), a story written while Seghers was in exile from Nazi Germany in Mexico in 1942–43, and Atom Egoyan's 1997 film *The Sweet Hereafter*, adapted from Russell Banks's 1991 novel of the same name. Both narratives, using cues specific to written and to cinematic narrative, suggest ways in which traumatic occurrences resist being presented in narrative form. But in other contexts, polychronic narration can be used to suggest that situations, entities, and events are anchored, in the storyworld itself, in more than one place in time. This is the sort of temporal indeterminacy at work in the third narrative considered here, D. M. Thomas's 1981 novel *The White Hotel*. Thomas's novel has been characterized as an example of magical realism, and with good reason. Arguably, its temporal structure is more ontologically destabilizing than the structures found in Seghers's tale or Egoyan's film. Interpreting Thomas's novel requires modeling a storyworld whose very history is polychronic; in that world, time does not unfold linearly. By contrast, in Seghers's story and Egoyan's film, polychrony serves mainly to inhibit the readers' or viewers' efforts to comprehend the (temporal structure of the) storyworld exhaustively. Countering the myth of total narration by means of narrative structure itself, Seghers's tale and Egoyan's film provide strategically vague cues for re-creation of their respective storyworlds. In all three cases, though, fuzzy temporal ordering forces interpreters to acknowledge that strategies for linearizing and narrativizing the action are just that—strategies for cognizing events some of which resist (or altogether deny) chronological ordering. Again, then, polychronic narration can be described as a specialized cognitive instrument. It is a narrative device that cues interpreters to rethink the scope and limits of narrative itself—specifically, to rethink its linearizing capacity viewed as both a discourse genre and a pattern of thought.[9]

Seghers's "Der Ausflug": Humble Narration

The title of Seghers's story already signals the paradoxical nature of the experiences that the tale recounts. An *Ausflug* or school excursion is difficult to reconcile with the idea of dead girls undertaking such a trip. Similarly, in the story as a whole Seghers forces readers to juxtapose, on the one hand, idyllic images of schoolchildren in the pastoral setting of the Rhinelands with, on the other hand, scenes from a later, war-torn Germany, in which the innocent-seeming schoolgirls and schoolboys have grown up to despise, betray, and literally murder one another. The narrative consists of an ongoing mediation of cultural through personal memory, as the feverish, weakened, displaced, only semi-reliable narrator memorializes the effects of the fascistic terror on the lives of her erstwhile companions, her childhood friends. In thus compelling readers to register, again and again, painful discrepancies between past and present, frightening contrasts between unspoiled schoolchildren and the victims or victimizers those children eventually become under the impress of a fascistic regime, Seghers's tale exemplifies the sort of deflationary irony that Paul Fussell (1975) has ascribed to texts written around the time of the First World War. Seghers's tale, too, seems to embody an irony in which prewar hopes and ideals give way to obscene wartime atrocities. Concomitantly, despair of ever being able to understand the world at all replaces an earlier, more optimistic *Weltanschauung.*

Even as it implies stark, ironic contrasts between past and present, however, Seghers's story makes it difficult to reconstruct a temporal continuum along which events might be arranged and labeled as earlier and later. From the outset, the frame tale surrounding "Der Ausflug" creates a pretext for polychrony, a mode of narration that purposely resists linearity by multiplying ways in which narrated events can be ordered. The frame tale projects both personal and collective history into the fantastic territory of what is, indistinguishably, remembrance, dream, and fever-induced hallucination. Set in Mexico, to which Seghers herself was exiled until the collapse of the Third Reich (LaBahn 1986: 5–32, 49–87), the frame begins with a Mexican tavern owner observing, with unconcealed fascination, the displaced narrator "als suche er Spuren meiner phantastischen Herkunft" 'as though he sought traces of my fantastic [European] descent' (Seghers 1980: 331).[10] Indeed, the narrator's geographical and cultural displacement, and its effects on her attempt to recount her own earlier experiences under the Nazis in Europe, produce some of the tale's more striking, even surrealistic, descriptions, including those of mountain ravines "[als] kahl und wild wie ein Mondgebirge" 'as barren and savage as a chain of lunar mountains' (331) and pepper trees that, glowing at the edge of a desolate gorge, "schienen eher zu brennen als zu blühen" 'appeared rather to burn than to bloom' (331). Here and now, where the telling of the past is to take place, anything seems possible; in such environs readers should perhaps expect the ordering of events *not* to be pegged to a straightforwardly sequential past, present, and future.

Expressionistic or quasi-Expressionistic elements of the frame tale create further possibilities for polychrony. Specifically, Seghers represents the perceiving subject—here, the narrator herself—not merely as registering but also as oneirically transforming and defamiliarizing the world at large. Having lain for months in the grip of a fever that has reached her even where the ravages of war could not (331–32), at the opening of the frame tale the narrator refers repeatedly to her own "Schwäche und Müdigkeit" 'weakness and exhaustion' (332), and remarks at one point that her "Augen vor Hitze und Müdigkeit brannten" 'eyes burned with heat and weariness' (332). Likewise, both in dividing the frame tale from her account of the *Ausflug* proper and in segmenting the various phases of the schoolgirls' excursion, the narrator repeatedly uses the same strange, glowing cloud of dust. This dust cloud is raised and lowered like an intangible curtain to reveal ever-changing scenes and configurations of the spectral dead-and-alive *Mädchen*. The narrator attributes its punctuating rise and fall now to her own weakness, now to some mysterious, vaguely atmospheric circumstance (332, 333, 339, 360–62). By thus stipulating that, in general, the perceptions on which readers must rely are, however, unreliable[11]—by alternating between the immediacy of objective experience and its (inescapable) mediation by subjective factors—the narrative introduces a constant play between the real and the imagined. Debatably, this play between perception and imagination transcends strictly Expressionistic concerns, for Seghers's narrator acknowledges that "ich nicht wußte, ob er [der flimmrigen Dunst . . . die alles vernebelte] aus Sonnenstaub bestand oder aus eigener Müdigkeit" 'I did not know whether [the glimmering haze . . . that beclouded everything] consisted of dust motes or my own weariness' (332), the text thereby embarking on an exploration of what constitutes accurate recounting, adherence to a veridical chronology, in the first place. Readers' attempts to reconstruct the (series of) incidents recounted by the narrator—the chains of events that constitute the narrative scaffolding of the tale—unfold within this same dialectic of description and projection, telling and creating. The most insistent question posed by this narrative: How to mark time in a story about the elusiveness of time and the polysemousness of its marks?[12]

My concern, then, is with the peculiar mode of temporality encoded in Seghers's story, the multiple sequencings it promotes—not just through a frame tale premised on cultural, geographical, and psychological disorientation, but also through the formal mechanisms of the narrative as a whole. At issue, more specifically, are the temporal displacements, the radically anachronistic effects, structuring Seghers's narrative of the dead German schoolgirls. Even as it cues readers to build a model of what went on in the narrator's past—that is, to reconstruct a storyworld temporally embedded within the storyworld of the present act of telling—the narrator's retrospective account suggests that whereas some situations and events recounted in her tale can be plotted on a time line, narrativized as earlier and later, others cannot be chronicled in that fashion. Temporally indeterminate, they exceed linear time without being timeless, disrupt chronology without being achronic. By figuring some events as resistant to linearization, Seghers's story both invokes and subverts reading conventions associated with narrative as a discourse genre. Seghers's formal experiments are hence only partly susceptible to analysis via classical, structuralist models for understanding narrative progression. Narratologists should explore how narratives such as Seghers's reflexively call into question the processing strategies that predispose recipients to read stories in sequential ways—indeed, to read narrative as the preeminent way of conceptualizing sequence itself (Mink 1978: 131–32).

My discussion of Seghers's tale is not solely an exercise in formal analysis, however. It also suggests how narrative theory can be an important tool for studying the relations between narrative structure and ideological (de)mystification. By resorting to temporally multiple situations and events, Seghers develops a strategy for countering, through narrative form itself, the fascistic ideology espoused by the Nazis. Specifically, Seghers's use of polychrony can be read in opposition to two major (and related) ideological components of German fascism. The first component is its tendency to search back through time for the eternal, *völkisch* basis of authentic German culture, even though no one stage of a culture, a thing continually and dynamically emergent in history, can be deemed true or authentic. The second component is its tendency to reduce complex historical situations to single causes—to overschematize and hyperlinearize time itself—by finding scapegoats for the obliquities of fate. By contrast, revealing the limits of narrative from within narrative itself, "Der Ausflug" orders and narrativizes but not absolutely, not once and for all. Engaging in fuzzy temporal ordering, that is, drawing on a multivalent temporal system, the tale offsets the presumptive, unself-questioning accounts whose putative finality forms the stuff of ideology. It substitutes for the arrogance of definitive narration a mode of telling that Seghers's narrator will go on to call *demütig—humble*.

Polychrony in "Der Ausflug"

Prima facie, and like other retrospective narratives (*Moby Dick*, *Heart of Darkness*), "Der Ausflug" opposes the present to the past or, more precisely, tries to reconstitute the past through an act of telling situated in the present. Another way of putting this would be to say that, typically, retrospective stories include (at least) two shifts of "deictic centers." Cognitively oriented narrative theorists have noted that, in ordinary discourse, deictic terms such as *here* and *now* refer to a specific conceptual location; but in the case of storytelling, "the deictic center often shifts from the environmental situation in which [the telling of the story] is encountered, to a locus within a mental model representing the world of the discourse" (Segal 1995: 15; cf. Ryan 1991: 13–30).[13] In Seghers's story, the frame tale prompts the first shift of deictic centers. If readers mean to participate at all in what Marie-Laure Ryan has called the "fictional pact" (1991: 26)—the set of conventions to which all participants in the game of fiction must adhere if that game is to proceed—they must relocate to a here and now situated in early 1940s Mexico. In signaling a transition from the frame tale to the framed narrative, however, the story triggers a second shift of deictic centers, this time from the one associated with Mexico to a here and now located in pre-WWII Germany. Yet as the narrative proceeds, it qualifies and to some extent undermines the second of the deictic shifts required for its processing.[14] Even as it distinguishes the frame tale from the story of the school excursion by centering the hypodiegetic narrative in a different, earlier here and now, the story erodes the basis for making that very distinction.

As I suggested earlier, Seghers's use of an exotic, dream-like (and perhaps dream-induced) setting helps trouble the boundary between past and present. Faced with this setting, readers hesitate between two strategies for deictic (re)centering. One strategy is to view the school excursion mainly or even totally as a figment of the narrator's feverish imagination. In this case "Der Ausflug" as a whole remains anchored in the here and now of the frame tale, a deictic center only partially and fitfully displaced by the here and now of an imagined Germany. The other strategy is to view the framed narrative as a genuinely retrospective recounting, memorializing a past that did, in fact, happen. In that case the story has two discrete deictic centers, straddles two different times and places, and must be interpreted as such. My claim is that, because of where and how it is told, the story prevents readers from fully embracing either interpretive option.

If the setting works mainly to ambiguate and pluralize the meaning of *here*, other features of the tale create a nonsingular *now*, yielding richly differentiated—and polychronic—temporal structures. At one level, "Der Ausflug" encodes polychrony through its verbal texture, by way of verb inflections and lexical choices, for example. But these discourse-level cues point to a more general way of characterizing the story's fuzzy temporal ordering. The narration indexes situations and events as temporally multiple by prompting readers to make causal inferences about them—to judge some things to be (prior) causes and other things to be (later) effects—at the same time that it brings the scope and validity of those same inferences into question. Seghers's work, then, is a narrative that both assumes the validity of *post hoc, ergo propter hoc* 'after which, therefore because of which' and dispels it as a fallacy—a fallacy whose systematic application Roland Barthes once equated with narrative itself (1977: 94). Or, to invoke terms that were introduced in earlier chapters and that surface again in my discussion of Egoyan's *The Sweet Hereafter* (see also note 28 in this chapter): the form of Seghers's tale cues readers to activate two preference rules that work against one another. The first rule: Use a bivalent temporal system to read later events as effects of earlier events and earlier events as causes of later ones. The second rule: Use a multivalent temporal system to read some events as indeterminate, that is, as occupying an inherently vague position on the chain of causes and effects undergirding the story, such that an effect might precede its cause.

At the level of verbal texture, Seghers exploits lexical and grammatical features of the German language to create temporal displacements (projections, retrogressions, and strange combinations of the two) whose effects cannot be situated on the continuum of any linear chronology, the dateline of any indisputable history. Consider, for example, some tokens of the noun *Spur* 'trace' and the verb *ahnen* 'to have a presentiment of, to suspect' found in the story. At one point the narrator is troubled to discover in the young Fräulein Sichel a few gray hairs, not "von jeher schneeweiß [hair], wie ich es in Erinnerung hatte" 'the snow-white [hair], that I had remembered her as having had at all times' (340), but rather just the trace (*Spur*) of her old age and of her later defilement for being Jewish (339–40). On one reading, based on the first of the two preference rules stated above, the story here foregrounds the deceptively creative power of memory, its tendency to project later eventualities onto their own conditions of emergence—to read the past in terms of the present. But on another reading, based on the second preference rule, the tale suggests that the trace of certain events can actually be detected even though, in the time frame that helps define the deictic center of the hypodiegetic narrative, the events themselves have not yet occurred. Events that did not yet happen have in some sense already occurred, but only within a multivalent temporal system whereby some events must be assigned the value of Indeterminate with respect to the NOW serving as a reference point in time. On this interpretation, "Der Ausflug" fuses, in the perspective of its perceiving, remembering, and/or dreaming narrator, the temporal coordinates of the (anterior) hypodiegetic events with those of the (posterior) diegetic events. The time of what is being recounted interweaves itself with the time of its recounting. Fräulein Sichel's experiences are not therefore presented as timeless, however. Rather, they are, as narrativized, temporally indeterminate: they have *both* already happened and *also* not yet happened in the time frame of the story-within-the-story. This is the time frame to which readers are prompted to shift by a narrator who is, to an indeterminate extent, constructing her experiences *while* remembering them. Or, to rephrase this last point, the narration is polychronic because of how the narrator positions herself in time; she narrates from an indeterminate location on the temporal continuum that stretches between the story and the story-within-the-story.

As the tale continues to unfold, the narrator detects in the face of a young Otto Fresenius who would later be killed in WWI "[d]ie Spur von Gerechtigkeit und Rechtlichkeit" 'the trace of righteousness and justness' (346). As in her account of the traces-before-the-fact of Fräulein Sichel's old age, the word *Spur* lexicalizes the temporal indeterminacy structuring the narrator's account. Already, and by means of an oddly subjunctive or counterfactual posteriority, traits of Otto, or rather traces of those traits, reveal aspects of his personality that *would have* prevented Otto from becoming (like Gustav Liebig) a member of the Nazi ss, even though Otto in fact dies in battle in 1914. As the narrator puts it: "Das wäre Otto Fresenius, selbst wenn er gesund aus dem Krieg gekommen wäre, nie geworden" 'Otto Fresenius would never have become [a member of the ss], even if he had returned from the [First World War] alive and well' (346). On one interpretation, this passage can be read as a counterfactual projection on the part of the narrator, a statement about what might have happened had history taken a different course. Having knowledge of how the future will turn out, the narrator can (retrospectively) discern traces of Otto's character that mark his relationship to events that could have happened to him in a future that, as it turns out, never unfolds. But the complexity of my paraphrase mirrors the complex temporality involved. By counterfactualizing the past, the narrator not only evaluates it by measuring it against what might have happened but did not;[15] she also reverses the direction of time's arrow, or rather makes it bidirectional. Effects of events that never will occur are narrativized as the causes of events that would have preceded them, had the later events in fact occurred. Otto dies before the righteousness whose traces the narrator discerns in the boy's face could possibly have been realized, though in fact his justness never will be realized. The boy thus bears, in the narrator's account, the unmistakeable signs of his rejection of a future guilt and complicity that Otto will never have the chance actually to spurn. Yet the structure of Seghers's tale does not license the inference that the traces of Otto's probity, or those of Fräulein Sichel's old age, actually precede the events that caused (or would have caused them) in the storyworld. This, as we shall see, is a more radical type of polychrony exploited in Thomas's magical realist narration in *The White Hotel*, but not in Seghers's tale or Egoyan's film. Instead, "Der Ausflug" warrants a more modest claim: namely, that in narrativizing what happened to Otto and Fräulein Sichel, the narrator's broadly retrospective account encodes certain objects and events as temporally indeterminate; such objects and events are vaguely rather than precisely situated on the chronology that the narrator's account *also* cues readers to attempt to reconstruct.

The narrator's use of the verb *ahnen*, again in the subjunctive mood, creates similarly polychronic effects.[16] Toward the end of her and her friends' excursion, and as she approaches her parents' house in her old home city or *Vaterstadt*, the narrator recognizes in herself a feeling of *Angst* perhaps all the more terrifying because of its temporal rootlessness. In this context, fear is not just temporally nomadic (it does not necessarily cease when the events that caused it have stopped happening) but also the result of one's inability to chronologize, to place one's own experiences and affects in time. The narrator recounts that "Ich hatte wieder einen Anflug von Angst, in meine eigene Straße zu biegen, *als ob ich ahnen würde, daß sie zerstört war*" 'I had once more a tinge of fear when it came time to turn down my own street, *as if I would have a presentiment that it had been destroyed*' (359, my emphasis). The result of hindsight that she has not yet had time to gain, the narrator locates her dread neither in the diegetic nor in the hypodiegetic universe, neither in the story nor in the story-within-the-story. It is, rather, an interstitial fear, a fear born between times, deriving from the ongoing process of narrativizing the past. The wartime devastation that retroactively causes the narrator's fear inhabits a past that, as told, makes it possible for her to comprehend the effects of war. Reshaped by a future that it has already shaped, the past is still underway. It lives on in the form of objects, situations, and events (fears, presentiments) that happen in time(s) without being reducible to any one temporal schematization, any one ordering.

As should already be apparent, "Der Ausflug" encodes polychrony—sets temporal indeterminacy into play—not merely through its verbal texture but also through the complicated inferences that such discourse-level features promote. More precisely, by activating both of the preference rules described above, the narrator's account prompts readers to fashion inferential chains—*a* caused *b*, *c* is an effect of *b*, etc.—but simultaneously undercuts readers' tendency to construe causes as anterior to effects. The story thus narrativizes while also pointing up the difficulty, in principle, of narrativization, of chaining together causes and effects to create a story. This is the key to what I am calling *humble narration*. The way the narrator tells about the small, characteristic wrinkle (*Falte*) on Leni's brow encapuslates the principle of narrative humility.[17] In Peircean terms, Leni's wrinkle is not just a symbol, a verbally realized sign that signifies what it does because of the conventions of the German language, but also an index, a sign that derives its semiotic status from its having been caused by something else—just as smoke signifies (as an index of) fire. Yet the narrator complicates the wrinkle's status as an index by allowing it to occupy a temporal span instead of just a point in time. To anticipate: whereas the arrogant narration associated with fascism does not hesitate to make one thing or event the index of another, dividing the storyworld into increments of Earlier and Later, Leni's wrinkle shows how humble narration places a question mark next to a whole complex of ideas—"index," "cause," "effect," "earlier," "later"—that other styles of storytelling assume as given.

When she first finds the young Leni and Marianne sitting on either end of a see-saw (we eventually learn that Marianne later contributes to the destruction of Leni and her family at the hands of the Nazis), the narrator characterizes Leni thus:

> Sie hatte mit zussamengezogenen dichten Brauen in ihrem runden Gesicht den entschlossenen, etwas energischen Ausdruck, den sie von klein auf bei allen schwierigen Unternehmungen annahm. Ich kannte die Falte in ihrer Stirn, in ihrem sonst spiegelglatten und runden Apfelgesicht, von allen Gelegenheiten, von schwierigen Ballspielen und Wettschwimmen und Klassenaufsätzen und später auch bei erregten Versammlungen und beim Flugblätterverteilen.... Die Falte in ihrer Stirn, die früher nur bei besonderen Gelegen-heiten entstand, wurde zu einem ständigem Merkmal, als man sie in Frauenkonzentrationslager im zweiten Winter dieses Krieges langsam, aber sicher an Hunger zugrunde gehen ließ. Ich wunderte mich, wieso ich ihren Kopf . . . bisweilen vergessen konnte, wo ich doch sicher war, daß sie selbst im Tod ihr Apfelgesicht mit der eingekerbten Stirn behalten hatte. (335)

> She had the determined, somewhat energetic expression that, with the thick brows of her round face drawn together, she assumed from a young age whenever she faced difficult undertakings. I recognized the crease in her brow, in a face otherwise mirror-smooth and round as an apple, at occasions ranging from difficult ball games to swim meets and class essays, and later, too, at excited meetings and during the distribution of pamphlets.... The wrinkle in her brow, which earlier revealed itself only during special occasions, became an enduring mark when she was allowed, in the second winter of the current war, to perish slowly but surely from hunger in a concentration camp for women. I wondered at how, up to now, I could have forgotten her [youthfully smooth] head, . . . when I

was sure that even in death she had retained an apple-like face with a deeply scored brow.

To be sure, in its transformation from an only intermittently apparent wrinkle to an indelible one, Leni's mark indexes more widespread, and more perfidious, sociopolitical changes. But again what the narrator's account foregrounds is how difficult it is to give the wrinkle and its changes an exact location on the timeline of causes and effects.

Note that classical narratology provides a way of describing the temporal structure of the passage quoted. In Genette's terms, the passage involves *paralepsis* (1980: 195–98). In recounting earlier events—events in which she participated as a younger, experiencing self—it is not just that Seghers's narrator tells the story as an older, remembering self. What is more, this homodiegetic narrator paraleptically imports back into her past experiences knowledge gained after the time of her actual participation in them.[18] Grounded in a linear unfolding of time that Seghers's narrator does not assume, however, the concept of paralepsis does not capture how the narrator's account cues readers to model aspects of the storyworld as temporally indeterminate. To say that the narrator's knowledge of the future colors her presentation of the past is to make a claim about the story that is globally true but undernuanced when it comes to local effects of humble narration. Narrative humility, as I have suggested, is a principle by which storytellers cognize earlier and later events as bidirectionally influencing one another—and recount them accordingly. Thus, Seghers's storyteller narrativizes Leni's wrinkle—assigns it indicial functions—by associating it with events that can be described as (incipient) causes only after the fact. As narrativized, as remembered, the indelible wrinkle is there before it was there, a sort of prefigurative index signifying the effects of causes that have not yet taken shape in the hypodiegetic universe. Conversely, the absence of the wrinkle indexes the desirability of the past only when one reads the past against the future, where the wrinkle finally becomes an enduring sign of cruelty and suffering. Here the narrator's knowledge of the storyworld's future does not merely "color" a preexistent past; it effectively constitutes that past by making it tellable *as* a past that led to the narrator's future. Yet her past remains, too, a horizon of the present. It is accessible only through a NOW—the NOW of the frame tale—in which the wrinkle functions, undecidably, as sign, effect, projection, dream, memory, or hallucination. Thus, represented as a fold where different times overlap, Leni's wrinkle obeys a multivalent temporal logic, ruled not by linearity but by reversibility. Snapping the inexorable chains of cause and effect, Leni's becomes, truly, a wrinkle in time. This temporal indeterminacy, this creasing of time, itself becomes a theme near the end of the story. Seghers's narrator, slowly and with all the bemused disorientation of the waking dreamer, begins to reinsert herself back into the deictic coordinates of the frame tale, wondering

> wie ich die Zeit verbringen sollte, heute und morgen, hier und dort, denn ich spürte jetzt einen unermeßlichen Strom von Zeit, unbezwingbar wie die Luft. Man hat uns nun einmal von klein auf angewöhnt, statt uns der Zeit demütig zu ergeben, sie auf irgendeine Weise zu bewältigen. (362)

> how I should spend the time, today and tomorrow, here and there, for I now discerned an immeasurable stream of time, imperturbable as the air. From a young age we had been taught to master time somehow, instead of humbly resigning ourselves to time.

Just by humbly resigning herself to time, the narrator can suture past, present, and future into a story that unfolds in time without claiming to be the story of time's unfolding. The same narrative humility—a way of telling rooted in an awareness of the limits as well as the possibilities of stories—accounts for the polychronic profile of "Der Ausflug." The tale does not purport to master time, to tell what happened once and for all. The search for a definitive order of events gives way to an exploration of what it means to create sequences. Because in some instances time can be run forward or backward, or rather in both directions at once, a thing is what it is not by virtue of the way it occupies a point in time, but rather by virtue of how it refuses or negates such temporal delimitation—how it moves around in time. The actions of little snub-nosed Nora, for example, must be situated in a temporal loop that circulates between her childhood adoration of Fräulein Sichel, on the one hand, and a later moment in which she spits on her former teacher and denounces her as a Jewish pig (*Judensau*), on the other hand (339–40). The narrator remembers Nora in terms of who she eventually becomes, but also, when she becomes that person, in terms of someone she used to be. Similarly, the narrator's account of Gerda draws on a multivalent temporal system. Gerda "war zur Krankenpflege und Menschenliebe geboren" 'was born to care for the sick and to love her fellow human beings' (342), but she can be defined neither by the indestructible traces (*[un]vertilgbar . . . Spuren*) of her earlier compassionate acts, nor by those acts themselves, nor by that final moment when, about to commit suicide because her husband has hung Nazi flags outside their home, she stands completely and hopelessly alone (343, 348). Rather, constituted even as it is being remembered, the story of Gerda resists schematization into an hypodiegetic before and a diegetic after. Polychrony thus goes hand in hand with a loss of certainty, but with a form of certainty that has never not been suspect. Seghers's story suggests that the arrogance of fascistic logic, based as it is on exclusion and absolute difference, can be countermanded by humble narration.

Remembering, an Infinite Task

If "Der Ausflug" focuses on the problems of storytelling, however, it also focuses on the potentials—indeed, the necessity—of telling stories. Just because situations and events cannot be definitively ordered, that does not mean that humans should stop trying to order them into stories. Of special importance here is the emphasis on brute particularity in Seghers's tale; important, too, is the tale's emphasis on memory as a vehicle for storing irreducible particulars in narrative form. Rather than commenting in general on a given event or state of affairs (death in a concentration camp, an act of complicity, an instance of heroism or of compassion), "Der Ausflug" resolutely historicizes it, anchoring it in the manifold of circumstances in which it took shape and that it continues to affect.[19] The tale's ongoing concern with memory likewise signals its commitment to the profound specificity of every experience. By foregrounding the always unfinished work of memorialization, the tale actively refuses to make things timeless, achronic. Instead, it indicates that the *raison d'être* of narrative is to remember things in time. Its business is to record for a present that is itself fugitive, vanishing, a past that is never fully narrativizable, that cannot be reduced to any single order, but that gains its meaning and order from people's attempts to tell stories about it.

The story persistently foregrounds the necessity of memory and, conversely, the negativity or evil of forgetting. "Der Ausflug" just *is* an effect of the will to remember. Seghers's rich lexicon of memory— *Gedächtnis* 'memory,' *erinnern* 'to remind,' *merken* 'to keep in mind, to make note of,' and, conversely, *vergessen* 'to forget'—includes words that can be found at nearly every juncture of the tale, in connection with nearly every character whom the narrator (re)encounters. For example, once again indefinitely situated somewhere between past and present, the narrator feels "als ob ich die höhere Pflicht hätte, mir auch die winzigsten Einzelheiten für immer zu merken" 'as if I had had the higher duty to make note of even the slightest particularities' of Fräulein Sichel while given the chance (340). Yet this higher obligation of memory is not simply diegetic in origin, issuing from the narrator's attempt to call up, in exile and *post hoc*, the fantastic traces of a past that must never be forgotten. The duty of remembrance also operates intradiegetically, issuing from Fräulein Sichel's suggestion, internal to the narrated events, that "weil ich gern fahre und weil ich gern Aufsätze schreibe, sollte ich für die nächste Deutschstunde eine Beschreibung des Schulausfluges machen" 'because I liked to travel and to write essays, I should for our next German class compose a description of the school excursion' (353). This description merges, kaleidoscopically, with the conduct of the diegesis itself.[20] Inversely, the narrator attributes to forgetfulness Nora's failure to feel any remorse for the way she later treats Fräulein Sichel: "hatte [Nora] Fräulein Sichels Platz sogar geschwind mit ein paar Jasminzweigen umwunden. . . . Das hätte die Nora sicher, wäre ihr Gedächtnis nicht ebenso dünn gewesen wie ihre Stimme, später bereut, als Leiterin der Nationalsozialistischen Frauenschaft unserer Stadt" '[Nora] had even wound around Fräulein Sichel's table setting, quickly, a couple of branches of jasmine. . . . Nora, if her memory had not become as thin as her voice, would certainly have regretted that later, as leader of the Nazi Women's Organization of our city' (339). The story of Nora serves as a cautionary tale; it makes of memory a moral imperative. And humble narration, enabled by polychrony, is memory mixed with the desire to remember better.

Limits of Order

Through its form as well as its themes, its structure as well as its vocabulary, Seghers's story thus prompts a rethinking of classical definitions of narrative as the representation of events in a time sequence. According to standard accounts, narrative is by and large factive in nature. Narratives characteristically (re)produce, from a stance of relative certainty, chains of singular past states and events. Recent work suggests, however, that this classical conception of narrative as factive—as a discourse type centering on strings of situations and events that have already definitely been accomplished—may not hold for all narratives or for every aspect of every narrative.[21] Some narrative subgenres—or some features of texts pertaining to the discourse genre *narrative*—may call into question the limits of applicability of classical definitions of narrative itself. Here two approaches present themselves. Either the standard definitions hold good, and stories that resist description in those terms are actually narrative paraphenomena—discourse (sub)types that are parasitic on real narratives, quasi-stories (or quasi-narrative features) comprehensible only against the backdrop of narrative modes that do, in fact, conform to the classical accounts. Or else, conversely, the classical accounts must be rethought as locally but not globally valid—as adequate for the description and analysis of many, perhaps even most, cases of narrative discourse, but certainly not all possible cases. In the present chapter, as in this book as a whole, I adopt the second of these two approaches.

I have argued that "Der Ausflug" encodes polychronic structures that both cue and disappoint expectations of narrative factivity; it both triggers and disables processing strategies geared to the interpretation of narratively organized sequences of events. Framed as a retrospective story, it nonetheless unmoors participants, situations, and events and sends them drifting into what Seghers calls the imperturbable stream of time—a fluid temporality in which past, present, and future do not have definite (or even definable) contours. Put briefly, the tale retrospectively portrays a past that is still in the making. It may be that classical models require only minor adjustments to handle such radicalized forms of anachrony. But then again, a wider sampling of polychronic narratives— coupled with an analysis of how polychrony pertains to (post)modern fictional techniques more generally—may lead to the fashioning of new, enriched models for studying order in stories. In any event, questions about polychrony bear on the whole system of norms supporting the design and interpretation of discourse we call narrative.

As I have already hinted at several points, this normative system extends beyond the confines of particular fictional genres or subgenres. It grounds itself in the broad, everyday use of stories to come to terms with—to define—the order of the real. Stories define the order of the real in both of the two operative senses: they define the domain of situations and events that counts as reality, and they define what modes of sequencing, what chains of cause and effect, are endemic to or indicative of that domain. Viewed from this perspective, narrative is not a discourse genre but an ideologeme—perhaps the ideologeme par excellence. A story is a unit that, when combined with other story units in a densely textured mosaic of narratives, helps constitute a culture's or a subculture's sense of reality. Correlatively, the study of narrative form should not be viewed as merely an examination of verbal design. It is also an inquiry into how modes of storytelling—in particular, strategies for ordering—help shape people's intutions about what is and is not the case.

Seghers's polychronic narration can be interpreted as a style of storytelling premised on an awareness of the power of stories to mold cultures, histories, worlds. Cognizant of this power, the tale points to the limits of order even as it orders. More precisely, even as its retrospective form works to reactivate an earlier, better time—to make its lost meaning live again—the tale highlights the impossibility of ever rediscovering *the* past of a now that is itself irreducibly plural. At the same time, even as it tells the story of what caused the moral or physical destruction of a whole generation, it articulates not a single reason but a network of factors—intersecting and highly ramified lines of causation that make it impossible to assign blame to *an* agent of destruction. When effects predate causes in the telling of what happened, the primary task is not to assign blame but to establish connections, not to find a scapegoat from the past for the deficiencies of the present but to see how prior situations and events are systematic with problems in the world at hand.[22] Thus, in contrast to the fascistic ideology whose destructiveness it portrays as unanchored in time, both the forms and themes of "Der Ausflug" are radically resistant to singular explanations. Unlike fascistic narratives that eventuate in simple answers to complex issues, Seghers's is a story whose unfolding opens up ever more complicated questions.

German fascism sought to ensure a glorious future by appealing to, fully reactivating, an authentic tradition and culture located in Germany's past. In building an ideology grounded in nostalgia, the Nazi regime drew on a variety of *völkisch* or populist movements that took rise in nineteenth-century Romanticism and that, unlike other, progressive forms of populism, fostered an ethnic-nationalist conception of German culture (Payne 1995: 52–53, 162). According to this conception, any modern-day cultural revolution must be "based on a regeneration of the Volk, a return to traditional values, and the restoration of a community in which a natural hierarchy would exist, an aristocracy of prophets and warriors" (Laqueur 1996: 24; cf. Hayes 1973: 20–22). As in the Romanticism of Rousseau, the creation of true culture depends on a return to origins, to the starting point of truth itself. At stake is a linear, if backward, movement to the beginning of a history that unfolds as a fall into inauthenticity, a corruption of truth by time. Seghers's polychronic narration presents, instead, an origin that cannot be reached because it contained, all along, signs of an emergent future. As remembered/constructed by the narrator, the original excursion of the schoolchildren is not a definite point in time but a cluster of relationships between different times.[23] Hence time is not the degradation but the medium of truth. A true past is a past that circulates with a present and a future, which take their truth in turn from that past. The recounting of temporally multiple situations and events enables and enhances this circulation between times.

Related to German fascism's retrospective account of pure, *völkisch* origins was its story about how the *Volk* came to be corrupted in the first place. The corruption of history is tantamount to racial and ethnic miscegenation over time, an adventitious mixing of other, inferior cultures with the original Germanic (or in some formulations Nordic) culture.[24] Thus, in writings such as Hitler's *Mein Kampf* (*My Struggle*), "[a]ll history was declared a history of racial struggle, the fundamental unit of human society being the race" (Payne 1995: 157; cf. Horkheimer and Adorno 1988: 168–208; Laqueur 1996: 25). Precedents for this view, integral to Nazi ideology, can be found in early-nineteenth-century theories of racial superiority—Fichte's, for example (Hayes 1973: 21). But the anti-Semitism of the fascists was designed to explain peculiarly modern ills. In particular, "It was the collapse of German society in 1918 and the following years which gave new life to anti-Semitisim. To the minds of the general public, right-wing propaganda about Jewish betrayal seemed a plausible explanation for the misfortunes which had overtaken Germany" (Hayes 1973: 29). As ideologemes of fascism, then, stories assumed a form that promoted highly reductive causal inferences. Narratives were so designed—ordered—as to reduce the most multifaceted events (the defeat of Germany in WWI and the economic and other hardships brought on by that defeat) to a single, racial/ethnic cause. In response to this hyperlinearization of history, "Der Ausflug der toten Mädchen" multiplies lines of causation, making them flow from effect to cause as well as from cause to effect. It counters stories of the original crime of race with a mode of narration that refuses to locate any single crime at the origin. Indeed, Seghers's tale suggests that the criminals of history are not those who disturb a predestined order of events, but those who seek to mask their own strategies for ordering as destiny itself.

Egoyan's *The Sweet Hereafter*: Desperate Narration

Like Seghers's "Der Ausflug," Atom Egoyan's film *The Sweet Hereafter* involves the reconstruction of a traumatic event from the past whose effects live on in and mold a present that in turn gives shape to that past. Polychrony in Seghers's story stems from a single narrator's indeterminate location between past and present; by only vaguely positioning herself (and hence readers) on the narrative timeline, the narrator inhibits attempts to build an exhaustive intepretation of what happened when, and what causes led to which effects, in the storyworld. By means of its temporal profile, Seghers's humble narration dissociates itself from the reductive, and destructive, stories that *do* purport to give an exhaustive account of what they tell about. Egoyan's *The Sweet Hereafter* also exploits temporal indeterminacy to contrast itself with reductive stories, but the film identifies a different source for the impulse to narrate in reductively linear ways. That source is not arrogance but desperation. Further, the film uses different narrative techniques to create polychronic effects, drawing on resources specific to the medium of film to prevent viewers from assigning a definite temporal position to elements in the storyworld.

From Written Narrative to Film Narrative

In the Russell Banks novel from which the film was adapted (Banks 1991), four narrators in five sections present their versions of the events preceding and following upon a school bus accident that kills most of the children living in Sam Dent, a small rural town in upstate New York. (To draw on the narratological terminology discussed in chapter 8, Banks's novel is a multiply focalized narrative, much like William Faulkner's *As I Lay Dying* [1987] though with fewer individual accounts. In both texts, many of the same events are seen and described from several different perspectives.) Dolores Drischoll, the driver of the school bus that crashed, narrates the first section. Then comes a section narrated by Billy Ansel, a Vietnam veteran who owns and operates a local garage. Billy is driving behind the bus waving to his two young children (the way he does each morning) when it slides off an icy road and falls through ice that has formed on the surface of water never drained from a quarry near town. Mitchell Stephens tells the third narrative; he is a successful New York City attorney who believes and tries to persuade others to believe that "there are no accidents" (Banks 1991: 91). Having in a sense lost his own daughter, Zoe, to drug addiction, Stephens uses the judicial system as a vehicle for displacing his own anger and desire for revenge. He has thus traveled to Sam Dent to convince the parents of the children who were killed that "some bungling corrupt state agency or some multinational corporation [has] cost-accounted the difference between a ten-cent bolt and a million-dollar out-of-court settlement and has decided to sacrifice a few lives for the difference" (91). Nichole Burnell, a teenager who survives the crash as a paraplegic and who ultimately thwarts the lawsuit by stating that Dolores, the bus driver, was speeding at the time of the accident, narrates the fourth section. The last narrative is told, once again, by Dolores Drischoll, who is given a fairly hostile reception when she attends the town fair with her husband late in the summer following the accident. Dolores's concluding account suggests that she, like Nichole's parents, may never fully come to terms with the accident and its consequences. Dolores takes a grossly inappropriate delight in watching "Boomer," a vehicle she once used to ferry the town's children to and from school, being driven in the demolition derby at the fair.

In adapting the novel, Egoyan chose to make Stephens's perspective function as, for the most part, the deictic center orienting the film's presentation of the storyworld. In the film version, many of the events associated with the accident emerge during Stephens's interviews with people whom he recruits for his lawsuit against school and town officials. Other events, never brought within the compass of Stephens's perceptions or knowledge, are presented directly in shots unmediated by Stephens in his role as the film's major center of consciousness. Still other events emerge by way of a conversation that Stephens has with Alison, a former friend of Zoe's, on a plane flight that takes place some two years after the accident. The episode on the plane is not a part of Banks's novel; by incorporating it into the film Egoyan effectively stretches out the narrative timeline, creating additional possibilities for both analepses (flashbacks) and prolepses (flashforwards). Indeed, because of these multiple sources of information and the plurality of time frames to which they are indexed, as the film unfolds it massively scrambles the order of events as they occurred in the storyworld. (Figure 9, presented below, indicates just how radically the film reorders storyworld events.) The sheer amount of scrambling involved serves to reinforce the difficulty of chaining together into a narrative traumatic occurrences located but not contained within the past. In other words, the film's temporal structure points up how painful events resist being modeled in the form of a chronological series or linear array.

The film thus models the very process of narrative modeling, not only by narrating antichronologically but also by exploiting fuzzy temporal ordering to engage in polychronic narration. Drawing on formal properties specific to film, it sets polychrony into play, first, by withholding contextual details that would enable viewers to assign various shots a definite position in time. Second, it creates polychronic effects by using what film theorists call asynchronous sound (Bordwell and Thompson 1997: 336–39), that is, sounds originating at a different point within storyworld chronology than the visual images with which those sounds are associated. In both respects the film's structure works to undermine the reductive style of narration—what I am calling *desperate narration*—that is one of its chief themes.[25]

From Anachrony to Polychrony

Figure 8 is a first attempt at schematizing the order of storyworld events insofar as their order can be reconstructed by virtue of cues included in the film. Letters of the alphabet represent narrative episodes (described below the diagram); vertical lines mark the location of episodes on a timeline that the viewer must reconstruct to build a semantic interpretation of the narrative presented by the film.[26] Double vertical lines enclosing asterisks indicate clusters of episodes about which the film does not give enough contextual detail for them to be arranged into ordered sets, though enough detail *is* given for them to be ordered with respect to other, singular episodes and to other such clusters. Episodes falling within these clusters, although not strictly speaking indeterminately

Figure 8. A Storyworld Chronology for Egoyan's *The Sweet Hereafter*

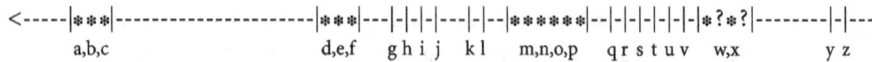

```
<-----|* * *|---------------------|* * *|---|-|-|-|---|-|--|* * * * * *|--|-|-|-|-|-|* ? *|--------|-|----
      a,b,c                       d,e,f     g h i j   k l  m,n,o,p      q r s t u v  w,x           y z
```

a = Stephens and Klara, his ex-wife, are sleeping with their daughter Zoe, at this time a very small child sharing their bed

b = Stephens and ex-wife drive Zoe to doctor; Stephens is ready to perform an emergency tracheotomy if necessary

c = Klara lifts Zoe as a child in a field; Zoe is laughing

d = With the camera occupying Billy Ansel's perspective, his twins run toward him, laughing with joy

e = Day marked by two episodes:

  e_1 = Nichole Burnell performs in a band on a stage at the fair, while her father, Sam, looks on approvingly

  e_2 = Sam and Nichole eat ice cream and watch Dolores Driscoll arrive at the fair with a busload of children

f = Night marked by three main episodes:

  f_1 = Nichole babysits Billy Ansel's twins, reading the tale of the Pied Piper to them

  f_2 = As Nichole babysits, Billy first plays his electric guitar at his garage and then walks across the street to meet Risa Walker in their usual room at the Bide-a-Wile motel, where they make love

  f_3 = After Billy returns and gives Nichole some of his dead wife's clothes, Sam picks up Nichole (his daughter), drives her home, and has sex with her in the hayloft in the barn

g = Dolores picks up children in the school bus on the morning of the accident (as she recounts during her interview with Stephens):

  g_1=Dolores picks up Bear Otto

  g_2=Dolores picks up Sean Walker

h = Moments before the bus accident, Billy Ansel drives behind the bus, calls to arrange a meeting with Risa that night, and waves at his children, who are turned around in their seats looking out the back window at their father as the bus moves forward

i = The accident: the bus slides off the road, breaks through the guardrail, careens down a hill, then sinks into the water that has collected in the unused quarry near town; the water has been covered over with a layer of ice that cannot sustain the weight of the bus

j = Billy identifies his dead children with two slight nods of his head

k = Stephens arrives in Sam Dent to pursue litigation in connection with the accident; Zoe reaches him on his cell phone just before he gets stuck in a carwash

l = Stephens arrives at the Bide-a-Wile motel and interviews Risa and Wendell Walker; in the middle of the interview Zoe calls Stephens again

continued on following page

Figure 8 *continued*

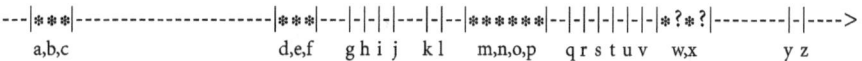

m = Stephens interviews Dolores Driscoll
n = Stephens meets with Hartley and Wanda Otto
o = Stephens visits Billy's garage to see the bus
    o_1 = Stephens films the interior of the bus with a videocamera
    o_2 = Stephens then tries unsuccessfully to get Billy to join the lawsuit
    o_3 = reaching her father on his cell phone after Billy has driven off, Zoe tells Stephens that she is HIV-positive
p = As Nichole Burnell lies in a hospital bed, the doctor touches Nichole's head and says, "The mind is kind"; Nichole's mother says, "You're so lucky," followed by Sam's "Don't even try remembering"
q = Billy meets Risa in their usual motel room and confronts her about the lawsuit
r = Nichole is driven home by her parents in the spring and finds in her room the computer Stephens has bought her, presumably to encourage her to testify in a manner that will help the lawsuit go forward
s = Stephens interviews Nichole
t = Billy visits the Burnells and tries to persuade Nichole's parents to drop the lawsuit
u = Deposition at the community center: Dolores Driscoll testifies
v = Deposition at the community center: Nichole Burnell testifies
w = At the fair Nichole smiles with a ferris wheel rotating above her head; alternatively this event could have occurred at a time nearer to d, e, and f or to y and z
x = Billy Ansel watches the damaged bus being lifted by a crane; it is difficult to know exactly where to place this scene on the timeline, though it does occur sometime after o since the bus is parked at Billy's garage when Billy confronts Stephens
y = two years after either the accident or Stephen's decision to terminate the case, Stephens takes a plane in another attempt to "rescue Zoe"; Alison, Zoe's former friend, is there and serves as an intradiegetic narratee to whom Stephens recounts incidents associated with b
z = Getting off his plane and into a cab, Stephens sees Dolores taking the tickets of passengers on the airport shuttle bus she now drives; Stephens and Dolores make eye contact

ordered in the context of the narrative as a whole, still cannot be arranged into a fixed sequence. They are, in other words, only partially ordered.

Figure 9 represents the order in which these episodes are presented as the film itself unfolds in time. Like figure 8, figure 9 is just a first attempt at schematization that must be refined (as we shall see) to accommodate temporally indeterminate episodes. Preliminarily, though, the array indicates the order in which viewers see episodes that they must then try to linearize as part of the process of interpreting the narrative, that is, of mentally modeling the storyworld that the film prompts them to reconstruct.

Together figures 8 and 9 suggest how the temporal structure of the film delinearizes and complicates what Stephens and some of the grieving parents instead try to hyperlinearize and oversimplify. Reeling from his own daughter's inexplicable and unpreventable slide into heroin addiction, Stephens tries to compensate by imposing a certain kind of narrative schema on the circumstances surrounding the accident—and by getting others to impose that same schema. Specifically, Stephens seeks to narrativize the accident as an easily reconstructed sequence of causally and chronologically linked occurrences, in which a specific agent or group of agents can be assigned blame for what both the film and novel, however, represent as a genuine accident. As represented by the film, however, the crash persistently thwarts the work of human understanding and memory; it is an incident figured as something whose fundamental character is that it could have happened otherwise or might very well not have happened at all. Thus, in her account of the accident in the novel, Dolores represents the storyworld as ontologically rather than temporally indeterminate, leaving it finally undecided whether a dog was or was not there to dart out onto the road and cause her to lose control of the bus (Banks 1991: 1–2). For his part, Stephens asks the Ottos why, given how many times Dolores had driven her bus route over the years, she just happened to have an accident on the morning in question. Rooted in contingency, happenstance, inexplicability, the accident leaves for some what is an intolerable legacy, given its brute resistance to explanation or even description by way of stories that might be used to establish culpability in a court of law.

Yet Stephens has made a life's work of telling the sorts of narratives from which the film structurally as well as thematically dissociates itself.

Figure 9. The Order in Which Episodes Are
Presented in Egoyan's *The Sweet Hereafter*

a, e$_1$, k, e$_2$, l, y, g$_1$, m, h, m, h, y, n, y, f$_1$, f$_2$, f$_1$, f$_2$, f$_3$, f$_1$, f$_3$, h, m, g$_2$, m, h, i, a, y, b, c, j, d, r, q, s, y, o$_1$, o$_2$, o$_3$, b, o$_1$, u, t, v, z, x, w, f$_1$

As an aggressive lawyer specializing in liability cases, Stephens can be expected to narrate opportunistically; but beyond this, as a father channeling his private grief into public action, Stephens has learned to cope by telling desperate stories. Such stories work to hide the ways in which traumatic events resist being linearized into recognizable narrative sequences. As Dolores individually names and weeps over the dead children during her deposition, for example, Stephens sits across from her impassively and asks: "And then what happened?" Stephens speaks colorlessly, numbly, his single-minded quest for definite causes a way of displacing and neutralizing his own sense of personal loss. Stephens's motives are further ironized when this shot segues into the episode (t) in which Billy confronts Nichole's parents about a lawsuit that has helped destroy the community he once knew. Remaining true to his own principle that there are no accidents, and using the cognitive schema that Mark Turner (1996: 26–47) describes under the rubric EVENTS ARE ACTIONS, Stephens promises the grief-stricken Ottos that he will reveal "who is responsible for this tragedy." He projects onto the accident a story in which someone can be assigned blame for what happened.

In turn, the film explicitly prompts its viewers to project onto Stephens's own storytelling habits the narrative of the Pied Piper, which Nichole reads as a bedtime story to Billy Ansel's children (at f$_1$) but which is not a part of Banks's novel. Like the Pied Piper enchanting first the town's rats and then its children with his music, Stephens mystifies the community of Sam Dent with his promise of a story in which *someone, somewhere*, will *somehow* be held accountable for the accident. Falling under Stephens's spell, Risa Walker desperately holds on to the belief that the guardrail was not built strongly enough to keep the bus from sliding off the road, and that someone has therefore been negligent. When Billy asks Risa whether she really believes this, Risa replies, "I have to." Asked why, Risa responds, tautologically, "Because I have to." Her comment reveals that Stephens's mode of narrativizing is a form of reassurance, a metaphysics or even a religion of blame, masking itself as a strategy for explanation. Hence when Risa implicates that the accident may have been caused by Nichole's wearing an item of clothing that once belonged to Billy's dead wife, Billy says, "Christ, it sounds like you're looking for a witch doctor not a lawyer. Maybe they're the same thing."

Billy here does propositionally what the film does structurally: comment on the dangers of the desperate narration in which Stephens engages and succeeds in getting others to engage. In effect, Stephens's style of narration is a synedoche; it stands for all modes of interpretation that tell more or less reductive stories about experiences whose painfulness consists in their refusal to be reduced in any such way. At issue are experiences that resist being cognized via prototypical narrative schemata of the sort THIS, THEN, BECAUSE OF THIS, THAT. Or rather, the film's narrative structure self-consciously models the process by which people rely on narrative to impart causal and chronological structure to both past and present events. The film's disruptions of linear chronology foreground narrative process over narrative product; forcing the viewer to resequence episodes into a linear or quasi-linear order, the movie's structure points up narrative in its profile as an activity rather than an object, a vehicle for comprehension rather than a thing to be comprehended. In brief, by virtue of its temporal structure, the film insists that stories are made, not found.

More than this, however, the film draws on a multivalent temporal system to create polychronic effects. It is not just that the viewer must actively work to construct a timeline for episodes presented nonchronologically or anti-chronologically; beyond this, some episodes in the film simply cannot be assigned a determinate location on the narrative timeline. Desperate narration like Stephens's, of course, cannot tolerate such temporal indeterminacy. It is based on a bivalent system in which every occurrence can be slotted into its own unique position along a chain of (earlier) Causes and (later) Effects. But Egoyan's film cues viewers to model the storyworld quite differently—more vaguely, in grays instead of blacks and whites, as a domain about which exhaustive knowledge is impossible.

Images, Sounds, and Temporal Indeterminacy

Here it is important to note a difference between film narratives and written narratives. Written narratives encode polychrony by *including* certain kinds of information linguistically—in Seghers's story, chiefly by way of nonindicative verbal moods and lexical items that occur in specific contexts. Films, however, encode polychrony by *leaving out* certain kinds of information (cf. Chatman 1978: 30, 106–7; 1990: 38–55). In a film such as *The Sweet Hereafter*, as figure 9 suggests, anachrony is the norm rather than the exception. Hence, to return to the terms used in my discussion of Seghers's story, viewers of the film must suspend what can be described as a default preference rule for interpreting narrative: If event B is presented after event A in the narrative, then unless told otherwise assume that in the storyworld itself B occurred after A. William Labov (1972a) describes this iconic matching of narrative clauses (or, in the present case, cinematic images) with storyworld events as a feature definitive of narrative itself (contrast Herman 1999c). Debatably, though, it is more appropriately characterized as a cognitive preference that can be suspended or deactivated in the context of particular narratives or narrative styles. In such contexts, where the preference for iconic matching is suspended by a more or less pervasive anachrony, interpreters of the narrative activate a preference rule based on the opposite principle: Unless told otherwise, assume an event B following event A in the narrative does NOT model a storyworld in which B follows A. The episodes represented in clusters in figure 8 are, I would argue, ambiguous on this score. There are not enough contextual cues for viewers to suspend the preference NOT to read the episodes as chronologically presented; but neither are there enough cues to *activate* this preference rule. Rather, the film leaves the order of the clustered episodes deliberately vague or, to use Edmund Husserl's word, "anexact"; it does not provide enough visual or auditory information for them to be linearized in a precise way relative to one another. Such temporal indeterminacy might be labeled *restricted* polychrony, since its scope does not include the entire timeline. Even restricted indeterminacy of this sort, however, helps create a narrative environment unfavorable to desperate narration. The environment is one in which viewers are cued to model portions of the storyworld as domains in which causal links between episodes cannot be definitively or even provisionally established.

Even more challenging for the viewer is the task of placing on the narrative timeline the two episodes that figure 8 tags with question marks, w and x. As already indicated in my list and description of the episodes, w is especially (if not absolutely) resistant to temporal indexing. The episode is indeterminately located somewhere on the large portion of the timeline that stretches from d,e,f to z. Again, this is because of a lack of contextual detail. All the viewer sees in w is Nichole smiling at dusk as the Ferris wheel turns above her; the film does not reveal whether or not she is in a wheelchair, or whether or not she is with her father on the day that she and he see Dolores Driscoll drop off the children at the fair (at e_2). Hence the episode could conceivably occupy several positions quite widely spaced along the narrative timeline. Similarly, the final image of the film resists being assigned a definite location in time. After the image of Nichole smiling at the fair, the film shifts to the night on which Nichole babysits Billy's two children (f_1). She closes the book containing the story of the Pied Piper, kisses the two children goodnight and turns off their lights, and then walks out of their bedroom and down to the end of the hallway, where she stands with her back to the camera and facing the window. The window is suddenly illuminated by intense flashes of light that eventually give way to a light that is equally intense but fixed. The light is of an ambiguous quality and source, however. It might be the flash of Billy's headlights as he returns home from his tryst with Risa Walker; or it might be Nichole's father's headlights as he arrives to pick her up; or, interpreted less naturalistically, the light might represent the massively accelerated passage of time itself, with night yielding to daylight that rapidly fills the window. The final shot provides insufficient detail for the viewer to choose between these interpretive options and establish a preference ranking, and in consequence the temporal position of the shot vis-à-vis the storyworld as a whole remains indeterminate. More generally, the film narrates polychronically by exploiting the potentials of the medium of film to present relatively decontextualized images, in contrast to the necessarily temporally contextualizing effects of, for example, verb tenses found in written narratives. Using the very absence of detail as a resource for polychronic narration, the film makes it impossible for viewers to form a semantic representation of the storyworld that would enable them to locate episode w or the final image at a determinate point in time. Such polychrony, as already suggested, gives the lie to Stephens's way of telling "the" story of the accident.

Another resource for polychronic narration in film is cinema's unique combination of two modes or "tracks" of information, auditory as well as visual.[27] As David Bordwell and Kristin Thompson note (1997: 337–39), sound and image are often synchronous; in other words, the temporal position of the sound in the storyworld often matches that of the image. But sound and image can also be asynchronous, yielding both sound flashbacks and sound flashforwards, that is, sounds that are earlier and sounds that are later in the storyworld than the image on screen. In addition to using synchronous sound, Egoyan's film features both sorts of asynchrony. For example, the episode involving Stephens and Zoe's former friend Alison on the plane (y) contains two sound flashbacks (as well as several visual ones). Stephens tells Alison how he and his ex-wife, Klara, drove Zoe to the doctor after she had been bitten by poisonous spiders, with Stephens singing lullabies to Zoe as he held her in his lap and kept his pen knife open in case he had to perform an emergency tracheotomy. At two different points, the sound of a man's voice singing a lullaby punctuates Stephens's telling of the story to Alison. The first occurrence of the sound is much lower in volume than the second. This exemplifies not only how sound flashbacks can be used to reveal subjective states of participants—that is, Stephens's memory of the incident gets more vivid as he continues to narrate what happened—but also how loudness correlates with the perceived spatial or temporal distance of objects, situations, or events (cf. Bordwell and Thompson 1997: 333–35).

A sound flashforward occurs during the episode in which Stephens meets with the Ottos and convinces them to participate in the lawsuit (n). After Stephens says to them, synchronously, "You see, I'm not just here to speak for your anger, but for the future as well," his voice is then heard saying offscreen: "I did everything that the loving father of a drug addict is supposed to do." Then the image track "catches up" with the sound track, moving forward in time to the conversation that Stephens has with Alison on the plane (at y). There are also combinations of the two types of asynchrony. For instance, in the episode on the plane Alison asks Stephens how Zoe is. Stephens does not respond verbally, but the image track shifts back in time to the scene (g_1) in which the Ottos are chatting with Dolores as they put their son, Bear, on the bus. Offscreen the viewer hears the sound of Dolores narrating the action being shown on the screen. This sound is a flashforward within a flashback; the image track again "catches up" to the episode in which Stephens interviews Dolores about what happened on the day of the accident (m).

In other cases, however, asynchronous sounds prove more difficult to locate in time. Figure 10 divides the image track (IT) from the sound track (ST) and represents several instances of asynchrony between them, using an @ sign to indicate what visual information the asynchronous sounds are being attached to. More precisely, the letters to the right of the @ sign designate the visual information to which sounds (designated by letters to the left of the @ sign) are indexed. As in figure 8, question marks are one indicator of temporal indeterminacy. Thus, at the end of episode o, after Zoe has called Stephens on his cell phone to tell him that she is HIV-positive, and after the image track moves back in time to Stephens's holding the infant Zoe in his lap (b), there is a second flashback to a point less distant in time (o_1). Here the viewer sees the footage of the interior of the bus that Stephens shot with his video camera prior to his encounter with Billy Ansel (at o_2). Associated with this footage are sounds of children laughing and shouting, sounds that then modulate into those of children sobbing. It is impossible to know exactly where in storyworld chronology these sound originate. The sounds of happy children might be indexed to h, the sounds of weeping children to i, but there is again insufficient contextual detail for the viewer to assign the sounds a determinate location in time. Here the asychronous sound creates another instance of restricted polychrony. It is true that the sounds can be (vaguely) located somewhere between between d,e,f, and i, and not earlier or later, but that is as much as can be said about them.

By contrast, the sound of Nichole reciting the tale of the Pied Piper to Billy's children does in fact originate at a definite point in time (i.e., f_1). But arguably, the sheer frequency with which it is flashed back to (asynchronously) serves to make its temporal boundaries become fuzzy or indeterminate as the film proceeds. The tale of Pied Piper is heard when Nichole's father is seen kissing her in the loft of the barn (f_3), just prior to Nichole's deposition at the community center (v), again during the deposition itself, in association with the image of Nichole smiling at the fair (w), and during the episode with Stephens and Alison on the plane (y). Attached to the visual track at multiple points, the story comments auditorily on several dimensions of the action being shown visually. The film projects the role of the Piper both onto Stephens and onto Nichole's father, but it also suggests, at y, that Zoe has herself been enchanted, sealed inside the magic mountain by a Piper exacting a form of payment

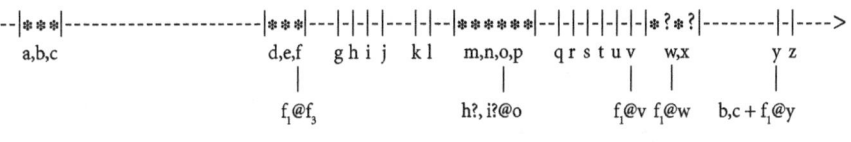

Figure 10. Asynchronous Sounds in Egoyan's *The Sweet Hereafter*

from her parents. Further, at f_3, when Nichole's father picks her up at Billy's house, it is not just that the sound of Nichole's voice heard off-screen reading the bedtime tale constitutes a sound flashback to f_1. More than this, the content of the portion of the tale being read points ahead in time to the accident and its effects on Nichole herself:

> Did I say all?
> No, one was lame
> and could not dance
> the whole of the way.
> And in afteryears
> if you would blame
> his sadness he was used to say:
> "It's dull in our town
> since my playmates left.
> I can't forget that I'm bereft
> of all the pleasant sights they see,
> which the Piper promised me."

As a sound flashback attached at multiple points to an image track moving both backward and forward in time and embedding at f_3 a proleptic comment on narrative information yet to be presented, Nichole's voice-over recitations of the tale of Pied Piper resist clear-cut temporal delimitation. Note, too, that the lines following those just quoted—

> For he led us, he said,
> to a joyous land
> joining the town
> and just at hand
> where the waters gushed
> and the fruit trees grew

> And flowers put forth
> a fair hue
> and everything was strange, and new"

—are heard offscreen both when the visual track shows Nichole's father kissing her and when, at w, it shows Nichole smiling at the fair. In this instance, asynchronous sound not only prompts the viewer to make a (partial) deictic shift back to an earlier point in time but also links two images separated by a quite long temporal interval in the image track. Egoyan's use of asynchronous sound thus crosscuts the syntagmatic logic of THIS, THEN, BECAUSE OF THIS, THAT with a paradigmatic logic of THIS, THOUGH LATER OR EARLIER THAN THAT, BEARS COMPARISON WITH THAT. Foregrounding the second sort of logic, even as it assumes that the viewer will use the logic of linearity as a resource for interpretation, *The Sweet Hereafter* builds into its very structure countermeasures to desperate narration.

As the image track shifts from Stephens getting off his plane and encountering Dolores driving the airport shuttle (z) to the temporally indeterminate image of Nichole smiling at the fair (w), the viewer hears the following voice-over narration addressed to Stephens by Nichole:

> As you see her, two years later, I wonder if you realize something. I wonder if you understand that all of us, Dolores, me, the children who survived, the children who didn't, that we're all citizens of a different town now. [The image track shifts here to x, another temporally indeterminate episode in which Billy watches as the school bus is lifted up in the air by a crane at his garage.] A place with its own special rules, special laws, a town of people living in the sweet hereafter.

Spatializing time, figuring the hereafter as an elsewhere, the aftermath of the accident as a "different town" where those affected by it now live, the very manner in which the film represents Nichole as addressing Stephens suggests why his desperate form of storytelling ultimately fails on its own terms: the lawsuit does not go forward. Asynchronous sounds and decontextualized images reveal that although the film itself opens an imaginary space for the sweet hereafter, that town's "special rules, special laws" are of a preeminently temporal character. It is a town ruled not by linear but by multilinear time. Its inhabitants experience not Earlier Causes and Later Effects but events that must be assigned *three* values: Earlier, Later, and Indeterminate.

Thomas's *The White Hotel*: Magical Narration

Another narrative featuring temporal indeterminacy but employing it for different, arguably more radical modeling purposes, is D. M. Thomas's *The White Hotel*. Thomas's novel has been characterized as a "boundary work" within the genre of magical realism (Foster 1995: 280). Originally used by Franz Roh (1925) to describe developments in post-Expressionist painting in German-speaking countries during the interwar period, the term *magical realism* later acquired currency in literary-historical contexts.[28] Specifically, it refers to texts that build on but also subvert representational techniques such as the ones used by nineteenth-century realistic writers (Dickens, Stendahl, Flaubert). More specifically still, magical realists such as Gabriel García Márquez, Toni Morrison, Salman Rushdie, and Derek Walcott employ "ontological disruption [to figure] political and cultural disruption: magic is often given as a cultural corrective, requiring readers to scrutinize accepted realistic conventions of causality, materiality, motivation" (Zamora and Faris 1995: 3). Radicalizing realist concerns with the nature of reality and its representation, magical realists traffic in hallucinatory scenes and events and deploy fantastic characters; they also reconfigure as gradient and reversible oppositions (real versus imaginary, self versus other, life versus death) that are binary and irreversible in more narrowly realistic genres. Magical realist texts thus fuse "possible worlds, spaces, systems" that would be irreconcilable in other fictional modes, situating themselves on a "liminal territory between or among those worlds—in phenomenal and spiritual regions where transformation, metamorphosis, and dissolution are common" (Zamora and Faris 1995: 6). Here I focus on polychrony as a resource for magical realist narration in *The White Hotel*; students of this narrative genre would do well to investigate fuzzy temporal ordering as one of its key structural markers.

More precisely, whereas Seghers's story and Egoyan's film introduce temporal indeterminacy into efforts to narrativize and comprehend past trauma, thus countering both arrogant and desperate styles of narration, Thomas's work engages in a form of *magical* narration that ascribes temporal indeterminacy to elements of the storyworld itself. Polychrony, here, impinges upon what is being recounted and not just the attempt to recount it. Hence the ontological contours of the storyworld look very different in *The White Hotel* than they do in "Der Ausflug" and *The Sweet Hereafter*. Events in the storyworld actually occur at more than one place on the narrative timeline, rather than being narrativized in a way that leaves their exact place in time an open question. Because of these temporally indeterminate events, the problem whose solution is typically construed as the motor of narrative—that is, *And then what happened?*—becomes a special limiting case of another problem with a much richer, much more complicated temporal structure: *How is what has not yet happened making its effects felt on what has already happened, is happening now, and is immediately about to happen?*

Against Freud: Feeling the Future

Of special interest in this connection is what John Burt Foster Jr. (1995) has described as Lisa Erdman's "physiological clairvoyance" in *The White Hotel*. (In magical realist texts more generally, argue Lois Parkinson Zamora and Wendy B. Faris, "historical narrative is no longer chronicle but clairvoyance" [1995: 6].) From the start Lisa experiences pains in her left breast and pelvic region that a fictitious version of Sigmund Freud reads as hysterical symptoms rooted in some original psychological trauma. Like his actual-world counterpart, Thomas's Freud is committed to an etiological, backward-looking method of interpretation.[29] Yet the temporal structure of the narrative as a whole gives the lie to Freud's diagnostic techniques. In the case study he reports as "Frau Anna G.," Freud hypothesizes that Lisa's complaints stem from repressed knowledge of her own homosexuality (Thomas 1981: 134–44)—knowledge that can only be brought to consciousness by way of psychoanalytic investigation into the past. As Freud puts it, "[E]very gift has its cost, and the price of freedom from intolerable knowledge had been an hysteria" (136). As the novel proceeds, though, it becomes evident that Anna's/Lisa's pain is not the trace of a past trauma, but rather the anticipatory illumination of a future one. What Freud construes as hysterical symptoms prove to be effects-before-the-fact of Lisa's own brutal rape and murder in a future that will unfold at Babi Yar, a ravine in Kiev where, beginning on 28 September 1941, over one hundred thousand Jews, Gypsies, and Soviet prisoners of war were exterminated by the Nazis.[30] For most of the novel, then, Lisa's pain is an effect of events that have not yet happened in the storyworld, a symptom that predates the condition it indexes.

Further, in contrast to Seghers's story, fuzzy temporal ordering cannot be ascribed to constraints on the narration of traumatic events involving both an experiencing and a remembering self. A polyphonic text closer in this respect to *The Sweet Hereafter* than to "Der Ausflug," *The White Hotel* features a plurality of voices and perspectives and hence many sources of cues for storyworld reconstruction—some of them yielding conflicting versions of the world figured by the text (Cross 1992; Newman 1989: 193). Adding to the complexity of the narration is the novel's use of multiple registers of discourse—poetic, epistolary, scientific, mock-autobiographical, historiographical, and prophetic-utopian—distributed between its various narrative voices. The result is a text that extends polychrony from the domain of personal remembrance into the realm of history itself. Put otherwise, the text authenticates fuzzy temporal ordering as part of the structure of the real, rather than as a strategy for coming to terms with events especially resistant to a remembering self's narration. This is what makes Thomas's narration not just polychronic but also magical realist. In moving from "Der Ausflug" and *The Sweet Hereafter* to *The White Hotel*, recipients move from an emphasis on the epistemological and affective dimensions of polychrony to an exploration of its ontological import. Putting this point still another way, the temporal structure of Thomas's novel prevents a naturalistic reading of the sort that Seghers's story and Egoyan's film still allow. Seghers's and Egoyan's narratives do use polychrony to inhibit an exhaustive reconstruction of the storyworlds they encode, but they impute merely vagueness, not a unique ontological structure, to the elements of the storyworld that they allow readers to model only "anexactly."

Recall that, in "Der Ausflug," Seghers relies largely on subjunctive verbal moods and lexical items to destabilize the ordering of events in a storyworld being built even as it is being remembered. *The Sweet Hereafter* uses decontextualized images and asynchronous sound to create similarly polychronic effects. In *The White Hotel*, what is particularly instrumental in creating a multivalent temporal system is the way the text parcels out information about Lisa's life history. Thus, in contrast to Seghers's use of temporal indeterminacy in written narrative, polychrony in Thomas's novel derives more from the juxtaposition of large-scale textual segments than from semantic information encoded in the morphology of individual verbs or the meaning of particular words. After some preliminary correspondence written mainly by "Freud," readers encounter, in the "Don Giovanni" and "The Gastein Journal" sections of the novel, phantasmagoric descriptions, images of violent sexual penetration, and a narratorial style marked in general by a superabundant sexual imagination. These sections are followed by the Freudian case study, "Frau Anna G.," in which Freud presents his theory of the causes of Anna's/Lisa's "symptoms." Then come sections detailing later phases of Lisa's life, her murder at Babi Yar, and finally her posthumous existence in "The Camp" in Palestine, all of which retrospectively confer a predictive or anticipatory significance on the pains that Freud construes as being caused by events buried in Lisa's past. Not just discredited by subsequent narrative developments, Freud's account figures as a stand-in for all interpretive models grounded in bivalent as opposed to multivalent temporal systems. Just as in *The Sweet Hereafter* Stephens is emblematic of all who tell desperate stories, Freud's case study is a synecdoche for all intepretive paradigms in which a line of causality stretches unidirectionally (if sometimes covertly) from Earlier to Later. To Freud's methods can be opposed modeling strategies according to which causality flows both forward and backward in time. Such strategies draw on a temporal system that allows interpreters to assign to some events the value of Indeterminate, neither definitely Earlier nor definitely Later than some NOW used as a point of reference in time.

True, Thomas's multivalent temporal system does unfold gradually over the course of the novel, taking time to reveal itself. But retrospectively that system supports a reading of the novel as representing events that are intrinsically temporally indeterminate, inherently vaguely positioned in time, and not just narrativized as such. The first section of the novel consists of a poem that Lisa has composed between the lines of the score of "Don Giovanni." Here Lisa writes of the affair she imagines herself having had with Freud's son—an affair redescribed heterodiegetically in the following section, entitled "The Gastein Journal."[31] The poem describes how

> no shame
> could make me push my dress down, thrust his hand
> away, the two, then three, fingers he jammed
> into me though the guard brushed the glass (15–16);

how one night "he almost burst my cunt apart" (18); and how

> pulling me upon him without warning,
> your son impaled me, it was so sweet I screamed
> but no one heard me for the other screams (19).

Supplementing these images of penetration, the journal describes how, at Bad Gastein, "When they [the two lovers] went down to dinner, her breasts felt like bursting" (64). The woman asks her lover, " 'Is my breast softer than the stone?' He nodded, resting his head on it to prove its softness. . . . He fondled her breast that was so much softer than flint" (41). In a Dali-esque fusion of the magical and the real, another passage in the journal reads:

> A Lutheran pastor said hesitantly that he had seen a breast flying through the yew trees when he had strolled up to the church one evening before dinner. . . . A heavily busted woman with greying hair said that she had recently had a breast removed because of a growth. . . . [The Bolshevik] Vogel, looking distinctly yellow, said he thought he had seen a petrified embryo floating in the lake shallows, but it could just as easily have been a piece of fossilized tree. His sister, beginning to weep, confessed to an abortion, ten years ago. (56)

The journal also mentions that after the baker reports that he has "seen a womb gliding across the lake" (57), an elderly nurse tells him that her grand-niece "had only a month ago undergone an operation for the removal of her womb" (58).

After being confronted with these phantasmagoric descriptions, readers are then forced to shift to a scientific register, the discourse of psychoanlysis, in Freud's case study of Lisa as "Frau Anna G." As part of his attempt to offer an etiology of Anna's/Lisa's condition, Freud remarks:

> In the autumn of 1919 I was asked by a doctor of my acquaintance to examine a young lady who had been suffering for the past four years from severe pains in her left breast and pelvic region, as well as a chronic respiratory condition. When making this request he added that he thought the case was one of hysteria, though there were certain counter-indications which had caused him to examine her very thoroughly indeed in order to rule out the possibility of some organic affection. (89)

The structure of the narrative as a whole confirms that the concept of the "organic" is more apt than Freud himself recognizes in his case study. The novel suggests that Lisa's life unfolds according to a sort of organic temporality, in which any given moment is organically related to, or systematic with, moments that are ostensibly earlier and later than the instant in question. Lisa could not be the person that she is without a future that has not yet happened but that is already organically affecting the times that are presumed to precede it. But given his own investigative procedures, Freud persists in his search for a "particular event which might have been instrumental in unleashing [Lisa's] hysteria" (130). Granted, Freud does read into Lisa's life a retrospective logic according to which what is about to happen in it shapes what came before. He writes that Lisa's happy memories extended only to her fifth summer, "for the shadow of the event which would bring a cruelly sudden expulsion from her paradise was already hanging over her—her mother's death" (93). Generally, though, causality for Freud moves only in a forward direction. Noting that Lisa's mother died in a hotel fire on a night when a storm is raging, Freud postulates that "[t]wo of her recent hallucinations in adult life—a storm at sea, and a fire at a hotel—clearly related to this tragic event" (93). Discounting what Anna/Lisa herself considers as her gift of prescience or "prediction" (111), Freud argues that "[w]hat she had in her consciousness was only a secret and not a foreign body. She both knew and did not know. . . . Clearly the child in Frau Anna's mind was telling us to look at her breast and her ovary: and precisely the left breast and ovary, for the unconscious is a precise and even pedantic symbolist" (99). By threatening termination of her treatment, Freud even "managed to drag from her the truth about her marriage" (123), during which Lisa/Anna experienced hallucinations whenever sexual intercourse took place. Two of those hallucinations involve falling from a great height and being buried by a landslide.

At this juncture, or rather when they reinterpret these incidents in light of Lisa's subsequent murder at Babi Yar, readers can detect pressures of a polychrony operating on the structures of the real as modeled via magical realist narration. For all of Freud's attempts to provide an explanation of Lisa's symptoms based on his theory that she has repressed knowledge about her own homosexuality, Lisa's hallucinations and physical problems prove to have a prospective or predictive significance, not a retrospective one. Their meaning does not become apparent until the penultimate section of the novel, "The Sleeping Carriage," in which Lisa and her husband's son Kolya are executed at Babi Yar. Lined up at the edge of a ravine, about to be cut down by bullets from a machine gun, Lisa grasps Kolya's hand and leaps down into the ravine (247). After the soldiers have covered over the corpses with dirt (in a manner prefigured by Lisa's hallucinations), Lisa's body will eventually be swamped by a "green, stagnant and putrid" lake created when engineers build a dam across the mouth of the ravine (252). Before this can happen, though, Kolya dies in the fall, and as Lisa herself lies dying, just before being savagely raped with a soldier's bayonet, the narration shifts from Lisa's to an external perspective:

> An ss man bent over an old woman lying on her side, having seen a glint of something bright. His hand brushed her breast when he reached for the crucifix to pull it free, and he must have sensed a flicker of life. Letting go the crucifix he stood up. He drew his leg back and sent his jackboot crashing into her left breast. She moved position from the force of the blow, but uttered no sound. Still not satisfied, he swung his boot again and sent it cracking into her pelvis. Again the only sound was the clean snap of the bone. Satisfied at last, he jerked the crucifix free. . . . The woman, whose screams had not been able to force a way through her throat, went on screaming. (248–49)

This passage indicates that Lisa's murder in 1941 is, in fact, the cause of physical and mental problems that she began experiencing a quarter of a century earlier, despite Freud's insistence that her problems are the effects or symptoms of still earlier events. What is more, when the ss man rips Lisa's crucifix from her neck, his action belies Freud's theory that Lisa fingers her crucifix (which was previously her mother's) whenever she is failing to be completely truthful with him during analysis (131). Lisa's pains and habit of touching the crucifix are not the signs of past events that she has more or less successfully concealed from herself but anticipations of events pertaining to a hidden future that is already impinging upon the present.[32] The pains that Lisa experiences in her breast and pelvis are in this sense temporally indeterminate in the context of the storyworld; they necessarily appear in time but cannot be located at some definite point along a chain of causes and effects that unfolds linearly in time. Indeed, the text suggests as much in describing the events at Babi Yar as occupying "no conceivable part of time" (246).

Nightmares of History

By the same token, the nightmare that Lisa has in 1929 in "The Health Resort" section of the novel, where Lisa is performing in an opera in Milan, proves to be the effect of a cause that has not yet occurred: "As dawn glimmered through the curtains she slept, and dreamed she was standing over a deep trench filled with many coffins. . . . As she mourned for [Vera, another opera singer], in a line of crying mourners, there was a rumble above her, and she knew a landslide was going to crash down and bury her" (163–64). The temporal position of the events in Lisa's dreams must be assigned the value of Indeterminate; anticipating the future that will prove to be their cause, the dreamed events can be categorized neither as Earlier nor as Later than Babi Yar, strictly speaking. They subsist, in the words of Walter Benjamin (1969), in " 'the time of the now' [*Jetztzeit*] which is shot through with chips of Messianic time" (263). Similarly temporally indeterminate are the events in the nightmare described in the opening paragraphs of "The Gastein Journal." On the train to Bad Gastein, the unnamed woman who will repeat the experiences that Lisa describes as her own in "Don Giovanni" is awakened by the ticket collector from a disturbing dream. (We learn in "Frau Anna G." that Lisa's trip to Bad Gastein occurred sometime in 1919, some twenty-two years before the massacre at Babi Yar.) A figure in her own nightmare, the woman

> stumbled over a root, picked herself up and ran on blindly. There was nowhere to run, but she went on running. The crash of foliage grew louder behind her, for they were men, and could run faster. Even if she reached the end of the wood there would be more soldiers waiting to shoot her, but these few extra moments of life were precious.... Then she looked up into the frightened face of a small boy. He was naked like her, and blood poured from a hundred gashes and scratches. "Don't be frightened, lady," he said. "I'm alive too." "Be quiet!" she told him. (31–32)

Rather than being a fantasy structure reworking events stored in the dreamer's memory, when read in the context of the novel as a whole this dream suggests that history itself is structured phantasmagorically. More precisely, it indicates that history's temporal profile mirrors that of dreams, organized analogically more than chronologically, with the relative posteriority or anteriority of a thing or event being less salient than the organic interconnectedness of items multiply and thus indeterminately situated in time. For the dream reprises events that again do not occur until Babi Yar, as described in the penultimate section of the novel:

> A woman did scramble up the ravine's side, after dark. It was Dina Pronicheva. And when she grasped hold of a bush to pull herself over, she did come face to face with a boy, clothed in vest and pants, who had also

inched his way up. He scared Dina with his whisper: "Don't be scared, lady! I'm alive too."

Lisa had once dreamt those words, when she was taking the thermal springs at Gastein with Aunt Magda. But it is not really surprising, for she had clairvoyant gifts and naturally a part of her went on living with these survivors: Dina, and the little boy who trembled and shivered all over. . . . Dina survived to be the only witness, the sole authority for what Lisa saw and felt.[33] (250–51)

It is important to note that the novel itself does not merely exploit but also thematizes an enriched temporality that resists being divided into Earlier and Later. Thematically as well as formally, the text prompts readers to model the storyworld not in terms of a linear array of causes followed by effects, but rather as a multilinear complex of vectors of causality moving both backward and forward in time. Minimally, by making temporality itself a problem, the novel defamiliarizes both the structure and the effects of time. At some points, time and causality do not seem to flow in any direction whatsoever, as in "The Gastein Journal," where the woman cannot be sure that a particular night is her second night with her lover because she "had lost all sense of time" (40). Similarly, later in the journal the guests at the white hotel are described as having "no idea what time it was. Time, that had raced during the evening, now dragged for Madame Cottin, lying open-eyed in the dark; and did not exist, in different ways, for the sleeping guests, for the dead down in the cool store rooms, and for the lovers" (61). At other points time accelerates, attaining an incredible velocity. At Babi Yar, as the people lined up for execution are stripped and beaten,

> Some became old in minutes. When Lisa's gift or curse of second sight had failed her so miserably and her husband was snatched away in the dark, her hair had gone grey overnight—the old saying was true. . . . [Now, at Babi Yar, Sonia's] raven hair turned grey in the time it took for her to be stripped and sent away to be shot. Lisa saw it happen again and again. (242)

At still other points, as in "The Health Resort" section, the novel more or less explicitly evokes polychrony as a theme. Here Lisa has moved to Kiev to marry Victor, Vera's husband, and become a mother to Kolya, Victor's and Vera's son. She visits a summer house on the grounds where she used to live as a child. With a distinctly Proustian emphasis on the way sensory experiences such as smells and tastes can unlock realms of memory that seem more like vast, open spaces than unidirectional chains of causes and effects, the narrator reports that Lisa

> had the feeling that she was no more than a spectre. Herself was unreal, the little boy was unreal. She was cut off from the past and therefore did not live in the present. But suddenly, as she stood close against a pine tree and breathed its sharp, bitter scent, a clear space opened to her childhood, as though a wind had sprung up from the sea, clearing a mist. It was not a memory from the past but the past itself, as alive, as real; and she knew that she and the child of forty years ago were the same person. . . . as she looked back through the clear space of her childhood, there was no blank wall, only an endless extent, like an avenue, in which she was still herself, Lisa. She was still there, even at the beginning of all things. And when she looked in the opposite direction, towards the unknown future, death, the endless extent beyond death, she was still there. It all came from the scent of a pine tree. (213–14)

To reach the promised land described in "The Camp" is to enter just this sort of magical temporality. In the camp there coexist situations and events that are ostensibly more or less widely spaced along the syntagmatic chain of historical occurrence—such as Freud's being sick with cancer, Lisa's mother's still being alive. Like the town by means of which Nichole Burnell figures the sweet hereafter as a place—the town where the voices of children who survived the bus accident mingle with those of the children who did not—the camp in *The White Hotel* occupies an imaginary space governed by "special rules, special laws" that are in fact temporal in nature. But whereas Nichole merely alludes to the town of the sweet hereafter, mentioning it in passing, Thomas devotes seventeen pages of heterodiegetic narration to what transpires in a place manifestly ruled by temporal indeterminacy. By so openly accommodating this indeterminacy within the world it represents as real (or as undecidably real/irreal), *The White Hotel* uses polychrony to accomplish a mode of narration that is not just humble or antireductive but is ontologically transgressive. This is magical narration.

In his case study of "Frau Anna G.," Freud suggests that because of the structure of the unconscious, memory is necessarily paraleptic in its functioning, illicitly importing information from the Later back into its attempts to reproduce an Earlier: "I have my doubts if we ever deal with a memory *from* childhood; memories *relating to* childhood may be all that we possess. Our childhood memories show us our earliest years not as they were but as they appeared at the later period when the memories were aroused" (109). The magical realism of *The White Hotel* derives from a kind of radicalization of Freud's theory; the novel makes paralepsis compulsory not just for psychical but also for historical processes. Thus, in Thomas's text, the Later is constantly migrating back into the Earlier, as attested by Lisa's nightmares as well as her clairvoyant physiology. Although they, too, draw on a multivalent temporal system, the historical paralepses of Thomas's novel therefore constitute a mode of fuzzy temporal ordering distinct from the modes found in Seghers's "Der Ausflug" and Egoyan's *The Sweet Hereafter*. Seghers and Egoyan use polychrony to warn against the danger of pursuing impossible totalities, wholly exhaustive stories, seamless and fully surveyable chains of causes and effects. Thomas uses polychrony to suggest that history itself may not be structured according to prototypical narrative schemata, such as THIS, THEN, BECAUSE OF THIS, THAT. Minimally, though, all three narratives show that the classical concepts of order developed by structuralist narratologists retain their validity, but only within certain limits. Narratologists must now reassess those limits and develop explanatory models for narrative phenomena—including polychrony—that prove resistant to earlier frameworks.[34]

7

Spatialization

This chapter examines the role of space in narrative, as well as the role that narrative plays in helping create mental representations of space. To be sure, as chapter 6 indicated, it is a basic function of narrative to situate things (more or less definitely) in time. As was well attested both by the Russian Formalists and by structuralist narratologists, stories, in fact, are marked by a complex, double temporality, being sequentially organized accounts of sequences of events (Chatman 1990). Yet narratives can also be thought of as systems of verbal or visual cues prompting their readers to *spatialize* storyworlds into evolving configurations of participants, objects, and places. Further, although A.-J. Greimas and his associates had already begun to make space a focal point of narratological research by the late 1960s, anticipating subsequent trends in fields such as linguistic semantics, discourse analysis, and cognitive science, most narratologists working in the classical, structuralist tradition failed to pick up on Greimas's lead. It is only now, when (socio)linguistic, cognitive, and narratological approaches to the study of narrative have finally started to converge, that Greimas's prescient observations on space can be extended and refined.

More precisely, narratology is now in a position to further Greimas's pathbreaking ideas partly because it can make use of research tools developed in studies of natural-language narratives, including oral narratives told in conversational or instructional settings or in response to questions asked by sociolinguistic and other interviewers. In recent years the study of such conversational storytelling has emerged as a vital field of cross-disciplinary research, spanning not just narratology but also linguistics, cognitive science, ethnography, and sociology (see, e.g., Bamberg 1997; Bruner 1986; Linde 1993; Polanyi 1989; Riessman 1993; Rubin 1995). In turn, narrative theorists such as Catherine Emmott (1997) and Monika Fludernik (1996) have shown how ideas deriving from the analysis of narrative in general can be brought to bear on literary narratives in particular.[1] Their work suggests that readers are able to interpret literary narratives because they rely on many of the same linguistic and cognitive parameters guiding interpretation of stories told in conversational contexts. The present chapter combines all of these resources—narratological, linguistic, cognitive-scientific, and other—to make a more specific claim about narrative: namely, that spatial reference plays a crucial, not an optional or derivative, role in stories. Indeed, throughout the chapter I use the locution *narrative domains* to emphasize that narratives should be viewed not just as temporally structured communicative acts but also as systems of verbal or visual prompts anchored in mental models having a particular spatial structure. More exactly, narratives represent the world being told about as one having a specific spatial structure.

The chapter begins by contrasting Roland Barthes's remarks on the spatiotemporal dimensions of narrative with Greimas's remarks, arguing that Greimas sketched more productive lines of inquiry in this connection. I then show how in recent years researchers working in a number of disciplinary traditions have devoted considerable attention both to the linguistic encoding of spatial relationships and to the way these linguistic reflexes of space bear on the interpretation of narrative discourse. In particular, I survey six key ideas growing out of work on language and space and sketch their applications for narrative analysis. Though the scope of the research based on these six concepts necessitates a fairly synoptic presentation here, the concepts can nonetheless be used to throw light on a variety of narrative texts. Conversely, the texts reveal the importance of incorporating literary and other written narratives into ongoing research on language, narrative, and space. Such narratives, particularly those associated with modernist and postmodernist modes of literary experimentation, often do not just rely on but also actively manipulate the signals and strategies by which spatial reference is accomplished in narrative domains.

Hence, the penultimate section of the chapter focuses on a single text, Flann O'Brien's 1967 novel *The Third Policeman* (1976), to demonstrate how the research tools surveyed previously can be used in concert to expose a rich structure of spatial reference in narrative. O'Brien's oneiric (indeed, nightmarish) landscapes sometimes make it difficult to situate objects in space or to track the movements of participants through it. Thus, the novel provides an important test case for studying how narratives enable (or in some cases inhibit) "cognitive mapping" (Downs and Stea 1977; Gould and White 1986; Ostroff 1995), the process by which things and events are mentally modeled as being located somewhere in the world. The chapter concludes with a discussion of how the ideas developed here bear on what can be called the *text-type approach* to narrative analysis (Chatman 1990; Schiffrin 1994; Virtanen 1992; Werlich 1975). In that approach, stories are distinguished from lists, descriptions, arguments, expositions, and so forth, on the basis of structural features associated with each text type. Yet the crucial role of spatial reference in narrative suggests the need to rethink features commonly assumed to constitute the textual prototype STORY, as well as standard assumptions about core versus peripheral properties of narrative and the relation between narrative and other text types, especially DESCRIPTION.

Early Approaches to Space: Barthes versus Greimas

In some of the early research on narrative, if space was discussed at all it was used negatively to mark off setting from story (Chatman 1978: 138–45), orientation from complicating action (Labov 1972a), description from narration proper (Genette 1976: 5–8; Hamon 1982; Kittay 1981b). This initial polarization of narrative and description may have been a legacy of what Jeffrey Kittay (1981a) characterizes as "the Aristotelian concept of action, which suggests that description be viewed as secondary, and purely functional, or merely decorative" (i; cf. Kittay 1981b). Indeed, a broad emphasis on action in narrative made it possible for description and story to be interdefined, such that each was viewed as the other's opposite, with description being construed as "[t]he representation of objects, beings, situations, or ... happenings in their spatial rather than temporal existence, their topological rather than chronological functioning, their simultaneity rather than succession" (G. Prince 1987: 19).[2]

Yet the expulsion of description to the frontiers of narrative did not go unquestioned—even by narrative theorists who at times seemed to assume the preeminence of temporal sequence in stories and the subordinate status of descriptions of people, places, and spaces. Thus, even though Philippe Hamon (1982) opposed narrative structures and descriptive systems, characterizing the one as an "oriented vector" leading to the inversion and transformation of elements of contents and the other as a network of semantic relationships (e.g., inclusion, resemblance, contiguity) (158–62), he also wrote that "[t]o map out a theory of the descriptive would be . . . to avoid localising it as an *anterior* practice . . . or reducing it to its transitivity by labelling it in such a way as to put it perpetually at the service of hierarchically superior instances of narration" (1981: 25–26). Similarly, even as Gérard Genette (1976) argued that "[e]very narrative includes two types of representation"— that is, "representations of actions and events, which constitute the narration properly speaking, and representations of objects or people, which make up the act of what we today call 'description'" (5)—he noted that these two types of representation "are blended together and always in varying proportions" in a given story (5). Hence "description could be conceivable independent of narration, but one never actually finds it in a free state" (6); hence, too, "[i]f description marks a boundary of narrative, it is an internal and rather ill-defined boundary" (7). For analogous reasons, in an excellent overview and rethinking of classical approaches to space in narrative, Gabriel Zoran (1984) argues that plot, commonly taken to be the sine qua non of narrative, "must be seen as more than simply a structure in time. It includes routes, movement, directions, volume, simultaneity, etc., and thus is an active partner in the structuring of space in the [narrative] text" (314). Here Zoran draws on M. M. Bakhtin's (1981b) notion of the *chronotope* or space-time complex to identify a *chronotopic* (as well as a *topographical* and a *textual*) level of spatial structuring in narrative. Whereas space is represented at the topographical level as a static entity and is structured at the textual level by virtue of being presented through the medium of language, space has structure imposed on it at the chronotopic level by events and movements within the world being told about, or what I am calling the storyworld (Zoran 1984: 315–322).[3]

At the end of the present chapter I revisit issues raised by Zoran's study, arguing that the chronotopic profile of stories requires a rethinking of approaches that divide NARRATIVE and DESCRIPTION into two distinct text types. For the moment, I wish to examine the treatment of space in one of the touchstones of structuralist narratology, Roland Barthes's 1966 "Introduction to the Structural Analysis of Narratives" (Barthes 1977, especially 91–97). This essay, for all of its other merits, exemplifies one unfortunate tendency within classical narratology: the tendency to view temporality as the hallmark of narrative and space as a more or less optional accompaniment. Barthes made a first cut between distributional (or syntagmatic) and integrational (or paradigmatic) units of narrative; he then further subdivided the distributional units into nuclei and catalyzers and the integrational units into indices and informants. Informants are the features of narration that serve "to identity, to locate in time and space," and they are paired with catalyzers insofar as "their functionality . . . is . . . weak without being nil" (1977: 96). As Barthes put it:

> Indices [which refer to "the character of a narrative agent, a feeling, an atmosphere . . . or a philosophy" (96)] always have implicit signifieds. Informants, however, do not, at least on the level of the story: they are pure data with immediate signification. Indices involve an activity of deciphering, the reader is to learn to know a character or an atmosphere; informants bring ready-made knowledge. . . . Whatever its 'flatness' in relation to the rest of the story, the informant . . . always serves to authenticate the reality of the referent, to embed fiction in the real world. Informants are realist operators and as such possess an undeniable functionality not on the level of the story but on that of the discourse. (96)

The last part of this passage reveals that, although Barthes had begun his essay by describing narrative as international, transhistorical, and transcultural, he based his discussion primarily on a certain class of written narrative texts. At issue are narratives in more or less conscious control of their "reality effects" (Barthes 1982); such effects are the product of conventional devices (e.g., the inclusion of ostensibly irrelevant, "luxurious" details about places, things, or participants) that serve to immerse the reader in the storyworld, creating an overriding impression of its realness or authenticity. Accordingly, for Barthes, the analyst should focus on how narratives use spatiotemporal information to graft fictional entities onto a paradoxically mythic order of the real, thereby making "the real" into a myth in its own right (cf. Barthes 1972). Despite its brilliance, Barthes's analysis lacks scope. Not just fictional narrative but *any* story about spatially or temporally nonproximate events—about things not happening in the here and now—will contain formal cues prompting the listener or reader to construe the storyworld as real, as actual. Indeed, as Marie-Laure Ryan has shown, the more such cues there are in a given story and the more systematically they operate, the more narrativity will that story possess, the more "narrative-like" will it seem (Ryan 1991: 125–27).

Further, by redescribing informants as *cues*, I mean to dispute Barthes's suggestion that informants are "pure data with immediate signification," textual features that are at best weakly functional and that fail to trigger inferencing procedures of any real complexity or importance (cf. G. Prince 1982: 32-33). Already in the late 1960s, Greimas and his colleagues began developing a quite different approach that anticipated more recent work on language and narrative (Greimas 1988; Greimas and Courtés 1983). The Greimassian approach, like the work that came after it, assumes that spatial reference involves quite complicated inferencing techniques and that it plays a crucial, not a weak or derivative, role in stories. For example, anticipating the concept of deictic shift discussed below, Greimas and Courtés (1983) argued that narratives, among other types of discourse, are made possible by spatiotemporal *disengagement*, that is, a "split which creates, on the one hand, the subject, the place, and the time of the enunciation and, on the other, the . . . spatial and temporal representation of the utterance" (88; cf. Greimas 1988: 22-23).[4] Furthermore, they detailed a process of spatial localization, whereby storytellers distribute storyworlds into spaces that they represent as being inhabited by particular characters (Greimas and Courtés 1983: 180-81; cf. Greimas 1988: 22-23; 79-83). Building on Meletinsky's (1970) distinction between familiar and alien spaces in Russian folktales, Greimas created a taxonomy that distinguished between topical (or relatively proximal) and heterotopical (or relatively distal) narrative spaces, further subdividing topical space into utopian and paratopical spaces that he associated with action and setting, respectively (Greimas 1988: 76-100; cf. Greimas and Courtés 1983: 180-82).

Indeed, for Greimas, all of these spatial zones and subzones are importantly interconnected with what is arguably the central concept in his narrative-theoretical framework—namely, the concept of "narrative program," defined as "an elementary syntagm [underlying] the surface narrative syntax, composed of an utterance of doing governing an utterance of state" (Greimas and Courtés 1983: 245; cf. Greimas 1988: 173-97). Narrative programs can be compared with what later researchers have termed *action structures* (Giora and Shen 1994; Herman 1997a, 2000a), previously discussed in chapters 2 and 3. Recall that action structures are a way of accounting for why narratives do not consist of mere bundles or agglomerations of sentences; instead, stories form *Gestalten*, psychological wholes, textual sequences whose coherence is supported by interpreters' inferences about participants engaged in activities over time, with a view to accomplishing particular goals. In other words, events in a story do not just happen one after another or in pairwise fashion; rather, they unfold as plan-based actions performed by participants who are attempting to bring about some desired state or event by solving problems or resolving conflicts. For their part, Greimas and Courtés (1983) distinguish between *base*, *instrumental*, and *annex* narrative programs. These three types of narrative programs correspond, respectively, to simple programs (e.g., buying some food), programs that must be implemented before some other program can be realized (getting a job in order to have money to buy food), and programs undertaken by a secondary participant to whom that task has been delegated by a primary participant (having a friend buy food in one's behalf) (246).[5] More to the point, all such narrative programs unfold not merely in time but also in space, necessitating *spatial* as well as *temporal programming* (Greimas and Courtés 1983: 246–48).

Spatial programming, in fact, operates at two levels. On the one hand, linguistically speaking, the discourse cues that evoke storyworlds also serve to "localize" narrative programs spatially, such that "partial spaces are syntagmatically strung together" in the clauses and sentences comprised by the discourse (Greimas and Courtés 1983: 247). On the other hand, in the storyworld itself "spatial programming is carried out by putting the programmed components of the subjects (of their narrative programs) into correlation with the segmented spaces that they use (cf. kitchen + dining room; bedroom + bathroom)" (247). Greimas's emphasis on spatial programming in narrative reveals problems with text-type approaches that make spatial reference a peripheral rather than core property of STORY construed as a textual prototype (see the final section of this chapter). But what is more, the notion of spatial programming prefigures an approach to narrative analysis that in a certain sense has become possible to develop and implement only now, with the help of research tools fashioned by linguists and cognitive scientists, among others. I discuss these tools in the next section.

Six Concepts from Recent Research on Language, Narrative, and Space

At issue most broadly is the way narratives encode emergent spatial relationships among participants, objects, and places. In this connection, recent work in narrative theory incorporating discourse-analytic and cognitive-scientific ideas has shown that grasping the *when*, *what*, *who*, and *where* of events being recounted is a matter of actively building and updating the mental representations termed *storyworlds* in the present study. Emmott (1997), for example, has developed the notion of "contextual frames" to discuss how readers of written narratives supplement text-based or propositional information with situation-based information (cf. Speelman and Kirsner 1990). When people read they do not automatically and iteratively assign referents to third-person pronouns, for instance, by attaching them to entities previously mentioned in the discourse. Rather, reference assignment is made possible when narrative texts cue readers to activate contextual frames, that is, knowledge representations that store specific configurations of characters located at specific space-time coordinates in the storyworld. Referring expressions thus evoke not just fictional individuals but whole contextual frames; pronouns such as *he* and *she* and definite descriptions such as *the city* and *the person I met today* are anchored not so much in particular entities as in the spatiotemporal contexts of those entities. Hence to know who or what is being referred to at a given point in a narrative text is to have the ability to build (or update) a mental model of where, within the storyworld, the thing referred to is located in time and space. More generally, Emmott's model, like Fludernik's (1996) emphasis on VIEWING and EXPERIENCING as basic cognitive parameters for telling and interpreting stories, suggests that framing representations of the *where* in a story is a major dimension of narrative processing. At stake is much more than simply filtering out descriptive detail to form interpretations of "core" narrative elements (e.g. who did what to whom and why).

To help underscore the critical role of spatial reference in narrative domains, I turn now to six key concepts emerging from recent work on language and space—research on which Emmott, Fludernik, and other narrative theorists have begun to draw, more or less directly. Listed below are the six ideas that are discussed, in the same order, in ensuing subsections:

> the notion of *deictic shift*, whereby a storyteller prompts his or her interlocutors to relocate from the here and now of the current interaction to the alternative space-time coordinates of the storyworld (i.e., the world being told about);

Spatialization 271

the distinction between *figure* and *ground*, alternatively described as *located object* versus *reference object*;

the notions of *regions*, *landmarks*, and *paths*, as developed by Landau and Jackendoff (1993);

the distinction between *topological* (or inherent) and *projective* (or viewer-relative) *locations*;

the deictic functions of *motion verbs* located on a semantic continuum whose poles, in English, are *come* and *go*;

and the distinction between the WHAT and WHERE systems of spatial cognition, proposed by Landau and Jackendoff (1993; see also Landau 1994, 1996).

Although in what follows I cannot hope to provide an exhaustive characterization of how these aspects of spatial reference function in narrative discourse, a few illustrative instances may point up ways in which space is integral to stories.

Deictic Shift

Researchers such as Zubin and Hewitt (1995) have discussed how storytelling involves a shift of deictic centers, whereby narrators prompt their interlocutors to relocate from the HERE and NOW of the act of narration to other space-time coordinates—namely, those defining the perspective from which the events of the story are recounted (see also Gerrig 1993; Greimas 1988: 22–23; Greimas and Courtés 1983: 88; Ryan 1991; Talmy 1995; Yuhan and Shapiro 1995). By means of linguistic devices expressing information about the participant structure, object structure, spatial structure, and temporal structure of the narrated events, narrative opens a "conceptual window through which the storyworld can be glimpsed" (Zubin and Hewitt 1995: 131), or rather deictically tracked, from the vantage of narratorial perspective.[6] In the case of fictional narrative, readers or listeners are openly prompted to make a deictic shift to an alternative possible world (Ryan 1991)—one where Richard Nixon might be a used car salesman or narratologists the most powerful group in society. But as deictic-shift theorists stress, *all* storytellers cue their audiences to transport themselves from the spatiotemporal parameters of the current interaction to those defining the storyworld. Even such minimal narratives (or quasi-narratives) as *John ate;*

then he slept require a deictic shift to the world in which the eating and the sleeping occur; and within that world, the temporal deictic *then* prompts a shift from one set of space-time coordinates to another.[7]

As discussed in connection with Anna Seghers's "The Excursion of the Dead Girls" in chapter 6, deictic shifts play an especially important role in what are commonly called framed narratives.[8] In Chaucer's *Canterbury Tales*, for example, readers must make an initial deictic shift from the space-time coordinates of the world in which the text is being read to the HERE and NOW of the springtime pilgrimage to Canterbury, that is, the fictional world in which individual pilgrims engage in telling their own tales. Cues for additional (more precisely, embedded) deictic shifts, which guide readers to relocate to the storyworlds presented by each teller, can be found in the so-called links or interchanges among the various pilgrims. (Recall that Seghers's story creates zones of temporal indeterminacy by means of a frame-tale that both cues and inhibits a secondary or embedded shift to the storyworld located in the protagonist-narrator's past.) In several instances Harry Bailey, the landlord of the Tabard Inn who has been charged with judging which pilgrim tells the best tale, also takes on the role of helping storytellers and their listeners (as well as Chaucer's readers) jointly enact such shifts, as in the case of the link preceding *The Pardoner's Prologue and Tale*:

"Thou bel ami, thou Pardoner," he said,
"Tel us some mirthe or japes right anoon."
"It shal be doon," quod he, "by Saint Ronion.
But first," quod he, "here at this ale-stake
I wol both drinke and eten of a cake." (1993: 165.30–34)

At once rooted in and representing traditions of oral narrative, Chaucer's *Tales* reveal the extent to which deictic shifts are interactionally accomplished, a function of cues being interpreted as such by an audience and used by them to reconstruct the spatiotemporal parameters of the storyworld. The passage just quoted, although it does not itself trigger a shift to a different HERE and NOW, prepares the Pardoner's audience and the reader to make such a shift. In other words, it eases relocation to the storyworld that will be hypocritically adduced by the greedy Pardoner as an exemplum, a narrative illustrating the dangers of being greedy.

Likewise, Joseph Conrad's *Heart of Darkness* dramatically enacts in its frame-tale a secondary deictic shift. Like participants in the story itself, readers must engage in this shift; otherwise, they will not be able to reconstruct the embedded storyworld presented by the character-narrator Marlow, who tells about how he was so profoundly affected by the experience of seeking out and then finding Kurtz in the Belgian Congo. The opening of the novel requires readers to make an initial deictic shift to a fictional HERE and NOW. An anonymous homodiegetic narrator recounts events that happened one night aboard the *Nellie*, a cruising yawl anchored on the Thames, when Marlow told about his "inconclusive experiences" to those listening to him in the darkness (Conrad 1996: 21). Conrad's readers, like Marlow's audience aboard ship, must then make a secondary shift to the embedded storyworld that Marlow homodiegetically presents. Periodically, by reporting incidents that happen during Marlow's telling of his story—"He [Marlow] was silent for a while" (42); " 'Try to be civil, Marlow,' growled a voice, and I knew there was at least one listener awake besides myself' " (50); "Marlow ceased, and sat apart, indistinct and silent, in the pose of a meditating Buddha" (95)—the primary narrator cues temporary shifts back from the embedded to the initial deictic center. In this way, the novel dramatizes the immersive power of narrative itself, its capacity to transport listeners and readers by way of deictic shifts to different space-time coordinates. Or rather, by using a two-step, layered deictic shift to simulate readerly immersion and then periodically reversing the direction of the shift to re-expose the frame-tale, Conrad's novel not only exploits but also comments on and thereby disrupts the immersive potential of stories. In turn, this structured interplay of shifts in space and time substitutes for a monolithic vision of the real, such as the one Kurtz sought to impose in the Congo, a plurality of perspectives on a world that refuses to be seen in any one way, from the vantage point afforded by any one set of contextual coordinates.

There are, to be sure, narratives requiring multiple, sometimes quite elaborate, deictic shifts. For example, one of the challenges posed by epistolary novels such as Tobias Smollett's *Humphry Clinker* (1985) is that readers have to use textual cues to establish a deictic center for each letter writer's contribution. More than this, readers have to accommodate deictic shifts prompted by exchanges between different correspondents as well as by changes in a given correspondent's spatiotemporal situation as it evolves over the course of the novel. Meanwhile, in George Foy's science fiction novel *The Shift* (Foy 1996), the protagonist-narrator is a designer of virtual reality systems who regularly plugs himself into an apparatus that transports him to a virtual world designed to simulate New York City as it existed in the nineteenth century. The reader must thus engage, along with the protagonist, in embedded deictic shifts of the sort found in Chaucer and Conrad. But in this case the shifts are more problematic because the protagonist constantly reminds the reader of the presence (and limitations) of the technology enabling the shifts, such as the treadmill that only approximates the experience of walking on sidewalks and streets in virtual reality.[9] Thematically the novel explores the possibility of a kind of ontological crossover effect, a technologically induced metalepsis that implants the simulated into the real. As the novel proceeds, elements of the virtual world designed by the protagonist appear to migrate into space-time coordinates defining the HERE and NOW of the fictional world, in contrast to those defining the virtual-within-the-fictional world.

In other, more formally ingenious texts, such as James Joyce's *Ulysses* or William Faulkner's *The Sound and the Fury*, the use of interior monologue to mirror the rapid, sometimes unpredictable, movements of thought results in a noticeable absence of customary prompts for deictic shifts, including temporal and spatial adverbs, prepositional phrases such as *at that time*, *in that place*, or their equivalents, shifts in verb tense, and so on. This helps explain why readers often feel that they must *reread* such narratives a second or third time to be able to follow (or anticipate) the shifts in space and time that are as much implied as formally marked by the text.

Figure versus Ground (Or Located Object versus Reference Object)

Research in the fields of linguistic semantics, cognitive linguistics, and artificial intelligence has led to the decomposition of apparently stable positions, places, or points into relational systems (Frawley 1992: 250–74; Herskovits 1986; Landau and Jackendoff 1993: 217–22). More specifically, the semantic structure of spatial expressions can be thought of as a dependency relation between two or more entities: a *located object* (or *figure*) and a *reference object* (or *ground*). Cataloging the various possible relationships between located and reference objects—such as coincidence, interiority, exteriority, anteriority, laterality—linguists have also examined ways languages encode these relationships (Landau and Jackendoff 1993: 223–29). At issue are locative adverbs (*forward*, *together*, *sideways*) and prepositions (*beyond*, *with*, *over*), which convey information about the geometric character of located and reference objects (volumes, surfaces, points, and lines). Such forms also encode information about objects' axial structure (top, bottom, right, left)—whether the objects in question have inherent axes like those of spheres or cylinders or contextually imposed ones like those that speakers of English attribute to a located object *on top of* or *under* a reference object (see the subsection below on topographical versus projective locations). Linguistic forms can be used to express, as well, information about the number of reference objects being used to identify a located object. For example, we say that a cat is *between* a pair of entities but *among* an aggregate of them.

Like deictic shifts, figure-ground relationships are basic to the process of narration. It would be impossible, arguably, to build or reconstruct a storyworld without an articulation of the perceptual field into focused-upon participants, objects, and places and a background against which those focused-upon entities stand out. But it can also be argued that storyworlds do not simply mirror an experiential domain prestructured into figure(s) and ground. Rather, by detaching specific incidents from the ongoing flux of experience and focusing narrators', listeners', and readers' attention on localized areas of concern, stories help humans structure the world into a foreground and a background to begin with, thereby making it cognizable, manipulable, liveable. Consider the following passage from George Eliot's *Daniel Deronda*. Here the narrator gives an account of Gwendolen Harleth's return to Offendene, after an absence prompted by her discovery that her fiancé, Grandcourt, has fathered two children with Lydia Glasher:

> But the slow drive was nearly at an end, and the lumbering vehicle coming up the avenue was within sight of the windows. A figure appearing under the portico brought a rush of new and less selfish feeling in Gwendolen, and when springing from the carriage she saw the dear beautiful face with fresh lines of sadness in it, she threw her arms round her mother's neck, and for the moment felt all sorrows only in relation to her mother's feeling about them.
>
> Behind, of course, were the sad faces of the four superfluous girls [i.e., Gwendolen's sisters], each, poor thing—like those other many thousand sisters of us all—having her peculiar world which was of no importance to anyone else, but all of them feeling Gwendolen's presence to be somehow a relenting of misfortune: where Gwendolen was, something inter-

esting would happen; even her hurried submission to their kisses, and "Now go away, girls," carried the sort of comfort which all weakness finds in decision and authoritativeness. (1986: 271)

To be sure, this account reveals the extent to which establishing figure-ground relationships enables local acts of perception. Yet it also shows how such relationships are inextricably interlinked with narrative, including the more or less explicit or tacit life stories in terms of which people conduct their everyday affairs and take up certain role relationships with respect to one another.

Initially, from the perspective of the extradiegetic narrator, as well as that of any observer who might indeed have caught a glimpse of Gwendolen's carriage from the windows mentioned at the end of the first sentence,[10] the approaching carriage is itself a figure set off against a ground consisting of reference objects situated in the surrounding landscape (the avenue, the house with the windows, etc.). In the first clause of the second sentence, however, there is a shift to Gwendolen's perspective; now her mother literally appears as a "figure" or located object standing in a particular type of dependency relation to the portico as reference object. Specifically, she stands to the portico in a relation of inferiority, as is encoded in the semantics of the word *under*. The second clause of this same sentence registers additional perspectival shifts or rather focusings-in, with first the mother's face and then the lines of sadness on her face assuming the status of located objects as the distance between Gwendolen and her mother diminishes. More precisely, the preposition *in* encodes the lines of sadness as interior to the face, while a basic assumption of relevance (Grice 1989: 22–40) licenses the inference that the "dear beautiful face" mentioned in the second clause belongs to the "figure" mentioned in the first clause. Overall, then, whereas the first paragraph of the quoted passage begins by establishing Gwendolen's carriage as a located object vis-à-vis the avenue, the house containing the windows, and other reference objects in the landscape, as it proceeds the paragraph mirrors the unfolding of Gwendolen's own perceptual activity. The paragraph enacts a dynamic process whereby smaller and smaller portions of what began as undifferentiated ground are focused on as figure, in the sequence HOUSE → MOTHER → MOTHER'S FACE → LINES OF SADNESS IN MOTHER'S FACE. Note, too, that these successive shifts in perceptual focus create a space for a parallel trajectory of emotional response. Over the course of the paragraph, as she gets spatially closer to her mother, Gwendolen likewise moves from the state of self-absorption that is quite typical for her at this point in the novel to an empathetic identification with her mother's feelings. Eliot's manipulation of figure-ground relationships in the second paragraph of the quoted passage, however, suggests that at this stage Gwendolen's capacity for selflessness and empathy may be as superficial as it is short-lived. Using a narratorial style ambiguous between the authorial and reflectorized modes (Stanzel 1971, 1984; Fludernik 1996), Eliot makes it hard to determine the source and status of the sentiment that the four sisters are so many reference objects serving to set Gwendolen off. It is not clear whether the claim that each sister has her own "peculiar world which was of no importance to anyone else" is an instance of narratorial commentary, a belief state of the four sisters themselves, a reflex of Gwendolen's view of her family, or perhaps the combined product of all these factors. In any event, the two paragraphs taken together indicate how figure-ground relationships structure narrative discourse at a number of different levels, which interact synergistically. Better, perhaps, the contrast between located and reference objects can be thought of as operating within autonomous but interconnected modules of narrative structure—perceptual, emotive, and thematic/conceptual—with the output of one module providing input for another. Thus, as even this brief passage demonstrates, emotional identification is enabled by perceptual discrimination, while expressions of empathy can in turn generate inferences about who is of primary as opposed to secondary importance on a given occasion or over an extended duration. In turn, changing judgments about what is important can lead to inversions of what counts as figure and what counts as ground in both the perceptual field and the realm of emotional response—as Gwendolen herself discovers over the course of the novel. On this view, narrative is not so much a textual chain on which these linked figure-ground modules are strung, as an overarching communicative, interactional, and cognitive environment thanks to which the modules can be brought into a systematic, mutually enabling and constraining relationship with one another.

Regions, Landmarks, and Paths

Building on the distinction between figure and ground, Barbara Landau and Ray Jackendoff (1993) have redescribed places as *regions* occupied by *landmarks* or reference objects, and *paths* as the routes one travels to get from place to place (223). The notion of paths is an especially important one in narrative domains, since paths imply motion from one place to another and thus dynamic or emergent spatial properties of the sort characteristic of narratives.

Consider the following news report on NATO forces' bombing of Serbia on the night of 16 April 1999, posted to CNN's Web site *(http://www.cnn.com)* at 5:22 A.M. (EDT) on that same date. News correspondents Brent Sadler, Alessio Vinci, Jim Clancy, and Bill Hemmer contributed to this report, which I present in abbreviated form and whose paragraphs I have numbered for ease of reference.

(a) BELGRADE, Yugoslavia (CNN) — Amid recriminations over an airstrike that killed fleeing Kosovar Albanians, NATO pressed on with airstrikes across Yugoslavia Friday, including an attack that hit a densely populated area of a Serb town near the Hungarian border, Serbian TV said.

(b) Serbian television and Belgrade radio said civilian areas were struck in the town of Subotica, about 9 miles (15 km) south of the Yugoslav-Hungarian border. It was the first reported attack in the town, and Serbian video showed damage to what appeared to be houses.

(c) Belgrade radio and TV reported a refugee complex housing Serbian refugees from Bosnia and Croatia was hit by three missiles in Paracin, about 75 miles (120 km) southeast of Belgrade. . . .

(d) Three missiles slammed into the country's main oil refinery in Pancevo and a chemical factory was struck, Serbian TV reported. Missile strikes reportedly hit an oil refinery in Novi Sad, Yugoslavia's second largest city that has sustained heavy bombings during Operation Allied Force.

(e) A bridge in Smederevo, about 25 miles (40 km) east of Belgrade, was damaged, Serb TV said. State-run television also reported NATO strikes around the Montenegran capital of Podgorica. . . .

(f) Earlier, Yugoslav government officials charged that NATO jets had struck the village of Srbica Thursday, killing seven ethnic Albanians including children.

(g) The village is west of Pristina, they said, promising to take journalists to the scene.

(h) That report came following an admission by NATO that one of its pilots, believing he was attacking a military vehicle at the head of a

Spatialization 279

convoy in southwestern Kosovo, may have mistakenly struck a civilian vehicle instead. . . .

(i) A refugee who arrived in Kukes, Albania, said a plane passed over his convoy, dropped a bomb, then returned and dropped another. He said he and his son hid beneath their tractor. His wife was killed.

A case could be made for construing the report as a list rather than a story (cf. Schiffrin 1994: 291–315), with paragraph (a) announcing a general topic or event category ("airstrikes across Yugoslavia Friday") subsequently exemplified by mentions of particular events falling within that category (Friday night's airstrikes on Subotica, Paracin, Pancevo, Novi Sad, Smederevo, Podgorica, and Srbica). As excerpted here, however, this report exhibits enough narrative structure to cue readers to form a mental representation of a series of events occurring in parallel but rooted in a single conflict between opposing groups of participants. Further, given that the military conflict ramifies unexpectedly and beyond anyone's control, with terrible human consequences (paragraphs [h] and [i]), the report displays the sort of tellability often taken to be a criterion for narrative (Labov 1972a, 1997). Landmarks, regions, and paths all play an important role in the report, facilitating cognitive mapping of the storyworld and, in particular, enabling the reader to chart the spatial trajectories along which the narrated events unfold.

Several items mentioned in this report serve as landmarks in the storyworld. For example, in paragraphs (a) and (b), the border between Yugoslavia and Hungary provides a landmark by which to fix the location of the town of Subotica, a particular region of which (i.e., "a densely populated area") is singled out in paragraph (a). Similarly, the city of Belgrade functions as a landmark in paragraphs (c) and (e), while the mention of the city of Pristina in paragraph (g) helps establish where the Kosovar refugees were killed. In general, the toponym *Yugoslavia* enables readers to identify the overall region of the conflict, whereas subsequent toponymic and more broadly geographical references allow the space of the conflict to be divided into subregions. In turn, by modeling the conflict space as one consisting of multiple subregions being attacked simultaneously, the report suggests the broad scale of the airstrikes—with NATO jets and missiles tracing a complex network of paths over the target area. On a smaller scale, and in a manner that points up the human toll exacted by the conflict, paragraph (i) describes how a jet pursues a deadly route through space only to reverse course and, horribly, retrace that same path. Note, too, the manipulation of figure-ground relationships that create, in paragraph (i), the same focusing-in effect found in the passage from *Daniel Deronda*. The convoy serves initially as a reference object by means of which the refugee communicates the location of the plane; but then a single tractor within the convoy becomes the ground against which he locates his son and himself during the bombing.

Topological versus Projective Locations

Also crucial for understanding the emergent spaces modeled and communicated by narratives is the distinction between topological and projective locations, discussed by researchers such as William Frawley (1992), William F. Hanks (1990: 293–351), and Stephen C. Levinson (1996). Whereas topology "is the study of the geometric properties of objects that are invariant under change of the object," projective locations are ones that "vary in value and interpretation depending on how they are viewed," thus relying on an orientative framework projected by the viewer (Frawley 1992: 254, 262; for a questioning of the topological-projective distinction, see Levinson 1996: 134–56). What counts as the *inside of* a cube is invariant and thus a topological location; but what counts as *in front of* a tree is a projective location, varying with one's angle of vision.

The following passage from Ernest Hemingway's *A Moveable Feast* demonstrates the interplay between topological and projective locations in narrative discourse, as well as the special importance of projectively located entities in narrative domains. At this point in the text, Hemingway is describing how he used to have to go hungry while still a young, struggling writer, doing his best to avoid the places in Paris that sold food and that thus might all too palpably remind him of his own hunger:

> After you came out of the Luxembourg [Gardens] you could walk down the narrow rue Férou to the Place St.-Suplice and there were still no restaurants, only the quiet square with its benches and trees. There was a fountain with lions, and pigeons walked on the pavement and perched on the statues of the bishops. There was the church and there were shops selling religious objects and vestments on the north side of the square.
>
> From this square you could not go further toward the river without

passing shops selling fruits, vegetables, wines, or bakery and pastry shops. But by choosing your way carefully you could work to your right around the grey and white stone church and reach the rue de l'Odéon and turn up to your right toward Sylvia Beach's bookshop and on your way you did not pass too many places where things to eat were sold. The rue de l'Odéon was bare of eating places until you reached the square where there were three restaurants. (1964: 69–70)

Note Hemingway's use of landmarks (the square at Place St.-Suplice, Sylvia Beach's bookshop, etc.) to help readers map his progress through subregions within the city of Paris. These landmarks also lend a sense of authenticity and credibility to the account Hemingway offers of past difficulties that might otherwise seem exaggerated, even romanticized. But furthermore, although the passage does locate entities in the storyworld topologically (e.g., by establishing that the shops selling religious items are located on the north side of the square at Place St.-Suplice), its dominant mode of spatial reference is projective. With the help of second-person narration, a mode that prompts identification with the character Hemingway as he moves through space, the passage works to position the reader in the spatiotemporal coordinates that define the protagonist-narrator's changing vantage point on the storyworld. In other words, the passage takes the reader on a tour through the streets of Paris, rather than encoding spatial representations that take the form of an aerial map, a static view of the city from above. The passage cues the reader to model the layout of the storyworld in terms of what could be seen if "you" walked down rue Férou to the Place St.-Suplice, thence toward the Seine, and finally up rue de l'Odéon to the square with the three restaurants.

The Hemingway passage thus manifests the same overall structure that Charlotte Linde and William Labov (1975) discovered in their study of residents' descriptions of apartment layouts. Linde and Labov found that their informants displayed a preference for projective description in talking about complex spaces; like Hemingway in his account of life in Paris, interviewees tended to describe their apartments by way of dynamic "tours" instead of static "maps" (cf. Tversky 1996). More generally, as a discourse genre and a cognitive style that relies fundamentally on perspective taking (Ochs et al. 1992), narrative is arguably one of the principal means of building and communicating projective locations—such locations being indexed to a particular perspective vis-à-vis the storyworld.[11] Chapter 8 offers a fuller account of the links between narration and perspective taking.

Motion Verbs

Motion verbs, too, are instrumental for the construction and updating of cognitive maps for storyworlds. At issue are the verbs that, in English, are located on a semantic continuum whose poles are *come* and *go* (Brown 1995: 108–24, 188–91; Landau and Jackendoff 1993; Zubin and Hewitt 1995). By encoding the directionality of movement, motion verbs express projective locations of entities being perceived by narrators, as well as paths taken by entities as they move or are moved from place to place. In the natural-language narratives Brown (1995) studied, verbs such as "*come, arrive, walk in* are used of entry into the space . . . which is nearest the observer . . . , whereas *go, walked off/out* and *leave* are used as characters leave that space" (190). Analogously, consider the following passage from Daniel Defoe's *Moll Flanders*, in which the protagonist-narrator gives an account of her encounter with the eldest son of the family for whom she is working as a servant, being at this time only about eighteen years old and relatively easily taken advantage of:

> It happened one day that he [the eldest son] *came running* upstairs, towards the room where his sisters used to sit and work, as he often used to do; and calling to them before he came in, as was his way too, I, being there alone, *stepped to* the door and said, "Sir, the ladies are not here; they *are walked down* the garden." As I *stepped forward* to say this he *was just got to* the door, and clasping me in his arms as if it had been by chance, "Oh, Mrs. Betty," says he, "are you here? That's better still; I want to speak with you more than I do with them"; and then, having me in his arms, he kissed me three or four times. (1964: 23, my emphases)

The motion verbs (more precisely, verbal phrases) that I have emphasized play an important role in this passage; they help readers build up representations of an action structure, a pattern of goal-directed actions and counteractions, on the basis of the participants' movements along pathways cutting through space and charted by the sequence of verbs. True, these verbs work in concert with other elements of the discourse serving to position participants in space and time. At the beginning of the passage, for example, the temporal descriptor *one day* and the definite description *the room where his sisters used to sit and work* jointly trigger a deictic shift and set the space-time coordinates of the deictic center to which the reader is prompted to relocate. In addition, the narrator uses figure-ground relationships to establish ever more precisely specified locations of the two main participants vis-à-vis first the room, then the door to the room, then one another. Yet motion verbs contribute crucial semantic information concerning the participants' *emerging* whereabouts in space—their spatial trajectories over the duration of the event sequence being narrated. The emphasized verbs thus do more than simply provide descriptive backdrop for the narrated action. By configuring the storyworld spatially as well as temporally, they enable readers to identify an action structure in which the eldest son enters the room containing the protagonist-narrator with the aim of seducing her, with the mature Moll Flanders representing herself as a passive, unsuspecting young woman at the time.

The son comes running upstairs to where Moll is seated alone. Moll then steps to the door to answer the son. Next, in telling the son that his sisters *are walked down* to the garden, Moll uses an archaic form of the verb *be* to express not a state or an ongoing action, but rather a perfective activity type—namely, a completed action as a result of which the sisters have left Moll alone (and vulnerable) in the room.[12] Meanwhile, at nearly the same moment Moll takes a path of motion terminating in her position near the door, the son *was just got to* that door. Here Moll again uses perfective *be* to express not a state or a durative activity type but instead a punctual, already accomplished action. Having reached the same door to which Moll's own path of motion takes her, the son clasps Moll in his arms and kisses her. Viewed as a whole, therefore, this sequence of verbal forms configures the storyworld in two stages. It first locates the son at the distal end of an axis whose proximal end is the vantage point of Moll herself. The sequence then charts the son's ever-increasing proximity to Moll until it results in direct bodily contact—this being, for a young woman of Moll's status, quite perilous. Retrospectively narrating the incident, Moll tracks the son's location by observing how his position changes relative to her own situation in space; she does not just record that he came upstairs into a particular room, but uses the locative adverb *towards* to transform simple motion in space into progress that leads to the terminus corresponding to her own vantage point on the storyworld. In short, the passage reveals how narratives encode directions of movement as viewer-relative. To put this last point another way, the passage demonstrates how motion verbs collocate with projective locations in narrative discourse.

The WHAT versus the WHERE Systems

In their research on spatial language and cognition, Landau and Jackendoff (1993; Landau 1994, 1996) have postulated a distinction between the WHAT and WHERE systems of human cognition, the WHAT system being concerned with objects (object shapes, names, and kinds), the WHERE system concerned with places. Although humans use thousands and thousands of count nouns to name objects and draw on a rich combinatorial system to describe object geometries, the relatively small number of spatial prepositions used to represent locations preserve only very basic geometric object properties—chiefly their main axes. We have extensive verbal resources for talking about species, sizes, attributes, and parts of cats, but more limited resources for talking about where they are in space, using prepositions and adverbs mainly to position them along a front-back axis and divide them bilaterally along an axis perpendicular to the first.

Several of the examples discussed in previous subsections reveal, on the one hand, a rich WHAT system based on object shapes, names, and kinds and, on the other hand, a WHERE system preserving much coarser geometric properties of objects. For instance, despite its brevity the passage taken from Eliot's *Daniel Deronda* details a storyworld richly furnished with driveways, carriages, houses, windows, porticos, family members, and faces marked with lines of sadness. By contrast, in building a WHERE rather than a WHAT system for the storyworld, Eliot draws on the grammatical resources of English mainly to map the position of participants and objects on a single axis corresponding to Gwendolen's line of sight. The passage contains a verbal phrase characterizing Gwendolen's carriage as *coming up* the driveway, while the preposition *behind* assigns the four sisters a position at the distal end of the axis whose midpoint is occupied by Gwendolen's mother.[13] Likewise, the passage from Hemingway's *A Moveable Feast* shows a contrast between a full WHAT and a minimal WHERE system. As already discussed, the protagonist-narrator establishes projective locations for multiple places and objects in Paris. Hemingway builds these projective representations with the help of motion verbs, many of them verbal phrases containing spatial prepositions, prepositional phrases, and locative adverbs—*came out of*, *walk down*, *go further toward*, and *work to your right around*. With the exception of the last-mentioned construction, which encodes a curvilinear trajectory of motion, these verb forms (like the forms in the passage from *Daniel Deronda*) encode a WHERE made up of linear paths corresponding to a distal-proximal axis cutting bidirectionally through space.

The Third Policeman: Toward an Integrative Analysis

The six key ideas synopsized in the previous section support the contention that, far from merely providing descriptive background or ornamentation for the primary action in a story, spatial reference helps *constitute* narrative domains. In the present section, to illustrate further how strategies for spatial reference often interact in narrative discourse, I offer a somewhat more detailed analysis of a single literary narrative, Flann O'Brien's *The Third Policeman*, published posthumously in 1967. Arguably, the point of this narrative is bound up with its protagonist-narrator's use of discourse strategies that at once trigger and inhibit readers' attempts to construct a cognitive map of the storyworld being recounted. In other words, O'Brien's is a narrative that foregrounds the necessity of spatialization even as it thwarts the readers' efforts to spatialize the storyworld it encodes. This tension helps define the "hellish otherworld" (Mazzullo 1995) to which the main character is consigned. *Hell*, in this context, names less a place than the cognitive dissonance caused by the narrator's efforts to model the otherworld *as* a place. To put this same point in a more general way, O'Brien's hell is one marked by a mismatch between basic parameters for spatial cognition and the regions in which the narrator finds himself, posthumously at least.[14]

In the terminology of Jurij Lotman and Boris Uspenskij (1986), literary works generally furnish a secondary modeling system that grounds itself in, or bases itself upon, features of the primary modeling system, that is, language itself. *The Third Policeman* can be viewed as a particular type of secondary modeling system in which the narrator's account throws light on the functioning of spatial cognition in (narrative) discourse. O'Brien's novel is, to be sure, an attempt to use narrative to imagine space otherwise, to situate its narrator in a radically otherworldly place. Yet even the most ingenious, the most fantastic, narrative imaginings remain bound by constraints associated with spatial reference and spatial thinking. Thus, far from being invalidated by (postmodern) narratives that work to construct atypical spaces, linguistic, discourse-analytic, and cognitive-scientific research can help illuminate these narratives' forms and functions. What gives experimental fiction its palpability, its salience, is the way it builds on shared cognitive and communicative systems to prompt its readers to reconsider the nature and scope of thinking and communicating. Conversely, analysis of texts like O'Brien's demonstrates the importance of developing an integrative approach to spatial reference in narrative domains—an approach that draws together the research paradigms that I have been reviewing in more or less piecemeal fashion up to now.

With John Divney, an underhanded schemer and unscrupulous opportunist, the nameless protagonist-narrator of O'Brien's novel conspires to murder and rob old Mathers, a retired cattle trader presumed to be wealthy. Divney's motive for the violent murder is bald-faced greed. But to ensure his co-conspirator's participation in the scheme, Divney appeals to the narrator's sense of the importance of his own scholarly pursuits, which have culminated in his composing a "definitive 'De Selby Index'" (O'Brien 1976: 14), a book collating previous commentators' writings on a bizarre "savant" named de Selby. The money stolen from old Mathers is supposed to subsidize the narrator's publication of his magnum opus. Meanwhile, the narrator incorporates de Selby's heterodox ideas into the telling of his own life story, presenting the ideas largely unironically and often in the form of highly discursive footnotes. Some of de Selby's "theories" suggest that the narrator may be engaging in special pleading with respect to his role in the murder—or, at best, that he is hopelessly (and comically) deluded about the significance of de Selby's contributions to science. For example, the narrator reports de Selby's view that houses have produced a "progressive predilection for interiors" that has in turn led to a "softening and degeneration of the human race," with the result that houses built without roofs and walls might be especially "therapeutic" (21). De Selby also theorizes that night is an effect of accumulations of black air produced by mysterious volcanic activities (32 n. 4, 116–18 n. 1); that the earth is not in fact spherical but rather sausage-shaped (93–96); that percussive sounds derive from the bursting of "atmosphere balls" (144 n. 1); that water is an essential component of happiness, with the result that de Selby himself drew some 80,000 gallons of water from the city water supply in a single week (144–48); and that what humans conceive of as sleep is in reality a series of brief fits or heart attacks (166 n. 1).

But other theories developed by de Selby—particularly, as we shall see, those pertaining to the nature of space—provide a kind of template for interpreting the narrator's experiences. Indeed, what the narrator experiences as hell may literally be a hell of his own making; the otherworld may be a projection of his own fears and obsessions onto what Marie-Laure Ryan (1991) would call the novel's textual actual world—the world that the narrator experiences as and assumes to be actual—after he and Divney have murdered old Mathers. (As is revealed at the end of the novel, O'Brien's anti-hero enters this hellish domain of semi-human bicycles and oddly configured police barracks when he reaches for the black box that supposedly contains old Mathers' money. Divney, as it turns out, has booby-trapped this box with explosives [23, 197], so as to avoid having to share the loot with the narrator.) To some extent, O'Brien's hell is the ontological corollary of psychosis; in it there is an erosion of the boundary between the real and the imagined, the world and the narrator's mental representations of that world. Thus, when he first enters the "mysterious townland," the narrator is accosted by a one-legged murderer who is arguably a figure for himself, an actualization of his own self-image (43–49). Similarly, the narrator's guilty conscience and fear of reprisal by the authorities may account for the otherworld's being populated chiefly by policemen. Oftentimes operating incomprehensible machinery (106–14, 128, 130–32, 151), these gigantic policemen seem to externalize and actualize the narrator's most profound anxieties—not only about his own culpability for the crime but also about the unintelligibility of experience and the mechanistic, robotic quality of his entire existence up to the time of murder.[15]

What makes hell particularly hellish, however, is the way it brings two incompatible frames of reference—or cognitive systems—into conflict. On the one hand, the narrator operates under the assumption that the otherworld has the same space-time characteristics of the world in which he used to live. But on the other hand, saturated with the de Selbian metaphysics that he has killed Mathers to publish and perpetuate, the narrator is doomed to live out the (counterintuitive) theories that his philosopher-hero seems to have foisted upon his devotees.[16] As the narrator reports, one of de Selby's more striking ideas is that " 'a journey is an hallucination'" (50). Even though his theory "seems to discount the testimony of human experience and is at variance with everything I have learnt myself on many a country walk" (50), de Selby's reasoning leads him to reject

> the reality or truth of any progression or serialism in life, [denying] that time can pass as such in the accepted sense and [attributing] to hallucinations the commonly experienced sensation of progression as, for instance, in journeying from one place to another or even "living." If one is resting at A, he explains, and desires to rest in a distant place B, one can only do so by resting for infinitely brief intervals in innumerable intermediate places. Thus there is no difference essentially between what happens when one is resting at A before the start of the "journey" and what happens when one is "en route," i.e., resting in one or other of the intermediate places. (50)

This is, of course, a modern-day version of Zeno's paradox, whereby motion is deemed impossible because the distance an arrow must travel to reach a target, for example, can be subdivided into infinitely many segments of space.[17] Like Zeno's, de Selby's anti-serialistic theory militates against basic parameters of spatial reference and spatial cognition, including those associated with deictic shifts, paths of motion, and figure-ground relationships. But as the quoted passage suggests, de Selby must rely on these same parameters—for example, he must differentiate between place A and place B as figure and ground—just to articulate a theory according to which the parameters fail to hold. Similarly, when de Selby posits that roads "point" in certain directions, asserting that it is better not to travel east on a road that is headed west (38; cf. 82, 83, 86, 143), his idea seems laughable precisely because it conflicts with what remains an assumed distinction between topological and projective descriptions or locations. De Selby's theory, that is, conflates intrinsic with contextually imposed spatial properties. Roads do not themselves point in any particular direction; rather, *objects* occupy viewer-relative positions, projectively pointing in certain directions along roads that can be redescribed as potential paths of motion for a perceiver/cognizer.

The narrator's punishment is to live out, for all eternity, the conflict between humans' shared strategies for spatialization and those that seem to be required to cognize de Selbian spaces. In other words, the narrator's torment is to be perpetually unable to adjust, because of basic and general structures of cognition, to the spatiotemporal makeup of the world as de Selby theorized it. Phenomena that the narrator continues to assume to be local and atypical violations of the space-time contours of ordinary existence prove, in fact, to be global and normal characteristics of his de Selbian hell. They are consequences of a mode of theorizing at odds with the manner in which humans typically experience their shared world. Further, as an unreliable narrator, the protagonist remains unaware of the extent to which his own de Selbian obsessions have been actualized in the otherworld—and thrown up as insuperable obstacles to his negotiation of hellish space.[18] What begins as a comic incongruity between the theory and the experience of space thus gives way, as the novel proceeds, to a sort of ominous cooptation of reality by theory. The result is a novel whose tone gets darker and more unsettling as it goes on.

Hence, the narrator's task is truly a Sissyphean one: to orient himself within a space that refuses to be spatialized with the help of parameters on which both he and O'Brien's readers have always relied to get their bearings. *The Third Policeman* is, as much as anything else, the record of the narrator's (unreliable) efforts to conduct this impossible mapping operation. Consider, for example, the passage recounting how the narrator sets off the explosive device with which Divney has booby-trapped old Mathers's cash box:

> I thrust my hand bodily into the opening [in the floor where Mathers's cash box has been placed] and just when it should be closing about the box, something happened.
>
> I cannot hope to describe what it was but it had frightened me very much long before I had understood it even slightly. It was some change which came upon me or upon the room, indescribably subtle, yet momentous, ineffable. It was as if the daylight had changed with unnatural suddenness, as if the temperature of the evening had altered greatly in an instant or as if the air had become twice as rare or twice as dense as it had been in the winking of an eye; perhaps all of these and other things happened together for all my senses were bewildered all at once and could give me no explanation...
>
> I heard a cough behind me, soft and natural yet more disturbing than any sound that could ever come upon the human ear.... the utterance of the cough seemed to bring with it some more awful alternation in everything, just as if it had held the universe standstill for an instant, suspend-

ing the planets in their courses, halting the sun and holding in midair any falling thing the earth was pulling toward it. (23)

Viewed in retrospect (i.e., in light of what is revealed in the final chapter of the novel), this passage lacks textual cues prompting the reader to make the deictic shift required to relocate to the narrator's posthumous vantage point. Or rather, the cues are ambiguous, hinting toward the need for some sort of reorientation, but one that is of indefinite nature and extent. The passage might even be construed (again retrospectively) as suggesting that the passage from life to death does not require the radical change of perspective commonly assumed. Hell, it seems, is an intensification and suspension, rather than a wholesale transformation, of the HERE and NOW. In any event, in its form the quoted passage mirrors the narrator's own lack of awareness that he must make a deictic shift to the space-time coordinates of the otherworld. Through the technique that Gérard Genette (1980) termed *paralipsis*, or the omission of information potentially available to the narrator of a retrospective account, O'Brien's anti-hero induces in the reader the same feelings of dis- or misorientation that he himself experienced at this stage.

Furthermore, although the exact nature of the "awful alternation" encountered by the narrator remains at this point unclear, some of its chief symptoms prove to be spatiotemporal. As he sits facing an apparently reincarnated Mathers, "[y]ears or minutes could be swallowed up with equal ease in that indescribable and unaccountable interval" (24), and oddly enough the sun both rises and sets in the east (36). Indeed, even though he is only a three-hour walk from home, the narrator "seemed to have reached regions which I had never seen before" (39), where a police barracks seems to lack depth or breadth, its two-dimensional appearance "leaving no meaning in the remainder" (53); where a policeman's geometric properties are unaccountably difficult to configure into an organized whole or *Gestalt*, seeming "to create together, by some undetectable discrepancy in association or proportion, a very disquieting impression of unnaturalness, amounting almost to what was horrible and monstrous" (54); where, when Policeman MacCruiskeen extracts a series of successively smaller chests from other, only barely perceptibly larger chests, "[q]ueerly enough they looked to me as if they were all the same size but invested with some crazy perspective" (73); where an ostensibly random configuration of cracks on a ceiling forms, instead, a representation of "every road and house I knew . . . , and nets of lanes and neighbourhoods that I did not know also," providing "a map of the parish, complete, reliable and astonishing" (123); and where "eternity," accessible by an elevator, " 'has no size at all,' the Sergeant explained, 'because there is no difference anywhere in it and we have no conception of the extent of its unchanging co-equality' " (133). In fact, when he takes the lift down to this netherworld-within-the-otherworld, the narrator sees objects that

> lacked an essential property of all known objects. I cannot call it shape or configuration since shapelessness is not what I refer to at all. I can only say that these objects, not one of which resembled the other, were of no known dimensions. They were not square or rectangular or circular or simply irregularly shaped nor could it be said that their endless variety was due to dimensional dissimilarities. Simply their appearance, if even that word is not inadmissible, was not understood by the eye and was in any event indescribable. (135)

As incidents such as these suggest, there is a fundamental mismatch between, on the one hand, what the narrator expects his world to be like—and, vicariously, what the reader expects the storyworld to be like—and, on the other hand, the characteristics that the world actually turns out to have.[19] Indeed, what Victor Shklovsky (1965) would characterize as the novel's defamiliarizing power, its ability to "make strange," derives in part from the way the text disappoints standard expectations about the disposition of objects in space. In other words, the novel defamiliarizes by evoking a storyworld in which some of the narrator's default assumptions about its spatial configuration are inapplicable. Other parameters or default assumptions, however, do seem to apply, creating a "mixed" space-time system in which the narrator cannot trust the evidence of his own senses. Therein lies its hellishness. But whereas the narrator tends to group together quite disparate spatiotemporal phenomena under headings such as *indescribable* and *incomprehensible*, the research concepts discussed in previous subsections provide a more nuanced vocabulary in this connection. As I have already begun to indicate vis-à-vis the notion of deictic shift, the concepts at issue can yield finer-grained categories by which to identify and diagnose several subtypes of cognitive dissonance at work in O'Brien's text.

Note that, from the start of his journey through hell, the narrator seems to have difficulty modeling the storyworld in terms of figures and grounds. Or, alternatively, regions of storyworld itself, given their de

Selbian profile, refuse to be modeled in terms of reference and located objects. For one thing, the narrator constructs certain portions of the storyworld as *intrinsically ground*. The result is a paradox undermining the very logic of the figure-ground distinction, which assumes a perceptual field only temporarily and provisionally structured into located and reference objects. Thus, commenting on the road that leads from Mathers's house to the barracks, the narrator remarks: "I found it hard to think of a time when there was no road there because the trees and the tall hills and the fine views of bogland had been arranged by wise hands for the pleasing picture they made when looked at from the road" (37). Similarly paradoxical, and similarly conflating spatial perception with causal reasoning, is the narrator's observation that a "house was quiet in itself and silent but a canopy of lazy smoke had been erected over the chimney to indicate that people were within engaged on tasks" (86). Later, again transposing the distinction between grounds and figures onto the one between causes and effects, the narrator comments that "[c]louds of white and grey pillowed [a distant hill] and on its soft shoulder trees and boulders were put pleasingly to make it true" (120). At another point, while walking through the landscape with Sergeant MacCruiskeen, the narrator notes blue mountains that seem to have been placed "at what you might call a respectful distance" from those observing them (77–78). The narrator thus seems to construe the mountains as reference objects constituting a sort of preestablished ground for located human activity. Yet he also complains that the mountains "kept hemming us in and meddling oppressively with our minds" (78), transforming the mountains into located objects (indeed, agents) in their own right. Here as elsewhere the protagonist's disorientation stems in part from the uncertain, shifting status of located objects vis-à-vis reference objects, as well as the fuzziness of the boundary between what counts as a figure and what can be taken to be a ground consisting of objects-in-the-world.[20] Even though he ought to know better, the narrator keeps on assuming that de Selbian spaces obey the logic governing figures and grounds in our shared world, and the result is a private, even custom-made hell.

Furthermore, it is not clear whether the narrator is consistent in distinguishing—or, alternatively, whether in this world a distinction *can* be made—between topological and projective descriptions. Take the problem of determining the size of objects. It remains unclear whether the narrator is able to (or should even try to) make allowances for apparent fluctuations in objects' size based on their relative proximity to his own vantage point on the storyworld. Hence, in the following passage it is unclear whether in O'Brien's otherworld changes in size do, in fact, correlate with the viewer-relative property of increased distance: "Far away near the sky tiny people were stooped at their turf-work, cutting out precisely-shaped sods with their patent spades and building them into a tall memorial twice the height of a horse and cart" (86). The same ambiguity operates in another panoramic view provided by the narrator: "Men who were notable for the whiteness of their shirts worked diminutively in the distant bog, toiling in the brown turf and heather. Patient horses stood near with their useful carts and littered among the boulders on a hill were tiny sheep at pasture" (125). Inversely, there is the problem of the enormous size of Policeman Fox in the novel's penultimate chapter (180). Fox's size again presents a fundamental interpretive difficulty. It can be interpreted, on the one hand, as a result of the narrator's conflating projective with inherent spatial attributes and more specifically as an Expressionistic or quasi-Expressionistic projection of his own anxieties about authority onto object geometries in the external world.[21] On the other hand, however, Fox's "overbearing policemanship, his massive rearing of wide strengthy flesh, his domination and his unimpeachable reality" (180) may be a function of the de Selbian makeup of hell itself. On this latter view, the enormity of Fox, the third policeman whose barracks is (impossibly) located in the interstices of the walls of Mathers's house, indexes a strangely relativistic/nonrelativistic spacetime system. In that system, objects are inherently large and small and roads have intrinsic directionality, yet matter is convertible into energy (106–14), and absolute serial progression through time or space is impossible—as de Selby theorized and as the narrator's iterated cycle of punishments confirms.

Emblematizing the unmappable nature of hell, its resistance to modes of perceiving and inferencing based on standard parameters for spatial cognition, is the narrator's attempt to navigate the spaces of Mathers's house, just prior to his final "arrest" by Policeman Fox (174–80). Like the labyrinthine interior spaces of Henry James's story "The Jolly Corner" (James 1996), Mathers's house may in fact represent the baroque complexities of consciousness itself, the twists and turns of a mind that only partly knows its own workings. But in any event, as the narrator first approaches the house, once again the border between located and reference objects is fuzzy, with the "dead man's empty house spreading its desolation far into the surrounding night" (174). Further, what appears to be the ordinary yellow light of an oil lamp burning in a window acquires, by some subtle shift of perspective, a "quality which was wrong, mysterious, alarming" (175). It is this mysterious light that leads the narrator to discover that it is impossible for him to construct a cognitive map of the house. Despite repeated attempts, he cannot locate exactly where in the house a light would have to be shining in order for it to cast the illumination that he sees "lying thickly on the misty night air and playing on the dark-green leaves of a tree that stood nearby" (177). Whatever room the narrator pinpoints as its most likely source, the light seems to issue either from the room to his right or the room to his left (177–78). Thus, the text implies that the source of the light is *inherently viewer-relative*, its position in the storyworld being unamenable to the distinction between topological and projective description, in much the same way certain regions seem intrinsically (and thus paradoxically) backgrounded.

In other respects, however, the storyworld *does* seem to be cognizable in terms of parameters standardly associated with spatial reference. This helps explain why the narrator keeps on experiencing so many unpleasant surprises. Since the otherworld has some of the space-time characteristics of his previous world (and arguably could not even be imagined if it did not), the narrator mistakenly infers that it is uniformly susceptible to his old strategies for spatialization. For example—and likely because of very general constraints on how space can be imagined, fictionally or otherwise—the contrast between a full WHAT and a minimal WHERE system holds even for the region containing Mathers's house. Thus, as he decides whether to proceed on his way or turn around and look back at the house, the narrator locates himself within a storyworld richly furnished with objects but charts his own movements along a single axis leading to and away from his vantage point on Mathers's place:

> I had turned away to go when a feeling came upon me that the house had changed the instant my back was turned. This feeling was so strange and chilling that I stood rooted to the road for several seconds with my hands gripping the bars of the bicycle, wondering painfully whether I should turn my head and look or go resolutely forward on my way. I think I had

made up my mind to go and had taken a few faltering steps forward when some influence came upon my eyes and dragged them round till they were again resting upon the house. They opened widely in surprise and once more my startled cry jumped out from me. A bright light was burning in a small window in the upper storey. (175)

Likewise, as in the example from Defoe's *Moll Flanders* discussed in the previous section, the narrator uses motion verbs to encode a deictic field in which paths of motion traverse a distal-proximal axis, the proximal end of which corresponds to the narrator's perspective on the storyworld. Hence, after the narrator has hurled a rock "about the size of a bicycle lamp" through the upper-story window with the mysterious light streaming from it,

> I turned and fled at top speed down the drive until I had again reached and made contact with the bicycle. . . . Suddenly a shadow appeared, blotting out the light on the whole left-hand side. . . . I was still gazing at the window when I heard soft sounds behind me. I did not look round. Soon I knew they were the footsteps of a very heavy person who was walking along the grass margin of the road to deaden his approach. Thinking he would pass without seeing me in the dark recess of the gateway, I tried to remain even more still than my original utter immobility. The steps suddenly clattered out on the roadway not six yards away, came up behind me and then stopped. . . . I swung round in amazement. Before me, almost blocking out the night, was an enormous policeman. (179–80)

The narrator goes away from the house, taking a path of motion along an axis paralleling the driveway; the locative adverb *down* marks the path as essentially linear. He establishes a new fixed vantage point once he reaches the bicycle. A shadow enters (*appears* within) the narrator's perceptual field at its distal boundary, defined now by the window. In conjunction with two occurrences of the spatial preposition *behind* (and the noun phrase *his approach*), the locutions *was walking along the grass margin of the road* and *came up* map Policeman Fox's progress through the region separating him and the narrator. As in the passage from Defoe, the narrator thus relies heavily on verbs of motion to track entities as they successively move closer to or get farther away from the vantage point of his narration. And once again the verbs collocate in a way that suggests a quite minimal WHERE system, preserving only very coarse geometric properties of the WHAT. That is, in representing place, the narrative expresses mainly the axial structure of objects, and more specifically the direction in which they are pointed along the paths that lead to and away from the site of the narrator's perceptual activity.

In short, the protagonist evokes (and tries to navigate) a storyworld that both does and does not conform to basic parameters for mentally modeling the location of objects in space. His problem—and it is a problem that will apparently torment him forever—is that he cannot be sure which of his principles for cognitive mapping can still be relied on in a hell of his and de Selby's making. Likewise, by destabilizing readers' assumptions about the space-time characteristics of the storyworld it cues them to reconstruct, O'Brien's novel temporarily traps its readers in an unsettling otherworld. Even as it makes its readers think twice about their strategies for spatialization, the narrative places a premium on the process of spatializing. It suggests that, in proportion with their resistance to spatial cognition, human beings' experiences becomes increasingly less tellable—and less liveable.

Spatialization and the Text-Type Approach

The present chapter is, of course, far from being an exhaustive account of how spatial reference functions in *The Third Policeman* or in the other narratives I have examined—let alone in narrative as such. Yet the analysis has, I believe, succeeded in showing spatial reference to be not an optional or peripheral feature of stories, but rather a core property that helps *constitute* narrative domains. This is as true of O'Brien's novel as it is of the other narratives discussed more cursorily. It is just that O'Brien's text displays greater self-consciousness about the critical role played by spatial reference in storyworld (re)construction. The novel creates, in this way, a secondary modeling system of a distinctly postmodernist stripe. In general, though, the narratives analyzed reveal that telling a story necessitates modeling and enabling others to model, an emergent constellation of spatially related entities. In turn, this conclusion has important ramifications for approaches to narrative analysis based on the concept of text types.

For example, Tuija Virtanen (1992) grounds her analysis of the NARRATIVE text type in previous research on cognitive prototypes (e.g., Rosch et al. 1976). Subdivided into "core" and "peripheral" features, prototypes are typically defined as stereotypical or "good" examples of the phenomena for which they are used as analogs or models. Prototypes can thus be thought of as models prestored in the mind in the form of knowledge representations of a certain kind.[22] For Virtanen, what William Labov (1972a) characterized as the *temporal juncture* is the minimal or core requirement for narrative in contradistinction to other text types, such as instruction, exposition, description, and argument. In Labov's original formulation, clauses can be categorized as narrative only if they are separated by a temporal juncture, such that the clauses form an ordered set, and "a change in their order will result in a change in the temporal sequence of the original semantic interpretation" of the story (360–61). Likewise, deploying a two-level typology that distinguishes between discourse types and text types, with narrative text sometimes subserving argumentative discourse or argumentative text sometimes subserving descriptive discourse (cf. Chatman 1990: 6–37; contrast Schiffrin 1994: 282–333), Virtanen (1992) claims that "the temporal juncture characteristic of the minimal narrative has to be present in a text that [realizes] the narrative discourse type"; inversely, narrative "cannot surface through a non-narrative type of text without a minimal narrative frame text" (304–5).

As the present chapter indicates, however, features that have been centrally associated with the prototype DESCRIPTION may have to be included among the core properties of narrative as well. As my examples suggest, narrators and readers engage in the joint construction of mental models not just temporally but also spatially structured. Relying crucially on such mechanisms as deictic shift and the building of projective locations for agents and objects, narrative entails a process of cognitive mapping that assigns referents not merely a temporal but a *spatio*temporal position in the storyworld. Hence Labov's notion of temporal junctures needs to be respecified; such junctures involve not ordered sets of events per se but more precisely the ordered distribution of event constituents in time and space. This respecification helps explain the intuition that, even if the events mentioned in the following example (taken from chapter 3) did occur, in fact, in the order mentioned and are thus separated by two temporal junctures, the sequence of actions and events does not qualify as a narrative:

> A monkey screeched in the jungle. Sunlight blazed down upon the Arctic Ocean. The rancher gazed proudly at his bison.

Specifically, the way these events (and their constituents) are distributed in space is what prevents their being construed as elements of a narrative. In other words, temporal sequence is a necessary but not a sufficient condition for narrative. An important topic for future research, therefore, is how temporal junctures must be meshed in a particular, highly structured way with spatial reference in order for a text to be assimilable to the prototype NARRATIVE and interpreted as such.

To phrase this last point otherwise: making spatial reference a core property of stories requires rethinking the place of NARRATIVE vis-à-vis DESCRIPTION in standard text typologies.[23] It may be misleading to say that descriptive text sometimes (i.e., optionally) subserves narrative discourse, or that peripherally narrative displays features that align it with peripheral features of description—the boundaries between these two text types being, as prototype theory predicts, fuzzy instead of sharp. Rather, given that narratives naturally and normally rely on deictic shifts, contrasts between figures and grounds, projective versus toplogical locations, motion verbs, and other strategies for encoding the spatial layout of storyworlds, a more radical realignment of narrative and description seems to be necessary. Indeed, a research model based on text types may take narrative theorists only so far. That model may be unable to capture how stories encode entities moving or being moved along narratively salient paths—that is, how spaces and trajectories can have more or less saliency in a story depending on the way agents and objects are temporally distributed over regions linked by paths (see Herman 1999f).

In any event, drawing on many of the cognitive and communicative resources typically associated with description, the narratives examined in this chapter build relationships between agents, objects, and places, thereby creating a rich blend of space and time, or what Bakhtin would characterize as a chronotopic structure (Bakhtin 1981b; Zoran 1984). No wonder, then, that the word *narrative* itself derives from the Sanskrit word *jnā:na-*, meaning "knowledge." It is not just that knowledge about space makes it possible to understand narratives; more than this, narrative is a pattern of thinking and communicating, a cognitive style as well as a discourse genre, on the strength of which humans spatialize and thereby comprehend the world. In this sense, narrative does not merely reflect spatial categorizations of experience but furthermore is one of the chief means by which people go about building spatial representations of a world that they could not otherwise begin to experience at all. It is thus a fundamental, not a specialized or derivative, mode of cognition. By the same token, narratology should no longer be viewed as mainly a literary-theoretical enterprise; it should instead assume its rightful place within the more general endeavor of cognitive science, under whose auspices any number of disciplines are now converging on the question of how humans build, revise, and communicate a broad range of mental representations, including storyworlds.

8
Perspectives

In the previous chapter, I characterized narrative as a discourse genre and a cognitive style that relies fundamentally on perspective taking. Situating participants and objects in an unfolding pattern of spatial relationships, stories exploit mental models based on a distinction between topological and projective locations. To put this last point more strongly: narrative is one of the principal means of building and communicating projective locations, such locations being indexed to a particular perspective vis-à-vis the storyworld. Spatialization in narrative is thus inextricably interlinked with the problem of perspective. And within the classical, structuralist tradition of narrative poetics, an extensive body of scholarship has grown up around the issue of perspective. Much of this research stems from pioneering insights of Gérard Genette, who first called for a more careful discrimination between the questions "Who sees?" and "Who speaks?" in narrative (1980: 186; cf. Bal 1985: 101). In distinguishing between these questions, Genette recognized that whereas the link between narration and perspective taking may be organic and indissoluble, it is also complex, with seeing and speaking standing in a heteromorphic rather than an isomorphic relation to one another. I can tell a story, build and communicate a storyworld, by adopting any number of vantage points, including that of a mute anonymous onlooker later recounting the action, one of the primary participants in the narrative sequence, or an omniscient narrator of the sort found in Henry Fielding's *Tom Jones* or George Eliot's *Middlemarch*. Conversely, the perspective I adopt does not determine which narrative style (e.g., what narrative temporalities) I might deploy. For example, regardless of my perspective, I can narrate events retrospectively, simultaneously, or prospectively, and I can present in a more or less chronological fashion the sequence of actions I am prompting you to reconstruct. In short, whereas the question "Who speaks?" pertains to narration, the question "Who sees?" pertains to what Genette proposed to call *focalization*.

Genette's original proposal was this: "To avoid the too specifically visual connotations of the terms vision, field, and point of view, I will take here the slightly more abstract term focalization which corresponds, besides, to Brooks and Warren's expression, 'focus of narration'" (1980: 189).[1] Ever since, the concept of focalization has figured as an important tool for narratological analysis. Like the earlier terms of art (point of view, perspective, etc.) upon which Genette meant to improve, focalization is a way of talking about perceptual and conceptual frames, more or less inclusive or restricted, through which participants, situations, and events are presented in a narrative.[2] Modes of focalization thus serve as markers of the way in which any mental model of narrated events will be perspectivally constrained, that is, built up in a projective fashion. Indeed, one of the defining features of narrative is its representation of human experience as invariably filtered through one perspective or another. As Monika Fludernik (1996: 129–77) has shown, even texts featuring the so-called omniscient narration of the high-realist novel—texts that approximate what Franz Karl Stanzel (1971, 1984) termed the *authorial* narrative situation—can be read or narrativized only by appeal to basic cognitive parameters that include VIEWING as well as EXPERIENCING, ACTING, and TELLING. As Fludernik puts it, "The authorial narrator's more extended omniscience regarding the space and time of the action does not pose any problems in relation to natural parameters: it can be accounted for easily within the traditional function of the historian as a compiler and accumulator of traditional lore and a recensor of earlier versions of the story" (1996: 167). More generally, in exploring the perspectival dimension of narrative, narrative theorists are dealing not with binary but with scalar phenomena. There is no such thing as an aperspectival or nonprojective story, but rather ways of presenting a narrative in which the exigencies of perspective taking are more or less accentuated.[3]

In fact, insofar as it accustoms interpreters to look less for the facts than for versions of the facts, teaching them to contextualize what happened by way of strategies for viewing and telling about what happened, narrative can be seen as a prototype for all perspective-taking, version-making activities (cf. Ochs et al. 1992). Yet it is important to emphasize that stories not only facilitate but also formally encode ways of seeing. The concept of focalization points up this modeling capacity of narrative. Thus, to say that an event or object or participant is focalized in a certain manner is to say that it is perspectivally indexed, structured so that it has to be interpreted as refracted through a specific viewpoint and anchored in a particular set of contextual coordinates. As I discuss in the next section, the formal indices of focalization include (in spoken and written narratives, at least) pronouns, definite and indefinite articles, verbs of perception and cognition, verbal tenses and moods, and evaluative lexical items and marked syntax.

After reviewing classical typologies of focalization and considering examples of the modes of focalization identified by structuralist narratologists, I turn my attention to a kind of focalization that the original typologies did not include. At issue is what I call "hypothetical focalization" (hereafter, HF), which entails the use of hypotheses, framed by the narrator or a character, about what might be or might have been seen or perceived—if only there were someone who could have adopted the requisite perspective on the situations and events at issue. I argue that the omission of HF from the standard typologies was not fortuitous; rather, its description (let alone explanation) requires conceptual resources largely unavailable to classical narratology. Accounting for HF, I contend, requires that we draw on ideas developed after, or at least independently of, the ensemble of linguistic and philosophical concepts on which the early narrotologists by and large relied. Specifically, ideas drawn from possible-worlds semantics—ideas first imported into narrative theory by such scholars as Lubomír Doležel (1976, 1979, 1980, 1983, 1998), Thomas Pavel (1986), and Marie-Laure Ryan (1991, 1992) — can help account for the form and functioning of HF. This conceptual framework helps spotlight the semantic or, in a sense I explain below, *intensional* aspects of narrative. By contrast, structuralist narratology was marked precisely by its preoccupation with narrative form, at the expense of the more recalcitrant and less readily formalizable domain of narrative meaning.[4] The present chapter, then, does not merely synopsize existing research on focalization. It also echoes earlier chapters (in particular, chapters 1, 4, and 7) in arguing that the specifically semantic dimensions of building and communicating storyworlds need to be studied further, with focalization providing a convenient point of access to key problems within the field of narrative semantics.

Focalization: Types and Markers

In his pathbreaking discussion of "the problems of analyzing narrative discourse according to categories borrowed from the grammar of verbs," Genette (1980) puts focalization in the category of *mood* (versus those of *tense* or *voice*) (30–31). For Genette narrative mood spans "modalities (forms and degrees) of narrative 'representation' " (31). In a footnote appended to this passage, Genette furthermore remarks that "[t]he term is used here with a sense very close to its linguistic meaning," citing the *Littré* dictionary's definition of *mood*: "Name given to the different forms of the verb that are used to affirm more or less the thing in question, and to express . . . the different points of view from which the life or the action is looked at" (31 n. 9). Under the heading of narrative mood Genette groups what he calls distance, which depends on the degree to which a narrative "shows" or else "tells" the events of the story, and perspective, which Genette rechristens focalization. Whereas Genette himself would later comment on "the obviously metaphorical nature of the paradigm tense/mood/voice" invoked in *Narrative Discourse* (Genette 1988: 41), one might dispute the need for any such (partial) recantation. It is not that the grammatical framework lacks descriptive adequacy in this context and should therefore be deprecated as a merely heuristic device. To the contrary, narrative theorists should arguably take the paradigm *more* seriously, drawing more extensively on the research model outlined by William Frawley (1992): "Speakers often qualify their statements with respect to believability, reliability, and general compatability with accepted fact. The area of semantics that concerns the factual status of statements is modality. . . . Modality affects the overall *assertability* of an expression," bearing "not only [on] objective measures of factual status but also [on] subjective attitudes and orientations toward the content of an expression by its utterer" (384–85). My discussion of HF stresses the importance of studying connections between modes of focalization, grammatical moods, and epistemic modalities, that is, degrees of certainty interpreters can have with respect to the objects, events, or states of affairs about which a narrative cues them to frame interpretations.

For the moment, though, it is worth exploring the potentials of the classical approach to focalization. In Genette's scheme, there are three types of narratives: internally focalized narratives, externally focalized narratives, and nonfocalized narratives, that is, narratives with zero focalization.[5] Stories told by omniscient narrators can be redescribed as narratives with zero focalization. As already indicated, it is perhaps misleading to speak of "zero" focalization in this context, given that readers inevitably interpret narratives by relying on what Fludernik (1996) specifies as the basic cognitive parameters of VIEWING. That said, however, the famous opening of Charles Dickens's *Bleak House*—

1. Fog everywhere. Fog up the river, where it flows among green aits and meadows; fog down the river. . . . Fog on the Essex marshes, fog on the Kentish heights. . . . Chance people on the bridges peeing over the parapets into a nether sky of fog (1964: 17)

—is narrated in a manner that does seem to transcend the limits of space and time, the constraints of an individualized point of view, thereby approximating zero focalization. Other narratives are marked by species of internal focalization, whether fixed, variable, or multiple. Patrick Modiano's *La Place de l'étoile* (The place of the star; 1968), despite its quasi-hallucinogenic shifts between past and present, Europe and Palestine, is focalized through a *fixed* center of consciousness. Hermann Broch's *Die Schlafwändler* (*The Sleepwalkers*; 1978) is by contrast *variably* focalized through several characters, all of them moving like sleepwalkers toward an all-encompassing sociohistorical apocalypse, different aspects of which are presented from the vantage point of each character. In William Faulkner's *As I Lay Dying* (1987) the *same* set of events gets *multiply* focalized through the incommensurable perspectives of the Bundrens, each family member attempting to come to grips, in highly disanalogous ways, with the legacy of Addie Bundren's death. Finally, what Genette called external focalization can be found in some of Dashiell Hammett's stories and novels, for example, since there "the hero performs in front of us without our ever being allowed to know his thoughts or feelings" (Genette 1980: 190)—or at least *all* of his thoughts or feelings.

What still needs to be specified, however, are the finer-grained features of narrative discourse that motivate categorizations such as the ones put forth in the previous paragraph. At issue are formal markers (technically, morphosyntactic elements of utterances contained in the discourse) that signal what sort of perspectival filtering is at work in a narrative—or at least in a portion of that narrative. In what follows I briefly catalogue some of these formal indices and discuss their functioning in specific narrative contexts. This preliminary discussion will set the stage for my subsequent remarks about HF and my argument that its description and analysis highlight the need for new tools for narratology. Such tools will be afforded by integrating narrative theory and language theory (including possible-worlds semantics) within a broader, cognitive-scientific approach to narrative viewed as a main strategy for viewing—a prime resource for taking perspectives, building up ways of seeing.

Pronouns

Although personal pronouns enable readers to distinguish between homodiegetic and heterodiegetic narration, they do not reliably index a story as focalized in one manner as opposed to another. Thus, gappy or paraliptic first-person narratives, such as Agatha Christie's *The Murder of Roger Ackroyd* (1976) or John Lanchester's *The Debt to Pleasure* (1996), can have elements of external focalization, in Genette's sense, whereas third-person narration can either be rigorously internally focalized, as in Franz Kafka's *Der Prozeß* (*The Trial*; 1986), or else focalized externally in Bal's and Rimmon-Kenan's sense (e.g., Tobias Smollett's *Roderick Random* [1927]). There is a similarly loose form-function correlation between possessive pronouns and modes of focalization. But demonstrative pronouns operate differently. Such pronouns can be used either literally to mark off a distal-proximal axis in space (*this* chair over here, but *that* one over there), or else figuratively to set up such an axis along a timeline or in conceptual space (I do it *this* way today, but I did it *that* way yesterday). To this extent, demonstrative pronouns invariably serve as indices of internal focalization, marking objects or actions as refracted through someone's perspective. The perspective-marking function of demonstrative pronouns is exemplified in passage 2, taken from Elizabeth Bowen's *The Death of the Heart*:

> 2. Portia, when Anna looked straight at her, immediately looked away. This was, as a matter of fact, the first moment since they came in that there had been any question of looking straight at each other. But during the conversation about Pidgeon, Anna had felt *those* dark eyes with a determined innocence steal back again and again to her face. (1966: 49, my emphasis)

Indefinite and Definite Articles

The use of indefinite (*a*, *an*, *one*) and definite (*the*) articles sets up a contrast in some ways analogous to the one set up by *this* and *that*.

In this case, however, choices between indefinite and definite articles create not a proximal-distal scale for elements in the storyworld, but rather a binary distinction between information that is given and information that is new vis-à-vis the discourse (cf. Firbas 1964, 1992; E. Prince 1981, 1992). Further, insofar as given and new information will be given or new from a particular perspective, the alternation between indefinite and definite articles, like choices between demonstrative pronouns, marks objects, participants, and events as filtered through someone's perspective. Thus David Lodge's (1996) analysis of Hemingway's "Cat in the Rain," which I have excerpted as passage 3, turns on the strategic omission of an article before the first word in the title of the story. As Lodge points out, the lack of an article in the title makes it impossible to decide definitively between two interpretations of the end of the story, where there is a shift from the wife's to the husband's perspective.

> 3. Someone knocked at the door.
> "Avanti," George said. He looked up from his book.
> In the doorway stood the maid. She held a big tortoise-shell cat. . . .
> (quoted in Lodge 1996: 34)

The end of the story is fundamentally ambiguous because the husband did not bother to get out of bed to look at the cat his wife saw, so when he uses the indefinite article *a* to mark the cat as new as opposed to given information, readers cannot be sure whether the cat is truly a new entity or just an entity that is new *from the husband's perspective*.

Verbs of Perception, Cognition, and Emotion

Now consider passage 4, taken from Ann Radcliffe's *The Italian*. Ellena has been imprisoned in a convent, and this passage describes the first time she hears the voice (and then sees the face) of the kindly sister Olivia:

> 4. Among the voices of the choir, was one whose expression immediately fixed her [Ellena's] attention; it *seemed to speak* a loftier sentiment of devotion than the others, and to be modulated by the melancholy of an heart, that had long since taken leave of this world. Whether it swelled with the high peal of the organ, or mingled in low and trembling accents with the sinking chorus, Ellena *felt* that she understood all the feelings of the breast from which it flowed; and she looked to the gal-

lery where the nuns were assembled, to discover a countenance, that might *seem to accord* with the sensibility expressed in the voice. (1968: 86, my emphases)

In this passage several verbs and verbal phrases index the narrated action as filtered (i.e., focalized internally) through Ellena's perspective, even though it is narrated in a pseudo-objective third-person style.[6] True, the vocabulary of sentiment and feeling pervades this passage and contributes to the gendering of the very different domains in which Ellena and Vivaldi, the male protagonist, are constrained to act in the novel. More than this, however, verbs of perception such as *seem* are deeply bound up with the Gothic conventions that Radcliffe herself helped establish. These conventions foreground the enigmatic nature of characters and events—characters and events whose decoding in a sense constitutes the main "action" of the novel itself. Verbs of perception, cognition, and emotion are thus used to signal the active, ongoing deciphering of what is being narrated, its refraction through some character-perceiver's or character-knower's perspective. Indeed, as I discuss below, when clustered together in higher concentrations, such verbs can serve to mark HF, a mode of focalization that highlights uncertainty, guesswork, or ignorance on the part of the focalizing agent.

Tenses and Verbal Moods

I discuss verbal moods extensively in my remarks on HF, which exploits non-indicative moods to register what might or could be seen, perceived, or in some way experienced, if only someone were there to engage in the focalizing activity that is recorded as having merely hypothetically occurred. Yet verb tenses, too, can be used to index perspectival constraints. Specifically, as Fludernik (1996) points out, they can be used to signal "the perception of a *current* state of affairs which is the result of a previous process" (194). Take, for example, the passage from Upton Sinclair's *The Jungle* excerpted as 5. Here the pluperfect tense marks how the scene appears to the novel's protagonist, Jurgis Rudkus, who is described a few sentences earlier as standing "upon the steps, bewildered" (1990: 172). Having just been released from jail, Jurgis lacks a wider context for the current weather conditions and must perform inferences based, presumably, on his own previous perceptual experience during past winters:

5. There *had been* a heavy snow, and now a thaw *had set in*; a fine sleety rain was falling, driven by a wind that pierced Jurgis to the bone. (172, my emphases)

In the first two clauses quoted, just by using the morphology of English verbs, the narrator of *The Jungle* can dramatize Jurgis's experience of emerging into the outside world and perceiving it anew, after having been pent up in jail.

Evaluative Lexical Items and Marked Syntax

Likewise, evaluatively colored lexical items (cf. Fludernik 1996: 200–201) can serve as indices of internal focalization in passages that might otherwise suggest an objective or external presentation. The same goes for atypical syntactic or discourse patterning. Take, for instance, the famous opening of James Joyce's *A Portrait of the Artist as a Young Man*:

6. Once upon a time and a very good time it was there was a moocow coming down along the road and this moocow that was coming down along the road met a nicens little boy named baby tuckoo....
   His father told him that story: his father looked at him through a glass: he had a hair face. (1964: 8)

In the first sentence of this passage, near-rhyming diminutives (*moocow ... tuckoo*) and nonstandard word formation (*nicens*) indicate that the action is being focalized by a child. The same effect is accomplished by the absence of conjunctions or subordinating connectives between the three clauses strung together in the second sentence. The very minimal syntax of all three clauses (apparently linked together by mere associative logic) also serves to index them as perspectivally filtered.

HF: Beyond the Classical Typologies

Having surveyed some of the types and markers of focalization amenable to classical description, I turn now to a mode of focalization not readily described in the terms provided by older frameworks. At issue are narratives whose interpretation provokes, in a more or less direct or explicit way, speculation about some non-existent focalizor. At issue, too, are narratives that prompt speculation about focalizing activity that someone who actually exists in the storyworld may or may not have performed. In other words, some narratives are focalized such that recipients gain, as it were, illicit access to the aspects of the storyworld—aspects not, in fact, focalized, or not focalizable even in principle, from the perspective encoded as the actual vantage point for narration.[7] Such narratives modalize, or rather virtualize, their own representation of events into counterfactual belief contexts—that is, (sets of) possible worlds or candidate mental models—in which the events *might* be represented as such. Further, although in the remainder of this chapter I limit my efforts to a partial description and analysis of HF, my account points to the need to rethink the nature and dynamics of focalization in general. The nonlocatability of HF within structuralist typologies indicates the limitations of classical models, or more precisely shows that those models achieve descriptive adequacy only within certain limits. In particular, HF suggests that researchers can gain new insights into narrative meaning by substituting for a discontinuous model based on the distinction between internal and external focalization, between "personal" and "impersonal" narration, a continuous model in which a range of perspective-taking strategies are distributed along a scale. These strategies, any number of which may collocate in a given narrative, encode different degrees of certainty with respect to objects, participants, and events in the storyworld.

Thus, in the remarks that follow I draw on work in linguistic semantics to argue that ways of focalizing a story can be redescribed as the narrative representation of propositional attitudes; that is, modes of focalization encode into narrative form various kinds of epistemic stances that can be adopted toward what is being represented in a narrative.[8] In narrative discourse what I am calling *hypothetical focalization*, or HF, is the formal marker of a peculiar epistemic modality, in which, to use the terminology of Frawley (1992), the *expressed world* counterfactualizes or virtualizes the *reference world* of the text. Frawley's *reference world* corresponds to that subset of propositions about the storyworld that can be used to express the facts of the storyworld. Thus, the reference world is made up of all those propositions having the value True in the possible world mentally modeled via storyworld reconstruction. The expressed world, by contrast, consists of propositions that display varying degrees of conformity (or, in the case of negation, total noncomformity) with the reference world.[9] Hence Frawley construes modality generally as an "epistemic version of deixis," asserting that "modality is the way a language encodes the *comparison of an expressed world with a reference* world. ... The *expressed world*, the state of affairs in the asserted proposition, is the modal equivalent of the deictic located point. The *reference world*, normally the actual world of speech, is the modal counterpart of the spatial and temporal reference point, the here-and-now" (387).[10] For example, in statements displaying a specifically negative modality, whose narrative counterpart may be what Jean Sareil (1987) has characterized as "negative description," the speaker's commitment to the truth of the expressed world with respect to the reference world is at the zero degree. If I say *the cat is not hungry*, I am, of course, not at all committed to the truth of the proposition "The cat is hungry" relative to my current belief context, my present reference world. Conversely, if I say *the cat went inside the house to eat*, the indicative mood of my statement, together with the absence of any negational adverb or particle (*never* went, did *not* go), signals that I am quite firmly committed to the truth of this proposition—more firmly than if I had said *the cat may have gone inside the house to eat* or *The cat could have gone inside the house to eat*. But the epistemic commitments signaled in narrative discourse via HF (e.g., *A concerned neighbor might* [would, could, must] *have surmised that the cat was hungry*) are more difficult to sort out. The relationship between the expressed world and the reference world is more complicated; for in hypothetically focalized narrative, it is harder to rewrite "the values for ... deictic points ... in terms of the speaker's state of belief" and to interpret "the relation between those points ... as degrees of commitment and likelihood of the actualization of states of affairs" (Frawley 1992: 388). To put it another way, HF marks more or less severe, more or less pervasive diegetic indecision over what counts as the actual versus what counts as merely possible worlds built up over the course of a narrative.[11]

Direct HF: The Counterfactual Witness

Two broad categories of narratives can be classed as hypothetically focalized. The first category contains narratives that explicitly appeal to a hypothetical witness, a counterfactual focalizor, in setting out the elements of the story. This first species of hypothetical focalization can be termed *direct* HF, by analogy with taxonomies of speech presentation in narrative (see chapter 5). Whereas direct HF entails explicit mention of a counterfactual observer or witness, *indirect* HF, as I discuss below, covers those stretches of narrative discourse the interpretation of which requires that readers *infer* the focalizing activity of a merely hypothetical onlooker. As an instance of direct HF, consider first a passage, excerpted as 7, that occurs near the opening of Edgar Allan Poe's "The Fall of the House of Usher." The narrator includes this description, or nondescription, of how Usher's house might appear to the gaze of a merely hypothetical observer:

> 7. Perhaps the eye of a scrutinizing observer might have discovered a barely perceptible fissure, which, extending from the roof of the building in the front, made its way down the wall in a zigzag direction, until it became lost in the sullen waters of the tarn. (1990: 1392)

The hypotheticality of this passage gets grammaticalized, first, by way of the lexical item *perhaps*, an adverb with both alethic and epistemic functions, indicating both possibility and doubt.[12] More precisely, *perhaps* is a sentential adverb that sets up a particular belief context, a candidate mental model. By virtue of this context or model the content of Poe's statement can be judged as one to whose truth the narrator is not firmly committed (cf. Frawley 1992: 385–86). Second, the grammar of the passage encodes hypotheticality by way of the subjunctive mood of the modal auxiliary *might*. In lieu of the word *would*, *might* again implies a lack of commitment to the truth of the expressed world relative to the reference world of the story. Above and beyond its grammatical profile, note that Poe's description is only hypothetically accessible to— focalizable by—a nonexistent or virtual spectator. The spectator occupies a space that is parasitical, ontologically speaking, on the entities and situations actually inhabiting Poe's narrative universe. In other words, the witness (or the witness's focalizing eye) acquires the status of an entity that is virtual with respect to the entities, states, and events actualized, or even *de jure* actualizable, over the course of Poe's narrative. It is a given of the tale, a *datum narratus*, that Poe's narrator is the only observer who *could* focalize the House of Usher when the story opens.

Similarly, Darl Bundren invokes a counterfactual observer in 8, which excerpts the opening lines of Faulkner's *As I Lay Dying*:

> 8. Jewel and I come up from the field, following the path in single file. Although I am fifteen feet ahead of him, anyone watching us from the cottonhouse can see Jewel's frayed and broken straw hat a full head above my own. (1987: 3)

Anyone, here, is not part of the ontological furniture of the universe that includes the participants, situations, and events of the novel. Instead, Faulkner's *anyone* signals what an observer can or could see, if such an observer, relegated to virtuality by the modal structure of the narrative itself, were there to do the focalizing only hypothetically accomplished by the (nonactual) spectator in the cottonhouse. And when in Conrad's *Heart of Darkness* Marlow describes the human heads that Kurtz has affixed to stakes planted around his hut—

> 9. "they were expressive and puzzling, striking and disturbing—food for thought and also for vultures if there had been any looking down from the sky" (1996: 74)

—Conrad's virtual vultures do not actually focalize the shrunken heads as food. They merely *would have* done so if they had been there, spectral spectators in a world significant aspects of which ultimately remain unfocalizable, "inscrutable," from any perspective whatsoever.

There are, it seems, what might be called stronger and weaker versions of the virtual or counterfactual witnesses invoked in direct HF. For example, in passage 10, excerpted from A. S. Byatt's *Possession*, the narrator's appeal to the counterfactual witness links up with the process of hypothesis formation itself:

> 10. An observer might have speculated for some time as to whether they [Roland Mitchell and Maud Bailey] were travelling together or separately, for their eyes rarely met, and when they did, remained guarded and expressionless. (1990: 297)

Byatt's narrator resorts to the "stronger" version of direct HF, calling upon a virtual spectator to focalize the protagonists on their voyage back into history; and history, here, is a prior sociotemporal context that begins to obtrude into, to absorb, the present precisely through the guesswork and speculation enacted by the novel's academic protagonists. The virtuality of Byatt's focalizor, then, reinforces the salient ontology of the novel's fictional world, stratified as it is into situations and events whose spatiotemporal complexity creates "a continuous hesitation between two frames of reference" (Pavel 1986: 62)—specifically, those of the nineteenth and twentieth centuries. The observer on the train both is and is not there, like the past whose possible modes of focalization, as it were, furnish the most abiding concern of Byatt's novel. Here the direct HF works less to make readers doubt whether Roland and Maud are in fact traveling together at this point in the novel than to signal that the fact of their traveling together might, in another frame of reference, be more difficult to establish, more problematic, than it is in the one that readers are ultimately encouraged to adopt. The format of Byatt's text therefore encodes that same proliferation of possible frames of reference—and *eo ipso* the multiplication of candidate models of a given situation or event—which is also its chief topic.

By contrast, the following passage from Kingsley Amis's *Lucky Jim* features a weaker version of direct HF. In passage 11, the hypothetical focalizors are not themselves virtual entities; rather, their acts of focalization (may) have virtual status in the reference world around which the narrative propositions center themselves. Because the focalizing acts are not subject to (dis)confirmation in the reference world of the narrative, those acts figure as hypotheses constructed by a protagonist engaged in self-experimentation from the start:

> 11. To look at, but not only to look at, they resembled some kind of variety act: Welch tall and weedy, with limp whitening hair, [James] Dixon on the short side, fair and round-faced, with an unusual breadth of shoulder that had never been accompanied by any special physical strength or skill. Despite this over-evident contrast between them, Dixon realized that their progress, deliberate and to all appearances thoughtful, *must seem rather donnish to passing students*.[13] (1961: 8, my emphasis)

In the last sentence of this passage, the narrator's use of the modal auxiliary *must* in *must seem* counterfactualizes not the students, whom the narrator presupposes as part of the reference world, but rather the focalizing that the students might or might not be doing at the moment they pass Welch and Dixon. Because of the relation between the expressed world and the reference world subtending Amis's text, the students cannot be assumed to be focalizors in this instance but merely hypothesized as such. It is not just that the subjunctive verbal mood grammatically encodes a non-assured epistemic stance; more than this, the text signals the modality of doubt by shifting the burden of focalization onto spectators only hypothetically aware of what is going on around them. The same goes for passage 12, taken from Russell Banks's *The Sweet Hereafter*. In Billy Ansel's homodiegetic account of the bus accident, direct HF enables Banks to portray Ansel and the other parents of the dead children as solipsistically sealed off from one another in their grief, forced to engage in guesswork about one another's perceptions and thoughts. Here Ansel attributes possible focalizing acts to onlookers so stunned by the accident (like Ansel himself) that *no* perceptual activity can be reliably ascribed to them:

12. The snow continued to fall, and from the perspective of Risa and the others back at the accident site, I must have disappeared into it, just walked straight out of their reality into my own. (1991: 72)

Yet both Amis's and Banks's are relatively weak versions of direct HF, for in each case the narrator merely imputes virtual acts to actual figures, instead of calling on one or more virtual figures to perform an equally virtual act of focalization. The hypotheticality of these two passages, as we might also put it, is less radical than it would be had the passages been focalized according to the stronger version of direct HF. In both examples the expressed world matches up more closely with the reference world than is the case in passage 10, excerpted from Byatt's *Possession*.

To extrapolate: Byatt's text participates in what Linda Hutcheon (1988) would call the (quintessentially postmodern) genre of historiographic metafiction, in which the nature and configuration of the novel's reference world, and its relation to the reference world(s) of historical discourse, form part of the very subject matter of the novel. By contrast, *Lucky Jim* can be construed (broadly) as a *Bildungsroman* and thus as part of a genre in which the protagonist must modify his or her orientation toward a world whose basic (ontological) contours are ultimately not in question. *The Sweet Hereafter*, using multiple focalization to explore how people differently narrativize and thereby come to terms with a traumatic event (as discussed in chapter 6), is closer to *Possession* than to *Lucky Jim* in its overt insistence on narrative as a strategy for cognizing or indeed constructing the past. Yet each of the five first-person narratives contained in Banks's novel encodes a version of the past in which quite definite claims can be made about the reference worlds subtending these accounts; it is the reader's juxtaposition of these different world versions that introduces uncertainty about a past in which Dolores Driscoll may or may not have been driving at fifty-five miles per hour when the bus crashed, and a present in which Wendell Walker is variously described by Dolores as "pleasantly withdrawn" (21), by Billy Ansel as "lazy and pretty dumb and pessimistic" (58), and by Mitchell Stephens as someone who "looked like a pushover, but . . . had an attitude. In the middle of a wrecked life, drowning in sadness, he was still able to hold his grudges" (107). Thus, the theory developed here predicts that within any of the novel's five subnarratives, the weaker variety of direct HF is more likely to occur than the stronger variety; only certain perceptual states of participants in the storyworld are encoded as doubtful or hypothetical, not the existence of those participants.

My larger point, however, is that more careful description of the stronger and weaker subtypes of direct (and, for that matter, indirect) HF may help capture *differentiae specificae* of narrative genres. It is not that the presence of either direct or indirect HF in a text is a sufficient condition for that text's being included in the post-, non-, or anti-realistic genres associated with such writers as Kafka, Gide, Faulkner, and those who came after them. Rather, there are grounds for making a more modest claim: namely, that among the repertoire of narrative devices typically exploited by texts that question or resist the norms and presuppositions of realistic genres, HF may upon further investigation prove to be a particularly important technique. In any case it warrants further study, given its omission from structuralist frameworks. I return to the question of HF and genre at the end of the chapter.

An Excursus on Concealed Hypotheticality

Before going on to examine indirect as opposed to direct HF, I should like to make a brief excursus on what might be termed the problem of concealed hypotheticality in the context of focalization. At issue is the way ostensibly nonhypothetical modes of focalization may nevertheless entail a sort of surreptitious virtuality. The problem of concealed hypotheticality arises because non-indicative grammatical moods are not the only linguistic resource for indexing modes of focalization as hypothetical. Take, for example, Haven Gillespie's lyrics for the 1934 song "Santa Claus Is Coming to Town." The chorus (as so memorably sung by Bing Crosby) features the following lines:

13. He sees you when you're sleeping,
He knows when you're awake;
He knows if you've been bad or good,
So be good for goodness' sake!

Passage 13 has three verbs in the indicative mood (*sees, knows, knows*) and one verb in the imperative mood (*be good*). The first three verb forms seem to mark correspondence or agreement between the expressed world and the reference world subtending the discourse—with the fourth, imperative form establishing a deontic versus epistemic modality, in which the grammatical mood encodes the "*imposition of an expressed world on a reference world*" (Frawley 1992: 420), but not doubt about the relation between those two worlds. Put otherwise, once listeners have resituated themselves within the reference world of the chorus—a world in which Santa Claus exists and is on his way to town to reward the good and not give any presents to the bad—the format of the discourse seems to suggest that Santa's seeing and knowing are actual, not virtual or hypothetical, modes of focalization.

Still, one might contend that the chorus constitutes part of a (directly) hypothetically focalized narrative; more exactly, it is an instance of narrative discourse exploiting the weaker version of direct HF. In this case, the hypotheticality of Santa's focalizing act derives not from doubtfulness encoded via the morphology of verbs, but rather from the durative force of the temporal conjunction *when*, which here has the sense of *whenever*. The quasi-aspectual (i.e., imperfective or progressive) force of the lexical item *when* suggests not an event, but rather a state or condition.[14] More precisely, the format of the chorus implies that all of us are in a condition of being focalized by Santa. Yet one can only hypothesize or infer that, during any one of the discrete temporal segments composing the (presumably temporally unbounded) state of being seen and known by Santa, Santa is *at that moment* scrutinizing people's minds and deeds and deciding whether they are worthy of presents or not. Otherwise the song would have to be interpreted as conferring on Santa the status of an omniscient deity, an interpretation that perhaps runs counter to the purpose and occasion of Gillespie's lyrics, if not to Santa's own religico-mythological heritage. To put the point more generally, a (perceptual) state is not necessarily analyzable into a set of constituent or atomic states, every one of which has the same structure as the global state. The condition of being enthralled allows for momentary fluctuations of interest; watching a movie does not exclude intermittent bouts of daydreaming. Yet the unwittingly sinister resonance of Gillespie's chorus hinges on some such conflation of the durative with the discrete; moreover, the temporal or rather aspectual conflation produces here a kind of paranoiac confusion of the virtual with the actual.[15] The lyrics code a punctual or temporally bounded situation type ("Santa sees you on occasion x, y, or z, during which time you are sleeping") as a durative situation type ("Santa sees you whenever and for as long as you might happen to be sleeping"). In consequence, what might happen on any given occasion passes itself off as what really does happen and happens all the time.

As the Santa Claus example suggests, the interrelations between narrative form, aspect, and (concealed) hypotheticality require more thorough investigation. But I shall at least postulate that an interesting subspecies of HF, potentially of either the direct or the indirect type, sometimes results when narrative discourse codes events as conditions—represents activities as states—or more accurately when it elides the difference between punctual and durative situation types. Debatably, this covert kind of HF couches itself in indicative verbal moods precisely so that readers or listeners will be led to construe as actual what, upon further interpretation, can only be deemed virtual. Study of nonliterary narrative and other discourse genres promises to turn up concealed hypotheticality in a number of different contexts; for example, in political propaganda ("Candidate X is watching out for your interests"), in advertisements ("Because of a low student-teacher ratio, students at University Y receive special, individualized attention from their instructors"), and in verbal attempts to enforce laws and regulations, such as the road signs that read "SPEED CHECKED BY RADAR." In the latter instance, the sign's elliptical format—"SPEED [is? might be? will probably be? occasionally? regularly? always?] CHECKED BY [one person? many people? operating] RADAR"—deletes information about both aspect and modality that ordinarily get coded in the grammar. Indeed, in its discourse *functions* if not its grammatical *form*, that is, in the epistemic modalities that its telegrammatic style works to suppress or occlude, the "SPEED CHECKED BY RADAR" sign furnishes an instance of what I now go on to characterize as (weak) indirect HF.

Indirect HF: The Inference to Virtuality

The second broad category of hypothetically focalized narratives includes all those stories featuring perspectives that an observer *could* adopt, though that hypothetical focalizor is not explicitly invoked, not directly thematized, by the narrative discourse itself. Instead, recipients must infer the presence or at least functioning of HF, if the narrative discourse falling under this heading is to make sense at all. As with narratives that explicitly appeal to a counterfactual witness, this second, relatively implicit variety of HF features verbal moods and adverbs that are the grammatical markers of doubt—or rather of the various epistemic modalities more or less assimilable to doubt.

For instance, at one point in Nadine Gordimer's *A Guest of Honour* (1970), the narrator describes the novel's protagonist and another character walking away from a house:

> 14. [Adam] Mweta was smaller and more animated than [James] Bray, and seen from the distance of the house, as they got further away their progress would have been a sort of dance. (73–74)

The locution *would have been* is what distinguishes HF, in this instance, from the simple external focalization corresponding to the so-called omniscient point of view. By substituting the latter mode of focalization for indirect HF, I could rewrite Gordimer's description such that Bray's and Mweta's progress, seen from the distance of the house, just *was* (or *appeared to be*) a sort of dance. Refocalized in that way, however, the passage would reposition the reader elsewhere along the continuum of epistemic modalities. Specifically, in moving from a subjunctive to an indicative grammatical mood in his context, the reader would likewise have to move from the modality of the doubtful or hypothetical to the modality of the known—of the confirmed or at least confirmable. In the refocalized version of the Gordimer passage, the expressed world would center itself more squarely on the reference world. The passage would reveal a greater commitment to the truth of the expressed world in its bid to detail the parameters of the reference world. Hence—and here the analogy between modes of focalization and propositional attitudes begins to assert itself (see the final section of this chapter)—the senses, the meanings, attaching to the differently focalized versions of the passage are fundamentally nonsubstitutable.

Likewise, Elizabeth Bowen's "Her Table Spread," excerpted in passage 15, resorts to indirect HF. At one point the narrator provides a glimpse of the sumptuous dining room table from what can be inferred to be the perspective of one of the sailors whom the story's protagonist has already cast in her own hypothetical dramas of rescue and romance:

> 15. Dinner was being served very slowly. Candles—*possible to see from the water*—were lit now. (1991: 313, my emphasis)

Here the momentary shift to a hypothetical perspective—the reorientation of the expressed world around the undecidably virtual or nonvirtual focalizing acts of the sailors on the water—is marked by the modal operator *possible*. *Possible* is in other words a textual cue, triggering an inference about the hypotheticality of the description, which encodes a perceptual act noncongruent with the reference world but not performed by any particular or at least confirmable witness. Furthermore, note that in the Bowen passage HF coincides with what is arguably a fragment of interior monologue. Given the vast importance of hypothesis and contrary-to-fact speculation in people's mental lives, HF can be predicted to play an especially important and prominent role in texts with a high concentration of interior monologue. Passage 16, taken from Bruce Sterling's *Islands in the Net*, furnishes an analogous example. Laura Webster, the novel's protagonist, speculates as follows:

> 16. What would it be like to attack this place [i.e., the Grenada of the year 2023]? Laura could imagine angry, hungry rioters with their pathetic torches and Molotov cocktails—wandering under those towers like mice under furniture. . . . Growing frightened as their yells were answered by silence—beginning to creep in muttering groups, into the false protection of the rocks and trees. *While every footstep sounded loud as drumbeats on buried microphones, while their bodies glowed like human candles on some gunner's infared screens.* (1989: 142–43, my emphasis)

The emphasized passage represents a complex or mixed usage of HF. The first clause involves indirect HF, the second, direct HF.

For a more extended example of indirect HF itself, consider passage 17, from Stephen Crane's "The Open Boat":

> 17. In the wan light the faces of the men must have been gray. Their eyes must have glinted in strange ways as they gazed steadily astern. Viewed from a balcony, the whole thing would, doubtless, have been weirdly picturesque. But the men in the boat had no time to see it, and if they had had leisure, there were other things to occupy their minds. . . . The process of the breaking day was unknown to them. . . . It was probably splendid, it was probably glorious, this play of the free sea, wild with lights of emeralds and white and amber.[16] (1990: 397)

Again the passage contains grammatical markers of doubt—specifically, those found in the locutions *must have been*, *would . . . have been*, *doubtless*, and *probably*, together with the conditional *if they had had leisure*. The grammar of the passage encodes a highly mediated relation between the expressed and the reference world; the narrator's focalization of the men in the boat roots itself in tenuousness, non-assurance, even manifest fictionality, such that the scene takes on the appearance of a play "viewed from a balcony." The metaphor of theatricalization reinforces, in the verbal texture of the passage, the way the narrative uses the grammar of English to structure and stage the scene, which is focalized by an audience only virtually in attendance. In effect, the narrative focalizes details that both are and are not part of the reference world: if someone had been there to focalize them the details would have been evident, but since, strictly speaking, someone was not there, the details simply could not be evident. Yet the narrative unfolds by focalizing the scene *as if* the grey faces and glinting eyes were, in fact, included in the ontology of the storyworld, *as if* such things formed part of the inventory of the actual. If, then, the expressed world is here patently incongruent with the reference world, nonetheless the grammar of the narrative troubles the border between actuality and virtuality. Arguably, Crane's narrative *constitutes* the reference world just by framing, in the expressed world, a series of hypotheses about what things might be like but are not.

Passage 18, from Salman Rushdie's *Haroun and the Sea of Stories*, also features a counterfactual conditional, but it encodes an even more complicated epistemic modality than the one operative in the Crane passage.

18. Miss Oneeta was standing on her upstairs balcony, shaking like a jelly; and if it hadn't been raining, Haroun might have noticed that she was crying. (1990: 21)

Here a hypothetical act of focalization is embedded within what Nicholas Rescher (1964) would call a *speculative* counterfactual conditional, as opposed to a *nomological* counterfactual conditional that merely specifies a covering law (e.g., "If I had not fed my cat so many treats, she would not have gotten so fat"). As Rescher puts it, "A purely speculative counterfactual conditional leads to paradox not because it is meaningless, but because it is overly meaningful, being so ambiguous as to admit of contrary, or at least discordant, interpretations, and doing so in a setting where no machinery for resolving this conflict is to be found" (36). Rushdie's text is likewise overly meaningful. It makes a problematic or belief-contravening supposition (= "Haroun focalizes Miss Oneeta crying") the consequent of a speculative counterfactual conditional whose antecedent (= "If it hadn't been raining") is itself an instance of indirect HF. To put the same point another way, Rushdie's discourse, by embedding doubt within doubt, exploits a whole syntax of uncertainty; the indirect HF set up by the counterfactual conditional creates, in turn, a merely hypothetical context for (weak) direct HF via Haroun.

Table 13. Some Modes of Focalization in Narrative

I. External = Involves a mode of perspective taking transcending ordinary limits of space and time; characteristic of texts with an "omniscient" narrator, i.e., Stanzel's (1984) authorial narrative situation

II. Internal = Involves perspective taking associated with a center of consciousness, i.e., with the perceptual activity of a storyworld participant; cf. Stanzel's figural narrative situation
   A. Fixed = the center of consciousness is singular, remaining constant throughout the narrative
   B. Variable = there is more than one center of consciousness over the course of the narrative, and each focalizes different spatiotemporal segments of the storyworld
   C. Multiple = there is more than one center of consciousness over the course of the narrative, and each focalizes the same (or at least overlapping) spatiotemporal segments of the storyworld

III. Direct HF = Involves explicit appeal to a hypothetical witness
   A. Strong direct HF = involves an observer (or group of observers) only counterfactually existent in the storyworld
   B. Weak direct HF = involves an actual observer whose focalizing acts are presented as contrary to fact

IV. Indirect HF = Involves implicit appeal to a hypothetical witness, whose focalizing activity must be inferred
   A. Strong indirect HF = involves an observer whose existence must be inferred, but whose focalizing acts resist (dis)confirmation
   B. Weak indirect HF = involves an inferred observer whose focalizing activity the discourse encodes as (to some degree) less doubtful than it is in the case of strong indirect HF

Rather than trying to write the grammar of doubt, however, I restrict myself to offering a partial classification of the ways uncertainty can enter narrative discourse via focalization. Table 13 lists all the types of focalization under discussion; I expand on some of the implications of this taxonomy in the remainder of the section, as well as in the section that follows. In this framework, Crane's text can be characterized as a "stronger" version of indirect HF than Bowen's. The sailors whose perspective Bowen's protagonist momentarily, and hypothetically, adopts

Table 14. A Classification of Some Hypothetically Focalized Narratives

	Strong	Weak
Direct HF	Byatt	Amis
Indirect HF	Crane	Bowen

are, in fact, part of the reference world of the story; only their focalization of the candles on the table is in doubt. In Crane's story, however, almost all of the circumstantial detail featured in the passage is in doubt; the description as a whole falls under the scope of a sort of extended (speculative) counterfactual conditional: "If the men in the boat had had more leisure and there were not other things occupying their minds at the time, they would have noticed such things as the weird picturesqueness of the scene and the splendor of the breaking day." Table 14 schematizes these conclusions.

This grid suggests possibilities for an enriched typology of focalization—one that shifts emphasis from the (quasi-primitive) distinction between internal and external focalization, personal and impersonal narration, to the discrimination between modes of focalization as ways of encoding epistemic modalities in narrative discourse. A narrative making explicit appeal to a counterfactual witness (Poe) encodes a different kind of uncertainty than does a story in which readers infer that some portion of a character's thoughts most likely involves hypothesis or speculation (Bowen). But narrative theory has only started to recognize that such differences are crucially connected with the meaning of narratives. More generally, narratology can be retooled by linking it up with language-theoretical approaches to meanings construed as intensions, affording new understandings of narrative mood, new perspectives on perspective.

HF, Possible Worlds, and Narrative Genres

I can now formulate more explicitly the argument I have been working up to over the course of this chapter: namely, that to start coming to terms with how narratives mean, theorists need to attach the semantics of focalization to the larger tradition of semantic analysis. Of special relevance here is the approach to semantic analysis that has stressed how meaning is always meaning-within-a-model-of-the-world, that is, intensional.

Thomas Pavel (1986) has shown that, by embracing a form of textual immanentism or "mythocentrism," structuralist narratologists effectively placed a "moratorium on referential issues" in the study of stories. Promulgating a "strongly antiexpressive aesthetics," classical narratology discouraged "reflection on those literary and artistic features that transcend purely structural properties: style, reference, representation, global meaning, expressiveness" (8). Put otherwise, in a manner at cross-purposes with their conscious aims, structuralist theorists helped drive a wedge between the study of (literary) narrative and broader trends in the study of language and discourse (cf. Pavel 1989; Herman 1995a). A development of crucial importance in the history of semantic inquiry, yet neglected until quite recently by theorists of narrative, is Gottlob Frege's (1969) distinction between the sense (*Sinn*) and the reference (*Bedeutung*) of propositions, later reformulated by Rudolf Carnap (1947) and others as a distinction between the intensional and extensional properties of expressions.[17]

According to this scheme, in the sentences *Mary likes Brussels* and *Mary likes the capital of Belgium*, the expressions *Brussels* and *the capital of Belgium* have the same extensions but not the same intensions. That is one way to account for why these expressions cannot be substituted for one another without altering the truth value of the resulting sentence. Mary might very well like Brussels because she thinks it is the capital of Holland, a country she champions. By the same token, if I hold that Brussels has good museums, and yet I have forgotten (or never learned) that Brussels is the capital of Belgium, I am not committed to the belief that Belgium's capital has good museums, even I believe the city of Brussels to be excellent in that respect. Such nonsubstitutability of sense, whereby the content of expressions cannot be distributed across different contexts of belief while preserving the truth values of those expressions, is what W. V. O. Quine (1980) went on to describe as referential opacity.[18] Possible-worlds (or, to use the more technical designation, "model-theoretic") semantics in its post-Fregean incarnation is a logico-epistemological apparatus for handling difficulties presented by the referential opacity of propositional attitudes (marked by verbs of believing, knowing, thinking, etc.). The possible-worlds framework was designed to handle propositions embedded in such modal contexts—propositions involving attributions of necessity, possibility, impossibility, and so on, to states of affairs. The present section outlines how this semantic paradigm can be fruitfully brought to bear on the description and analysis of HF as well.

In a possible-worlds framework, intensions can be conceived of as the meanings of propositions whose truth value is positive in some possible world, though not necessarily in the world speakers and their interlocutors are wont to deem actual. Intensions are thus relativized meanings, that is, meanings-within-some-model-of-the-world. Hence, the intensional properties of an expression are just those properties that do not remain constant when that expression is invoked in different contexts of belief, different conditions of use. In one possible world, or alternatively one context of belief, the expression *Brussels* might be used to mean, say, a place with good museums; in this case, the proposition "X believes that Brussels is a place with good museums" is T, has a positive truth value, whereas the statement "X believes that Brussels is the capital of Belgium" could be T, F, or indeterminate, depending on the belief state of X at a given moment. To generalize, what people mean by the expressions they use depends crucially on the contexts in which they use them. Accordingly, attitudes of knowing, believing, hoping, concluding, and hypothesizing will not remain constant across changes of context ("I hope to go to Brussels$_{capital}$" versus "I hope to go to Brussels$_{museum}$"), or in the face of more or less embedded contexts ("John believes that Mary knows that Peter hopes that Brussels is worth visiting"). A meaning is, rather, an intensional function or operator; it is a device for mapping the semantic content of expressions from the contexts of belief in which the expressions might possibly occur—from those possible worlds in which the expressions have the value True—into the reference world that speakers and their interlocutors model and remodel during a discourse situation. When the discourse situation at issue happens to be narrative in nature, then part of the meaning of the discourse will depend on how readers, viewers, or listeners contextualize—interpret—the propositional attitudes encoded in the narrative as modes of focalization.

In suggesting that there is an analogy, more or less exact, between modes of focalization and propositional attitudes, I am suggesting that focalization itself can be redescribed as the narrative transcription of attitudes of seeing, believing, speculating, and so forth, anchored in particular contexts or frames, that is, particular models of the way the world is. Likewise, as discussed in connection with the instance of indirect HF found in passage 14, the extract from Gordimer's *A Guest of Honour*, differently focalized narrative representations will not be interchangeable, substitutable, without changes in the meaning of the narrative or narratives in question. Rather, types of focalization can be interpreted as scalar phenomena, ranked incrementally along a continuum of epistemic modalities. In other words, by studying how language theorists have drawn on the semantics of possible worlds to map grammatical moods into epistemic modalities, and vice versa, narratologists can work toward a richer, better typology of focalization. As suggested by figure 11, the older narratological categories can be plotted within a system, or rather along a scale, of epistemic deixis.

The upper boundary of the scale is marked by the authorial narrative situation, involving omniscience or, in Genette's terms, zero focalization. The analogue of what Rimmon-Kenan (1983) calls external focalization, zero focalization is just a name for an epistemic stance in which a focalizor has absolute faith in the veracity, the actualness or actualizability, of the states of affairs detailed in the narrative. This boundary corresponds with maximal certainty in narration, an epistemic stance encoding congruence between the expressed world and the reference world subtending the narrative. Species of internal focalization might be plotted lower down the scale, with fixed focalization describable as a belief context anchored in a particular possible world (that is, a particular mental model of the real), variable focalization as the alternation or conjoining of such belief contexts, and multiple focalization as the embedding or at least layering of belief contexts. In general, now only partly congruent with the reference world, the expressed world when focalized internally features different modes and degrees of doubt, which figures even more prominently in that elliptical focalizing that Genette (versus Bal and Rimmon-Kenan) called external. At or near the lower boundary of the continuum are the species of focalization associated with HF, which signals the doubt about the very grounds for doubt. It involves a more or less severe mismatch between reference world and expressed world—a mismatch persisting for a longer or shorter duration within the narrative discourse, as the case might be. In hypothetically focalized narratives, doubt attaches now to the status of narrative agents (are they there or not?), now to that of their thoughts and behavior (do they

Figure 11. Modes of Focalization on a Scale of Epistemic Deixis

<--->
      SHF   WHF EFG   IF   EFR-K/ZF

SHF = "Strong" Hypothetical Focalization
WHF = "Weak" Hypothetical Focalization
EFG = External Focalization in Genette's terms
IF = Internal Focalization (including fixed, variable, and multiple subtypes)
EFR-K = External Focalization in Rimmon-Kenan's terms
ZF = Zero Focalization (the equivalent of EFR-K)

---

do/think/perceive that or not?), now to that of their circumstances (is their world like that or not?). The stronger and weaker versions of direct and indirect HF mark different distributions of doubt and doubtfulness with respect to the entities, situations, and events being focalized—different ways of ranking claims about the storyworld according to their place on the continuum of epistemic modalities.

Granted, as Genette remarks, "Since the function of narrative is not to give an order, express a wish, state a condition, etc., but simply to tell a story and therefore to 'report' facts (real or fictive), its one mood, or at least its characteristic mood, strictly speaking can be only the indicative" (1980: 161). Thus narrative discourse exploits grammatical moods other than the indicative—and *eo ipso* the epistemic modalities affiliated with doubt—only at its own peril. A story rich in hypotheticality can lack or rather actively destroy that assurance that Gerald Prince (1988) describes as the hallmark of narrative itself: "Narrative, which is etymologically linked to knowledge, lives in certainty (this happened then that; this happened because of that; this happened and it was related to that) and dies from (sustained) ignorance and indecision" (4). The use of HF in narrative, then, marks the exception more than the rule; it is perhaps less a narrative than a counter-narrative device. But all narratives encode different degrees of certainty with respect to what is narrated. Exploiting the same epistemic modalities operative in discourse at large, narrative discourse characteristically indicates how much credence readers should place in any one proposition found in the text.

Debatably, extended narrative discourse has evolved into the preeminent resource for perspective taking precisely because it accommodates such a wide range of epistemic stances, chaining together in a single discourse propositions more or less widely spaced along the scale by which degrees of certainty are encoded in discourse.[19]

I do not mean to suggest that the present analysis has thrown new light on *all* of the narrative phenomena discussed in earlier research on focalization. My purpose has been only to give some initial indications of how narrative theorists might embark on such a redescription. In this connection, HF is, I believe, an especially diagnostic problem domain; it shows that, in order to come to terms with the cognitive dimensions of narrative perspective, researchers need to bridge narratological accounts of focalization and ideas drawn from semantic theory. Further, although this chapter has merely started to sketch the forms and functions of HF, it has at least begun to indicate how HF might help analysts rethink differences between narrative genres.

To be sure, hypotheticality in discourse need not *always* have the function of conveying uncertainty or doubt. In their study of the instructional register of coaching, Shirley Brice Heath and Juliet Langman (1994) found that "eventcasts," or hypothetical descriptions of what might happen in game situations, are an important instrument for building the knowledge repertoire of team members. *If-then* conditionals, for example, allow coaches and players to engage in contrary-to-fact speculation on what might happen at the end of a close game not currently being played. Yet the perspectival indices that cluster around HF are often the formal markers of skepticism, detachment, even paranoia. Thus the model developed here predicts that the distributions and modalities of HF will differ across different genres—that HF will function differently in realistic narrative genres than in other sorts of genres. In principle, of course, HF can appear in any narrative, regardless of genre, such as passage 19, an extract from *Jane Eyre*. When Jane narrates how, having fled from Thornfield Hall, she seeks the solitary comforts of "the universal mother, Nature," her account resorts first to the stronger version of direct HF and then, in its emphasis on the hypothetical incredulity and suspiciousness of unspecified virtual witnesses, to the stronger version of indirect HF.

19. a chance traveller might pass by; and I wish no eye to see me now: strangers would wonder what I am doing, lingering here at the sign-post,

evidently objectless and lost. I might be questioned: I could give no answer but what would sound incredible, and excite suspicion. (Brontë 1960: 325)

Or consider passage 20 from *Vanity Fair*. Here William Thackeray's obtrusive narrator, embedding the weaker version of direct HF within a satirical apostrophe to the reader, which is in turn embedded within a counterfactual conditional, calls attention to the absurd ephemerality of fashions in "Vanity Fair."

20. Her [Becky Sharp's] complexion could bear any sunshine as yet; and her dress, though if you were to see it now, any present lady of Vanity Fair would pronounce it to be the most foolish and preposterous attire ever worn, was as handsome in her eyes and those of the public, some five-and-twenty years since, as the most brilliant costume of the most famous beauty of the present scene. (1963: 461)

In writers such as Brontë and Thackeray, however, HF does not compromise basic epistemological presuppositions and norms. Debatably, in passages 19 and 20, HF helps keep the virtual in the service of the actual, marking momentary derangements of a modal structure in which the known and the real vastly exceed the unknown and the irreal. Such derangements are edifying; readers pass through salutary doubts to achieve greater certainties. But in texts of a different genre—and this in part contributes to their recognizably different generic status—HF helps put the actual in the service of the virtual, formally marking doubts about whether human beings can determine, in every case, where they stand in a world they only thought they knew.

Furthermore, attempting to characterize the epistemic modality (or modalities) indexed by HF indicates why broader traditions in linguistic (here, semantic) inquiry are so invaluable for the study of narrative. The semantics of focalization presents an especially good opportunity for researchers to use semantic models to throw light on the intensional properties of narrative discourse. If narrative theorists are to begin measuring narrative mood against epistemic modality, they need to establish, in a more principled way, routes of transfer between work on propositional attitudes, the semantics of possible worlds, and the analysis of focalization in narrative discourse. Though each of these theoretical toolkits is quite sophisticated in its own right, it will take their combined power and expressiveness to capture the mental operations required to build storyworlds, which are both perspectivally constrained and perspective-affording constructs. Again, then, a process as natural and seemingly automatic as figuring out the perspective from which a story is presented proves, on further inspection, to be a complex modeling process. This chapter is only a first step toward building the richly integrative approach required to make sense of how people make sense of narrative perspectives.[20]

9
Contextual Anchoring

A story is like a letter. *Dear You*, I'll say. Just *you*, without a name. Attaching a name attaches *you* to the world of fact, which is riskier, more hazardous: who knows what the chances are out there, of survival, yours? I will say *you*, *you*, like an old love song. *You* can mean more than one.
You can mean thousands.
MARGARET ATWOOD, *The Handmaid's Tale*

The last design principle to be considered in this book bears on a process that I refer to as *contextual anchoring*. Just as narratives cue interpreters to build temporal and spatial relationships between items and events in the storyworld, and just as they constrain readers, viewers, and listeners to take up perspectives on the items and events at issue, stories trigger recipients to establish a more or less direct or oblique relationship between the stories they are interpreting and the contexts in which they are interpreting them. Or rather, the format of a story can sometimes prompt interpreters to reassess the relation between two types of mental models involved in narrative understanding. On the one hand, interpreters build models as part of the process of representing the space-time profile, participant roles, and overall configuration of storyworlds. On the other hand, interpreters rely on analogous, model-based representations of the world(s) in which they are trying to make sense of a given narrative. Contextual anchoring is my name for the process whereby a narrative, in a more or less explicit and reflexive way, asks its interpreters to search for analogies between the representations contained within these two classes of mental models. There can be many or few representations involved, and the projection relations that the text cues readers to build between them can be more or less dense or multiplex.

In parallel with previous chapters, I argue here that existing narratological frameworks need to be enriched if researchers are to capture how stories anchor themselves in particular contexts of interpretation.

To make that task more tractable, I focus on two important—and interrelated—aspects of contextual anchoring in narrative, deictic reference and mechanisms of address. In linguistic research, as I discuss in more detail below, *deixis* refers to all the resources of language that anchor it to essential points in context (Frawley 1992: 274–83), including temporal adverbs like *now* and *afterward*, locative adverbs of the sort investigated in chapter 7 (*here, there, yonder*), honorific terms and particles that index interlocutors' social status (*sir, Dr. Herman*), and other forms that attach utterances to the occasions in which they are designed and interpreted. The present chapter focuses more specifically on person deixis, accomplished in English by pronoun usage (*I, we, you*), among other resources (e.g., conjugations of verbs). Even more specifically, the chapter examines processes of contextual anchoring in second-person narration, which provides an interesting case study in how stories can at once rely on and challenge the border between text and context. Narrative *you* taken as a special case of person deixis also raises the question of how mechanisms of address impinge on the process of contextual anchoring. In some cases, at least, narrative *you* does not simply or even mainly refer to storyworld participants but also (or chiefly) addresses the interpreter of the narrative. And sometimes a single instance of narrative *you* both refers and addresses. The result then is a fitful and self-conscious anchoring of the text in its contexts, as well as a storyworld whose contours and boundaries can be probablistically but not determinately mapped, the inventory of its constituent entities remaining fuzzy rather than fixed.

Contexts for Contextual Anchoring

Narrative theorists have already developed descriptive vocabularies—vocabularies oriented around the constructs "narratee," "implied reader," "audience," and related notions—that capture important aspects of the process I am calling contextual anchoring. Arguably, though, these vocabularies can be rethought in productive ways if they are seen as bearing on particular dimensions of the process by which a text attaches itself to a context of interpretation, and further the vocabularies would all benefit from being brought into closer contact with relevant linguistic research on the text-context interface. Hence, as with the other aspects of narrative discussed in this book, the study of contextual anchoring calls for not just a new synthesis of narrative-theoretical approaches but also for a new interlinking of narratological and linguistic theories.[1] For example, narratologists have distinguished between intradiegetic and extradiegetic narratees, or narratees represented as characters and narratees not so represented (G. Prince 1987: 57; cf. G. Prince 1980b, 1982, 1985; Genette 1980, 1988). Both sorts of narratees can be described as textual constructs, or rather as textually encoded reception positions with which the position of a current reader can be more or less analogous. But since intradiegetic narratees are themselves portrayed as participants in the storyworld, they are as a rule less likely than extradiegetic narratees to be close analogues for the reader; that is, the projection relations between reader and narratee are likely to be denser in the case of extradiegetic narratees than in the case of intradiegetic ones. Admittedly, I can find broad analogies between my own situation and that of the intradiegetic narratees who are listeners to Marlow's tale aboard *The Nellie* in *Heart of Darkness* (Conrad 1996); such analogies enable me to interpret Conrad's text as an instance of framed or embedded narrative in the first place. Or again, in the case of *The Odyssey*, my ability to "naturalize" a fictional storytelling situation in terms of my own analogous experiences of listening to stories is what allows me to construe the members of the Phaiákian court as intradiegetic narratees for Odysseus's tales about the hedonistic Lotus Eaters, the brutal Kyklopês, the bewitching Kirkê, and so on (Homer 1999: books 9–12). In both of these cases, however, the projection relations I establish between myself and the intradiegetic or storyworld-internal narratees will be thinner, less dense, than the ones I establish between myself and the extradiegetic narratee of such fictions as Edith Wharton's *The House of Mirth* (1994) or Virginia Woolf's *To the Lighthouse* (1989). Because in the latter instances the narratee is not characterized as a specific storyworld participant, I can more easily ascribe to the narratee the reception position I myself currently occupy. There is less to block the ascription of my own mental models to the narratee. Putting this same point another way, all other things being equal, the more underspecified the reception position encoded in the text of a narrative, the more likely I as reader will be able to project models of my own current reading environment into that position.

But all other things are usually *not* equal. That is why narrative theorists have developed finer discriminations between reception positions encoded in (or assumed by) narratives, their work illuminating the variable nature of contextual anchoring. Pertinent here is Wayne C. Booth's (1983) influential concept of the "implied reader," that is, the reader who shares the assumptions, beliefs, and norms of the "implied author," construed as the source of those tacit assumptions, beliefs, and norms that organize what sort of information is revealed, withheld, accentuated, or downplayed during the telling of a story (cf. Chatman 1978, 1990; Rimmon-Kenan 1983). For example, the implied author of James Joyce's *Ulysses* (1986) includes bathroom matters among the events relevant for narration, whereas the implied author of George Eliot's *Daniel Deronda* (1986) does not. (Note that both texts rely mainly on extradiegetic, uncharacterized narratees as opposed to intradiegetic, characterized ones, so that they cannot be saliently contrasted on that dimension.) Further, as Booth recognized, the structure of a narrative determines how closely a current reader can approximate the reception position of the implied reader; conversely, the degree to which current reception positions can be projected onto ideal or textually presupposed ones provides a useful way of talking about how strategies for narrative processing can change over time. In 1922, the first readers of *Ulysses* were faced with a narrative whose narratee is extradiegetic, as are readers of the novel today. But today's readers are likely to establish denser projection relations between themselves and Joyce's narratee than were readers in the early 1920s. In Booth's terms, this is because the stance of today's readers more closely approximates that of the text's ideal reader than did the stance of *Ulysses'* first interpreters, some of them sharing Virginia Woolf's (1925) view that Joyce's important work could nonetheless be "difficult and unpleasant" (151), others actively helping bring about the early ban on the novel's publication and sale in the United States. Indeed, as Hans Robert Jauss's (1996) reception-theoretical approach suggests, it is not just that one and the same text can generate radically different processes of contextual anchoring at different times. What is more, fictions like Joyce's can help reshape their own contexts of reception, bringing successive groups of interpreters into closer and closer alignment with the implied reader presupposed by a text that continues to be read and reread. Part of story logic, then, is its power to create new possibilities for projection; narrative itself can work to readjust the contextual parameters in terms of which people produce and understand stories.

Further, at a given point in the history of its reception, a narrative can use an intradiegetic or characterized narratee to complicate the projection relations between interpreters and storyworlds. Conversely, complicated modes of contextual anchoring can be used to trigger inferences about the structure of a narrative and the status of its narrator. In Henry James's "The Jolly Corner" (1996), for example, Alice Staverton is the intradiegetic narratee to whom Spencer Brydon recounts at least part of what his long-deferred return to the United States has meant for him. As a relatively fully characterized storyworld participant, Staverton might be assumed to have a profile disanalogous with that of most (if not all) possible readers. Arguably, however, her ironic reactions to Brydon's self-absorbed remarks provide paradigms for interpretation, affording clues for contextual anchoring. Specifically, Staverton as an intradiegetic narratee complements the story's extradiegetic one, giving interpreters a stereoscopic vantage point on Brydon as a somewhat ridiculous egoist as well as the adventurous pursuer and then prey of the self he never actually became. (See chapter 4 for a fuller discussion of James's story.) The narrative's formal design thus necessitates a dual response of "irony" and "sympathy," a crosshatching of thinner and denser projection relations between interpreters and the storyworld. Using narrative strategies generated by the later James's modernist aesthetic—an aesthetic that replaced certainties with ambiguities in a bid to reevaluate the capacity of stories to represent human experience—"The Jolly Corner" resists being anchored in contexts of interpretation in any singular or monolithic way. The irreducible complexity of contextual anchoring is part of the *point* of James's narrative, not just a byproduct of attempts to interpret it.

Meanwhile, in his 1977 article "Truth in Fiction," Peter J. Rabinowitz (1996) refined Booth's scheme to distinguish between and characterize several reception positions that interpreters of narrative must regularly—and simultaneously—occupy.[2] The result is an audience-based approach to narrative comprehension that again underscores the complexity of contextual anchoring. Or rather, in a manner that directly parallels the fictional experiments conducted by James, Joyce, and other innovators in story logic, Rabinowitz's account presents a sort of "exploded view" of the factors involved in the anchoring process. The convergence of these factors can be construed as merely a special case or variety of contextual anchoring rather than its necessary foundation or corollary. In particular, Rabinowitz differentiates between actual, authorial, and narrative audiences. Whereas the first category comprises current, flesh-and-blood readers, the authorial audience comprises the hypothetical audience for which an author writes, and the narrative audience comprises an "imaginary... audience for which the narrator is writing," that is, an "imitation audience [possessing] particular knowledge" not necessarily possessed by the authorial audience (Rabinowitz 1996: 215). In cases of reliable narration—such as *Daniel Deronda* or *To the Lighthouse*—the authorial and narrative audiences are convergent. In these two cases the *degree* of contextual anchoring (i.e., the density of projection relations) may vary across particular readings, depending on interpreters' abilities and predilections, but the same *sort* of anchoring strategies will be involved. By contrast, in instances of unreliable narration—such as that of the butler, Mr. Stevens, in Kazuo Ishiguro's *The Remains of the Day* (1990)—the authorial and narrative audiences diverge, producing a split or bifurcated anchoring process. Indeed, a narrator's unreliability is perceptible only *because* of this divergence or bifurcation. An account such as Stevens's can be recognized as unreliable precisely when its interpretation requires one to entertain assumptions, beliefs, or norms that conflict with those required for one's full participation in the authorial audience.[3] This dual anchoring strategy is clearly of a different kind than the one structuring comprehension of narratives like Eliot's or Woolf's.

Although previous narratological research centering around narratees, implied readers, and audiences thus throws light on the interface between stories and their interpreters, the rest of my chapter outlines other ways to investigate the role of contextual anchoring in stories. Using a second-person narrative as my tutor text, and drawing on linguistic theories of person deixis and of the address functions of personal pronouns, I further test the intuition that stories not only assume a relation between texts and contexts but sometimes work to reshape it. Moving toward a finer-grained approach to the text-context interface, I show that in second-person fiction quite different anchoring processes can be triggered by separate occurrences of the pronoun *you* in a single narrative. Although it is oriented around just one narrative, the approach sketched here does afford, I believe, glimpses of how interpreters rely on story logic to make moment-by-moment decisions concerning what constitutes text and what constitutes context. Conversely, story logic is in part based on those same moment-by-moment decisions.

Storyworld Construction and the Ontology of Narrative *You*

In his groundbreaking investigation "Narrative 'You' in Contemporary Literature," Bruce Morrissette (1965) opens his analysis by citing the Sartrean dictum "that every novelistic technique implies a metaphysical attitude on the part of the author" (1). Arguably, the same proposition applies, at one remove, to the various descriptions put forth by Morrissette himself and by other, later students of second-person narration.[4] That said, researchers need further specification of the metaphysics—more precisely, the ontology—of narrative *you*. At issue, more precisely still, is the ontological status of the entity or entities to which readers ascribe certain properties when, in constructing a mental model corresponding to some emergent (portion of a) narrative text, they come upon the lexical item *you* in that textual domain (cf. Webber 1991: 110–11). Study of narrative *you*, in other words, can illuminate the process by which specific types of narrative structure trigger readers to anchor storyworlds in particular contexts of interpretation. A principled account of the discourse functions of the second-person pronoun in narrative contexts may thus yield not only new tools for the poetics of second-person fiction but also new insights into the broader role of contextual anchoring in narrative comprehension.

To this end, the rest of the chapter examines Edna O'Brien's 1970 novel *A Pagan Place* (1984) as an illustrative instance of how stories anchor themselves in particular interpretive contexts. I explore O'Brien's narrative techniques in light of linguistic theories of (person) deixis, those theories having emerged historically from more broadly pragmatic theories concerning the situatedness of utterances in contexts. Ludic fictional techniques of the sort used by O'Brien both illuminate and are illuminated by recent work on deixis—notably, the theories about modes of participation in discourse and about culturally saturated deictic fields developed by William Hanks (1990). Drawing on such research to sketch the forms and functions of textual *you* in O'Brien's novel—a narrative told entirely in the second person and anchored in the world of a (nameless) preadolescent girl coming of age in rural Ireland during World War II—I at the same time describe aspects of the interface between storyworlds and interpreters working to reconstruct them. One of my hypotheses is that in second-person fictions like O'Brien's, the deictic force of textual *you* sometimes helps decenter what

Marie-Laure Ryan would term the modal structure of the narrative universes built up by those fictions (Ryan 1991: 109–23; cf. Pavel 1986: 43–113). In some cases at least, narrative *you* produces an ontological hesitation between what is actual and what is virtual within the storyworld. More precisely, *you* can induce hesitation between reference to entities, situations, and events internal to the storyworld and reference to entities, situations, and events external to the storyworld. As a result, narrative understanding unfolds within the emergent spatiotemporal parameters of competing mental models of the narrated domain.

To revert to terms introduced in chapter 6: certain occurrences of narrative *you* function in an indeterminate or "fuzzy" way, making it impossible to decide exactly where those tokens of *you* fall on the continuum that stretches between reference to storyworld participants and address to readers.[5] In this way, just as polychronic narration provides a higher-order modeling system with which to reassess stories' capacity to order things in time, second-person narration affords novel perspectives on the way interpreters make sense of stories by situating them in contexts.

Virtual, Actual, and Indeterminate *You*: A First Approach

One of the chief difficulties connected with the study of second-person fiction in general, until recently at least, is the lack of narratological tools precise enough to capture the sophistication of fictional practice (but see Fludernik 1993a, 1994a, 1994b, 1996: 223–49). Even a cursory examination of textual *you* in *A Pagan Place* reveals a rich diversity of functions attaching to the pronoun. Refinement of the poetics of second-person fiction—and, more generally, the development of an adequate theory of contextual anchoring in narrative—requires a nomenclature that can capture the sometimes fugitive elements of the phenomenology of reading *you*. (Also at stake is the phenomenology of the Reading You.)

In particular, second-person fictions like *A Pagan Place* engage in what Brian McHale (1987) would describe as a quintessentially postmodernist foregrounding of ontological issues—a playing with or transgression of boundaries assumed to separate the actual and the virtual, the fictional and the real (3–40; cf. Herman 1993). My chief concern here is to provide new investigative tools for studying such boundary work.

Contextual Anchoring 339

In this vein, note that previous accounts of narrative *you* can be preliminarily divided into two types, based on the sort of mental models they ascribe to interpreters working to assign referents to the pronoun *you* in narrative discourse. As Monika Fludernik (1993c) puts it in her discussion of the "naturally occurring text type paradigms that second-person fiction utilizes in its attempt to ease the reader into a story form that seems to contradict expectations of customary patterns of verisimilitude" (220; cf. Fludernik 1996: 222–49), "Discourse models for possible second-person narration can be divided roughly into those that highlight a prominent address function (which in actual second-person fiction, is then supplemented by an existential component, i.e. involvement in the story), and those that portray a *you's* experiences in combination with a latent situation of address" (230). Thus, in the context of a second-person fiction like O'Brien's, one species of discourse model prompts readers to assume that the entity evoked by *you* exists in the world of the narrative—as the fictional protagonist who addresses to herself a narrative of which she is in turn the (intradiegetic) narratee. On this model, the reader construes the referent of *you* as having an actuality-status of *virtual* (= storyworld-internal) with respect to the world in which the narrative is being read.[6] By contrast, in adopting the other type of mental model, interpreters postulate that textual *you* evokes an entity—namely, the interpreter himself or herself—that is actual or at least actualizable (= storyworld-external) in his or her world and hence virtual in the world of the narrative.

By working toward a third, enriched kind of discourse model, one that incorporates both of the models just outlined and yields what amounts to a three-valued modal logic, my analysis attempts to redress a lacuna noted by Fludernik: "Previous research [on second-person fiction] has either focussed on the use of the second-person pronoun in reference to a fictional protagonist or on the address function of second-person texts, but ignoring the central issue of the combination of these two aspects" (1993c: 218; cf. Fludernik 1993a: 445–46). Fludernik (1993c) herself proposes a suggestive new typology (spanning the categories *homocommunicative*, *heterocommunicative*, and *homoconative*) by means of which narrative theorists can rethink the relations between fictional reference and address in the context of second-person fiction (224; cf. Fludernik 1996: 244–49). The typology yields a finer-grained specification of "the communicative level" vis-à-vis "the story level of the fiction" (224), distinguishing between several varieties of second-person (self-)address run together in the older typologies (221–23). Taking a different approach to the problem of contextual anchoring in second-person narration, my discussion situates both the referential and address mechanisms of *you* amid an array of discourse functions attaching to the pronoun, in a more or less accentuated fashion, in different narrative contexts. In this subsection I give a preview of the functions of *you* in *A Pagan Place*, providing a more detailed analysis of each function in the penultimate section of the chapter.

What I have termed the referential mechanisms associated with textual *you* pertain to one functional subtype of the pronoun, a subtype marked by an uncoupling of the grammatical form of *you* from its deictic functions. In this way *you* refers to O'Brien's narrator-protagonist by a process of what Uri Margolin (1984) has termed deictic transfer, another species of which produces the functional subtype known as impersonal or generalized *you*. Deictic transfer is evident in passage 1, taken from the opening of the novel:

> 1. Manny Parker was a botanist, out in all weathers, lived with his sister that ran the sweetshop, they ate meat Fridays, they were Protestants. Your mother dealt there, found them honest. (O'Brien 1984: 3)

Here, arguably, the second-person possessive pronoun presents no special interpretive difficulties. Interpreters can take *your* to refer to the fictional protagonist of *A Pagan Place*, a protagonist who, as (intradiegetic) narrator, is also, over the course of the novel as a whole, her own intradiegetic narratee—that is, a narratee included in the diegetic situation whose product is the narrative itself. A similar interpretation can be sketched out for the token of *your* found in passage 2, also part of O'Brien's introductory account of the narrator-protagonist-narratee's fictional circumstances:

> 2. Your mother could not bear to see and hear stray cattle dispersing all over the fields because she had a presentiment that they were going to be there forever, fattening themselves for free. (5)

The other subtype of *you* that uncouples grammatical form and deictic function is the impersonal or generalized *you*—the "pseudo-deictic" *you* (Furrow 1988: 372)—that often plays a prominent role not only in second-person literary narratives but also in (the language of) proverbs, maxims, recipes, VCR instructions, song lyrics and, though they might tell you otherwise, astrologers' prognostications. Thus, in a string like passage 3—

3. When you're hot, you're hot—

"the second-person pronouns are impersonal: non-deictic in that their interpretation does not depend directly on any feature of the non-linguistic context of the utterance" (Anderson and Keenan 1985: 260).[7] As I discuss below, use of a generalized *you* is rare in O'Brien's novel, in part because of its thematic focus—that is, its insistence on particularizing a narrator-protagonist in search of an identity for herself.

Meanwhile, the address mechanisms of narrative *you*—discourse functions that differ in degree, not kind, from the functions I have called referential—can be respecified as a convergence between the grammar of *you* and its deictic profile. This convergence between the form and functioning of *you*, like their uncoupling, yields two functional subtypes: what I shall term *fictionalized* address, which entails address to or by the members of some fictional world and thus constitutes "horizontal" address; and *actualized* address or apostrophe, which as I construe it here entails address that exceeds the frame (or ontological threshold) of a fiction to reach the audience, thus constituting "vertical" address.[8] Taking fictionalized address first, note that syntactic inversion is often a marker of the Anglo-Irish idiolect associated with (and in fact used to characterize) the narrator-protagonist's father. Thus the inverted locution at the end of passage 4 signals indirect discourse, in which *you* figures as a term of address uttered *by* the father *to* his daughter, as subsequently reported (to herself) by the daughter. Here *you* functions as part of what I am calling fictionalized (or horizontal) address:

4. The women brought you into the bedroom that led off the kitchen and while you were vomiting your father called in to know if it was vomiting you were. (41)

Similarly, setting itself off against the background of the ongoing (unmarked) narration, periphrasis is a (marked) stylistic figure whose emphatic quality suggests not self-address, but rather the self-addressed report of *someone else's* address, as in passage 5.

5. Your mother said they would not force *you*, they were not believers in force. (193, my emphasis)

As for the difference between fictionalized and actualized address, or horizontal and vertical address, Margolin (1984) suggests that this is a distinction that will not always be clear-cut. Margolin points out that "in the absence of clear textual indicators, the speech situation [in second-person narration] may become ambiguous . . . : is its narrator t[he] narratee, or rather a narratee's response embedded in the narrator's utterance, or is it genuine self-address?" (189). Margolin's hermeneutic inventory—note that his questions concern the exact *scope* of the address functions attaching to textual *you*—can be extended. Take passage 6, for example:

> 6. The squeals of each particular pig [being slaughtered by the father] reached you no matter where you hid, no matter where you happened to crouch, and it was heart-rending as if the pig was making a last but futile appeal to someone to save him. (19)

Here, arguably, the chain of empathic identification stretches beyond the diegetic situation of the novel—beyond that virtual *you* who, in O'Brien's fictional world, addresses to herself comments regarding her own inability to ignore the pigs' final appeal—and reaches those fragments of our world(s) in which pity for pigs is actually to be found. Similar difficulties of determining the scope of *you* manifest themselves in passage 7:

> 7. Alone for the first time in the street, you were conscious of your appearance. Your coat was ridiculous compared with other people's coats. (172)

In passage 7, textual *you* functions not (or not only) as discourse particle relaying and linking the various components of a fictional protagonist's self-address, but (also) as a form of address that exceeds the frame of the fiction itself. *You*, as used in passages 6 and 7, designates anyone who has ever been or might conceivably be upset by the slaughter of animals, or embarrassed by the homeliness of her coat when she stands alone for the first time on a crowded city street.

Yet another discourse function, or rather blend of functions, triggered by *you*, arguably of crucial importance to second-person fictions like *A Pagan Place*, is more difficult to situate (or at least to situate exactly) amid the other functions just sketched. Less a discrete, autonomous discourse function than a hybridized combination of the other functional subtypes, this usage of narrative *you* is what I refer to as *double deixis*. It is a mode of pronoun usage that draws attention to and so de-automatizes processes of contextual anchoring. To anticipate: in some instances at least, O'Brien's textual *you* functions neither as a coded reference to an *I* (a fictional protagonist) or to an indefinite *one* (Laberge 1980; Laberge and Sankoff 1979); nor as a term of (horizontal) address in the fictional world built up by the novel; nor yet as a vehicle for apostrophic, vertical address to the reader. Rather, on some occasions *you* functions as a cue for superimposing two or more deictic roles, one internal to the storyworld represented in or through the diegesis and the other(s) external to that storyworld. (As should already be apparent, however, the heuristic constructs *internal* and *external* have to be rethought in this connection.)

Consider passage 8, in which the narrator recounts the panting of a masturbator in the hotel room next to the one the protagonist and her mother have rented when they travel to Dublin to visit Emma:

8. . . . you heard panting from the next room, the amateur actor's room. It was like something you had heard before, distantly, a footprint on your mind, you didn't know from where. (169–70)

Here the second-person pronoun would seem to encode reference to an addressee—that is, a participant in the discourse situation represented in the narrative. The absence of direct discourse, it is true, prevents readers from interpreting *you* as a term of address in the strict sense; the narrative does not represent someone uttering *you* to someone else. Still, the *you* is arguably anything but generalized or impersonal. Interpreting *you* as generalized would amount to ignoring the richness of the contextual information encoded in the description via, for example, the definite noun phrases *the next room* and *the amateur actor's room*. The form of these locutions suggests information already given, not new (in the sense specified by Firbas [1964, 1992] and E. Prince [1981, 1992]), vis-à-vis the discourse situation at issue. More precisely, in its use of a definite rather than indefinite noun phrase, the passage anchors the description in what might be termed a specific perceptual frame, particularized by the first occurrence of the verb *heard* and associated here with the protagonist herself. Within that perceptual frame, the room next door is a live issue, a current concern, rather than some adventitious or detachable discourse topic. To resort to a classical narratological vocabulary: the passage's selection of a particular syntactic option (*the next room* versus *a neighboring room*) signals internally focalized narrative discourse. The *you* functions as a pronominal stand-in for an *I* through whom are filtered the situations and events being recounted, in turn, to an equally particularized intradiegetic narratee (who, according to one broad approach to second-person narration, is just the protagonist-narrator herself). *You* picks out *this particular* fictional protagonist in the act of self-address.

Yet the second sentence of the quoted passage—"It was like something you had heard before, distantly, a footprint on your mind, you didn't know from where"—complicates the foregoing interpretation. Here the *you* hovers somewhere between an apostrophic term of address, an instance of the deictic transfer constituting fictional reference, and generalized or pseudo-deictic *you*. Depending on whether your mind had, has, or might yet have (or could in your own view be described, figuratively, as having) a footprint of sexuality inscribed upon it, you will find yourself more or less within the discourse context both presupposed and elaborated by the description at issue. Thus, some elements of the passage create a specific and highly particularized perceptual frame, thereby prompting interpreters to virtualize the discourse referent of *you* (i.e., locate it inside the storyworld). Yet other elements of passage 8 cue recipients to actualize the *you* (i.e., locate its referent outside the storyworld) via experiential repertoires they themselves may or may not have acquired. The deictic coordinates orienting the description of the Dublin hotel begin to obtrude into the world occupied by readers; conversely, the HERE and NOW of the act of interpretation begins to orient the building of a storyworld. As Jürgen Habermas (1988) puts it in his reading of Calvino's *If on a Winter's Night a Traveler*:

> Der Roman in der zweiten Person macht den Leser zu einem Mitspieler, der zwischen einer fiktiven Welt und seiner realen schwebt, der zugleich drinnen and drauĕn ist: drinnen als eine unter mehreren fingierten Personen, aber zugleich drauĕn, weil die Figur des gelesenen auf den wirklichen Leser verweist und insofern eine Referenz über das Buch hinaus herstellt. (256)

> The novel in the second person makes of the reader a fellow player, who is suspended between a fictive world and his own real world, and who stands simultaneously inside and outside the fiction: inside it as one among several fictitious personages, but at the same time outside it, because the figure of the "read" reader refers back to the real reader and, to that extent, produces a reference that points beyond the fiction itself.

Contextual Anchoring 345

In doubly deictic contexts such as passage 8, in other words, the audience will find itself more or less subject to conflation with the fictional self addressed by *you*. The deictic force of *you* is double; or to put it more precisely, the scope of the discourse context embedding the description is indeterminate, as is the domain of participants in principle specified or picked out by *you*.

Closer study of this superimposition of deictic roles via textual *you* can, I believe, help theorists fruitfully redescribe the oftentimes disorienting, sometimes uncanny experience of reading second-person fictions, one of whose most characteristic formal gambits is "to try to put the reader in the text" (Kacandes 1993a: 139) and thereby abolish the boundary between the textual and the extra-textual, the fictive and the real, the virtual and the actual (cf. McHale 1987: 222–27; Phelan 1994; Richardson 1991: 312). Arguably, a discourse model that accommodates doubly deictic *you* will (on occasion) assign *both* virtuality *and* actuality to the entity or entities indexed by narrative *you*. Or, to put the point another way, double deixis is a name for the ontological interference pattern produced by two or more interacting spatiotemporal frames—none of which can be called primary or basic relative to the other(s)—set more or less prominently into play when interpreters read fictions written in the second person.

Even this initial survey of *you* in *A Pagan Place* indicates the complexity and variety of the discourse functions attributable to the pronoun. At issue are (at least) four functional types of textual *you*, along with a fifth, hybridized type that combines features of the other four and that I am calling doubly deictic *you*:

(a) generalized *you*

(b) fictional reference

(c) fictionalized (= horizontal) address

(d) apostrophic (= vertical) address

(e) doubly deictic *you*

These functions of textual *you* must be accommodated by any theory of contextual anchoring in second-person narration, and I examine the five functions in more detail below. First, however, I discuss how linguistic theories of deixis can facilitate a more principled investigation of contextual anchoring in the case of narrative *you*.

Deixis, Person Deixis, and Narrative *You*

Working within a research tradition that extends back (at least) to Karl Bühler's (1965) pathbreaking discussion of deixis in *Sprachtheorie* (originally published in 1934), most linguists would agree that deictic expressions can be defined as "linguistic elements whose interpretation in simple sentences makes essential reference to properties of the extralinguistic context of the utterances in which they occur" (Anderson and Keenan 1985: 259). Thus deixis designates "the way an expression is anchored to some essential point *in context*" (Frawley 1992: 274), with deictic expressions constituting "that aspect of the linguistic form because of which it can figure in the given, concrete context, because of which it becomes a sign adequate to the conditions of the given, concrete situation" (Vološinov 1973: 68). As Stephen C. Levinson (1983) puts it, "[D]eixis concerns the ways in which languages encode or grammaticalize features of the *context of utterance* or *speech event*, and thus also concerns ways in which the interpretation of utterances depends on the analysis of that context of utterance" (54).[9]

Language theorists have developed a variety of explanatory models to account for this grammaticalization of context through deixis. Roman Jakobson (1971), for example, invokes the concept of "shifters": "Any linguistic code contains a particular class of grammatical units which Jespersen labeled *shifters*: the general meaning of a shifter cannot be defined without reference to the message.... shifters are distinguished from all other constituents of the linguistic code solely by their compulsory reference to the given message" (131–32). Oswald Ducrot and Tzvetan Todorov (1979) similarly emphasize the message-specific character of deictic terms: "Deictics are expressions whose referent can only be determined with respect to the interlocutors.... E. Benveniste has shown that deictics constitute an irruption of discourse within language, since their very meaning ... , even though it depends on language, can only be defined by allusion to their use" (252). Meanwhile, in a book-length study of the deictic complexity of narrative texts, Gisa Rauh (1978) draws on the later Wittgenstein's conception of meaning as use to characterize deictic expressions:

> Deiktische Ausdrücke haben nicht die Funktion, Gegenstände, auf die mit ihrer Verwendung verwiesen wird, zu charakterisieren. Ihre Bedeutung kann nicht unabhängig von ihrer Verwendung beschrieben werden, sondern sie ist abhängig von der Situation eines Sprechereignisses, dem

auërsprachlichen Kontext einer Äußerung. Die Bedeutung deiktischer Ausdrücke verändert sich mit dem Äußerer einer Äußerung und dessen Position in Raum und Zeit. (30) Deictic expressions do not have the function of characterizing objects to which these expressions, in being used, will refer. Their meaning cannot be described independently of their use, but is rather dependent on the situation of a speech event, the extralinguistic context of an utterance. The meaning of deictic expressions changes with the utterer of an utterance and with his or her position in space and time.

Further, as I discussed in a different connection in chapter 7, linguists and cognitive scientists have in recent years developed new tools for describing and analyzing "deictic centers" and "deictic shifts" in narrative. For Zubin and Hewitt (1995), narrative understanding requires interpreters to construct a deictic center from which to view the unfolding story events, using "this deictic center as we would use the 'I' of face-to-face interaction to anchor our comprehension of the text" (131). Deictic shifts are thus accomplished "by decoupling the linguistic marking of deixis from the speech situation, and reorienting it to the major characters, the locations, and a fictive present time of the story world itself" (131).

For their part, discourse analysts and researchers in the field of linguistic pragmatics have identified what appear to be at least five different kinds or rather dimensions of deixis. In addition to *spatial* deixis (*The cat slept* over there), *temporal* deixis (After that *I got really bored*), and *person* deixis (She's *smarter than I am*), theorists have also identified forms of *social* and *discourse* deixis. Socially deictic expressions encode "social distinctions that are relative to participant-roles" (Levinson 1983: 63; Brown and Yule 1983: 50–58). For example, in English I will use a different term of address according to my social position relative to the addressee (I would say *Mr. President*, but the attorney general might say *George*); other languages encode social distinctions through their personal pronoun systems (familiar *tu* and *du* versus formal *vous* and *Sie* in French and German, respectively). Finally, discourse deixis encodes references to "portions of the unfolding discourse in which the utterance (including the text referring expression) is located" (Levinson 1983: 62). Examples would include expressions such as *as I just said* or *as will become clearer in a moment*.

For any study of the way narrative *you* bears on processes of contextual anchoring, research on person deixis is, of course, especially salient. Ever since the work of Bühler (1965: 107) and then Émile Benveniste (1966: 225–36, 251–58), theorists have used the idea of participant roles to ground a distinction between first- and second-person pronouns, on the one hand, and third-person pronouns, on the other hand.[10] According to this research tradition, *I* and *you*, by grammatically encoding the roles of addressor/speaker and addressee/hearer, typically designate participants in a current discourse situation. By contrast, *he*, *she*, and *they* typically designate not participants in the current discourse, but rather elements of the (extralinguistic) context of the discourse.

Indeed, it seems that all languages encode through their personal pronoun systems reference to (at least) the speaker, the hearer or addressee, and the nonspeaker or nonhearer. These three persons, along with their different numbers (i.e., singular *I* and *you* versus plural *we* and *you* [*all*]), can be construed as "the set of contextual anchors for deictic reference to speech act participants" (Frawley 1992: 280). More precisely, "The nonparticipant forms signal that the referent is neither the current animator nor the current receiver, but some third party(s). Whereas the Spkr and Adr forms encode that the referent they identify is *identical* to some participant in the current indexical field of interaction, the nonparticipant forms signal a *disjunction* between coparticipants and the referent(s)" (Hanks 1990: 179).[11] If then a language were to encode in the addressee form *you* both actual and potential parties to the discourse—both addressees and overhearers, participants and nonparticipants—it would risk conflating the "field of interaction" with the larger context in which the interaction occurs, the coparticipants *in* the current discourse with the referents *of* the discourse. Such a language would include not just deictic but also doubly deictic expressions. Users of the language in question—like interpreters of second-person narratives—might find themselves to be oddly nonvirtual participants in discourses from which they are nevertheless spatiotemporally removed.

I am hinting that second-person narratives such as O'Brien's call attention to the conditions and limits of participation in—that is, the contextual anchoring of—narrative discourse generally. Significantly, similar concerns manifest themselves in Jakobson's (1971) account of the shifters incorporated into the grammar of languages by way of their personal pronoun systems. Commenting on acts of narrative communication in particular, Jakobson writes: "*Person* characterizes the participants of the narrated event with reference to the participants of the speech event. Thus first person signals the identity of a participant of the narrated event with the performer of the speech event, and the second person, the *identity with the actual or potential undergoer* of the speech event" (134, my emphases). In hedging on the question of whether the entity indexed by narrative *you* matches up with an actual or merely a potential undergoer of the speech event, Jakobson likewise hedges on whether *you* refers to an item in the storyworld with which I might only potentially identify or else me, the reader or listener.[12] In such cases, where it is no longer possible to clearly demarcate participation in a discourse from nonparticipation in that discourse, contextual anchoring has become a dominant rather than a latent concern in the narrative.

Likewise, narrative *you* in *A Pagan Place* produces a double deixis mirrored in Jakobson's uneasy distribution of *you* between actual and potential undergoers, real and virtual participants. More precisely, O'Brien's text sometimes telescopes into one grammatical form— *you*—deictic functions associated with both participant-centered and nonparticipant-centered pronouns. In some narrative contexts, textual *you* thus yields a superimposition of deictic roles, a blended or double form of person deixis encompassing both the addressee and what Benveniste (1966) specified as the "non-personne"—that is, the "persons and entities which are neither speakers nor addressees of the utterance in question" (Levinson 1983: 62).[13] Putting this last point another way, although in narratives such as O'Brien's *you* has the morphosyntactic profile of the second-person pronoun in English, and thus prima facie seems to encode the role of the addressee into narrative discourse, nonetheless in some instances the deictic functions of *you* are only partly in agreement with the word's grammatical form.[14] Functionally speaking, *you* in those cases superimposes the deictic role of the audience or overhearer (in this instance the reader) onto the deictic role(s) spatiotemporally anchored in the storyworld. The grammatical profile of *you* thus drastically underdetermines its deictic functions; the text projects itself into a range of contexts that cannot be strictly delimited. Indeed, doubly deictic *you*, like relatively recent developments in the field of linguistic pragmatics, compels readers as well as theorists to question the idea that texts and contexts are separate things—to dispute "the idea that a linguistic string (a sentence) can be fully analysed without taking 'context' into account" (Brown and Yule 1983: 25; cf. Bar-Hillel

1954; Green 1989: 17–35; Schiffrin 1990b). To this extent, second-person fictions such as *A Pagan Place* should be construed not just as doubly deictic but also as metadeictic. Such fictions, by formally encoding (features of) the contexts in which they are or might be read, in turn prompt reflection on how contexts permeate and modify the narrative structures anchored in them, like the tendrils of a plant growing through porous stone.

Narrative *You* and Contextual Anchoring in *A Pagan Place*

Concepts formalized in linguistic theory thus furnish new ways of describing narrative practice in texts such as *A Pagan Place*. Adapting the terminology of Lotman and Uspenskij (1986), second-person fictions such as O'Brien's furnish a secondary modeling system that grounds itself in, or bases itself upon, the deictic features and address mechanisms of the primary modeling system, language itself. Narrative *you* provides new perspectives on the forms and functions of deixis and address in a variety of discourse situations—not just those created by the interpretation of narrative discourse but also those embedded in or figured by stories. As already indicated, contextual anchoring in second-person narrative requires situating instances of *you* along a continuum; at one end of the continuum the pronoun takes on strictly referential functions, and at the other, strictly the function of address. Because scalar or gradient (*more or less*) rather than binary (*either/or*) processes are involved here, some occurrences of the pronoun will blend the referential and address functions, producing double deixis. In such cases narrative *you* resists being assigned an exact or determinate position on the continuum. Further, although I am focusing on second-person narration as a case study, arguably the model outlined here can be extended to account for contextual anchoring in narrative generally. My approach assumes that narrative comprehension requires, in part, monitoring how closely and in what ways a storyworld matches the contexts in which it is being reconstructed. Use of narrative *you* is a technique by means of which stories can denaturalize this monitoring process and transform it from an automatic into a conscious interpretive activity. But that, too, is a (reflexive or second-order) process of contextual anchoring. Studying the gamut of techniques that enable, reinforce, thematize, or disrupt contextual anchoring remains an important task for future narrative-theoretical research.

For my present purposes, it is important to note that O'Brien's emphasis on role-playing in human interaction helps pluralize the referent of narrative *you* into a cluster of roles, actual (or storyworld-external), virtual (or storyworld-internal), and actual-virtual (or indeterminately located vis-à-vis the storyworld). For example, O'Brien persistently favors similes of a theatrical provenance—"He [the protagonist's father] touched her wrist and begged her forgiveness. It was like a gesture in a play"(107)—thereby figuring discourse participants as performers in front of an audience (cf. 23, 29, 73, 79). Further, in a passage such as 9, the text momentarily shifts to a first-person pronoun to sketch a typical scene of confession. In consequence the novel emphasizes that even utterances ostensibly authenticated by a speaking *I* are just another species of illocutionary acts, communicative performances, the accomplishment of which entails playing a particular role in a particular speech situation:

> 9. You went to the curate because the parish priest was deaf and the sins had to be shouted at him. The same set of sins every week. I cursed, I told lies, I had bad thoughts. (42)

Or consider the extraordinary account of how the protagonist and Della, a girl in the neighborhood suffering from tuberculosis, play a game in which one of them takes on the role of a film star. In passage 10, the shift to a third-person pronoun represents not just make-believe embedded within an already fictive situation, but also a ludic transposition of gender roles:

> 10. Clark Gable was the first to speak. He asked why she [Della] went motoring with Robert Donat. She said she liked Robert Donat's car. . . . Then Clark Gable said he'd box her ears if she ever did that again. She said to Clark Gable What about Dorothy Lamour then, what about her. He said Dorothy Lamour was just a bon-bon compared with her, Della, and then he asked her if she loved him and she shrugged and said she didn't know and when he pressed for an answer she said A teeny bit. Then he took her wrists and squeezed them very tight and she pleaded for mercy and he would not let go until she kissed him and the kiss was on the lips and very passionate. You knew it was passionate because you were Clark Gable and Robert Donat and Dorothy Lamour and all of those characters. (63)

Here, identity itself reduces to a series of enunciatory and behavioral roles performed with the help of pronominal shifts and their attendant deictic displacements. To cite a remark made by Édouard Morot-Sir in a somewhat different context, "Les déictiques identifiés par le linguiste sont, au niveau de la performance, les indices d'une des grandes fatalités du langage: être personne (et l'on peut donner à cet énoncé ses deux significations opposées: être tout, être rien) par procuration déictique" 'one can be anyone (and here that locution can be assigned two opposed meanings: one can be everyone possible, and one can be no one in particular) by way of deictic proxy' (131). A more precise characterization of the principles and effects of such "procuration déictique" is what I am working toward in this chapter.

As already outlined, O'Brien's novel features at least five distinct usages of *you*—usages that researchers need to sort out if they are to begin specifying the dynamics of contextual anchoring in second-person narration and, by extension, narrative generally. In effect, each usage marks a different relation between the grammatical form and the deictic functions of *you*. To recapitulate: in that usage of the second-person pronoun that involves full agreement between the form of *you* and its functions, *you* encodes the participant role of an addressee. There are two functional subtypes of this usage: fictionalized or horizontal address and apostrophic or vertical address. Alternatively, another usage of *you* involves complete disagreement between morphosyntactic form and deictic function, resulting in deictic transfer(s). Once again, there are two functional subtypes in this case: *you* creates the displaced deixis of an *I* → *you* deictic transfer, or by a different species of transfer, *you* takes on the role of an impersonal or generalized or colloquial (= pseudo-deictic) *you*, in which *you* and *your* virtually lose their deictic force and become, instead, what Melissa Furrow (1988) has termed "colloquial stand-ins for the indefinite pronoun *one*" (370). Finally, there is the usage that entails neither complete concord nor complete discord between grammatical form and deictic functioning, but instead a merely partial (dis)agreement between the form and functions of *you*. This is the usage that I am categorizing as doubly deictic. Doubly deictic *you* ambiguates virtualized and actualized discourse referents, or rather superimposes the deictic roles of nonparticipants and participants in the discourse, thus reweighting both terms in the text-context relation itself. As such, the notion of double deixis can help account for the para-

Figure 12. A Scalar Model of Narrative *You*

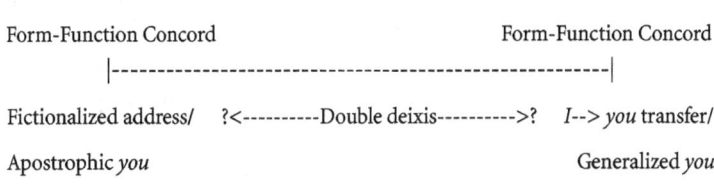

doxical reading position that at least some modes of second-person narration compel interpreters to occupy. As James Phelan (1994) succinctly puts it, "When the second-person address to a narratee-protagonist both overlaps with and differentiates itself from an address to actual readers, those readers will simultaneously occupy the positions of addressee and observer" (351).

Figure 12 provides an initial schematization of narrative *you*, with the degree of concord between the grammatical form and the deictic functions of the pronoun decreasing as one moves from left to right along the scale. Further, just as I used question marks to represent fuzzy temporal ordering in Egoyan's *The Sweet Hereafter* in chapter 6 (see figures 8 and 10), the question marks in figure 12 indicate the indeterminate boundaries—the shifting form-function relations—characteristic of doubly deictic *you*. Additional refinements of this scheme—refinements enabling representation of the modal status of the discourse referents corresponding to each functional subtype of *you*—will need to be introduced (see tables 15 and 16 below). First, though, some further illustrative instances from *A Pagan Place* will help concretize the model outlined thus far, positioning it in the context of previous research on second-person narrative.

Form-Function Discord: Deictic Transfer and Generalized *You*

The functions of narrative *you* located on the right-hand portion of the scale in figure 12 correspond to an uncoupling of its grammatical form from its deictic functions. Following Butor (1964: 67), these subtypes of *you* might be called the "déplacements des personnes" 'displacements of persons'; or, better still, to use Margolin's (1984: 198; 1986/87: 190–99) term, form-function discord in narrative *you* enables *deictic transfer*.

One subtype of this second usage of *you* is the displacement or transfer from *I* to *you* already discussed at some length above. (Strictly speaking, both *I → you* and *he/she → you* transfers should be included in this category, but I simplify matters by assuming that O'Brien's narrator is also the fictional protagonist.) This sort of deictic transfer operates in passages such as 11:

> 11. You had to pass your own gates to go to your aunt's. (189)

In such contexts the highly localized nature of the fragment of the world evoked by the discourse precludes generalized *you* while the address functions of *you* remain relatively latent. As Margolin (1986/87) points out, furthermore, "If... the [*I → you (tu/vous)*] transfer is in the past tense, we are dealing with... a case of what Bühler has termed '*deixis am Phantasma*.' In it, the speaker conjures up a past version of himself and talks to and about it as if it were present in his immediate deictic field, while distinguishing it from his present identity through the difference in tense and person" (196). Note, too, that the *I → you* deictic transfer is, as Katherine Passias (1976) points out, the prevalent usage of *vous* in what may be the single most influential second-person fiction, Butor's 1957 novel *La Modification:* "No matter how involved he may be in a narrative, there is an underlying awareness that the message is about 'the other.' The surface modulations of the pronoun in *La Modification* do not change the underlying relationship, namely that the narrator is someone outside of the reader's personal experiences, addressing him and attributing to him experiences that are not his" (200–201).[15]

The other subtype of *you* that uncouples grammatical form and deictic function is the impersonal or generalized *you*—the "pseudo-deictic" *you* (Furrow 1988: 372)—already illustrated in passage 3.

> 3. When you're hot, you're hot.

I should underscore here that the possibilities and limits of this impersonal usage of *you* are to some extent language-specific. For example, the grammar of a language like modern Hebrew, in which second-person pronouns, in both the singular and plural numbers, encode information about the gender of the addressee (Anderson and Keenan 1985: 269), does not underdetermine the deictic functions of those pronouns to the degree that the grammar of English underdetermines their English counterparts.[16] Translated into Hebrew, passage 3 would encode information about both gender and number that its English version

Contextual Anchoring 355

leaves wholly unspecified.[17] Hence narrative *discourse* such as O'Brien's exploits the *language* in which it is rooted; the (deictic) effects of second-person fiction will not necessarily be transferable *in toto* across different languages.

In any event, in *A Pagan Place*, generalized or impersonal *you* manifests itself quite rarely. The *you* of the narrative is not the *you* of fortune cookies and newspaper horoscopes; readers are not encouraged to depersonalize this *you* who, caught in the interstices between childhood and adulthood, is herself searching for an identity—familial, social, and sexual.[18] Some of the narrator-protagonist's recountings begin with what seems like an impersonal and pseudo-deictic *you*—"You always ran home from school. Your friends jeered" (11)[19]—but are then inflected with information firmly anchored in the discourse context furnished by a personal history—"Called you sutach, called you suck-suck, called you diddums and spoilsport and clown and pissabed" (11). An account of tea roses in a vase on the table, represented in passage 12, perhaps comes closer to generalized *you*:

> 12. When you looked into them without blinking it was like getting drawn into them, it was like a spell, getting drawn into folds and folds of red. They were different near the base, had different shadings, different gradations of color and all had unique centers. (200)

What are perhaps the only indisputable instances of generalized *you*, however, are the occurrences of *you* in the moral that the protagonist's mother draws from the story of the man merely shipped off to Australia for shooting and killing a woman who refused to serve him another drink—

> 13. The man was deported to Australia instead of getting jailed and he was never heard of again and your mother said that was destiny for *you* (20, my emphasis)

—and later on in the verses offered by the father when he sees some mice in his shoe:

> 14. There's going to be a race,
> Five asses and a ginnet
> And I bet you two to one
> That the Father's ass will win it.[20] (134)

Ostensibly, the species of deictic transfer evident in examples such as passages 11, 12, 13, and 14 bear out Brian Richardson's (1991) interpretation of the novel as an instance of "standard," versus the "subjunctive" or "autotelic," forms of second-person fiction. For Richardson, one of the indices of the standard mode is its use of a narrative *you* convertible to the first or third person (319). At issue is a *you* referentially grounded in some fictional narrator or protagonist and derived from the first or third person forms by a (narratologically reconstructible) series of pronominal transformations and displacements:

> Second-person narrative may be defined as any narration that designates its protagonist by a second-person pronoun. This protagonist will usually be the sole focalizer, and is generally the work's narratee as well. In most cases, the story is narrated in the present tense. . . . The most common type of second-person narrative, what I will term the "standard" form, is also the closest to more traditional forms of narration. In it, a story is told, usually in the present tense, about a single protagonist who is referred to in the second person; the "you" also designates the narrator and the narratee as well, though as we will see there is frequently some slippage in this unusual triumvirate.[21] (311)

According to this argument, in a passage such as 15—

> 15. In one of the fields there was an old bus with two hairy fellows living in it and although they never accosted you, you thought they might (O'Brien 1984: 80)

—one recognizes the *modus operandi* of O'Brien's novel as a whole. To judge from examples such as 15, *A Pagan Place* is a text in which "the narrator, focalizer and narratee are in fact one person" (Richardson 1991: 316). Here the customary address functions of *you* subordinate themselves to the referential (one might well say "anaphoric") functions of the pronoun. *You* now operates as a sort of syncategorematic term or discourse particle, whose chief function is to establish cohesion among the various narrative units uttered, lived, and interpreted, in closed-circuit diegesis, by the fictional protagonist herself.

In short, although it allows for "some slippage" in this connection, by and large the discourse model subtending Richardson's interpretation of *A Pagan Place* as a standard second-person fiction confers an actuality-status of *virtual* (= storyworld-internal) on the entities evoked by textual *you*. As in Michel Butor's early definition of the second person in fictional contexts as "celui à qui l'on raconte sa propre histoire" 'that person to whom one relates one's own life story' (66), in Richardson's scheme textual *you* in *A Pagan Place* designates a personage or entity actual only within the storyworld. By definition, that personage or entity is unreal or irreal with respect to the world in which readers perform acts of "fictional recentering," that is, the acts on the strength of which interpreters relocate to the storyworlds evoked by fictions such as O'Brien's (Ryan 1991: 21–23). Some such discourse model informs, too, Genette's understanding of second-person narration, given that Genette defines "second-person narrating" as "the identity *between narratee and hero*" (1988: 133; cf. G. Prince 1987: 84). The character-you and the narratee-you (G. Prince 1982: 20) coincide, and in turn the character/narratee-you coincides with the narrator. As Prince puts it, "Sometimes, the narratee-character of a given account may be, at the same time, its narrator. In this case, the latter addresses this account to no one else than himself" (21). Yet what Richardson deems the typical profile of standard second-person fictions, and what Butor, Genette, and Prince construe as the index of second-person fiction *per se*, is better conceived of as a special, limiting case of a particular strategy for reading *you*. As Gerald Prince's formulation in particular suggests (but see G. Prince 1985: 302), this model backgrounds the address functions of the second-person pronoun in the interest of constructing a modally homogeneous interpretation of textual *you*—that is, an interpretation of *you* as designator of the virtual.

There are, however, occurrences of *you* in O'Brien's novel that require more or less complicated adjustments in this initial approach—though perhaps not a wholesale abandonment of the discourse model that posits a sort of diegetic solidarity (in Hjelmslev's sense) between narrator, focalizing protagonist, and narratee.[22] For example, in passage 16, an account of how her father and mother first met, the self-address of the narrator-protagonist is inflected by intermittent representation of her father's patterns of speech; the narrative thus embeds free indirect discourse within the protagonist's self-address, loosening the diegetic links that connect narrator, protagonist-focalizor, and narratee to a single node, as it were, of the virtual or irreal.[23]

16. Your father met your mother at that dance *but didn't throw two words to her*. Your mother was *all dolled up*, home from America on holiday, had a long dress and peroxide in her hair. Your mother *put the eye on him* then and got her brother to invite him up to their house to walk the land. (7, my emphases)

Later on in the novel, after Emma's pregnancy is discovered, the self-address again constitutes, too, reported speech, this time by way of indirect discourse:

> 17. Your father said all the private shit was over and that it was now in the public domain. (130)

The self-address is here complex or mixed, opening itself to address by others—and *a fortiori* address to others. At the very least, the discourse functions performed by *you* have already begun to complicate the modal status of what the term designates, given that the pronoun has begun to embed virtuality within virtuality—to insert address by other fictional personages within the ongoing self-address of the protagonist.

In fact, O'Brien relies on a variety of grammatical and rhetorical resources to signal forms of represented speech and thought in the context of second-person narration. Such formal features help readers negotiate instances of *you* that deviate from what might be deemed the default interpretation of the second-person pronoun in *A Pagan Place*—that is, the assumption that, unless otherwise indicated, *you* is a pronominal stand-in for an *I* who figures as the protagonist of a narrative that she addresses to herself and that we eavesdropping readers (quasi-voyeuristically) overhear. Above, in connection with passage 4, I discussed how syntactic inversion is often a marker of the Anglo-Irish idiolect associated with (and used to characterize) the narrator-protagonist's father. Inverted locutions can thus mark where the narrator's self-address gives way to speech reports taking the form of indirect discourse. Then again, a subjunctive grammatical mood can indicate where both narration and reported speech give way to reported thought, as in passage 18.

> 18. You would go away from them, far, far away, where no conveyance could bring them to you. (222)

Passage 18 represents a strangely hybrid form of self-address, combining elements of the self-address that sometimes occurs within the quoted monologues representing consciousness in third-person contexts (Cohn 1978: 90–91) with elements of those representations of consciousness in first-person contexts in which "a first person compulsively buttonholes a second person who seems to be simultaneously inside and outside the fictional scene, inside and outside the speaking self" (Cohn 1978: 178).

Contextual Anchoring 359

My larger point is that, even within the framework of the discourse model that assigns a virtual, storyworld-internal referent to O'Brien's *you*, distinctions need to be drawn between species of self-address; self-address containing (what are postulated as "factual") reports of address by other fictitious personages; self-address featuring beliefs, desires, and intentions never actualized in the world of the novel and thus acquiring the status of second-order fictions; and so on. Still, a case can be made for the view that, in the instances of *you* just considered, O'Brien includes enough textual indicators (verbal moods, speech styles, rhetorical signatures, etc.) for interpreters to assort all these modalities of *you*—to situate their various discourse referents within the storyworld affiliated with the novel.

Form-Function Concord: Fictionalized and Apostrophic Address

However, there are other instances of *you* in which the form of the expression specifies instead of conflicting with its function, producing either fictionalized or apostrophic address. Especially in the case of apostrophic address, the second discourse model typically brought to bear on the study of second-person fiction begins to make its relevance felt. Unlike the first model, which informs accounts such as Genette's, Gerald Prince's, and Richardson's, the second model prompts me not to virtualize, but rather to actualize the entity referenced by *you*. More specifically, the model prompts me to interpret *you* neither as an instance of (self-)address nor as reference to O'Brien's fictional protagonist, but rather as an address to the actual audience—to me, the reader of this very text.

Note that insofar as interpretation of O'Brien's text activates this second discourse model at all, Richardson's classification of *A Pagan Place* as a standard versus "autotelic" second-person fiction is in jeopardy. Given that "The defining criterion of . . . 'the autotelic' . . . is the direct address to a 'you' that is at times the actual reader of the text and whose story is juxtaposed to, and can merge with, the characters of the fiction" (1991: 320)—and given that in such autotelic fictions "the 'you' continues to move, shift, double back, and change again, addressing alternately the real reader, the implied reader, and the narratee" (321)—O'Brien's novel might qualify as a "mixed" second-person fiction, one that oscillates between the standard and autotelic modes. Indeed, in *A Pagan Place* such oscillation is sometimes accelerated, as it were, whereby a single instance of the second-person pronoun (versus its pattern of usage in the fiction as a whole) cues readers both to actualize and to virtualize the entity designated by *you*—to construe *you* as doubly or indeterminately deictic, that is, as a form of direct address *and* as a reference (or address) to a fictional character. I return to doubly deictic *you* in my next subsection.

As for the subtype of narrative *you* entailing fictionalized address, its use is restricted to contexts of direct discourse. (Fictionalized *self*-address, however, can be only partly assimilated to contexts involving direct discourse. See note 23.) In such contexts a tag clause specifies that the *you* is being represented as an *utterance* issued by some participant in the discourse and thus as an actual term of address, rather than as a generalized or impersonal *you*, as a *you* standing in for an *I*, or as a *you* whose referent is ambiguous between fictional addressee and audience.

Passage 19 represents the mother's response to the news that the protagonist's sister, Emma, is pregnant.

19. [The mother] supplied a proverb: Sharper than a serpent's tooth is a thankless child. Then she looked at you and said Not *you* darling. (127-28, my emphasis)

Here the shift from the language of proverbs to direct discourse is in itself significant. After all, proverbial utterances either explicitly or implicitly invoke an impersonal *you*, and the generalized *you* of proverbs marks a different relation between grammatical form and deictic function than the relation marked by *you* operating strictly as a term of address. Later, when the narrator and her mother visit Emma in Dublin and the narrator finds Emma in a café, the narrator again uses *you* as a term of address, though in this case, it is true, the utterance forms part of a merely imagined scenario.

20. They played a waltz. It was slow and alluring and you longed to say to Emma Will *you* dance. (174, my emphasis)

Note that, because O'Brien omits quotation marks throughout the novel, in both passages 19 and 20 the author's use of an uppercase letter in midsentence typographically signals the advent of the direct discourse that in turn delimits the deictic functions of *you*. Such capitalization is not obligatory, however; the novel does not make things that easy for its readers. Thus, when the priest gets back from his missionary work in the South Seas and attempts to seduce the protagonist on a houseboat, readers have to infer just where direct discourse attaches a specific and localized addressee to *you*, that is, just where the *you* forms the representation of an interlocutor's utterance:

> 21. He sat on the edge of your seat, touched your knees a few times, then he unlaced your shoes, removed them, then your ankle socks. He said hadn't *you* better come down from *your* perch. (202, my emphases)

The other species of textual *you* characterized by agreement between grammatical form and deictic function is apostrophic *you*. Here, though, the address operates vertically instead of horizontally, directed toward an actual (storyworld-external) versus fictionalized (storyworld-internal) addressee. Indeed, an interpretive schema for actualizing *you* has been in place ever since the classical rhetoricians identified the figure of *apostrophe*. Its name derived from the Greek verb ἀποστρέφω— literally, "to turn away or aside"—the rhetorical figure of apostrophe designates those moments when "[t]he orator suddenly breaks off to address someone or something" (Dupriez 1991: 58). Originally, "[t]he term . . . referred to any abrupt 'turning away' from the normal audience to address a different or more specific audience, whether present (e.g., one person out of the assemblage) or absent" (Perrine 1974: 42). Here I opt for a somewhat more restricted sense of *apostrophe*, using *fictionalized address* to cover all modalities of address except those in which an apostrophic *you* directly designates the audience comprising readers of (or listeners to) a fiction. Those modalities of *you* ingeniously characterized by Irene Kacandes under the rubric of "literary performatives," in which "to *read* the address is to perform what one reads" (1993a: 141), may constitute the limit-case of apostrophic *you* (cf. Kacandes 1993b). As opposed to Calvino's *If on a Winter's Night a Traveler* (Kacandes 1993a; cf. Habermas 1988), however, in *A Pagan Place* strict apostrophic *you* is rare, perhaps even non-existent. Thus the two passages from O'Brien bearing on the slaughter of the pigs and on the embarrassment caused by your ridiculous coat, that is, examples 6 and 7, are arguably instances not of apostrophic *you*, in the strict sense, but rather of doubly deictic *you*, in which there is a superimposition of deictic roles. In this conflation of roles, as discussed in my next subsection, *you* compromises the boundary between the (virtual) fictional protagonist and the (actual) reader, rather than pointing beyond the fictional world to address those trying to make sense of it.

So far as I can tell, in *A Pagan Place* there is only one instance of *you* that could be classed, on a first reading at least, as apostrophic you. Example 22 represents the passage in question.

> 22. This is to warn you. Read this carefully.
> You received two anonymous letters. One said that a letter had been sent to inform the mistress of novices of the type of family you had come from. . . . The other begged you, implored you not to go [to the convent]. . . . (225)

The first sentence of passage 22 apparently has as its addressee the actual reader being warned and admonished to read (these very words) carefully. Felicitous interpretation of the sentence, it would seem, requires the enactment of what Kacandes (1993a) would call a literary performative, in which "[o]ne experiences the shock of being 'talked to' by the text" (147). Yet the rest of the quoted passage helps interpreters contextualize the first sentence as a (quoted) fictionalized address—as words anonymously written to the protagonist and now cited by her in retrospective narration—instead of a vertical address to the audience.

Though the passage therefore fails to support the initial reading of the *you* as apostrophic (in my restricted sense of that term), it does provide an occasion to mention an important issue connected with the concepts of apostrophe and address themselves. Bernard Dupriez (1991) observes that "[i]t also happens [in apostrophe] that addresses are made to a second person in the hope that they will be overheard by a third party, as when a mother asks her two-year-old child to look for the scissors, knowing that her husband is not far away. This produces a double actualization of the receiver" (59). The result—a more or less obvious substitution of an addressee for an audience also privy to the current speech situation—yields what might be termed covert apostrophe (or, alternatively, specious address). Yet Herbert H. Clark and Thomas B. Carlson (1982) have argued that in all speech situations involving more than two participants, *every* utterance achieves, more or less successfully, the "double actualization" described by Dupriez as a special case of apostrophic *you*. For Clark and Carlson all illocutionary acts performed in multiparty conversational situations derive (in terms of logical priority, not temporal sequence) from a class of metaperformative utterances "added to inform the participants of what is being performed" (1982: 361). Clark and Carlson call these metaperformative speech acts *informatives*, further defined as acts performed "by the speaker to make it known to the participants [i.e., "third parties" to the discourse such as the husband in Dupriez's example] what illocutionary act he is performing for the addressees" (350). Informatives are what account for interlocutors' ability to signal (without laboriously and egregiously explaining) to fellow conversationalists which utterances are designed to elicit a response from which participants when, such that the intended respondents can issue their rejoinders felicitously and so contribute to the ongoing collaborative construction of a discourse.

Would one thus be warranted in claiming that, in general, the illocutionary acts comprised by second-person fictions have the status of Clark and Carlson's informatives? Is not the (self-)address in second-person contexts specious address or covert apostrophe—address apparently confined to fictionalized addressees but in actual fact directed toward all the parties engaged in the communicative situation, including the readers who function as an audience in cases of fictionalized address? This hypothesis is interesting enough to call for a fuller investigation, particularly since O'Brien's novel, for example, thematizes the (meta-)illocutionary dynamics of informatives.[24] Thus at one point Emma "addressed you but it was for your mother to register" (119). When it comes to the illocutionary profile of the novel as a whole, however, the instances of narrative *you* that I am calling doubly deictic could be said to function not as an informatives but precisely as antiinformatives. Double deixis marks illocutionary overload, as it were, and instead of fostering strategic discriminations between specious and actual addressees, doubly deictic *you* is part of a (postmodern) discourse strategy that constructs addressee and audience, participant and nonparticipant, as deeply and irremediably interlinked (cf. Herman 1993: 183–86).

Form-Function Fuzziness: Double Deixis

The fifth usage of *you* to be considered here—doubly deictic *you*—is actually a hybridized usage blending the other discourse functions of the pronoun. Thus the perceptibility of doubly deictic *you* as a stylistic figure derives from its (fluctuating) position relative to a ground comprising the other functional subtypes already described. Neither a term of address nor *not* a term of address, doubly deictic *you* ranges over the middle portion of a continuum whose lower and upper limits, respectively, are marked by the two limit-cases of virtualized and actualized *you* (see figure 12). Hovering between these two extremes, double deixis ontologically destabilizes a modal system that can no longer be neatly divided into the virtual and the actual—into what is internal to the storyworld and what is external to it. Double deixis thus marks a more radical kind of ontological destabilization than does the phenomenon of *Deixis am Phantasma* (Bühler 1965: 133; Margolin 1984: 200, 1986/87: 197). Instead of a here-and-now speaker's imaginary and temporary relocation to an alternative system of space-time coordinates, double deixis produces an interference pattern between two or more competing deictic fields, none of which can fully orient the deictic transfers. Hence there is no longer any ultimate (non-imaginary) reference point anchoring localized and recognizably phantasmagoric shifts in space and time. To put this point another way, given that in its doubly deictic usage the grammatical form of *you* only partly specifies its deictic functions, such that the scope of the agreement between the form and function of *you* is in this case fuzzy or indeterminate, the second-person pronoun grafts the text *more or less* onto its context(s), superimposing the fictional protagonist/addressee *more or less* onto the audience. Thus double deixis might be described as a jointly derealized and devirtualized narrative *you*.

Consider the combination of particularized (and thus virtualized) with nonparticularized (and thus actualizable) experiences in passage 23, which describes a (non-) conversation between the protagonist and her sister:

> 23. Each time you were on the point of saying something to Emma the words got caught in your throat and you could neither say them nor forget them and you could not utter them. You were like someone with a muzzle. Emma must have thought it was enmity, because she stuck her tongue out at you. (119)

Like passage 8, the instance of doubly deictic *you* discussed above, passage 23 contains similes—in 8: "It was like something you had heard before"; in 23: "You were like someone with a muzzle." In both examples the comparisons more or less explicitly connect (or at least suggest the possibility of connecting) the particularized occurrences with more general experiences. Indeed, in cases of metaphor, where explicit markers of comparison are suppressed, what might otherwise be construed as a jointly particularizing and departicularizing effect of the second-

Contextual Anchoring 365

person pronoun is sometimes attenuated noticeably, even dissipated altogether, as in passage 24.

24. The sun and your heartbeat were far apart, the sun was a great gold fleshy orb, and your heart was a pump attending to its own bloodstream.[25] (141)

Here the metaphors, creating quite idiosyncratic conceptual blends (Turner 1996), give a particularizing force to *you*.

Contrast passage 25, in which an "as if" construction toward the end of the passage again functions as a cue for the doubly deictic projection of a fictional *you* onto the audience and vice versa:

25. You were saying goodbye to fields and to trees, and even to headlands of fields where a plow never got and where not an ear of barley had chanced to grow. In all these corners there were bits of things, machinery, broken delft, cowhorns that had served as funnels, machine oil tins and the rags and remnants that the scarecrows wore.

You felt a terrible burden as if something inanimate might speak or something motionless might get up and move. (231-32)

Again, the *you* in this passage cannot be *completely* reduced to the *you* encoding, either through reference to the fictional protagonist or through self-address, a participant who is located somewhere in the indexical field defining the storyworld. Yet the *you* does not stand in for *one*, either, since the amount of circumstantial detail built into the description—the inventory of the "bits of things" left in the corners of the fields, the partitioning of the scene into fields, trees, and headlands of fields—cannot be reconciled with the notion of an impersonal or generalized *you*, nor for that matter with an apostrophic *you* in the strict sense. Arguably, the deictic scope of the *you* encompasses more than a particularized addressee or storyworld participant, but stops short of including anyone whatsoever. The scope of *you* is modalized, as it were, such that it covers anyone who *might conceivably be* a participant in the discourse; *you* ranges over any context that *might be* activated and brought to bear on the discourse.

By the same token, interpreting doubly deictic *you* requires that both readers and narrative theorists abandon what William Hanks (1990) has characterized as the "assumption of egocentricity" in previous models for understanding deixis. A second-person fiction such as O'Brien's highlights, instead, "the sociocentricity of deictic reference" (Hanks 1990: 7; cf. Anderson and Keenan 1985: 277; Frawley 1992: 280; and

Levinson 1983: 64). For Hanks, referential practice reveals how "the speaking 'ego' [is itself] a social construction, [and how] the act of deictic reference is in important ways grounded on the relation between interlocutors," given that "interaction puts in play the reciprocity of perspectives, the production of mutual knowledge, conflict, and asymmetry" (7; cf. 192–254). Thus, "Deictic reference is a communicative practice based on a figure-ground structure joining a socially defined indexical ground, emergent in the process of interaction, and a referential focus articulated through culturally constituted schematic knowledge. To engage in referential practice is to locate oneself in the world, to occupy a position, however fleetingly, in one or more sociocultural fields" (514).

The doubly deictic *you* of second-person narration, similarly, forces interpreters to resituate deixis in an indexical field that shows itself to be culturally and communicatively saturated from the start. Extending the contextual parameters of discourse beyond the spatiotemporal coordinates occupied by current speaker and current addressee, doubly deictic *you* suggests that discourse participation is in some sense a more primitive notion than that of discourse participant. Thus, in processing O'Brien's narrative discourse, we (the audience) are able to adopt the role of participant precisely because discourse in general encodes reference to a set of potential addressees even when pointing to an actual addressee. The doubly deictic *you* of second-person narratives suggests that there *can be* an addressee just because there *could be* other addressees (cf. Bakhtin 1986: 99). In other words, what interlocutors and readers deem to be actual speech situations are just part of a larger network of (more or less) virtualized speech situations, toward which any current discourse is constantly tending and from which it never ceases to emerge. In this economy of speech, hearing can no longer be neatly distinguished from overhearing. We are eavesdroppers on the discourse that addresses us and beckoned by discourse addressed to others.

Table 15 sketches correlations between subtypes of narrative *you*, on the one hand, and the modal status of the discourse referents evoked by each usage, on the other hand. As table 15 begins to suggest, contextual anchoring in the case of second-person narration requires parsing occurrences of *you* and assigning—if the interpreter is working with a simplified, two-valued modal logic—virtual (storyworld-specific) or ac-

Table 15. Some Initial Parameters for Parsing Narrative *You*

	Virtualized (Storyworld-Internal Referent)	Actualized (Storyworld-External Referent)
Deictic transfer	*I* —> *you* transfer	Generalized *you*
Address	*You* as fictional address	Apostrophic *you*

Table 16. Additional Parameters for Parsing Narrative *You*

	Form /function concord*	Modal status**
I —> *you* transfer	-	-
Generalized *you*	-	+
Fictionalized address	+	-
Apostrophic *you*	+	+
Double deixis	+/-	+/-

* a negative value signifies disagreement; a positive value, agreement
** a negative value signifies virtuality; a positive value, actuality

tual (audience-specific) status to referents indexed by the pronoun. But this grid needs to be refined to reflect, first, the gradient way in which interpreters assign an actuality-status to referents of *you* and, second, the indeterminate modal status of some of those referents. For example, generalized *you* prompts recipients to actualize (i.e., assign a value of actual to) the pronoun's discourse referent to a greater degree than do instances of *I* → *you* deictic transfer (or self-address) enacted by a fictional protagonist. Thus, the discourse referent of *when you're hot, you're hot* is arguably more readily assimilated to the domain of the actual than the entity evoked by *you* in "Jewel was the teacher's pet the way *you* were your mother's" (O'Brien 51). But neither of these usages of *you* cues interpreters to actualize the referent of the pronoun to the degree that apostrophic *you* does. What is more, since it assumes a two-valued modal logic, table 15 cannot represent the position of doubly deictic *you* vis-à-vis the other four usages of the pronoun. As suggested by figure 12, instances of narrative *you* involving double deixis cannot be assigned an exact position on the scale that stretches from a fully virtualized to a fully actualized *you*, that is, from the referential to the address functions of the pronoun. Table 16, although it does not capture the scalar profile of the actuality-status assigned to any referent of *you*, does at least represent all five usages of narrative *you* along the two dimensions of form/function concord and modal status. As the "±" symbol indicates, the schema is based on a three-valued modal logic encompassing actual, virtual, and indeterminate.

Narrative, Narrative *You*, and Deictic Systems of a Higher Order

I have already suggested that the story logic of *A Pagan Place*, rich in implications for the study of deixis in language and narrative, involves not just double deixis but also metadeixis. Like linguistic theories of deixis, narrative *you* makes an issue of how texts attach themselves to—depend for their meaning on—contexts of interpretation (cf. Green 1989; Grice 1989; Levinson 1983). More specifically, the perceptibility and force of doubly deictic *you* derive from the way the pronoun calls attention to the nonrigidity, the permeability, of the border between texts and contexts. O'Brien's shifting usage of narrative *you* reveals that contexts of interpretation are dynamic and, as it were, vegetal, living and growing with the multiplicity of linguistic forms that they embed and in which they are embedded. Contexts thus resemble the lichen that you sometimes see growing on and through a wall, lichen that may have "passed into the body of the stone and . . . become part of it. There was white and green and rust-colored lichen and there were queer shapes, all wavery at the edges, like the borders of countries on the school map" (110).

This blurring of the border between texts and contexts, enacted both by linguistic research and by second-person narration, raises a question that has been implicitly orienting my discussion in this chapter. The question is this: Given that narrative *you* functions as part of a secondary modeling system, a higher-order deictic system that illuminates ways in which languages grammaticalize contexts, how does the study of second-person fiction bear on existing narratological theories? The short answer is that, like other narrative modes investigated in this book (e.g., polychronic narration, hypothetical focalization), second-person narration underscores the need to develop new tools for narratology,

Contextual Anchoring 369

particularly linguistic and discourse-analytic tools. Integrating such tools is a first step toward describing processes of contextual anchoring in narrative comprehension, let alone explaining them.

A fuller response to the question would necessitate taking into account issues broached by Brian Richardson in his work on second-person fiction. For Richardson, "a thorough poetics of fiction" written in the second person "could destroy the dream of a universal narratology" (1991: 314; cf. Richardson 1994, 1998). In arguing this claim, however, Richardson reproduces a distinction made by Russian Formalists (e.g., Shklovsky 1990) between poetic and practical uses of language, though with a terminological shift whereby *fictional* stands in for *poetic* and *factual* stands in for *practical*:

> For those theorists attempting to construct a universal narratology, capable of embracing all narratives, both factual and fictional, . . . [a] problem appears. First and third person novels have obvious non-fictional counterparts in autobiography and biography, but second person is an exclusively and distinctively literary phenomenon, its only non-fictional analogues being the pseudo-narrative forms of the cookbook, the travel guide and the self-help manual. The typical discourse of the standard second-person novel . . . has no precise non-fictional equivalent, and theories that ignore the distinction between fictional and factual narratives may bear their own refutation within them if they allow such a category in their analysis.[26] (Richardson 1991: 313–14)

Fludernik (1993c) has adduced evidence suggesting that second-person narration is not in fact "an exclusively and distinctively literary phenomenon," but one might dispute Richardson's claims in principle. Debatably, what distinguishes factual from fictional uses of discourse cannot be specified by recourse to an inventory of linguistic devices pertaining, unequivocally, to fictional but not factual discourse (cf. Pratt 1977). Factual and fictional uses of discourse are, rather, just that—uses of a single stock of linguistic resources but within different speech genres (Bakhtin 1986) marked by different conditions of production and reception. From this perspective, the (sub)genres "nonliterary narrative" and "literary narrative" involve different configurations of functional constraints placed on one and the same set of formal elements. Accordingly, the task for researchers is to develop narratological models comprehensive enough to accommodate, in one explanatory framework, natural-language as well as literary narratives. Avant-garde literary narratives such as *A Pagan Place* do afford specialized or higher-order modeling systems that illuminate the way narrative communication grounds itself in the structures of language. As I see it, however, the onus is on those critical of "universal narratology" to demonstrate that fundamentally different cognitive processes are indeed involved during the comprehension of narratives in different speech genres—such as oral narratives versus written ones, or literary narratives versus written but nonliterary ones, or relatively sophisticated literary narratives versus relatively unsophisticated ones.[27] That said, researchers would do well to study processes of contextual anchoring across all these narrative formats, for the investigation of new problem domains can only facilitate the building of a richer, more integrative narratology of the sort proposed in this book.

In any event, rather than jeopardizing the project of a universal narratology, the formal innovations characteristic of second-person fiction can be seen as enabling that project, compelling researchers to enrich the study of narrative discourse with state-of-the-art theories about discourse in general. If anything, description and analysis of narrative *you* require a *strengthened* commitment to investigating the relations between narrative form and universal grammar—between the stylistic innovations of texts such as *A Pagan Place*, on the one hand, and theories about the deictic profile and address functions of linguistic expressions, on the other hand. I would thus reinflect in a more positive way Margolin's (1984) comments about what he terms the "low narrative intelligibility of modernist and postmodernist narratives" (184), given the manner in which they sometimes purposely impede or disrupt the process of contextual anchoring. Granted, varieties of narrative *you* sometimes undercut interpreters' attempts to co-create storyworlds, making it difficult or even impossible for them to establish the exact position of those storyworlds vis-à-vis the here-and-now of the act of interpretation. It is a different question, though, whether such narrative techniques contribute to a wholesale "denarrativisation of the domain of reference," yielding "an unordered, free floating set of possible world states" (184). Which formulation is preferable: that the mercurial profile of narrative *you* in second-person fictions results in low intelligibility, a diminishment of their overall narrativity, or rather, that use of an irreducibly plural *you* enhances stories' ability to signal the problems and possibilities of narrative itself, giving them a higher capacity for secondary modeling? Are these formulations semantically equivalent, the narratological counterpart to saying that the glass is half empty or the glass is half full? Such questions, though they have emerged from my inquiry into contextual anchoring, also form part of the general horizon for narratology after structuralism, defining boundary conditions for future frameworks for narrative analysis. Indeed, the primary of aim of the present chapter, like this book as a whole, has been to sketch out just these horizons of inquiry. My hope is that this chapter and the preceding ones have helped chart directions for further research on what sort of thing (or, better, process) a story is; what linguistic or semiotic formats narrative requires, prefers, and disprefers; and how stories enable human beings to make sense of themselves, one another, and the world.

Notes

INTRODUCTION

1. See chapter 3 for a discussion of some of this artificial-intelligence-oriented work on narrative.

2. See the papers collected in Mateas and Sengers (1999) for an assessment of the challenges involved. See also Murray (1997) and Ryan (2000) for additional information on relevant technical and conceptual issues.

3. Hence, in my usage, the term *storyworld* can be defined as a specialized discourse model, making it possible to interpret discourse as narratively organized; storyworlds can be distinguished from other sorts of discourse models used to interpret other kinds of discourse, including syllogistic arguments, exchanges of insults, recipes, sermons, and essays. *Storyworld* and *discourse model* should therefore *not* be construed as cognate terms for what narratologists like Seymour Chatman (1978), inspired by the work of Gérard Genette (1980), have called *story* and *discourse*—i.e., *what* is being told about and the *way* it is told. See the subsequent discussion for a fuller account of the story/discourse distinction, as well as a fuller specification of storyworlds as a particular type of discourse model.

4. In this study, I argue for probabilistic, preference-based correlations between (sets of) textual cues and the storyworlds that they prompt interpreters to reconstruct. In other words, whereas I agree that the surface structure of a text does not *define* that text as a narrative, my working assumption is that there are principled, nonrandom relations between textual cues and the processing strategies that make a text or a discourse recognizably narrative in nature.

5. Hence, for Mandler (1984), a story grammar should be distinguished from a story schema: "A story grammar is a rule system devised for the purpose of describing the regularities found in one kind of text. The rules describe the units of which stories are composed, that is, their constituent structure, and the ordering of the units, that is, the sequences in which the constituents appear. A story schema, on the other hand, is a mental structure consisting of sets of expectations about the way in which stories proceed" (18).

6. See chapter 4, for instance, for an effort to use ideas from functional grammar and linguistic semantics to outline constraints on the variable patterning of storyworld participants with narrative-pertinent roles.

7. I defer until chapter 4 a discussion of the parallels between storyworlds and what A. J. Greimas (1983) called "semantic microuniverses." Constituted in part by the set of participant roles structuring a given story, Greimas's semantic microuniverses are manageable, cognizable models of the world that narrative enables language users to carve out of the "immanent semantic universe," which consists of a limitless combinatorial matrix of sememes—i.e., minimal units of meaning based on various contrastive relations.

8. Chapters 6, 7, and 9 all revisit, from different perspectives, the functions of deixis in narrative, with deixis broadly definable as the anchoring of language (via expressions such as *here, I, now*) to specific contexts of utterance. All three chapters explore narrative-theoretical implications of the notions of *deictic center* and *deictic shift* in particular.

9. See Doležel (1998: 16–24) and Ronen (1994) for accounts of the differences between the possible worlds of logic and philosophy and the fictional worlds of literature.

10. See Doležel (1999: 256–61) for an account of the contrasts between the "macromorphologies" of fictional and historical worlds. For example, whereas fiction makers can call into existence a world of any type, historical worlds are restricted to those that are physically possible.

11. For his part, Philip E. Agre (1997), in a study that bears importantly on many of the issues explored in this book, critiques what he terms "the cult of cognition" (3) in computational theories of action developed under the auspices of research in the field of artificial intelligence (or AI). Agre's stated aim is "to orient research in AI away from cognition—abstract processes in the head—and toward *activity*—concrete undertakings in the world" (4). Here, however, I assume that the mental models supporting narrative comprehension require interpreters to construe storyworld entities and individuals *as situated*—i.e., as embroiled in a space-time context that is at once physically, historically, and socially or interactionally constituted. Hence a commitment to studying the cognitive dimensions of story logic does not, in my view, entail blind obedience to a cult of cognition.

12. For Johnson-Laird (1983), however, what can be called "the principle of finitism" constraining mental models serves to distinguish them from the possible worlds associated with model-theoretic semantics, for example. The principle of finitism, based on the assumption that the brain is a finite organism with considerable but not unlimited processing power, dictates that "[a] mental model must be finite in size and cannot directly represent an infinite

domain" (398; cf. 433–35). By contrast, the set of possible worlds does constitute an infinite domain.

But as Johnson-Laird acknowledges (167–81), possible-worlds theory can supplement a mental-models approach to the semantics of natural language. Specifically, "model-theoretic semantics should specify what is computed in understanding a sentence, and psychological semantics should specify how it is computed" (167). Thus, in chapter 8, I return to ideas drawn from possible-worlds semantics to suggest the complexity of the information that interpreters must sometimes compute in order to reconstruct how a storyworld is perspectivally filtered.

13. Actually, as Rolf A. Zwaan (1996: 243–45) notes, much recent work on language comprehension assumes that texts can be understood on three levels during and after comprehension: the *surface structure*, or a "verbatim representation of the surface form of the text" (243), thought to be a transient phenomenon during the process of comprehension; the propositional *textbase*, or a representation of the semantic meaning of the text; and the *situation model*, or a representation of the situation that the text is about, and "an amalgamation of information obtained from the text and inferences constructed by the reader" (244; cf. Kronfeld 1990). In this scheme, the notion of *mental model* would be congruent with that of *situation model*. Cf. Johnson-Laird (1983: 407).

14. McKoon et al. (1993: 58) draw a distinction between models of (relations between) entities explicitly mentioned in a discourse and mental models taken in a broader sense—i.e., models supporting inferences about (relations between) entities *not* explicitly mentioned. In this book, I construe discourse models as a type of mental model. See Walker, Joshi, and Prince (1998) for other recent attempts to fix the scope of discourse models and to specify the nature and relations between discourse entities. Also, chapter 9 returns to the idea of discourse models in discussing the nature of the entities evoked by textual *you* in second-person narration.

15. For a theory of narrative understanding based not on mental (or discourse) models but on strategies for problem solving, see, for example, Trabasso and van den Broek (1985), Trabasso and Sperry (1985), and Fletcher, van den Broek, and Arthur (1996). In this last-mentioned study, the authors argue that "the meaning of a narrative text is represented in long-term memory as a network. The nodes of this network represent the individual clauses of the text, whereas the links represent causal and enabling relations among those clauses. . . . This model assumes that comprehension is a problem-solving process. Understanding an individual clause requires that the reader discover its causal antecedents and consequences. . . . Understanding the text

as a whole requires that the reader find a causal path that links its opening... to its final outcome" (142-44).

16. For a fuller synopsis of Emmott's important—indeed, pathbreaking—account, see Herman (1998e).

17. In this sentence I use the phrase *narrative imagining* in the sense specified by Mark Turner (1996: 26-37) and spelled out in greater detail in chapter 1. In this context narrative imagining means the use of familiar story patterns to conceptualize more or less novel situations.

18. See Herman (1998c), however, for arguments against overvaluing the logic that stories *are* vis-à-vis the logic that stories *have*. Both dimensions of story logic deserve careful study.

19. Similarly, in David Francis and Christopher Hart's (1997) account, "Ethnomethodological studies of texts have analysed them as situated accomplishments of commonsense knowledge" (123; cf. Hester and Eglin 1997; Polkinghorne 1988: 13-36, 125-55; Schiffrin 1994: 232-39). Herman (in preparation) examines the story logic of oral narratives, using ethnomethodological concepts (among other analytical tools) to explore the situated production of narratives that *do* emerge from face-to-face interaction.

1. STATES, EVENTS, AND ACTIONS

1. As discussed below, there are grounds for dividing not states from events, but rather stative from nonstative *types* of events. In turn, actions can be characterized as a specific sort of (executable and deliberately initiated) event. Further, even though it makes actions a crucial part of narrative, I believe that the account offered here avoids the androcentrism that Susan Sniader Lanser (1991) has detected in (classical) narratology. Lanser's argument is that action-oriented models of plot do not provide adequate descriptive (let alone explanatory) tools for many narratives written by women—given that these narratives often focus on the inability of participants to act. In this book, however, I define *action* in the rather narrow sense used in linguistic semantics and philosophical theories of action, i.e., as any intendedly begun and executable event, more or less temporally bounded or unitized. From this perspective, the concept of action is a way of capturing the rich semantic profile of storyworlds, whose changes of state can be coded via several types of nonstative propositions (e.g., causes and motions, as well as actions).

2. Richard J. Gerrig (1993), however, reports recent empirical work suggesting that even though everyone makes inferences about causality in interpreting stories, "readers [or listeners] are not automatically keeping a character's goals active in the moment-by-moment experience of a narrative world" (36; cf. 53-63).

3. Like Ray Jackendoff (1983: 128–58; cf. Lerdahl and Jackendoff 1983; Jahn 1997, 1999), William Frawley (1992: 56–58) associates preference rules with gradient and prototypical situations, properties, and relations, as opposed to absolute, "either-or" situations, properties, and relations. Thus, taking the (gradient) semantic property of punctuality as an example, Frawley defines a preference rule as "a statement in probabilistic form of the relative strength of two or more items for interpretation relative to some property or properties. To be interpreted punctually, *wink* is preferred over *punch*, which in turn is preferred over *slide off*, notationally, *wink punch slide off*" (57).

In his own, pathbreaking account of the ubiquity of preference-rule systems, which can be seen to operate in areas as apparently diverse as musical compositions, taxonomical classifications, and the grammar of verbs, Jackendoff (1983) identifies five symptoms of systems of preference rules: "(1) judgments of graded acceptability and of family resemblance; (2) two or more rules, neither of which is necessary, but each of which is under certain conditions sufficient for a judgment; (3) balancing effects among rules that apply in conflict; (4) a measure of stability based on rule applications; (5) rules that are not logically necessary used as default values in the face of inadequate information" (152). Preference-rule systems thus require a shift from the idea of *necessary and sufficient conditions* associated with binarized, either-or judgments about a thing's membership in a class or its possession of particular attributes, to *typicality conditions* that work in a gradient way. Thus, it is typical but neither necessary nor sufficient for members of the class "bird" to have the attribute "capable of flight." In the chapters that follow, I discuss genre-based preference rankings for several aspects of narrative structure, including degrees of boundedness of states, actions, and events (this chapter); degrees of explicitness of action representations (chapter 2); and degrees of probability for the fusing of two or more participant roles in one storyworld entity (chapter 4).

4. See Herman (1999a) for a synopsis and critique of Turner's model.

5. For her part, Marie-Laure Ryan (1991: 129–35) makes a threefold distinction between *happenings*, *actions*, and *moves*, with moves being a specific type of action. While actions are deliberately targeted toward a goal and have a voluntary human or human-like agent, happenings occur accidentally, having a patient but not an animated agent. Moves, further, are conflict-solving actions "with a high-priority goal and a high risk of failure" (130). In Ryan's scheme, moves bear the focus of narrative interest and should be distinguished from incidental or habitual doings.

6. Davidson (1985) suggests that there is no way to answer this question, even in principle: "I think that by and large how we put the world together is

how it is put together, there being no way, error aside, to distinguish between these constructions" (172).

7. To this extent, Vendler's approach can be aligned with other developments in twentieth-century language theory that hearken back to the great speculative grammars developed by medieval scholars such as Thomas of Erfurt in the early fourteenth century. These grammars assumed a correspondence between *res* (things), *vox* (voice, language), and *intellectus* (mind). See Herman (1995a: 4–34) for details.

For a more ontologically parsimonious approach, which denies that events are basic items in the universe, see Jonathan Bennett's (1988) arguments for the view that events are "supervenient," i.e., so constituted that "all the truths about them are logically entailed by and *explained* or made *true by* truths that do not involve the event concept" (12). Terence Parsons (1990: 12–19) reviews evidence in favor of the (counter)argument that events exist, including the behavior of grammatical modifiers, the nature of perceptual idioms, and the tendency of people to engage in more or less explicit talk about events. For her part, Judith Felson Duchan (1986) points to communicative disorders that derive from an inability to use tense and aspectual markers, conjunctions, and other grammatical resources to describe, sequence, and causally link events.

8. In a subsequent refinement of his model, Labov (1997) introduces the new concept of sequential clause, defined as a particular type of independent clause whose head must indicate a specific time domain and that identifies sequential time relations. A narrative clause can then be said to consist of a sequential clause with all the subordinate clauses that are dependent on it. Labov acknowledges that the past progressive tense (i.e., an imperfective tense) can head sequential clauses; as a result, accomplishments and not just achievements might be categorized as constituents of narrative clauses. Yet Labov defines sequential clauses in a manner that still seems to suggest a preference for punctual verbs: "In English, sequential clauses are headed by verbs in the preterit tense, past progressive, or the present tense with the semantic interpretation of a preterit (historical present)" (1997: 400).

9. I have edited out transcriptional details in presenting this example, e.g., some of those designed to capture intonational patterns and stress. See Herman (2000a) for a fuller discussion and more detailed transcription.

10. For an account of the ideological dimensions of such coding strategies, see the work of Norman Fairclough (1989, 1995) and other proponents of critical discourse analysis.

11. I am grateful to Brian McHale for drawing my attention to the important issues that I have tried to address (or at least allude to) in this paragraph.

12. William Frawley (1992) distinguishes between "pure processes in which entities change states, or enter into a new state from an old one—*inchoatives*—and processes that necessarily come to an end—*resultatives*" (183).

13. Frawley (1992: 146) notes that his own list of event types is meant to be representative rather than exhaustive, there being other (more or less language-specific) classes of events besides acts, states, causes, and motion.

14. Frawley (1992: 149–95) proposes several diagnostic tests for the difference between actives and statives in English. For example, actives tend to allow the progressive, whereas statives do not (*Joe was stealing the money* versus *Joe was being involved in the stealing of the money*). Other tests include sensitivity to pseudo cleft constructions (*What X did was Y*), the what-happened question, the imperative, and the adverbs *carefully* and *deliberately*. For his part, Jan van Voorst (1988) argues that states are not processes going on in time, in contrast to nonstative activities. As van Voorst puts it, "Nonstative constructions mark an event and exhibit event structure. Stative constructions do not mark an event but imply the predication of a property" (15).

15. Thus, in a footnote (148 n. 2) Frawley remarks that actives, insofar as they are characterized by internal heterogeneity and boundedness in time (= "unitized"), can be likened to entities conceptually and to count nouns (*tree, woman*) grammatically. By contrast, statives are characterized by internal homogeneity and continuousness and are unbounded in time just like mass nouns are unbounded in space (e.g., *water, space*).

16. In this connection, see van Voorst's (1988) attempt to analyze events not by way of time schemata but spatially, as grammatically coded phenomena delimited by a spatially located object of origin or actualization and a parallel object of termination.

17. By "naturalistic," I mean to suggest, not the conventions associated with French or American Naturalism, but rather storyworlds in which natural or physical laws can be assumed to be valid.

18. See Mark Turner's (1996: 140–68) argument that humans' capacity to use language originated not through a process of genetic specialization, but rather through principles of narrative imagining or, in Turner's scheme, parable.

19. See Herman (2001b) for arguments along these lines. No blanket judgment, however, can be made about the scalability of linguistic constructs vis-à-vis higher, discourse-level structures. In some cases, cognitive processes brought to bear on clause- and sentence-level structures *do* seem to be scalable—i.e., extendable to higher levels of narrative structure. Thus chapter 4 argues that theories about the semantic roles of clause and sentence elements

capture important dimensions of the process by which interpreters make inferences about (emergent) participant roles in stories.

20. I delivered an earlier version of a portion of this chapter at the 1999 meeting of the Modern Language Association, for a session on "Cognitive Linguistics and the Future of Linguistic Criticism." I am grateful to Marie-Laure Ryan, Joyce Tolliver, Mark Turner, and especially Brian McHale for comments on my talk. Also, several members of the audience whose names I do not know made suggestions that helped me improve the chapter.

2. ACTION REPRESENTATIONS

1. Indeed, as Therese Budniakiewicz (1992) notes, "The differentiation between events-processes and events-actions is one of the most difficult and complex tasks faced by theories of human behavior, theories built within the social sciences, philosophy, psychology, and logic" (40).

2. Hence, though the same information could in principle be expressed propositionally, a film might rely solely on images of a person with a wobbly gait to represent his or her being in a (temporary) state of drunkenness. Without any assistance from the sound track, the viewer of the film is perfectly able to process this sequence of images as encoding the person's current state. Similarly, a prior sequence might visually encode the action(s) that led from an initial state of sobriety to a terminal state of drunkenness, and a later sequence might cue reconstruction of events associated with being drunk, e.g., an onset of slurred speech or a loss of decision-making capabilities.

3. In Frawley's (1992) terms, entities can be "viewed as relatively atemporal individuals in conceptual space, typically, but not necessarily, taking the forms of nouns," whereas "events, [or] temporally sensitive relations in conceptual space, [include] states, processes, acts, and conditions of existence, again typically, but not necessarily, surfacing as verbs" (197). In chapter 4, I again draw on Frawley's work and other linguistic research to explore how entities or individuals can carry out or, more generally, play a role in events in storyworlds.

4. See, in this connection, Arthur C. Danto's (1985: 238–45) contrast between the "explanation sketches" used in scientific investigations of general physical laws and the "narrative explanations" used to account for particularized actions and sequences of actions performed by agents in history.

5. Labov groups together negatives, questions, imperatives, and hypotheticals under the category of *comparators*, which he contrasts with constructions falling within three other categories of evaluative devices, *intensifiers*, *correlatives*, and *explicatives* (1972a: 378–93).

6. Similarly, the *Beowulf* poet helps the audience measure the significance

of Beowulf's death by poignant allusions to what will *not* be done with the treasures once guarded by the dragon that Beowulf and Wiglaf barely manage to slay: "These shall the fire devour, flames enfold—no earl to wear ornament in remembrance, nor any bright maiden add to her beauty with neck-ring; but mournful-hearted, stripped of gold, they [the Geats] shall walk, often, not once, in strange countries—now that the army-leader has laid aside laughter, his game and his mirth" (1993: 66).

7. My use of the term *open* is different from Umberto Eco's usage in *The Open Work* (1989). For Eco a work is open to the degree that it is purposely designed to require an interpreter or performer or addressee to bring it to completion. Meanwhile, the (gradient) distinction of open/specified outlined here is closer in spirit to Lubomír Doležel's (1998: 169–84) idea of saturated/ unsaturated than Eco's notion of open/closed. Degrees of openness, for me, refer to the extent to which a narrative enables readers, listeners, or viewers to "fill in" action representations that are intrinsically underspecified by textual cues. No narrative totally and exhaustively encodes actions; they all require readers to co-construct the story. But some stories make it easier than others to reconstruct parameters of action not explicitly specified via textual cues.

8. See chapter 5 for more on Grice's pragmatic theories.

9. I do not mean to imply, in this paragraph, that people cannot share general concepts of act-types—e.g., those of changing a tire, borrowing money, or insulting a supervisor at work. Denying the existence of such general concepts would be tantamount to radical relativism of a sort inconsistent with the claims set out in chapter 3, for example. What I *am* hypothesizing is that *shared styles of narrative imagining* do much to account for people's ability to carve up the flux of experience into commonly recognized (sequences of) actions.

10. Note that by equating biography with life *description*, von Wright to some extent begs the question of the relation between narrative and description. See Chatman (1990); Genette (1976); Hamon (1981, 1982); Herman (forthcoming); Kittay (1981a, 1981b); and chapter 7 of this book.

11. Along these lines, accounts of both the *Anchluss* and Edna Pontellier's awakening would no doubt have to be accounted for by way of molecular versus atomic narratives—even though for the sake of simplicity I presented both of these examples as if they lent themselves to explanation by way of atomic narratives.

12. Discussions with R. Michael Young have helped me articulate the ideas developed in this paragraph. For relevant research, see Young (1996, 1997, 1999a, 1999b) and Young, Pollack, and Moore (1994).

13. Monika Fludernik (1996: 26–35, 311–33), for example, defines narrativ-

ity as a scalar property by virtue of which texts will be more or less amenable to the process of "narrativization," or the "re-cognization of a text as narrative" (313). Further, Fludernik situates narrativity "in an organic frame of embodied and evaluative experientiality" (322), such that texts in which it is least possible to discern (or impute) some sort of evaluation of the *experiential quality* of the occurrences being narrated will display the least narrativity. Chapter 3 presents a different account of (degrees of) narrativity.

3. SCRIPTS, SEQUENCES, AND STORIES

1. As the closing paragraphs of chapter 2 indicated, sequences of actions (in the strict sense) must be interwoven with states and events to qualify as narrative. Thus, when I refer to *action sequences* or *sequences of events* I use that phrase as shorthand for *sequences of actions intermixed with states and events*.

2. Over the course of this chapter, the term *script* in fact takes on a number of meanings, spanning not only the narrower sense originally imputed to it by researchers in cognitive science and AI, but also a broader sense (or range of senses) stemming from my efforts to map the script concept into narrative- and literary-theoretical contexts. In its narrower sense, I use *script* to denote the stereotyped sequences of actions that form a crucial part of human beings' knowledge about the world. In a broader usage, the term *script* highlights the links between prestored, dynamic knowledge representations bound up with everyday life (e.g., those associated with switching on a computer or ordering French fries) and the stereotypic plot structures that readers use to anticipate the unfolding story logic of literary works written in different periods and genres. Hence this chapter aims not only to enrich narrative theory with research on scripts but also to enrich the script concept by exploring its applicability to central problems of narrative and literary theory.

3. For ontogenetic accounts of the growth of humans' ability to use and understand narratives, see, for example, Michael G. W. Bamberg (1987, 1997b) and Carole Peterson and Allyssa McCabe (1983). For a phylogenetic account of the emergence of narrative abilities in the human species, see Lynda MacNeil (1996).

4. For an ambitious and illuminating synthesis of the synchronic/cognitive and diachronic/literary-historical approaches, see Fludernik's *Towards a 'Natural' Narratology* (1996), a watershed publication in the field of narratology after structuralism.

5. Heating instructions are for Red Baron Premium 4-Cheese Frozen Pizza.

6. Teun A. van Dijk's (1981) characterization of episodes as discourse units

can be compared with AI accounts of scripts, as can Mandler's (1984) account of episodes as elements of *story schemas*, or mental structures "consisting of sets of expectations [specifically] about the way in which stories proceed" (18; cf. Arthur C. Graesser, Scott P. Robertson, and Patricia A. Anderson 1981; Graesser and Leslie F. Clark 1985: 189–244; Tom Trabasso and Linda L. Sperry 1985; and Trabasso and Paul van den Broek 1985). Mandler makes a further distinction between story schemas and *story grammars*, or rule systems "devised for the purpose of describing the regularities" found in narratives (18). For more on the possibilities and limits of story grammars and schemas, see, for example, John B. Black and Gordon H. Bower (1980: 223–50), Bertram Bruce (1978, 1980, 1983), Nancy L. Stein (1982), Perry W. Thorndyke (1977), Robert Wilensky (1982). (See also note 13 below.) Branigan (1992: 1–32) provides a useful overview of much of this work.

For more on the history of the concepts of *schema*, *script*, and *frame* in the context of AI research, see Philip E. Agre (1997), Daniel Crevier (1993), and Roger C. Schank (1990). For information on recent developments in AI-based approaches to text interpretation, see Bruce K. Britton and Arthur C. Graesser (1996) and Paul S. Jacobs and Lisa F. Rau (1993).

7. Along with researchers such as Black and Bower (1980), Bruce (1980, 1983), Rachel Giora and Yeshayahu Shen (1994: 450–51), Thomas Pavel (1985a: 14, 17–24), Propp (1968: 25–65), and Ryan (1991: 124–47), I hold that being able to process sequences of actions and events as narratives requires more than just the ability to situate reportable occurrences against a background of stereotypic knowledge. Narrative processing arguably requires, too, the ability to make textually cued inferences about participants' ongoing motivations, goals, and plans (cf. Herman 2000a). Richard J. Gerrig (1993), however, describes some empirical experiments whose results may militate against this claim (36, 53–63).

8. See chapter 4 for a more extensive treatment of the potentials and problems of Greimas's theory of actants.

9. For her part, Emma Kafalenos (1995, 1997, 1999) has engaged in an illuminating attempt to reduce Propp's scheme to eleven functions that better reveal "the general situations underlying the specific conditions of the stories [Propp] studied" (1995: 119). Kafalenos (1999) suggests that events can be assigned an interpretation by virtue of their place within a larger configuration of events. But the question remains (and, as suggested by William O. Hendricks 1967, it seems to be a version of the classic bootstrapping problem): how do interpreters assemble events into narratively organized configurations, since the meaning of individual events cannot be known without knowledge of an overarching configuration (cf. Bruner 1991: 7–11)?

10. In her discussion of some of the limitations of narrative grammars developed in the broadly Proppian tradition, Ryan (1991: 211–22) has shown how a system of plot representation devised by Wendy Lehnert (1981), an AI researcher, better captures the functional polyvalence of narrative events.

11. Although at times my discussion invokes the somewhat broader concepts of "world knowledge" and "world models," which encompass both script-like (dynamic) and frame-like (static) knowledge structures, my primary focus throughout the chapter is on standardized *sequences* of events.

12. For Schank and Abelson (1977) novel situations require more general planning mechanisms built into human intelligence. See, also, Ralph Grishman (1986: 146–47) and, for a plan-based model of discourse production and processing, R. Michael Young (1996, 1997, 1999b).

13. This same example bears out Robert Scholes's (1974) claim that "narrative, as an experience for the audience, is teleological. It is the target which has provoked the arrow and not the arrow which has sought the target" (100).

14. Problems of this sort motivate Wilensky's (1982) critique of the "story grammar enterprise" and his arguments for dissociating narrative from language. This book argues instead that the notion "story" refers to mental objects that tend probabilistically to collocate with certain classes of linguistic—or, more broadly, semiotic—objects. The textual or semiotic objects consist of cues for the reconstruction of the mental objects making up storyworlds.

15. From this perspective, frequently recurring plots may be redescribed as canonical sequences (i.e., configurations of states, events, and actions) with an especially high degree of tellability. Not all versions or instantiations of those plots, however, will possess equal degrees of narrativity. As discussed in chapter 2, Ryan (1991: 148–74) argues that a plot gains in tellability in proportion with the number of virtual embedded narratives it contains.

16. On the basis of empirical studies involving 103 high-school-age subjects of both sexes, Giora and Shen (1994) have argued that degrees of narrativity can be correlated with the type of organizational principle that predominates within a given (narrative) text. At issue are three such principles—action structure, causal structure, and temporal structure—and Giora and Shen's results suggest "that readers judge narratives which exhibit Causal connectivity as better examples of narrative than the ones which exhibit Temporal connectivity, and that they prefer texts which exhibit Action structure over both Temporal and Causal structures" (451). Giora and Shen's model owes much to AI-oriented research on narrative, insofar as the "psychological whole termed here Action structure is typically characterized as consisting of a goal-oriented/Problem-solving structure" (450–51). Cf. Black and Bower (1980), Bruce (1980, 1983), Mandler (1984), Pavel (1985a), and Ryan (1991).

17. Here, as in chapter 2, I echo Giora and Shen (1994) in defining an action structure as "a higher-order organization which hierarchically connects not only adjacent events . . . but also events which are remote from one another on the temporal axis of a given discourse. Thus a story . . . is more than pairwise relationships among events, but rather, a string of events combined into a psychological whole" (450; cf. Rummelhart 1975).

18. Prince's point is that narratives may be expressed in different media (film, dance, language, etc.), and conversely that nonnarratives can also be expressed in such media. Furthermore, given that "a narrative, a non-narrative poem, or an essay may deal with the same subjects and develop the same themes" (1980a: 51), what Hjelmslev would call the substance of the content side does not define narrative as such, either.

19. See the important work of May Charles (1995), who has studied how readers draw on world knowledge and text models to construct fictional worlds.

20. Thus Diderot's text at times displays the kind of radical uncertainty promoted through the narrative techniques of later writers such as Kafka (1984a, 1986; cf. Herman 1995a: 124–38). Both Diderot's and Kafka's texts trace the *lower* limit of narrativity characterized in the previous section. Bounding narrative, on this side, are sequences of states, events, and actions that refuse to be configured into action structures supporting narrative comprehension. Such sequences represent not just "breaches" of canonical patterns of behavior, but rather a concerted, pervasive undermining of the scripts and frames on which those canons are based.

21. This point can be put the other way around: it is because 17 relates in certain ways to a certain class of scripts that readers give it the generic label of autobiography.

22. I am grateful to Emma Kafalenos, Harold Mosher Jr., Susan Moss, Thomas Pavel, Gerald Prince, and Marie-Laure Ryan for their invaluable feedback on earlier versions of this chapter. Special thanks to Eric Wirth for helping me revise, quite extensively, a later version. In the meantime, the chapter has benefited from discussions of planning, computation, and related matters with R. Michael Young.

4. PARTICIPANT ROLES

1. A preliminary methodological note: The placement of the present chapter suggests that I conceive of participant roles and relations as narrative microdesigns, but as the chapter proceeds it will confirm that the microdesign/macrodesign distinction itself serves mainly a heuristic function in my account—here as elsewhere in the book. It is true that, within any tem-

poral slice of a storyworld, a participating individual or entity is precisely that—*an* individual or entity, and hence a local rather than global aspect of the storyworld. Part of the point of my chapter, however, is that tracking participants through storyworlds emergent in time involves a sorting and matching procedure that bears on three sets of inferences: (a) those concerning participants' roles and relations in a current time slice; (b) those pertaining to their roles and relations in a previous phase of the storyworld; and (c) those framed to anticipate the roles and relations more or less likely to obtain in a future time slice. Thus participant roles and relations are based on a reciprocity of microdesigns and macrodesigns, or parts and wholes, in narrative. They have a particular current status because of their history and their future.

2. Gerald Prince (1982: 71) anticipates some of these lines of connection.

3. As discussed in chapter 1, narrative-pertinent distinctions need to be drawn between processes and events and between different types of events (e.g., unbounded events versus deliberately initiated actions). Thus, in characterizing participants as individuals or entities involved in processes, I am speaking in a shorthand way of modes of participation that will need to be specified more finely. Sydney M. Lamb (1999: 159), furthermore, distinguishes between events as instances of processes and processes as categories of events. Events are realized linguistically as clauses, processes as verbs.

4. Thus, to state the focus of the present chapter more precisely, I am in principle concerned with three sets of roles and relations: relations between various participants in a storyworld, relations between participants and nonparticipants or circumstances, and relations between various nonparticipants.

5. As these comments indicate, the approach that I develop in this chapter borrows from Catherine Emmott's (1997) suggestive account of characters in narrative as entity representations of a special sort. As Emmott discusses, although recipes are like stories insofar as both require updating of entity representations (e.g., eggs might have to be represented as intact initially but then as split into the yolk and the white), "characters [in narratives] require more complex representations in view of the fact that they have intentions and awareness, as well as past histories and personalities and relations to other characters" (38).

6. As indicated by the example of discourse anaphora just mentioned, I make a further assumption: namely, that not only are clause- and sentence-level processing strategies capable of being *scaled to* the discourse level, but they also *interact with*, and are in part *determined by*, processes required to make sense of extended discourse. Further, I refer here (and throughout) to theories of clauses *and* sentences because linguists disagree about which of

these two units of grammatical organization should be the primary focus of analysis. A basic definition of *clause* is David Crystal's (1997): a unit smaller than the sentence, but larger than phrases, words, or morphemes (62).

7. Indeed, Greimas sometimes equivocates on this issue, remarking at one point that "[a]n actor functions as an actant only when it is put into play by *either narrative syntax or linguistic syntax*" (1987: 114, my emphasis).

8. Herman (2000b) situates structuralist theories of actants in a larger complex of cultural and intellectual forces, including an Existentialist distrust of psychology as a resource for explaining human behavior.

9. To get a sense of just how influential Propp's text was, see, for example, Bremond (1973) and Todorov (1977a, 1977b). For more recent work drawing inspiration from Propp, see Emma Kafalenos's (1995, 1997, 1999) function-analytic approach to narrative interpretation. On the Aristotelian subordination of character to plot, see Aristotle (1971: 52) and Rimmon-Kenan (1983: 34).

10. As Barthes (1977) put it in his 1966 "Introduction to the Structuralist Analysis of Narratives," noting that in Aristotelian poetics "the notion of character is secondary, entirely subsidiary to the notion of action," "[s]tructural analysis, much concerned not to define characters in terms of psychological essences, has so far striven, using various hypotheses, to define a character not as a 'being' but as a 'participant'" (104, 106).

11. Greimas (1987), positing a distinction "between *actants*, having to do with narrative syntax, and *actors*, which are recognizable in the particular discourses in which they are manifested" (106), made the further claim that "an articulation of actors constitutes a particular *tale*; a structure of actants constitutes a *genre*" (1983: 200).

12. Actually, the term that Tesnière uses in this connection is *le noeud verbal* 'the verbal knot.' For Tesnière (1976: 11–21), structural syntax studies the phrase, which can be defined as an organized ensemble whose constituent elements are words. What Tesnière calls structural connections define hierarchical dependency relations between dominant and subordinate elements in the phrase, with each such relation forming a "knot" (14). Indeed, as Budniakiewicz notes (1992: 29), Tesnière's conception of the verbal knot can be viewed as an important precursor to the notion of *predicators*, a term introduced by Charles Fillmore (1968) in his use of the predicate calculus to articulate a theory of case grammar (cf. Lyons 1977). As I go on to discuss in more detail in my next subsection, *predicates* can be defined as operators with one or more *arguments*, or terms related to one another in various ways by virtue of those predicates. *Predicators* is a term designed to distinguish this logico-semantic theory of predication from ideas of the predicate deriving

from traditional grammar (Budniakiewicz 1992: 28). Hence predicators are most simply defined as "verbs and other argument-taking lexical items" (Levin and Hovav 1996: 506 n. 1).

13. Greimas invokes Tesnière's theatrical metaphor at the beginning of chapter 10 of *Structural Semantics*, "Reflections on Actantial Models" (1983: 197–221).

14. Greimas (1987) suggested that, in principle, a theory of character must include not just a typology of actantial roles but also an account of how actants manifest themselves in the "discoursive structures" of stories—structures built up through "relational figurative network[s] that can be strung out over entire sequences" as well as through individual narrative utterances (115; 113–19; cf. Greimas and Courtés 1983: 5–8; Margolin 1987: 107, 1990b: 844).

15. Throughout, in order to highlight the difference between actors and actants, I capitalize the names of the six actantial roles identified by Greimas. Further, to underscore the parallels between Greimas's actantial model and recent work in linguistic semantics and functional grammar, in subsequent sections I capitalize the names of the participant roles (Actor, Goal, Patient, etc.) identified in recent linguistic research.

16. Note here the interesting parallels between Greimas's critique of Propp and Souriau and Ray Jackendoff's (1987: 378–79) remarks on problems with linguistic theories that merely "annotate" syntactic structures with a list of thematic roles such as *Theme*, *Agent*, and so on. Broaching issues that I discuss in more detail in my next subsection, Jackendoff argues that merely drawing up a list of role-based annotations of syntax fails to provide any independent motivations for the thematic analyses thereby generated. Similarly, for Greimas "[i]t is not the individual actants nor a list of them that matter but the semantic structure that interrelates them" (Budniakiewicz 1998b: 7).

17. As early as 1973, however, Greimas recognized the importance of just these sorts of inferences. Thus, in his revised version of the theory of actants, Greimas remarks that actantial models "constitute an attempt to account for instances and trajectories of meaning that generate discourse. But their importance is also pragmatic. They have to be considered as models of predictability, as hypotheses presented in the form of logical articulations that, once projected onto texts, can enhance their readability" (1987: 113).

18. For an insightful early treatment of how participant relations can be used to define the "mind styles" of fictional narrators and characters, see Leech and Short's account (1981: 29–34, 187–208). Leech and Short base their remarks, in part, on previous research by Halliday (1971) and Roger Fowler (1977). See, in this same connection, the second part of my next chapter.

19. As Liliane Haegeman (1994: 49–55) discusses in her overview of Government and Binding Theory, the dominant syntactic model during the 1980s and on into the early 1990s (cf. Chomsky 1981), the terms *thematic roles, theta roles*, and *g-roles* were introduced in this framework in order to specify the semantic relationship between verbs and their respective arguments. *Arguments*, in this context, can be defined as entities, persons, or things picked out from a universe of discourse and related to one another by virtue of the predicate-argument structure encoded in a verb (Haegeman 1994: 43). As an example of a two-place predicate, Haegeman cites the verb *kill*: "We say that the verb *kill* takes two arguments to which it assigns a theta role: it assigns the role AGENT to the subject argument of the sentence, and the role PATIENT to the object argument" (49). So-called *theta grids*, further, can be used to specify not only the number of arguments of a predicate but also the type of semantic roles those arguments have (51). See also note 29 below.

20. Halliday (1976) identifies interrogative constructions as a linguistic probe that can be used to distinguish participants and nonparticipants or circumstances. Specifically, "participants are questioned by *what* or *who* (or a nominal group with WH-determiner, e.g. *which line*, *whose hat*), as in *what was he throwing stones at?*, whereas circumstances are questioned by *when*, *where, how* or *why*, e.g. *where was he throwing stones?*" (160). Frawley makes a similar point: "[Participant roles] are the roles of arguments necessitated by the predication itself, those that generally answer the question, 'Who did what to whom?' [Nonparticipant roles] are optional roles necessitated by the semantic context more than by the predication. They generally answer the question, 'Why, where, when, and how?' " (1992: 201–2). Further, in his most recent synopsis of functional grammar, Halliday (1994: 151) identifies nine types of circumstance that can be encoded in the structure of a clause: Extent (e.g., distance, duration), Location (place, time), Manner (means, quality, comparison), Cause (reason, purpose, behalf), Contingency (condition, concession, default), Accompaniment (addition), Role (guise, product), Matter, and Angle.

21. See J. R. Martin (1996a) for an interesting comparison and contrast of Halliday's approach with the theory of case grammar developed by Charles Fillmore (1968, 1971, 1977; cf. Cook 1989). Historically speaking, the problems as well as the potentials of Fillmore's case grammar influenced research on theta roles, i.e., semantic roles assigned to the arguments of verbs, in the Government and Binding model of syntax (Chomsky 1981), which in turn influenced more recent research on thematic roles (Frawley 1992; Jackendoff 1987; Malmkjaer 1991).

22. As Halliday (1967) puts it, "A system is a set of features one, and only

one, of which must be selected if the entry condition to that system is satisfied; any selection of features formed from a given system network constitutes the 'systemic description' of a class of items" (37). In his early work, Halliday distinguishes between the transitivity system network, which centers around process types and the way they are encoded in the structures of the clause, and the theme system network, *theme* being "a general term for all those choices involving the distribution of information in the clause" (37). In the more comprehensive model outlined in his recent textbook on functional grammar, Halliday (1994: 33) distinguishes between three systems bearing on the structures of the clause. In one system, the functions of the grammatical subject of a clause are determined by the way the clause functions as a *message*; here the subject functions as a theme or "quantum of information." In another system, the subject takes on functions because of the way the clause is structured as part of an *exchange*; here the subject "is the element [that] the speaker makes responsible for the validity of what he is saying." Third, when the clause is construed as a *representation*, the subject takes on the role of a participant, with the clause functioning as "a construal of some process in ongoing human experience." The approach to participant roles and relations that I draw on here is thus only one component of what evolved into a much larger theory about the jointly informational, communicative, and representational dimensions of grammar.

23. The idea of process types bears interesting affinities with what René Dirven and Marjolijn Verspoor (1998: 81–102) characterize in cognitive-linguistic terms as *event schemata*, or conceptual schemata of recurrent types of events. A schema of this sort "combines a type of action or state with its most salient participants, which may have different 'roles' in the action or state" (82). Dirven and Verspoor identify seven event schemata (*Being, Happening, Doing, Experiencing, Having, Moving,* and *Transferring*) and discuss how they and their participants "are 'linguistically framed' into the linear and hierarchical structure of a sentence" (101).

24. The table also suggests grounds for rethinking Monika Fludernik's (1996) claim that the factor chiefly responsible for making narrative interpretable as narrative is human experientiality, or "the evocation of consciousness [in terms of] cognitive schema of embodiedness that relates to human existence and human concerns" (12–13). By contrast, table 9 indicates that the role of Experiencer (and the mental process type that specifies participants as Experiencers and Phenomena) figures only more or less centrally, depending on the narrative genre.

25. In this sense, a functionalist approach to narrative participants provides support for Mark Turner's (1996: 140–68) suggestion that grammar may

be a complex product of narrative imagining, rather than a system for meaning making that precedes narrative and makes it possible. Conceivably, ways of telling stories, each way having contrastive preference rankings for process types, may have generated analogous clause- and sentence-level strategies for encoding actions and events as distinct types of processes specifying different kinds of participants.

26. Since Fillmore's (1968) initial formulation of his case grammar, linguists have disagreed over how many case roles are required exhaustively to map the syntax-semantics interface—i.e., to capture all the predicate-argument relations that can be grammatically encoded. Frawley (1992: 201) found anywhere from eighteen to twenty-five case roles in the literature he surveyed.

27. A perusal of James's story turned up very few sentence-level instantiations of the roles labeled Reason and Purpose. The paucity of entities explicitly coded as Reasons and Purposes in the storyworld underscores the extent to which Brydon's motivations and aims remain obscure, even or especially to himself. Since the story is an instance of what Stanzel (1971, 1984) would call *figural narration*—i.e., *Er*-narration refracted through the perceptions and thoughts of a storyworld participant—James's refusal to code entities as Reasons and Purposes accentuates for readers both the necessity and the difficulty of framing inferences about what Brydon's motivations and aims might really be.

28. Hence, although the notions of "setting" and "nonparticipants" partially overlap, the latter notion is broader than the former. Setting typically denotes time and place, but not motivations, aims, or means.

29. Examples of this sort suggest problems with one of the fundamental principles of the Government and Binding approach to syntactic analysis, i.e., the *theta criterion*, a simplicity condition on predication that can be formulated as follows: "Every argument in a predication must be assigned one and only one thematic role" (Frawley 1992: 232). As Jackendoff (1987) noted, however, "The correspondence between syntax and ϑ-roles must be stated in somewhat less rigid terms, in particular admitting the real richness of thematic roles" (383).

30. Thus, the way a narrative assigns storyworld entities the role of Locative is inextricably interlinked with the way it prompts interpreters to spatialize the microuniverse (or microuniverses) that the narrative encodes. See chapter 7.

31. As Frawley notes, however, the Actor-Undergoer hierarchy suggests ways of developing broad, typological classifications of languages: "The Actor/Undergoer Hierarchy . . . leads to the general morphosyntactic pre-

diction that there will be a range of languages typologically: those that prefer to code one or another end of the hierarchy more productively" (239). In a language such as English, for example, the morphological coding of Actor seems relatively undifferentiated, in contrast to the richer coding of the Undergoer. In describing the peregrinations of Lisa, the traveling ichthyologist, speakers can evoke the roles of Source, Path, Goal, and so on, as ways of coding the Undergoer at issue, using such locutions as *from Florida*, *to Florida*, *in Florida*, *across Florida*, *inside Florida*, etc. But there are fewer coding options when it comes to the Actor: cf. *the ichthyologist* traveled from Florida, *the ichthyologist* traveled to Florida, *the ichthyologist* traveled in Florida, etc. The situation seems to be the inverse in a language such as Tagalog, in which a whole system of verbal prefixes distinguishes kinds of actors, e.g., volitional versus nonvolitional actors (Frawley 1992: 239; cf. Foley and Van Valin 1984; J. R. Martin 1996b).

32. As Frawley (1992) puts it, whereas canonical forms lie at each end of the Actor-Undergoer hierarchy, "[l]ess canonical, or fuzzy, forms are found in the middle: that is, some predicates ought to be variable as to whether sources or goals [for example] are actors or undergoers" (236). Thus, the preference-rule system underlying the Actor-Undergoer hierarchy specifies more and less canonical realizations of macroroles, not one-to-one correspondences between types of participants and macroroles. This point is especially important when I turn to ways in which the Actor-Undergoer hierarchy can be used to highlight the interconnections between participant logic and narrative genres.

33. As the poet puts it, when Beowulf learns that the surging flames vomited by the dragon have melted his own home, "[h]is breast within boiled with dark thoughts—as was not for him customary. . . . His mind was mournful, restless and ripe for death" (56, 58).

34. Fludernik uses the term *narrativity* to designate what makes a story (interpretable as) a story. In chapter 3 I use the term *narrativehood* to designate membership criteria for the class of objects or events categorizable as instances of "narrative," reserving the term *narrativity* for the constellation of formal and contextual factors making a story more or less readily processed *as* narrative.

5. DIALOGUES AND STYLES

1. By contrast, some researchers working in the sociolinguistic tradition of narrative analysis have tended to divorce speech action from the "complicating actions" (Labov 1972a) reported by properly narrative clauses. In the coding scheme developed by Livia Polanyi (1985), for example, speech acts

are not classed among the events that have to be included in a summary or paraphrase of what happened in the storyworld that is being discussed. Rather, they are coded as evaluative (or metanarrative) *comments on* the events that constitute the gist of the story being told.

2. Monika Fludernik's (1993a) monumental study of free indirect discourse should be singled out for its comprehensiveness and methodological rigor. See also note 26 below.

3. For critiques of Pratt's earlier work on its own terms, see Pratt (1986) and Herman (1995a: 158–67). An important precedent for my analysis—one predating *both* Grice's and Pratt's work—was outlined by Jan Mukařovský (1977). A number of later studies falling under the rubric of poetics are relevant to the analysis offered here; these studies include Roger Fowler's chapter on dialogue in *Linguistic Criticism* (1986); Geoffrey Leech and Michael Short's (1981) investigation of conversation in the novel (288–317); Dick Leith's (1988) study of ballad dialogue; Norman Page's (1973) and Short's (1988) studies of speech presentation in the novel; Elizabeth Closs Traugott and Mary Louise Pratt's (1980) chapter titled "Speech Acts and Speech Genres"; and Kathleen Wales's (1988) essay on dialogue and the dialogic.

4. Mutt and Jute's dialogue spans pp. 16–18 of the text. More precisely, and to conform to the standard citational practice of providing both page and line numbers for references to the *Wake*, the interchange runs from 16.10 to 18.16. According to David Hayman (1990: 142), Joyce drafted part 1, chapter 1 (and thus the Mutt and Jute episode) of *Finnegans Wake* in September of 1926.

5. A few terminological points: In this chapter, my usage of *text* parallels that of Gillian Brown and George Yule (1983), who define *text* as "the verbal record of a communicative act" (6). Further, I parallel Schiffrin (1988) in distinguishing between *discourse* ("any unit of language beyond the sentence") and *conversation* ("any discourse which is produced by more than one person"); but for the purposes of my analysis I do not wish to restrict *conversation* to "just spoken dialogue," with *discourse* covering "both dialogic and monologic forms in either spoken or written modes" (253). To avoid monotony, I sometimes use *text* and *discourse* where the context sufficiently indicates (I hope) that strictly speaking I am referring to *conversation*.

6. For background on and justifications of this distinction, see Brown and Yule (1983: 19–26); Ralph Fasold (1990: 141–42); Gerald Gazdar (1979: 157–59, 161–68); Stephen C. Levinson (1983: 18–21); and Ellen Prince (1988: 166–67). However, see Wallace Chafe et al. (1992) for a discussion of how the "concept of grammar as emergent suspends provision for fixed structure" (366), thereby casting doubt on the saliency of the sentence-utterance distinction itself.

7. As Pratt (1977) notes, "Grice adopts the general term implicature to refer to the various kinds of calculations by which we make sense of what we hear" (154; see 154–200). To use Grice's (1989) classic example, if my letter of recommendation for a job candidate comments only on his or her regular attendance in class, then my letter can be construed as *implicating* that I do not fully support the recommendee's candidacy.

8. See Schiffrin (1988) for an overview of the major arguments and an extensive bibliography.

9. See Schiffrin (1994) for a useful overview of recent trends in discourse analysis, including variationist, conversation-analytic, speech-act-theoretical, interactional-sociolinguistic, ethnographic, and pragmatics-inspired trends.

10. In this connection, a number of theorists have argued that we need to distinguish between what Ellen Prince (1988) calls broadly "*interactive* competence" and what she terms "pragmatic *linguistic* competence" (167; cf. Schiffrin 1988: 256; Blakemore 1988: 230–31). Presumably, not all of the processing skills interlocutors bring to bear on conversational interaction and negotiation involve knowledge of the way context licenses particular interpretations of utterances cast in particular formats. "The difficulty for conversational analysts," as Schiffrin (1988) puts it, "is to integrate the contribution which language makes with the contribution of non-linguistic social processes" (252).

11. Kimberly Devlin (1983) characterizes Mutt and Jute as members of the same (very large) set of self/other dichotomies in the *Wake* "that are undermined by clues suggesting that self and other are similar, interconnected" (38; cf. 36, 39; and Eckley 1985: 182). For Bernard Benstock (1963: 26) this set encompasses such pairs as Shem and Shaun, Caddy and Primas, Jerry and Kevin, Dolph and Kev, Mick and Nick, Glugg and Chuff, Butt and Taff, Mutt and Jute, Muta and Juva, St. Patrick and the Archdruid, Tristopher and Hilary, Fester King and Pegger Festy, the Mookse and the Gripes, the Ondt and the Gracehoper, Burrus and Caseous, Justius and Mercius, time and space, and a tree and a stone. Other scholars (e.g., Begnal 1988; Glasheen 1977; Tindall 1969) interpret Mutt and Jute as the incarnation of still other literary teams, including Vladimir and Estragon in Beckett's *Waiting for Godot* (24), who also "swop hats" (16.8), Caliban and Stephano-Trinculo in Shakespeare's *The Tempest*, and Polyphemous and Odysseus in Homer's *The Odyssey*.

12. See David Hayman (1990) in this connection: "Chapter I.I functioned from the start as an overture chapter, brilliantly, though hardly transparently, synthesizing all the book's major themes and conflicts" (13).

13. As Bishop (1986) puts it, "Reconstructing the return of its 'retro-

spectable fearfurther' (288.F7) to the condition of Vico's aboriginal men, the first chapter of the Wake is densely clustered with images of giants and 'astoneaged' cave men (18.15)—Neanderthal men (18.22, 19.25), Cromagnon men (20.7), Heidelberg men (18.23), Mousterian men (15.33), Piltdown men (10.30), and the paleolithic characters 'Mutt and Jute'" (194; cf Hayman 38–40). In the same connection, see James S. Atherton (1960: 218–20) on the (ancient) Nordic elements of the episode.

14. For Roman Jakobson (1960), utterances performing a *phatic* function serve primarily "to establish, to prolong, or to discontinue communication, to check whether the channel works . . . , to attract the attention of the interlocutor or to confirm his continued attention" (355).

15. See the entry for "Anglo-Saxons" in the eleventh edition of the *Encyclopedia Britannica*, to which Joyce had access: "We need not doubt that the Angli and the Saxons were different nations originally; but from the evidence at our disposal it seems likely that they had practically coalesced in very early times, perhaps even before the invasion" of Britain (vol. 2: 38). Under "Jutes" in the same edition of the *Encylopedia*, this entry can be found: "the third of the Teutonic nations which invaded Britain in the 5th century, called by Bede *Iutae* or *Iuti*," and deriving, apparently, from Jutland, which, "though embracing several islands as well as a peninsula, may be said to belong to the continental portion of the kingdom of Denmark" (vol. 15: 609).

16. However, for criticisms of the descriptive, let alone explanatory, adequacy of these and other discourse-analytic categories, see John Searle (1992).

17. As M. Thomas Inge (1990) notes, "Bud Fisher's *Mutt and Jeff* beginning on November 15, 1907 was the first regularly published comic strip" (79), as well as the longest running daily American comic strip (82–84), published as recently as 1971 (Glasheen 1977: 202). The strip yielded a number of lexical innovations in English. Thus "*Mutt and Jeff* gained currency as apt names for tall and short couples (Fisher also popularized *fall guy*, *inside stuff*, *got his goat* . . .)" (Inge 1990: 23; cf. Daniels 1971: 4).

18. See Mukařovský (1977) for a number of pertinent observations in this connection. Mukařovský contrasts *conversational* with *personal* and *situational* types of dialogue; in the case of the conversational mode, "[a] pure play of meanings is both its aim and its extreme limit. Its prerequisite is a concentration of attention on the dialogue itself as a chain of semantic reversals" (91). Further, noting that "[u]nlike monologic discourse, which has a single and continuous contexture, several or at least two contextures interpenetrate and alternate in dialogic discourse," Mukařovský goes on to argue that "[t]he more vivid the dialogue, the shorter the individual replies, and the more distinct the collision of contextures. Thus arises a special semantic effect for which stylistics has even created a term: stichomythia" (87–88).

19. Commenting on the word *mahan* in this passage, Roland McHugh (1991) lists "*AngI* mahan: bear," but see, too, the entry for "Brian" in the eleventh edition of the *Encyclopedia Britannica*: "Brian (926–1014), king of Ireland, known as Brian Boru, Boroma, or Boroimhe (from *boroma*, an Irish word for tribute), . . . passed his youth in fighting against the Danes, who were constantly ravaging Munster. . . . In 976 his brother, Mathgamhain or *Mahon*, . . . was murdered; Brian avenged this deed, became himself king of Munster in 978" (vol. 4: 515, my emphasis). This historical information provides part of the interpretive context for Mutt and Jute's later remarks, as I discuss in this chapter.

20. AI researchers and computational linguists, however, have made important recent advances in computational approaches to discourse production and comprehension (see, e.g., Moser and Moore 1996; Young 1996, 1997; and Young, Pollack, and Moore 1994).

21. Some of these cues correspond to what, in spoken discourse, linguists refer to as "prosodic" features. In J. J. Gumperz's (1982) account, "'Prosody' here includes: (a) intonation, i.e. pitch levels on individual syllables and their combination into contours; (b) changes in loudness; (c) stress, a perceptual feature generally comprising variations in pitch, loudness and duration; (d) other variations in vowel length; (e) phrasing, including utterance chunking by pausing, accelerations and decelerations within and across utterance chunks; and (f) overall shifts in speech register. These are conceptual conflations of variations in the three basic phonological dimensions of frequency, amplitude and duration" (100).

22. Although the simplest systematics assumes that conversation's "turn-taking organization (and thus conversational activity per se) operates independently of . . . what occupies its turns, [or] the topic(s) in them," the systematics does concern itself with the *size* of turns, for whereas "the system does not define maximum turn size, . . . the turn-constructional component does determine minimal turn size" (Sacks, Schegloff, and Jefferson 1974: 710, 709; cf. 730).

23. See Östen Dahl (1974), František Daneš (1974), and Jan Firbas (1992) for more information on these and related conceptual pairs.

24. Actually, Blakemore's (1988) essay falls within the post-Gricean tradition of Relevance Theory, which was initiated by Deirdre Wilson and Dan Sperber and which seeks to reduce the number of Gricean conversational maxims to just one, *Be relevant*. Wilson and Sperber (1991) define relevance in terms of the technical notion of "contextual implications," which are the by-product obtained "when the addition of a proposition to a context modifies the context in a way that goes beyond the mere incrementation of that context with the proposition itself and all its logical implications" (381).

25. Contrast Bakhtin's (1986) integrative account of both literary and nonliterary genres in his essay "The Problem of Speech Genres," written in the mid-1950s.

26. Even earlier precedents for my approach include Sumner Ives's 1950 article on literary representations of dialect (1971) and Lubomír Doležel and Richard W. Bailey's (1969) edited collection of essays taking a statistical approach to stylistic analysis. See, more particularly, Leech and Short's (1981) richly functionalist account of style in fiction, especially the sections on levels of style (119–47) and on speech and thought representation in the novel (159–73, 318–51; cf. Semino, Short, and Culpeper 1997); Fludernik's (1993a) study of the jointly linguistic and fictional dimensions of free indirect discourse; Michael Toolan's (1996) integrational approach to language use generally; and Sara Mills's (1992) Marxist feminist analysis of how literary styles interpellate or position readers within certain socio-ideological roles. See, also, Roger Shuy's (1981) suggestive analysis of the thematic and characterological functions of code switching in *Lady Chatterley's Lover*.

27. Not all linguists would use the terms *style*, *dialect*, and *register* in the way that I use them here, and some have proposed alternative vocabularies for describing and explaining the phenomena I go on to discuss. For example, in the functionalist model of M. A. K. Halliday, which has strongly influenced linguists working in the United Kingdom, the term *field* is used to cover what North American linguists tend to refer to as *register* (= ways of speaking associated with particular activities), and *tenor* to cover what the present chapter designates as *style*. Further, drawing a distinction between first-order (or language-independent) and second-order (or language-dependent) social roles, Halliday (1978) conceives of the study of tenor as the study of systematic patterns of relationship between first- and second-order roles (144). Hence the dimension of tenor bears on the selection of interpersonal options during verbal interaction, i.e., the options available "in the systems of mood, modality, person, key, intensity, evaluation and comment and the like" (144). These options both determine and are determined by the role relationships of the participants involved.

See Michael Gregory and Susanne Carroll (1978) for an excellent overview of the Hallidayan scheme and its applicability to the sorts of discourse phenomena explored in this chapter. Further, see Norman Page (1973: 51–89) for an early and still useful account of dialect representation as a resource for fictional characterization.

28. Analogously, see Herman (1999e) for an account of how Wharton's novel, despite its anti-Semitic treatment of Simon Rosedale, undercuts essentialist notions of ethnicity as a bedrock of the self.

398 Notes to Pages 200–212

29. See Schiffrin's (1994: 386–405) discussion of the code-based, inferential, and interactional models of communication informing recent work in discourse analysis and, in particular, her account of how, in the interactional model, intersubjectivity is a locally managed effect of communication rather than its cause, basis, or medium.

30. Analogously, Shuy (1981) discusses how Oliver Mellors, in the 1928 work *Lady Chatterley's Lover*, shifts between standard and nonstandard dialects of British English in order to establish distance from or intimacy with Constance Chatterley during various phases of their relationship.

31. As Walt Wolfram and Natalie Schilling-Estes (1998: 62–66) note, the notion of "slang" includes linguistic items marked by a complex of sociopsychological attributes that it might be better to analyze separately, including informality, strong group identity associations, a flouting of maxims for usage that call for more conventional synonyms for the slang items (e.g., *vomit* instead of *barf*), and a relatively short life span. See also Connie Eble (1996).

32. It is, after all, a *word* that Selden believes will make all things clear between Lily and him (301).

33. Later, however, Lily is refreshed by Rosedale's honesty and directness, and Rosedale himself tries to help Lily by a plain business arrangement, "such as one man would make with another" (279).

34. I am grateful to Harold F. Mosher Jr., Elizabeth Traugott, Katie Wales, and two anonymous readers (one for *Style*, the other for *Language and Literature*) for comments on earlier versions of portions of this chapter.

6. TEMPORALITIES

1. For a concise exposition—and critique—of fuzzy logic, see Susan Haack's (1978: 162–69) discussion of Zadeh's model. As Haack explains, "Whereas in classical set theory an object either is or is not a member of a given set, in fuzzy set theory membership is a matter of degree; the degree of membership of an object in a fuzzy set is represented by some real number between 0 and 1, with 0 denoting *no* membership and 1 *full* membership" (165). Haack, however, argues against Zadeh's radical extension of fuzziness to the predicates True and False (169), and she also points out (167) that fuzzy logic has difficulty handling concerns traditionally viewed as central to the field of logic itself, including axiomatization, proof procedures, consistency, and completeness.

Yet Aristotle already had reservations about bivalent logics (Haack 1978: 204–20; cf. Rescher 1969). The earliest many-valued logical systems—e.g., systems encompassing the value Indeterminate, or Possible, as well as True and False—go back to Jan Lukasiewicz's 1920 essay on three-valued logic

(1967) and a study published by Emil Post the following year (1921). Along the same lines, in this chapter, I use the term *fuzzy temporality* synonymously with *multivalent temporal system* (more specifically, *three-valued temporal system*). Such a system requires adding, to the values Earlier-than-some-temporal-reference-point and Later-than-some-temporal-reference-point, the value Indeterminately-situated-with-respect-to-some-temporal-reference-point.

2. See, for example, Genette (1980: 25–32); Kafalenos (1995: 135 n. 7); G. Prince (1987: 21, 91); Rimmon-Kenan (1983: 3).

3. Barbara Herrnstein Smith (1981) makes this argument. For counterarguments, see G. Prince (1995).

4. Harry Shaw (1995a) takes up these terms proposed by Chatman (1990) but disputes Chatman's claim that narrators cannot inhabit both discourse space and story space at the instant of narration. For additional discussion of this issue, see Chatman (1995), Phelan (2000), Philp (1997), and Shaw (1995b).

5. To put this point another way, narrative theorists have used the story/discourse distinction to combine formal with functional analysis, showing how aspects of textual design affect story comprehension.

6. In this connection, G. Prince (1982) ascribes media-specific properties to stories, arguing that prolepsis can be handled less clumsily in print than in film narratives (50).

7. I use the word *inexactness*, but a more appropriate choice in this context might be Edmund Husserl's term *anexactitude*, a word Husserl uses to characterize concepts that are intrinsically fuzzy because they are "essentially and nonaccidentally inexact" (cited by Jacques Derrida 1989: 123). At issue are concepts such as those designated by the words *notched*, *indented*, and *lens-shaped*. In some contexts (e.g., contexts requiring the quick identification of an object being pointed to from a distance), these concepts are more useful than precise specifications of shape would be.

8. Thus, polychronic structures—temporally indefinite situations and events—should be distinguished from what Genette calls *syllepses*, or "anachronic groupings governed by one or another kinship (spatial, temporal, or other)" (1980: 85 n. 119). Rather than being temporally related departures from chronological sequence, as when, for example, one analepsis spawns other analepses that reach back to the same period of time, polychrony involves departures that lack any such (obvious) governing principle. Such departures compel readers or viewers to forge unexpected analogies and relationships between situations and events in the storyworld. Closer to polychrony is a phenomenon noted by Seymour Chatman, i.e., narratives that feature multiple story strands, each with its own "temporal center of gravity,"

"its own NOW" (1978: 66). (Cf. my discussion of deictic centers in the next section.) But whereas narratives of this kind involve "constant crosscutting" between the various story strands, in Seghers's story and Egoyan's film there is a kind of interpenetration of the deictic coordinates orienting earlier and later narrative "strands." In the story strands woven together in *The White Hotel*, NOW ceases to be a temporal center of gravity at all.

9. For Roland Barthes (1971a), the readability of classical narrative is ensured by its insistence on an irreversible order of events, with the consequence that "narrative undermines itself as it intensifies the attempts at reversibility in its general structure" (14). Hence Barthes distinguishes between the art of narrative and a fundamentally new art that he calls *narrative transgression* (13–14). The transition from narrative to narrative transgression involves a shift from "simple readability, characterized by a stringent irreversibility of actions (of the classical type), to a complex readability (precarious), subject to the forces of dispersion and to the reversibility of symbolic elements which destroy both time and logic" (14; cf. Barthes 1974). In Barthes's terms, polychronic narration could be characterized as a vehicle for narrative transgression. However, as I stress in the present chapter, the quality and magnitude of its transgressive force are variable, being dependent on how polychrony works in concert with a constellation of other factors within a particular narrative context.

10. All translations from Seghers's German are my own.

11. Seghers provides textual cues for interpreting the *Ausflug* not only as remembrance stimulated in part by weakness or hallucination but also as an extended dream. Thus, in the frame-tale, Seghers's narrator tries to follow with her eyes "den Teil des Weges . . . der aus dem Dorf in die Wildnis führte. Der Weg war so weiß, daß er in die Innenseiten der Augenlider geritzt schien, *sobald ich die Augen schloß*" 'the part of the path . . . which led from the village into the wilderness. The path was so white that it seemed etched into the inner side of my eyelids, *as soon as I shut my eyes*' (1980: 332, my emphasis).

12. Compare Gerald Prince's entry for *narrative* in his *Dictionary*: "by marking off distinct moments in time and setting up relations between them, by discovering meaningful designs in temporal series, by establishing an end already partly contained in the beginning and a beginning already partly containing the end, by exhibiting the meaning of time and/or providing it with meaning, narrative deciphers time and indicates how to decipher it. In sum, narrative illuminates temporality and humans as temporal beings" (1987: 60).

13. For an anticipation of some elements of this "deictic shift theory," see Käte Hamburger's discussion of the problem of the fictive present in *The Logic*

of *Literature* (1973: 89–98). Further, one of Hamburger's comments on the "fictional presentification" of past events (cf. G. Prince 1982: 28–29) helps corroborate the interpretation of Seghers's story that I go on to develop: "in personal memory vivid mental representation falls together with the feeling of the Then, of the Before, and when this image is reproduced from memory it in turn coincides with the temporal Now of the act of remembering and reliving" (100–101).

14. See chapter 9 for an account of how second-person narratives such as Edna O'Brien's *A Pagan Place* (1984) both promote and impede the *other* deictic shift just mentioned—the initial one that leads from the reader's here and now to the here and now orienting the diegesis. Second-person narration can produce an ontological hesitation between the fictional and the actual, compromising the border between the narrated world and the world in which the narrative is interpreted.

15. Here the narrator uses a device that Labov (1972a) would call a *comparator*; for Labov, this device provides an important resource for narrative evaluation, i.e., signaling the *point* of a story. As Labov puts it, "Comparators, including negatives, compare the events which did occur to those which did not occur," thus providing "a way of evaluating events by placing them against the background of other events which might have happened, but which did not" (381; cf. von Wright 1966 for an analogous account of *acting situations*, as discussed in chapter 2). Also, compare the narrator's account of Otto with what Gerald Prince discusses under the heading of the *disnarrated*, which "covers all the events that *do not* happen though they could have and are nonetheless referred to (in a negative or hypothetical mode) by the narrative text" (1992: 30; cf. chapter 8 in this book).

16. For other occurrences of *ahnen* in the story (not all of them as temporally problematic as the present instance), see Seghers (1980: 340, 345, 346, 347, and 350).

17. Walter Grossman (1962) also discusses Leni's wrinkle in connection with (the effects of) time. As Grossman (1962) puts it, "Die Falte war bereits dem Schulmädchen Leni eigen, und Anna Seghers sagt aus, was das Leben gemacht hat: es hat die Falte, die es auch hätten glätten können, vertieft und verhärtet" 'Leni already had the wrinkle as a schoolgirl, and Anna Seghers states what life has made of the wrinkle: whereas life could have smoothed the wrinkle away, in fact it deepened it and made it more severe' (128).

18. The term *paralepsis* pairs with what Genette calls *paralipsis*, in which a narrator tells *less* about events than he or she is "authorized" to by virtue of his or her own participation in them.

19. Compare Grossman's perceptive remarks on Seghers's substitution, in

every case, of an "individuellen Dasein" 'individual existence' for any "allgemeine Antwort" 'general answer' about the fate(s) of the German populace during the war (1962: 129).

20. See in this connection, too, the last sentences of the tale: "Plötzlich fiel mir der Auftrag meiner Lehrerin wieder ein, den Schulausflug sorgfältig zu beschreiben. Ich wollte gleich morgen oder noch heute abend, wenn meine Müdigkeit vergangen war, die befohlene Aufgabe machen" 'Suddenly my teacher's instructions—that I should carefully describe the school excursion—struck me once again. I wanted the next morning or even that very evening, once my weariness had passed, to fulfil the task that had been assigned me' (Seghers 1980: 362).

21. See chapter 8 in this book; Herman (1995a: 124–38; 1999c; Margolin (1999); G. Prince (1992: 28–38); and Ryan (1991: 149–74).

22. Even as the tale thwarts straightforward inferences about how the past caused the present, "Der Ausflug" thematizes the destructive dynamics of blame. Thus Marianne, who never really recovers from Otto Fresenius's death in World War I, may have betrayed Leni because of her resentment over Leni's good fortune in finding a husband and having a child (Seghers 1980: 346–47). See also Seghers's description of Ida, whose fiancé likewise dies at Verdun: "und wenn sie auch in jetzigen Krieg keinen Bräutigam hatte, ihr Wunsch nach Rache, ihre Erbitterung waren immer noch wach" 'and although she had had no fiancé in the present war, her wish for revenge, her resentment was still alive' (341–42).

All the same, I do not mean to imply that Seghers's tale is designed in a way that exempts its readers from the need to explore causes for fascism and other social evils. Rather, it prompts reflection on the very idea of cause and on the nature and scope of relations of consequentiality. Conversely, I am not arguing that stories centering around single causes are *ipso facto* fascistic. It all depends on how much explanatory force is concentrated in a given cause and how narrowly circumscribed that cause is. Telling a story about how a thief stole a bicycle or someone committed a murder is manifestly different, of course, from telling a story about how a single group is responsible for everything that is wrong with the world.

23. In this respect, Seghers's polychronic technique counters not just fascistic ideology but also the reductive form of historicism critiqued by Walter Benjamin (1969) in one of his "Theses on the Philosophy of History," a text composed just a few years before "Der Ausflug" was written: "Historicism contents itself with establishing a causal connection between various moments in history. But no fact that is a cause is for that reason historical. It became historical posthumously, as it were, through events that may be sepa-

rated from it by thousands of years. A historian who takes this as his point of departure stops telling the sequence of events like the beads of a rosary. Instead, he grasps the constellation which his own era has formed with a definite earlier one" (263).

24. As Payne (1995) points out, "Hitler was not, strictly speaking, a mere German nationalist, for the concept of the [superior] Nordic race, as he privately admitted, extended to certain other peoples—or sectors of other peoples—in central and northern Europe" (157).

25. Desperate narration is also the subject of criticism in the lyrics of "Courage," a song composed by The Tragically Hip and included as a prominent part of the film's sound track. Cf., for example, the lines: "So there's no simple explanation / for anything important any of us do." From the album *Fully Completely* (MCA Records Inc., Canada, 1992).

26. With respect to the temporal distance between episodes (i.e., how long after one episode the next occurred), this diagram is only very roughly proportional. Also, note that whereas I use subscripts to subdivide some of the more complicated narrative episodes, in principle every episode in the film could be similarly subdivided (and the ones that are currently subdivided could be analyzed further). Hence my diagram is structured around an implicit criterion of narrative relevance; I represent only those sub-episodes that seem to me especially salient in the context of the overall temporal and thematic structure of the film.

27. See Seymour Chatman's (1999) analysis of voice-over narration for a discussion of how film's ability to combine visual and auditory information requires a rethinking of a key claim made by structuralist narratologists. At issue is their claim that specific properties of the various media in which a story can in principle be told do not affect the (semantic) "content" of the story itself, such that one and the same story can be told in both a novel and film.

28. As Irene Guenther (1995: 33) notes, as a label for post-Expressionist painting, Roh's term *Magischer Realismus* was quickly eclipsed by the term *Neue Sachlichkeit* 'new objectivity,' coined by German museum director Gustav Hartlaub and used in connection with a 1925 exhibition. At issue in this trend was not so much a particular subject matter as "the fastidious depiction of familiar objects, [a] new way of seeing and rendering the everyday"— in short, "a new definition of the object, clinically dissected, coldly accentuated, microscopically delineated" (Guenther 1995: 36). As Guenther puts it, "Over-exposed, isolated, rendered from an uncustomary angle, the familiar became unusual, endowed with an *Unheimlichkeit* (uncanniness) which elicted fear and wonder" (36). Guenther goes on to discuss early extensions of

magical realism/new objectivity into literary writing (e.g., Alfred Kubin's 1909 *Die andere Seite* 'The Other Side' [1967] and Alfred Döblin's 1929 *Berlin Alexanderplatz* [1931]), as well as its suppression by the Nazis.

29. In this connection, *The White Hotel* raises the question of how the theoretical predispositions of Thomas's Freud relate to those of the actual Sigmund Freud. As Brent D. Slife (1993: 62–68) has shown, the actual Freud's approach to temporality was of a complex or "mixed" sort, combining features of a Lockean, objectivist view of time with a Kantian, subjectivist view. Moreover, whereas Freud was committed to a deterministic, linear model of time, whereby past events eventuate in present behaviors, he also thought of the unconscious as timeless, viewing the id as a repository of instincts rooted in "some primaeval phylogenetic experience" (Freud 1969: 64). For Freud, the id is an archaic heritage that, existing in some sense beyond or outside of the order of linear time, is recapitulated or instantiated ontogenetically, by particular individuals caught up in the temporal flux. Nonetheless, like Thomas's fictitious Freud, the actual Freud seems to have made no provision for radical temporal indeterminacy of the sort characterizing the storyworld of *The White Hotel*, in which "later" events can figure as causes of "earlier" effects.

30. Thomas acknowledges using material from Anatoli Kuznetsov's *Babi Yar* for the section of the novel entitled "The Sleeping Carriage" (221–53). For additional historical information, see the entry for Babi Yar at the website maintained by the Simon Wiesenthal Online Multimedia Learning Center, which can be found at *http://motlc.wiesenthal.com/pages/t004/t00412.html* (last accessed 5 April 2001).

31. Freud interprets Anna's/Lisa's journal as a sort of polymorphous opera in its own right: "Anna herself is (at times) the opera singer; but also the prostitute without a breast, the pale, thin invalid without a womb, the dead mistress in the common grave. Sometimes the 'voices' are distinct, but more often they blend, melt into each other" (142).

32. In one instance, even Freud hedges on the question of whether Lisa's symptoms point forward or backward in time: "It remained uncertain why the pains attacked the left side of her body. An hysteria not seldom attaches itself to a physical weakness in the constitution, provided it fits in with the primary symbolism; and it may be that there was *a propensity to illness* in the patient's left breast and ovary, which would become manifest later in life. On the other hand, perhaps the left-sidedness arose from a memory that was never brought to the surface. No analysis is ever complete; the hysterias have more roots than a tree" (140, my emphasis).

33. Compare, too, the narrator's account of Lisa's thoughts before she takes Kolya's hand and leaps into the ravine with him: "When it got dark, she would

find Kolya and they would crawl up out of the ravine, slip into the woods and make their escape" (247).

34. I am grateful to Emma Kafalenos, Uri Margolin, Michael Ossar, Don Palmer, James Phelan, and Marie-Laure Ryan for helpful feedback on earlier versions of this chapter. Specifically, Phelan's insightful remarks helped me reword a number of key passages; Kafalenos's and Ryan's searching criticisms helped me rethink my whole approach to the problem of time in narrative; and Margolin carefully read and provided detailed comments on a later version of the chapter (as I indicate in my introductory section). Margolin also pointed me to several invaluable linguistic and philosophical treatments of the problem of time. For his part, Palmer provided helpful reminders about Freud's Platonism.

7. SPATIALIZATION

1. Conversely, Herman (1999c) shows how ideas developed by narratologists studying literary narrative can be used to study conversational narratives. See also Herman (1999f).

2. Philippe Hamon (1982) goes so far as to argue that "the fundamental characteristic of realist discourse is to deny, to make impossible, the narrative, any narrative. This is because the more it becomes saturated with descriptions, the more it is concomitantly forced to multiply its empty thematics and its redundancies, and the more it becomes organized and repetitious, thus becoming increasingly a closed system: instead of being referential, it becomes purely anaphoric; instead of evoking the real ('things' and 'events') it constantly evokes itself" (170).

3. Zoran's insightful account anticipates many of the issues explored by subsequent researchers and presented in my next section, including the distinction between topographical and projective locations and the deictic and semantic functions of verbs of motion (*go, come*, etc.).

4. Well before Greimas developed the notion of disengagement, Bühler (1965) had discussed the phenomenon of *Deixis am Phantasma*, whereby entities not present in the immediate deictic field of a current communicative act are treated as if they were, as when a speaker makes an apostrophe to an absent (or even dead) interlocutor. See chapter 9.

5. As Greimas and Courtés (1983) put it, "Whether it concerns a simple NP [= narrative program] or an ordered series of NPs including the instrumental NP and, if there are any, annex NPs, the syntagmatic set thus recognized corresponds to the performance of the subject, on condition, however, that the subjects of doing and the subjects of state be syncretized in a given actor and that the subjects of the annex NPs be identical with the subject of the principal doing, or, at least, delegated and governed by that subject" (246).

6. See chapter 9 for a fuller characterization of recent linguistic work on deictic features of utterances.

7. By contrast, G. Prince (1987) uses this example to claim that "it is possible to narrate without referring to the story space, the space of the narrating instance, or the relations between them" (88).

8. My being obliged to discuss deictic shifts both in the previous and in the present chapter underscores the jointly temporal and spatial dimensions of deixis itself. Thus deictic terms such as *here* and *now* (or *there* and *then*) can be interpreted only by reference to the *where* and *when* coordinates defining the contexts in which the terms are uttered.

9. The title of Foy's book alludes to similar problems with the technology used in the novel to support immersion in virtual worlds. Technicians struggle to find both hardware and software solutions for a glitch they call *the shift*, which refers to a more or less noticeable lag between a user's manipulation of the virtual reality system and the effect within the virtual world that the user's manipulation is supposed to produce.

10. In the absence of any report that a storyworld participant actually perceived Gwendolen's carriage through those windows, the narrator's remark that the carriage is "within sight of the windows" affiliates this passage with instances of "hypothetical focalization" discussed in chapter 8.

11. Indeed, for Elinor Ochs et al. (1992), everyday storytelling can be characterized as an experience in theory building, wherein children acquire the ability to recognize and express different points of view, to see stories metacognitively as versions, to evaluate these discrepant versions of events, and to distinguish protagonists' from narrators' versions.

12. For more on the convergence of present tense *be* forms and perfective functions, as well as the role of that convergence in dialects of English spoken today, see Walt Wolfram (1996). See also Mays Rydén and Sverker Brorström's (1987) book-length study.

13. By contrast, the verbal phrase that characterizes Gwendolen as *springing from* the carriage encodes a trajectory of motion that can be inferred to be roughly perpendicular to Gwendolen's line of sight—assuming that her carriage conformed to the prototype with doors opening outward from one side.

14. To this extent, *The Third Policeman* lends support both to Fredric Jameson's (1988) claim that cognitive mapping is a quintessentially postmodernist concern and to Jean-François Lyotard's (1984) account of postmodernism itself as "that which, in the modern, puts forward the unpresentable in presentation itself" (81).

15. The word *mechanically* and its cognates occur frequently in the text. This, for example, is the narrator's account of how he killed old Mathers: "I

went forward mechanically, swung the spade over my shoulder and smashed the blade of it with all my strength against the protruding chin" (16; see also 22, 23). A short while later, as the narrator sits facing a dead Mathers apparently come alive again, "[w]ords spilled out of me as if they were produced by machinery" (26). O'Brien may have conflated mechanical with the unintelligent (and unintelligible) because he composed *The Third Policeman* at a time when research of the sort conducted by Alan Turing on intelligent machines (Turing 1950) had not yet been widely reported. Nonetheless, given that the novel affiliates itself with key developments in the scientific theory of its day, as documented by Charles Kennitz (1985) and Mary A. O'Toole (1988), one suspects that the motif of the black cash box may be an elaborate pun on the notion of "black-box explanations" (cf. Geminiani, Carassa, and Bara 1996). At issue are causal explanations of phenomena that try to work backward from observed effects to the processes (housed figuratively in "black boxes") that must have operated on certain preconditions to produce said effects.

16. Kemnitz (1985) argues that, prior to his death, the narrator lives in a world with the space-time characteristics that Albert Einstein assigned to what he called "'the zone of middle dimensions,' the realm of our daily experience where Newtonian physics and Euclidean geometry continue to be useful" and where the notion that "solid bodies [move] through empty space" remains a valid or operational one (59). This zone is to be contrasted with the parish of the three policemen, the hellish otherworld that lies beyond the zone of middle dimensions and contains phenomena postulated in connection with quantum mechanics and relativity theory (60). My own discussion of the novel suggests, instead, that the narrator must attempt to navigate simultaneously both classical and post- or nonclassical space-time systems. Thus the narrator's account, under the influence of de Selbian theory, encodes a storyworld that both does and does not conform to what Frawley (1992) characterizes as "the backdrop of a canonical and naive conception of space and physics, or the mentally projected world of space" against which spatial reference and spatial cognition unfold. The tension that results—the way the text triggers strategies for spatialization that in some instances prove untenable—is my chief concern here.

17. De Selby articulates this paradox in a distinctly Nietzschean way. Although O'Brien's narrator nowhere mentions Nietzsche, his account of de Selby's theory of the impossibility of progression recalls Nietzsche's argument, in his essay "On Truth and Lies in a Nonmoral Sense" (1979), that humans perceive the world not as it is but in terms of metaphors that enable them

to negotiate what remains a fundamentally inscrutable environment. What Nietzsche recognizes that de Selby does not, however, is that assimilating particular instances under general concepts (e.g., by storing them in the form of script- or frame-like mental representations) is a survival mechanism built into the human cognitive system.

18. Part of the reason the narrator can be deemed unreliable is that, over and over again, he re-experiences his entry into the disturbingly disorienting "country" of the policemen as wholly new. Thus, as the main character heads back toward the police barracks at the end of the novel (198–99), O'Brien incorporates into his homodiegetic narration the very same sentences—indeed, whole paragraphs—used to recount his initial impressions of this region of the storyworld (cf. pp. 52–54). He has not learned, readers can infer, from hellish experiences already undergone.

19. Or, to express the paradox better, the narrator does not recognize the extent to which the space-time characteristics of the otherworld are a projection of his own de Selbian fantasies. Nor does he recognize the extent to which such fantasies militate against the very possibility of spatial cognition.

20. At another point in his account, the narrator seems to suggest that certain regions of the storyworld resist categorization as either figure or ground: "The sky was a light blue without distance, neither near nor far. I could gaze at it, through it and beyond it and see still illimitably clearer and nearer the delicate lie of its nothingness" (151).

21. On this reading, whereby Policeman Fox's exaggerated size can be construed as a projection of the narrator's own feelings of inferiority, O'Brien's novel bears comparison with Franz Kafka's *The Trial*. In particular, as the "case" against Joseph K. gathers momentum, and he finds it increasingly difficult to function in his capacity as chief clerk at the bank, K. engages in a similar projection of his feelings of inadequacy, with his peers at one point seeming to have acquired the proportions of "giants" (1984a: 131). More generally, there are strong parallels between K.'s conflict with a hyperbureaucratized judicial system in *The Trial* and *The Third Policeman*'s use of policemen and police barracks to explore issues of guilt, institutionalized authority, technologies of surveillance, and so on.

22. To use the cognitive-scientific vocabulary sketched in chapter 3, prototypes are mental representations of a frame-like or static type, as opposed to representations of a script-like or dynamic type.

23. Chatman (1990) observes: "For narratology, Description is the most interesting of the other text-types because its relation to Narrative is the most subtle and complex" (15).

8. PERSPECTIVES

1. Later, though, Genette (1988) would go on to say that "My only regret is that I used a purely visual, and hence overly narrow, formulation. . . . There would have been no point in taking great pains to replace point of view with focalization if I was only going to fall right back into the same old rut; so obviously we must replace *who sees?* with the broader question *who perceives?*"—or rather, with the question "*where is the focus of perception?*" (64). Shlomith Rimmon-Kenan (1983) makes the same point: "It seems to me that the term 'focalization' is not free of optical-photographic connotations, and— like point of view—its purely visual sense has to be broadened to include cognitive, emotive and ideological orientation" (71). Mieke Bal (1985) had already taken a step in this direction by defining focalization as "the relation between the vision ['of the fabula"] and that which is 'seen,' *perceived*" (100, my emphasis).

2. Hence Gerald Prince's (1987) definition of *focalization*: "The perspective in terms of which the narrated situations and events are presented; the perceptual or conceptual position in terms of which they are rendered (Genette)" (31).

3. What leads me to categorize perspective as a macrodesign principle is the way narrative imagining is tantamount to adopting (and cuing listeners, viewers, or readers to adopt) a perspective or range of perspectives on the storyworld at issue. Perspective taking is, in this sense, a global constraint on narrative structure; as just stated, there can be no aperspectival or nonperspectival story. Of course, narratives do accommodate significant shifts in perspective during their unfolding, and the present chapter goes on to identify a number of linguistic markers that can be used to index such perspectival shifts at a local level. Nonetheless, as I use the term here, *perspective* denotes chiefly the overall ecology of perspective taking in (and made possible by) narrative.

4. As G. Prince (1991) puts it: "It is unquestionable that, in its classical period, because of textocentrism, because of the influence exerted by structural and even generative linguistics, because, too, of the temptation of the scientific and the difficulty of formally mastering the semantic, narratology mainly studies narrative syntax and narrative discourse, achieving its most striking results in these areas" (547).

5. In Rimmon-Kenan's scheme, external focalization corresponds to Genette's zero focalization (see figure 11 later in the chapter). In this chapter, except where the context indicates otherwise, I use the term *external focalization* in Rimmon-Kenan's, not Genette's, sense. For his part, Seymour Chatman (1990) proposes the terms *slant* and *filter* to capture the difference be-

tween, on the one hand, "the narrator's attitudes and other mental nuances appropriate to the report function of discourse" and, on the other hand, "the much wider range of mental activity experienced by characters in the story world—perceptions, cognitions, attitudes, emotions, memories, fantasies, and the like" (143). In this way, "[t]he external-internal tangle that 'focalization' gets into would be resolved because, by definition, a term such as 'filter' would be recognized as internal to the story world and 'slant,' by contrast, as external to it" (148). The varieties of hypothetical focalization that I examine later in this chapter, however, may trouble the boundary between slant and filter. They entail perceptual and conceptual filtration of events through an agent not actually in the storyworld, yet nonetheless imagined as counterfactually present by interpreters. Similarly, HF suggests a blending of the *Ich-* and *Er-* (I- and He-) forms of narration that Lubomír Doležel (1980) described as distinct types: "Introducing hypotheses, conjectures, guesses, i.e., non-authentic motifs, is a privilege of the Ich-form narrator not available to the anonymous Er-form narrator" (19 n. 16; cf. Doležel 1998: 145–68).

6. See Wallace Chafe and Johanna Nichols (1986) for information on how verbs such as *seemed*, adverbs such as *perhaps*, modal auxiliaries such as *might have* or *would have*, and other grammatical forms function as *evidentials*. Evidentials include a large repertoire of devices by means of which languages encode attitudes toward knowledge, or rather degrees of certainty toward what is known.

7. Thus, HF might be construed as a special case of what Genette (1980) terms "paralepsis," i.e., "giving more [information] than is authorized in principle in the code of focalization governing the whole" (195). Genette (1988) later described paralepsis as "an infraction, intentional or not, of the modal position of the moment" (74–75). My purpose here is to analyze in detail the paraleptic effects of HF specifically—effects that may suggest less the infraction of a code than grounds for rethinking the principles on which the code itself is based.

8. John Lyons (1977) defines propositional attitudes as "verbs denoting belief, doubt, intention, etc." (190). As Jaakko Hintikka (1971: 148 n. 9) writes, the term itself apparently derives from Bertrand Russell's *An Inquiry into Meaning and Truth*, originally published in 1940. See Hans Kamp (1990) for a thorough survey of major issues in the study of propositional attitudes and contexts of belief. For an early attempt at formalization of concepts in this research domain, see Alonzo Church (1990). Ralph Grishman (1985: 96–100) discusses how propositional attitudes, among other phenomena, pose challenges to the effort to develop computational models of natural language processing.

9. In distinguishing between the expressed world and the reference world, Frawley builds on the work of Sandra Chung and Alan Timberlake (1985), who make a correlative distinction between *event world* and *actual world* (241–55). Chung and Timberlake use the distinction to describe how "[l]anguages often have a verbal morphology that encodes the epistemological status of an event" (244; cf. Chafe and Nichols 1986).

10. It may be helpful to cite Frawley's account at greater length: "Modality is an epistemic version of deixis, with the values for the deictic points rewritten in terms of the speaker's state of belief and the relation between those points interpreted as degrees of commitment and likelihood of the actualization of states of affairs. When the reference world coincides with the expressed world, we get actual modality, or *realis*. When the reference world does not coincide with the [expressed] world, we get nonactual modality, or *irrealis*. This basic dichotomy is a scale, and thus the factual status of a proposition depends on the extent to which the two epistemic deictic points diverge; this divergence is translated into possibility, evidence, obligation, commitment and so on" (388).

11. Arguably, although there are some prefigurations of what I am calling HF in earlier narratological accounts (e.g., Genette 1980: 202–3; Rimmon-Kenan 1983: 79), those accounts are vitiated by an insufficiently developed narrative semantics. One of my research hypotheses is that internal and external focalization can be redescribed as relatively imprecise (or at least portmanteau) labels for the gamut of formal devices—among them, notably, verbal moods—that help encode epistemic stances in narrative discourse.

12. On alethic and epistemic modalities, see Doležel (1998: 114–32), Rescher (1964: 57), and Ryan (1991: 109–23).

13. In fact, *Lucky Jim* is a text rich in instances of HF, something that is perhaps to be expected given the novel's persistent emphasis on self-consciousness, role-playing, and self-theatricalization, with Dixon constantly trying out possible identities. See, for example, Amis (1961: 154, 179, 195, and 204).

Further, this passage and the one quoted subsequently from *The Sweet Hereafter* point up affinities between what I am calling HF and what Monika Fludernik (1996) has termed "figuralization," another way of characterizing blends between personal (or *Ich*-form) and impersonal (or *Er*-form) narration. For Fludernik, figuralization involves the "implicit evocation of an observer figure on the story level," i.e., the suggestion "of a deictic centre which is located on the scene but cannot be identified with one of the main characters" (192; cf. 197–201). As described here, HF, like figuralization, reduces to "linguistic signals [evoking] a perceiver and experiencer, a consciousness (or

SELF) on the story level" (197). But distinguishing between four subtypes of HF may yield finer discriminations between figuralizing modes, with *strong direct HF* involving an observer (or group of observers) only counterfactually existent in the storyworld, *weak direct HF* an actual observer whose focalizing acts are presented as contrary to fact, *strong indirect HF* an observer whose existence must be inferred, but whose focalizing acts resist (dis)confirmation, and *weak indirect HF* an inferred observer whose focalizing activity the discourse encodes as (to some degree) less doubtful than in the case of strong indirect HF. See table 13 and the ensuing discussion.

14. I write "quasi-aspectual" because, as Suzanne Fleischman (1990) argues in her treatment of aspect, strictly speaking "aspect refers only to grammatical means of expressing such notions as 'completion,' 'durativity,' and 'iterativity' " (20), not to *lexical* means for expressing those same notions.

15. Indeed, what might be termed Gillespie's panoptical Santa—further glimpsed in the verse that runs "He's making a list, / Checking it twice; / He's gonna find out / Who's naughty and nice"—suggests that study of HF might be articulated with Michel Foucault's (1979: 195–28) famous account of Jeremy Bentham's panopticon, an innovation in penal architecture by virtue of which prisoners are encouraged to infer than an observer or set of observers, who can in principle see everything going on in the prison, is at every moment seeing everything that is going on in every prisoner's cell. Virginia and William Herman kindly transcribed Gillespie's lyrics for me.

16. In point of fact, this passage, like 16, exemplifies "mixed" HF. The first three sentences of 17, like its final sentence, involve indirect HF. However, the counterfactual conditional found in the fourth sentence—"But the men in the boat had no time to see it, *and if they had had leisure*, there were other things to occupy their minds"—suggests (weak) direct HF of the sort used in the passage from Amis's *Lucky Jim* (passage 11). Like the Amis passage, the fourth sentence of 17 codes the men in the boat as actual storyworld participants, portraying as virtual only the focalizing activity that they might have engaged in but did not.

17. Hintikka (1971), however, suggests that the very distinction between meaning and reference is "profoundly misleading" (145). Hintikka develops arguments for the view that "what is often thought of as the theory of meaning is better thought of as the theory of reference for certain more complicated conceptual situations" (165; cf. Putnam 1990).

18. As Quine (1980) puts it, "a name may occur referentially in a statement S and yet not occur referentially in a longer statement which is formed by embedding S in the context 'is unaware that . . .' or 'believes that. . . .' To sum up the situation in a word, we may speak of the contexts 'is unaware that . . .'

and 'believes that...' as *referentially opaque*. The same is true of the contexts 'knows that...,' 'says that...,' 'is surprised that...,' etc.... It will next be shown that referential opacity afflicts also the so-called *modal* contexts 'Necessarily...' and 'Possibly...'" (142–43; cf. Roberts 1993).

19. To speak again with Genette (1980), "there are not only differences between affirming, commanding, wishing, etc., but there are also differences between degrees of affirmation; and... these differences are ordinarily expressed by modal variations, be they the infinite and subjunctive of indirect discourse in Latin, or, in French, the conditional that indicates information not confirmed.... one can tell *more* or *less* what one tells, and can tell it *according to one point of view or another*; and this capacity, and the modalities of its use, are precisely what our category of *narrative mood* aims at" (161–62).

20. In working on this chapter, I have benefited from the comments of Dorrit Cohn, James Phelan, and Marie-Laure Ryan, who provided helpful feedback on several earlier drafts.

9. CONTEXTUAL ANCHORING

1. In this respect, the present chapter seeks to build on recent work by Monika Fludernik (1996) and Michael Kearns (1999). Particularly relevant is Fludernik's discussion of "the strategic expansion of deictic options" in experimental fictions, which call into question both the theoretical category of *person* (as it is used by narrative theorists such as Genette and Stanzel) and the cognitive frame of *personhood* (see 222–49, especially 244–49). For his part, Kearns provides a careful and inspiring synthesis of narratological, rhetorical, and speech-act-theoretical approaches to questions also addressed in this chapter, including the chief question of how narrative texts pertain to their contexts of interpretation.

2. See Phelan (1994) for a discussion of the commonalities and contrasts between the (largely structuralist) notion of "narratee," on the one hand, and Rabinowitz's (rhetorical) notion of "narrative audience," on the other hand.

3. For a typology of modes of unreliability in narrative—one that draws on Ishiguro's novel as its tutor text—see Phelan and Martin's (1999) important study.

4. There is by now a considerable amount of critical argumentation for the view that second-person fiction is no mere literary-historical curiosity, destined, like other stylistic oddities, for an early and ignominious obsolescence. For early statements, see, in addition to Morrissette (1965), Michel Butor (1964) and Francisco Ynduráin (1969). For an overview of more recent work, see Fludernik (1994a).

5. Thus, in parallel with the three-valued temporal logic that I discussed in

chapter 6 and that encompasses the values *Earlier*, *Later*, and *Indeterminate*, the present chapter describes and analyzes narrative *you* in terms of a three-valued modal logic encompassing the values *Virtual* (= storyworld-internal), *Actual* (= storyworld-external), and *Indeterminate*.

6. For accounts of why intradiegetic narratees are more readily interpreted as virtual or storyworld-specific than extradiegetic narratees, see Genette (1980: 260; 1988: 131). See also G. Prince (1985: 301; 1987: 57).

7. As Anderson and Keenan (1985) go on to point out, however, the grammar of some languages encodes a distinction between personal and impersonal *you*, so that "[i]n Breton, for example, impersonal forms are given a distinct verbal inflection" (260).

8. Provisionally, I use the terms *audience*, *overhearer*, and *nonparticipant* interchangeably, and in contradistinction to *addressee*, *hearer*, and *participant*, respectively. I say "provisionally" because, as I go on to discuss, second-person fictions such as *A Pagan Place* call into question classical frameworks for understanding modes of participation in discourse. Likewise, in the arena of linguistic theory, researchers such as Goffman (1981) and Hanks (1990: 145–54) attempt to work past these constellations of terms toward a finer-grained specification of participant roles in discourse. See also Clark (1992) and Clark and Carlson (1982).

9. For a humorous representation of the difficulties, not to say impossibility, of framing a language entirely devoid of deictic expressions, see Bar-Hillel (1954: 367–69). For a somewhat questionable assimilation of *all* linguistic items to deictic expressions, see Vološinov (1973): "The meaning of a word is determined entirely by its context" (79).

10. Here, of course, I invoke a notion of participant roles different from the one developed in chapter 4. There my concern was with ways in which storyworld entities and individuals participate in—or rather, can be mentally projected as participating in—events around which a narrative centers. By contrast, the present chapter focuses on the concept "participation in discourse," i.e., ways in which interlocutors, ratified but unaddressed recipients, bystanders, overhearers, etc., orient themselves toward an ongoing discourse, and more specifically an ongoing discourse that is narratively organized. Hence as I use the term in this context, *participants* is synonymous with the *participant statuses* into which Erving Goffman (1981: 124–59) analyzed *participation frameworks*, or environments for participating in talk.

11. For more on participant frames and roles, see Brown and Yule (1983: 38–50), Goffman (1981), Hanks (1990: 137–91), Levinson (1983: 72), and Schiffrin (1987: 27) and (1994: 97–136).

12. Jakobson's hedged definition may derive from the functional perspec-

tive on language developed by Jakobson, Mukařovský, and other members of the Prague School in the interwar years and afterward. Indeed, Prague School functionalism is better described as polyfunctionalism: for the Prague School, the (hierarchical) relation between the poetic, cognitive, practical, and other functions always copresent in a given utterance *could always have been otherwise* at any given time and are always subject to different configurations of dominance and latency over time (see Herman 1995a: 154–68).

13. Cf. Benveniste (1966): "dans la classe formelle des pronoms, ceux dits de 'troisième personne' sont entièrement différents de *je* et *tu*, par leur fonction et par leur nature ... la 'troisième personne' est bien une 'non-personne'" 'in the formal class called pronouns, those terms of the "third person" are entirely different than *I* and *you*, in both their function and their nature. ... the "third person" is indeed a "nonperson"' (256).

14. I am hedging here ("some instances") because unlike Fludernik (1993c, 1994b) and Richardson (1991, 1994), for example, I do not try to catalogue possible subgenres of second-person fiction (e.g., according to the relative frequency or prominence of doubly deictic *you*) but instead focus on the richness and complexity of the discourse functions of narrative *you* in a single fiction.

15. Note furthermore that Morrissette (1965), writing early in the history of experimentation with this narrative technique, construes Butor's *La Modification* as a paradigm case for second-person fiction generally. Morrissette thus interprets the traits associated with *I → you* deictic transfer as an index of the "pure" form of narrative *you*, "in which the pronoun, while retaining its moralizing tonality in a rhetoric of self-judgment (or judgment by an outside 'voice' which must nevertheless be audible to the narrator o[r] hero), is used to recount individual, specific, past actions devoid of any general or typical implications" (13). Hence Morrissette's approach appertains to that species of discourse model that calls for the virtualization of storyworld items evoked by narrative *you*.

16. Likewise, the highly elaborate system of honorifics in Japanese, for example, encodes into the personal pronoun system information about the relative rank or respect level of the discourse participants—information not built into the grammar of English (Levinson 1983: 90–94; Anderson and Keenan 1985: 275). *A Pagan Place* would thus look very different indeed in a Japanese translation.

17. Kacandes (1993a: 147), like McHale (1987: 256), makes a similar observation about the *you* of the original Italian version of Calvino's *If on a Winter's Night a Traveler*, as opposed to the uninflected *you* of the English translation. However, in an e-mail communication to the author (6 June 1994), Chanita

Goodblatt pointed out that "in Hebrew the second-person, masculine plural effectively can function in many contexts as the impersonal, English *you*—and in some cases the second-person, masculine singular can also do so." Cf. Laberge (1980) and Laberge and Sankoff (1979).

18. In this connection, see Richardson's (1991) illuminating remarks concerning "O'Brien's creative narrative strategy for representing issues of language, gender, and silence," and his suggestion that "O'Brien's technique liberates the novel from the tyranny of an all-encompassing 'I' that for many resonates patriarchal values; at the same time, it discloses a female subject position that has historically been suppressed and denied" (317).

19. Here the durative (quasi-aspectual) force of *always* militates against the punctuality and specificity conferred on *you* by the past tense (perfective), which typically marks a singular, unrepeatable action.

20. Laberge and Sankoff (1979: 429) and Laberge (1980: 80–81) identify the formulation of truisms and morals as one of the major contexts of use in which speakers of Montréal French regularly substitute *tu* and *vous* for indefinite *on* (cf. some prescient remarks by Morrissette 1965: 8–9). The authors construe such pronominal displacement as evidence for the "migration [of *tu* and *vous*] across morphological categories, from the definite to the indefinite system" (439). One wonders whether, more generally, a correlation could be established between the relatively recent morphological migration of second-person pronouns and the fact that "[t]he huge bulk of second-person fiction . . . dates from the past fifteen years" (Fludernik 1993c: 217).

21. Richardson (1991) points out, however, that O'Brien's novel "is one of the very few second-person texts narrated almost entirely in the past tense" (316). Actions and events narrated in the past tense (more precisely: those narrated in the past tense and by way of verb forms having a perfective rather than imperfective aspect) are spatiotemporally bounded in nature, given that they are represented as having already occurred or been brought to completion. This makes past-tense second-person narration such as O'Brien's an especially favorable discourse environment for what I go on to characterize as doubly deictic narrative *you*. In doubly deictic *you*, the deictic field(s) orienting relatively *particularized* accounts of storyworld participants get superimposed on the deictic field(s) orienting a current interpreter's sense of place, time, and overall situation.

22. Compare this discourse model with the notion of "meaning as soliloquy" that Derrida (1973) identifies in Husserl's *Logical Investigations* and elsewhere in Husserlian phenomenology: "The subject does not have to pass forth beyond himself to be immediately affected by his expressive activity. My words are 'alive' because they seem not to leave me: not to fall outside me, outside my breath, at a visible distance" (76).

23. Arguably the phenomenon of self-address constitutes a kind of hybridized category that combines features of *I* → *you* deictic transfer with features of fictionalized or horizontal address. To put this same point another way, self-address intertwines the referential and address functions of narrative *you* but without cuing recipients to actualize that *you*. Self-address involves a fictional *I* addressing to herself, homodiegetically, propositions bearing on her own prior actions, during the performance of which the acting *I* is retrospectively designated as *you*. My subsequent discussion presupposes this (relatively vague) definition of self-address.

24. Though I can only allude to Clark and Carlson's (1982) powerful analysis here, future research on second-person fiction specifically, and contextual anchoring more generally, would do well to take into account Clark and Carlson's characterization of informatives, as well as their comments on, for example, lateral versus linear indirect addressees (336–38), unknown versus known overhearers (344–46), and complex indirect speech acts (364–65). See Clark (1992) for further information on "Discourse as a Collaborative Process" (101–97) and "Audience Design in Language Use" (199–297).

25. This is not to say, however, that all instances of doubly deictic *you* involve similes. The point is, rather, that similes create a favorable environment for double deixis. For doubly deictic contexts that do not feature comparisons, see O'Brien (1984: 98, 109, 167).

26. Note that the distinctions factual/fictional and literary/nonliterary are really crosscutting. There can be literary treatments of factual situations and events, such as Truman Capote's *In Cold Blood* (1966). Conversely, there can be nonliterary fictions, as when a gifted storyteller orally relays the legendary lore of a particular community.

27. See Fludernik (1996) for arguments that a core set of cognitive principles and parameters supports comprehension of both oral and written narratives.

Bibliography

Adams, Hazard, and Leroy Searle, eds. 1986. *Critical Theory since 1965*. Tallahassee: Florida State University Press. (Now available from University Press of Florida.)
Agre, Philip E. 1997. *Computation and Human Experience*. Cambridge: Cambridge University Press.
Allwood, Jens, Lars-Gunnar Andersson, and Östen Dahl. 1977. *Logic in Linguistics*. Cambridge: Cambridge University Press.
Amis, Kingsley. 1961. *Lucky Jim*. London: Penguin.
Anderson, Stephen R. and Edward L. Keenan. 1985. "Deixis." In Timothy Shopen, ed., *Language Typology and Syntactic Description*, vol. 3: *Grammatical Categories and the Lexicon*, pp. 259–308. Cambridge: Cambridge University Press.
Aristotle. 1971. *Poetics*. In Hazard Adams, ed., *Critical Theory since Plato*, pp. 48–66. San Diego: Harcourt Brace Jovanovich.
Atherton, James S. 1960. *The Books at the Wake: A Study of Literary Allusions in James Joyce's Finnegans Wake*. New York: Viking Press.
Atwood, Margaret. 1985. *The Handmaid's Tale*. New York: Fawcett Crest.
Austin, J. L. 1962. *How to Do Things with Words*. Cambridge: Harvard University Press.
Bakhtin, M. M. 1981a. "Discourse in the Novel." In Michael Holquist, ed., Caryl Emerson and Michael Holquist, trans., *The Dialogic Imagination: Four Essays*, pp. 259–422. Austin: University of Texas Press.
———. 1981b. "Forms of Time and of the Chronotope in the Novel: Notes towards a Historical Poetics." In Michael Holquist, ed., Caryl Emerson and Michael Holquist, trans., *The Dialogic Imagination: Four Essays*, pp. 84–258. Austin: University of Texas Press.
———. 1984. *Problems of Dostoevsky's Poetics*. Trans. Caryl Emerson. Minneapolis: University of Minnesota Press.
———. 1986. "The Problem of Speech Genres." In Caryl Emerson and Michael Holquist, eds., Vern W. McGee, trans., *Speech Genres and Other Late Essays*, pp. 60–102. Austin: University of Texas Press.
Bal, Mieke. 1985. *Narratology: Introduction to the Theory of Narrative*. Trans. Christine van Boheemen. Toronto: University of Toronto Press.

Bamberg, Michael G. W. 1987. *The Acquisition of Narratives: Learning to Use Language*. Berlin: Mouton de Gruyter.
——, ed. 1997a. "Oral Versions of Personal Experience: Three Decades of Narrative Analysis." Special issue of *Journal of Narrative and Life History* 7:1–415.
——, ed. 1997b. *Narrative Development: Six Approaches*. Mahwah NJ: Lawrence Erlbaum.
Banfield, Ann. 1982. *Unspeakable Sentences: Narration and Representation in the Language of Fiction*. Boston: Routledge and Kegan Paul.
Banks, Russell. 1991. *The Sweet Hereafter*. New York: HarperCollins.
Bar-Hillel, Yehoshua. 1954. "Indexical Expressions." *Mind* 63:359–79.
Barnes, Djuna. 1961. *Nightwood*. New York: New Directions.
Barry, Jackson G. 1990. "Narratology's Centrifugal Force: A Literary Perspective on the Extensions of Narrative Theory." *Poetics Today* 11.2:295–307.
Barthes, Roland. 1971a. "Action Sequences." In Joseph Strelka, ed., *Patterns of Literary Style*, pp. 5–14. University Park: Pennsylvania State University Press.
——. 1971b. "The Structuralist Activity." In Hazard Adams, ed., *Critical Theory since Plato*, pp. 1196–99. San Diego: Harcourt Brace Jovanovich.
——. 1972. *Mythologies*. Trans. Annette Lavers. New York: Hill and Wang.
——. 1974. *S/Z*. Trans. Richard Miller. New York: Hill and Wang.
——. 1977. "Introduction to the Structural Analysis of Narratives." In *Image Music Text*, trans. Stephen Heath, pp. 79–124. New York: Hill and Wang.
——. 1982. "The Reality Effect." In Tzvetan Todorov, ed., Ronald Carter, trans., *French Literary Theory Today*, pp. 11–17. Cambridge: Cambridge University Press.
——. 1996. "To Write: An Intransitive Verb?" In Philip Rice and Patricia Waugh, eds., *Modern Literary Theory*, pp. 41–50. London: Arnold.
Bartlett, Frederick. 1932. *Remembering: A Study in Experimental and Social Psychology*. Cambridge: Cambridge University Press.
Bavelas, Janet B., L. Edna Rogers, and Frank E. Millar. 1985. "Interpersonal Conflict." In Teun A. van Dijk, ed., *Handbook of Discourse Analysis*, vol. 4, pp. 9–26. Orlando FL: Academic Press.
Begnal, Michael H. 1988. *Dreamscheme: Narrative and Voice in Finnegans Wake*. Syracuse: Syracuse University Press.
Bell, Allan. 1984. "Language Style as Audience Design." *Language in Society* 13:145–204.
Benjamin, Walter. 1969. "Theses on the Philosophy of History." In Hannah Arendt, ed., Harry Zohn, trans., *Illuminations*, pp. 253–64. New York: Schocken Books.

Bennett, Jonathan. 1988. *Events and Their Names*. Indianapolis: Hackett Press.

Benstock, Bernard. 1963. "The Quiddity of Shem and the Whatness of Shaun." *James Joyce Quarterly* 1:26–33.

Benveniste, Émile. 1966. *Problèmes de linguistique générale*. Paris: Gallimard.

Beowulf. 1993. In M. H. Abrams, ed., *The Norton Anthology of English Literature*, vol. 1, 6th ed., pp. 27–68. New York: W. W. Norton.

Bernard, Kenneth. 1994. *The Baboon in the Nightclub*. Santa Maria CA: Asylum Arts.

Biber, Douglas. 1988. *Variation across Speech and Writing*. Cambridge: Cambridge University Press.

———. 1994. "An Analytical Framework for Register Studies." In Biber and Finegan (1994b), pp. 31–56.

Biber, Douglas, and Edward Finegan. 1994a. "Introduction: Situating Register in Sociolinguistics." In Biber and Finegan (1994b), pp. 3–12.

———, eds. 1994b. *Sociolinguistic Perspectives on Register*. Oxford: Oxford University Press.

Bishop, John. 1986. *Joyce's Book of the Dark*. Madison: University of Wisconsin Press.

Black, John B., and Gordon H. Bower. 1980. "Story Understanding as Problem Solving." *Poetics* 9:223–50.

Black, Max. 1937. "Vagueness: An Exercise in Logical Analysis." *Philosophy of Science* 4:427–55.

Blakemore, Diane. 1988. "The Organization of Discourse." In Frederick J. Newmeyer, ed., *Linguistics: The Cambridge Survey*, vol. 4, pp. 229–50. Cambridge: Cambridge University Press.

Bloom, Paul, Mary A. Peterson, Lynn Nadel, and Merrill F. Garrett, eds. 1996. *Language and Space*. Cambridge: MIT Press.

Bobrow, Daniel G., and Donald A. Norman. 1975. "Some Principles of Memory Schemata." In Daniel G. Bobrow and Allan Collins, eds., *Representation and Understanding: Studies in Cognitive Science*, pp. 131–49. New York: Academic Press.

Bockting, Ineke. 1994. "Mind Style as an Interdisciplinary Approach to Characterisation in Faulkner." *Language and Literature* 3:157–74.

Booth, Wayne C. 1983. *The Rhetoric of Fiction*. 2nd ed. Chicago: University of Chicago Press.

Bordwell, David, and Kristin Thompson. 1997. *Film Art: An Introduction*. 5th ed. New York: McGraw-Hill.

Borges, Jorge Luis. 1964. *Labyrinths*. Ed. Donald A. Yates and James E. Irby. New York: New Directions.

Bouissac, Paul, ed. 1998. *Encyclopedia of Semiotics*. Oxford: Oxford University Press.
Bowen, Elizabeth. 1966. *The Death of the Heart*. London: Penguin.
———. 1991. "Her Table Spread." In William Trevor, ed., *The Oxford Book of Irish Short Stories*, pp. 311–18. Oxford: Oxford University Press.
Bradley, A. C. 1965. *Shakespearean Tragedy*. London: Macmillan.
Branigan, Edward. 1992. *Narrative Comprehension and Film*. London: Routledge.
Bremond, Claude. 1973. *Logique du récit*. Paris: Seuil.
———. 1980. "The Logic of Narrative Possibilities." Trans. Elaine D. Cancalon. *New Literary History* 11:387–411.
Britton, Bruce K., and Arthur C. Graesser, eds. 1996. *Models of Understanding Text*. Mahwah NJ: Lawrence Erlbaum.
Broch, Hermann. 1978. *Die Schlafwändler*. Frankfurt am Main: Surhkamp-Verlag.
Brontë, Charlotte. 1960. *Jane Eyre*. New York: New American Library.
Brown, Gillian. 1995. *Speakers, Listeners and Communication: Explorations in Discourse Analysis*. Cambridge: Cambridge University Press.
Brown, Gillian, and George Yule. 1983. *Discourse Analysis*. Cambridge: Cambridge University Press.
Brown, Penelope, and Stephen C. Levinson. 1987. *Politeness: Some Universals in Language Usage*. Cambridge: Cambridge University Press.
Bruce, Bertram. 1978. "What Makes a Good Story?" *Language Arts* 55:460–66.
———. 1980. "Analysis of Interacting Plans as a Guide to the Understanding of Story Structure." *Poetics* 9:195–311.
———. 1983. "Plans and Discourse." TEXT 3:253–59.
Bruner, Jerome. 1986. *Actual Minds, Possible Worlds*. Cambridge: Harvard University Press.
———. 1991. "The Narrative Construction of Reality." *Critical Inquiry* 18:1–21.
Buck, R. A. 1996. "Reading Forster's Style: Face Actions and Social Scripts in *Maurice*." *Style* 30.1:69–94.
Budniakiewicz, Therese. 1992. *Fundamentals of Story Logic: Introduction to Greimassian Semiotics*. Amsterdam: John Benjamins.
———. 1998a. "Actants." In Bouissac (1998), pp. 5–8.
———. 1998b. "Actantial Model." In Bouissac (1998), pp. 8–11.
———. 1998c. "Narrative Structures." In Bouissac (1998), pp. 437–43.
———. 1998d. "Greimas, Algirdas-Julien." In Bouissac (1998), pp. 271–74.
Bühler, Karl. 1965. *Sprachtheorie*. Stuttgart: Fischer.
Burke, Kenneth. 1969. *A Grammar of Motives*. Berkeley: University of California Press.

Butor, Michel. 1957. *La Modification*. Paris: Minuit.
———. 1964. "L'Usage des pronoms personnels dans le roman." In *Répertoire*, vol. 2, pp. 61–72. Paris: Minuit.
Byatt, A. S. 1990. *Possession*. New York: Vintage Books.
Cameron, Deborah, and Jennifer Coates. 1988. "Some Problems in the Sociolinguistic Description of Sex Differences." In Jennifer Coates and Deborah Cameron, eds., *Women in Their Speech Communities*, pp. 13–26. London: Longman.
Cameron, Deborah, Fiona McAlinden, and Kathy O'Leary. 1988. "Lakoff in Context: The Social and Linguistic Functions of Tag Questions." In Jennifer Coates and Deborah Cameron, eds., *Women in Their Speech Communities*, pp. 74–93. London: Longman.
Capote, Truman. 1966. *In Cold Blood*. New York: Random House, 1966.
Carnap, Rudolf. 1947. *Meaning and Necessity*. Chicago: University of Chicago Press.
Cervantes, Miguel de. 1964. *Don Quixote*. Trans. Walter Starkie. New York: Signet.
Chafe, Wallace. 1998. "Things We Can Learn from Repeated Tellings of the Same Experience." *Narrative Inquiry* 8:269–85.
Chafe, Wallace, and Johanna Nichols, eds. 1986. *Evidentiality: The Linguistic Coding of Epistemology*. Norwood NJ: Ablex.
Chafe, Wallace, Elinor Ochs, Deborah Schiffrin, Paul J. Hopper, and Jane Anne Edwards. 1992. "Discourse." In William Bright, ed., *International Encyclopedia of Linguistics*, vol. 1, pp. 355–71. Oxford: Oxford University Press.
Charles, May. 1995. "A Postmodern Challenge to Reference-World Construction: Gilbert Sorrentino's Mulligan Stew." *Style* 29.2:235–61.
Charniak, Eugene, and Drew McDermott. 1985. *Introduction to Artificial Intelligence*. Reading MA: Addison-Wesley.
Chatman, Seymour. 1978. *Story and Discourse: Narrative Structure in Fiction and Film*. Ithaca: Cornell University Press.
———. 1990. *Coming to Terms: The Rhetoric of Narrative in Fiction and Film*. Ithaca: Cornell University Press.
———. 1995. "How Loose Can Narrators Get? (And How Vulnerable Can Narratees Be?)." *Narrative* 3.3:303–6.
———. 1999. "New Directions in Voice-Narrated Cinema." In Herman (1999d), pp. 315–39.
Chaucer, Geoffrey. 1993. *The Pardoner's Prologue and Tale*. In M. H. Abrams, ed., *The Norton Anthology of English Literature*, vol. 1, pp. 164–79. New York: Norton.

Cheshire, Jenny. 1992. "Register and Style." In William Bright, ed., *International Encyclopedia of Linguistics*, pp. 324-27. New York: Oxford University Press.

Chomsky, Noam. 1965. *Aspects of the Theory of Syntax*. Cambridge: MIT Press.

———. 1981. *Lectures on Government and Binding*. Dordrecht, Netherlands: Foris.

Chopin, Kate. 1993. *The Awakening*. Ed. Nancy A. Walker. Boston: Bedford Books.

Christie, Agatha. 1976. *The Murder of Roger Ackroyd*. New York: Garland.

Chung, Sandra, and Alan Timberlake. 1985. "Tense, Aspect, and Mood." In T. Shopen, ed., *Language Typology and Syntactic Description*, vol. 3: *Grammatical Categories and the Lexicon*, pp. 202-58. Cambridge: Cambridge University Press.

Church, Alonzo. 1990. "Intensional Semantics." In A. P. Martinich, ed., *The Philosophy of Language*, 2nd ed., pp. 40-47. Oxford: Oxford University Press.

Clark, Herbert. 1992. *Arenas of Language Use*. Chicago and Stanford: University of Chicago Press and The Center for the Study of Language and Information.

Clark, Herbert H., and Thomas B. Carlson. 1982. "Hearers and Speech Acts." *Language* 58:332-73.

Coates, Jennifer. 1993. *Women, Men and Language*. 2nd ed. London: Longman.

Coetzee, J. M. 1988. *Foe*. Harmondsworth UK: Penguin.

Cohn, Dorrit. 1978. *Transparent Minds: Narrative Modes for Presenting Consciousness*. Princeton: Princeton University Press.

———. 1999. *The Distinction of Fiction*. Baltimore: Johns Hopkins University Press.

Conrad, Joseph. 1996. *Heart of Darkness*. Ed. Ross C. Murfin. Boston: Bedford Books.

Cook, Walter A. 1989. *Case Grammar Theory*. Washington DC: Georgetown University Press.

Coste, Didier. 1989. *Narrative as Communication*. Minneapolis: University of Minnesota Press.

Couperie, Pierre, et al. 1968. *A History of the Comic Strip*. Trans. Eileen B. Hennessy. New York: Crown.

Craik, Kenneth H. 1943. *The Nature of Explanation*. Cambridge: Cambridge University Press.

Crane, Stephen. 1990. "The Open Boat." In R. V. Cassill, ed., *The Norton Anthology of Short Fiction*, 4th ed., pp. 395-416. New York: W. W. Norton.

Crevier, Daniel. 1993. *AI: The Tumultuous History of the Search for Artificial Intelligence*. New York: Basic Books.

Cross, Richard K. 1992. "The Soul Is a Far Country: D. M. Thomas and the White Hotel." *Journal of Modern Literature* 18:19–47.

Crystal, David. 1997. *A Dictionary of Linguistics and Phonetics*. 4th ed. Oxford: Basil Blackwell.

Culler, Jonathan. 1975a. *Structuralist Poetics: Structuralism, Linguistics, and the Study of Literature*. Ithaca: Cornell University Press.

———. 1975b. "Defining Narrative Units." In Roger Fowler, ed., *Style and Structure in Literature: Essays in the New Stylistics*, pp. 121–45. Oxford: Basil Blackwell.

Dahl, Östen, ed. 1974. *Topic and Comment, Contexual Boundedness and Focus*. Hamburg: Helmut Buske Verlag.

Daneš, František, ed. 1974. *Papers on Functional Sentence Perspective*. Prague: Academia.

Daniels, Les. 1971. *Comix: A History of Comic Books in America*. New York: Bonanza Books.

Danto, Arthur C. 1985. *Narration and Knowledge* (including the integral text of *Analytical Philosophy of History*). New York: Columbia University Press.

Davidson, Donald. 1980. *Essays on Actions and Events*. Oxford: Clarendon Press.

———. 1985. "Reply to Quine on Events." In Ernest LePore and Brian P. McLaughlin, eds., *Actions and Events: Perspectives on the Philosophy of Donald Davidson*, pp. 172–76. Oxford: Basil Blackwell.

Davis, Lawrence H. 1979. *Theory of Action*. Englewood Cliffs NJ: Prentice Hall.

Defoe, Daniel. 1964. *Moll Flanders*. New York: New American Library.

Derrida, Jacques. 1973. *Speech and Phenomena and Other Essays on Husserl's Theory of Signs*. Trans. David B. Allison. Evanston: Northwestern University Press.

———. 1989. *Edmund Husserl's* Origin of Geometry: *An Introduction*. Trans. John P. Leavey Jr. Lincoln: University of Nebraska Press.

Devlin, Kimberly. 1983. "Self and Other in *Finnegans Wake*: A Framework for Analyzing Versions of Shem and Shaun." *James Joyce Quarterly* 21:31–50.

Dickens, Charles. 1964. *Bleak House*. New York: New American Library.

Diderot, Denis. 1986. *Jacques the Fatalist*. Trans. Michael Henry. London: Penguin Books.

Dirven, René, and Marjolijn Verspoor. 1998. *Cognitive Exploration of Language and Linguistics*. Amsterdam: John Benjamins.

Döblin, Alfred. 1931. *Alexanderplatz, Berlin: The Story of Franz Biberkopf*. Trans. Eugene Jolas. New York: Viking Press.

Doležel, Lubomír. 1972. "From Motifemes to Motfs." *Poetics* 4:55–90.
———. 1973. *Narrative Modes in Czech Literature*. Toronto: University of Toronto Press.
———. 1976. "Narrative Modalities." *Journal of Literary Semantics* 5:5–15.
———. 1979. "Extensional and Intensional Narrative Worlds." *Poetics* 8:193–211.
———. 1980. "Truth and Authenticity in Narrative." *Poetics Today* 1:7–25.
———. 1983. "Intensional Function, Invisible Worlds, and Franz Kafka." *Style* 17:120–41.
———. 1990. *Occidental Poetics: Tradition and Progress*. Lincoln: University of Nebraska Press.
———. 1998. *Heterocosmica: Fiction and Possible Worlds*. Baltimore: Johns Hopkins University Press.
Doležel, Lubomír, and Richard W. Bailey, eds. 1969. *Statistics and Style*. New York: Elsevier.
Donovan, Josephine. 1998. "Beyond the Net: Feminist Criticism as a Moral Criticism." In Keesey (1998), pp. 235–45.
Dosse, François. 1997. *History of Structuralism*. Vols. 1 and 2. Trans. Deborah Glassman. Minneapolis: University of Minnesota Press.
Downs, Roger M., and David Stea. 1977. *Maps in Minds: Reflections on Cognitive Mapping*. New York: Harper and Row.
Dowty, David. 1979. *Word Meaning and Montague Grammar*. Dordrecht, Netherlands: Reidel.
Dreiser, Theodore. 1997. *Sister Carrie*. New York: Doubleday.
Duchan, Judith Felson. 1986. "Learning to Describe Events." *Topics in Language Disorders* 6.4:27–36.
Duchan, Judith F., Gail A. Bruder, and Lynne E. Hewitt, eds. 1995. *Deixis in Narrative: A Cognitive Science Perspective*. Hillsdale NJ: Lawrence Erlbaum.
Ducrot, Oswald, and Tzvetan Todorov. 1979. *Encyclopedic Dictionary of the Sciences of Language*. Trans. Catherine Porter. Baltimore: Johns Hopkins University Press.
Dupriez, Bernard. 1991. "Apostrophe." In Albert W. Halsall, trans. and ed., *A Dictionary of Literary Devices*, pp. 58–60. Toronto: University of Toronto Press.
Eble, Connie. 1996. *Slang and Sociability: In-group Language among College Students*. Chapel Hill: University of North Carolina Press.
Eckley, Grace. 1985. *Children's Lore in* Finnegans Wake. Syracuse: Syracuse University Press.
Eco, Umberto. 1989. *The Open Work*. Trans. Anna Cancogni. Cambridge: Harvard University Press.
Egoyan, Atom. 1997. *The Sweet Hereafter*. Fine Line Cinema.

Eliot, George. 1986. *Daniel Deronda*. Ed. Barbara Hardy. London: Penguin.
Emmott, Catherine. 1994. "Frames of Reference: Contextual Monitoring and the Interpretation of Narrative Discourse." In Malcolm Coulthard, ed., *Advances in Written Text Analysis*, pp. 157–66. London: Routledge.
———. 1997. *Narrative Comprehension: A Discourse Perspective*. Oxford: Oxford University Press.
Fairclough, Norman. 1989. *Language and Power*. London: Longman.
———. 1995. *Critical Discourse Analysis: The Critical Study of Language*. London: Longman.
Fasold, Ralph. 1990. *Sociolinguistics of Language*. Oxford: Basil Blackwell.
Fauconnier, Gilles. 1985. *Mental Spaces*. Cambridge: MIT Press.
Faulkner, William. 1987. *As I Lay Dying*. New York: Vintage International.
Fawcett, Robin P. 1980. *Cognitive Linguistics and Social Interaction*. Heidelberg: Julius Groos Verlag.
Ferguson, Charles. 1994. "Dialect, Register, and Genre: Working Assumptions about Conventionalization." In Biber and Finegan (1994b), pp. 15–30.
Fillmore, Charles. 1968. "The Case for Case." In Emmon Bach and Robert T. Harms, eds., *Universals in Linguistic Theory*, pp. 1–88. New York: Holt, Rinehart, and Winston.
———. 1971. "Some Problems for Case Grammars." In Richard J. O'Brien, ed., *Georgetown University Roundtable on Languages and Linguistics 1971*, pp. 35–56. Washington DC: Georgetown University Press.
———. 1977. "The Case for Case Reopened." In Peter Cole and Jerrold Sadock, eds., *Syntax and Semantics*, vol. 8, pp. 59–81. New York: Academic Press.
Firbas, Jan. 1964. "On Defining the Theme in Functional Sentence Analysis." *Travaux linguistiques de Prague* 1:267–80.
———. 1992. *Functional Sentence Perspective in Written and Spoken Communication*. Cambridge: Cambridge University Press.
Flaubert, Gustave. 1992. *Madame Bovary: Patterns of Provincial Life*. Trans. Francis Steegmuller. New York: Vintage Books.
Fleischman, Suzanne. 1990. *Tense and Narrativity: From Medieval Performance to Modern Fiction*. Austin: University of Texas Press.
Fletcher, Charles R., Paul van den Broek, and Erik J. Arthur. 1996. "A Model of Narrative Comprehension and Recall." In Britton and Graesser (1996), 141–63.
Fludernik, Monika. 1993a. *The Fictions of Language and the Languages of Fiction*. London: Routledge.
———. 1993b. "Narratology in Context." *Poetics Today* 14:729–61.
———. 1993c. "Second-Person Fiction: Narrative You as Addressee and/or Protagonist." *AAA—Arbeiten aus Anglistik und Amerikanistik* 18:217–47.

———, ed. 1994a. "Second-Person Narrative." Special issue of *Style* 28.

———. 1994b. "Introduction: Second-Person Narrative and Related Issues." *Style* 28:281–311.

———. 1996. *Towards a "Natural" Narratology*. London: Routledge.

Foley, William A., and Robert D. Van Valin Jr. 1984. *Functional Syntax and Universal Grammar*. Cambridge: Cambridge University Press.

Forster, E. M. 1927. *Aspects of the Novel*. New York: Harcourt Brace.

Foster, John Burt, Jr. 1995. "Magical Realism, Compensatory Vision, and Felt History: Classical Realism Transformed in The White Hotel." In Lois Parkinson Zamora and Wendy B. Faris, eds., *Magical Realism: Theory, History, Community*, pp. 267–83. Durham: Duke University Press.

Foucault, Michel. 1979. *Discipline and Punish: The Birth of the Prison*. Trans. Alan Sheridan. New York: Vintage Books.

Fowler, Roger. 1977. *Linguistics and the Novel*. London: Methuen.

———. 1986. *Linguistic Criticism*. Oxford: Oxford University Press.

Fox, Barbara A. 1987. *Discourse Structure and Anaphora*. Cambridge: Cambridge University Press.

Foy, George. 1996. *The Shift*. New York: Bantam Books.

Francis, David, and Christopher Hart. 1997. "Narrative Intelligibility and Membership Categorization in a Television Commercial." In Stephen Hester and Peter Eglin, eds., *Culture in Action: Studies in Membership Categorization Analysis*, pp. 123–51. Lanham MD: University Press of America.

Frawley, William. 1992. *Linguistic Semantics*. Hillsdale NJ: Lawrence Erlbaum.

Frege, Gottlob. 1969. "On Sense and Reference." In Peter Geach and Max Black, trans. and eds., *Translations from the Philosophical Writings of Gottlob Frege*, pp. 56–78. Oxford: Basil Blackwell.

Freud, Sigmund. 1969. *An Outline of Psycho-Analysis*. Trans. James Strachey. New York: W. W. Norton.

Frye, Northrop. 1974. "Allegory." In Alex Preminger, Frank J. Warnke, and O. B. Hardison Jr., eds., *The Princeton Encyclopedia of Poetry and Poetics*, pp. 12–15. Princeton: Princeton University Press.

Furrow, Melissa. 1988. "Listening Reader and Impotent Speaker: The Role of Deixis in Literature." *Language and Style* 21:365–78.

Fussell, Paul. 1975. *The Great War and Modern Memory*. Oxford: Oxford University Press.

Galbraith, Mary K. 1995. "Deictic Shift Theory and the Poetics of Involvement in Narrative." In Duchan, Bruder, and Hewitt (1995), pp. 19–59.

Garfinkel, Harold. 1967. *Studies in Ethnomethodology*. Englewood Cliffs NJ: Prentice Hall.

Garnham, Alan, and Jane Oakhill. 1996. "The Mental Models Theory of Language Comprehension." In Britton and Graesser (1996), pp. 313–39.

Gazdar, Gerald. 1979. *Pragmatics: Implicature, Presupposition and Logical Form*. New York: Academic Press.

Geminiani, Giuliano C., Antonella Carassa, and Bruno G. Bara. 1996. "Causality by Contact." In Jane Oakhill and Alan Garnham, eds., *Mental Models in Cognitive Science: Essays in Honour of Phil Johnson-Laird*, pp. 275–303. East Sussex UK: Psychology Press.

Genette, Gérard. 1976. "Boundaries of Narrative." *New Literary History* 8:1–13.

———. 1980. *Narrative Discourse: An Essay in Method*. Trans. Jane E. Lewin. Ithaca: Cornell University Press.

———. 1988. *Narrative Discourse Revisited*. Trans. Jane E. Lewin. Ithaca: Cornell Univ. Press.

———. 1997. *Palimpsests: Literature in the Second Degree*. Trans. Channa Newman and Claude Doubinsky. Lincoln: University of Nebraska Press.

Gerrig, Richard J. 1993. *Experiencing Narrative Worlds: On the Psychological Activities of Reading*. New Haven: Yale University Press.

Gibbon, Edward. 1932. *The Decline and Fall of the Roman Empire*. 3 vols. New York: Modern Library.

Gilbert, Sandra. 1998. "The Second Coming of Aphrodite: Kate Chopin's Fantasy of Desire." In Keesey (1998), pp. 354–70.

Giora, Rachel, and Yeshayahu Shen. 1994. "Degrees of Narrativity and Strategies of Semantic Reduction." *Poetics* 22:447–58.

Gilman, Charlotte Perkins. 1980. *The Charlotte Perkins Gilman Reader*. Ed. Ann J. Lane. New York: Pantheon Books.

Givón, Talmy. 1993. *English Grammar: A Function-Based Introduction*. Vol. 1. Amsterdam: John Benjamins.

Glasheen, Adaline. 1977. *Third Census of Finnegans Wake: An Index of the Characters and Their Roles*. Berkeley: University of California Press.

Goffman, Erving. 1955. "On Face-Work: An Analysis of Ritual Elements in Social Interaction." *Psychiatry* 18:213–31.

———. 1974. *Frame Analysis: An Essay on the Organization of Experience*. New York: Harper and Row.

———. 1981. *Forms of Talk*. Philadelphia: University of Pennsylvania Press.

Goldman, Alvin I. 1970. *A Theory of Human Action*. Englewood Cliffs NJ: Prentice Hall.

Gordimer, Nadine. 1970. *A Guest of Honour*. London: Penguin.

Gordon, Peter. 1994. "Names, Pronouns, and Discourse Coherence." Paper presented to the Triangle Linguistics Club, National Humanities Center, February, Research Triangle Park NC.

Gould, Peter, and Rodney White. 1986. *Mental Maps*. 2nd ed. Boston: Allen and Unwin.

Grabes, Herbert. 1978. "Wie aus Sätzen Person werden." *Poetica* 10:404–28.

Graesser, Arthur C., and Leslie F. Clark. 1985. *Structures and Procedures of Implicit Knowledge*. Norwood NJ: Ablex.

Graesser, Arthur C., Scott P. Robertson, and Patricia A. Anderson. 1981. "Incorporating Inferences in Narrative Representations: A Study of How and Why." *Cognitive Psychology* 13:1–26.

Green, Georgia M. 1989. *Pragmatics and Natural Language Understanding*. Hillsdale NJ: Lawrence Erlbaum.

Gregory, Michael, and Susanne Carroll. 1978. *Language and Situation: Language Varieties and Their Social Contexts*. London: Routledge and Kegan Paul.

Greig, Andrew. 1994. *Western Swing*. Newcastle upon Tyne UK: Bloodaxe Books.

Greimas, Algirdas-Julien. 1983. *Structural Semantics: An Attempt at a Method*. Trans. Danielle McDowell, Ronald Schleifer, and Alan Velie. Lincoln: University of Nebraska Press.

——. 1987. "Actants, Actors, and Figures." In *On Meaning: Selected Writings in Semiotic Theory*, pp. 106–20. Trans. Paul J. Perron and Frank H. Collins. Minneapolis: University of Minnesota Press.

——. 1988. *Maupassant: The Semiotics of Text*. Trans. Paul Perron. Amsterdam: John Benjamins.

——. 1990a. "On Scientific Discourse in the Social Sciences. In *The Social Sciences: A Semiotic View*, trans. Paul Perron and Frank H. Collins, pp. 11–36. Minneapolis: University of Minnesota Press.

——. 1990b. "The Pathways of Knowledge." In *The Social Sciences: A Semiotic View*, trans. Paul Perron and Frank H. Collins, pp. 37–58. Minneapolis: University of Minnesota Press.

Greimas, Algirdas-Julien, and Joseph Courtés. 1983. *Semiotics and Language: An Analytical Dictionary*. Trans. Larry Crist, Daniel Patte, James Lee, Edward McMahon II, Gary Phillips, and Michael Rengstorf. Bloomington: Indiana University Press.

Grice, Paul. 1989. *Studies in the Way of Words*. Cambridge: Harvard University Press.

Grishman, Ralph. 1986. *Computational Linguistics: An Introduction*. Cambridge: Cambridge University Press.

Grossman, Walter. 1962. "Die Zeit in Anna Seghers' 'Der Ausflug der toten Mädchen.'" *Sinn und Form* 14:120–43.

Grosz, Barbara, and Candace Sidner. 1986. "Attention, Intentions, and the Structure of Discourse." *Computational Linguistics* 12:175–204.

Guenther, Irene. 1995. "Magic Realism, New Objectivity, and the Arts during the Weimar Republic." In Lois Parkinson Zamora and Wendy B. Faris, *Magical Realism: Theory, History, Community*, pp. 33-73. Durham: Duke University Press.

Gumperz, John J. 1982. *Discourse Strategies*. Cambridge: Cambridge University Press.

Haack, Susan. 1978. *Philosophy of Logics*. Cambridge: Cambridge University Press.

Habermas, Jürgen. 1988. *Nachmetaphysisches Denken: Philosophische Aufsätze*. Frankfurt am Main: Suhrkamp Verlag, 1988.

Haegeman, Liliane. 1994. *Introduction to Government and Binding Theory*. 2nd ed. Oxford: Basil Blackwell.

Halliday, M. A. K. 1967. "Notes on Transitivity and Theme in English (Part I)." *Journal of Linguistics* 3:37-81.

———. 1971. "Linguistic Function and Literary Style: An Inquiry into William Golding's *The Inheritors*." In Seymour Chatman, ed., *Literary Style: A Symposium*, pp. 330-65. Oxford: Oxford University Press.

———. 1976. "Types of Process." In Gunther Kress, ed., *Halliday: System and Function in Language*, pp. 159-73. Oxford: Oxford University Press.

———. 1978. *Language as Social Semiotic: The Social Interpretation of Language and Meaning*. London: Edward Arnold.

———. 1994. *An Introduction to Functional Grammar*. 2nd edition. London: Edward Arnold.

Halliday, M. A. K., and Ruqaiya Hasan. 1976. *Cohesion in English*. London: Longman.

Hamburger, Käte. 1973. *The Logic of Literature*. Trans. Marilyn J. Rose. Bloomington: Indiana University Press.

Hamilton, Heidi Ehernberger. 1994. *Conversations with an Alzheimer's Patient: An Interactional Sociolinguistic Study*. Cambridge: Cambridge University Press.

Hamon, Philippe. 1981. "Rhetorical Status of the Descriptive." In "Towards a Theory of Description." Special issue of *Yale French Studies* 61:1-26.

———. 1982. "What Is a Description?" In Tzvetan Todorov, ed., R. Carter, trans., *French Literary Theory Today*, pp. 147-78. Cambridge: Cambridge University Press.

Hanks, William F. 1990. *Referential Practice: Language and Lived Space among the Maya*. Chicago: University of Chicago Press.

Hayes, Paul M. 1973. *Fascism*. New York: Free Press.

Hayman, David. 1990. *The 'Wake' in Transit*. Ithaca: Cornell University Press.

Heath, Shirley Brice, and Juliet Langman. 1994. "Shared Thinking and the Register of Coaching." In Biber and Finegan (1994b), pp. 82-105.

Hejinian, Lyn. 1991. *Oxota: A Short Russian Novel*. Great Barrington MA: Figures.

Hemingway, Ernest. 1964. *A Moveable Feast*. New York: Charles Scribner's Sons.

Hendricks, William O. 1967. "On the Notion 'Beyond the Sentence.'" *Linguistics* 37:12–51.

———. 1977. "'A Rose for Emily': A Syntagmatic Analysis." *PTL* 2:257–95.

Herman, David. 1993. "Modernism versus Postmodernism: Towards an Analytic Distinction." In Joseph Natoli and Linda Hutcheon, eds., *A Postmodern Reader*, pp. 157–92. Albany: SUNY Press.

———. 1994a. "The Mutt and Jute Dialogue in Joyce's *Finnegans Wake*: Some Gricean Perspectives." *Style* 28:219–41.

———. 1994b. "Hypothetical Focalization." *Narrative* 2:230–53.

———. 1994c. "Textual *You* and Double Deixis in Edna O'Brien's *A Pagan Place*." *Style* 28:378–410.

———. 1995a. *Universal Grammar and Narrative Form*. Durham: Duke University Press.

———. 1995b. "Autobiography, Allegory, and the Construction of Self." *British Journal of Aesthetics* 35:351–60.

———. 1997a. "Scripts, Sequences, and Stories: Elements of a Postclassical Narratology." *PMLA* 112:1046–59.

———. 1997b. "Toward a Formal Description of Narrative Metalepsis." *Journal of Literary Semantics* 26:132–52.

———. 1998a. "Limits of Order: Toward a Theory of Polychronic Narration." *Narrative* 6:72–95.

———. 1998b. "Dialogue in a Discourse Context: Discourse-Analytic Models and Woolf's *To the Lighthouse*." *Virginia Woolf Miscellany* 52:3–4.

———. 1998c. "Narrative, Science, and Narrative Science." *Narrative Inquiry* 8.2:379–90.

———. 1998d. "Theories of Fiction and the Claims of Narrative Poetics." *Poetics Today* 19:597–607.

———. 1998e. Book Notice of Catherine Emmott's *Narrative Comprehension: A Discourse Perspective*. *Language* 74:869–71.

———. 1999a. "Parables of Narrative Imagining." *Diacritics* 29.1:20–36.

———. 1999b. "Narratologies: An Introduction." In Herman (1999d), pp. 1–30.

———. 1999c. "Towards a Socionarratology: New Ways of Analyzing Natural-Language Narratives." In Herman (1999d), pp. 218–46.

———, ed. 1999d. *Narratologies: New Perspectives on Narrative Analysis*. Columbus: Ohio State University Press.

———. 1999e. "Economies of Essence in Edith Wharton's *The House of Mirth*." *Edith Wharton Review* 16.1:6–10.

———. 1999f. "Spatial Cognition in Natural-Language Narratives." In Mateas and Sengers (1999), pp. 21–25.

———. 2000a. "Pragmatic Constraints on Narrative Processing: Actants and Anaphora Resolution in a Corpus of North Carolina Ghost Stories." *Journal of Pragmatics* 32.7:959–1001.

———. 2000b. "Existentialist Roots of Narrative Actants." *Studies in Twentieth-Century Literature* 24:257–69.

———. 2001a. "Style Shifting in Edith Wharton's *The House of Mirth*." *Language and Literature* 10:61–77.

———. 2001b. "Sciences of the Text." *Postmodern Culture*. http://www.iath.virginia.edu/pmc/text-only/issue.501/11.3herman.txt (date of access: 1 September 2001).

———. Forthcoming. "Spatial Reference in Narrative Domains." TEXT.

———. In preparation. *Narrative as Cognitive Artifact*.

Hernadi, Paul. 1972. "Dual Perspective: Free Indirect Discourse and Related Techniques." *Comparative Literature* 24: 1–23.

Herskovits, Annette. 1986. *Language and Spatial Cognition*. Cambridge: Cambridge University Press.

Hester, Stephen, and Peter Eglin. 1997. "Membership Categorization Analysis: An Introduction." In Stephen Hester and Peter Eglin, eds., *Culture in Action: Studies in Membership Categorization Analysis*, pp. 1–23. Lanham MD: University Press of America.

Hintikka, Jaakko. 1971. "Semantics for Propositional Attitudes." In Leonard Linsky, ed., *Reference and Modality*, pp. 145–67. Oxford: Oxford University Press.

Hjelmslev, Louis. 1954. "La Stratification du langage." *Word* 10:163–88.

———. 1961. *Prolegomena to a Theory of Language*. Trans. Francis J. Whitfield. Madison: University of Wisconsin Press.

Homer. 1999. *The Odyssey*. Trans. Robert Fitzgerald. In Sarah Lawall, ed., *The Norton Anthology of World Masterpieces: The Western Tradition*, vol. 1, pp. 209–514. New York: W. W. Norton.

Horkheimer, Max, and Theodor Adorno. 1988. *Dialect of Enlightenment*. Trans. John Cumming. New York: Continuum.

Hutcheon, Linda. 1988. *A Poetics of Postmodernism*. London: Routledge.

Hymes, Dell. 1974. *Foundations in Sociolinguistics: An Ethnographic Approach*. Philadelphia: University of Pennsylvania Press.

Inge, M. Thomas. 1990. *Comics as Culture*. Jackson: University of Mississippi Press.

Iser, Wolfgang. 1978. *The Act of Reading: A Theory of Aesthetic Response*. Baltimore: Johns Hopkins University Press.

Ishiguro, Kazuo. 1990. *The Remains of the Day*. New York: Knopf.
Ives, Sumner. 1971. "A Theory of Literary Dialect." In Juanita V. Williamson and Virginia M. Burke, eds., *A Various Language: Perspectives on American Dialects*, pp. 145–77. New York: Holt, Rinehart and Winston.
Jackendoff, Ray. 1983. *Semantics and Cognition*. Cambridge: MIT Press.
———. 1987. "The Status of Thematic Relations in Linguistic Theory." *Linguistic Inquiry* 18:369–411.
Jacobs, Paul S., and Lisa F. Rau. 1993. "Innovations in Text Interpretation." *Artificial Intelligence* 63:143–91.
Jahn, Manfred. 1997. "Frames, Preferences, and the Reading of Third-Person Narratives: Towards a Cognitive Narratology." *Poetics Today* 18:441–68.
———. 1999. "'Speak, Friend, and Enter': Garden Paths, Artificial Intelligence, and Cognitive Narratology." In Herman (1999d), pp. 167–94.
Jakobson, Roman. 1960. "Closing Statement: Linguistics and Poetics." In Thomas A. Sebeok, ed., *Style in Language*, pp. 350–77. Cambridge: MIT Press.
———. 1971. "Shifters, Verbal Categories and the Russian Verb." In *Selected Writings*, vol. 2, pp. 130–47. The Hague: Mouton.
James, Henry. 1992. *The Portrait of a Lady*. New York: Vintage Books.
———. 1996. "The Jolly Corner." In *Complete Stories, 1898–1910*, pp. 697–731. New York: Library of America.
Jameson, Fredric. 1988. "Cognitive Mapping." In Cary Nelson and Lawrence Grossberg, eds., *Marxism and the Interpretation of Culture*, pp. 347–57. Urbana: University of Illinois Press.
Jauss, Hans Robert. 1996. "Literary History as a Challenge to Literary Theory." In Philip Rice and Patricia Waugh, eds., *Modern Literary Theory: A Reader*, 3rd ed., pp. 82–89. London: Arnold.
Jespersen, Otto. 1922. *Language: Its Nature, Development, and Origin*. London: Allen and Unwin.
Johnson-Laird, P. N. 1983. *Mental Models: Towards a Cognitive Science of Language, Inference, and Consciousness*. Cambridge: Harvard University Press.
Joyce, James. 1939. *Finnegans Wake*. New York: Penguin Books.
———. 1964. *A Portrait of the Artist as a Young Man*. New York: Penguin Books.
———. 1986. *Ulysses*. New York: Vintage Books.
Kacandes, Irene. 1993a. "Are You in the Text? The 'Literary Performative' in Postmodernist Fiction." *Text and Performance Quarterly* 13:139–53.
———. 1993b. "Can You Talk Back? Toward a Typology of Second-Person Fiction." Paper presented at the session on "Second-Person Poetics" at the MLA Convention, December, Toronto, Canada.

Kafalenos, Emma. 1995. "Lingering along the Narrative Path: Extended Functions in Kafka and Henry James." *Narrative* 3:117–38.

———. 1997. "Functions after Propp: Words to Talk about How We Read Narrative." *Poetics Today* 18:469–94.

———. 1999. "Not (Yet) Knowing: Epistemological Effects of Deferred and Suppressed Information in Narrative." In Herman (1999d), pp. 33–65.

Kafka, Franz. 1984a. *The Trial*. Trans. Willa and Edwin Muir; revised by E. M. Butler. New York: Schocken Books.

———. 1984b. *Metamorphosis*. Trans. Willa and Edwin Muir. New York: Limited Editions Club.

———. 1986. *Der Prozeß*. Frankfurt am Main: Fischer Taschenbuch Verlag.

Kamp, Hans. 1990. "Prolegomena to a Structural Account of Belief and Other Attitudes." In C. Anthony Anderson and Joseph Owens, eds., *Propositional Attitudes: The Role of Content in Logic, Language, and the Mind*, pp. 27–90. Stanford: Center for the Study of Language and Information.

Kearns, Michael. 1999. *Rhetorical Narratology*. Lincoln: University of Nebraska Press.

Keesey, Donald, ed. 1998. *Contexts for Criticism*. 3rd ed. Mountain View CA: Mayfield.

Kemnitz, Charles. 1985. "Beyond the Zone of Middle Dimensions: A Relativistic Reading of *The Third Policeman*." 15:56–72.

Kiefer, Ferenc. 1992. "Case." In William Bright, ed., *International Encyclopedia of Linguistics*, pp. 217–18. New York: Oxford University Press.

Kiesling, Scott, and Natalie Schilling-Estes. 1998. "Language Style as Identity Construction: A Footing and Framing Approach." Paper presented at the Conference on New Ways of Analyzing Variation in English, Athens GA.

Kittay, Jeffrey. 1981a. Introduction. In "Towards a Theory of Description." Special issue of *Yale French Studies* 61:i–v.

———. 1981b. "Descriptive Limits." In "Towards a Theory of Description." Special issue of *Yale French Studies* 61:225–43.

Kolodny, Annette. 1986. "Dancing through the Minefield: Some Observations on the Theory, Practice, and Politics of a Feminist Literary Criticism." In Adams and Searle (1986), pp. 499–512.

Korte, Barbara. 1987. "Das Du im Erzähltext." *Poetica* 19:168–89.

Kosko, Bart. 1986. "Fuzzy Cognitive Maps." *International Journal of Man-Machine Studies* 24:65–75.

———. 1992. *Neural Networks and Fuzzy Systems: A Dynamical Systems Approach to Machine Intelligence*. Englewood Cliffs NJ: Prentice Hall.

———. 1993. *Fuzzy Thinking: The New Science of Fuzzy Logic*. New York: Hyperion.

Kronfeld, Amichai. 1990. *Reference and Computation: An Essay in Applied Philosophy of Language*. Cambridge: Cambridge University Press.

Kubin, Alfred. 1967. *The Other Side: A Fantastic Novel*. Trans. Denver Lindley. New York: Crown.

LaBahn, Kathleen J. 1986. *Anna Seghers' Exile Literature: The Mexican Years (1941–1947)*. New York: Peter Lang.

Laberge, Suzanne. 1980. "The Changing Distribution of Indefinite Pronouns in Discourse." In Roger W. Shuy and Anna Shnukal, eds., *Language Use and the Uses of Language*, pp. 76–87. Washington DC: Georgetown University Press.

Laberge, Suzanne, and Gillian Sankoff. 1979. "Anything *You* Can Do." In Talmy Givón, ed., *Syntax and Semantics 12: Discourse and Syntax*, pp. 419–20. New York: Academic Press.

Labov, William. 1972a. "The Transformation of Experience in Narrative Syntax." In *Language in the Inner City*, pp. 354–96. Philadelphia: University of Pennsylvania Press.

———. 1972b. "Rules for Ritual Insults." In David Sudnow, ed., *Studies in Social Interaction*, pp. 120–69. New York: Free Press.

———. 1972c. "The Isolation of Contextual Styles." In *Sociolinguistic Patterns*, pp. 70–109. Philadelphia: University of Pennsylvania Press.

———. 1997. "Some Further Steps in Narrative Analysis." In Bamberg (1997), pp. 395–415.

Labov, William, and Joshua Waletzky. 1967. "Narrative Analysis: Oral Versions of Personal Experience." In June Helm, ed., *Essays on Verbal and Visual Arts*, pp. 12–44. Seattle: University of Washington Press.

Lafayette, Madame de. 1994. *The Princess of Clèves*. Trans. John D. Lyons. New York: W. W. Norton.

Lakoff, Robin. 1975. *Language and Woman's Place*. New York: Harper and Row.

Lamb, Sydney M. 1999. *Pathways of the Brain: The Neurocognitive Basis of Language*. Amsterdam: John Benjamins.

Lanchester, John. 1996. *The Debt to Pleasure*. New York: Henry Holt.

Landau, Barbara. 1994. "Object Shape, Object Name, and Object Kind: Representation and Development." *Psychology of Learning and Motivation* 31:253–304.

———. 1996. "Where's What and What's Where: The Language of Objects in Space." In Lila Gleitman and Barbara Landau, eds., *The Acquisition of the Lexicon*, pp. 259–96. Cambridge: MIT Press.

Landau, Barbara, and Ray Jackendoff. 1993. "'What' and 'Where' in Spatial Language and Cognition." *Behavioral and Brain Sciences* 16:217–65.

Lanser, Susan Sniader. 1981. *The Narrative Act: Point of View in Prose Fiction*. Princeton: Princeton University Press.

———. 1991. "Toward a Feminist Narratology." In Robyn Warhol and Diane Price Herndl, eds., *Feminisms: An Anthology*, pp. 610–629. New Brunswick NJ: Rutgers University Press.

Laqueur, Walter. 1996. *Fascism: Past, Present, Future*. Oxford: Oxford University Press.

Leech, Geoffrey N., and Michael H. Short. 1981. *Style in Fiction: A Linguistic Introduction to English Fictional Prose*. London: Longman.

Lehnert, Wendy. 1981. "Plot Units and Narrative Summarization." *Cognitive Science* 4:293–332.

Leith, Dick. 1988. "A Pragmatic Approach to Ballad Dialogue." In Willie van Peer, ed., *The Taming of the Text: Explorations in Language, Literature and Culture*, pp. 35–60. London: Routledge.

Lejeune, Philippe. 1988. *On Autobiography*. Trans. Katherine M. Leary. Minneapolis: University of Minnesota Press.

Lerdahl, Fred, and Ray Jackendoff. 1983. *A Generative Theory of Tonal Music*. Cambridge: MIT Press.

Levin, Beth, and Malka Rappaport Hovav. 1996. "Lexical Semantics and Syntactic Structure." In Shalom Lappin, ed., *The Handbook of Contemporary Semantic Theory*. Oxford: Basil Blackwell.

Levinson, Stephen C. 1983. *Pragmatics*. Cambridge: Cambridge University Press.

———. 1996. "Frames of Reference and Molyneux's Question: Crosslinguistic Evidence." In Bloom et al. (1996), pp. 109–69.

Lévi-Strauss, Claude. 1986. "The Structural Study of Myth." In Adams and Searle (1986), pp. 809–22.

Linde, Charlotte. 1993. *Life Stories: The Creation of Coherence*. Oxford: Oxford University Press.

Linde, Charlotte, and William Labov. 1975. "Spatial Networks as a Site for the Study of Language and Thought." *Language* 51:925–39.

Lodge, David. 1996. "Analysis and Interpretation of the Realist Text." In Philip Rice and Patricia Waugh, eds., *Modern Literary Theory*, pp. 24–41. London: Arnold.

Longacre, Robert E. 1983. *The Grammar of Discourse*. New York: Plenum Press.

Lotman, Jurij, and B. A. Uspenskij. 1986. "On the Semiotic Mechanism of Culture." Trans. George Mihaychuk. In Adams and Searle (1986), pp. 410–22.

Lukasiewicz, Jan. 1967. "On 3-Valued Logic." In Storrs McCall, ed., *Polish Logic*, pp. 16–18. Oxford: Clarendon Press.

Lyons, John. 1977. *Semantics.* Vol. 2. Cambridge: Cambridge University Press.

Lyotard, Jean-François. 1984. *The Postmodern Condition: A Report on Knowledge.* Trans. Geoff Bennington and Brian Massumi. Minneapolis: University of Minnesota Press.

MacBride, Maud Gonne. 1983. *A Servant of the Queen.* Suffolk UK: Boydell Press.

MacNeil, Lynda D. 1996. "Homo Inventans: The Evolution of Narrativity." *Language and Communication* 16.4:331–60.

Malmkjaer, Kirsten. 1991. "Case Grammar." In Kirsten Malmkjaer and James M. Anderson, eds., *The Linguistics Encyclopedia*, pp. 65–70.

Mandler, Jean Matter. 1984. *Stories, Scripts, and Scenes: Aspects of Schema Theory.* Hillsdale NJ: Lawrence Erlbaum.

Mandler, Jean M., and Nancy S. Johnson. 1977. "Remembrance of Things Parsed: Story Structure and Recall." *Cognitive Psychology* 9:111–51.

Margolin, Uri. 1984. "Narrative and Indexicality: A Tentative Framework." *Journal of Literary Semantics* 13:181–204.

———. 1986. "The Doer and the Deed: Action Basis for Characterization in Narrative." *Poetics Today* 7:205–26.

———. 1986/87. "Dispersing/Voiding the Subject: A Narratological Perspective." *Texte* 5/6:181–210.

———. 1987. "Introducing and Sustaining Characters in Literary Narrative: A Set of Conditions." *Style* 21:107–24.

———. 1990a. "The What, the When, and the How of Being a Character in a Literary Narrative." *Style* 24:453–68.

———. 1990b. "Individuals in Narrative Worlds: An Ontological Perspective." *Poetics Today* 11:843–71.

———. 1995. "Characters in Literary Narrative: Representation and Signification." *Semiotica* 106:373–92.

———. 1999. "Of What Is Past, Is Passing, or to Come: Temporality, Aspectuality, Modality, and the Nature of Narrative." In Herman (1999d), pp. 142–66.

Martin, J. R. 1996a. "Metalinguistic Diversity: The Case from Case." In Ruqaiya Hasan, Carmel Cloran, and David Butt, eds., *Functional Descriptions: Theory in Practice*, pp. 325–74. Amsterdam: John Benjamins.

Martin, J. R. 1996b. "Transitivity in Tagalog: A Functional Interpretation of Case." In Margaret Berry, Christopher Butler, Robin Fawcett, and Guowen Huang, eds., *Meaning and Form: Systemic Functional Interpretations*, pp. 229–96. Norwood NJ: Ablex.

Martin, Wallace. 1986. *Recent Theories of Narrative.* Ithaca: Cornell University Press.

Mateas, Michael, and Phoebe Sengers, eds. 1999. *Narrative Intelligence: Papers from the 1999 AAAI Fall Symposium*. Technical Report FS-99-01. Menlo Park CA: American Association for Artificial Intelligence Press.

May, John R. "Local Color in *The Awakening*." In Keesey (1998), pp. 133–38.

Mazzullo, Concetta. 1995. "Flann O'Brien's Hellish Otherworld: From *Buile Suibhne* to *The Third Policeman*." *Irish University Review* 25:318–27.

McDowell, John H. 1985. "Verbal Duelling." In van Dijk (1985a), pp. 203–11.

McHale, Brian. 1978. "Free Indirect Discourse: A Survey of Recent Accounts." *PTL* 3:249–88.

———. 1987. *Postmodernist Fiction*. New York: Methuen.

———. 1998. "Telling Stories Again: On the Replenishment of Narrative in the Postmodernist Long Poem." Paper presented at the Annual Meeting of the Society for the Study of Narrative Literature, April, Northwestern University, Chicago.

McHugh, Roland. 1991. *Annotations to* Finnegans Wake. 2nd ed. Baltimore: Johns Hopkins University Press.

McKoon, Gail, Gregory Ward, Roger Ratcliff, and Richard Sproat. 1993. "Morphosyntactic and Pragmatic Factors Affecting the Accessiblity of Discourse Entities." *Journal of Memory and Language* 32:56–75.

Meletinsky, Eleazar M. 1970. "Problèmes de la Morphologie Historique du Conte Populaire." *Semiotica* 2:128–35.

Mercadal, Dennis. 1990. *A Dictionary of Artificial Intelligence*. New York: Van Nostrand Reinhold.

Merivale, Patricia, and Susan Elizabeth Sweeney, eds. 1999. *Detecting Texts: The Metaphysical Detective Story from Poe to Postmodernism*. Philadelphia: University of Pennsylvania Press.

Metzger, John. 1998. "Tales That Tell: An Ethnographic Approach to Conversational Narratives." Unpublished ms.

Mills, Sara. 1992. "Knowing Your Place: A Marxist Feminist Stylistic Analysis." In Michael Toolan, ed., *Language, Text and Context: Essays in Stylistics*, pp. 182–205. London: Routledge.

Milne, A. A. 1926. *Winnie-the-Pooh*. New York: E. P. Dutton.

Mink, Louis. 1978. "Narrative Form as Cognitive Instrument." In Robert H. Canary and Henry Kozicki, eds., *The Writing of History: Literary Form and Historical Understanding*, pp. 129–49. Madison: University of Wisconsin Press.

Minsky, Marvin. 1975. "A Framework for Representing Knowledge." In Patrick Winston, ed., *The Psychology of Computer Vision*, pp. 211–77. New York: McGraw-Hill, 1975.

———. 1988. *The Society of Mind*. New York: Touchstone.

Modiano, Patrick. 1968. *La Place de l'étoile*. Paris: Gallimard.
——. 1978. *Rue des boutiques obscures*. Paris: Gallimard.
Morgan, Charles G. 1998. "Fuzzy Logic." In Edward Craig, ed., *The Routledge Encylopedia of Philosophy*, vol. 3, pp. 822–24. London: Routledge.
Morot-Sir, Édouard. 1982. "Texte, Référence et Déictique." *Texte* 1:113–42.
Morrissette, Bruce. 1965. "Narrative 'You' in Contemporary Literature." *Comparative Literature Studies* 2:1–24.
Moser, Megan, and Johanna D. Moore. 1995. "Using Discourse Analysis and Automatic Text Generation to Study Discourse Cue Usage." Paper presented at the AAAI Spring Symposium on Empirical Methods in Discourse Interpretation and Generation.
Moser, Megan, and Johanna D. Moore. 1996. "Toward a Synthesis of Two Accounts of Discourse Structure." *Computational Linguistics* 22.3:409–420.
Mukařovský, Jan. 1977. "Two Studies of Dialogue." In John Burbank and Peter Steiner, trans. and eds., *The Word and Verbal Art*, pp. 81–115. New Haven: Yale University Press.
Muldoon, Paul. 1991. *Madoc: A Mystery*. New York: Farrar, Straus and Giroux.
Murray, Janet H. 1997. *Hamlet on the Holodeck: The Future of Narrative in Cyberspace*. New York: Free Press.
Newman, Robert D. 1989. "D. M. Thomas' The White Hotel: Mirrors, Triangles, and Sublime Repression." *Modern Fiction Studies* 35:193–209.
Nieraad, Jürgen. 1978. "Pronominalstrukturen in realistischer Prosa." *Poetica* 10:485–506.
Nietzsche, Friedrich. 1979. "On Truth and Lies in a Nonmoral Sense." In Daniel Breazeale, trans. and ed., *Philosophy and Truth: Selections from Nietzsche's Notebooks of the Early 1870s*, pp. 79–91. Atlantic Highlands NJ: Humanities Press.
O'Brien, Edna. 1984. *A Pagan Place*. Port Townsend WA: Graywolf Press.
O'Brien, Flann. 1976. *The Third Policeman*. New York: Plume.
Ochs, Elinor, Carolyn Taylor, Dina Rudolph, and Ruth Smith. 1992. "Storytelling as Theory-Building Activity." *Discourse Processes* 15:37–72.
Olsen, Tillie. 1989. *Tell Me a Riddle*. New York: Delta.
Ostroff, Susan. 1995. "Maps on My Past: Race, Space, and Place in the Life Stories of Washington D.C. Area Teenagers." *Oral History Review* 22:33–53.
O'Toole, Mary A. 1988. "The Theory of Serialism in The Third Policeman." *Irish University Review* 18:215–25.
Page, Norman. 1973. *Speech in the English Novel*. London: Longman.
Paris, Bernard. 1998. "The Uses of Psychology" [excerpt from *A Psychological Approach to Fiction*]. In Keesey (1998), pp. 226–34. Mountain View CA: Mayfield.

Parsons, Terence. 1985. "Underlying Events in the Logical Analysis of English." In Ernest LePore and Brian P. McLaughlin, eds., *Actions and Events: Perspectives on the Philosophy of Donald Davidson*, pp. 235-67. Oxford: Basil Blackwell.
——. 1990. *Events in the Semantics of English: A Study in Subatomic Semantics*. Cambridge: MIT Press.
Pascal, Roy. 1977. *The Dual Voice*. Manchester: Manchester University Press.
Passias, Katherine. 1976. "Deep and Surface Structure of the Narrative Pronoun *Vous* in Butor's *La Modification* and Its Relationship to Free Indirect Style." *Language and Style* 9:197-212.
Pavel, Thomas G. 1985a. *The Poetics of Plot: The Case of English Renaissance Drama*. Minneapolis: University of Minnesota Press.
——. 1985b. "Literary Narratives." In Teun A. van Dijk, ed., *Discourse and Literature*, pp. 83-104. Amsterdam: John Benjamins.
——. 1986. *Fictional Worlds*. Cambridge: Harvard University Press.
——. 1989. *The Feud of Language: A History of Structuralist Thought*. Trans. Linda Jordan and Thomas G. Pavel. Cambridge: Basil Blackwell.
Payne, Stanley G. 1995. *A History of Fascism, 1914-1945*. Madison: University of Wisconsin Press.
Perrine, Laurence. 1974. "Apostrophe." In Alex Preminger, ed., *The Princeton Encyclopedia of Poetry and Poetics*, p. 42. Princeton: Princeton University Press.
Peterson, Carole, and Allyssa McCabe. 1983. *Developmental Psycholinguistics: Three Ways of Looking at a Child's Narrative*. New York: Plenum.
Phelan, James. 1989. *Reading People, Reading Plots: Character, Progression, and the Interpretation of Narrative*. Chicago: University of Chicago Press.
——. 1994. "Self-Help for Narratee and Narrative Audience: How I—and You?—Read 'How.'" *Style* 28:350-65.
——. 1996. *Narrative as Rhetoric: Technique, Audiences, Ethics, Ideology*. Columbus: Ohio State University Press.
——. 2001. "Why Narrators Can Be Focalizers—and Why It Matters." In Will van Peer and Seymour Chatman, eds., *Narrative Perspective*, pp. 51-64. Albany: SUNY Press.
Phelan, James, and Mary Patricia Martin. 1999. "The Lessons of 'Weymouth': Homodiegesis, Ethics, and *The Remains of the Day*." In Herman (1999d), pp. 88-109.
Philp, Michael. 1997. "Building the Ideologue: New Perspectives on Focalization in Film and Print Narratives." Master's thesis, North Carolina State University.
Piwowarczyk, Mary Ann. 1976. "The Narratee and the Situation of Enunciation: A Reconsideration of Prince's Theory." *Genre* 9:161-77.

Poe, Edgar Allan. 1990. "The Fall of the House of Usher." In R. V. Cassill, ed., *The Norton Anthology of Short Fiction*, 4th ed., pp. 1390–1405. New York: W. W. Norton.

Polanyi, Livia. 1985. "Conversational Storytelling." In van Dijk (1985a), pp. 183–201.

———. 1989. *Telling the American Story: A Structural and Cultural Analysis of Conversational Storytelling*. Cambridge: MIT Press.

Polkinghorne, Donald E. 1988. *Narrative Knowing and the Human Sciences*. Albany: SUNY Press.

Post, Emil. 1921. "Introduction to a General Theory of Elementary Propositions." *American Journal of Mathematics* 43:163–85.

Pratt, Mary Louise. 1977. *Towards a Speech Act Theory of Literary Discourse*. Bloomington: Indiana University Press.

———. 1986. "Ideology and Speech-Act Theory." *Poetics Today* 7:59–73.

Preston, Dennis. 1991. "Sorting out the Variables in Sociolinguistic Theory." *American Speech* 66:33–56.

Prince, Ellen F. 1981. "Toward a Taxonomy of Given-New Information." In Peter Cole, ed., *Radical Pragmatics*, pp. 223–56. New York: Academic Press.

———. 1988. "Discourse Analysis: A Part of the Study of Linguistic Competence." In Frederick J. Newmeyer, ed., *Linguistics: The Cambridge Survey*, vol. 2, pp. 164–82. Cambridge: Cambridge University Press.

———. 1992. "The ZPG Letter: Subjects, Definiteness, and Information-Status." In William C. Mann and Sandra A. Thompson, eds., *Discourse Description: Diverse Linguistic Analyses of a Fund-Raising Text*, pp. 295–325. Amsterdam: John Benjamins.

Prince, Gerald. 1973. *A Grammar of Stories*. The Hague: Mouton.

———. 1980a. "Aspects of a Grammar of Narrative." *Poetics Today* 1:49–63.

———. 1980b. "Introduction to the Study of the Narratee." In Jane P. Tompkins, ed., *Reader-Response Criticism*, pp. 7–25. Baltimore: Johns Hopkins University Press.

———. 1982. *Narratology: The Form and Functioning of Narrative*. Berlin: Mouton.

———. 1983. "Narrative Pragmatics, Message, and Point." *Poetics* 12:527–36.

———. 1985. "The Narratee Revisited." *Style* 19:299–302.

———. 1987. *A Dictionary of Narratology*. Lincoln: University of Nebraska Press.

———. 1988. "The Disnarrated." *Style* 22:1–8.

———. 1991. "Narratology, Narrative, and Meaning." *Poetics Today* 12:543–552.

———. 1992. *Narrative as Theme: Studies in French Fiction*. Lincoln: University of Nebraska Press.

———. 1995. "Narratology." In Raman Selden, ed., *The Cambridge History of Literary Criticism*, vol. 8, pp. 110–30. Cambridge: Cambridge University Press.

Propp, Vladimir. 1968. *Morphology of the Folktale*. 2nd ed. Trans. Laurence Scott; revised by Louis A. Wagner. Austin: University of Texas Press.

Putnam, Hilary. 1990. "Meaning and Reference." In A. P. Martinich, ed., *The Philosophy of Language*, 2nd ed., pp. 308–15. Oxford: Oxford University Press.

Quine, Willard Van Orman. 1960. *Word and Object*. Cambridge: MIT Press.

———. 1980. *From a Logical Point of View*. 2nd ed. Cambridge: Harvard University Press.

Rabinowitz, Peter J. 1996. "Truth in Fiction: A Reexamination of Audiences." In David H. Richter, ed. *Narrative/Theory*, pp. 209–26. White Plains NY: Longman.

Radcliffe, Ann. 1968. *The Italian*. Oxford: Oxford University Press.

Rauh, Gisa. 1978. *Linguistische Beschreibung deiktischer Komplexität in narrativen Texten*. Tübingen: Narr.

Reddy, Michael J., 1979. "The Conduit Metaphor." In Andrew Ortony, ed., *Metaphor and Thought*, pp. 284–324. Cambridge: Cambridge University Press.

Reilly, Rick. 1998. "Last Call." *Sports Illustrated* 88.19:32–52.

Reinhart, Tanya. 1983. *Anaphora and Semantic Interpretation*. London: Croom Helm.

Rescher, Nicholas. 1964. *Hypothetical Reasoning*. Amsterdam: North-Holland.

———. 1966. "Aspects of Action." In Nicholas Rescher, ed., *The Logic of Decision and Action*, pp. 215–19. Pittsburgh: University of Pittsburgh Press.

———. 1969. *Many-Valued Logic*. New York: McGraw-Hill.

Rhys, Jean. 1993. *Wide Sargasso Sea*. Harmondsworth UK: Penguin.

Richardson, Brian. 1991. "The Poetics and Politics of Second-Person Narrative." *Genre* 24:309–30.

———. 1994. "I Etcetera: On the Poetics and Ideology of Multipersoned Narratives." *Style* 28:312–28.

———. 1998. "A Postclassical Narratology." PMLA 113:288–89.

Riessman, Catherine Kohler. 1993. *Narrative Analysis*. Newbury Park CA: Sage.

Rickford, John, and Faye McNair-Knox. 1994. "Addressee- and Topic-Influenced Style Shift: A Quantitative Sociolinguistic Study." In Biber and Finegan (1994b), pp. 236–76.

Rilke, Rainer Maria. 1983. *The Notebooks of Malte Laurids Brigge*. Trans. Stephen Mitchell. New York: Random House.

Rimmon-Kenan, Shlomith. 1983. *Narrative Fiction: Contemporary Poetics*. London: Methuen.

———. 1989. "How the Model Neglects the Medium: Linguistics, Language, and the Crisis of Narratology." *Journal of Narrative Technique* 19:157–66.

Robbe-Grillet, Alain. 1957. *La Jalousie*. Paris: Éditions de Minuit.

Roberts, Lawrence D. 1993. *How Reference Works: Explanatory Models for Indexicals, Descriptions and Opacity*. Albany: SUNY Press.

Robinson, Lillian S. 1986. "Treason Our Text: Feminist Challenges to the Literary Canon." In Adams and Searle (1986), pp. 572–82.

———. 1994. "The Traffic in Women: A Cultural Critique of *The House of Mirth*." In Wharton (1994), pp. 340–58.

Roh, Franz. 1925. *Nach-Expressionismus, Magischer Realismus: Probleme der neuesten Europäischen Malerei*. Leipzig: Klinkhardt and Biermann.

Romaine, Suzanne. 1999. *Communicating Gender*. Mahwah NJ: Lawrence Erlbaum.

Ronen, Ruth. 1994. *Possible Worlds in Literary Theory*. Cambridge: Cambridge University Press.

Rosch, Eleanor, Carolyn B. Mervis, Wayne D. Gray, David M. Johnson, and Penny Boyes-Braem. 1976. "Basic Objects in Natural Categories." *Cognitive Psychology* 8:382–439.

Rubin, David C. 1995. *Memory in Oral Traditions: The Cognitive Psychology of Epic, Ballads, and Counting-Out Rhymes*. Oxford: Oxford University Press.

Rummelhart, David E. 1975. "Notes on a Schema for Stories." In Daniel G. Bobrow and Allan Collins, eds., *Representation and Understanding: Studies in Cognitive Science*, pp. 211–36. New York: Academic Press.

Rushdie, Salman. 1990. *Haroun and the Sea of Stories*. London: Granta Books.

Ryan, Marie-Laure. 1979. "Linguistic Models in Narratology: From Structuralism to Generative Semantics." *Semiotica* 28.1/2:127–55.

———. 1991. *Possible Worlds, Artificial Intelligence, and Narrative Theory*. Bloomington: Indiana University Press.

———. 1992. "Possible Worlds in Recent Literary Theory." *Style* 26:528–553.

———. 1997. "Postmodernism and the Doctrine of Panfictionality." *Narrative* 5:165–87.

———. 1999. "Cyberage Narratology: Computers, Metaphor, and Narrative." In Herman (1999d), pp. 113–41.

———. 2000. *Narrative as Virtual Reality: Immersion and Interactivity in Literature and Electronic Media*. Baltimore: Johns Hopkins University Press.

———. Forthcoming. "Fiction and Its Other: How Trespassers Help Defend the Border." *Semiotica*.

Rydén, Mays, and Sverker Brorström. 1987. *The Be/Have Variation with Intransitives in English*. Stockholm: Almqvist and Wiksell.

Sacks, Harvey, Emanuel A. Schegloff, and Gail Jefferson. 1974. "A Simplest Systematics for the Organization of Turn-Taking for Conversation." *Language* 50:696-735.
Salmon, Nathan. 1992. "Temporality." In William Bright, ed., *International Encyclopedia of Linguistics*, vol. 4, pp. 141-44. New York: Oxford University Press.
Sapir, Edward. 1921. *Language: An Introduction to the Study of Speech*. New York: Harcourt Brace.
Sareil, Jean. 1987. "La Description négative." *Romanic Review* 78:1-9.
Sartre, Jean-Paul. 1938. *La Nausée*. Paris: Gallimard.
———. 1964. *Nausea*. Trans. Lloyd Alexander. New York: New Directions.
———. 1965. "The Humanism of Existentialism." In Wade Baskin, ed., *The Philosophy of Existentialism*, pp. 33-57. New York: Philosophical Library.
Schank, Roger C. 1990. *Tell Me a Story: A New Look at Real and Artificial Memory*. New York: Charles Scribner.
Schank, Roger C., and Robert P. Abelson. 1977. *Scripts, Plans, Goals and Understanding: An Inquiry into Human Knowledge Structures*. Hillsdale NJ: Lawrence Erlbaum.
Schegloff, Emanuel A. 1981. "Discourse as an Interactional Achievement." In Deborah Tannen, ed., *Analyzing Discourse: Text and Talk*, pp. 71-93. Washington DC: Georgetown University Press.
———. 1997. "'Narrative Analysis' Thirty Years Later." In Bamberg (1997), pp. 97-106.
Schiffrin, Deborah. 1985. "Everyday Argument: The Organization of Diversity in Talk." In van Dijk (1985a), pp. 35-46.
———. 1987. *Discourse Markers*. Cambridge: Cambridge University Press.
———. 1988. "Conversation Analysis." In Frederick J. Newmeyer, ed., *Linguistics: The Cambridge Survey*, vol. 4, pp. 251-76. Cambridge: Cambridge University Press.
———. 1990a. "The Principle of Intersubjectivity in Communication and Conversation." *Semiotica* 80:121-51.
———. 1990b. "Between Text and Context: Deixis, Anaphora, and the Meaning of *Then*." TEXT 10:245-70.
———. 1994. *Approaches to Discourse*. Cambridge MA: Basil Blackwell.
Scholes, Robert. 1974. *Structuralism in Literature: An Introduction*. New Haven: Yale University Press.
Scollon, Ron, and Suzanne Wong Scollon. 1995. *Intercultural Communication: A Discourse Approach*. Oxford: Basil Blackwell.
Searle, John R. 1969. *Speech Acts*: An Essay in the Philosophy of Language. Cambridge: Cambridge University Press.

———. 1992. "Conversation." In Herman Parret and Jef Verschueren, eds., (*On*) *Searle on Conversation*, pp. 7–29. Amsterdam: John Benjamins.
Segal, Erwin M. 1995. "Narrative Comprehension and the Role of Deictic Shift Theory." In Judith F. Duchan, Gail A. Bruder, and Lynne E. Hewitt, eds., *Deixis in Narrative: A Cognitive Science Perspective*, pp. 3–17. Hillsdale NJ: Lawrence Erlbaum.
Seghers, Anna. 1980. "Der Ausflug der toten Mädchen." *Erzählungen, 1926–1944. Gesammelte Werke in Einzelausgaben*, vol. 9, pp. 330–62. Berlin: Aufbau-Verlag.
Segre, Cesare. 1995. "From Motif to Function and Back Again." In Claude Bremond, Joshua Landy, and Thomas Pavel, eds., *Thematics: New Approaches*, pp. 21–32. Albany: SUNY Press.
Semino, Elena, Mick Short, and Jonathan Culpeper. 1997. "Using a Corpus to Test a Model of Speech and Thought Presentation." *Poetics* 25:17–43.
Shaw, Harry. 1995a. "Loose Narrators." *Narrative* 3:95–116.
———. 1995b. "Thin Description: A Reply to Seymour Chatman." *Narrative* 3:307–14.
Shklovsky, Victor. 1965. "Art as Technique." In Lee T. Lemon and Marion J. Reis, eds., *Russian Formalist Criticism*, pp. 3–24. Lincoln: University of Nebraska Press.
———. 1990. *Theory of Prose*. Trans. Benjamin Sher. Elmwood Park IL: Dalkey Archive Press.
Short, Michael. 1988. "Speech Presentation, the Novel and the Press." In Willie van Peer, ed., *The Taming of the Text: Explorations in Language, Literature and Culture*, pp. 61–81. London: Routledge.
Showalter, Elaine. 1977. *A Literature of Their Own: British Women Novelists from Brontë to Lessing*. Princeton: Princeton University Press.
———. 1993. "Tradition and the Female Talent: *The Awakening* as a Solitary Book." In Chopin (1993), pp. 169–89.
Shuy, Roger. 1981. "Code-Switching in *Lady Chatterley's Lover*." *York Papers in Linguistics* 9:223–40.
Sinclair, Upton. 1990. *The Jungle*. New York: Signet Classic.
Sklar, Lawrence. 1998. "Time." In Edward Craig, ed., *Routledge Encyclopedia of Philosophy*, vol. 9, pp. 413–17. London: Routledge.
Slife, Brent D. 1993. *Time and Psychological Explanation*. Albany: SUNY Press.
Smith, Barbara Herrnstein. 1981. "Narrative Versions, Narrative Theories." In W. J. T. Mitchell, ed., *On Narrative*, pp. 209–32. Chicago: University of Chicago Press.
Smith, Quentin. 1998. "Tense and Temporal Logic." In Edward Craig, ed., *Routledge Encyclopedia of Philosophy*, vol. 9, pp. 303–7. London: Routledge.

Smollett, Tobias. 1927. *Roderick Random*. New York: Dutton.
———. 1985. *Humphry Clinker*. London: Penguin Books.
Souriau, Étienne. 1950. *Les Deux cent milles situations dramatiques*. Paris: Flammarion.
Spark, Muriel. 1961. *The Prime of Miss Jean Brodie*. New York: Plume.
Speelman, Craig P., and Kim Kirsner. 1990. "The Representation of Text-Based and Situation-Based Information in Discourse Comprehension." *Journal of Memory and Language* 29:119–32.
Spenser, Sir Edmund. 1981. *The Faerie Queene*. Ed. Thomas P. Roche Jr. and C. Patrick O'Donnell Jr. New Haven: Yale University Press.
Stange, Margit. 1998. "Personal Property: Exchange Value and the Female Self in *The Awakening*." In Keesey (1998), pp. 505–16.
Stanzel, Franz Karl. 1971. *Narrative Situations in the Novel*: Tom Jones, Moby-Dick, The Ambassadors, Uysses. Trans. J. P. Pusack. Bloomington: Indiana University Press.
———. 1984. *A Theory of Narrative*. Trans. Charlotte Goedsche. Cambridge: Cambridge University Press.
Stein, Nancy L. 1982. "The Definition of a Story." *Journal of Pragmatics* 6:487–507.
Sterling, Bruce. 1989. *Islands in the Net*. New York: Ace Books.
Sternberg, Meir. 1978. *Expositional Modes and Temporal Ordering in Fiction*. Baltimore: Johns Hopkins University Press.
Stevenson, Robert Louis. 1905. *The Merry Men and Other Tales: Strange Case of Dr. Jekyll and Mr. Hyde*. New York: Charles Scribner.
Stevenson, Rosemary J. 1996. "Mental Models, Propositions, and the Comprehension of Pronouns." In Jane Oakhill and Alan Garnham, eds., *Mental Models in Cognitive Science: Essays in Honour of Phil Johnson-Laird*, pp. 53–76. East Sussex UK: Psychology Press.
Talmy, Leonard. 1995. "Narrative Structure in a Cognitive Framework." In Duchan, Bruder, and Hewitt (1995), pp. 421–60.
Tannen, Deborah. 1989. *Talking Voices: Repetition, Dialogue, and Imagery in Conversational Discourse*. Cambridge: Cambridge University Press.
Tannen, Deborah, and Cynthia Wallat. 1993. "Interactive Frames and Knowledge Schemas in Interaction: Examples from a Medical Examination/Interview." In Deborah Tannen, ed., *Framing in Discourse*, pp. 57–76. New York: Oxford University Press.
Tesnière, Lucien. 1976. *Éléments de syntaxe structurale*. 2nd ed. Paris: Klinksieck.
Thackeray, William Makepeace. 1963. *Vanity Fair*. Boston: Houghton Mifflin.
Thalberg, Irving. 1977. *Perception, Emotion, and Action*. Oxford: Basil Blackwell.

Thomas, D. M. 1981. *The White Hotel*. New York: Penguin.
Thorndyke, Perry W. 1977. "Cognitive Structures in Comprehension and Memory of Narrative Discourse." *Cognitive Psychology* 9:77–110.
Tindall, William York. 1969. *A Reader's Guide to Finnegans Wake*. New York: Farrar, Straus and Giroux.
Todorov, Tzvetan. 1968. "La Grammaire du récit." *Langages* 12:94–102.
——. 1969. *Grammaire du "Décaméron."* The Hague: Mouton.
——. 1977a. "The Methdological Heritage of Formalism." In *The Poetics of Prose*, pp. 247–67. Trans. Richard Howard. Ithaca: Cornell University Press.
——. 1977b. "Narrative Transformations." In *The Poetics of Prose*, trans. Richard Howard, pp. 218–33. Ithaca: Cornell University Press.
——. 1990. *Genres in Discourse*. Trans. Catherine Porter. Cambridge: Cambridge University Press.
Toolan, Michael. 1996. *Total Speech: An Integrational Linguistic Approach to Language*. Durham: Duke University Press.
Trabasso, Tom, and Linda L. Sperry. 1985. "Causal Relatedness and Importance of Story Events." *Journal of Memory and Language* 24:595–611.
Trabasso, Tom, and Paul van den Broek. 1985. "Causal Thinking and the Representation of Narrative Events." *Journal of Memory and Language* 24:612–30.
Traugott, Elizabeth Closs, and Mary Louise Pratt. 1980. *Linguistics for Students of Literature*. New York: Harcourt Brace Jovanovich.
Turing, Alan. 1950. "Computing Machinery and Intelligence." *Mind* 59:433–60.
Turner, Mark. 1996. *The Literary Mind*. New York: Oxford University Press.
Tversky, Barbara. 1996. "Spatial Perspective in Descriptions." In Bloom et al. (1996), pp. 463–91.
Vachek, Josef. 1966. *The Linguistic School of Prague*. Bloomington: Indiana University Press.
Van Dijk, Teun A. 1972. *Some Aspects of Text Grammars: A Study in Theoretical Linguistics and Poetics*. The Hague: Mouton.
——. 1976. "Philosophy of Action and Theory of Narrative." *Poetics* 5:287–338.
——. 1981. "Episodes as Units of Discourse Analysis." In Deborah Tannen, ed., *Analyzing Discourse: Text and Talk*, pp. 177–95. Washington DC: Georgetown University Press.
——, ed. 1985a. *Handbook of Discourse Analysis*. Vol. 3. Orlando FL: Academic Press.
——. 1985b. "Introduction: Discourse Analysis as a New Cross-Discipline." In van Dijk (1985a), pp. 1–10.

Van Dijk, Teun A., and Walter Kintsch. 1983. *Strategies of Discourse Comprehension*. New York: Academic Press.

Van Valin, Robert D., Jr. 1993. "A Synopsis of Role and Reference Grammar." In Robert D. Van Valin Jr., ed., *Advances in Role and Reference Grammar*, pp. 1–164. Amsterdam: John Benjamins.

Vattimo, Gianni, and Pier Aldo Rovatti, eds. 1988. *Il Pensiero debole*. Milan: Feltrinelli, 1988.

Vendler, Zeno. 1967. *Linguistics in Philosophy*. Ithaca: Cornell University Press.

Virtanen, Tuija. 1992. "Issues of Text Typology: Narrative—A 'Basic' Type of Text?" *TEXT* 12:293–310.

Vološinov, V. N. 1973. *Marxism and the Philosophy of Language*. Trans. Ladislav Matjeka and I. R. Titunik. New York: Seminar Press.

von Wright, Georg Henrik. 1966. "The Logic of Action—A Sketch." In Nicholas Rescher, ed., *The Logic of Decision and Action*, pp. 121–36. Pittsburgh: University of Pittsburgh Press.

———. 1983. *Philosophical Papers*. Vol. 1: *Practical Reason*. Ithaca: Cornell University Press.

Voorst, Jan van. 1988. *Event Structure*. Amsterdam: John Benjamins.

Wales, Kathleen. 1988. "Back to the Future: Bakhtin, Stylistics and Discourse." In Willie van Peer, ed., *The Taming of the Text: Explorations in Language, Literature and Culture*, pp. 176–92. London: Routledge.

Walker, Marilyn A., Aravind K. Joshi, and Ellen F. Prince, eds. 1998. *Centering Theory in Discourse*. Oxford: Oxford University Press.

Webber, Bonnie Lynn. 1979. *A Formal Approach to Discourse Anaphora*. New York: Garland.

———. 1991. "Structure and Ostension in the Interpretation of Discourse Deixis." *Language and Cognitive Processes* 6:107–35.

Werlich, Egon. 1975. *Typologie der Texte: Entwurf eines textlinguistischen Modells zur Grundlegung einer Textgrammatik*. Heidelberg: Quelle and Meyer.

Wharton, Edith. 1994. *The House of Mirth*. Ed. Shari Benstock. Boston: Bedford Books.

White, Hayden. 1996. "The Value of Narrativity in the Representation of Reality." In Susan Onega and José Angel García Landa, eds., *Narratology: An Introduction*, pp. 273–85. London: Longman.

Whorf, Benjamin Lee. 1956. *Language, Thought, and Reality: Selected Writings of Benjamin Lee Whorf*. Ed. John B. Carroll. Cambridge: MIT Press.

Wilde, Oscar. 1998. *The Picture of Dorian Gray*. Ed. Norman Page. Peterborough ON: Broadview Press.

Wilensky, Robert. 1982. "Story Grammars Revisited." *Journal of Pragmatics* 6:423–432.

Wilson, Deirdre, and Dan Sperber. 1991. "Inference and Implicature." In Stephen Davis, ed., *Pragmatics: A Reader*, pp. 377–92. Oxford: Oxford University Press.

Wittgenstein, Ludwig. 1922. *Tractatus Logico-Philosophicus*. London, Kegan Paul, Trench, Trubner.

———. 1969. *The Blue and Brown Books*. 2nd ed. Oxford: Basil Blackwell.

Wolff, Cynthia Griffin. 1998. "Thanatos and Eros: Kate Chopin's *The Awakening*." In Keesey (1998), pp. 263–77.

Wolfram, Walt. 1996. "Delineation and Description in Dialectology: The Case of Perfective *I'm* in Lumbee English." *American Speech* 71:5–26.

Wolfram, Walt, and Clare Dannenberg. 1999. "Dialect Identity in a Tri-Ethnic Context: The Case of Lumbee American Indian English." *English World-Wide* 20:179–217.

Wolfram, Walt, and Natalie Schilling-Estes. 1998. *American English: Dialects and Variation*. Oxford: Basil Blackwell.

Woolf, Virginia. 1925. "Modern Fiction." In *The Common Reader*, pp. 146–54. New York: Harcourt, Brace.

———. 1989. *To the Lighthouse*. New York: Harcourt Brace Jovanovich.

Wright, Richard. 1993. *Native Son*. New York: Harper Perennial.

Yaeger, Patricia S. "'A Language Which Nobody Understood': Emancipatory Strategies in *The Awakening*." In Keesey (1998), pp. 433–49.

Ynduráin, Francisco. 1969. *Clásicos modernos: Estudios de crítica literaria*. Madrid: Gredos.

Young, Katharine Galloway. 1987. *Taleworlds and Storyrealms: The Phenomenology of Narrative*. Dordrecht, Netherlands: Martinus Nijhoff.

———. 1999. "Narratives of Indeterminacy: Breaking the Medical Body into Its Discourses: Breaking the Body out of Postmodernism." In Herman (1999d), pp. 197–217.

Young, R. Michael. 1996. "Using Plan Reasoning in the Generation of Plan Descriptions." *Proceedings of the National Conference on Artificial Intelligence*, pp. 1075–80. Portland OR, 4–8 August. Cambridge:MIT Press.

———. 1997. "Generating Descriptions of Complex Activities." Ph.D. thesis, University of Pittsburgh.

———. 1999a. "Toward a Computational Model of Suspense." Paper presented at Interactive Frictions: A National Conference on Interactive Narrative, June, Los Angeles, University of Southern California.

———. 1999b. "Notes on the Use of Plan Structures in the Creation of Interactive Plot." In Mateas and Sengers (1999), pp. 164–67.

Young, R. Michael, Martha E. Pollack, and Johanna D. Moore. 1994. "Decomposition and Causality in Partial Order Planning." *Proceedings of the Six-*

teenth Annual Conference on AI and Planning Systems, pp. 188–93. Chicago: n.p.

Yuhan, Albert Hanyong, and Stuart C. Shapiro. 1995. "Computational Representation of Space." In Duchan, Bruder, and Hewitt (1995), pp. 191–226.

Zadeh, Lofti A. 1965. "Fuzzy Sets." *Information and Control* 8:338–53.

Zamora, Lois Parkinson, and Wendy B. Faris. 1995. "Introduction: Daiquiri Birds and Flaubertian Parrot(ie)s." In Zamora and Faris, eds., *Magical Realism: Theory, History, Community*, pp. 1–13. Durham: Duke Univeristy Press.

Zoran, Gabriel. 1984. "Towards a Theory of Space in Narrative." *Poetics Today* 5:309–335.

Zubin, David A., and Lynne E. Hewitt. 1995. "The Deictic Center: A Theory of Deixis in Narrative." In Duchan, Bruder, and Hewitt (1995), pp. 129–55.

Zwaan, Rolf A. 1996. "Toward a Model of Literary Comprehension." In Britton and Graesser (1996), pp. 241–55.

Index

actantial roles: Greimas's taxonomy of, 93, 125–33; possibility of syncretism of, 93, 129–33, 137–38; syncretism of as basis for generic typologies, 130–31. *See also* participant roles

actants: vis-à-vis actors (*acteurs*), 123, 124, 125, 126–27, 129–30, 135; as antipsychological approach to character, 125, 387 n. 8 n.10; as based on unstated interpretive glosses, 131–32; as deriving from an Aristotelian subordination of character to plot, 119, 122–23, 133, 387 n.9 n.10; vis-à-vis French Existentialism, 387 n.8; Greimas's theory of, 11, 93, 115, 118, 120, 121–22, 123–33, 387 n.7 n.11, 388 n.13 n.14 n.16 n.17; as prerequisite for Greimas's "semantic microuniverses," 121–22, 126, 132, 374 n.7; and Propp's "spheres of action," 123, 124, 125; and the question of gender, 112; and Souriau's dramatic theories, 126; and Tesnière's syntactic theories, 115, 118, 121, 124–25, 387 n.7; as uncoupling the predicate of "humanness" from participants, 123. *See also* narrative sequences; participant roles; participants; scalability

acting situations: as accounting for the narrative interest of characters' actions, 56–57, 58, 380–81 n.6; across narrative genres, 59–60; vis-à-vis Bremond's logic of narrative possibilities, 56–57; as contrasted with the results of actions, 55–56, 57, 58–59, 60–61, 63; as contributing to the life situation of an agent, 74–75; vis-à-vis the disnarrated, 57, 380–81 n.6, 401 n.15; as expressible via counterfactual conditional statements, 56, 57, 74, 94; vis-à-vis Labov's comparators, 58, 380–81 n.6, 401 n.15; as opportunities for action, 14, 56; place of in von Wright's theory of action, 73–75; and Ryan's virtual embedded narratives, 58; as the state in which the world would have been, 56; and tellability, 58–59, 94. *See also* comparators; conflict; preference rules

action descriptions, 54, 55–56, 62–64, 68–73. *See also* narrative descriptions

action representations: correlation of with textual cues, 62, 66, 67, 68–69; as mentally projected modes of behaving, 53, 62; as narrative microdesigns, 53; preferred types of in different narrative genres, 63–66; as requirement for creating and comprehending storyworlds, 55; scalar model of, 64–65, 72. *See also* contexts; explicit texture; mental models; underspecification

actions: action theorists' decomposition of, 54, 61–64, 74; as explainable in terms of reasons, 70; as fundamental ingredient of narrative, 27, 28, 41, 73, 377 n.5; individuation of, 70–73; as opposed to descriptions of actions, 70; relation of to agents' biographies, 51, 54, 69, 74–75; and Ryan's concept of moves, 377 n.5; as subtype of events, 6, 38–39, 40, 42, 44–45, 53, 82, 376 n.1; taxonomies of, 55, 69–73; as way of accounting for relations between states, 74. *See also* action descriptions; action representations; acting situations action structures: as anchored in inferences about participants' beliefs, desires, and intentions, 75, 83, 85, 90–91, 376 n.2, 383 n.7, 384 n.16; as definitive of stories vs. mere strings of sentences, 54; and degrees of narrativity, 101–3, 104, 384 n.16, 385 n.20; as enabling sequences of events to be construed as molecular narratives, 82–84, 85; as grounded in inferences about participant roles, 116; as mental models accommodating blends of stereotypical and nonstereotypical knowledge, 85; as more or less fine-grained, 113; as principles of organization enabling nonadjacent events to be coherent wholes, 6, 27, 54, 75–76, 83, 385 n.17. See also mental models; motion verbs; narrativehood; narrative programs; narrativity, scripts

action theory: austere, moderate, and prolific versions of, 69–73; as benefiting from integration with cognitive-scientific research, 54, 72–73, 82–84; central questions of, 54, 380 n.1; compared with storytelling, 55; and the question of ontological parsimony, 66, 69–73; as resource for narrative theory, 27, 54–66, 69–82; use of stories in as explanatory device, 54–55, 76, 77; as wider in scope than the study of verb semantics, 51. See also narrative

Actor-Undergoer hierarchy, the. See participant roles

act-tokens: versus act-types, 55, 62, 63, 70–71; basic vs. nonbasic kinds of, 70; and Goldman's theory of level-generation, 70–71

adjacency pairs. See discourse analysis

Agre, Philip E., 374 n.11, 383 n.6

allegory, 47–48, 65, 88, 145, 146. See also *The Faerie Queene*

Allwood, Jens, Lars-Gunnar Andersson, and Östen Dahl, 148

Die andere Seite (Kubin), 404 n.28

Anderson, Stephen R., and Edward L. Keenan, 341, 346, 354, 365, 414 n.7, 415 n.16

anexactitude, 245, 253, 399 n.7. See also polychronic narration

anti-Semitism: in "Der Ausflug der toten Mädchen," 226, 231; in German fascism, 236, 402 n.22, 403 n.24; in *The House of Mirth*, 397 n.28

apostrophe, 362, 405 n.4. See also *Deixis am Phantasma*; narrative *you*

arguments. See participant roles; predicates

Aristotle, 119, 133, 265, 385 n.9

artificial intelligence (AI): background on, 383 n.6; and "narrative intelligence," 1, 373 n.2; vis-à-vis narrative theory, 1, 85, 89–90, 97–113, 373 n.1 n.2, 374 n.11, 382 n.2, 384 n.10, 384 n.16; vis-à-vis situated knowledge and practice, 374 n.11. See also discourse models; narrative sequences

As I Lay Dying (Faulkner), 237, 305, 312–13. See also hypothetical focalization; multiple focalization

asynchronous sound in film: definition of, 239, 246–47; as enabling polychronic narration, 239, 248–50, 253; in *The Sweet Hereafter*, 247–50, 253

Atherton, James S., 395 n.13

atomic narratives, 54, 73, 80, 381 n.11. See also molecular narratives

audience. See contextual anchoring; narrative audience

"Der Ausflug der toten Mädchen," 213, 220–37, 251–52, 253, 261, 272, 400 n.10 n.11, 401 n.13 n.15 n.16, 401–2 n.19, 402 n.20 n.22 n.23. See also anti-Semitism; fascism; narrative levels; paralepsis; polychronic narration

Austin, J. L., 177

autobiography, 35, 110, 111–12

avant-garde narratives, 22, 64, 65, 72, 91, 100, 103–4, 110, 112–13, 147, 174, 234, 251, 264, 285–99, 329, 335, 369–70, 385 n.20, 413 n.1. See also modeling systems

The Awakening (Chopin), 56–58, 59, 60, 61–62, 63–64, 65, 68, 69, 74, 78, 79, 81, 127, 381 n.11. See also gender

Babi Yar (Kuznetsov), 404 n.30

Bakhtin, M. M., 172, 194–95, 266, 298,

366, 369, 397 n.25. See also genres; speech styles; storyworlds; stylistics
Bal, Mieke, 301, 326, 409 n.1
Bamberg, Michael, 31, 263, 382 n.3
Banfield, Ann, 172
Bar-Hillel, Yehoshua, 349–50, 414 n.9
Barry, Jackson G., 85
Barthes, Roland, 3, 45, 49, 81, 87, 95–96, 106, 111, 117, 119, 122, 123–25, 146, 199, 225, 264, 266–67, 387 n.10, 400 n.9. See also narrative sequences; narrative transgression; reality effects; scalability; scripts; spatialization
Bartlett, Frederick, 89, 97
Bavelas, Janet B., L. Edna Rogers, and Frank E. Millar, 185
Begnal, Michael H., 394 n.11
Bell, Allan, 197
Benjamin, Walter, 258, 402–3 n.23
Bennett, Jonathan, 378 n.7
Benstock, Bernard, 180, 394 n.11
Benveniste, Émile, 346, 348, 349, 415 n.13
Beowulf, 36, 46, 130, 145, 166, 167, 380–81 n.6, 392 n.33
Berlin Alexanderplatz (Döblin), 404 n.28
Bernard, Kenneth, 104
Biber, Douglas, 182, 196
Bildungsroman, 315
biographies: complexity of in multiperson narrative worlds, 75; versus histories, 75; in von Wright's sense, 54, 73, 75–76, 77, 381 n.10
Bishop, John, 180, 394–95 n.13
Black, John B., and Gordon H. Bower, 383 n.6 n.7, 384 n.16
Black, Max, 212
black-box explanations, 407 n.15
Blakemore, Diane, 175, 191, 394 n.10, 396 n.24
Bleak House (Dickens), 305
Bobrow, Daniel G., and Donald A. Norman, 89
Bockting, Ineke, 205
Booth, Wayne C., 171, 334, 335
Bordwell, David, and Kristin Thompson, 239, 246–47
Borges, Jorge Luis, 165

Index 455

Bradley, A. C., 119
Branigan, Edward, 85, 106, 383 n.6
breach of expectations: as characterized by Bruner, 7, 85; as criterion for narrative, 83–84, 90–91, 103; and tellability, 84, 90–91; versus stereotypic knowledge, 103. See also conflict; narrativehood; narrativity
Bremond, Claude, 3, 56–57, 87, 93, 94, 96–97, 106, 387 n.9. See also acting situations; functions; logic of narrative possibilities (in Bremond's sense), narrative sequences; scripts
Britton, Bruce K., and Arthur C. Graesser, 383 n.6
The Brothers Karamazov (Dostoyevsky), 127
Brown, Gillian, 20, 282
Brown, Gillian, and George Yule, 20, 177, 178, 191, 347, 349, 393 n.5, 393 n.6, 414 n.11
Brown, Penelope, and Stephen C. Levinson, 197, 200
Bruce, Bertram, 87, 383 n.6 n.7, 384 n.16
Bruner, Jerome, 7, 85, 133, 263, 383 n.9
Buck, R. A., 106, 200
Budniakiewicz, Therese, 115, 118, 122, 123, 129, 132, 148, 380 n.1, 387–88 n.12, 388 n.16
Bühler, Karl, 346, 348, 364, 405 n.4
Burke, Kenneth, 63
Butor, Michel, 353, 356, 413 n.4. See also *La Modification*

Cameron, Deborah, and Jennifer Coates, 202
Cameron, Deborah, Fiona McAlinden, and Kathy O'Leary, 202, 203
The Canterbury Tales (Chaucer), 272. See also spatialization
Carnap, Rudolf, 324
case roles. See participant roles
"Cat in the Rain" (Hemingway), 307
causality. See narrative, polychronic narration
Chafe, Wallace, 214
Chafe, Wallace, and Joanna Nichols, 410 n.6, 411 n.9

456 Index

Chafe, Wallace, Elinor Ochs, Deborah Schiffrin, Paul J. Hopper, and Jane Anne Edwards, 393 n.6
characters: as ideological constructs, 119; as individuals in possible worlds, 120; vis-à-vis narrative actants, 115; narratological accounts of, 115, 118–22; Phelan's approach to, 119–20; semiotic vs. mimetic approaches to, 119; as subset of participants in storyworlds, 115. *See also* actants; participant roles; participants
Charles, May, 385 n.19
Charniak, Eugene, and Drew McDermott, 89
Chatman, Seymour, 8, 13, 43, 98, 119, 214, 245, 263, 265, 297, 334, 373 n.3, 381 n.10, 399 n.4, 399–400 n.8, 403 n.27, 408 n.23, 409–10 n.5. *See also* focalization; hypothetical focalization
Cheshire, Jenny, 197
Chicago Bulls, 28
children's fiction, 110–11
Chomsky, Noam, 49, 389 n.19 n.21
Chung, Sandra, and Alan Timberlake, 411 n.9
Church, Alonzo, 410 n.8
circumstances: and nonparticipant roles, 116, 150, 389 n.20; as opposed to participants, 7, 115, 150, 386 n.4, 389 n.20; and Tesnière's notion of *circonstants*, 115, 124, 128, 134. *See also* participant roles; participants
Clark, Herbert H., 414 n.8, 417 n.24
Clark, Herbert H., and Thomas B. Carlson, 362–63, 414 n.8, 417 n.24
class. *See* speech styles; style shifts
Coates, Jennifer, 202–3
cognitive mapping. *See* spatialization
cognitive narratology: Manfred Jahn's approach to, 4–5; Monika Fludernik's approach to, 4, 302
cognitive science: as informing deictic shift theory, 14–15, 224; as overarching framework for narrative theory, 2, 5, 6, 38, 85–86, 89–92, 97–113, 115, 121–22, 171, 172–73, 299, 305–6; and the study of spatial reference in narrative, 263, 269–85, 286, 298–99. *See also* artificial intelligence (AI); discourse models; mental models; spatialization; storyworlds
Cohn, Dorrit, 16, 172, 204, 358, 413 n.20
comic strips. See *Mutt and Jeff*
comparators, 58, 380 n.5, 401 n.15
conduit metaphor, 19
conflict: and narrativity, 102; as prototypically required for narrative, 76, 84, 90–91; and tellability, 84, 90–91. *See also* breach of expectations; narrativehood; narrativity
contexts: criteria for the relevance of, 186–87; as determining appropriate action representations, 66, 71–73; as determining what counts as a "turn" in conversational exchanges, 189; in Emmott's sense, 20; as factor responsible for discourse coherence, 174–75, 177–80, 190–91; as licensing inferences about the meaning of utterances, 175–80, 394 n.10; as necessary for the interpretation of deictic expressions, 332, 346–50; as required for the recognition of discourse topics, 191–93; and speech registers, 195–96; vis-à-vis speech styles and social identities, 195, 205; as what gets paired with sentences to produce utterances, 175–76. *See also* contextual anchoring; discourse analysis; film narrative; linguistic pragmatics; narrativehood; narrativity
contextual anchoring: as anchoring storyworlds in current contexts of interpretation, 8–9, 22, 211, 331–32, 333–36, 337, 370; and Booth's notion of the implied reader, 334; vis-à-vis the concept of deictic shift, 401 n.14; as dimension of narrative understanding, 8–9, 22, 211, 331–32, 333–36, 350, 370; as encompassing issues explored separately in earlier approaches, 332–36, 413 n.1; in *Heart of Darkness*, 333; in "The Jolly Corner," 335; vis-à-vis linguistic mechanisms of address, 332, 362–63; vis-à-vis linguistic theories of deixis, 332, 338, 345–50, 368; and narrative *you*, 336,

345, 370; in *The Odyssey*, 333; in *A Pagan Place*, 337–346, 350–68; as principle for macrodesigning narratives, 211, 331; and Rabinowitz's theory of audiences, 335–36; vis-à-vis the reception history of particular texts, 334; in *The Remains of the Day*, 336; in second-person narration, 332, 336, 338, 345, 350, 368, 370; and speech-act participants, 348–49, 362–63; and the text-context interface, 8–9, 211, 331–32, 336, 368; vis-à-vis theories of the narratee, 333–335, 336; two classes of mental models involved in, 331, 333; in *Ulysses*, 334. *See also* double deixis; informatives; narrative *you*; second-person narration; story logic

contextual frames: as mental representations of participants, places, and times, 20–21, 270; and referring expressions, 270; vis-à-vis storyworlds, 21, 270

contextual monitoring: in Emmott's theory, 21; and the reconstruction of storyworlds, 21

conversational narrative: vis-à-vis literary narratology, 4, 23–24, 30–32, 33–35, 263–64, 272, 369–70, 378 n.9, 405 n.1, 417 n.27; sociolinguistic perspectives on, 23–24, 30–32, 33–35, 263, 376 n.19, 392–93 n.1. *See also* speech representation

Cook, Walter A., 116, 389 n.21

Cooperative Principle, the, 176–77, 178, 186, 190. *See also* implicatures; linguistic pragmatics

Coste, Didier, 129

Craik, Kenneth H., 17

Crevier, Daniel, 383 n.6

critical discourse analysis. *See* fictional dialogues; speech styles

Cross, Richard K., 253

Crystal, David, 387 n.6

Culler, Jonathan, 3–4, 67–68, 69, 94, 106, 125

Dahl, Östen, 396 n.23
Danes, Frantisek, 396 n.23
Daniel Deronda (Eliot), 275–77, 280, 284,

Index 457

285, 334, 336, 406 n.10 n.13. *See also* hypothetical focalization; spatialization

Daniels, Les, 395 n.17

Danto, Arthur, 54, 55, 73, 77–82, 85, 380 n.4

Davidson, Donald, 28, 29, 51, 53, 54, 70, 71, 377–78 n.6

Davis, Lawrence H., 54, 55, 69–70, 71

The Death of the Heart (Bowen), 306

The Debt to Pleasure (Lanchester), 216, 306

The Decameron (Boccaccio), 2

deictic center. *See* deictic shift

deictic shift, 5, 9, 14–15, 224–25, 270, 271–74, 290, 347, 374 n.8, 400–401 n.13, 406 n.8. *See also* contextual anchoring; double deixis; epistolary novels; framed narratives; interior monologue; polychronic narration; spatialization; storyworlds

deixis, 332, 346–50, 374 n.8, 406 n.8, 414 n.9, 415 n.13. *See also* contexts; contextual anchoring; deictic shift; double deixis

Deixis am Phantasma, 364, 405 n.4. *See also* contextual anchoring; deictic shift; deixis; double deixis

Derrida, Jacques, 399 n.7, 416 n.22

description. *See* narrative; text-type approach

detective fiction, 65, 144, 145, 146, 165–66

Devlin, Kimberly, 180, 394 n.11

dialects. *See* language varieties; speech representation; speech styles

Dirven, René, and Marjolijn Verspoor, 390 n.23

discourse analysis: as concerned with units of language beyond the sentence, 177, 393 n.5; and the construct of adjacency pairs, 184–87; Goffman's approach to, 179, 199–200; and "male" vs. "female" styles of discourse, 201–5, 206–7; recent trends in, 394 n.9, 398 n.29; Searle's critique of, 395 n.16; and the study of spatial reference in narrative, 263, 270, 271–74, 286; and the study of talk as an interactional achievement, 178–79; and topic shifts,

458 Index

discourse analysis (*continued*)
191–93, 197, 396 n.23; and turn-taking in conversation, 179, 184, 187–91, 396 n.22. *See also* footing; participation frameworks (in Goffman's sense); speech styles; style shifts
discourse coherence, 174–75, 176–78, 179–80, 182. *See also* contexts; linguistic pragmatics
discourse models: as blueprints communicated in discourse, 19; in cognitive approaches to language understanding, 5, 19–20, 375 n.14; computational approaches to, 396 n. 20; vis-à-vis narrative *you*, 339, 375 n.14, 415 n.15; as resources for assigning referents to textual cues, 20–21, 375 n.14. *See also* mental models; narrative *you*; storyworlds
discourse topics, 182, 191–93, 197. *See also* contexts; discourse analysis
disnarrated, the, 57, 401 n.15
Doctor Jekyll and Mr. Hyde (Stevenson), 130
Doležel, Lubomír, 4, 15, 16, 54, 66, 67–68, 75, 94, 172, 303, 374 n.9 n.10, 381 n.7, 410 n.5, 411 n.12
Doležel, Lubomír, and Richard W. Bailey, 397 n.26
Donovan, Josephine, 79
Don Quixote (de Cervantes), 107, 108, 109
Dostoyevsky, Fyodor, 172. *See also The Brothers Karamazov*
double deixis: as combining functional subtypes of narrative *you*, 342, 345, 363; and the concept of deictic shift, 401 n.14; as conflating speech-act participants with discourse referents, 348, 349, 363, 365, 414 n.8; as cue for superimposing storyworld-internal and -external referents, 343, 345, 349, 360, 361, 363–68, 370, 401 n.14, 413–14 n.5; as deautomatizing the process of contextual anchoring, 324, 349–50, 370, 401 n.14; as more or less prominent feature of second-person narration, 345; in similes vs. metaphors, 364–65, 417 n.25; and verb tense and aspect, 416 n.21. *See also* contextual anchoring; narrative *you*; ontological indeterminacy; second-person narration
Downs, Roger M., and David Stea, 265
Dowty, David, 39
Duchan, Judith Felson, 39, 65, 378 n.7
Ducrot, Oswald, and Tzvetan Todorov, 346
Dujardin, Eduoard, 172
Dupriez, Bernard, 361, 362, 363
duration (in Genette's sense). *See* temporal ordering

Eble, Connie, 398 n.30
Eckley, Grace, 394 n.11
Eco, Umberto, 381 n.7
Einstein, Albert, 407 n.16
Emmott, Catherine, 5, 10, 20–21, 263, 270, 376 n16, 386 n.5
Encyclopedia Brittanica, 395 n.15, 396 n.19
Enlightenment, the, 108
epic, 36, 41, 46, 48, 91, 145, 146, 162, 166, 167, 169
epistemic modalities: complexity of in hypothetical focalization, 311, 320–21, 326–27; as degrees of certainty encoded in narrative discourse, 304, 326–29; as encoding comparison of an expressed world with a reference world, 310–11, 312, 314, 315, 316–17, 319–21, 326, 411 n.9 n.10; and negation, 311; scale of correlated with varieties of focalization, 326–29. *See also* evidentials; focalization; hypothetical focalization
epistolary novels, 273
ethnomethodology, 23, 376 n.19. *See also* narrative
events: as basic constituent of narrative, 27, 43–45; as instantiations of more general processes, 134, 386 n.3; as resource for narrative microdesigns, 6, 27, 33; vis-à-vis states in narrative, 44, 376 n.1. *See also* actions; event types; process types; UNDERSTAND EVENTS AS ACTIONS
event schemata. *See* process types
event types: alternations between as narrative technique, 32–33; as coding strategy in discourse, 29–30, 32–33, 36–37,

39–49, 50, 53, 379 n.12; defined in terms of time-schemata, 30–31, 38; defined in spatial terms, 379 n.16; preferred combinations of in narrative genres, 45–49, 50, 86; stative vs. nonstative, 40–41, 379 n.14 n.15 evidentials, 410 n.6. *See also* epistemic modalities
experiential repertoires. *See* frames; schemata; scripts
explicit texture: as opposed to zero texture, 69; relation of to action representations, 69; relation of to tellability, 69
Expressionism, 222
external focalization (in Genette's sense), 305, 326, 409 n.5. *See also* epistemic modalities; gappiness of narratives
external focalization (in Rimmon-Kenan's sense): classified by Genette as zero focalization, 304–5, 409 n.5; in *Bleak House*, 305; as epistemic modality, 326. *See also* focalization

face wants. *See* speech styles
Fairclough, Norman, 121, 202, 205, 206, 378 n.10
The Faerie Queene (Spenser), 46, 47–48, 145
"The Fall of the House of Usher" (Poe), 312
fascism: ideological components of, 223–24, 232, 235–37, 402 n.22, 403 n.24; as portrayed in "Der Ausflug der toten Mädchen," 221, 226–33. *See also* anti-Semitism; polychronic narration
Fasold, Ralph, 175, 176, 393 n.6
Faulkner, William, 172. See also *As I Lay Dying*, *The Sound and the Fury*
Fawcett, Robin P., 115
feminist interpretations of narrative. *See* gender
feminist narratology. *See* narratology
Ferguson, Charles, 196, 197
fictional dialogues: and the canonical situation of utterance, 181; discourse analysis as approach to, 174–75, 177–80, 182–93, 199–207, 393 n.3 n.5; ideological dimensions of, 206–7; interactional dimensions of, 173–74, 182–93; and issues of class and gender, 199–207; linguistic pragmatics as approach to, 173–80, 182, 393 n.3; metacommunicative profile of, 7, 173–74, 179–80, 182–93, 183–84, 193; as models of hypothetical discourse situations, 174, 183, 189, 193; Mukařovský's approach to, 393 n.3, 395 n.18; and phatic utterances, 182–83, 395 n.14; and prosodic features of spoken discourse, 396 n.21; and social scripts, 106; sociolinguistic perspectives on, 194–95, 198–207; speech-act theory as approach to, 174; and the status of the "Mutt and Jute" episode in *Finnegans Wake*, 180–81, 190; as underexplored area in critical discourse analysis, 205–7; and the use of typographical cues, 188–91; and verbal dueling, 185–86. *See also* discourse analysis; linguistic pragmatics; speech representation; speech styles; style shifts
fiction vs. nonfiction, 15–16, 35, 67–68, 224, 271–72, 417 n.26
figural narration, 160, 391 n.27. *See also* narrative situations (in Stanzel's sense)
Fillmore, Charles, 116, 121, 149, 164–65, 387 n.12, 389 n.21, 391 n.26
film narrative: and Egoyan's adaptation of Banks's *The Sweet Hereafter*, 237–39; and the withholding of contextual details in individual shots, 239, 245–46, 250, 253; vis-à-vis written narrative, 244–45, 246, 399 n.6; 403 n.27. *See also* polychronic narration
Finnegans Wake (Joyce), 65, 72, 91, 171, 173, 174, 179–93, 393 n.4, 394 n.11 n.12, 395–96 n.13. *See also* "Mutt and Jute"
Firbas, Jan, 101, 307, 343, 396 n.23
Fisher, Bud, 185, 395 n.17. See also *Mutt and Jeff*
Fleischmann, Suzanne, 30, 412 n.14
Fletcher, Charles R., Paul van den Broek, and Erik J. Arthur, 375–76 n.15
Fludernik, Monika, 4–5, 33, 85, 106, 168–69, 171, 172, 263, 270, 277, 302, 305, 308, 309, 338, 339–40, 369, 381–82 n.13, 382 n.4, 390 n.24, 392 n.34, 393 n.2, 397

460 Index

Fludernik, Monika (*continued*)
  n.26, 411–12 n.13, 413 n.1 n.4, 415 n.14, 416 n.20, 417 n.27. *See also* cognitive narratology; hypothetical focalization; narrativity
focalization: and aspectuality, 317–18, 412 n.14; and the authorial narrative situation (in Stanzel's sense), 302; vis-à-vis Chatman's notions of slant and filter, 410–11 n.5; defined in terms of perceptual and conceptual frames, 302, 409 n.2; as encoding epistemic stances toward narrated worlds, 310–23, 325–29, 411 n.11; and evaluative lexical items and marked syntax, 309; formal markers of, 8, 303, 305, 306–9, 312; Genette's original definition of, 301, 409 n.1; and indefinite and definite articles, 306–7; and linguistic theories of modality, 304, 310–11, 312, 314, 315, 316–17, 319–21, 411 n.9 n.10, 413 n.19; and perspectival constraints on mental models, 302–3; and pronouns, 306; and propositional attitudes, 310–11, 319, 325–26, 329; Rimmon-Kenan's broad conception of, 409 n.1; and sentential adverbs, 312, 318–19, 320; structuralist typologies of, 303–6; and verbs of perception, cognition, and emotion, 307–8; and verb tenses and moods, 308–9, 312, 314, 316–17, 318–19, 320. *See also* epistemic modalities; hypothetical focalization; narrative perspective; perspective taking
Foley, William A., and Robert D. Van Valin, Jr., 157, 392 n.31
footing: in Goffman's sense, 199–200; and gender roles, 200, 201–5
Forster, E. M., 98
Foster, John Burt, Jr., 251, 252
Foucault, Michel, 412 n.15
Fowler, Roger, 195, 205, 388 n.18, 393 n.3
framed narratives, 272–73
frames: as analogous to prototypes, 408 n.22; as encoding stereotypic knowledge, 85, 89; as knowledge representations of a relatively static sort, 85, 89; as opposed to relatively dynamic scripts, 85, 89; types of bearing on notions of the self, 112–13. *See also* scripts
Francis, David, and Christopher Hart, 376 n.19
Frawley, William, 12, 23, 29, 30, 39–40, 41, 42, 53, 116, 134, 149, 150–51, 156, 157, 158, 159, 160, 164, 274, 280, 304, 310–11, 312, 317, 332, 346, 348, 365, 377 n.3, 379 n.12 n.13 n.14 n.15, 380 n.3, 389 n.20 n.21, 391 n.26 n.29, 391–92 n.31, 392 n.32, 407 n.16, 411 n.10. *See also* participant roles; verb semantics
free indirect discourse. *See* speech representation
Frege, Gottlob, 324
frequency (in Genette's sense). *See* temporal ordering
Freud, Sigmund, 252, 253–54, 255–57, 260–61, 404 n.29 n.31 n.32, 405 n.34, 404 n.29
Frye, Northrop, 48
functional grammar. *See* participant roles; process types
functions: as defined by Propp, 123; Bremond's probabilistic account of, 94; Kafalenos's rethinking of, 383 n.9, 387 n.9; Propp's determinist model of, 93–94. *See also* hermeneutic composability
Furrow, Melissa, 340, 352, 354
Fussell, Paul, 221
fuzzy logic: versus classical, two-valued logics, 212, 398 n.1; history of, 212, 398–99 n.1; as paradigm for understanding narrative *you*, 413–14 n.5; as paradigm for understanding indeterminate temporal ordering in narrative, 212–14, 399 n.1; potential limitations of, 398 n.1. *See also* double deixis; narrative *you*; polychronic narration; temporal ordering
fuzzy temporality. *See* fuzzy logic; temporal ordering

Galbraith, Mary K., 5, 15
gappiness of narratives: in Doležel's sense, 66, 67–69; and external focalization (in Genette's sense), 306; in Iser's sense, 67; and Genette's concept of paralipsis, 216, 290, 306, 401 n.18. *See also* action rep-

resentations; implicit information in narrative; underspecification
Garfinkel, Harold, 23
Garnham, Alan, and Jane Oakhill, 18, 19
Gazdar, Gerald, 393 n.6
Geminiani, Giuliano C., Antonella Carassa, and Bruno G. Bara, 407 n.15
Genette, Gérard, 2, 3, 27, 53, 82, 171, 212, 214–19, 230, 265, 266, 290, 301–2, 303–5, 326, 327, 333, 357, 373 n.3, 381 n.10, 399 n.2 n.8, 401 n.18, 409 n.1 n.2 n.5, 410 n.7, 411 n.11, 413 n.19 n.1, 414 n.6. *See also* gappiness of narratives; narrative hypertexts; narrative hypotexts; paralepsis; speech representation; temporal ordering
gender: in *The Awakening*, 56–57, 59, 61–62, 74, 75, 79; empirical research on, 202–3; and feminist interpretations of narrative, 79, 107–8, 112, 201–5, 206–7; in *The House of Mirth*, 195, 199–200, 201–5, 207; in *The Portrait of a Lady*, 46; in *The Princess of Clèves*, 107–8; in *A Servant of the Queen*, 112; and slang, 201–2, 203, 204; vis-à-vis ways of communicating, 199–200, 201–5, 207. *See also* actants; footing; speech styles; style shifts
genres: as associated with preferred process types, 139–40, 143–48; and Bakhtin's theory of speech genres, 397 n.25; as codified sets of scene-building strategies, 165–69; as correlated with distinct sorts of processing strategies, 110; of narrative, 6, 33, 35–38, 40–42, 45, 45–49, 59–60, 63–66, 69, 72, 82–83, 86, 91, 104, 105, 107, 110–13, 130–31, 133, 136, 139–40, 143–48, 162, 164–69, 220, 233–34, 251, 252, 255, 256, 264–65, 272–73, 285, 315, 316, 328–30, 385 n.21, 414 n.14; as sets of properties corresponding with ideal types, 36; Todorov's definition of, 35–36; and typicality judgments, 167–68. *See also individual names of genres*; actantial roles; event types; hypothetical focalization; narrativehood; narrative sequences; paralepsis; participant roles; preference rules; process types; scenes (in Fillmore's sense); scripts
Gerrig, Richard J., 16, 271, 376 n.2, 383 n.7
Gibbon, Edward, 80
Gilbert, Sandra, 60, 64, 65, 79
Giora, Rachel, and Yeshayahu Shen, 28, 268, 383 n.7, 384 n.16, 385 n.17
given and new information, 101, 103, 104, 307, 343
Givón, Talmy, 39, 42–43, 44, 45
Glasheen, Adaline, 394 n.11, 395 n.17
goals. *See* action structures
Goffman, Erving, 65, 143, 179, 199–200, 414 n.8 n.10 n.11. *See also* discourse analysis; footing; participation frameworks (in Goffman's sense)
Goldman, Alvin I., 54, 57, 70–71
Goodblatt, Chanita, 415–16 n.17
Gothic novels and tales, 88, 105
Gould, Peter, and Rodney White, 265
Graesser, Arthur C., and Leslie F. Clark, 383 n.6
Graesser, Arthur C., Scott P. Robertson, and Patricia A. Anderson, 383 n.6
grammaticality judgments. *See* narrativehood; preference rules
Green, Georgia M., 5, 19, 175, 350, 368
Gregory, Michael, and Susanne Carroll, 397 n.27
Greig, Andrew, 104
Greimas, Algirdas-Julien, 3, 8, 11, 93, 115, 118, 120, 121–22, 123–27, 128–33, 135, 137, 143, 147, 149, 150, 157, 263, 264, 268, 269, 271, 374 n.7, 387 n.7 n.11, 388 n.13 n.14 n.15 n.16 n.17, 405 n.4. *See also* actantial roles; actants; narrative programs; participants; scalability; spatialization
Greimas, Algirdas-Julien, and Joseph Courtés, 8, 115, 123, 268, 269, 271, 388 n.14, 405 n.5
Grice, H. P., 58, 67, 173, 174, 175, 176–80, 190, 191, 276, 368, 381 n.8, 393 n.3, 394 n.7, 396 n.24 *See also* Cooperative Principle, the; fictional dialogue; linguistic pragmatics; principle of minimal departure; tellability
Grishman, Ralph, 89, 384 n.12, 410 n.8

Grossman, Walter, 401 n.17, 401–2 n.19
Grosz, Barbara and Candace Sidner, 5
Guenther, Irene, 403–4 n.28
A Guest of Honour (Gordimer), 319, 326
Gumperz, John J., 177, 182, 396 n.21

Haack, Susan, 398 n.1
Habermas, Jürgen, 344, 361
Haegeman, Liliane, 389 n.19
Halliday, M. A. K., 115, 134, 136–48, 203, 388 n.18, 389 n.20 n.21, 389–90 n.22, 397 n.27
Hamburger, Käte, 400–401 n.13
Hamilton, Heidi, 65
Hamlet (Shakespeare), 12, 14, 127
Hammett, Dashiell, 166, 305
Hamon, Philippe, 265–66, 381 n.10, 405 n.2
The Handmaid's Tale (Atwood), 331
Hanks, William F., 280, 337, 348, 365–66, 414 n.8 n.11
Haroun and the Sea of Stories (Rushdie), 321
Hayes, Paul M., 236
Hayman, David, 393 n.4, 394 n.12, 395 n.13
Heart of Darkness (Conrad), 272–73, 313, 333. See also contextual anchoring; hypothetical focalization; spatialization
Heath, Shirley Brice, and Juliet Langman, 197, 328
Hejinian, Lyn, 104
Hendricks, William O., 11, 84, 131, 383 n.9
hermeneutic composability: as defined by Bruner, 133; and Hendricks's critique of Propp's notion of functions, 383 n.9
Hernadi, Paul, 172
Herskovits, Annette, 274
"Her Table Spread" (Bowen), 319–20, 322–23
Hester, Stephen, and Peter Eglin, 376 n.19
Hintikka, Jaakko, 410 n.8, 412 n.17
historiographic metafiction. See hypothetical focalization
history. See paralepsis; polychronic narration
Hjelmslev, Louis, 13, 95, 104, 357, 385 n.18
Horkheimer, Max, and Theodor Adorno, 236

The House of Mirth (Wharton), 32–33, 173, 194, 195, 198–207, 333, 397 n.28, 398 n.32 n.33. See also anti-Semitism; gender; speech styles
Humphry Clinker (Smollett), 273
Husserl, Edmund, 245, 399 n.7, 416 n.22
Hutcheon, Linda, 315
Hymes, Dell, 196
hypothetical focalization: anticipations of in structuralist research, 411 n.11; in "As I Lay Dying," 312–13; vis-à-vis Chatman's notions of slant and filter, 409–10 n.5; and counterfactual conditionals, 321; as cuing the construction of candidate mental models, 310, 312, 314; in *Daniel Deronda*, 406 n.10; definition of, 8, 303; in "The Fall of the House of Usher," 312, 323; and Fludernik's concept of figuralization, 411–12 n.13; and Foucault on Bentham's panopticon, 412 n.15; vis-à-vis Genette's concept of paralepsis, 410 n.7; in *A Guest of Honour*, 319, 326; in *Haroun and the Sea of Stories*, 321; in *Heart of Darkness*, 313; in "Her Table Spread," 319–20, 322–23; and historiographic metafiction, 315; and interior monologue, 320; in *Islands in the Net*, 320; in *Jane Eyre*, 328–29; in *Lucky Jim*, 314, 315, 411 n.13; as mode of focalization not included in structuralist typologies, 303, 309–10; and narrative genres, 316, 328–30; vis-à-vis narrativity, 327; in "The Open Boat," 320–21, 322–23; in *Possession*, 313–14; as representation of events in terms of counterfactual belief contexts, 310, 312, 321; as requiring conceptual tools unavailable to structuralist narratologists, 303, 305–6, 309, 323–30; in "Santa Clause is Coming to Town," 316–18; in *The Sweet Hereafter* (print version), 314–16; in *Vanity Fair*, 329; varieties of, 311–23, 411–12 n.13, 412 n.16. See also epistemic modalities; focalization; ontological indeterminacy; perspective taking; possible-worlds semantics

If on a Winter's Night a Traveler (Calvino), 119, 344, 415 n.17

The Iliad (Homer), 42, 46, 166
implicatures, 67, 394 n.7. *See also* linguistic pragmatics
implicit information in narrative, 5–6, 66, 67–69, 97–105, 113. *See also* gappiness of narratives; principle of minimal departure; scripts; underspecification
implied reader, 332, 334. *See also* contextual anchoring
In Cold Blood (Capote), 417 n.26
informants (in Barthes's sense). *See* spatialization
informatives: versus double deixis, 363; as metaperformative speech act in multiparty talk, 362–63, 417 n.24; as thematized in *A Pagan Place*, 363. *See also* double deixis; narrative *you*
Inge, M. Thomas, 395 n.17
intensional vs. extensional meaning, 303, 324–26, 329, 412 n.17. *See also* possible worlds; possible-worlds semantics; propositional attitudes; referential opacity
interior monologue, 274, 320. *See also* hypothetical focalization
internal focalization: as defined by Genette, 304, 305, 306; as epistemic modality, 326; fixed, variable, and multiple varieties of, 305, 326. *See also* epistemic modalities; focalization; multiple focalization
intertextuality, 92, 385 n.19. *See also* genres; scripts
Iser, Wolfgang, 67, 106
Islands in the Net (Sterling), 320
The Italian (Radcliffe), 307–8
Ives, Sumner, 397 n.26

Jackendoff, Ray, 116, 377 n.3, 388 n.16, 389 n.21, 391 n.29
Jacobs, Paul S., and Lisa F. Rau, 383 n.6
Jacques the Fatalist (Diderot), 108, 385 n.20
Jahn, Manfred, 4–5, 85, 106, 377 n.3
Jakobson, Roman, 3, 182, 346, 348–49, 395 n.14, 414–15 n.12
Jameson, Fredric, 406 n.14
Jane Eyre (Brontë), 16, 328–29

Jauss, Hans Robert, 334
Jespersen, Otto, 202
Johnson-Laird, P. N., 11, 17, 18, 374–75 n.12, 375 n.13
"The Jolly Corner" (James), 127–28, 129, 142, 144, 148, 151–56, 160–65, 167, 293, 335, 391 n.27. *See also* contextual anchoring; participant roles
Jordan, Michael, 28
Joyce, James, 172. *See also* *Finnegans Wake*; *A Portrait of the Artist as a Young Man*; *Ulysses*
The Jungle (Sinclair), 308–9

Kacandes, Irene, 345, 361, 362, 415 n.17
Kafalenos, Emma, 84, 94, 383 n.7, 385 n.22, 387 n.9, 399 n.2, 405 n.34
Kamp, Hans, 410 n.8
Kearns, Michael, 413 n.1
Kennitz, Charles, 407 n.15 n.16
Kiefer, Ferenc, 116
Kiesling, Scott, and Natalie Schilling-Estes, 199
Kittay, Jeffrey, 265, 381 n.10
Kolodny, Annette, 79
Kosko, Bart, 212
Kronfeld, Amichai, 375 n.13

LaBahn, Kathleen J., 221
Laberge, Suzanne, 343, 416 n.17, 416 n.20
Laberge, Suzanne, and Gillian Sankoff, 343, 416 n.17, 416 n.20
Labov, William, 30, 31, 33, 56, 58, 87, 185, 197, 265, 279, 297, 378 n.8, 380 n.5, 392 n.1, 401 n.15. *See also* comparators; narrative
Labov, William, and Charlotte Linde, 281
Labov, William, and Joshua Waletzky, 30–31, 87, 103, 245
Lady Chatterley's Lover (Lawrence), 397 n.26, 398 n.30
Lakoff, Robin, 202
Lamb, Sydney M., 134, 386 n.3
Lanchester, John, 6
Landau, Barbara, 271, 284
Landau, Barbara, and Ray Jackendoff, 271, 274–75, 277–78, 282, 284
language varieties, 173, 196, 197. *See also* speech representation; speech styles

464 *Index*

Lanser, Susan Sniader, 376 n.1
Laqueur, Walter, 235–36
Leech, Geoffrey N., and Michael H. Short, 174, 195, 205, 388 n.18, 393 n.3, 397 n.26
Lehnert, Wendy, 384 n.10
Leith, Dick, 393 n.3
Lerdahl, Fred, and Ray Jackendoff, 377 n.3
Levin, Beth, and Malka Rappaport Hovav, 388 n.12
Levinson, Stephen C., 177, 181, 184, 188, 193, 280, 346, 347, 349, 366, 368, 393 n.6, 414 n.11
Lévi-Strauss, Claude, 3, 93, 131
Linde, Charlotte, 31, 263
linguistic pragmatics: and conversational implicatures, 177; vis-à-vis Relevance Theory, 396 n.24; as study of the use of context to make inferences about utterance meanings, 175, 176–77, 394 n.10. *See also* fictional dialogues; implicatures; speech styles
linguistics: as resource for narrative theory, 2–5, 7, 29, 31–32, 38, 39, 49, 101–3, 106, 115–18, 121, 123–35, 136–69, 172–80, 184–93, 195–98, 263–65, 269–85, 286, 303, 304, 306–30, 332–33, 339–50, 365–66, 369, 374 n.6, 380 n.3; use of by structuralist narratologists, 2–3, 49, 115, 124–25, 303, 303–4, 324, 388 n.13. *See also* actants; contextual anchoring; discourse analysis; fictional dialogues; linguistic pragmatics; linguistic semantics; narrative *you*; participant roles; participants; possible-worlds semantics; process types; speech representation; speech styles; style shifts; stylistic; syntax
linguistic semantics: as concerned with the truth-conditional meaning of sentences, 175–76; and issues of narrative perspective, 303, 304, 310–11, 312, 314, 315, 316–17, 319–21, 323–30; and the study of spatial reference in narrative, 263, 274–77. *See also* epistemic modalities; focalization; intensional vs. external meaning; participant roles; participants; possible-worlds semantics; predicates; propositional attitudes; spatialization; verb semantics

literary transduction, 16
Lodge, David, 307
logic of action, 61. *See also* acting situations; action descriptions; actions; action theory
logic of narrative possibilities (in Bremond's sense), 56–57. *See also* acting situations; comparators; disnarrated, the
Longacre, Robert E., 185
Lost Highway (Lynch), 117
Lotman, Jurij, and B. A. Uspenskij, 218, 285, 350
Lucky Jim (Amis), 314, 315, 411 n.13, 412 n.16
Lukasiewicz, Jan, 398–99 n.1
Lyons, John, 387 n.12, 410 n.8
Lyotard, Jean-François, 406 n.14

MacNeil, Lynda D., 86, 382 n.3
Madame Bovary (Flaubert), 6, 108–9
magical realism, 220, 251, 252, 255, 256, 403–4 n.28. *See also* ontological indeterminacy; polychronic narration
Malmkjaer, Kirsten, 116, 389 n.21
Mandler, Jean Matter, 10, 85, 373 n.5, 383 n.6, 384 n.16
Mandler, Jean M., and Nancy S. Johnson, 94
Margolin, Uri, 4, 120, 121, 213, 340, 341–42, 353, 354, 364, 370, 388 n.14, 402 n.21, 405 n.34
Martin, J. R., 115, 389 n.21, 392 n.31
artin, Wallace, 106
Mateas, Michael, and Phoebe Sengers, 373 n.2
May, John R., 60
Mazzullo, Concetta, 285
McDowell, John H., 185
McHale, Brian, 103, 171–72, 338, 345, 378 n.11, 380 n.20, 415 n.17
McHugh, Roland, 396 n.19
McKoon, Gail, Gregory Ward, Roger Ratcliff, and Richard Sproat, 5, 19–20, 375 n.14
Mein Kampf (Hitler), 236
Meletinsky, Eleazar M., 268
mental models: and contextual anchoring,

331, 333, 337; defining features of, 17; and deictic shifts, 14–15, 224; and discourse models, 19–20; Johnson-Laird's typology of, 17; as resource for text processing, 18–19, 270, 375 n.13; role of in narrative understanding, 1, 5–6, 17, 19, 64, 116, 211, 263, 264–65, 375–76 n.15; and spatialization, 211, 263–65, 270, 301; as standing in a one-many and many-one relation to textual cues, 11–12, 62, 66, 68–69, 129–31, 151, 156, 157, 373 n.4; status of in functional grammar, 136; of temporally ordered events, 218, 242, 244–50, 252, 253, 254, 255–56, 260–61; of varieties of communicative behavior in storyworlds, 171, 172, 173, 179–80, 184, 193–94, 195. *See also* action structures; contextual anchoring; discourse models; hypothetical focalization; modeling systems; motion verbs; narrative domains; participant roles; possible worlds; process types; scenes (in Fillmore's sense); spatialization; storyworlds
Mercadal, Dennis, 89
Merivale, Patricia, and Susan Elizabeth Sweeney, 165
metalepsis. *See* ontological indeterminacy
Metamorphoses (Ovid), 45, 116
The Metamorphosis (Kafka), 44, 45, 46, 48, 116–17
metaphysical detective fiction, 147, 165–66
Metzger, John, 214
Mills, Sara, 397 n.26
mindstyle. *See* participant roles; speech styles
Mink, Louis, 223
minor narratives, 104
Minsky, Marvin, 85, 89, 98, 99, 103
modality. *See* epistemic modalities; focalization
modeling systems: and avant-garde narratives, 369–70; Lotman and Uspenskij's conception of, 285, 350; narrative as secondary type of, 218, 285; and polychronic narration, 218, 220; and second-person fictions, 350, 368–70; vis-à-vis spatialization in postmodern fiction,

285–86, 296. *See also* polychronic narration; second-person narration
Modiano, Patrick, 165. See also *La Place de l'étoile*
La Modification (Butor), 354, 415 n.15
molecular narratives, 54, 73, 80–81, 82, 85, 381 n.11. *See also* action structures; atomic narratives
Moll Flanders (Defoe), 282–84, 295. *See also* motion verbs; spatialization
Morgan, Charles G., 212
Morot-Sir, Édouard, 352
Morrissette, Bruce, 337, 413 n.4, 415 n.15, 416 n.20
Moser, Megan, and Johanna D. Moore, 396 n.20
Mosher, Harold, Jr., 385 n.22, 398 n.34
Moss, Susan, 385 n.22
motion verbs: as enabling identification of action structures, 283; as encoding directionality of movement, 282–84, 295; as expressing nonstative events, 40; as indexing perspectives on narrated events, 282–84, 295; as instrumental for the construction and updating of cognitive maps for storyworlds, 282; in *Moll Flanders*, 282–84, 295. *See also* spatialization
A Moveable Feast (Hemingway), 280–81, 284–85
Mukařovský, Jan, 393 n.3, 395 n.18, 415 n.12
Muldoon, Paul, 104
multiple focalization: in *As I Lay Dying*, 237, 305; in *The Sweet Hereafter* (print version), 237–38, 315
The Murder of Roger Ackroyd (Christie), 306
Murray, Janet H., 373 n.2
Mutt and Jeff, 184–85, 395 n.17
"Mutt and Jute," 173, 174, 179–93, 394 n.11 n.12, 394–95 n.13, 395 n.15, 396 n.19
narratee, 332–336, 413 n.2, 414 n.6. *See also* contextual anchoring;, narrative audience
narrative: and causality, 223–24, 225, 234–37, 242–44, 245, 252, 254, 256, 257, 259, 261, 375–76 n.15, 376 n.2, 402 n.22,

466 Index

narrative (*continued*)
402–3 n.23, 404 n.29; vis-à-vis description, 265–66, 283, 381 n.10, 405 n.2, 408 n.23; as discourse genre or text type, 1, 87–89, 90, 105, 220, 223, 233–34, 265, 266, 268, 269, 279, 297, 301; as etymologically related to "knowledge," 298; flexibility of as cognitive frame and communicative mode, 48–49, 60, 277, 328; as ideologeme, 234–35, 236; as inextricably linked with perspective taking, 281–82, 301, 302–3, 406 n.11; Labov's conception of, 30–32, 245, 378 n.8; as means for cognizing events-in-sequence, 218, 220, 223, 233, 263, 265–66; as means for cognizing spatially structured environments, 263, 264–65, 266, 267–85, 298–99, 301; pervasiveness of, 23, 49; as resource for structuring and comprehending experience, 21, 24, 28, 121–22, 149, 164–65, 218, 263, 264–65, 275, 277, 296, 298–99, 301, 328, 371, 374 n.7; as root concept of Danto's theory of action, 77; as situated practice describable in ethnomethodological terms, 23–24, 376 n.19; as systematic application of the fallacy *post hoc, ergo propter hoc*, 225; as underanalyzed concept in action theory, 76, 77; undesirability of according to Sartre, 109. *See also* narrativehood;, narrativity; polychronic narration; text-type approach
narrative acquisition: ontogenetic approaches to, 382 n.3; phylogenetic approaches to, 382 n.3
narrative and trauma. *See* polychronic narration; temporal ordering
narrative audience: vis-à-vis actual and authorial audiences, 336; vis-à-vis contextual anchoring, 335–36, vis-à-vis the narratee, 413 n.2. *See also* contextual anchoring
narrative competence, 104–5
narrative descriptions: in Danto's sense, 77; as analog for action descriptions in von Wright's sense, 77
narrative domains, 264, 286, 296. *See also* mental models; spatialization; storyworlds

narrative explanations: as comparable with action descriptions, 78; as constitutive of actions, 79–80; versus explanation sketches, 78, 380 n.4; as focus of Danto's theory of actions, 77–81; as particularized but making appeal to general laws, 78. *See also* action descriptions; action theory
narrativehood: as binary predicate, 90; defined as what makes a story a story, 86, 90; as determined by the form of the content side of language, 104, 385 n.18; as a function of the relation between scripts and departures from them, 86, 90, 91, 113; and genre, 105; vis-à-vis grammaticality judgments concerning sentences, 49–50, 117; of narratively vs. nonnarratively organized sequences of actions and events, 73, 75–76, 87, 89, 99–100, 101–2, 382 n.1; vis-à-vis narrativity, 86, 91, 100, 101–2, 385 n.20, 392 n.34; and patterns of expectation, 84, 86, 90; problems with Propp's approach to, 94–95; as a product of both formal and contextual factors, 94–96, 97–105. *See also* action structures; breach of expectations; conflict; narrativity; recipes vs. stories; space; spatialization; temporal junctures; text-type approach
narrative hypertexts (in Genette's sense), 214–15
narrative hypotexts (in Genette's sense), 214–15
narrative imagining: as defined by Turner, 28, 34, 376 n.17, 379 n.18; styles of vis-à-vis modes of action representation, 72, 79–80, 381 n.9. *See also* action representations; UNDERSTAND EVENTS AS ACTIONS
narrative levels: in "Der Ausflug der toten Mädchen," 224–25, 226, 228, 230, 402 n.20; in retrospective homodiegetic narration, 224–25
narrative macrodesigns, 7–9, 73, 105, 147, 211, 385–86 n.1. *See also* contextual anchoring; perspective taking; spatialization; temporal ordering

narrative macroroles, 160–69. *See also* participant roles
narrative microdesigns, 6–7, 27, 53, 73, 105, 147, 171, 385–86 n.1. *See also* action representations; events; participants
narrative perspective: as complex modeling process, 330, 375 n.12; and the concept of focalization, 301–3; need for richer approaches to, 303, 304, 323, 329–30, 375 n.12; structuralist approaches to, 301–6. *See also* focalization; hypothetical focalization; perspective taking; spatialization
narrative point, 103
narrative predicates (in Danto's sense), 77–78, 81–82
narrative programs: as comparable to action structures, 268–69; as defined by Greimas and Courtés, 268–69, 405 n.5; as involving both spatial and temporal programming, 269
narrative progression, 74, 150, 151, 155, 160–63, 164–68
narrative sequences: AI-oriented conceptions of, 89–92; Barthes's conception of, 95–96; Bremond's conception of, 96–97; as constituted by a network of actantial roles, 93; as embedded in larger discourse contexts, 99; as mediated by encounters with previous sequences, 104, 105; as probabilistic vs. deterministic in nature, 94, 108; structuralist conceptions of, 87, 89, 92–97; Todorov's definition of, 95. *See also* narrative; narrativehood; narrativity; sequences
narrative situations (in Stanzel's sense), 160, 302. *See also* figural narration; focalization
narrative versions, 214–15
narrative *you*: and apostrophe or "vertical" address, 341, 343, 352, 359–60, 361, 362, 367; and aspectuality, 416 n.19 n.21; and the concept of "informatives," 362–63; in the context of speech and thought reports, 357–59, 360–61, 417 n.23; continuum of discourse functions attaching to, 338–45, 350–68; and deictic transfer, 340, 352, 353–54, 356–57, 367, 415 n.15, 417 n.23; discourse models for the interpretation of, 339, 356–57, 359; and double deixis, 342–43, 344–45, 349–50, 352–53, 363–68; and fictionalized or "horizontal" address, 341, 343–44, 352, 359, 360–61; functions of as language-specific, 354–55, 414 n.7, 415 n.16, 415–16 n.17; gradient vs. binary processing mechanisms associated with, 350, 352–53, 363–64, 367–68; and Hanks's theory of deictic reference as sociocentric, 365–66; as involving a three-valued modal logic, 413–14 n.5; and linguistic theories of person deixis, 347–49; and the phenomenology of reading, 338, 353; as potentially blending referential and address functions, 332, 348–49, 350, 353, 360, 361, 414 n.8, 417 n.23; and pseudo-deictic or generalized *you*, 340–41, 343, 352, 354–55, 367; in second-person narration, 332, 337, 338, 414 n.8; in *A Pagan Place*, 337, 340–45, 350–68; and verb tense, 416 n.21. *See also* contextual anchoring; double deixis; discourse models; fuzzy logic; informatives; second-person narration
narrativity: as affected by the form of the expression side of language, 104; defined as measure of how readily a story can be processed as a story, 86, 87, 91, 100, 104, 381–82 n.13, 385 n.20; vis-à-vis formal and contextual variables, 104; as a function of human experientiality for Fludernik, 168–69, 382 n.13, 390 n.24; as a function of the variable contrast between scripts and stories, 86, 91–92; increments on the scale of, 91, 100–105, 385 n.20; vis-à-vis participant roles, 168–69; as reaching a maximum in proportional blends of the stereotypic and the nonstereotypic, 91, 103, 164; as scalar or fuzzy predicate, 84, 86, 91, 100, 381–82 n.13. *See also* hypothetical focalization; narrativehood; preference rules; second-person narration; spatialization; tellability

468 *Index*

narratology: after structuralism, 4–5, 27, 84, 85, 92, 97, 104, 113, 212–14, 217–20, 223, 233–34, 261, 263, 264, 299, 310–11, 323–30, 331–32, 332–33, 368–71; feminist rethinkings of, 376 n.1; rhetorical approaches to, 335–36, 413 n.1 n. 2; structuralist conceptions of, 2–4, 84, 85, 92, 93–97, 211, 212, 214–17, 223, 230, 261, 263, 264, 265–69, 301–3, 304–5, 387 n.10, 409 n.4. *See also* gender; speech styles; style shifts

Native Son (Wright), 89, 93, 94

naturalization. *See* scripts

natural-language narratives. *See* conversational narratives

La Nausée (Sartre), 109

Newman, Robert D., 253

news stories, 36, 41, 46–47, 60, 65, 66, 91, 278–80. *See also* spatialization

Nietzsche, Friedrich, 407–8 n.17

Nightwood (Barnes), 65, 112–13

1984 (Orwell), 119

Nixon, Richard, 271

nonparticipant roles. *See* circumstances; participant roles; setting

North Carolina ghost stories, 33–35, 37, 41–42, 48

The Notebooks of Malte Laurids Brigge (Rilke), 36–37, 38, 41–42

Nouveau Roman, 65

novel, the: vis-à-vis the anti-novel, 108; vis-à-vis the metanovel, 109; portrayed by Diderot as source of outworn scripts, 108. *See also individual forms of the novel*

Ochs, Elinor, Carolyn Taylor, Dina Rudolph, and Ruth Smith, 281, 302, 406 n.11

The Odyssey (Homer), 36, 46, 130, 145, 167, 333. *See also* contextual anchoring

ontological indeterminacy: in "Der Ausflug der toten Mädchen," 222, 224–25, 226–28, 230–31, 400 n.11; and double deixis, 344–45, 349, 351, 353, 360, 363–68, 370; as a function of competing mental models of the narrated domain, 338; as hallmark of magical realism, 220, 251–52, 256, 260; and hypothetical focalization, 311, 313–14; and metalepsis, 274; in *A Pagan Place*, 344, 361, 363–68; in second-person narration, 332, 338, 401 n.14, 413–14 n.5; in *The Shift*, 274; in *The Sweet Hereafter*, 242; in *The Third Policeman*, 287–96; in *The White Hotel*, 220, 251–52, 256, 260–61. *See also* double deixis, narrative *you*, polychronic narration

"The Open Boat" (Crane), 320–21, 322–23

Ossar, Michael, 405 n.34

Ostroff, Susan, 265

O'Toole, Mary A., 407 n.15

A Pagan Place (O'Brien), 8, 337–45, 349–68, 370, 401 n.14, 415 n.16, 416 n.18 n.19 n.21, 417 n.25. *See also* contextual anchoring; double deixis; informatives; narrative *you*; ontological indeterminacy

Page, Norman, 195, 393 n.3, 397 n.27

Palmer, Don, 405 n.34

paralepsis: as defined by Genette, 230; and Freud's theory of the unconscious, 260–1; as the opposite of paralipsis, 401 n.18; vis-à-vis polychronic narration in "Der Ausflug der toten Mädchen," 230; and *The White Hotel*'s magical-realist vision of history, 261. *See also* gappiness of narratives; hypothetical focalization

paralipsis. *See* gappiness of narratives

The Pardoner's Tale (Chaucer), 1, 24, 272

Paris, Bernard, 119

Paris School of Semiotics, 122, 132

Parsons, Terence, 29, 39, 378 n.7

participant frameworks (in Goffman's sense), 414 n.10 n.11

participant roles: and the Actor-Undergoer hierarchy, 148, 157–69, 392 n.32; and case, thematic, or ϑ-roles, 116, 134, 149–69, 389 n.19 n.21, 391 n.26 n.29; and cohesive links between episodes, 117; default vs. marked assignments of, 159–60, 162, 165–69; as dimension of narrative understanding, 7, 116–17, 126–28, 135–36, 146–47, 149–50, 386 n.5; and Fillmore's theory of meaning as relativized to scenes, 121, 164–65; Frawley's taxonomy of, 150–56; functional grammar as approach to, 136–48; fusions of as explainable in terms of predicate-argument relations, 149–51, 155–56, 158–69; vis-à-vis grammatical roles, 134, 157, 158–60; in "The Jolly Corner," 151–56, 158, 160–65; and language typology, 157–58, 391–92 n.31; as mental models, 117; and mindstyles, 388 n.18; as "moderately plural," 146–47; and narrative genres, 143–48, 162, 165–69, 392 n.32; as resource for managing change-of-state predicates in narrative understanding, 20, 116–17, 151, 155–56; as scalable from clauses and sentences to narratives, 143, 148, 149–50, 151, 152–55, 156, 157, 160, 379–80 n.19; and semantic macroroles, 148, 157–69, 392 n.32; semantic theories of predication as approach to, 148–69, 387–88 n.12; tiered approach to, 157–69; Van Valin's scalar or continuous model of, 157–61. *See also* genres; hermeneutic composability; narrativity; participants; process types; spatialization; style shifts

participants: as constituents of contextual frames, 21, 386 n.5; as crucial ingredient of storyworlds, 116; defined as individuals involved in processes, 115, 120, 137, 380 n.3, 386 n.1, 391 n.22; and functional grammar, 115, 116, 389 n.20 n.21, 389–90 n.22, 390–91 n.22; vis-à-vis Greimas's theory of actants, 11, 115, 118, 120, 125, 126, 137–38, 143, 148, 149, 150, 151, 157, 388 n.15 n.16; and interactions between the syntax and semantics of clauses and sentences, 115, 125, 133–40; at the level of clauses and sentences, 116, 136–43, 148–55, 156, 158–60; as narrative microdesigns, 53; vis-à-vis nonparticipants, 115, 116, 129, 134, 135, 150, 152–56, 163, 386 n.4, 389 n.20; and semantic theories of predication in natural language, 116, 148–49. *See also* actants; characters; contextual frames; participant roles; process types

Pascal, Roy, 172
Passias, Katherine, 354
Pavel, Thomas, 4, 15, 18, 28, 125, 303, 313, 324, 338, 383 n.7, 384 n.16, 385 n.22
Payne, Stanley G., 235, 403 n.24
Peirce, C. S., 228–29
Perrine, Laurence, 361
perspectives. *See* external focalization (in Genette's sense); external focalization (in Rimmon-Kenan's sense); focalization; hypothetical focalization; internal focalization; narrative; narrative perspective; perspective taking; spatialization

perspective taking: as dimension of narrative understanding, 8, 22, 211, 375 n.12; as involving scalar vs. binary phenomena, 302, 310, 323, 411 n.11; as principle for macrodesigning narratives, 211, 409 n.3; as prototypically embodied in narrative, 302, 406 n.11; textual cues enabling, 8, 306–9. *See also* focalization; hypothetical focalization; narrative perspective; spatialization

Peterson, Carole, and Allyssa McCabe, 382 n.4
Phelan, James, 74, 119, 345, 353, 399 n.4, 405 n.34, 413 n.20 n.2
Phelan, James, and Mary Patricia Martin, 413 n.3
phenomenology of reading, the, 215
Philp, Michael, 399 n.4
The Picture of Dorian Gray (Wilde), 130
La Place de l'étoile (Modiano), 117, 305
plans. *See* scripts
Plato, 171
Polanyi, Livia, 31–32, 263, 392–93 n.1
Polkinghorne, Donald E., 376 n.19
polychronic narration: as accomplished via medium-specific properties of film, 237, 239, 243, 244–50; as accomplished via the formal texture of written narrative, 225–28, 245, 253; as accomplished via the juxtaposition of large-scale textual segments, 253–61; as antidote to desperate ways of telling stories, 237, 242–44, 246, 250; in "Der Ausflug der toten Mädchen," 213, 220–37, 261; and

470 Index

polychronic narration (*continued*)
Barthes's concept of narrative transgression, 400 n.9; and Benjamin's concept of historicism, 402–3 n. 23; and Benjamin's concept of *Jetztzeit*, 258; conceived as inexact coding of events' temporal position, 213, 220, 222–23, 224–25, 226, 227, 237, 244, 261; conceived as coding of events as inherently temporally indeterminate, 213, 220, 227, 251–52, 256, 261; and the concept of "organic" temporality, 255–56, 258; defined generally in terms of fuzzy or interdeterminate temporal ordering, 22, 212–14; as device used to explore the scope and limits of narrative itself, 218, 220, 223, 228, 229, 231, 244, 251, 261; vis-à-vis full, random, multiple, and partial temporal ordering, 213; versus Genette's concept of syllepsis, 399 n.8; as highlighting the difficulty of narrativizing traumatic experiences, 219–20, 237, 242–44, 253; as a "humble" way of telling stories, 224, 228, 229, 230, 231–32, 233, 235–37; and Husserl's concept of the anexact, 245, 253; and magical realism, 220, 251, 252, 256, 260; and the nature of history, 253, 258; and the need to remember, 232–33; as ontologically destabilizing, 251–52, 256, 260; and the problem of causality, 218, 219, 223, 225, 228–31, 235–37, 242–44, 245, 250, 252, 254, 256, 257, 259, 261, 402 n.22, 402–3 n.23, 404 n.29; as a product of inhibited or partial deictic shifts, 224–25, 226, 228, 237, 272, 399–400 n.8; as a strategy for countering fascistic ideology, 223–24; in *The Sweet Hereafter*, 213, 214, 220, 237–50, 261; in *The White Hotel*, 213, 220, 251–61. *See also* fuzzy logic; modeling systems; paralepsis; postmodern fiction; preference rules; temporal ordering
polychrony. *See* polychronic narration
The Portrait of a Lady (James), 46, 166–67
A Portrait of the Artist as a Young Man (Joyce), 309
Possession (Byatt), 217, 313–14, 315

possible worlds: and fiction, 15; vis-à-vis fictional worlds, 374 n.9; and hypothetical focalization, 310, 324–26; vis-à-vis mental models, 18, 374–75 n.12; and nonfiction, 15–16, 374 n.10. *See also* epistemic modalities; focalization; mental models; possible-worlds semantics; storyworlds
possible-worlds semantics: as resource for analyzing hypothetical focalization, 303, 305–6, 324–26, 375 n.12; as spotlighting the intensional aspects of narrative, 303, 324–26. *See also* intensional vs. extensional meaning; propositional attitudes; referential opacity
Post, Emil, 399 n.1
postmodern fiction: as challenge to canons of tellability, 100, 113; as evoking but then refusing generic templates, 147; and the need for an integrative approach to spatial reference in narrative, 286; and polychronic narration, 234. *See also* modeling systems; spatialization
Prague School functionalism, 414–15 n.12
Pratt, Mary Louise, 174, 369, 393 n.3, 394 n.7
predicates: binary vs. gradient types of, 45, 48; as connected to arguments via case, thematic, or ϑ-roles, 116, 149–50, 151, 389 n.19 n.21, 391 n.26 n.29; as element of propositional structure, 148–49; as operating on (or "taking") one or more arguments, 148–49; 387–88 n.12, 389 n.19. *See also* narrative predicates; participant roles
predication. *See* participant roles
preference rankings. *See* preference rules
preference rules: for assigning roles to participants in storyworlds, 116, 136, 143–48, 157, 161–69; for blends of acting situations and results, 59–60; definitions of, 23, 377 n.3; for event types in narrative, 31, 33–38, 41–42, 45–49; and grammaticality judgments about sentences vs. narratives, 49–50; impact of narrative experimentation on, 64–65; and the logic that stories have, 22–23;

and narrative genres, 6, 22, 33, 35–38, 40–42, 45–49, 59–60, 63–66, 72, 91, 143–48, 162, 164–69, 234, 377 n.3, 392 n.32; and narrative media, 12; and narrativity, 168–69; and overlap among participant roles, 133, 137–40, 143–48, 159–60, 161–69; as probabilistic vs. deterministic, 12, 28, 377 n.3; for ratios of stereotypic to nonstereotypic actions and events, 91–92; for storyworld reconstruction, 21–22, 41–42, 245; for temporal ordering, 225, 226, 228, 245, 250; and typicality conditions, 377 n.3; and the variable patterning of mental and linguistic objects, 12. *See also* action representations; process types; tellability, UNDERSTAND EVENTS AS ACTIONS
Preston, Dennis, 197
The Prime of Miss Jean Brodie (Spark), 217
Prince, Ellen F., 101, 307, 343, 393 n.6, 394 n.10
Prince, Gerald, 3, 13, 44, 49, 56, 67, 94, 103, 104, 123, 214, 265, 268, 327, 333, 357, 385 n.18 n.22, 386 n.2, 399 n.2 n.3 n.6, 400 n.12, 401 n.13 n.15, 402 n.21, 405 n.7, 409 n.2 n.4, 414 n.6
The Princess of Clèves (de Lafayette), 107–8
principle of minimal departure, 68, 106
process types: as coding strategies in storyworlds, 143–48; as constraining possibilities for role overlap, 136, 137–40, 143–48; vis-à-vis "event schemata," 390 n.23; Halliday's theory of, 136–47; instantiation of in events, 120, 134, 386 n.3; as major innovation of functional grammar, 138; vis-à-vis narrative genres, 136, 139–40, 143–48, 390 n.24; as scalable from clauses and sentences to discourse, 139–40, 143; as specifying inventories of participant roles, 116, 136, 137–43; as specifying preferences for assigning roles to participants, 136, 136, 137–48, 390–91 n.22; and transitivity systems, 136–38. *See also* genres; participant roles; participants
propositional attitudes, 324–25, 329, 410

Index 471

n.8. *See also* intensional vs. extensional meaning; focalization; possible-worlds semantics; referential opacity
Propp, Vladimir, 13, 28, 84, 87, 93–94, 118, 122–23, 124, 125, 131, 133, 211, 383 n.7 n.9, 384 n.10, 387 n.9, 388 n.16. *See also* actants; functions; hermeneutic composability; narrativehood
prototypes, 408 n.22. *See also* frames
psychological novels and tales, 36–37, 41, 46, 60, 120, 144, 145, 162, 166–67, 169
Putnam, Hilary, 412 n.17

Quine, Willard Van Orman, 29, 324, 412–13 n.18

Rabinowitz, Peter J., 335–36, 413 n.2
Rauh, Gisa, 346–47
Realist novel, the, 45, 60, 65, 91, 108–9, 145–46
reality effects, 267
A la Recherche du temps perdu (Proust), 215, 216, 218–19
recipes vs. stories, 88, 89
Reddy, Michael J., 19
referential opacity, 324–25, 412–13 n.18. *See also* intensional vs. extensional meaning; possible-worlds semantics
registers. *See* speech styles
reportability. *See* tellability
reported thought. *See* speech representation; speech styles
Reilly, Rick, 28
The Remains of the Day (Ishiguro), 336
Rescher, Nicholas, 54, 62–63, 321, 398 n.1, 411 n.12
Rhys, Jean, 16
Richardson, Brian, 345, 355–56, 356–57, 359, 369, 415 n.14, 416 n.18 n.21
Rickford, John, and Faye McNair-Knox, 197
Riessman, Catherine Kohler, 263
Rimmon-Kenan, Shlomith, 4, 44, 119, 123, 129, 216, 326, 327, 334, 387 n.9, 399 n.2 n.3, 409 n.1 n.5, 411 n.11
Robbe-Grillet, Alain, 64, 65, 91, 100
Roberts, Lawrence D., 413 n.18
Robinson, Lillian S., 79, 201

472 Index

Roderick Random (Smollett), 306
Roh, Franz, 251
Romaine, Suzanne, 202
Ronen, Ruth, 374 n.9
Rosch, Eleanor, Carolyn B. Mervis, Wayne D. Gray, David M. Johnson, and Penny Boyes-Braem, 296
Rousseau, Jean Jacques, 236
Rubin, David C., 263
Rummelhart, David E., 11, 54, 385 n.17
Russell, Bertrand, 410 n.8
Russian Formalists, the, 13, 119, 211, 263
Ryan, Marie-Laure, 4, 14, 15, 16, 20, 28, 32, 33, 35, 56, 58, 59, 85, 94, 106, 172, 224, 267, 271, 303, 338, 357, 373 n.2, 377 n.5, 380 n.20, 383 n.7, 384 n.10 n.15 n.16, 385 n.22, 402 n.21, 405 n.34, 411 n.12, 413 n.20. *See also* acting situations; actions; virtual embedded narratives
Rydén, Mays, and Sverker Brorström, 406 n.12

Sacks, Harvey, Emanuel A. Schegloff, and Gail Jefferson, 179, 184, 187, 188, 189, 190, 396 n.22
Salmon, Nathan, 213
"Santa Claus Is Coming to Town" (Gillespie), 316–18, 412 n.15
Sapir, Edward, 28
Sareil, Jean, 311
saturation. *See* gappiness of narratives; implicit information in narrative; underspecification
Saussure, Ferdinand de, 3, 194, 195
scalability: vis-à-vis Barthes's definition of stories as long sentences, 117; of clause- or sentence-level structures to discourse-level structures, 49, 117–18, 143, 148, 149–50, 379–80 n.19, 386–87 n.6; and Greimas's theory of actants, 118; in contrast to isomorphism, 118. *See also* participant roles
scenes (in Fillmore's sense), 121, 149, 164–65. *See also* genres; participant roles
Schank, Roger C., 85, 97, 383 n.6
Schank, Roger C., and Robert P. Abelson, 85, 89–90, 97, 98, 384 n.10
Schegloff, Emanuel, 178, 179

schemata (as synonym for frames or framelike structures), 89. *See also* frames
Schiffrin, Deborah, 101, 178, 179, 183, 185, 200, 265, 279, 297, 350, 376 n.19, 393 n.5, 394 n.8 n.9 n.10, 398 n.29, 414 n.11
Scholes, Robert, 384 n.13
Scollon, Ron, and Suzanne Wong Scollon, 200
scripts: anticipations of in Barthes's work, 95–96; anticipations of in Bremond's work, 96–97; anticipations of in Culler's work, 106; bearing of on notions of the self, 112–13; and degrees of narrativity, 7, 86, 102–5; and differences among narrative genres, 86, 92, 105, 109–113, 382 n.2, 385 n.21; and discourse comprehension, 90; as encoding stereotypic knowledge about sequences of events, 7, 85, 89, 90, 382 n.2; as forming backdrop for tellable actions and events, 85; and the historical development of narrative techniques, 86, 92, 105, 107–9, 382 n.2; and intertextuality, 92, 105, 385 n.19; as knowledge representations of a relatively dynamic sort, 85, 89; and literary narrative, 106–13, 382 n.2; and Mandler's concept of episodes, 383 n.6; as means for naturalizing texts, 106; and narrative comprehension, 97–113, 382 n.2; and narrativehood, 85, 86; as opposed to relatively static frames, 85, 89; versus plans, 384 n.12; and reader response, 106; as reducing the complexity of various processing tasks, 89–90, 97; Schank and Abelson's definition of, 97; and van Dijk's concept of episodes, 382–83 n.6
Searle, John, 177, 395 n.16
second-person narration: background on, 413 n.4; and degrees of narrativity, 370; and the increasing use of *you* in the indefinite sense of "one," 416 n.20; as metadiectic, 350, 368; vis-à-vis narrative theory, 368–71; as reflexive exploration of contextual anchoring in narrative, 332, 337, 348, 349–50, 350–51, 368–70, 401 n.14. *See also* contextual

anchoring; double deixis; modeling systems; narrative *you*; ontological indeterminacy
Segal, Erwin M., 5, 14–15, 224
Segre, Cesare, 106–7
semantic microuniverses. *See* actants
Semino, Elena, Mick Short, and Jonathan Culpeper, 397 n.26
sentences vs. utterances, 175–77, 393 n.6. *See also* contexts; linguistic pragmatics; linguistic semantics
sequences: of actions, 73–84, 107–8, 110, 112, 113; and conversational openings, 87–88. *See also* action structures; narrative sequences; temporal ordering; temporal sequence
A Servant of the Queen (MacBride), 111–12
setting, 391 n.28
Shakespeare, 119
Shaw, Harry, 399 n.4
The Shift (Foy), 273–74, 406 n.9
Shklovsky, Victor, 13, 95, 211, 291, 369
Short, Michael, 393 n.3
Showalter, Elaine, 79
Shuy, Roger, 397 n.26, 398 n.30
Sister Carrie (Dreiser), 42
Sklar, Lawrence, 213
The Sleepwalkers (Broch), 305
Slife, Brent D., 404 n.29
Smith, Barbara Herrnstein, 399 n.3
Smith, Quentin, 213
sociolinguistics. *See* conversational narrative; discourse analysis; fictional dialogues; footing; language varieties; participation frameworks; speech representation; speech styles; style shifts
The Sound and the Fury (Faulkner), 274
Souriau, Etienne, 118, 126, 388 n.16
space: vis-à-vis narrative temporality, 263, 265–68; as obligatory vs. optional in narrative, 264, 265, 275, 283, 296–99, 406 n.7; in structuralist treatments of narrative, 265–69. *See also* spatialization; temporal sequence
spatialization: and Barthes's ideas about space in narrative, 264, 266–68; as both triggered and impeded in *The Third Policeman*, 264–65, 285–96, 407 n.16, 408 n.19; in *The Canterbury Tales*, 272; and cognitive mapping, 8, 279, 281, 285, 297, 406 n.14; as creating possibility for empathy with participants, 276–77; in *Daniel Deronda*, 275–77, 284; and degrees of narrativity, 267; and deictic shifts, 270, 271–74; as dimension of narrative understanding, 7–8, 22, 211, 263, 264–65, 270, 296, 298; and the distinction between topological and projective locations, 271, 280–82, 288, 292–93; as the encoding and reconstruction of spatially structured environments, 263, 265, 301; and the figure-ground distinction, 271, 274–77, 280, 291–92, 293–94, 408 n.20; and Greimas's work on space in narrative, 263, 268–69; in *Heart of Darkness*, 272–73; inhibited modes of in postmodern narratives, 22, 264–65, 285, 406 n.14; links of with perspective taking, 281–82, 301, 306; in *Moll Flanders*, 282–84, 295; and motion verbs, 271, 282–84, 406 n.13; in *A Moveable Feast*, 280–81, 284; and narrativehood, 297–98; in news stories, 278–80; and the nonparticipant role of Locative, 391 n.30; and the notions of regions, landmarks, and paths, 271, 277–80; and the preference for dynamic "tours" over static "maps," 281; as principle for macrodesigning narratives, 211; vis-à-vis recent research on language and spatial cognition, 264, 269–99; and the WHAT vs. WHERE systems of spatial cognition, 271, 284–85, 294–95, 295–96 *See also* contextual frames; motion verbs; narrative domains; narrative programs; participant roles; perspective taking; temporal junctures
speech acts. *See* contextual anchoring; double deixis; informatives
speech-act theory. *See* fictional dialogues
speech registers. *See* speech styles
speech representation: as both indexing and creating participants' identities, 173, 199–207, 397 n.27; in conversational narrative, 392–93 n.1; and di-

speech representation (*continued*)
alects or language varieties, 173; and the distinctions "scene vs. summary" and "telling vs. showing," 171; free indirect discourse as particular mode of, 172, 393 n.2, 397 n.26; Genette's foundational work on, 171; as link between language theory and literary experimentation, 182, 205–7; as narrative microdesign, 171; McHale's scalar model of, 171–72; vis-à-vis the "no-narrator" theory, 172; and Plato's distinction between mimesis and diegesis, 171; sociolinguistic perspectives on, 173, 194–207; subtypes of, 172; vis-à-vis thought representation, 172, 204–5, 397 n.26; verbal texture of, 173, 194–207. *See also* fictional dialogues; narrative *you*; speech styles; style shifts

speech styles: Bakhtin's approach to, 194–95; as both cause and effect of social roles, 205; vis-à-vis class and gender, 195, 197, 201–5, 206–7; and code switching, 397 n. 26, 398 n.30; conceived as intraspeaker vs. interspeaker variation, 197; in the context of fictional dialogues, 199–205, 206–7, 397 n.26; and critical discourse analysis, 205–7; empirical research on, 202–3; ideological dimensions of, 206–7; internalized as mindstyles, 205; and linguistic theories of politeness, 197, 200, 202, 204, 206–7; as means for creating identities, 194; vis-à-vis patterns of conflict in society at large, 204, 207; relation to other levels of narrative structure, 194; vis-à-vis reported thought, 204–5; representation of as metacommunicative dimension of narrative, 193–94, 195, 207; versus registers and language varieties (or dialects), 196–98, 206–7, 397 n.27; role of in *The House of Mirth*, 194, 195, 198–205, 206–7; and slang, 201–2, 203, 204, 206, 398 n.31; as socially distinctive ways of speaking, 195; and style shifting, 173, 195, 199–205, 206–7; as subdomain of sociolinguistic research, 194–98; as transdisciplinary object of study, 195. *See also* gender; slang; style shifts; stylistics

Speelman, Craig P., and Kim Kirsner, 18, 270

spoken vs. written discourse, 181–82

Stange, Margit, 79

Stanzel, F. K., 277, 302, 322, 391 n.27, 413 n.1

Star Trek, 68

Stein, Nancy L., 94, 383 n.6

stereotypic knowledge. *See* frames; schemata; scripts

Sternberg, Meir, 214

Stevenson, Rosemary J., 18

story. *See* narrative

story-discourse distinction, 13, 44, 104, 211, 214–20, 399 n. 2 n. 3 n.4 n.5. *See also* storyworlds

story grammars: Johnson-Laird's critique of, 11; Mandler's conception of, 10–11, 373 n.5, 383 n.6; versus story schemata, 10, 373 n.5, 383 n.6; Wilensky's objection to, 10, 384 n.14

story logic: vis-à-vis contextual anchoring, 334, 336; diachronic approaches to, 86, 87, 107–9, 382 n.4; as the logic that stories have, 22–23, 376 n.18; as the logic that stories are, 23–24, 376 n.18; vis-à-vis participant roles and relations, 116; synchronic approaches to, 86, 87, 107, 109–13, 382 n.4

storyworlds: and acting situations, 14; actuality status of, 67; as applicable in both fictional and nonfictional contexts, 16; and Bakhtin's notion of the chronotope (or space-time complex), 266, 298; as both perspectively constrained and perspective-affording, 329–30; and deictic shift theory, 14–15; vis-à-vis contextual frames, 21, 270; vis-à-vis discourse models, 5, 9–10, 20, 373 n.3; and the ecology of narrative interpretation, 13–14, 16–17; as an environment for individuating actions, 72–73; immersive potential of, 16–17, 273, 276–77; and narrative comprehension, 5–6, 14, 21, 373 n.4; and narrativity, 102; vis-à-vis the narratological construct of "story," 13–14, 16, 373 n.3; and possible worlds, 15–16, 120, 374 n.9, 375 n.12; reconstruction of as primary target for narrative analysis, 5; as type of mental model, 5–6, 9–13, 17, 19, 49, 116, 218, 263, 264–65, 270, 299, 329–30, 373 n.3, 384 n.14. *See also* acting situations; contextual anchoring; contextual frames; discourse models; fiction vs. nonfiction; hermeneutic composability; mental models; narrative domains; participant roles; possible worlds; preference rules; process types; spatialization

style shifts: and class bias in *The House of Mirth*, 201; versus essentialist theories about "women's language," 202; as marking patterns of alignment and opposition between storyworld participants, 199–205, 206–7, 398 n.30; as indexing (and creating) class- and gender-based identities, 195, 199–205, 206–7; as revealing mutually constitutive relation between style and identity, 195, 200–205, 397 n.27; and social status, 200–201; as transitions between distinct social styles, 195, 200–201. *See also* speech representation; speech styles

stylistics: Bakhtin's call for a sociological approach to, 194–95; as benefitting from incorporation of recent sociolinguistic research, 195–98, 205–7; challenges posed to by novelistic polyphony, 194; conceived as part of the study of style in language generally, 194–95, 205–7; conceived as the analysis of style in fiction, 194–95; statistical approaches to, 397 n.26

surrealism, 87, 221–22

The Sweet Hereafter (Egoyan), 213, 214, 220, 225, 237–50, 251–52, 253, 254, 261, 314–15, 315–16, 353, 411 n.13. *See also* film narrative; hypothetical focalization; multiple focalization; ontological indeterminacy; polychronic narration; UNDERSTAND EVENTS AS ACTIONS

syntax: absence of in narratives vs. clauses and sentences, 49–50; vis-à-vis semantics at the clause and sentence level, 133–40; and structuralist theories of actants, 124–25, 387 n.7. *See also* actants; participant roles; participants; predicates

tales of the supernatural, 144–45, 146, 167, 169. *See also* North Carolina ghost stories

Talmy, Leonard, 271

Tannen, Deborah, 201

Tannen, Deborah, and Cynthia Wallat, 199

tellability: changing threshold of in the face of narrative experimentation, 64–65, 113; and Grice's Maxim of Relation, 58–59; and narrativehood, 279; versus narrativity, 100, 384 n.15; of recurrent plot elements, 59; as scalar predicate, 100; as synonym for reportability, 100. *See also* acting situations; explicit texture; narrativehood; narrativity; postmodern fiction; virtual embedded narratives

temporal junctures: as defined by Labov, 31, 297; vis-à-vis space in narrative, 297–98; viewed by Virtanen as core requirement for the narrative text type, 297

temporal ordering: vis-à-vis duration (in Genette's sense), 215–16, 217; vis-à-vis frequency (in Genette's sense), 215–16, 217; fuzzy or indeterminate modes of in narrative, 7, 12, 22, 33, 82, 212–14, 217–20, 223–33, 234, 235–37, 239–42, 244–50, 251–52, 254–61; Genette's approach to, 216–19; as the hallmark of narrative, 400 n.12; Margolin's analysis of, 213; as principle for macrodesigning narratives, 211; and the scrambled narrative timeline in *The Sweet Hereafter*, 239, 242, 244, 245; vis-à-vis temporal junctures, 31; and traumatic experiences, 239. *See also* fuzzy logic; narrative; polychronic narration

temporal sequence: construed as definitive of narrative, 263, 266–67; as contrasted with spatial description, 265–

temporal sequence (*continued*)
66, 267. *See also* narrative; space; spatialization; temporal ordering
Tesnière, Lucien, 115, 118, 122, 124, 132, 134, 387 n.12, 388 n.13
text-type approach: as definining core vs. peripheral features of narrative, 265, 296–97; and the overlap between core features of narrative and description, 265, 266, 269, 270, 297–98; as strategy for positioning narrative among other discourse genres, 265. *See also* narrative; temporal junctures
Thalberg, Irving, 71
thematic roles. *See* participant roles
The Third Policeman (O'Brien), 22, 264–65, 285–96, 406 n.14, 406–7 n.15, 407 n.16, 407–8 n.17, 408 n.18 n.19 n.20 n.21. *See also* black-box explanations; ontological indeterminacy; spatialization
Thomas of Erfurt, 378 n.7
Thorndyke, Perry W., 383 n.6
Tindall, William York, 180, 394 n.11
Todorov, Tzvetan, 2, 3, 35–36, 49, 84, 95, 110, 122, 387 n.9. *See also* genres; narrative sequences
Tolliver, Joyce, 380 n.20
Toolan, Michael, 397 n.26
topic. *See* discourse analysis; discourse topics
To the Lighthouse (Woolf), 333, 336
Trabasso, Tom, and Linda L. Sperry, 375 n.15, 383 n.6
Trabasso, Tom, and Paul van den Broek, 375 n.15, 383 n.6
The Tragically Hip, 403 n.25
transformational-generative grammar, 49
Traugott, Elizabeth Closs, 398 n.34
Traugott, Elizabeth Closs and Mary Louise Pratt, 181, 182, 393 n.3
The Trial (Kafka), 12, 306, 385 n.20, 408 n.21
Turing, Alan, 407 n.15
turn taking. *See* discourse analysis
Turner, Mark, 28, 34, 37, 38, 41, 48, 243, 365, 376 n.17, 377 n.4, 379 n.18, 380 n.20,

390–91 n.25. *See also* narrative imagining; UNDERSTAND EVENTS AS ACTIONS
Tversky, Barbara, 281

Ulysses (Joyce), 167, 274, 334
underspecification: of action representations, 63–64, 66–69, 381 n.7; and the relative saturation of fictional worlds, 67, 68, 69, 381 n.7; and distributions of "zero texture" in narrative discourse, 68. *See also* gappiness of narratives; implicit information
UNDERSTAND EVENTS AS ACTIONS: as preference rule in narrative contexts, 28, 76; as preference rule more or less applicable to specific types of events, 28, 34–35, 37–38, 41–42, 48; in *The Sweet Hereafter*, 243
unreliable narration, 336, 408 n.18, 413 n.3

Van Dijk, Teun A., 54, 97, 174, 191, 382–83 n.6
Van Dijk, Teun A., and Walter Kintsch, 18, 85
Vanity Fair (Thackeray), 329
Van Valin, Robert D., 116, 152, 157–63, 165–69
Vattimo, Gianni, 103
Vattimo, Gianni, and Pier Aldo Rovatti, 104
Vendler, Zeno, 29–30, 31, 33, 37, 38, 61, 378 n.7
verb semantics: Frawley's approach to, 39–42; Givón's approach to, 42–49; implications of for storyworld reconstruction, 29, 40–42; as microdesign principle in narrative, 27; as part of a broader cognitive capacity required for narrative understanding, 53; and the problem of matching textual formats with mental representations, 50–51, 53; as resource for drawing distinctions between types of events, 29, 38–45, 53; Vendler's approach to, 29–31, 38, 378 n.7
Virtanen, Tuija, 265, 296–97
virtual embedded narratives: as defined by Ryan, 58–59; as directly propor-

tional with tellability, 58–59, 384 n.15. *See also* acting situations; tellability
Volosinov, V. N., 172, 346, 414 n.9
Von Wright, Georg Henrik, 14, 54, 55–56, 58, 61, 63, 72, 73–76, 77, 78, 94, 401 n.15
Voorst, Jan van, 39, 379 n.14 n.16
vraisemblance, 106, 108

Waking Ned Devine, 83–84
Wales, Kathleen, 393 n.3, 398 n.34
Walker, Marilyn A., Aravind K. Joshi, and Ellen F. Prince, 375 n.14
weak narrativity, 103–4. *See also* narrativity
Webber, Bonnie Lynn, 5, 19, 337
Werlich, Egon, 265
White, Hayden, 133
The White Hotel (Thomas), 213, 220, 227, 251–61, 404 n.29 n.30 n.31 n.32, 404–5 n.33. *See also* Freud, Sigmund; ontological indeterminacy; paralepsis; polychronic narration
Whorf, Benjamin Lee, 28
The Wife of Bath's Tale (Chaucer), 216
Wilensky, Robert, 10, 11, 383 n.6, 384 n.14
Wilson, Deirdre, and Dan Sperber, 396 n.24
Winnie-the-Pooh (Milne), 110–11, 112
Wirth, Eric, 385 n.22
Wittgenstein, Ludwig, 29, 346
Wolff, Cynthia Griffin, 60
Wolfram, Walt, 406 n.12

Wolfram, Walt, and Clare Dannenberg, 196
Wolfram, Walt, and Natalie Schilling-Estes, 196, 197, 198, 398 n.31
Woolf, Virginia, 117, 172, 334. *See also To the Lighthouse*
world models. *See* frames; schemata; scripts

Yaeger, Patricia S., 79
"The Yellow Wallpaper" (Gilman), 130–31
Yndurái̇n, Francisco, 413 n.4
Young, Katharine, 16, 65
Young, R. Michael, 381 n.12, 384 n.12, 385 n.22, 396 n.20
Young, R. Michael, Martha E. Pollack, and Johanna D. Moore, 381 n.12, 396 n.20
Yuhan, Albert Hanyong, and Stuart C. Shapiro, 271

Zadeh, Lofti A., 7, 212, 398 n.1. *See also* fuzzy logic
Zamora, Lois Parkinson, and Wendy F. Faris, 251, 252
Zeno's paradox, 288
zero focalization. *See* external focalization (in Rimmon-Kenan's sense)
zero texture. *See* explicit texture; underspecification
Zoran, Gabriel, 266, 298, 405 n.3
Zubin, David A., and Lynne E. Hewitt, 5, 15, 271, 282, 347
Zwaan, Rolf A., 375 n.13

In the Frontiers of Narrative series:

Story Logic: Problems and Possibilities of Narrative
by David Herman

Talk Fiction: Literature and the Modern Talk Explosion
by Irene Kacandes

www.ingramcontent.com/pod-product-compliance
Lightning Source LLC
Chambersburg PA
CBHW071432300426
44114CB00013B/1401